CHINA FINANCIAL POLICY REPORT

# 中国金融政策报告

## 2021

主　　编　　吴晓灵　陆　磊
执行主编　　何海峰

中国金融出版社

责任编辑：张菊香
责任校对：潘　洁
责任印制：程　颖

图书在版编目（CIP）数据

中国金融政策报告.2021/吴晓灵，陆磊主编.—北京：中国金融出版社，2021.5
ISBN 978 – 7 – 5220 – 1169 – 1

Ⅰ.①中…　Ⅱ.①吴…②陆…　Ⅲ.①金融政策—研究报告—中国—2021　Ⅳ.①F832.0

中国版本图书馆 CIP 数据核字（2021）第 099960 号

中国金融政策报告.2021
ZHONGGUO JINRONG ZHENGCE BAOGAO.2021

出版　中国金融出版社
发行
社址　北京市丰台区益泽路 2 号
市场开发部　（010）66024766，63805472，63439533（传真）
网上书店　www.cfph.cn
　　　　　（010）66024766，63372837（传真）
读者服务部　（010）66070833，62568380
邮编　100071
经销　新华书店
印刷　保利达印务有限公司
尺寸　185 毫米 × 260 毫米
印张　35
字数　300 千
版次　2021 年 5 月第 1 版
印次　2021 年 5 月第 1 次印刷
定价　126.00 元
ISBN 978 – 7 – 5220 – 1169 – 1
如出现印装错误本社负责调换　联系电话（010）63263947
编辑部邮箱：jiaocaiyibu@126.com

# 编委会

主　　　编：吴晓灵　陆　磊

执行主编：何海峰

顾　　　问（按姓氏笔画排列）：

邢　炜　朱　民　阮　路　李　扬

何艳春　张晓晶　陆　磊　陈共炎

范文仲　赵　红　洪　磊　聂伟迅

屠光绍　解　冬　潘光伟　霍学文

理查德·库珀　哈尔·斯科特

# 前　言

《中国金融政策报告 2021》由清华大学国家金融研究院与中国社会科学院金融政策研究中心联合组织编写。作为国内第一本金融政策类大型年度报告，在 2011 年诞生之初，《中国金融政策报告》就确立了"立足中国、沟通世界"的使命与原则。十一年来，我们始终秉承和坚持这一定位，全面、准确地反映了中国金融政策领域年度重大主题和政策动态，努力传递了中国金融发展的真实图景和中国金融政策的全面影响，得到了业界的肯定与认可，更增添了我们的信心、责任和担当。

2020 年是极不平凡的一年。面对严峻复杂的国际形势、艰巨繁重的国内改革发展稳定任务，特别是新冠肺炎疫情的严重冲击，中国统筹疫情防控和经济社会发展取得重大成果。根据国家统计局初步核算，2020 年全年国内生产总值为 101.6 万亿元，比上年增长 2.3%；全年人均国内生产总值为 72447 元，比上年增长 2.0%。从经济上看，面对历史罕见的冲击，中国扎实做好"六稳"工作，全面落实"六保"任务，经济运行逐季改善、逐步恢复常态，在全球主要经济体中唯一实现经济正增长，脱贫攻坚战取得全面胜利，决胜全面建成小康社会取得决定性成就。从金融上看，中国实施稳健的货币政策，坚决做好疫情防控金融服务，全力支持稳企业保就业，持续打好防范化解重大金融风险攻坚战，高风险金融机构和重点领域风险得到有序处置，进一步深化金融改革开放，资本市场总体保持了稳健发展势头，创业板改革并试点注册制、新三板改革、健全退市机制等一批标志性改革落地实施。2020 年实现了"十三五"圆满收官。《中国金融政策报告》项目与新华财经联合完成了第二届（2020）"十大金融政策"评选，发布了"国际十大金融政策""中国十大金融政策""（中国）区域与地方十大金融政策"榜单，涵盖了海内外对经济金融发展、金融市场培育、金融深化改革等方面具有重要影响力与促进作用的金融政策。

2021 年是"十四五"开局之年，中国将开启全面建设社会主义现代化国家新征程。同时，2021 年是中国共产党百年华诞。要巩固拓展疫情防控和经济社会发展成果，更好统筹发展和安全，扎实做好"六稳"工作，全面落实"六保"任务，科学精准实施宏观政策，努力保持经济运行在合理区间，坚持扩大内需战略，强化科技战略支撑，扩大高水平对外开放，保持社会和谐稳定，确保"十四五"开好局起好步，以优异成绩庆祝中国共产党成立100周年。这对2021年的金融政策提出了新要求——稳健的货币政策要灵活精准、合理适度，完善绿色金融政策框架和激励机制，进一步提升金融服务整体效能，加快完善宏观审慎政策框架，切实加强对互联网平台金融活动的监管，大力规范整治重点业务，扎实推进全面深化资本市场改革开放落实落地，保持复杂环境下资本市场稳健发展势头，稳慎推进人民币国际化，以及持续改进外汇管理和服务，等等。

《中国金融政策报告2021》延续了一贯的框架结构，包括两大模块即主题报告和动态报告。主题报告以"在变局中开新局——迈向新阶段的中国金融政策"为题目，回顾总结了"应对变局的金融政策实践"，全面展望了"以高质量发展开新局"的中国金融未来。同时，报告还收集了2020年金融政策两篇代表性的专题文章——《从传统货币理论与现代货币理论的分歧看财政政策与货币政策的协调》和《后疫情时期的科技创新与经济金融变革》。

在"2020年度中国金融政策动态"部分，我们先后对货币政策、汇率与国际收支相关政策、银行业市场发展政策、股票市场发展政策、保险市场发展政策、债券市场发展政策、证券投资基金市场发展政策、货币市场发展政策、信托与财富管理市场发展政策、金融衍生产品市场发展政策、商品期货市场发展政策、外汇市场发展政策、黄金市场发展政策、中国人民银行主要监管政策、中国银行业主要监管政策、中国证券业主要监管政策、中国保险业主要监管政策进行了回顾与分析，也相应给出了对政策的评价与展望。

此外，我们继续以"专栏"形式，反映中国金融政策的相关热点。这18个专栏既有金融改革发展，也有金融对外开放；既有金融行业市场，也有区域与地方金融；当然，还有金融科技等涉及金融创新的专栏。

2018年底和2019年初，作为《中国金融政策报告》系列的《金融政策信息》月刊和周报分别面世，以更加全面、及时地反映中国金融政策的最新发展和动态变化。我们将继续坚持"整理政策信息、评论利弊得失、促进法规完善、走向法治国家"的理念宗旨，努力推动《中国金融政策报告》项目"立足中国、沟通世界"。

《中国金融政策报告2021》作为集体研究的结果，作者团队主要由来自金融管理部门、金融业界机构、高校和学术机构等的专业人员构成，但并不代表他们所任职单位或机构的观点。最后由吴晓灵、陆磊、何海峰对报告全文进行了修改和定稿。先后参加各部分撰稿的执笔人是：吴晓灵、陆磊、何海峰、张岸元、马昀、张玉龙、臧赢舜、李佩珈、何晓贝、沈奕、马强、赵庆明、赵湘怀、梁超逸、任小勋、周昆平、赵亚蕊、余金馨、刘宇、徐克非、王未、荣艺华、杨超、蔡恒培、解学成、刘勇、张宸、李青云、王勤淮、刘思达、刘甲、甘正在、史广龙、尚昕昕、张燕生、罗江、郭荆璞、朱小川、童浩翔、周金飞、张伟、蒋健蓉、谢云霞、杜书明、谈亮、徐倩倩、刘学庆等。丁羽茜、余粤对英文译稿进行了校对。《中国金融政策报告》项目（课题组）实习同学搜集整理了2020年金融政策信息等资料。我们感谢中国金融出版社王效端主任、张菊香编辑的认真和严谨工作。

我们一如既往地期盼读者的批评和建议。

中国社会科学院金融政策研究中心主任
何海峰（代序）
2021年5月10日

## 2020 年度全球十大金融政策

| 序号 | 政策名称 | 发布时间 | 发布/制定机构 |
|---|---|---|---|
| 1 | 美联储宣布"无上限"量化宽松政策 | 3月23日 | 美联储 |
| 2 | 全球最大自贸协定——《区域全面经济伙伴关系协定》（RCEP）成功签署 | 11月15日 | RCEP成员国（东盟10国与中国、日本、韩国、澳大利亚、新西兰） |
| 3 | 世界银行和国际货币基金组织宣布提供最高达120亿美元与500亿美元应对新冠肺炎疫情，世卫组织提供约6.75亿美元以启动应对新型冠状病毒疫情的战略准备和应对方案 | 3月3-4日、2月5日 | 世界银行、国际货币基金组织，世界卫生组织 |
| 4 | 国际清算银行（BIS）和全球七大央行共同发布《央行数字货币》报告 | 10月4日 | BIS、美联储、欧洲央行、日本银行、英格兰银行、加拿大银行、瑞士国家银行、瑞典央行 |
| 5 | 欧洲央行采取一揽子措施应对疫情影响 | 3月12日 | 欧洲央行 |
| 6 | 国际货币基金组织发布《全球金融稳定报告》，探讨经济复苏的可能性 | 10月 | 国际货币基金组织 |
| 7 | 世界贸易组织携手6家多边开发银行支持贸易融资 | 7月6日 | 世界贸易组织、国际金融公司、欧洲复兴开发银行、亚洲开发银行、非洲开发银行、国际伊斯兰贸易金融公司和美洲开发银行 |
| 8 | 拜登提名美联储前主席耶伦出任财政部长，将创造历史 | 11月30日 | 美国政府 |
| 9 | 特朗普签署新一轮支出法案应对疫情恶化 | 12月27日 | 美国政府 |
| 10 | 中欧投资协定谈判完成 | 12月30日 | 中国、欧盟 |

## 2020 年度中国十大金融政策

| 序号 | 政策名称 | 时间 | 制定/发布机构 |
|---|---|---|---|
| 1 | 《〈中共中央关于制定国民经济和社会发展第十四个五年规划和二〇三五年远景目标的建议〉辅导读本》刊发"一行两会"领导的署名文章 | 12月3日 | 中共中央 |
| 2 | 《创业板改革并试点注册制总体实施方案》审议通过，证监会出台系列规则 | 4月27日 | 中央全面深化改革委员会会议、证监会 |
| 3 | 资本市场对外开放加快推进，将原来规定的2021年取消证券、期货、寿险外资股比限制等提前至2020年完成 | 自1月1日起 | 国务院、中国人民银行、中国银保监会、中国证监会 |
| 4 | 《关于进一步提高上市公司质量的意见》 | 10月5日 | 国务院 |

续表

| 序号 | 政策名称 | 时间 | 制定/发布机构 |
|---|---|---|---|
| 5 | 多部门出台金融抗疫系列与专题政策 | 2月9日、6月1日 | 财政部、国家发展改革委、工信部、中国人民银行、审计署、中国银保监会、中国证监会、国家外汇管理局、国家市场监管总局 |
| 6 | 《关于实施金融控股公司准入管理的决定》、《金融控股公司监督管理试行办法》和《金融控股公司董事、监事、高级管理人员任职备案管理暂行规定（征求意见稿）》发布，金融控股公司正式纳入监管 | 9月11日、9月11日、11月2日 | 国务院、中国人民银行、中国人民银行 |
| 7 | 《中华人民共和国商业银行法（修改建议稿）》、《中华人民共和国中国人民银行法（修订草案征求意见稿）》发布 | 10月16日、10月23日 | 中国人民银行 |
| 8 | 国务院金融稳定发展委员会第四十三次会议召开，研究规范债券市场发展、维护债券市场稳定工作 | 11月21日 | 国务院金融稳定发展委员会 |
| 9 | 《网络小额贷款业务管理暂行办法（征求意见稿）》 | 11月2日 | 中国银保监会、中国人民银行 |
| 10 | 沪深两市发布退市新规，推动退市改革 | 12月14日、12月31日 | 上海证券交易所、深圳证券交易所 |

## 2020年度区域与地方十大金融政策

| 序号 | 政策名称 | 时间 | 制定/发布机构 |
|---|---|---|---|
| 1 | 《关于金融支持粤港澳大湾区建设的意见》 | 4月24日 | 中国人民银行、中国银保监会、中国证监会、国家外汇管理局 |
| 2 | 《关于进一步加快推进上海国际金融中心建设和金融支持长三角一体化发展的意见》 | 2月14日 | 中国人民银行、中国银保监会、中国证监会、国家外汇管理局、上海市人民政府 |
| 3 | 我国金融科技创新监管试点实现全面落地 | 全年 | 中国人民银行 |
| 4 | 《国务院关于深化北京市新一轮服务业扩大开放综合试点建设国家服务业扩大开放综合示范区工作方案的批复》 | 8月28日 | 国务院 |
| 5 | 数字人民币试点多城落地 | 4月17日 | 中国人民银行数字货币研究所 |
| 6 | 《成渝地区双城经济圈建设规划纲要》正式印发 | 11月18日 | 中共中央、国务院 |
| 7 | 《关于加大金融支持科创企业健康发展的若干措施》 | 1月10日 | 北京市地方金融监督管理局、中国人民银行营业管理部、中国银保监会北京监管局、中国证监会北京监管局 |

续表

| 序号 | 政策名称 | 时间 | 制定/发布机构 |
|---|---|---|---|
| 8 | 各地多部门联合出台行动方案，对前期金融支持疫情防控和经济社会发展等一系列措施进一步升级和强化 | 7月 | 中国人民银行北京营业管理部等部门、中国人民银行上海总部等部门、中国人民银行天津分行、中国人民银行重庆营业管理部等部门 |
| 9 | 多地出台地方金融监督管理条例 | 全年 | 上海市人民代表大会常务委员会、浙江省人民代表大会常务委员会、内蒙古自治区人民代表大会常务委员会、广西壮族自治区人民代表大会常务委员会、江西省人民代表大会常务委员会 |
| 10 | 《关于设立北京金融法院的方案》 | 12月30日 | 中央全面深化改革委员会 |

# 目　　录

## 上篇　主题报告与专题文章

**主题报告：在变局中开新局——迈向新阶段的中国金融政策** ⋯⋯⋯⋯⋯⋯⋯ 3
    一、导语 ⋯⋯⋯⋯⋯⋯⋯⋯⋯⋯⋯⋯⋯⋯⋯⋯⋯⋯⋯⋯⋯⋯⋯⋯⋯⋯⋯ 3
    二、应对变局的金融政策实践 ⋯⋯⋯⋯⋯⋯⋯⋯⋯⋯⋯⋯⋯⋯⋯⋯⋯⋯⋯ 4
    三、以高质量发展开新局 ⋯⋯⋯⋯⋯⋯⋯⋯⋯⋯⋯⋯⋯⋯⋯⋯⋯⋯⋯⋯⋯ 8
    四、结论 ⋯⋯⋯⋯⋯⋯⋯⋯⋯⋯⋯⋯⋯⋯⋯⋯⋯⋯⋯⋯⋯⋯⋯⋯⋯⋯⋯ 12

**专题文章一：从传统货币理论与现代货币理论的分歧看财政政策与货币政策的**
            **协调** ⋯⋯⋯⋯⋯⋯⋯⋯⋯⋯⋯⋯⋯⋯⋯⋯⋯⋯⋯⋯⋯⋯⋯⋯⋯⋯ 13

**专题文章二：后疫情时期的科技创新与经济金融变革** ⋯⋯⋯⋯⋯⋯⋯⋯⋯⋯ 16

## 下篇　2020年度中国金融政策动态

**宏观金融政策** ⋯⋯⋯⋯⋯⋯⋯⋯⋯⋯⋯⋯⋯⋯⋯⋯⋯⋯⋯⋯⋯⋯⋯⋯⋯⋯ 23
    一、货币政策 ⋯⋯⋯⋯⋯⋯⋯⋯⋯⋯⋯⋯⋯⋯⋯⋯⋯⋯⋯⋯⋯⋯⋯⋯⋯ 23
    二、汇率与国际收支相关政策 ⋯⋯⋯⋯⋯⋯⋯⋯⋯⋯⋯⋯⋯⋯⋯⋯⋯⋯⋯ 33

**主要金融市场发展政策** ⋯⋯⋯⋯⋯⋯⋯⋯⋯⋯⋯⋯⋯⋯⋯⋯⋯⋯⋯⋯⋯⋯ 42
    一、银行业市场发展政策 ⋯⋯⋯⋯⋯⋯⋯⋯⋯⋯⋯⋯⋯⋯⋯⋯⋯⋯⋯⋯⋯ 42
    二、股票市场发展政策 ⋯⋯⋯⋯⋯⋯⋯⋯⋯⋯⋯⋯⋯⋯⋯⋯⋯⋯⋯⋯⋯⋯ 55
    三、保险市场发展政策 ⋯⋯⋯⋯⋯⋯⋯⋯⋯⋯⋯⋯⋯⋯⋯⋯⋯⋯⋯⋯⋯⋯ 76
    四、债券市场发展政策 ⋯⋯⋯⋯⋯⋯⋯⋯⋯⋯⋯⋯⋯⋯⋯⋯⋯⋯⋯⋯⋯⋯ 110
    五、证券投资基金市场发展政策 ⋯⋯⋯⋯⋯⋯⋯⋯⋯⋯⋯⋯⋯⋯⋯⋯⋯⋯ 119

六、货币市场发展政策 …………………………………………………… 126
七、信托与财富管理市场发展政策 ……………………………………… 132
八、金融衍生品市场发展政策 …………………………………………… 142
九、商品期货市场发展政策 ……………………………………………… 149
十、外汇市场发展政策 …………………………………………………… 155
十一、黄金市场发展政策 ………………………………………………… 159

**主要金融监管政策** ………………………………………………………… 165
　一、中国人民银行主要监管政策 ………………………………………… 165
　二、中国银行业主要监管政策 …………………………………………… 171
　三、中国证券业主要监管政策 …………………………………………… 180
　四、中国保险业主要监管政策 …………………………………………… 197

# 上 篇

主题报告与
专题文章

主题报告：

# 在变局中开新局

## ——迈向新阶段的中国金融政策①

## 一、导语

2020年是极不平凡的一年。面对新冠肺炎疫情叠加全球经贸争端的双重压力，我国金融业在变局中开新局、在危机中育新机，统筹疫情防控和经济社会发展，较好完成了"十三五"时期金融改革的各项任务，为开启"十四五"新征程，实现高质量发展奠定了坚实基础。

（一）"十三五"时期金融改革取得重大进展

"十三五"期间，我国金融业发展坚持稳中求进工作总基调，以改革创新为动力，深化金融供给侧结构性改革，着力处理好长期矛盾和短期挑战，圆满完成了"十三五规划"涉及的各项金融改革任务，金融业综合实力稳步增强，金融风险趋于收敛，成功应对新冠疫情冲击，为实体经济高质量发展发挥了十分重要的作用。

货币政策+宏观审慎政策双支柱调控框架不断完善。我国在全球范围内率先建立了"货币政策+宏观审慎政策"双支柱调控框架，更好地实现货币稳定和金融稳定。货币政策价格型调控框架逐步成型，积极培育以回购利率（DR）为主的货币市场基准利率体系，构建利率走廊引导货币市场利率运行，启动贷款市场报价利率（LPR）改革。完善宏观审慎管理体系，加强对系统重要性金融机构、金融控股公司与金融基础设施的统筹监管，引导金融机构加大对经济薄弱环节的支持力度。

银行业综合实力和竞争力再上新台阶。银行业资产规模稳步增长，总资产规模由2015年末的199.34万亿元增至2020年末的319.74万亿元，年复合增长率为9.9%。信贷结构持续优化，2020年金融机构普惠小微贷款余额达15.1万亿元，大型商业银行普惠小微企业贷款余额增速连续多年在30%以上。截至2020年末，我国银行业金融机构数量已超过4500家，多层次商业银行体系逐步成熟。

我国资本市场改革助推市场稳健发展。克服疫情等各种不利因素影响，我国资本市场实现正常开市和常态化运行。市场容量不断扩大，2020年末股票市场总市值约80万

---

① 作者：吴晓灵、陆磊、何海峰、张岸元、张玉龙、臧赢舜、马昀、李佩珈。

亿元，债券托管余额约114万亿元，均居全球第二位。多层次资本市场体系渐趋完备，创业板改革、注册制试点、新三板改革、健全退市机制等一批标志性改革落地实施。对外开放力度持续加大，互联互通机制不断完善，全球投资者参与度显著提高。2020年末，境外机构和个人投资者持有境内人民币金融资产共计8.98万亿元，比2015年末增加了5.38万亿元，增幅近150%。

防范化解金融风险攻坚战取得决定性胜利。金融监管框架持续优化，逐步形成"一委一行两会一局"为主、地方分工负责的金融监管架构，现代金融监管体系初具雏形。持续整治金融乱象，规范金融机构发展，影子银行规模较历史峰值下降约20万亿元，P2P平台全部清零，金融控股公司经营逐步走向规范。积极加快银行不良资产处置，2020年商业银行不良贷款率为1.84%，不良比率近年来首次下降。

（二）2020年我国金融业成功应对疫情和外部不确定性冲击

新冠肺炎疫情叠加经济摩擦使金融业面临错综复杂的局面。当前世界正处于百年未有之大变局，全球经济增长动力不足，保护主义、地缘政治风险上升，尤其是新冠肺炎疫情对全球经济金融的影响极为深远，全球感染者超过1.5亿人次。疫情对经济的冲击不仅是短期的也是中长期的，不仅是需求侧的也是供给侧的，不仅是总量的也是结构性的。作为现代经济的核心，金融业将持续受到影响。从实体经济层面看，尽管全球主要国家正在加速推进疫苗的生产和接种，全球经济复苏的不确定性仍然很大，经济基本面并不牢固，对金融稳定构成了新挑战。另一方面，应对疫情冲击过度依赖无限量宽松货币政策，导致主要经济体的货币宽松被迫长期持续，全球金融资产泡沫化风险值得警惕，对经济稳定构成了政策约束。疫情加剧了全球经济债务负担，全球杠杆率上升加剧了金融系统脆弱性。据国际金融协会（IIF）数据，新冠疫情使2020年全球债务较2019年增加24万亿美元，达到创纪录的281万亿美元；全球债务与GDP之比较2019年上升35个百分点，达到355%，增幅远超2008年全球金融危机期间10~15个百分点的增幅。

金融政策及时有效助力我国成功应对疫情。面对新冠疫情暴发和全球蔓延，党中央、国务院果断决策部署，统筹疫情防控和经济社会发展。金融管理部门迅速行动、多措并举、综合施策，实施了一系列金融支持政策，不仅为疫情防控提供直接融资支持，同时着眼宏观层面稳增长、保就业、保民生需要，积极发挥金融要素服务实体经济的功能，创设微观直达融资工具支持企业特别是中小微企业渡难关，推动金融体系让利实体经济1.5万亿元，为企业复工复产提供重要的金融支撑，使我国成为2020年全球主要经济体中唯一实现正增长的国家。

## 二、应对变局的金融政策实践

新冠肺炎疫情暴发伊始，党中央、国务院果断决策部署，统筹疫情防控和经济社会发展，2020年4月提出了"保居民就业、保基本民生、保市场主体、保粮食能源安全、保产业链供应链稳定、保基层运转"。对比前期的"六稳"目标，疫情期间"六保"任务更强调底线思维。在国务院金融稳定发展委员会的统一领导下，金融管理部门多措并举、综合施策，采取了一系列宏观和微观、短期和长期的金融政策，落实"六稳"工作、落实"六保"任务。这不仅为疫情防控提供了直接的融资支持，同时也有效发挥了金融要素服务实体经济功能，通过创设微观直达融资工具支持企业特别是中小微企业渡过难关，推动金融体系让利实体经济1.5万亿元，运用货币金融宏观逆周期政策工具保就业、保民生、稳增长。同时，综合平衡好发展和安全、改革和稳定的关系，不搞大水漫灌的强刺激，着力打好防范化解金融风险三年攻坚战，精准处置重点领域风险事件，守住不发生系统性金融风险的底线。

（一）多措并举直接支持疫情防控融资需要

新冠肺炎疫情发生以来，金融监管部门迅速响应，积极开展疫情防控工作，出台多项政策支持抗疫企业融资，为疫情期间重点物资的供应以及人民生活保障提供重要支撑，为企业复工复产提供新动力。

金融政策保障抗疫物资跨境流通便利。新冠疫情以来，我国外贸先后遭受国内疫情和海外疫情的双重冲击。金融监管部门对重要医用物资和重要生活物资的骨干企业实行名单制管理，开辟绿色通道；建立外汇政策绿色通道，放宽疫情防控相关资本项目收入结汇支付的事前单证要求；进一步便利和满足疫情防控相关跨境融资，对于确有跨境融资需要的企业，取消借用外债限额限制并可线上办理。加强对进出口企业的融资安排与支持，为重要医用物品和生活物资进口开辟绿色通道。

金融体系加大对抗疫领域的融资支持力度。在疫情防控期间，人民银行通过3000亿元专项再贷款向金融机构提供低成本资金，通过全国性的商业银行以及部分疫情严重地区的地方商业银行，向重要医用物品和生活物资生产、运输和销售的重点企业提供优惠信贷支持。同时，通过加强金融机构与有关医院、医疗科研单位和相关企业的服务对接，提供足额信贷资源，全力满足相关单位和企业卫生防疫、医药用品制造及采购、公共卫生基础设施建设等融资需求。

畅通金融基础设施服务保障金融抗疫渠道。抗疫伊始，人民银行会同银保监会、证监会、外汇局等金融监管部门采取果断措施，从工作机制、人员配备、办公场所、系统运维、技术支持等方面强化金融市场基础设施的服务保障能力，确保发行、交易、清算、结算等业务正常运转，尽可能实施全流程、全链条线上操作。制订应急预案，对突发事件快速响应、高效处理。各市场机构、金融基础设施之间密切配合、相互协作，保持业务系统联通顺畅。

表1　　　　　　　　我国支持抗疫企业融资政策

| 日期 | 政策名称 | 发布部门 | 内容 |
| --- | --- | --- | --- |
| 2020.2.14 | 《关于进一步做好疫情防控金融服务的通知》 | 银保监会 | 紧紧围绕疫情防控需求，全力做好治疗药物、疫苗研发等卫生医疗重点领域，以及重要物资生产、运输物流等相关企业的融资支持。用足用好中央政策，专设机制、充分授权、主动对接，降低融资成本，提供优惠利率和优质金融服务，支持企业恢复产能和扩大生产。鼓励保险机构结合自身情况，为身处疫情防控一线的工作人员提供意外、健康、养老、医疗等优惠保险服务。 |

续表

| 日期 | 政策名称 | 发布部门 | 内容 |
|---|---|---|---|
| 2020.2.9 | 《关于应对新型冠状病毒肺炎疫情帮助中小企业复工复产共渡难关有关工作的通知》 | 工信部 | 推动落实国家对防疫重点企业的财税支持政策。鼓励在中央贷款贴息的基础上，地方财政再予以进一步支持。 |
| 2020.2.1 | 《关于支持金融强化服务做好新型冠状病毒感染肺炎疫情防控工作的通知》 | 财政部 | 对2020年新增的疫情防控重点保障企业贷款，在人民银行专项再贷款支持金融机构提供优惠利率信贷的基础上，中央财政按人民银行再贷款利率的50%给予贴息，贴息期限不超过1年，贴息资金从普惠金融发展专项资金中安排。 |
| 2020.1.31 | 《关于进一步强化金融支持防控新型冠状病毒感染肺炎疫情的通知》 | 人民银行、财政部、银保监会、证监会、外汇局 | 对疫情防控相关领域的企业，以及重要生活物资的骨干企业实行名单制管理，人民银行通过专项再贷款向金融机构提供低成本资金，支持金融机构对名单内的企业提供优惠利率的信贷支持，支持开发性、政策性银行加大对上述市场化融资有困难的企业的资金支持。 |

资料来源：银保监会、中国人民银行、财政部、中信建投。

(二) 聚焦实体经济"稳增长" 强化逆周期金融调控

2020年以来，新冠肺炎疫情给我国经济社会发展带来严重冲击，第一季度GDP同比下降6.8%。我国金融监管部门及时加大货币金融政策的逆周期调控力度，稳中求进、精准施策、优化结构、让利实体，推动经济运行稳定恢复，使我国成为2020年全球唯一实现经济正增长的主要经济体。

货币信贷政策及时响应营造适宜货币金融环境。2020年，人民银行通过降准、中期借贷便利、再贷款、再贴现等工具，共推出9万多亿元的货币支持措施。到2020年末，广义货币（$M_2$）同比增长10.1%，社会融资规模存量同比增长13.3%，均保持合理增长。前瞻性引导中期借贷便利和公开市场操作中标利率下降30个基点，带动市场利率中枢下行，1年期贷款市场报价利率（LPR）同步下行。2020年企业综合融资成本明显下降，12月企业贷款加权平均利率为4.61%，较上年同期下降0.51个百分点，创有统计以来新低。

创新金融结构政策精准支持稳企业保就业。根据疫情防控形势和经济发展需要，分层次、有梯度出台三批次合计1.8万亿元的再贷款、再贴现政策。2020年6月1日，人民银行创设"普惠小微企业贷款延期支持工具"和"普惠小微企业信用贷款支持计划"两项直达实体经济的货币政策工具，进一步完善结构性货币政策工具体系，增强对稳企业、保就业的金融支持力度。总体来看，2020年信贷结构持续优化，年末普惠小微贷款和制造业中长期贷款余额同比分别增长30.3%和35.2%。

深化利率、汇率形成机制等金融领域重点改革。改革畅通货币政策传导，按照市场化、法治化原则顺利完成存量浮动利率贷款定价基准转换，推动银行将LPR嵌入内部转移定价（FTP）体系，坚决打破贷款利率隐性下限，促进利率传导效率明显提升，引导金融资源更多配置至小微、民营企业，降低贷款实际利率水平。继续推进汇率市场化改革，完善人民币汇率形成机制，增强汇率弹性，活跃银行间外汇市场交易，降低了微观经济主体的汇兑成本，促进我对外贸易和投资自由化便利化。

推动高水平金融开放，服务贸易投资自由化便利化。金融监管部门紧扣"稳住外贸外资基本盘"，配合其他宏观调控部门出台了一系列稳外贸的金融政策。出台支持涉外业务发展的一揽子外汇便利化政策，助力跨境电子商务等贸易新业态发展，提升跨境贸易投融资便利化水平。发挥中国出口信用保险公司与中国进出口银行的金融服务功能，运用全产品线出口信用保险和专项融资服务优势，为出口企业提供全方位金融支持。充分发挥政策性金融合力，帮助企业应对新市场开发、订单取消、出运拒收、款项支付等风险，切实缓解企业出口融资困难，帮助企业拓市场、保订单、保市场。

（三）积极推进资本市场改革与发展

2020年，资本市场统筹防控疫情和改革发展要求，注重发挥市场内生机制作用，统筹推进投资端和融资端改革，通过深化改革稳市场稳预期，保持资本市场稳健发展势头。

我国资本市场改革明显加速。2020年，创业板改革和试点注册制成功落地，创业板、新三板改革等一批标志性的改革举措相继推出，健全退市机制、提高上市公司质量等监管举措有效实施，资本市场重大改革取得了显著进展。

资本市场的法治建设和生态环境不断完善。指导银行等金融机构采用综合授信方式，对生产经营基本面良好、具备发展空间的上市公司予以支持。推进商业银行设立理财子公司，壮大机构投资者队伍，引导优质资金入场。针对疫情冲击，适时对资管新规进行微调预调，允许适当延长存量资管业务整改过渡期，减轻了对金融体系的冲击，稳妥有序完成存量资管业务规范整改工作。

支持符合条件的保险公司投资资本市场。对偿付能力较强、资产负债匹配情况较好的保险公司，赋予其更多投资自主权，提高其权益类资产投资，更好地发挥保险资金的长期投资、价值投资优势。这一举措有助于提高权益投资比重，促进资本市场长期稳定健康发展。

（四）稳妥有序化解金融风险、增强金融机构风险防范能力

补充资本金帮助中小银行对冲疫情影响。2020年7月，国务院常务会议首次提出在新增地方政府专项债限额中安排一定额度，允许地方政府依法依规通过认购可转换债券等方式，探索合理补充中小银行资本金的新途径。同时，优先支持具备可持续市场化经营能力的中小银行补充资本金，以此推动改革、转换机制。这不仅增强了中小银行服务中小微企业的能力，同时也有利于其完善治理、健全内控机制，进一步深化中小银行改革。

处置高风险中小金融机构方案顺利实施。克服疫情对金融环境的负面影响，2020年推动高风险中小金融机构处置取得关键进展和重要阶段性成果。恒丰银行、锦州银行等重点金融机构的改革重组方案顺利实施，包商银行破产清算各项工作稳妥有序进行。高

风险金融机构的顺利处置,确保了关键敏感时期金融体系的平稳运行,守住了不发生系统性金融风险的底线。

我国资本市场韧性和抗风险能力增强。资本市场经受住疫情冲击等外部风险事件影响,实现了正常开市和常态化运行。按照"控增量、消存量"的思路,做好防范化解上市公司股票质押流动性风险的相关工作,上市公司股票质押风险化解取得实质性成效,债券违约、私募基金等重点领域风险总体收敛。

(五)牢牢把握金融高质量发展的两大新着力点

着力发展绿色金融。这是我国基于推动构建人类命运共同体的责任担当和实现可持续发展的内在要求作出的重大战略决策。2020年习近平总书记在第75届联合国大会一般性辩论上宣布,我国二氧化碳排放力争于2030年前达到峰值,努力争取2060年前实现碳中和。党的十九届五中全会和2020年中央经济工作会议要求,加快推动绿色低碳发展,做好碳达峰、碳中和工作。2020年以来,金融部门通过金融资源配置、风险管理和碳价格发现,逐步完善绿色金融标准体系、监管和信息披露要求、政策激励、产品和市场体系、国际合作等绿色金融体系五大支柱建设。截至2020年第三季度末,我国本外币绿色贷款余额超过11万亿元,居世界首位。

着力完善支持创新的金融体系。习近平总书记指出,我国要强盛、要复兴,就一定要大力发展科学技术,努力成为世界主要科学中心和创新高地。科技创新需要高质量金融体系的支持。通过畅通科技型企业国内上市融资渠道,增强科创板"硬科技"特色,提升创业板服务成长型创新、创业企业功能,鼓励发展天使投资、创业投资,更好地发挥创业投资引导基金和私募股权基金作用。鼓励金融机构发展知识产权质押融资、科技保险等科技金融产品,开展科技成果转化贷款风险补偿试点。

## 三、以高质量发展开新局

2020年是"十三五"圆满收官之年,是确定"十四五"时期金融改革发展各项目标的关键一年。"十三五"时期金融政策实践的宝贵经验是树立底线思维,准确识变、科学应变、主动求变,善于在危机中育先机、于变局中开新局,以推动高质量发展为主题,以深化供给侧结构性改革为主线,以改革创新为根本动力,通过金融业高质量发展应对各种内外部风险挑战,为助力新发展格局的构建贡献金融力量。

(一)着力提升我国金融治理体系和治理能力现代化

《中共中央关于制定国民经济和社会发展第十四个五年规划和二〇三五年远景目标的建议》指出,要健全以国家发展规划为战略导向,以财政政策和货币政策为主要手段,就业、产业、投资、消费、环保、区域等政策紧密配合,目标优化、分工合理、高效协同的宏观经济治理体系,为完善宏观经济金融治理体系提供了根本遵循。为此,需着力推进以下改革任务。

保持宏观金融政策的连续性、稳定性和可持续性。在当前全球疫情尚未得到全面控制的情况下,宏观金融政策的首要目标是保就业和保市场主体。要持续加强和改进现代中央银行制度和货币调控机制，搞好跨周期政策设计，促进经济总量平衡、结构优化、内外均衡。坚持稳字当头、合理适度，不急转弯，执行好稳健的货币政策，保持人民币汇率在合理均衡水平上的基本稳定，促进经济平稳健康运行。要保持物价基本稳定，特别是关注大宗商品价格走势。中长期，要着眼于健全现代货币政策框架和完善货币供应调控机制，完善中央银行调节银行货币创造的流动性、资本和利率约束的长效机制，保持货币供应量和社会融资规模增速与反映潜在产出的名义国内生产总值增速基本匹配。以深化利率市场化改革为抓手，疏通货币政策传导机制，完善以公开市场操作利率为短期政策利率和以中期借贷便利利率为中期政策利率的中央银行政策利率体系，深化贷款市场报价利率改革，破除贷款利率隐性下限。

持续优化财政政策和货币政策之间的协调配合。中央银行要实现币值稳定目标，需要以市场化方式对银行体系货币创造过程进行调控，保持资产负债表的健康可持续。为此，必须实行独立的中央银行财务预算管理制度，防止财政赤字货币化，在财政和中央银行两个"钱袋子"之间建起"防火墙"。同时，要防止中央银行资产负债表承担企业信用风险，最终影响人民币信用。进一步明确财政政策和货币政策分工，财政政策在进行逆周期总量调控的同时，可以充分发挥其优化经济结构的优势，货币政策在营造适宜货币金融环境同时，要注重引导金融资源优化配置。二者各自发挥特长，充分显示我国的制度优势。

（二）构建金融有效支持实体经济的体制机制

服务实体经济是金融的天职。习近平总书记强调，金融要为实体经济服务，满足经济社会发展和人民群众需要。"十四五"时期，深化金融供给侧结构性改革必须贯彻落实新发展理念，强化金融服务功能，找准金融服务重点，充分体现服务实体经济、服务人民生活的宗旨和定位。

全面提升金融服务实体能力。着力推进金融支持稳企业保就业。加大对普惠金融的支持力度，继续加大对民营、小微、"三农"等领域的支持力度，实现包容性增长。促进小微企业融资实现"量增、价降、面扩"，加大对制造业中长期贷款的支持力度，实施普惠小微企业贷款延期还本付息政策和普惠小微信用贷款支持政策，稳定市场预期。全力做好收官阶段金融精准扶贫工作。巩固提升贫困地区基础金融服务质量，助力贫困县全部摘帽。持续加大对乡村振兴领域的资源投入。优化农村产权制度改革金融服务，发展壮大集体经济，推广农村承包土地的经营权抵押贷款业务。

加大对构建国民经济关键环节的支持力度。坚持扩大内需这一战略基点，聚焦生产、分配、流通、消费各环节循环畅通。按照产业协调、区域协调、城乡协调的内在要求，不断助力疏通内循环体系。顺应全球产业链和价值链的重构趋势，加大对高端制造业、新基建等的支持力度。从供需两端做好消费金融服务，助力形成强大的国内市场。大力发展绿色金融，从健全绿色金融标准体系、完善金融机构监管和信息披露要求、构建政策激励约束体系、不断完善绿色金融产品和市场体系、加强绿色金融国际合作五个方面，逐步完善绿色金融体系。

深化金融区域改革推动金融业开放创新。按照党中央、国务院的决策部署，将区域金融改革推向纵深，围绕供给侧结构性改革，探索培养竞争新优势。有步骤、有重点、有针对性地深入推进自贸区金融开放创新、绿色金融、农村金融、普惠金融等改革试点工作。促进区域协调发展，加强对京津冀、长三角、粤港澳大湾区、海南自贸区、成渝双城经济圈等国家区域发展战略的支持力度。及时梳理总结各地改革试点经验，合理把握新增试点区域的布局，推动区域金融改革工作迈上新台阶，增强金融服务改革开放和经济发展能力。

(三) 加快建立与金融强国地位相适应的现代金融体系

按照市场化、法治化、国际化原则，健全具有高度适应性、竞争力、普惠性的现代金融体系。

推动多层次资本市场体系健康发展。科学把握多层次资本市场定位，完善差异化的制度安排，畅通转板机制，形成错位发展、功能互补、有机联系的市场体系。持续推进关键制度创新，以多层次资本市场体系为不同企业提供多样化的融资服务。切实办好科创板，研究推出制度创新、相关产品和工具，支持更多"硬科技"企业利用资本市场发展壮大。借鉴国际最佳实践，不断总结科创板、创业板试点注册制的经验，稳步在全市场推行以信息披露为核心的注册制。推进商业银行设立理财子公司，支持符合条件的保险公司投资资本市场，壮大机构投资者队伍，引导优质资金入场。深入推进债券市场创新发展，完善债券发行注册制，深化交易所与银行间债券市场基础设施的互联互通。

大力发展绿色金融。研究修订《银行业存款类金融机构绿色金融业绩评价方案》，支持符合条件的金融机构积极探索更加精准、更低成本的方式，向低碳绿色项目提供支持。积极参与绿色金融标准体系建设，探索绿色金融国家标准和行业标准，推进绿色金融规范发展。推动碳金融市场全面规范发展，提升碳金融市场定价的权威性和交易效率。强化绿色金融数字基础设施建设，缓解资金供求双方的气候和环境信息不对称，化解绿色识别难题，为精准施策提供依据。

有序推动金融业高水平开放。充分利用国际国内两个市场、两种资源，不断提高金融服务实体经济的质量和效率。有序推进金融业双向开放，完善"沪港通"、"深港通"和"债券通"的相关制度安排，深化境外投资者与我国金融市场的联系。增强中国市场、中国资产的全球交易和定价能力，提高我国金融体系的国际竞争力。加大跨境金融业务创新，提高中资金融机构的全球竞争力和服务能力，提高对"走出去"中资企业的金融服务水平。

(四) 守住不发生系统性金融风险的底线

坚持总体国家安全观，强化底线思维，统筹好发展和安全之间的关系，筑牢金融安全堤坝，维护好国家安全和发展利益。

加强对金融的集中统一领导。充分发挥国务院金融稳定发展委员会的统筹协调作用，进一步完善符合我国国情的金融监管体系。着眼维护国家安全和发展利益需要，强化对中央金融事权监管能力建设，持续完善现代金融监管体系，补齐监管制度短板，健全风险全覆盖监管框架，提高金融监管市场化、法治化、国际化和透明度。优化地方金融监管体系，支持引导地方金融机构专注主业，坚持服务当地、服务小微企业、服务城乡居民的定位，促进地区金融供需结构平衡。坚持属地管理的原则，金融监管部门要加强对地方政府的指导，相互协作，形成合力。同时，充分发挥地方政府在属地金融机构资本管理和风险处置中的主体责任，对违法违规行为"零容忍"。

构建及时高效的金融风险处置机制。加强逆周期、跨市场的金融宏观审慎管理，加强宏观审慎与微观审慎监管的配合，制定和完善跨市场、跨业态、跨区域的金融风险监测、识别、预警和处置体系。建立了逆周期资本缓冲机制，初步构建起金融控股公司监管制度框架，完善系统重要性金融机构监管框架。加强风险识别，做到风险早发现、早介入、早防范。完善对突发性金融风险的应急管理和处置预案，健全市场化风险处置和救助机制。优化退出机制，允许风险可控但经营不善的金融机构破产出清。

完善金融机构的微观治理和监管体系。金融监管部门加强对金融机构的股东和实际控制人、风险集中度、关联交易、数据真实性等的监管，强化资本充足、监督检查和市场约束，补齐制度短板和监管漏洞，提升监管效率，做到全覆盖。强化监管追责问责，严肃查处金融监管失职渎职等行为。地方金融机构完善公司治理，加强风险管理，强化审慎经营，不过度追求规模扩张和发展速度。提高金融从业人员的专业素质和职业操守，明确行为底线，提高金融机构违法成本，约束"一把手"行为。

维护公平高效透明的金融生态环境。推动金融业履行社会责任，强化普惠金融、绿色金融，防止脱实向虚、投机套利。在支持金融创新的同时，严防垄断、维护市场秩序，促进公平竞争。建立健全以保护金融消费者权益为核心的最佳行为监管实践，完善金融消费者和投资者权益保护事前、事中、事后监管机制。坚决打击非法集资、非法吸储和金融诈骗，对各种变相违规的投融资活动予以坚决打击，切实维护人民群众的财产安全和社会稳定。

积极参与国际金融治理体系建设。构建海外利益保护和风险预警防范体系，建立国家金融安全审查机制，优化外商投资国家安全审查、反垄断审查等制度，筑牢金融风险防范的安全堤坝，为开放上好"保险阀"。

(五) 提升金融科技水平和监管能力

面对金融科技的持续快速发展，坚持既鼓励创新又守牢底线的积极审慎态度，在促进科技赋能金融的同时重视风险管理，在鼓励金融科技发展和防范金融风险积聚之间实现动态平衡和最优组合，切实解决好面临的新问题新挑战。

积极稳妥发展金融科技。加强对大数据、云计算、人工智能、区块链和移动互联等新技术的研究。加快金融机构数字化转型，重新塑造银行的IT基础设施，重新认识和构建银行的生态及企业价值链，以金融科技降低经营成本。多措并举，推动资本市场金融科技有序健康发展，开展资本市场金融科技创新试点，积极开展区块链在资本市场的应用探索，尝试打造资本市场监管链，提高资本市场服务实体经济的质量和效率。

打造审慎包容的监管环境。金融科技未改变金融的风险属性。应遵循"同样业务同样监管"原则，按照实质重于形式，落实穿透式监管，保持监管政策取向、业务规则和标准的大体一致，坚决防止监管套利。加大对垄断行为的处罚力度，通过立法加强数据信息保护，完善金融科技监管框架，防止监管套利和风险交叉传染。在公正监管、平等准入、公平竞争市场环境下，推动金融科技在资本合理扩张、保持创新活力和保护公众权利之间实现有序平衡，做到科技向善。

## 四、结论

习近平总书记指出，当今世界正在经历百年未有之大变局，新冠肺炎疫情全球大流行使这个大变局加速变化。2020年的金融政策实践经验充分证明，我国金融业在"十三五"时期的高质量发展在有力有效支持实体经济应对疫情和内外风险挑战中发挥了积极作用，在推动金融业更高质量发展中奠定了坚实基础。

展望"十四五"时期，金融政策实践将立足新发展阶段，贯彻新发展理念，更好地服务于新发展格局，我国的各项金融政策制定和执行将始终坚持高质量发展主题，围绕金融供给侧结构性改革主线，以改革创新为根本动力，全面增强金融服务实体经济能力。在宏观政策上，不断完善宏观经济治理体系，健全现代货币政策框架，持续优化财政政策和货币政策之间的协调配合。在体制机制上，加大对国民经济重点领域和关键环节的支持力度，推进金融区域改革开放，守住不发生系统性金融风险的底线。在创新发展上，着力建设现代金融体系，健全多层次资本市场体系，大力发展绿色金融，有序推动金融业高水平开放。在监管政策上，积极稳妥发展金融科技，打造审慎包容的监管环境，充分发挥金融在资源配置、价格发现和风险分散上的积极作用，统筹金融发展与金融安全。

金融是国家重要的核心竞争力，要正确把握金融本质和规律，学习借鉴外国有益经验，立足中国实际，走有中国特色的金融发展之路，推动"十四五"时期金融业高质量发展。

专题文章一：

# 从传统货币理论与现代货币理论的分歧
# 看财政政策与货币政策的协调[①]

## 第一，现代货币理论和传统货币理论的分歧

现代货币理论本来是一个很边缘的理论，但是近年来由于许多国家实施量化宽松的货币政策并没有导致通货膨胀，又由于金融危机和新冠疫情导致许多国家的财政日益拮据，财政债务上限屡受冲击，财政债务问题备受争议，于是财政赤字货币化问题引起了较大关注，对财政政策与货币政策的关系也提出了新的视角。世界经济复苏的不确定性日益增加，地缘政治日益复杂，各国经济均面临着国际产业链重构和结构性调整的困难，传统经济和以信息技术为代表的新经济交融发展。

我们有必要关注现代货币理论和数字货币对传统货币理论和经济实践的影响，注重货币政策与财政政策的协调及路线。现代货币理论认为货币是一种政府债务凭证，政府的税收权决定了法定货币的地位。公众由于交税的需求而接受货币，税收推动货币的发行、流通。政府债务是调节利率的手段。在独立的主权货币制度下，只要政府没有承诺以固定汇率兑换外币或黄金，政府财政赤字可以是无限的，政府不可能破产。因为政府可以通过货币发行偿还债务，同时可以通过提高税收或举债收回多余的货币。这里和传统货币最大的分歧就在于，传统货币认为货币的产生是交易的需求，因而有多种货币，但是最终能够成为法定货币的一定是靠政府的权力和政府的税收权。在这一点上其实传统货币理论和现代货币理论是有共同点的。但是在货币的本源上，传统货币被认为是媒介，还有更多的其他货币。现代货币理论特别注重财政，认为货币起源于财政的税收和法权，因而不太注重货币政策，只注重财政政策，提出了功能财政的概念。

所谓功能财政是说，如果国内收入水平过低、税收占比过低，政府就要增加支出，失业就是最充分的例证。出现失业就意味着政府支出过低。如果本国的利率水平过高的话，政府就需要多花钱、多提供基础货币来降低利率。功能财政的创始人勒纳拒绝稳健财政的概念。勒纳认为正确的赤字比例是充分就业的比例，正确的债务比例是与实现利率目标相一致的比例，利用市场利率水平和就业率水平确定整个的财政政策。

---

[①] 作者：吴晓灵，清华大学五道口金融学院理事长、中国人民银行原副行长。

### 第二，央行可在结构性调整中发挥作用

前一段时间大家在讨论财政赤字化是什么意思，认为只有央行在一级市场上购买财政债券才叫财政赤字货币化，如果在二级市场买好像就不是。实际上不论是在一级市场还是二级市场，购入财政债券其实都是财政赤字货币化。在信用货币制度下，法定货币是永远不需要偿还的债务。在这点上传统货币银行学和现代货币理论是有共识的。而且现代货币理论也不否认中央银行体制，也觉得即使是财政直接创造货币，用支付来创造货币，也要走中央银行的支付体系。所以从这点上来说，财政赤字货币化和信用货币的创造、法定货币的创造是同一个问题。

问题演变成谁来主导央行资产方的运用，因为支出都是通过央行的资产负债表。现代货币理论也不认为政府要直接发钞票买东西，也是政府通过央行支出，支付命令下达取决于财政的主动启动，或者是财政跟央行借1000亿元，借了之后财政就有1000亿元可以花了，或者是发1000亿元国债由央行买进，通过债务凭证的方式用出去。这个时候，如果央行的资产负债主要是黄金和财政的债券，那货币创造的使用主动权在谁手里——在财政手里。尽管在二级市场上买的时候，在数量上和利率上央行有一定的调控权，但是主动权都在财政手里，因为是财政把这些钱花了。如果是央行的资产负债结构里有再贷款，再贷款就是中央银行直接给商业银行贷款，商业银行有了基础货币就可以去创造其他货币了。在这里，中央银行是有自主权的。中央银行自主扩张资产，货币发行主动权在央行手里。

西方国家原来都是通过财政，但是这次金融危机之后，通过一些量化宽松的货币政策，央行直接买入非金融机构的资产，其实是做了结构性的调整。中国央行一直有结构性调整的做法，我们的教科书上都是说货币政策管总量，财政政策管结构。但是如果从货币创造的本质来说，央行对资产负债表的结构有调整的余地，或者是有很大的主动权。其实是央行可以通过对自己资产的运用来引导市场结构的一些调整。过去人民银行经常说这是阶段性的任务，现在看来不一定是阶段性的任务，而是在比较是财政直接支配钱的效率高，还是通过央行渠道支配钱的效率高、约束力更强。我觉得在中国，财政预算制度不是特别完善，而且必要的经济支出与最基本的公共支出界限不是很清楚，有一些涉及经济建设方面的内容，通过央行基础货币去引导可能是比较好的选择。

### 第三，关注预算的质量比关注预算赤字更重要

在信用货币制度下，一个主权国家的货币发行，从技术上是无限的，但是从经济上看是有限的，有通货膨胀率的限制。通货膨胀要是高了，确实会对老百姓的生活产生很大影响。但是，现代货币理论认为浮动汇率下的主权货币政府赤字是可以无限的，前提是要有有效的公共目标预算和保障充分就业的预算，其中特别强调预算问题。因为预算是财政创造货币，所以就要有有效的公共目标预算和保障充分就业的预算。约束政府支出的并不是政府偿付能力，而是其产生的意外影响，比如资源从效率更高的部门流出、

过度保障带来的道德风险等。预算案将会提供一种有效的项目管理和评估机制，确保预算用于公共目的。我们一直想建立财政效绩评估，但是到现在为止，中国并没有建立比较好的财政效绩评估。

对于财政赤字，各国政府都是非常担心的。欧盟成立时定出了3%的赤字率和60%的债务率，但现在来看欧盟的货币政策和财政政策是不搭配的，出现了债务的国家问题就比较严重。2008年时，欧盟没有发欧盟债来帮助南欧四国解决债务问题，2020年疫情期间就发行了7500亿欧元的复苏基金，其中有3900亿欧元是无偿的纾困基金，剩下的是低息贷款。领导人还达成了未来7年1.074万亿欧元的财政预算案，欧盟不得不用财政预算的方式来解决现在面临的经济问题。日本没有外债，都是本地债，所以赤字率和债务率很高的，赤字率基本上在6%，债务率都已经200%多了，但是没有对金融市场产生大的冲击。

对于中国来说，现在财政预算对于赤字是有控制的，政府用3%和60%来约束。我认为这其实是对社会公众的一种约束，3%和60%并不是非要守的自然限制。如果我们非要守这个限制，而不顾科学财政预算对经济积极推动的作用，带来的将是行为扭曲。我们现在公布的债务率是3.6%，但是地方专项债和中央发的特种国债都已经违背了特种国债和专项债的本意。特种国债和专项债要有本金的回收能力和利息的偿付能力，但是地方政府缺的是经常项目的支出，并不是缺建设的钱。发这样的债的后果，或者是钱根本用不出去，或者是变相地用。变相地用就是替代了商业银行的一些贷款，这些专项债的利率确实低于政策性贷款和商业银行贷款，所以起到了一个挤出效应。我们死守3%的赤字率，额外发2万多亿元特别债和地方债，最后就形成了一种扭曲的结果。还不如我们就承认6.1%的赤字率，赤字债该解决什么问题就解决什么问题。现在要"六保"，其实钱是不够的。地方政府现在不缺建设的钱，缺的是日常支出的钱。信用货币制度下的赤字率、债务率对于一个国家来说都不是固定的，要真正地不忘初心，为老百姓把钱花好、把钱用好、把经济搞好。

专题文章二：

# 后疫情时期的科技创新与经济金融变革[①]

**要点**：伴随着疫情期间的宏观"托底"政策、新兴科技创新动力和更为长期的数字化进程，经济结构的内在调整势所必然，由此引发了一系列经济学和经济政策思考。

2020年新冠肺炎疫情是深刻改变全球政治经济格局的大事件，从需求和供给两个维度带来了堪比20世纪30年代大萧条的总量冲击，对人类社会的生产、交流方式以及世界经贸活动产生了前所未有的影响。新冠肺炎疫情冲击更是经济长周期维度上的结构性冲击，将加速催化新知识和新技术在世界范围内的有效运用，使数字化发展成为后疫情时期推动经济复苏、改变交流方式和促进理论发展的重要因素，并将深刻影响国际政治经济关系，成为百年未有之大变局的催化剂。

## 一、原有模式与新兴动力推动后疫情时期经济金融新格局

2020年以来，新冠肺炎疫情"黑天鹅"事件对全球经济社会运行造成剧烈冲击，主要经济体基本都采取了两种必要的应对手段。一是短期政策应对——通过必要的政策工具，管理冲击造成的经济下行和系统性金融风险；二是长期结构调整——在致力于解决或部分解决冲击根源性问题的同时，使类似冲击转化为危机的概率得以降至最低，形成新的生产方式和要素组织模式。过去一个时期的长期结构调整范例，是人们在应对气候变化中致力于化石能源的替代性运用。所以，判断疫情之后的经济和金融运行形势，需要研究短期应对政策的有效性及其成本，以及疫情后的长期结构调整。

短期来看，政策和预期调整有效推动了全球经济触底反弹。疫情使经济运行的供给和需求两侧受到剧烈冲击，但随着财政、货币政策的发力，居民和企业逐步明确了病毒特性，有效调整了预期和投资决策，实现了不同程度的触底反弹。根据国际货币基金组织（IMF）2021年4月的预测，2020年全球经济增长-3.3%，2021年全球经济有望增长6%，较上年10月的预测值分别上调1.1个和0.8个百分点。从实际运行看，美国实际国内生产总值（GDP）于2020年同比萎缩3.5%，2021年第一季度环比折年率出现6.4%的较快增速；欧元区实际GDP于2020年同比萎缩6.6%，2021年第一季度收窄至

---

[①] 作者：陆磊，国家外汇管理局副局长。

同比萎缩 1.8%。中国经济表现最为突出，中国成为 2020 年全球唯一实现正增长的主要经济体，2021 年第一季度 GDP 同比大幅增长 18.3%。然而，经济复苏也存在宏观杠杆率上升和宏观政策空间压缩等成本。继 2008 年之后世界主要经济体再次进入全面量化宽松的时代。2020 年以来，全球 40 多个国家和地区的央行先后降息。其中，美联储实行平均通胀目标制，宣布开放式量化宽松政策扩大货币市场流动性便利规模，不限量按需买入债券和抵押贷款证券（MBS）。各国的一系列政策取向推动全球进入"宽货币、低利率"时期。在金融市场上，由于公开市场金融交易较少受到人员往来影响且受市场预期和情绪的快速影响，主要金融市场都在陡然下行后出现快速反弹。

从历史角度看，大的冲击后往往伴随着人类社会科技进步的加速。700 年前，14 世纪的黑死病在欧洲蔓延后，现代医学、生理学在欧洲发端并取得快速发展，欧洲走向文艺复兴以及后来的工业革命。100 年前，20 世纪初的西班牙大流感的暴发，导致全球死亡人数达到 2000 万～5000 万人，同时催生了病菌学、防疫学、药品研发的迅速发展，推动了物理学、化学与生命医学的深度融合，也催生出后来抗生素的发现、X 射线用于医学诊断等一大批影响人类社会的科技创新，在更好地保护人类健康的同时，也对社会经济活动的繁荣起到了重要的推动作用。此次疫情冲击下的科技创新也一样。截至 2020 年 11 月，处于临床测试阶段的疫苗有 48 种，包括基于脂质纳米颗粒的 mRNA 疫苗、DNA 疫苗、佐剂蛋白疫苗、灭活病毒颗粒疫苗、非复制型病毒载体疫苗等，还存在 164 种处于临床测试阶段的药物。可以预计，病毒及其影响将被控制在社会经济可承受的范围内。因此，经济和金融的逐步恢复得到了传统意义上的政策和新兴科学研究动力的双重加持。

## 二、要素革命：数字化进程是后疫情时期的重大要素转换

后疫情时期是一个怎样的时代？有充分证据显示，数字化进程是不可逆转的时代潮流。

疫情之前，数字经济规模增长迅速，已经占据全球经济四成比例。中国信息通信研究院 2020 年 10 月发布的《全球数字经济新图景（2020 年）》显示，2019 年全球数字经济规模达 31.8 万亿美元，占全球 GDP 比重达 41.5%，同比增长 5.4%，高于同期 GDP 名义增速 3.1 个百分点。2019 年，我国数字经济规模达 35.8 万亿元，占 GDP 比重达 36.2%，同比增长 15.6%，高于同期 GDP 增速 7.9 个百分点。胡润研究院发布的 2020 年胡润全球独角兽榜显示，全球 586 家独角兽企业中，电子商务企业有 89 家，人工智能和金融科技企业有 63 家，软件服务企业有 53 家，共享经济企业有 33 家，健康科技企业有 28 家，大数据企业有 20 家，数字经济相关企业占据了半壁江山。

新冠肺炎疫情在全球蔓延，推动数字经济加速发展。2020 年初暴发的新冠肺炎疫情的，导致社交接触受限，许多企业被迫将业务转到线上，数字化运营成为企业维持业务至关重要的方式。2020 年 9 月《福布斯》报道称，Twilio 咨询公司的调研数据显示，97% 的企业表示新冠肺炎疫情加速了其数字化转型；同时估测，疫情将全球数字化进程

至少提前了5~7年。

越来越多迹象表明,数据已经成为新的生产要素。同传统生产要素一样,数据质和量的提升可以提高数字经济产品的质量和数量,数据成为生产函数的自变量之一。从劳动、土地,到生产性资本,再到数据,人类生产活动中使用的生产要素的接触性和竞争性越来越弱,而生产要素所产生的规模经济、网络效应和范围经济效应却越来越强。例如,数字金融的发展可以推动金融更好地服务实体经济,资产管理和风险管理中基于大数据、人工智能的模型已经在各类金融机构中落地,基于大数据、区块链的先进管理技术也在中国金融监管部门中不断探索完善。

### 三、面向结构调整的理论和政策思考

伴随着疫情期间的宏观"托底"政策、新兴科技创新动力和更为长期的数字化进程,经济结构的自发调整势所必然,由此引发了一系列经济学和经济政策思考。

一是从宏观经济学角度探索货币理论和宏观政策。2021年乃至今后若干年,货币"寻锚"进程仍将持续,实际利率是关键指标。一方面,怎样以及在什么时点实施货币政策正常化,是各国宏观调控当局势必需要认真研究的问题。这里有两种可能:一是就业指标恢复正常推动的政策主动退出;二是债务率高企和系统性金融风险推动的被动出清。另一方面,结合上述的数字化进程分析,当数字化在政府部门、企业部门、金融部门普及达到一定程度后,流动性投放的传导路径可能将会发生改变。例如,货币政策部门可能基于数字化技术实现精准高效的货币投放,解决货币政策传导机制不畅的问题。届时,无限量宽松、金融风险等问题或许将迎刃而解。另一个更具有理论挑战性的问题是货币理论的重塑,比如数字$M_0$的推出与智能合约的结合,有可能导致任何不必要的流动性储备均将趋向于零。那么,早年凯恩斯提出的基于交易动机、投机动机和谨慎动机的货币需求理论就有可能被改写。什么是货币均衡,怎样实现货币均衡等问题,将成为未来研究的重大理论课题。

二是从微观经济学角度研究未来经济金融与数字化的融合发展。从福利经济学的角度看,数字技术创新以及与经济社会活动的深度融合,无论是在私人品层面还是在公共品层面,都可能成为促进社会福利增加的工具。从私人品角度看,人类未来将依托数字技术创新,在能够获得和处理更多信息的基础上,在衣、食、住、行、医疗、养老、储蓄等方面作出更精准的决策;同时,企业也能在获得授权和保护隐私的前提下对个人信息的处理提供定制化服务。数字货币的普及将降低社会经济活动主体的现金储备需求,提高收益性需求,从而实现传统储备现金的收益化。从公共品角度看,政府在合法范围内科学合理应用社会大数据,在宏观调整、货币财政政策决策方面,能够更精准、高效履行提供公共品的职能。如基于社会和经济领域的大数据,实现更加精准地研判宏观经济形势、预测经济拐点、社会突发事件等,辅助决策者科学、前瞻性地制定政策,更加高效、稳健地调控社会、经济运行。从微观经济学出发,需要特别关注数字经济与数字金融的定价问题。比如,差别化定制是否意味着产品的差异;如果产品是同质的,那么

价格差异是属于完全价格歧视还是因信息带来成本降低进而导致供给曲线向左方平移？前者意味着消费者剩余的消失，后者则意味着福利。这也是一个需要研究的学术问题。

三是从规制的角度研究数据生态中存在的问题。大型平台公司的垄断式发展、大数据"杀熟"、个人隐私泄露等问题，需要监管和立法部门紧跟形势变化，不断完善体制机制建设和法律制度框架。要加大对垄断行为的处罚力度，通过立法加强数据信息保护，完善金融科技监管框架，防止监管套利和风险交叉传染。当前经济社会的数字化进程仍面临诸多共同挑战，有理由期待数字规制理论和实践的伟大创新。

# 下 篇

## 2020年度中国金融政策动态

# 宏观金融政策

## 一、货币政策[①]

2020年新冠肺炎疫情对全球经济造成了巨大冲击，各国均实施大幅的降息和多种非常规货币政策来纾困经济和维护金融市场稳定。中国人民银行也实施了降准、下调公开市场操作等政策工具，推出了多项抗疫信贷政策，包括再贷款、再贴现和创新的直达实体经济的货币政策。总体而言，人民银行在保留货币政策空间的基础上，发挥了货币政策灵活精准的滴灌作用，对于下半年我国经济的强劲复苏起了重要作用。2021年全球经济复苏速度仍然面临高度不确定性，大国的货币政策和财政政策可能对我国产生溢出效应，因此2021年的货币政策制定面临更为错综复杂的内外部环境。

（一）2020年货币政策的主要内容

1. 公开市场操作

（1）公开市场操作

2020年3月30日，人民银行将公开市场操作7天逆回购利率从2.40%下调至2.20%，随后全年维持不变。截至2020年末，人民银行累计开展逆回购操作15.04万亿元，较2019年翻倍。其中，7天期操作累计11.59万亿元，是2019年（5.21万亿元）的两倍。

（2）央行票据互换工具（CBS）

2020年以来，人民银行共开展12期CBS操作，以每月一次的频率稳定开展。累计操作量610亿元，四个季度分别操作了160亿元、150亿元、150亿元和150亿元。期限均为3个月，费率均为0.10%。CBS操作对于提升银行永续债的二级市场流动性、支持银行特别是中小银行发行永续债补充资本发挥了积极作用，有助于增强金融服务实体经济的能力。

2. 中期借贷便利（MLF）和常备借贷便利（SLF）

（1）中期借贷便利（MLF）

2020年2月17日，人民银行将中期借贷便利1年期利率从3.25%下调了10个基点

---

[①] 作者：何晓贝，清华大学国家金融研究院金融与发展研究中心宏观金融负责人、《中国金融政策报告》项目（课题组）研究员。沈奕，清华大学国家金融研究院金融与发展研究中心研究人员。

至3.15%，4月15日又下调20个基点至2.95%。2020年，人民银行累计开展中期借贷便利操作5.15万亿元，均为1年期，投放量较2019年增长约40%，期末余额为5.15万亿元，比年初增加1.46万亿元。

（2）常备借贷便利（SLF）

2020年4月10日，人民银行下调SLF各期限利率30个基点，隔夜、7天、1个月利率分别降至3.05%、3.20%、3.55%。其中第一季度累计操作1027亿元，全年累计开展常备借贷便利操作共1862亿元，期末余额为198亿元。

3. 存款准备金率和超额存款准备金利率

（1）存款准备金率

2020年全年中国人民银行共三次降低存款准备金率，分别为一次全面降准、一次普惠定向降准和一次定向降准。具体而言，2020年1月6日，人民银行下调金融机构（不含财务公司、金融租赁公司和汽车金融公司）存款准备金率0.5个百分点，释放长期资金8000多亿元。2020年3月6日，人民银行实施普惠金融定向降准，根据机构在2019年度考核达标情况，相应给予0.5个或1.5个百分点的降准优惠，释放长期资金4000亿元，额外释放1500亿元用于发放普惠金融贷款。2020年4月3日，人民银行宣布下调农村信用社、农村商业银行、农村合作银行、村镇银行和仅在本省级行政区域内经营的城市商业银行的存款准备金率1个百分点，分别于4月15日和5月15日依次下调0.5个百分点，共释放长期资金约4000亿元。三次降低存款准备金率释放了1.75万亿元长期资金。

（2）超额存款准备金利率

超额存款准备金利率作为利率走廊的下限，从2008年11月以来一直维持在0.72%。2020年第一季度人民银行释放流动性后，存款类机构质押式回购利率（DR007）在3月一度下降到1.13%。为了打开市场利率下行的空间、鼓励银行投放贷款和减少超额存款准备金，2020年4月7日起人民银行将金融机构在人民银行的超额存款准备金利率从0.72%下调至0.35%。这是自2008年金融危机以来的首次下调。

4. 对冲新冠疫情影响的货币信贷政策

（1）再贷款再贴现

为支持抗疫保供，人民银行于2020年1月31日春节期间安排3000亿元专项再贷款定向支持疫情防控重点领域和重点企业；2月26日，新增再贷款再贴现额度5000亿元用于支持企业有序复工复产，并下调支农、支小再贷款利率0.25个百分点至2.5%；4月20日，再次新增再贷款再贴现额度1万亿元用于支持经济恢复发展。共计发放再贷款1.8万亿元。

截至2020年6月末，3000亿元专项再贷款基本发放完毕，支持有关银行向7597家全国性和地方性重点企业累计发放优惠贷款2834亿元，加权平均利率为2.49%，财政贴息50%后，企业实际融资利率约为1.25%；5000亿元再贷款、再贴现发放完毕，支持地方法人银行向59万家企业累计发放优惠利率贷款4983亿元，加权平均利率为

4.22%。截至2020年12月末，1万亿元普惠性再贷款、再贴现全部发放完毕，引导地方法人银行支持了158万家企业，加权平均利率为4.67%。

此外，针对疫情防控和复工复产的特殊信贷政策还包括贷款临时延期。3月1日，银保监会与人民银行等五部门联合印发《关于对中小微企业贷款实施临时性延期还本付息的通知》，鼓励遇到困难的中小微企业申请临时性延期还本付息。

（2）直达实体经济的货币政策工具

为了支持中小企业发展，2020年6月1日，人民银行创设两个直达实体经济的货币政策工具：普惠小微企业贷款延期支持工具和普惠小微企业信用贷款支持计划。这两项创新的货币政策工具完善了结构性货币政策工具体系，增强了对稳企业、保就业的金融支持力度。

普惠小微企业贷款延期支持工具提供400亿元资金，以通过特定目的工具（SPV）与地方法人银行签订利率互换协议的方式，向地方法人银行提供激励，激励资金约为地方法人银行延期贷款本金的1%。截至2020年末，全国银行业金融机构共对7.3万亿元贷款本息实施延期。普惠小微企业贷款延期支持工具按月操作，支持其6—12月对普惠小微企业贷款延期本金共计8737亿元，加权平均延期期限为12.8个月，减轻了小微企业阶段性还本付息压力。

为缓解小微企业缺乏抵质押担保的难点痛点，人民银行创设普惠小微企业信用贷款支持计划，提供4000亿元资金，通过SPV与地方法人银行签订信用贷款支持计划合同，向地方法人银行提供优惠资金支持。普惠小微企业信用贷款支持计划按季操作，支持其3—12月发放小微企业信用贷款共计4808亿元，有效缓解了小微企业融资难问题。2020年，银行业金融机构累计发放普惠小微信用贷款3.9万亿元，比上年多发放1.6万亿元。

5. 结构性货币政策

（1）抵押补充贷款（PSL）

2020年人民银行发放抵押补充贷款共202亿元，同比减少92%。截至2020年末，PSL期末余额为32350亿元，同比减少3224亿元。上半年，人民银行对政策性银行和开发性银行净收回抵押补充贷款共283亿元，其中第二季度净收回485亿元。

（2）定向中期借贷便利（TMLF）

2019年人民银行首次开展TMLF操作，目标是通过市场化的方式激励银行增加对民营、小微企业的信贷投放，降低民营、小微企业融资成本。2020年1月和4月，人民银行分别开展定向中期借贷便利操作，金额分别为2405亿元和561亿元，期限均为1年，利率为2.95%。TMLF年末余额为2966亿元。全年累计到期TMLF共5260亿元，其中4000亿元以中期借贷便利的形式续作。

（3）普惠金融

2020年是我国全面脱贫完成建设小康社会目标的一年。人民银行以"精准脱贫"为目标，积极运用扶贫再贷款、支农再贷款、支小再贷款、再贴现和抵押补充贷款等工具，引导金融机构加大对小微、民营企业、"三农"、扶贫等国民经济重点领域和薄弱环节的支持力度。

自2020年7月1日起，下调支农再贷款、支小再贷款、再贴现利率25个基点。调整后，3个月、6个月、1年期支农再贷款、支小再贷款利率分别为1.95%、2.15%和2.25%，再贴现利率为2%。2020年四个季度分别发放专项扶贫再贷款63亿元、80亿元、72亿元、79亿元，年末专项扶贫再贷款余额为370亿元。2020年末，全国支农再贷款余额为4572亿元，支小再贷款余额为9756亿元，扶贫再贷款余额为2153亿元，再贴现余额为5784亿元。

2020年的政府工作报告提出，"大型商业银行普惠型小微企业贷款增速要高于40%"。截至2020年底，普惠小微贷款余额为15.1万亿元，同比增长30.3%，较2019年末提高7.2个百分点；支持小微经营主体3228万户，同比增长19.4%。2020年，普惠小微贷款增加3.5万亿元，同比多增1.4万亿元。

6. 利率市场化改革

2020年以来，人民银行持续推进贷款市场报价利率（LPR）改革。自2020年1月1日起新发放贷款不再参考贷款基准利率定价。2020年3月至8月，按照市场化、法治化原则顺利完成存量浮动利率贷款定价基准转换。截至8月末，存量贷款定价基准转换率达92.4%。银行将LPR嵌入内部转移定价（FTP）体系，是打破贷款基准利率的隐性下限，推动银行实施市场化的利率定价的关键步骤。

LPR有效实现了利率的传导。2020年2月17日人民银行下调MLF利率10个基点，2月20日发布的1年期、5年期以上LPR则分别下调5个基点至4.05%和3.75%。4月15日1年期MLF下调20个基点，4月20日1年期和5年期的LPR报价分别再降20个基点和10个基点至3.85%和4.65%。

7. 货币市场和信贷市场利率

（1）货币市场利率

2020年货币市场利率全年走势呈U形。随着第一季度和第二季度的政策利率下调和降准措施，市场流动性逐渐宽裕，第二季度货币市场利率达到全年的最低位。随着更多直达实体经济的货币政策出台，人民银行在下半年没有再降息降准，因此第三、第四季度货币市场利率稳步回升。银行间市场存款类机构7天期质押回购利率（DR007）四个季度均值分别为2.11%、1.66%、2.15%、2.16%。7天质押式回购利率（R007）四个季度均值分别为2.49%、1.86%、2.50%、2.84%。R007在12月底达到4.0%左右。上海银行间市场同业拆放隔夜利率（Shibor）四个季度均值分别为1.60%、1.33%、1.82%、1.60%。

（2）贷款加权平均利率

货币政策有效传导到了实体经济。2019年第四季度贷款加权平均利率为5.44%，2020年第一季度已经下降到5.08%，全年保持相对稳定，第四季度为5.03%，创2009年以来的新低。2020年末较2019年末贷款加权平均利率下降了53个基点。

### 8. 人民银行数字货币

数字化人民币稳步推进。2016 年人民银行明确了发行数字货币的战略目标，启动了基于区块链和数字货币的数字票据交易平台原型研发工作。2017 年人民银行成立数字货币研究所。2020 年人民银行启动在深圳、苏州、雄安、成都以及冬奥会场景等地进行封闭测试。

（二）货币政策和宏观审慎政策在防范金融风险方面的操作

2020 年 10 月 23 日，中国人民银行就《中华人民共和国中国人民银行法（修订草案征求意见稿）》公开征求意见。本次修订是该法自 2003 年以来时隔 17 年的首次立法工作。本次修订填补了宏观审慎政策的制度空白，从法律上确立了"货币政策和宏观审慎政策双支柱调控框架"，明确了人民银行制定和执行宏观审慎政策的职责定位。

### 1. 宏观审慎评估（MPA）

2020 年以来，宏观审慎评估（MPA）继续发挥在优化信贷结构和促进金融供给侧结构性改革中的作用。一是进一步提高了小微、民营企业融资和制造业融资的考核权重，设立"再贷款运用"临时性考核指标，引导金融机构加大对国民经济重点领域和薄弱环节的支持，确保新增融资重点流向制造业、中小微企业。二是完善 LPR 运用相关考核。自 8 月 20 日起，不再统计贷款利率参照基准利率浮动情况，改为统计在 LPR 基础上加减点的情况。释放 LPR 改革降低贷款利率的潜能，推动银行加快存量浮动利率贷款定价基准转换工作，推动企业综合融资成本明显下降。

### 2. 房地产贷款集中度管理

为了防范房价过快上涨造成的系统性金融风险，2020 年 12 月 31 日，中国人民银行和中国银保监会联合发布《关于建立银行业金融机构房地产贷款集中度管理制度的通知》，该通知旨在控制房地产贷款的占比。通知将国有大型银行的房地产贷款占比上限设为 40%，中型银行、小型银行和非县城农合机构、县城农合机构、村镇银行分别为 27.5%、22.5%、17.5% 和 12.5%，并设立了 2 年以上的过渡期。

### 3. 建立逆周期资本缓冲机制

为了增强银行在经济周期波动中的抗风险能力，2020 年 9 月中国人民银行、中国银保监会联合发布《关于建立逆周期资本缓冲机制的通知》（银发〔2020〕233 号），明确建立逆周期资本缓冲机制，同时设置银行业金融机构初始逆周期资本缓冲比率为零。未来，中国人民银行、银保监会将综合考虑宏观经济金融形势、宏观杠杆率水平、银行体系稳健性及系统性金融风险表现等因素适时评估和调整逆周期资本缓冲比率。

### 4. 推动金融控股公司规范发展

为了防范企业向金融业盲目扩张进而累积风险，2020 年 9 月，国务院公布《关于实施金融控股公司准入管理的决定》（国发〔2020〕12 号，以下简称《准入决定》），中国人民银行公布《金融控股公司监督管理试行办法》（中国人民银行令〔2020〕第 4 号，以下简称《金控办法》），以并表为基础，按照全面、持续、穿透的原则，对非金融企业投资控股形成的金融控股公司依法准入并实施监管，规范金融控股公司的经营行为。《准入决定》和《金控办法》的实施,继续坚持金融业总体分业经营为主的原则,有利于金融控股公司持续健康发展,防范风险交叉传染,进一步促进经济金融良性循环。

5. 调整跨境融资宏观审慎管理

2020年3月12日,为进一步扩大利用外资,便利境内机构跨境融资,降低实体经济融资成本,根据当前宏观经济和国际收支状况,中国人民银行、国家外汇管理局决定将《中国人民银行关于全口径跨境融资宏观审慎管理有关事宜的通知》(银发〔2017〕9号)中的宏观审慎调节参数由1上调至1.25,有利于境内机构扩大跨境融资规模。

随着下半年人民币的升值,企业外币融资迅速增长,外债余额同步增加。为防范风险,12月14日,中国人民银行、国家外汇管理局决定将金融机构的跨境融资宏观审慎调节参数从1.25下调至1。

(三) 汇率和金融市场改革

1. 汇率形成机制

2020年美国和其他发达国家推出史无前例的货币宽松政策,而中国维持在常规货币政策区间,人民币兑美元汇率由年中7.1的低点逐步升值到年末的6.5。全年人民币汇率弹性增强,市场预期平稳,跨境资本流动有序,外汇市场运行保持稳定。为此,中国人民银行决定自2020年10月12日起,将远期售汇业务的外汇风险准备金率从20%下调为0,保持人民币汇率在合理均衡水平上的基本稳定。

2. 离岸人民币市场

2020年,人民银行继续在香港常态化发行央行票据。全年共发行12期计1550亿元人民币央行票据。四个季度分别发行400亿元、400亿元、400亿元和350亿元,各自包含3个月期、6个月期和1年期这三个品种。在港常态化发行人民币央行票据有利于丰富离岸市场中人民币产品,提升人民币离岸市场活跃度,推动人民币国际化的发展。2020年,除香港人民币央行票据以外的离岸人民币债券发行量超过1300亿元,比2019年增长30%。

3. 货币互换协议

2020年,人民银行先后与13个国家和地区(分别为埃及、老挝、瑞士、巴基斯坦、智利、蒙古国、阿根廷、新西兰、匈牙利、韩国、冰岛、俄罗斯和中国香港)签署了双边本币互换协议,并与其中4个国家和地区(巴基斯坦、智利、韩国和中国香港)扩大了互换规模。

(四) 2020年货币政策执行效果及评价

2020年爆发的新冠疫情,使全球陷入重大公共卫生和经济危机。全球主要经济体纷纷启动大规模的纾困措施,美联储一次性下调150个基点的利率,并启动了多项紧急流动性支持措施以稳定金融市场。

面对复杂的国内外经济形势和疫情反复的不确定性,我国的货币政策在保留正常货币政策空间的同时稳步发力。除了推出多项抗疫信贷政策和创新的货币政策,人民银行全年下调公开市场操作7天逆回购利率20个基点和MLF利率30个基点，整体引导市场利率下降。截至2020年12月底，一般贷款加权平均利率较2019年底下降40个基点至5.03%，创10年以来最低。

货币政策的调整有效传导到了实体经济。2020年全年新增社会融资规模34.86万亿元，同比上升13.3%，比上年多增9.28万亿元。其中，2020年3月社融规模达到51.84亿元，创单月历史新高。新增人民币贷款全年增长20.03万亿元，同比多增3.15万亿元。2020年广义货币供应量（$M_2$）余额为218.68万亿元，全年平均同比增速为10.33%。

在信贷规模增长的同时，信贷结构持续优化，制造业中长期贷款和小微企业贷款较快增长。2020年末，企（事）业单位贷款比年初增加12.2万亿元，同比多增2.7万亿元；制造业中长期贷款增速为35.2%，增速连续14个月上升；普惠小微贷款余额同比增长30.3%。

人民银行应对疫情影响的积极措施取得了十分有效的成果。2020年第一季度的GDP增长为-6.8%，随后便逐步回升，全年达到2.3%，明显高于市场预期。我国成为全球主要经济体中唯一一个正增长的经济体。2020年通胀很大程度上受到猪肉价格上涨的影响，但全年仍然保持在了温和的区间。消费者物价指数（CPI）在2020年初达到顶峰后逐渐回落，全年同比上涨2.51%。在国际金融市场波动增大的环境下，人民币汇率在合理均衡水平上保持稳定，汇率弹性有所增强，发挥了平衡内外部经济的自动稳定器的作用。2020年末中国外汇交易中心（CFETS）人民币汇率指数报94.84，较上年末升值3.78%。

（五）2021年货币政策展望

2021年全球经济的复苏前景很大程度上取决于新冠疫苗的生产和推广使用速度。主要发达国家都推出了史无前例的货币和财政刺激政策，随着隔离政策的逐步解除，消费和投资的回升很可能带动发达国家的通胀上升。美联储宣布采用平均目标通胀制，意味着美联储将允许通胀超过目标通胀率一段时期而不收紧货币政策。然而大国的货币财政政策将对中国产生一定的外溢效应，需要防范资本大规模流动带来的金融风险。而更有弹性的汇率将有助于吸收外部冲击。

后疫情时期国内的金融风险也在累积。2020年的抗疫信贷政策使得我国宏观杠杆率（实体经济债务占GDP比重）从2019年底的246%上升到2020年第三季度的271%，上升25个百分点，是2010年以来最快的上升幅度。随着第四季度经济加速复苏，2020年底宏观杠杆率保持稳定并小幅下降到270%。

展望2021年，只要我国经济维持稳定增长，"稳杠杆"的目标比较容易实现，并不意味着需要货币政策的明显转向。因此预计2021年货币政策不会"急转弯"。由于基数的原因，2021年的名义GDP增速会显著高于正常水平，因此$M_2$和社会融资规模的增速与"潜在"增速相匹配将更有助于维持稳健的货币政策。

2021年利率市场化改革也将不断深化。抗疫期间人民银行推出了多项创新的货币政策，但人民银行仍不遗余力地推动货币政策框架从数量型向价格型的转型。例如，人民银行明确表示,"首先要看政策利率是否发生变化,主要是央行公开市场7天期逆回购操作利率是否变化,而不应过度关注公开市场操作数量"。同时,存款基准利率将继续发挥整个利率体系"压舱石"的作用,人民银行通过加强存款利率自律管理,压降不规范存款创新产品,维护存款市场竞争秩序。

2020年习近平总书记宣布我国将在2060年实现"碳中和"目标。在此背景下,未来一段时期人民银行的重点任务之一是完善绿色金融政策框架,建立激励约束机制,用结构性货币政策工具引导金融机构按照市场化原则支持绿色低碳发展。

## 附表

**2020年中国货币政策大事记**

| 日期 | 内容 |
| --- | --- |
| 1月6日 | 中国人民银行下调金融机构存款准备金率0.5个百分点(不含财务公司、金融租赁公司和汽车金融公司) |
| | 中国人民银行与老挝人民民主共和国银行签署双边本币合作协议,允许在两国已经放开的所有经常和资本项下交易中直接使用双方本币结算 |
| 1月31日 | 中国人民银行发布《关于发放专项再贷款支持防控新型冠状病毒感染的肺炎疫情有关事项的通知》(银发〔2020〕28号),向主要全国性银行和湖北等10个重点省(市)的部分地方法人银行提供总计3000亿元低成本专项再贷款资金,支持抗疫保供 |
| 2月10日 | 中国人民银行与埃及中央银行续签规模为180亿元人民币/410亿埃及镑的双边本币互换协议 |
| 2月26日 | 中国人民银行发布《关于加大再贷款、再贴现支持力度促进有序复工复产的通知》(银发〔2020〕53号),增加再贷款再贴现专用额度5000亿元,同时,下调支农、支小再贷款利率25个基点至2.5%,为企业有序复工复产提供低成本、普惠性的资金支持 |
| 3月16日 | 中国人民银行实施普惠金融定向降准,对普惠金融领域贷款占比考核达标银行给予0.5个或1.5个百分点的存款准备金率优惠,并对此次考核中得到0.5个百分点存款准备金率优惠的股份制商业银行额外降准1个百分点 |
| 4月3日 | 中国人民银行决定下调农村信用社、农村商业银行、农村合作银行、村镇银行和仅在本省级行政区域内经营的城市商业银行存款准备金率1个百分点,分4月15日和5月15日两次实施。中国人民银行决定自4月7日起将金融机构在人民银行的超额存款准备金利率从0.72%下调至0.35% |
| 5月20日 | 中国人民银行与老挝中央银行签署规模为60亿元人民币/7.6万亿老挝基普的双边本币互换协议 |
| 6月1日 | 中国人民银行发布《关于普惠小微企业贷款延期支持工具有关事宜的通知》(银发〔2020〕124号),创设普惠小微企业贷款延期支持工具 |
| | 中国人民银行发布《关于普惠小微企业信用贷款支持计划有关事宜的通知》(银发〔2020〕125号),创设普惠小微企业信用贷款支持计划 |
| 6月29日 | 中国人民银行决定,从2020年7月1日起下调再贷款、再贴现利率。其中,下调支农再贷款、支小再贷款利率0.25个百分点。调整后,3个月、6个月和1年期支农再贷款、支小再贷款利率分别为1.95%、2.15%和2.25%。下调再贴现利率0.25个百分点至2%。下调金融稳定再贷款利率0.5个百分点。调整后,金融稳定再贷款利率为1.75%,金融稳定再贷款(延期期间)利率为3.77% |
| 7月31日 | 中国人民银行和巴基斯坦中央银行签署双边本币互换修订协议,将互换规模扩大为300亿元人民币/7200亿巴基斯坦卢比 |

续表

| 日期 | 内容 |
|---|---|
| 7月31日 | 中国人民银行和智利中央银行签署双边本币互换修订协议,将互换规模扩大为500亿元人民币/56000亿智利比索 |
| | 中国人民银行和蒙古国中央银行续签规模为150亿元人民币/6万亿蒙古图格里克的双边本币互换协议 |
| 8月6日 | 中国人民银行和阿根廷中央银行续签规模为700亿元人民币/7300亿阿根廷比索的双边本币互换协议,同时签署规模为600亿元人民币的双边本币互换补充协议 |
| 8月22日 | 中国人民银行和新西兰中央银行续签规模为250亿元人民币的双边本币互换协议 |
| 9月13日 | 中国人民银行公布《金融控股公司监督管理试行办法》(中国人民银行令〔2020〕第4号) |
| 9月17日 | 中国人民银行和匈牙利中央银行签署规模为400亿元人民币的双边本币互换补充协议 |
| 9月25日 | 中国证监会、中国人民银行、国家外汇管理局联合发布《合格境外机构投资者和人民币合格境外机构投资者境内证券期货投资管理办法》(中国证监会 中国人民银行 国家外汇管理局令第176号) |
| 9月30日 | 中国人民银行、中国银保监会联合发布《关于建立逆周期资本缓冲机制的通知》(银发〔2020〕233号) |
| | 中国人民银行与印度尼西亚银行签署《关于建立促进经常账户交易和直接投资本币结算合作框架的谅解备忘录》,推动使用本币进行双边贸易和直接投资结算 |
| | 中国人民银行、中国银保监会联合发布《关于建立逆周期资本缓冲机制的通知》(银发〔2020〕233号) |
| 10月10日 | 中国人民银行决定自2020年10月12日起,将远期售汇业务的外汇风险准备金率从20%下调为0 |
| 10月11日 | 中国人民银行和韩国中央银行签署双边本币互换展期与修订协议,将互换规模扩大为4000亿元人民币/70万亿韩元 |
| 10月19日 | 中国人民银行和冰岛中央银行续签规模为35亿元人民币/700亿冰岛克朗的双边本币互换协议 |
| 10月27日 | 部分人民币对美元中间价报价行基于自身对经济基本面和市场情况的判断,陆续主动将人民币对美元中间价报价模型中的逆周期因子淡出使用 |
| 11月23日 | 中国人民银行和俄罗斯中央银行续签规模为1500亿元人民币/17500亿卢布的双边本币互换协议 |
| | 中国人民银行和香港金融管理局签署双边本币互换修订协议,将互换规模扩大为5000亿元人民币/5900亿港元 |
| 12月3日 | 中国人民银行、中国银保监会联合发布《系统重要性银行评估办法》(银发〔2020〕289号),建立了我国系统重要性银行的评估框架 |
| 12月11日 | 为进一步完善全口径跨境融资宏观审慎管理,引导金融机构市场化调节外汇资产负债结构,中国人民银行、国家外汇管理局决定将金融机构的跨境融资宏观审慎调节参数从1.25下调至1 |
| 12月31日 | 中国人民银行、中国银保监会联合发布《关于建立银行业金融机构房地产贷款集中度管理制度的通知》(银发〔2020〕322号) |
| | 中国人民银行会同银保监会、财政部、国家发展改革委、工业和信息化部印发《关于继续实施普惠小微企业贷款延期还本付息政策和普惠小微企业信用贷款支持政策有关事宜的通知》(银发〔2020〕324号),将普惠小微企业贷款延期还本付息政策和普惠小微企业信用贷款支持政策的实施期限延长至2021年3月31日 |
| | 中国人民银行决定,从2021年1月1日起,信用卡透支利率由发卡机构与持卡人自主协商确定,取消信用卡透支利率上限和下限管理 |

资料来源:http://www.pbc.gov.cn/zhengcehuobisi/125207/125227/125963/4190884/index.html。

专栏 1

## 强化宏观审慎监管　着力金融治理现代化①

2020年10月23日，中国人民银行公布《中华人民共和国中国人民银行法（修订草案征求意见稿）》，此前10月16日已公布了《中华人民共和国商业银行法（修改建议稿）》。"两法"新修稿面向社会公开征求意见，为期一个月。基于中国的有益做法与国际的良好经验，此次修法，强化了宏观金融审慎监管和系统性金融风险防范，明确了金融体系的定位是"服务实体经济"，突出了中国人民银行在维护国家金融稳定和防范系统性金融风险工作中的职权与责任，彰显了中国金融治理的法治化思维、现代化决心与全球化态度。

改革开放以来，中华人民共和国成立后的第一部金融大法是1995年3月颁布实施的《中国人民银行法》，本次修订是继2003年修订17年来首次大修。而1995年颁布实施的《中华人民共和国商业银行法》，已经于2003年和2015年两次修改，2020年建议稿是第三次修改。需要特别说明的是，此次两法新修，《中国人民银行法》是"修订"，属于"全面性""原则性"修正，着力健全金融法治顶层设计；《商业银行法》是"修改"，属于"创新性"调整和"实践性"补充，着力增强资本约束能力、公司治理能力与金融服务实体经济能力。

《中国人民银行法（修订草案征求意见稿）》共9章73条。本次修订，一是明确了中国人民银行制定和执行宏观审慎政策的职责，明确了金融体系的定位是"服务实体经济"。二是增加了中国人民银行的职权，从13项拓宽到19项，包括制定和执行宏观审慎政策、拟订金融业重大法律法规草案、组织实施国家金融安全审查等。三是构建货币政策和宏观审慎政策双支柱调控框架。以加强逆周期调节和穿透式监管为重点，健全宏观审慎政策工具箱。四是明确"三个统筹"，即统筹系统重要性金融机构监管，统筹金融控股公司监管和统筹重要金融基础设施监管。五是强化维护金融稳定和处置系统性金融风险职责。六是完善人民币管理规定。正名数字货币，警惕虚拟货币风险。七是完善中央银行治理与监督制度，包括不向地方政府提供贷款、财务预算制度保持公开透明等。八是健全人民银行的履职手段，加大对金融违法行为的处罚力度。

《商业银行法（修改建议稿）》共11章127条。新增加了两章共32条，整合后新设或充实了4个章节，分别涵盖公司治理、资本与风险管理、客户权益保护、风险处置与市场退出。本次修改的重点和意图，一是完善商业银行类别。明确村镇银行法律地位，为未来出现的新型商业银行预留法律空间。二是建立分类准入和差异化监管机制。完善商业银行市场准入条件，强化股东监管。三是基于中国的有益做法与国际的良好经验，完善商业银行公司治理。四是强化资本管理。落实《巴塞尔协议Ⅲ》资本监管要求，确立资本约束原则，明确宏观审慎管理与风险监管要求。五是完善业务范围与经营规则，突出金融服务实体经济。明确区域性商业银行的本地化经营要求，回归本源。六是加强

---

① 作者：马强，上海市银行同业公会常务副会长、《中国金融政策报告》项目（课题组）高级研究员。

行为管理，规范客户权益保护。新设一章，专门对商业银行营销、信息披露、风险分级与适当性管理、个人信息保护、收费管理等客户保护规范作出具体规定。七是健全风险处置与市场退出机制。参考国际准则，总结我国银行业处置经验，建立风险评级和预警、早期纠正、重组、接管、破产等有序处置和退出机制，规范处置程序，严格处置条件，完善职能分工。八是加大违法处罚力度。

修订《中国人民银行法》作为深化金融供给侧改革的国家战略部署，旨在健全完善现代中央银行制度、强化宏观审慎管理和系统性金融风险防范，加强中国人民银行的职权与职责。商业银行是现阶段我国金融体系的关键性主体。修订《商业银行法》，充分审视了近年来银行业的多元化、专业化、国际化发展趋势，体现了差异化风险监管的政策取向。

## 二、汇率与国际收支相关政策[①]

2020年是极不平凡的一年，面对新冠肺炎疫情的严重冲击和错综复杂的国际形势，中国人民银行和国家外汇管理局坚决贯彻落实党中央、国务院决策部署，在积极落实疫情防控要求的同时，更加突出服务实体经济、推进改革开放和防范化解风险，全力做好"六稳""六保"工作，维护了外汇市场平稳运行和国际收支基本平衡。

（一）2020年人民币汇率及我国国际收支情况概述

1. 人民币对一篮子货币汇率小幅升值，名义和实际有效汇率均有所升值

2020年末，中国外汇交易中心（CFETS）人民币汇率指数报94.84，较上年末升值3.78%；参考特别提款权（SDR）货币篮子的人民币汇率指数报94.23，较上年末升值2.64%；参考国际清算银行（BIS）货币篮子的人民币汇率指数报98.68，较上年末升值3.78%。

根据国际清算银行的测算，2019年末至2020年末，人民币名义和实际有效汇率分别升值4.05%和3.33%。2005年人民币汇率形成机制改革以来至2020年末，人民币名义有效汇率升值37.67%，实际有效汇率升值51.32%。

2. 人民币对美元汇率先贬后升，弹性进一步增强

2020年人民币对美元汇率呈现先贬后升的走势，全年在岸和离岸人民币即期汇率分别收于6.5398元/美元和6.5030元/美元，较上年分别升值6.62%和7.05%。全年在岸人民币即期汇率最高价与最低价相差6617个基点，振幅高达9.67%，较上年提高2.21个百分点，低于同期日元对美元和欧元对美元分别为10.19%和14.61%的振幅。2020年，人民币对美元汇率年化波动率为4.5%，略高于上年度的4.0%。

2020年初，人民币对美元汇率延续上年第四季度以来的走势，一度升值至6.85元/美元附近。此后，在新冠疫情迅速蔓延以及国际外汇市场美元汇率上涨的双重压力下，人民币汇率开始走弱并再度破"7"。5月27日，在岸市场人民币即期汇率一度跌至7.1765元/美元的

---

[①] 作者：赵庆明，北京金融衍生品研究院原副院长。

年内最低点。此后，随着中国经济加快恢复以及国际市场上美元汇率走低，人民币对美元汇率重新回到7以内，并持续升值。到2020年底，人民币对美元汇率升至6.52元/美元附近，为过去两年半的最高水平。

2020年，人民币对美元汇率中间价最高为6.5236元，最低为7.1316元，243个交易日中140个交易日升值、103个交易日贬值。最大单日升值幅度为1.00%（670点），最大单日贬值幅度为0.76%（530点）。2020年末，人民币对美元汇率中间价较2019年末升值6.92%。2005年人民币汇率形成机制改革以来至2020年末，人民币对美元汇率中间价累计升值26.84%。

3. 人民币对其他国际主要货币汇率走势分化

2020年末，人民币对欧元、英镑、日元汇率中间价分别为1欧元兑8.0250元人民币、1英镑兑8.8903元人民币、100日元兑6.3236元人民币，分别较2019年末贬值2.61%、升值2.92%和升值1.34%。

2005年人民币汇率形成机制改革以来至2020年末，人民币对欧元汇率累计升值24.79%，对日元汇率累计升值15.53%。

4. 国际收支继续保持较好自主平衡，外债规模保持平稳增长

2020年，我国经常账户顺差2989亿美元，与同期国内生产总值（GDP）的比例为2.0%，上年这一比例为1.2%。其中，货物贸易顺差5338亿美元，比上年增加1085亿美元；服务贸易逆差1453亿美元，比上年收窄1158亿美元。服务贸易逆差大幅收窄，主要是受疫情影响跨境出行受限，旅行收支逆差出现大幅萎缩。据统计，2020年，旅行逆差1162亿美元，比上年收窄1026亿美元。资本和金融账户中，直接投资顺差1034亿美元，储备资产增加280亿美元。

2020年末，外汇储备余额为32165.22亿美元，比上年末增加1085.98亿美元。

外债规模继续保持平稳增长，外债风险总体可控。截至2020年12月末，我国全口径外债余额为24008亿美元，比2019年末增加3435亿美元。其中，短期外债余额为13164亿美元，比上年末增加1109亿美元，占外债余额的55%，较2019年末回落2个百分点。

5. 跨境人民币业务快速增长，在香港发行人民币央行票据常态化

2020年，跨境人民币收付金额合计28.4万亿元，同比增长44%，增速比上年度加快21个百分点。其中，实收14.1万亿元，实付14.3万亿元，净流出0.2万亿元，上年度是净流入0.3万亿元；收付比为1:1.01，上年度为1:0.97，流出流入更加均衡。经常项目跨境人民币收付金额合计6.8万亿元，同比增长13%，其中，货物贸易收付金额4.8万亿元，服务贸易及其他经常项目收付金额2万亿元。资本项目人民币收付金额合计21.6万亿元，同比增长59%。

2020年，中国人民银行总共在港发行12期共计1550亿元人民币央行票据，发行期数与上年相同，发行金额比上年增加50亿元。在香港常态化发行人民币央行票据，不仅丰富了香港市场人民币投资产品和流动性管理工具，而且带动了境内外市场主体在离岸市场发行人民币债券及开展人民币业务创新，对提升人民币离岸市场活跃度和促进离

岸人民币市场持续健康发展均具有积极作用。据统计，2020年，除香港人民币央行票据以外的离岸人民币债券发行量超过1300亿元，比2019年增加30%。中银香港于2021年1月27日启动香港人民币央行票据回购做市机制，这将提高香港人民币央行票据二级市场流动性。

6. 外汇市场交易量同比小幅增长，交易主体持续扩展

2020年，银行间外汇市场人民币直接交易成交较为活跃，流动性平稳，降低了微观经济主体的汇兑成本，促进了双边贸易和投资。2020年，人民币外汇即期交易累计成交金额折合8.4万亿美元，同比增长5.6%；人民币外汇掉期交易累计成交金额折合16.3万亿美元，同比减少0.2%，其中隔夜美元掉期交易累计成交金额9.5万亿美元，占总成交金额的58.3%；人民币外汇远期交易累计成交金额折合1044亿美元，同比增长37.4%。"外币对"累计成交金额折合8109亿美元，同比增长70.5%，其中成交最多的产品为欧元对美元，市场占比为57.2%。

外汇市场交易主体持续扩展。2020年末，银行间外汇市场共有即期市场会员735家，比上年末增加24家；远期、外汇掉期、货币掉期和期权市场会员分别为266家、259家、213家和163家，均比上年末有所增加。即期市场做市商30家，远掉期市场做市商27家，与上年末保持不变。

7. 境外货币当局动用货币互换协议下人民币金额明显增加

货币互换对促进双边贸易投资发挥了较好作用。2020年末，在中国人民银行与境外货币当局签署的双边本币互换协议下，境外货币当局动用人民币余额为500.32亿元，较上年末增加171.10亿元，增幅高达51.97%；中国人民银行动用外币余额折合5.16亿美元，较上年末减少17.38亿美元。

（二）2020年主要汇率及国际收支政策分析

1. 继续推进汇率市场化改革，保持人民币汇率在合理均衡水平上的基本稳定

2020年，中国人民银行和国家外汇管理局继续推进汇率市场化改革，完善以市场供求为基础、参考一篮子货币进行调节、有管理的浮动汇率制度，保持人民币汇率弹性，发挥汇率调节宏观经济和国际收支自动稳定器的作用。同时，注重预期引导，保持人民币汇率在合理均衡水平上的基本稳定。

进入2020年下半年后，随着我国宏观经济加快恢复，市场预期趋于平稳，跨境资本流动有序，外汇市场供求平衡运行平稳。为此，中国人民银行决定自2020年10月12日起，将远期售汇业务的外汇风险准备金率从20%下调为0。2020年10月27日，中国外汇市场自律机制秘书处公开表示，部分人民币对美元中间价报价行基于自身对经济基本面和市场情况的判断，陆续主动将人民币对美元中间价报价模型中的"逆周期因子"淡出使用。

2. 针对新冠疫情对经济的不利影响，外汇管理领域迅速反应，推出多项措施，便利贸易和投资，促进宏观经济恢复

一是为保障防疫物资及捐赠资金及时到位，简化相关购付汇业务流程。2020年1月27日至第二季度末，全国通过"绿色通道"办理货物贸易收付汇业务1.4万笔，涉及

金额49亿美元。二是阶段性放宽疫情防控相关资本项目收入结汇支付的事前单证要求。2020年1月27日至3月27日，全国共办理4895笔资本项目收入便利化支付，金额约9亿美元。三是便利和满足疫情防控相关跨境融资。对确有需要的企业可取消借用外债限额，并可线上申请外债登记。2020年1月27日至3月27日，共办理线上外债签约登记742笔，合计370亿美元。

此外，为推动企业复工复产，便利境内机构跨境融资，降低实体经济融资成本，根据当时的宏观经济和国际收支状况，2020年3月11日，中国人民银行、国家外汇管理局发布《关于调整全口径跨境融资宏观审慎调节参数的通知》（银发〔2020〕64号），将全口径跨境融资宏观审慎调节参数由1上调至1.25。政策调整后跨境融资风险加权余额上限相应提高，有助于便利境内机构特别是中小企业、民营企业充分利用国际国内两种资源、两个市场，多渠道筹集资金，缓解融资难、融资贵等问题，推动企业复工复产，服务实体经济发展。到了2020年第四季度，随着我国经济基本恢复到疫情前水平，出于宏观审慎管理需要，分步退出上述政策。2020年12月11日，中国人民银行、国家外汇管理局决定将金融机构的跨境融资宏观审慎调节参数由1.25下调至1。2021年1月7日，中国人民银行、国家外汇管理局决定将企业的跨境融资宏观审慎调节参数由1.25下调至1。

3. 继续提升贸易收支便利化水平

一是继续扩大贸易外汇收支便利化试点地区。截至2020年9月末，试点范围已扩大至全国19个地区的56家试点银行及374家企业。二是助力贸易新业态创新发展。2020年5月20日，国家外汇管理局出台《关于支持贸易新业态发展的通知》（汇发〔2020〕11号），优化外贸综合服务企业与跨境电商资金收付等流程，以加快跨境电子商务等贸易新业态发展。三是清理优化经常项目外汇法规。2020年8月，国家外汇管理局发布《关于印发〈经常项目外汇业务指引（2020年版）〉的通知》（汇发〔2020〕14号），实现经常项目外汇业务办理"一本通"，大幅精简法规数量和冗余条款，废止法规29件。四是提升服务贸易对外付汇便利水平。2020年11月1日，国家外汇管理局上线试运行全国范围服务贸易付汇税务备案信息的网上核验功能，持续推动服务贸易付汇税务备案电子化工作。

4. 推进个人外汇业务规范创新

2020年2月13日，为促进个人本外币兑换特许业务合规、有序发展，国家外汇管理局印发《关于修订〈个人本外币兑换特许业务试点管理办法〉的通知》（汇发〔2020〕6号）。主要内容有：一是优化"引进来"用汇环境，推动境外个人境内小额消费便利化试点和在华外籍高端人才薪酬购付汇便利化试点；二是便利"走出去"个人用汇，扩大线上办理不占用年度便利化额度的留学购付汇业务试点；三是推进中资企业驻外员工薪酬便利化结汇。

5. 继续扩大金融领域双向开放

一是放宽外资对我国金融机构的股比限制。证监会自2020年1月1日起在全国范围内取消期货公司外资股比限制，自4月1日起在全国范围内取消证券公司、基金管理公司外资股比限制。

二是扩大金融市场双向开放，取消合格境外机构投资者（QFII）和人民币合格境外机构投资者（RQFII）投资额度限制，简化境内证券期货投资资金管理，常态化发放合格境内机构投资者（QDII）额度。2020年5月，中国人民银行、国家外汇管理局发布《境外机构投资者境内证券期货投资资金管理规定》（中国人民银行 国家外汇管理局公告〔2020〕第2号），取消境外机构投资者额度限制，明确并简化境外机构投资者境内证券期货投资资金管理要求，进一步便利境外投资者参与我国金融市场。

三是推动债券市场对外开放。2020年3月，人民银行指导相关金融基础设施优化交易结算安排，在银行间债券市场推出循环结算服务和灵活结算周期服务，满足境外机构投资者多样化需求，进一步提升境外机构投资者操作便利度。2020年9月，人民银行、证监会、国家外汇管理局共同起草《关于境外机构投资者投资中国债券市场有关事宜的公告（征求意见稿）》，明确中国债券市场对外开放的整体性制度安排，就进一步便利境外机构投资者配置人民币债券资产有关安排征求市场意见。2020年9月，富时罗素公司宣布中国国债将于2021年10月被纳入富时世界国债指数（WGBI）。至此，全球三大债券指数提供商都已经计划将中国债券纳入相关指数，充分反映了国际投资者对于中国经济长期健康发展、金融持续扩大开放的信心。

四是扩展外债便利化试点，支持高新技术企业跨境融资。将北京中关村国家自主创新示范区外债便利化试点范围扩大至上海、湖北、广东及深圳等地，允许符合一定条件的高新技术企业在一定额度内自主借用外债。

6. 加强外汇市场监管，切实维护外汇市场秩序

在疫情防控常态化条件下，统筹疫情防控与防范化解金融风险关系，持续打好外汇领域防范化解重大金融风险攻坚战，进一步完善外汇市场"宏观审慎＋微观监管"两位一体管理框架，强化跨境资金流动风险监测与分析，突出打击地下钱庄、跨境赌博和网络炒汇等非法金融活动，为"六稳""六保"工作保驾护航。据统计，2020年，共查处外汇违规案件2440起，罚没款9.4亿元。全力打击外汇违法犯罪行为，严厉查处和公开通报典型案件，形成了震慑，维护了外汇市场健康良性的秩序。

（三）下一阶段政策展望

综合来看，下一阶段中国人民银行和国家外汇管理局在汇率和国际收支方面的重点工作有以下几方面。

一是稳步深化人民币汇率市场化改革。完善以市场供求为基础、参考一篮子货币进行调节、有管理的浮动汇率制度，保持人民币汇率弹性，发挥汇率调节宏观经济和国际收支自动稳定器作用。稳定市场预期，引导企业和金融机构树立"风险中性"理念，保持人民币汇率在合理均衡水平上的基本稳定。

二是稳慎推进人民币国际化。着眼于服务实体经济，顺势而为，促进贸易投资便利化。完善人民币使用相关政策制度。继续推动金融市场高质量双向开放。促进本外币、离岸在岸市场的良性协调发展。

三是防范跨境资本异常流动风险。加强外汇形势监测评估，密切关注疫情等外部冲击影响，引导金融机构和企业坚持风险中性原则，打击外汇投机行为，加强市场预期管理和宏观审慎管理，避免外汇市场无序波动。

四是深化外汇领域改革开放。以金融市场双向开放为重点，稳妥有序推进资本项目开放。完善境外机构境内发行股票、债券资金管理，推进私募股权投资基金跨境投资试点，改革外债登记管理，促进跨境投融资便利化。扩大贸易外汇收支便利化试点，促进贸易新业态发展。建设开放多元、功能健全的外汇市场，支持金融机构推出更多适应市场需求的外汇衍生品。支持企业合理审慎运用外汇衍生品管理汇率风险。

五是完善外汇市场"宏观审慎+微观监管"两位一体管理框架。以加强宏观审慎为核心改善跨境资本流动管理，以转变监管方式为核心完善外汇市场微观监管。完善以风险评估为导向的分类管理信用体系建设。加强非现场监管能力建设。以"零容忍"态度严厉打击地下钱庄、跨境赌博等外汇领域违法违规活动，维护外汇市场健康秩序。

六是完善中国特色外汇储备经营管理。集约高效做好外汇储备经营管理，维护外汇储备规模基本稳定。坚持市场化原则，前瞻性地做好战略配置，动态优化投资组合。保障外汇储备资产安全、流动和保值增值。

七是夯实外汇管理基础工作。深入研究"十四五"时期外汇管理改革思路，推进"数字外管"和"安全外管"建设，完善国际收支统计体系，做好常态化疫情防控工作。

## 附表

**2020年主要汇率政策和国际收支政策汇总**

| 日期 | 政策名称 | 主要内容 |
| --- | --- | --- |
| 1月13日 | 国家外汇管理局关于完善银行间债券市场境外机构投资者外汇风险管理有关问题的通知（汇发〔2020〕2号） | 进一步便利银行间债券市场境外机构投资者管理外汇风险 |
| 2月14日 | 中国人民银行 中国银行保险监督管理委员会 中国证券监督管理委员会 国家外汇管理局 上海市人民政府关于进一步加快推进上海国际金融中心建设和金融支持长三角一体化发展的意见（银发〔2020〕46号） | 支持上海国际金融中心建设的系列新举措 |
| 2月13日 | 国家外汇管理局关于修订《个人本外币兑换特许业务试点管理办法》的通知（汇发〔2020〕6号） | 在保持现有个人本外币兑换特许业务许可范围与个人结售汇管理原则不变的基础上，完善相关管理政策，便利个人本外币兑换 |
| 3月11日 | 《中国人民银行 国家外汇管理局关于调整全口径跨境融资宏观审慎调节参数的通知》（银发〔2020〕64号） | 将全口径跨境融资宏观审慎调节参数由1上调至1.25，以降低实体经济融资成本，扩大利用外资 |
| 3月19日 | 国家外汇管理局扩展外债便利化试点 支持高新技术企业跨境融资 | 将相关外债便利化政策试点范围扩大至上海（自由贸易试验区）、湖北（自由贸易试验区及武汉东湖新技术开发区）、广东及深圳（粤港澳大湾区）等省、市。同时，进一步提高北京市中关村科学城海淀园区的外债便利化水平 |

续表

| 日期 | 政策名称 | 主要内容 |
| --- | --- | --- |
| 4月10日 | 国家外汇管理局关于优化外汇管理 支持涉外业务发展的通知（汇发〔2020〕8号） | 简化外汇业务办理流程，优化外汇业务服务，提升跨境贸易投资便利化水平，积极支持企业复工复产 |
| 4月24日 | 中国人民银行 中国银行保险监督管理委员会 中国证券监督管理委员会 国家外汇管理局关于金融支持粤港澳大湾区建设的意见（银发〔2020〕95号） | 促进粤港澳大湾区跨境贸易和投融资便利化，提升本外币兑换和跨境流通使用便利度等 |
| 5月7日 | 境外机构投资者境内证券期货投资资金管理规定（中国人民银行 国家外汇管理局〔2020〕第2号） | 明确并简化境外机构投资者境内证券期货投资资金管理要求，进一步便利境外投资者参与我国金融市场 |
| 5月20日 | 国家外汇管理局关于支持贸易新业态发展的通知（汇发〔2020〕11号） | 优化贸易新业态外汇政策，支持贸易新业态发展 |
| 6月29日 | 中国人民银行 香港金融管理局 澳门金融管理局关于在粤港澳大湾区开展"跨境理财通"业务试点的联合公告 | 在粤港澳大湾区开展"跨境理财通"业务试点 |
| 8月28日 | 国家外汇管理局关于印发《经常项目外汇业务指引（2020年版）》的通知（汇发〔2020〕14号） | 全面整合经常项目外汇业务现有法规，精简部分业务流程和办理业务所需材料，同步废止法规29件 |
| 9月2日 | 中国人民银行 中国证监会 国家外汇管理局关于《境外机构投资者投资中国债券市场有关事宜的公告（征求意见稿）》公开征求意见的通知 | 进一步加强中国债券市场对外开放的系统性、整体性、协同性，便利境外机构投资者配置人民币债券资产 |
| 9月18日 | 国家外汇管理局综合司关于印发《对外金融资产负债及交易统计业务指引（2020年版）》的通知（汇综发〔2020〕71号） | 进一步完善对外金融资产负债及交易统计申报，便利申报主体更加准确地理解具体报送要求 |
| 9月21日 | 中国人民银行 国家外汇管理局关于《境外机构投资者投资中国债券市场资金管理规定（征求意见稿）》公开征求意见的通知 | 推动中国债券市场整体开放，统一境外机构投资者投资中国债券市场资金管理，进一步便利投资交易 |
| 9月22日 | 国家外汇管理局关于印发《通过银行进行国际收支统计申报业务实施细则》的通知（汇发〔2020〕16号） | 进一步规范申报主体通过境内银行进行涉外收付款国际收支统计申报 |
| 10月10日 | 中国人民银行决定将远期售汇业务的外汇风险准备金率下调为0 | 中国人民银行决定自2020年10月12日起，将远期售汇业务的外汇风险准备金率从20%下调为0 |
| 10月29日 | 国家外汇管理局关于印发《境内银行涉外及境内收付凭证管理规定》的通知（汇发〔2020〕17号） | 明确境内银行涉外及境内收付凭证管理要求 |
| 11月30日 | 国家外汇管理局综合司关于印发《国家外汇管理局信息系统代码标准管理规定》的通知（汇综发〔2020〕91号） | 进一步规范外汇信息系统代码标准化工作 |
| 12月11日 | 中国人民银行、国家外汇管理局调整跨境融资宏观审慎调节参数 | 将金融机构的跨境融资宏观审慎调节参数从1.25下调至1，此举是对3月12日政策的逆周期调整 |

续表

| 日期 | 政策名称 | 主要内容 |
|---|---|---|
| 12月14日 | 国家外汇管理局关于印发《对外金融资产负债及交易统计核查规则（2020年版）》的通知（汇综发〔2020〕94号） | 进一步提高对外金融资产负债及交易统计数据的准确性 |

资料来源：根据中国人民银行和国家外汇管理网站公开资料整理而成。

专栏2

## 《"十四五"规划建议》辅导读本出版，"一行两会"领导阐述金融体系改革方向①

2020年11月3日，党的十九届五中全会通过和发布《中共中央关于制定国民经济和社会发展第十四个五年规划和二〇三五年远景目标的建议》（以下简称《建议》）。随后出版的《〈建议〉辅导读本》刊发"一行两会"主要领导文章，解读和阐释《建议》中有关金融工作的重要规划和目标。

### 一、建设现代中央银行制度

人民银行行长易纲在署名文章《建设现代中央银行制度》中指出，建设现代中央银行制度，是推进国家治理体系和治理能力现代化的重大任务，推动高质量发展的内在需要，应对国际中央银行制度演变挑战的必然要求。目标是建立有助于实现币值稳定、充分就业、金融稳定、国际收支平衡四大任务的中央银行体制机制，管好货币总闸门，提供高质量金融基础设施服务，防控系统性金融风险，管控外部溢出效应，促进形成公平合理的国际金融治理格局。

### 二、完善现代金融监管体系

人民银行党委书记、银保监会主席郭树清在署名文章《完善现代金融监管体系》中指出，中外金融监管史表明，货币经济绝不能背离实体经济，将本求利是商业活动的正常状态，收益永远和风险成正比，要持续建设法治和诚信环境，把握好金融创新的边界，管好货币总闸门，坚决抑制房地产泡沫，紧紧抓住公司治理"牛鼻子"。需认真吸取以上经验教训，正确认识现阶段金融形势，因势利导地采取有针对性的措施。不断健全风险预防、预警、处置、问责制度体系，持续完善权责一致、全面覆盖、统筹协调、有力有效的现代金融监管体系。

### 三、提高直接融资比重

证监会主席易会满在《提高直接融资比重》署名文章中指出，提高直接融资比重，对于深化金融供给侧结构性改革，加快构建新发展格局，实现更高质量、更有效率、更加公平、更可持续、更为安全的发展，具有十分重要意义。必须从经济金融全局的高度

---

① 作者：赵湘怀，光大证券企划与经营管理部总经理、《中国金融政策报告》项目（课题组）研究员；梁超逸，光大证券企划与经营管理部高级经理；任小勋，光大证券企划与经营管理部资深经理。

加强统筹谋划，有效发挥市场主体、监管机构、宏观管理部门、新闻媒体等各方合力，努力促进直接融资和间接融资协调发展，进一步完善直接融资配套制度，构建有利于提高直接融资比重的良好市场生态。

综合来看，三位领导的署名文章分别从间接融资和直接融资的不同角度出发，前瞻性地解读了《建议》中金融重点发展目标和规划。一是深刻阐明了建设现代中央银行制度的内涵。完善货币供应调节机制，保持政策的连续性和可持续性，着力稳固经济，推动向好。建立现代金融机构体系，推进金融双向开放。二是提出金融支持实体经济发展举措。全面实行股票发行注册制，引导金融企业合理让利，使中小微企业融资更便利、融资成本做到稳中有降。健全中国特色多层次资本市场体系，推动上市公司提高质量，进一步完善直接融资配套制度。三是强调建设市场化、法制化和国际化的现代金融体系。为健全市场体系、保护投资者权益、保障实体经济发展指明了方向。

表　　　　　　　　　　　　　"一行两会"领导文章内容概要

| 署名文章及作者 | 解读《建议》中的规划和目标 | 重大举措和重点任务 |
| --- | --- | --- |
| 《建设现代中央银行制度》作者易纲 | 建设现代中央银行制度，完善货币供应调控机制，稳妥推进数字货币研发，健全市场化利率形成和传导机制。推进金融双向开放。 | 1. 完善货币供应调控机制。<br>2. 构建金融有效支持实体经济的体制机制。<br>3. 建立现代金融机构体系。<br>4. 推进金融双向开放。<br>5. 健全金融风险预防、预警、处置、问责制度体系。 |
| 《完善现代金融监管体系》作者郭树清 | 完善现代金融监管体系，提高金融监管透明度和法治化水平，完善存款保险制度，健全金融风险预防、预警、处置、问责制度体系，对违法违规行为零容忍。构建金融有效支持实体经济的体制机制，提升金融科技水平，增强金融普惠性。深化国有商业银行改革，支持中小银行和农村信用社持续健康发展，改革优化政策性金融。 | 1. 全面加强党对金融工作的集中统一领导。<br>2. 促进经济社会发展开创新局。<br>3. 建立高效的监管决策协调沟通机制，提高金融监管透明度和法治化水平。<br>健全宏观审慎、微观审慎、行为监管三支柱。<br>4. 构建权威高效的风险处置制度安排。<br>强化金融基础设施对监管的支持保障。<br>5. 积极参与国际金融治理框架重塑。<br>6. 培育忠诚干净担当的监管干部队伍。 |
| 《提高直接融资比重》作者易会满 | 全面实行股票发行注册制，建立常态化退市机制，提高直接融资比重，构建金融有效支持实体经济的体制机制，增强金融普惠性。 | 1. 全面实行股票发行注册制，促进直接融资和间接融资协调发展，拓宽直接融资入口。<br>2. 健全中国特色多层次资本市场体系，增强直接融资包容性，构建有利于提高直接融资比重的良好市场生态。<br>3. 推动上市公司提高质量，夯实直接融资发展基石，进一步完善直接融资配套制度。<br>4. 深入推进债券市场创新发展，丰富直接融资工具。加快发展私募股权基金，突出创新资本战略作用。<br>5. 大力推动长期资金入市，充沛直接融资源头活水。 |

# 主要金融市场发展政策

## 一、银行业市场发展政策[①]

（一）2020年中国银行业市场发展政策主要内容

2020年，面对严峻复杂的国内外形势尤其是新冠肺炎疫情的严重冲击，银行业市场发展的政策重点在提升金融服务实体经济质效，扎实做好"六稳"工作，全面落实"六保"任务，竭力帮助企业渡过难关。虽然国内经济逐步复苏，但全球疫情依然蔓延，国内外经营环境更加复杂多变，"防范金融风险，坚决打赢防范化解金融风险攻坚战"也依然是监管工作重点。

1. 抗击疫情，全力支持经济社会恢复发展

一是全力做好疫情防控金融服务。自疫情暴发以来，党中央依据疫情形势发展对统筹疫情防控和经济社会发展工作作出了系列重要部署。监管等部门出台了一系列政策措施引导银行业支持企业复工复产、促进经济稳定运行。2020年1月26日，银保监会印发了《关于加强银行业保险业金融服务 配合做好新型冠状病毒感染的肺炎疫情防控工作的通知》（银保监办发〔2020〕10号），从银行保险机构自身落实疫情防控要求、保障金融服务顺畅、开辟金融服务绿色通道、强化疫情防控金融支持、做好受困企业金融服务等五个方面提出了具体措施。1月29日，银保监会印发了《关于动员系统各级党组织和党员干部积极投身新型冠状病毒感染肺炎疫情防控阻击战的通知》（银保监党办发〔2020〕3号），指导银行保险机构全力配合做好金融服务。1月31日，人民银行会同财政部、银保监会等部门又出台了《关于进一步强化金融支持防控新型冠状病毒感染肺炎疫情的通知》（银发〔2020〕29号），就加大货币信贷支持力度、合理调度金融资源、保障金融服务、维护金融市场平稳有序运行等做了进一步强调，该通知是金融系统贯彻落实党中央、国务院决策部署，主动作为，扎实工作的重要举措。2月1日，人民银行会同银保监会等四部门印发《关于做好春节假期后金融服务工作的通知》（银发〔2020〕30号），切实加强金融部门疫情防控，做好春节假期后金融服务工作，确保金融市场平稳有序运行。

2月7日，人民银行、财政部等多部门先后印发了《关于疫情防控期间金融机构发

---

[①] 作者：周昆平，交通银行发展研究部资深专家、《中国金融政策报告》项目（课题组）高级研究员；赵亚蕊，交通银行发展研究部高级研究员。

行债券有关事宜的通知》（银市场〔2020〕5号）、《关于打赢疫情防控阻击战 强化疫情防控重点保障企业资金支持的紧急通知》（财金〔2020〕5号），引导金融机构支持疫情防控，强化疫情防控重点保障企业资金支持。2月14日，银保监会印发《关于进一步做好疫情防控金融服务的通知》（银保监办发〔2020〕15号），从做好金融服务、加强科技应用、完善制度机制等多个方面，推动银行业保险业做好新冠肺炎疫情防控金融服务。3月26日，银保监会印发了《关于加强产业链协同复工复产金融服务的通知》（银保监办发〔2020〕28号），针对企业复工复产以来，产业链上下游部分企业面临的现金流压力问题，就引导银行保险机构增强金融支持和服务、畅通产业链资金流、提升产业链协同复工复产整体效应等方面提出了具体措施。5月18日，银保监会联合工业和信息化部等六部门发布《关于进一步规范信贷融资收费 降低企业融资综合成本的通知》（银保监发〔2020〕18号），进一步规范信贷融资各环节收费与管理，维护企业知情权、自主选择权和公平交易权，降低企业融资综合成本。8月5日，银保监会等七部门发布《关于做好政府性融资担保机构监管工作的通知》（银保监发〔2020〕39号），建立健全政府性融资担保体系，促进政府性融资担保机构发挥作用，扎实做好"六稳"工作，全面落实"六保"任务。9月9日，银保监会印发《银行保险机构应对突发事件金融服务管理办法》（中国银保监会令2020年第10号），进一步落实习近平总书记针对新冠肺炎疫情应对工作提出的"抓紧补短板、堵漏洞、强弱项"。9月18日，人民银行联合工业和信息化部等八部门印发《关于规范发展供应链金融 支持供应链产业链稳定循环和优化升级的意见》（银发〔2020〕226号），做好金融支持稳企业保就业工作，精准服务供应链产业链完整稳定，提升整体运行效率，促进经济良性循环和优化布局。

二是加强小微企业金融支持力度。由于新冠疫情对小微企业带来重大影响，金融相关部门出台了一系列针对小微企业的政策措施，加大对受困小微民营企业扶持力度。3月1日，银保监会等五部门联合印发《关于对中小微企业贷款实施临时性延期还本付息的通知》（银保监发〔2020〕6号），重点帮扶前期经营正常、受疫情影响遇到暂时困难、发展前景良好的中小微企业，进一步纾解中小微企业困难，推动企业有序复工复产，提高金融服务的针对性、有效性。4月7日，国家税务总局与银保监会联合印发《关于发挥"银税互动"作用助力小微企业复工复产的通知》（税总办发〔2020〕10号），针对疫情期间小微企业更加迫切的资金需求，加大税收信用贷款支持力度，努力帮助小微企业复工复产渡过难关。5月26日、6月1日，人民银行联合银保监会等多部门，先后下发了《关于进一步强化中小微企业金融服务的指导意见》（银发〔2020〕120号）、《关于进一步对中小微企业贷款实施阶段性延期还本付息的通知》（银发〔2020〕122号）、《关于加大小微企业信用贷款支持力度的通知》（银发〔2020〕123号），推动中小微企业（含个体工商户和小微企业主，不含地方政府融资平台）融资规模明显增长、融资结构更加优化，推动加快恢复正常生产生活秩序，支持实体经济高质量发展。6月29日，银保监会印发《关于印发商业银行小微企业金融服务监管评价办法（试行）的通知》，进一步做好"六稳"工作，落实"六保"任务，更加有效地运用监管政策手段，引导和督促商业银行全面提升小微企业金融服务能力和水平，缓解小微企业融资难融资贵。

总体来看，自新冠疫情以来，监管部门及时出台了多项金融支持政策措施，对银行保险机构支持疫情防控、强化金融服务提出了明确要求。从坚持完善政策支持、提供差异化的优惠金融信贷支持、有效降低融资成本、提高金融服务效率和水平等多个方面加大金融支持，有力地支持了疫情防控和经济社会发展。

2. 政策精准发力，有效支持实体经济稳步发展

一是加大普惠、"三农"等薄弱领域支持力度。2020年是《推进普惠金融发展规划（2016—2020年）》的收官之年，也是脱贫攻坚决胜之年，更面临突如其来的新冠肺炎疫情，监管部门出台了多项政策支持普惠金融，助力银行业打赢脱贫攻坚战。3月10日，为促进银行业金融机构改善金融服务结构、提升金融服务效率、扩大普惠金融覆盖面，银保监会印发《关于优化银行业金融机构分支机构变更营业场所事项的通知》（银保监办发〔2020〕25号）。同一天，银保监会发布《关于进一步加大"三区三州"深度贫困地区银行业保险业扶贫工作力度的通知》（银保监办发〔2020〕24号），对进一步做好"三区三州"深度贫困地区银行业保险业扶贫工作作出安排部署。4月9日，银保监会发布《关于做好2020年银行业保险业服务"三农"领域重点工作的通知》（银保监办发〔2020〕31号），围绕补齐"三农"领域短板等重点工作，加大信贷投入力度，提高风险保障水平，助力补齐"三农"领域全面建成小康社会的突出短板，确保如期打赢脱贫攻坚战。6月24日，银保监会联合财政部等四部门印发《关于进一步完善扶贫小额信贷有关政策的通知》（银保监发〔2020〕28号），充分发挥扶贫小额信贷作用，助力高质量打赢脱贫攻坚战。

二是继续强化对国家区域经济战略的政策支持。在国内大循环为主体、国内国际双循环相互促进的新发展格局背景下，监管机构出台多项政策，推动银行业金融机构加强对国家重大战略区域的支持力度。2月14日，人民银行、银保监会等部门联合印发《关于进一步加快推进上海国际金融中心建设和金融支持长三角一体化发展的意见》（银发〔2020〕46号），从积极推进临港新片区金融先行先试、在更高水平加快上海金融业对外开放和金融支持长三角一体化发展等方面提出30条具体措施，这不仅有利于进一步加快推进上海国际金融中心建设和长三角一体化发展，也对引领全国高质量发展、加快现代化经济体系建设具有重大战略意义。4月24日，人民银行、银保监会等四部门联合印发《关于金融支持粤港澳大湾区建设的意见》（银发〔2020〕95号），从促进粤港澳大湾区跨境贸易和投融资便利化、扩大金融业对外开放、促进金融市场和金融基础设施互联互通、提升粤港澳大湾区金融服务创新水平、切实防范跨境金融风险等五个方面提出26条具体措施，进一步提升粤港澳大湾区在国家经济发展和对外开放中的支持引领作用。6月29日，人民银行、香港金融管理局、澳门金融管理局印发《关于在粤港澳大湾区开展"跨境理财通"业务试点的联合公告》，促进粤港澳大湾区居民个人跨境投资便利化。

### 3. 多措并举，防范化解高风险金融机构和重点领域风险

在全力支持经济社会恢复发展的同时，监管部门多措并举，抓好各种存量风险化解和增量风险防范。

一是有序推进中小银行风险化解。2020年，监管机构稳妥推进高风险中小银行等金融机构风险处置。5月23日，人民银行和银保监会发布《关于延长包商银行股份有限公司接管期限的公告》，加强对包商银行等风险的处置化解。12月30日，银保监会印发《关于进一步推动村镇银行化解风险改革重组有关事项的通知》（银保监办发〔2020〕124号），进一步督促主发起行落实风险处置牵头责任，推动村镇银行改革重组，加快村镇银行补充资本，强化风险处置。

二是加强信用风险防控与化解。在疫情影响下，不良资产暴露压力逐步增大，监管部门着力推动商业银行拓宽不良资产处置渠道并加大处置力度。6月15日，人民银行、国家发展改革委、证监会三部门联合印发《关于公司信用类债券违约处置有关事宜的通知》，建立健全债券违约处置机制、提升违约处置效率，有效防范化解债券市场风险。9月7日，银保监会印发《关于加强小额贷款公司监督管理的通知》（银保监办发〔2020〕86号），规范小额贷款公司经营行为，防范化解相关风险。12月18日，人民银行和银保监会联合印发《关于建立银行业金融机构房地产贷款集中度管理制度的通知》（银发〔2020〕322号），建立了银行业金融机构房地产贷款集中度管理制度，增强银行业金融机构抵御房地产市场波动的能力，防范金融体系对房地产贷款过度集中带来的潜在系统性金融风险，提高银行业金融机构的稳健性。

三是加强银行宏观审慎监管。监管部门对银行业金融机构可能存在的风险隐患也及时做了防范和治理。3月5日，人民银行、国家发展改革委等六部门联合印发了《统筹监管金融基础设施工作方案》，加强金融基础设施建设，强化宏观审慎管理，提高服务实体经济水平和防控金融风险能力。9月30日，人民银行、银保监会发布《关于建立逆周期资本缓冲机制的通知》，明确了我国逆周期资本缓冲的计提方式、覆盖范围及评估机制等内容，进一步促进银行业金融机构稳健经营，提升宏观审慎政策的逆周期调节能力，缓解金融风险顺周期波动和突发性冲击导致的负面影响，维护我国金融体系稳定运行。12月3日，人民银行和银保监会联合印发《系统重要性银行评估办法》（银发〔2020〕289号），进一步完善我国系统重要性金融机构监管框架，建立系统重要性银行评估与识别机制。

### 4. 加强经营规范整治，助力银行业稳健经营

2020年1月14日，银保监会发布《银行业保险业消费投诉处理管理办法》，切实维护银行业保险业消费者合法权益，进一步规范银行保险机构消费投诉处理工作。2月20日，银保监会印发《关于预防银行业保险业从业人员金融违法犯罪的指导意见》，进一步完善银行业保险业从业人员金融违法犯罪预防工作机制，防控银行保险机构案件风险，促进银行业保险业健康发展。5月22日，银保监会印发《关于印发银行保险机构涉刑案件管理办法（试行）的通知》（银保监发〔2020〕20号），进一步规范和加强银行

保险机构涉刑案件的管理工作，建立责任明确、协调有序的工作机制，依法、及时、稳妥处置案件。6月15日，银保监会印发《中国银保监会行政处罚办法》（中国银保监会令2020年第8号），统一规范机构改革后银行业和保险业行政处罚程序，提升金融违法违规成本，严肃整治金融市场乱象，防范化解金融风险。6月23日，银保监会印发《关于开展银行业保险业市场乱象整治"回头看"工作的通知》（银保监发〔2020〕27号），进一步巩固拓展乱象整治成果，坚决打赢防范化解金融风险攻坚战。7月14日，银保监会向系统内各级派出机构和银行保险机构印发《关于近年影子银行和交叉金融业务监管检查发现主要问题的通报》，通报了近年来对相关机构监管检查中发现的影子银行和交叉金融业务领域的突出问题，并提出了规范整改的工作要求，进一步巩固深化影子银行和交叉金融业务整治成果。7月17日，银保监会印发《全国非法集资监测预警体系建设规划（2020—2022年）》，旨在构建线上线下紧密结合、央地平台互联互通的监测预警体系，强化科技赋能，促进关口前移，阻止非法集资风险蔓延放大，切实保护人民群众财产安全。12月30日，人民银行组织起草了《金融机构反洗钱和反恐怖融资监督管理办法（修订草案征求意见稿）》，有效防范化解金融风险，提高反洗钱监管有效性，提升金融机构反洗钱工作水平。12月30日，银保监会印发《关于深化银行业保险业"放管服"改革 优化营商环境的通知》（银保监办发〔2020〕129号），有效推进银行业保险业简政放权、优化服务，更大激发市场活力，推动营商环境持续改善。

5. 加快补齐制度短板，推动业务转型升级

2020年，监管政策持续从制度上抓紧补短板、堵漏洞、强弱项，引导金融机构实现业务经营的转型升级。2月14日，证监会、财政部等四部门联合印发《关于商业银行、保险机构参与中国金融期货交易所国债期货交易的公告》（证监会公告〔2020〕12号），丰富国债期货投资者，促进国债期货市场健康有序发展。5月20日，银保监会下发《关于保险资金投资银行资本补充债券有关事项的通知（银保监发〔2020〕17号）》，进一步拓宽银行资本补充渠道。6月5日，人民银行下发《关于规范商业汇票信息披露的公告（征求意见稿）》，加强商业汇票信用体系建设，建立完善市场化约束机制，保障持票人合法权益。6月24日，人民银行出台了《标准化票据管理办法》（中国人民银行公告〔2020〕第6号），规范标准化票据融资机制，更好地服务中小企业和供应链融资。7月3日，人民银行、银保监会等四部门联合印发《标准化债权类资产认定规则》（中国人民银行 中国银保监会 中国证监会 国家外汇管理局公告〔2020〕第5号），规范金融机构资产管理产品投资，强化投资者保护，促进直接融资健康发展，有效防控金融风险。7月31日，监管部门明确资管新规采取"过渡期适当延长（由2020年延长至2021年）+个案处理"的政策安排，进一步缓解金融机构整改压力，推动资管存量业务整改平稳进行。9月15日，人民银行印发《金融消费者权益保护实施办法》（中国人民银行令〔2020〕第5号），规范金融机构提供金融产品和服务的行为，维护公平、公正的市场环境，促进金融市场健康稳定运行。12月18日，人民银行印发《商业承兑汇票信息披露有关事宜公告》（中国人民银行公告〔2020〕第19号），进一步加强商业承兑汇票

信用体系建设，完善市场化约束机制。12月19日，人民银行印发《规范人民币现金收付行为有关事项公告》（中国人民银行公告〔2020〕第18号），进一步普及现金收付规范要求，共建多元化支付条件下的现金和谐流通环境。12月25日，银保监会发布了《商业银行理财子公司理财产品销售管理暂行办法（征求意见稿）》，规范商业银行理财子公司理财产品销售业务活动，保护投资者合法权益，促进理财业务健康发展。同日，人民银行、国家发展改革委、证监会三部门联合发布《公司信用类债券信息披露管理办法》（中国人民银行　国家发展和改革委员会　中国证监会公告〔2020〕第22号），完善公司信用类债券信息披露制度，促进我国债券市场持续健康发展。12月31日，人民银行、国家发展改革委等多部门联合印发《关于进一步优化跨境人民币政策　支持稳外贸稳外资的通知》（银发〔2020〕330号），进一步贯彻落实党中央、国务院关于扎实做好"六稳"工作、全面落实"六保"任务的决策部署，推动形成以国内大循环为主体、国内国际双循环相互促进的新发展格局，发挥跨境人民币业务服务实体经济、促进贸易投资便利化的作用。

6. 加快银行业数字化转型，推动金融科技有序发展

近年来，阿里、腾讯等大型互联网科技公司发展迅猛，不断向金融领域渗透发展，同时也带来了一定的潜在风险。2020年以来，监管层多次公开指出要对金融科技监管进行顶层设计，加快推动银行业数字化转型。5月9日，银保监会印发《商业银行互联网贷款管理暂行办法（征求意见稿）》，并于7月12日印发正式稿，进一步规范商业银行互联网贷款业务经营行为，促进互联网贷款业务平稳健康发展。10月21日，人民银行发布《金融科技创新应用测试规范》、《金融科技创新安全通用规范》、《金融科技创新风险监控》三项金融科技创新规范，支撑金融科技创新监管。10月26日，人民银行印发《关于规范代收业务的通知》（银发〔2020〕248号），规范代收业务，保障当事人合法权益，防范支付业务风险。11月2日，银保监会和人民银行就《网络小额贷款业务管理暂行办法（征求意见稿）》公开征求意见，规范小额贷款公司网络小额贷款业务，防范网络小额贷款业务风险。

7. 加强银行业金融机构公司治理，完善约束机制

完善公司治理，实现科学稳健发展，仍旧是2020年监管的工作重点。7月4日，银保监会官网首次公开银行保险机构重大违法违规股东名单。8月17日，银保监会发布《健全银行业保险业公司治理三年行动方案（2020—2022年）》（银保监发〔2020〕40号），推动我国银行业保险业进一步加强党的领导，借鉴吸收国际先进经验，切实提升公司治理质效。9月11日，国务院印发《关于实施金融控股公司准入管理的决定》（国发〔2020〕12号），同日，人民银行印发《金融控股公司监督管理试行办法》（中国人民银行令〔2020〕第4号），对公司治理关键环节提出了监管要求，有效加强对非金融企业、自然人等主体控股或者实际控制金融机构的监督管理，规范金融控股公司行为。10月16日，人民银行印发《关于〈中华人民共和国商业银行法（修改建议稿）〉公开征求意见的通知》，新设商业银行公司治理章节，完善约束机制。11月2日，人民银行

印发对《金融控股公司董事、监事、高级管理人员任职备案管理暂行规定（征求意见稿）》公开征求意见的通知，规范金融控股公司运作，防范经营风险。

8. 进一步提升开放水平，持续深化金融领域改革开放

2020年以来，我国金融业对外开放步伐进一步加快。5月7日，人民银行、国家外汇管理局制定了《境外机构投资者境内证券期货投资资金管理规定》，规范境外机构投资者境内证券期货投资管理。5月27日，国务院金融稳定发展委员会办公室发布11条金融改革措施，其中涉及金融对外开放等重要内容。9月21日，人民银行、国家外汇管理局起草了《境外机构投资者投资中国债券市场资金管理规定（征求意见稿）》，有效推动中国债券市场整体开放，统一境外机构投资者投资中国债券市场资金管理，进一步便利投资交易。12月31日，为贯彻党中央、国务院关于扩大金融业对外开放的决策部署，明确外国保险集团公司和境外金融机构准入标准，银保监会决定对《中华人民共和国外资保险公司管理条例实施细则》部分条款予以修改。

（二）2020年中国银行业市场发展政策效果

1. 2020年银行业市场发展政策在多方面取得积极成效

2020年是全面建成小康社会和"十三五"收官之年，中央和地方层面的多个政策持续落地。在多项政策的影响和推动下，银行业市场总体运行稳健，各项指标处于合理区间。总体来看，我国银行业呈现以下积极变化。

第一，资产规模平稳增长，利润降幅有所放缓。2020年，新冠疫情冲击下，货币政策逆周期调节政策持续加码，银行业资产规模增速稳步提升。第四季度末，我国银行业金融机构本外币资产为319.7万亿元，同比增长10.1%。其中，大型商业银行本外币资产为128.4万亿元，占比40.2%，资产总额同比增长10%；股份制商业银行本外币资产为57.8万亿元，占比18.1%，资产总额同比增长11.7%。受疫情影响，商业银行净利润增速呈下降趋势，下半年随着国内疫情好转，净利润增速降幅有所放缓。2020年商业银行累计实现净利润1.94万亿元，同比下降2.7%，降幅较前三季度收窄5.6个百分点。

第二，信用风险进一步释放，资产质量基本稳定。2020年，商业银行内外部经营环境更加复杂多变，疫情进一步加速了经济下滑，银行业不良贷款有所上升。受国内经济好转以及多项信用风险化解政策的出台等多因素影响，信用风险整体处于可控水平。第四季度末，商业银行贷款余额为144万亿元。其中，正常类贷款余额为140万亿元，关注类贷款余额为3.8万亿元。不良贷款余额为2.7万亿元，较上季末减少1336亿元；不良贷款率为1.84%，较上季末下降0.12个百分点。

第三，风险抵补能力相对充足。尽管受疫情影响，商业银行净利润增速和资产质量持续承压，但商业银行通过发行优先股、永续债、二级资本债等工具补充了资本1.34万亿元，银行业新提取拨备1.9万亿元，同比多提取1139亿元。年末，商业银行贷款损失准备余额为5万亿元，较上季末减少1164亿元；拨备覆盖率为184.5%，较上季末上升4.58个百分点；贷款拨备率为3.39%，较上季末下降0.14个百分点。商业银行风险

抵御能力也始终保持在较高水平。第四季度末，商业银行（不含外国银行分行）核心一级资本充足率为10.72%，较上季末上升0.28个百分点；一级资本充足率为12.04%，较上季末上升0.36个百分点；资本充足率为14.7%，较上季末上升0.29个百分点。

2020年，面对严峻复杂的国内外形势特别是新冠肺炎疫情的严重冲击，银行业金融机构严格落实党中央、国务院和国务院金融稳定发展委员会的决策部署，在支持实体经济、提升金融服务质效以及深化改革发展等多个方面取得明显成效。

一是坚决做好疫情防控金融服务。银行业保险业在金融机构疫情期间做好各项金融服务，2020年紧急提供专项信贷5.3万亿元，全力支持武汉、湖北打赢疫情防控保卫战，累计为中小微企业和外贸企业实施延期还本付息6.6万亿元，发放应急贷款242.7亿元。

二是服务实体经济质效持续提高。2020年，人民币贷款增加19.6万亿元，同比多增2.8万亿元。民营企业、制造业贷款分别增加5.7万亿元、2.2万亿元。普惠型小微企业贷款、科学研究和技术服务业贷款、信息技术服务业贷款同比分别增长30.9%、20.1%、14.9%。

三是有效化解重点领域风险。2020年，包商银行等中小银行金融机构风险处置稳妥推进。信用风险持续化解，银行业不良资产全年处置3.02万亿元。高风险影子银行业务得到进一步拆解。房地产贷款增速8年来首次低于各项贷款增速。配合地方党委政府化解大型企业集团债务风险得到进一步推进。

四是银行业改革开放迈出坚实步伐。2020年以来，银行业改革工作持续深入推进。积极推动发行2000亿元地方政府专项债补充中小银行资本。持续推进各类银行保险机构的体制机制改革。出台健全公司治理三年行动方案。持续推动多项对外开放措施落地见效。

2. 银行业市场发展政策在部分领域仍存在完善空间

2020年，在多项监管政策举措推动下，银行业总体运行稳健，经营改革取得积极成效，但部分领域仍需要政策出台加以规范引导。

一是金融风险防范任务依然艰巨。2020年以来，中小银行风险得到有序处置，信用风险、影子银行风险等也得到一定化解。但国际经济金融形势仍然复杂严峻，国内外疫情变化和外部环境存在诸多不确定性，国内经济恢复基础尚不牢固。我国防范疫情输入和国际经济金融风险的压力仍然较大，不良贷款上升等信用风险可能滞后显现，区域性金融风险隐患仍然存在，未来这些领域仍需加以重点关注。

二是银行业金融机构公司治理机制仍需进一步完善。在过去一年监管和行业的持续努力下，我国银行业金融机构的公司治理建设和改革取得了积极成效，但仍然存在部分领域有待完善。具体包括，部分银行业金融机构股权结构不透明，股权代持、隐形股东问题较为突出，股东行为越位错位，有的大股东直接干预机构经营，对董事会和高管层进行幕后操纵，通过违规关联交易进行利益输送，肆意侵占机构利益。董事会运作不规范，部分非执行董事存在不能、不敢或者不愿履职的现象，少数董事的独立性和专业性严重欠缺。信息披露不规范，对包括金融消费者在内的利益相关者权益保障不足等。

三是互联网金融监管工作有待进一步提升。在前期出台的多项政策约束下，网络借贷领域风险形势已发生根本好转。但总体来看网贷机构存量风险处置和网贷风险监管长效机制尚未建立，互联网金融活动的常态化监测和监管需要进一步加强，恶意逃废债行为依然存在，民间违法金融活动滋生的苗头依然存在。

（三）2021年中国银行业市场发展政策展望与建议

展望2021年，作为全面建设社会主义现代化国家新征程开启之年，以及"十四五"开局之年，结合中央经济工作会议最新会议精神和2021年重点任务部署，贯彻新发展理念、构建新发展格局、持续深化金融供给侧结构性改革、着力提升服务实体经济质效、深入推进改革开放、切实防范化解金融风险等仍将是金融监管政策重点。建议未来监管政策重点完善以下方面。

一是为构建新发展格局提供有力支持，进一步提升金融服务整体效能。党的十九届五中全会明确提出要加快构建以国内大循环为主体、国内国际双循环相互促进的新发展格局，并作出重大工作部署。未来的监管重点应当全力支持国内国际双循环发展，积极探索促进科技创新的各种金融服务，持续促进扩大内需，同时稳步推进银行业保险业高水平对外开放。在后疫情时期，要助力提升经济恢复支持力度和金融服务整体效能，尤其是要强化对中小微企业、民生等领域的金融支持。

二是持续防范化解金融风险，加强部分领域金融监管。2021年，防范化解金融风险仍是监管工作重中之重，未来建议监管政策重点是继续紧盯高风险城商行和农村金融机构等高风险机构的风险防范处置、房地产贷款集中度管理制度和重点房地产企业融资管理规定等落实情况、不良资产处置等领域。同时，建议做好外部风险冲击的防范工作，切实加强对互联网平台金融活动的监管，包括加强对银行保险机构与互联网平台合作开展金融活动的监管，以及要坚决遏制垄断和不正当竞争行为等。

三是要持续深化金融供给侧结构性改革，提升公司治理和内控管理水平。商业银行体制机制改革当前已经取得积极成效，在此基础上，建议2021年监管政策举措重点关注银行金融机构体系改革优化、中小银行补充资本、村镇银行改革和兼并重组、推动大型银行向中小银行输出风控工具和技术等。同时进一步加快完善公司治理监管制度体系。建议抓紧出台银行保险机构公司治理准则、大股东行为监管、关联交易管理、董事监事履职评价等监管规制。健全商业银行股权托管机制，完善股东中长期分类惩戒处置机制，持续开展公司治理监管评估，完善公司治理监管信息系统，提高监管的信息化水平等。

## 附表

### 2020 年中国银行业市场主要发展政策

| 日期 | 政策名称 | 发文单位 |
| --- | --- | --- |
| 1月14日 | 银行业保险业消费投诉处理管理办法（中国银保监会令2020年第3号） | 银保监会 |
| 1月26日 | 关于加强银行业保险业金融服务 配合做好新型冠状病毒感染的肺炎疫情防控工作的通知（银保监办发〔2020〕10号） | 银保监会 |
| 1月29日 | 关于动员系统各级党组织和党员干部积极投身新型冠状病毒感染肺炎疫情防控阻击战的通知（银保监党办发〔2020〕3号） | 银保监会 |
| 1月31日 | 关于进一步强化金融支持防控新型冠状病毒感染肺炎疫情的通知（银发〔2020〕29号） | 人民银行、财政部、银保监会、证监会、国家外汇管理局 |
| 2月1日 | 关于做好春节假期后金融服务工作的通知（银发〔2020〕30号） | 人民银行、银保监会、证监会、国家外汇管理局 |
| 2月7日 | 关于疫情防控期间金融机构发行债券有关事宜的通知（银市场〔2020〕5号） | 人民银行 |
| 2月7日 | 关于打赢疫情防控阻击战 强化疫情防控重点保障企业资金支持的紧急通知（财金〔2020〕5号） | 财政部、国家发展改革委、工业和信息化部、人民银行、审计署 |
| 2月14日 | 关于进一步做好疫情防控金融服务的通知（银保监办发〔2020〕15号） | 银保监会 |
| 2月14日 | 关于进一步加快推进上海国际金融中心建设和金融支持长三角一体化发展的意见（银发〔2020〕46号） | 人民银行、银保监会、证监会、国家外汇管理局、上海市人民政府 |
| 2月14日 | 关于商业银行、保险机构参与中国金融期货交易所国债期货交易的公告（证监会公告〔2020〕12号） | 证监会、财政部、人民银行、银保监会 |
| 2月14日 | 关于《标准化票据管理办法（征求意见稿）》公开征求意见的通知 | 人民银行 |
| 2月20日 | 关于预防银行业保险业从业人员金融违法犯罪的指导意见 | 银保监会 |
| 3月1日 | 关于对中小微企业贷款实施临时性延期还本付息的通知（银保监发〔2020〕6号） | 银保监会、人民银行、国家发展改革委、工业和信息化部、财政部 |
| 3月5日 | 统筹监管金融基础设施工作方案 | 人民银行、国家发展改革委、财政部、银保监会、证监会、国家外汇管理局 |
| 3月10日 | 关于优化银行业金融机构分支机构变更营业场所事项的通知（银保监办发〔2020〕25号） | 银保监会 |
| 3月10日 | 关于进一步加大"三区三州"深度贫困地区银行业保险业扶贫工作力度的通知（银保监办发〔2020〕24号） | 银保监会 |
| 3月18日 | 保险资产管理产品管理暂行办法（中国银保监会令2020年第5号） | 银保监会 |
| 3月26日 | 关于加强产业链协同复工复产金融服务的通知（银保监办发〔2020〕28号） | 银保监会 |

续表

| 日期 | 政策名称 | 发文单位 |
|---|---|---|
| 4月7日 | 关于发挥"银税互动"作用助力小微企业复工复产的通知（税总办发〔2020〕10号） | 国家税务总局、银保监会 |
| 4月9日 | 商业银行小微企业金融服务监管评价办法（试行）（征求意见稿） | 银保监会 |
| 4月9日 | 关于做好2020年银行业保险业服务"三农"领域重点工作的通知（银保办发〔2020〕31号） | 银保监会 |
| 4月24日 | 关于金融支持粤港澳大湾区建设的意见（银发〔2020〕95号） | 人民银行、银保监会、证监会、国家外汇管理局 |
| 5月7日 | 境外机构投资者境内证券期货投资资金管理规定（中国人民银行 国家外汇管理局公告〔2020〕第2号） | 人民银行、国家外汇管理局 |
| 5月9日 | 商业银行互联网贷款管理暂行办法（征求意见稿） | 银保监会 |
| 5月18日 | 关于进一步规范信贷融资收费 降低企业融资综合成本的通知（银保监发〔2020〕18号） | 银保监会、工业和信息化部、国家发展改革委、财政部、人民银行、市场监管总局 |
| 5月20日 | 关于保险资金投资银行资本补充债券有关事项的通知（银保监发〔2020〕17号） | 银保监会 |
| 5月22日 | 关于印发银行保险机构涉刑案件管理办法（试行）的通知（银保监发〔2020〕20号） | 银保监会 |
| 5月23日 | 关于延长包商银行股份有限公司接管期限的公告 | 银保监会 |
| 5月26日 | 关于进一步强化中小微企业金融服务的指导意见（银发〔2020〕120号） | 人民银行、银保监会、国家发展改革委、工业和信息化部、财政部、市场监管总局、证监会、国家外汇管理局 |
| 6月1日 | 关于进一步对中小微企业贷款实施阶段性延期还本付息的通知（银发〔2020〕122号） | 人民银行、银保监会、财政部、国家发展改革委、工业和信息化部 |
| 6月1日 | 关于加大小微企业信用贷款支持力度的通知（银发〔2020〕123号） | 人民银行、银保监会、财政部、国家发展改革委、工业和信息化部 |
| 6月5日 | 关于《关于规范商业汇票信息披露的公告（征求意见稿）》公开征求意见的通知 | 人民银行 |
| 6月15日 | 中国银保监会行政处罚办法（中国银保监会令2020年第8号） | 银保监会 |
| 6月15日 | 关于公司信用类债券违约处置有关事宜的通知 | 人民银行、国家发展改革委、证监会 |
| 6月23日 | 关于开展银行业保险业市场乱象整治"回头看"工作的通知（银保监发〔2020〕27号） | 银保监会 |
| 6月24日 | 标准化票据管理办法（中国人民银行公告〔2020〕第6号） | 人民银行 |
| 6月24日 | 关于进一步完善扶贫小额信贷有关政策的通知（银保监发〔2020〕28号） | 银保监会、财政部、人民银行、国务院扶贫办 |
| 6月29日 | 关于印发商业银行小微企业金融服务监管评价办法（试行）的通知 | 银保监会 |

续表

| 日期 | 政策名称 | 发文单位 |
|---|---|---|
| 6月29日 | 关于在粤港澳大湾区开展"跨境理财通"业务试点的联合公告 | 人民银行、香港金融管理局、澳门金融管理局 |
| 7月3日 | 标准化债权类资产认定规则（中国人民银行 中国银保监会 中国证监会 国家外汇管理局公告〔2020〕第5号） | 人民银行、银保监会、证监会、国家外汇管理局 |
| 7月12日 | 商业银行互联网贷款管理暂行办法（中国银保监会令2020年第9号） | 银保监会 |
| 7月14日 | 关于近年影子银行和交叉金融业务监管检查发现主要问题的通报 | 银保监会 |
| 7月17日 | 全国非法集资监测预警体系建设规划（2020—2022年） | 银保监会 |
| 8月5日 | 关于做好政府性融资担保机构监管工作的通知（银保监发〔2020〕39号） | 银保监会、国家发展改革委、工业和信息化部、财政部、农业农村部、商务部、人民银行 |
| 8月17日 | 关于印发健全银行业保险业公司治理三年行动方案（2020—2022年）的通知（银保监发〔2020〕40号） | 银保监会 |
| 9月7日 | 关于加强小额贷款公司监督管理的通知（银保监办发〔2020〕86号） | 银保监会 |
| 9月9日 | 银行保险机构应对突发事件金融服务管理办法（中国银保监会令2020年第10号） | 银保监会 |
| 9月11日 | 关于实施金融控股公司准入管理的决定（国发〔2020〕12号） | 国务院 |
| 9月11日 | 金融控股公司监督管理试行办法（中国人民银行令〔2020〕第4号） | 人民银行 |
| 9月15日 | 金融消费者权益保护实施办法（中国人民银行令〔2020〕第5号） | 人民银行 |
| 9月18日 | 关于规范发展供应链金融 支持供应链产业链稳定循环和优化升级的意见（银发〔2020〕226号） | 人民银行、工业和信息化部、司法部、商务部、国资委、市场监管总局、银保监会、国家外汇管理局 |
| 9月21日 | 关于《境外机构投资者投资中国债券市场资金管理规定（征求意见稿）》公开征求意见的通知 | 人民银行、国家外汇管理局 |
| 9月30日 | 关于建立逆周期资本缓冲机制的通知 | 人民银行、银保监会 |
| 10月16日 | 关于《中华人民共和国商业银行法（修改建议稿）》公开征求意见的通知 | 人民银行 |
| 10月21日 | 金融科技创新风险监控规范（JR/T 0120—2020） | 人民银行 |
| 10月26日 | 关于规范代收业务的通知（银发〔2020〕248号） | 人民银行 |
| 11月2日 | 关于《金融控股公司董事、监事、高级管理人员任职备案管理暂行规定（征求意见稿）》公开征求意见的通知 | 人民银行 |
| 11月2日 | 关于《网络小额贷款业务管理暂行办法（征求意见稿）》公开征求意见的公告 | 银保监会、人民银行 |

续表

| 日期 | 政策名称 | 发文单位 |
|---|---|---|
| 12月3日 | 系统重要性银行评估办法（银发〔2020〕289号） | 人民银行、银保监会 |
| 12月18日 | 商业承兑汇票信息披露有关事宜公告（中国人民银行公告〔2020〕第19号） | 人民银行 |
| 12月18日 | 关于建立银行业金融机构房地产贷款集中度管理制度的通知（银发〔2020〕322号） | 人民银行、银保监会 |
| 12月19日 | 规范人民币现金收付行为有关事项公告（中国人民银行公告〔2020〕第18号） | 人民银行 |
| 12月23日 | 完善银行间债券市场现券做市商管理有关事宜（中国人民银行公告〔2020〕第21号） | 人民银行 |
| 12月25日 | 公司信用类债券信息披露管理办法（中国人民银行 国家发展和改革委员会 中国证监会公告〔2020〕第22号） | 人民银行、国家发展改革委、证监会 |
| 12月25日 | 关于《商业银行理财子公司理财产品销售管理暂行办法（征求意见稿）》公开征求意见的通知 | 银保监会 |
| 12月30日 | 关于深化银行业保险业"放管服"改革 优化营商环境的通知（银保监办发〔2020〕129号） | 银保监会 |
| 12月30日 | 金融机构反洗钱和反恐怖融资监督管理办法（修订草案征求意见稿） | 人民银行 |
| 12月30日 | 关于进一步推动村镇银行化解风险改革重组有关事项的通知（银保监办发〔2020〕124号） | 银保监会 |
| 12月31日 | 关于《中国银保监会关于修改〈中华人民共和国外资保险公司管理条例实施细则〉的决定（征求意见稿）》公开征求意见的通知 | 银保监会 |
| 12月31日 | 关于进一步优化跨境人民币政策 支持稳外贸稳外资的通知（银发〔2020〕330号） | 人民银行、国家发展改革委、商务部、国资委、银保监会、国家外汇管理局 |

**专栏3**

### 评述《网络小额贷款业务管理暂行办法（征求意见稿）》①

2020年11月2日，银保监会同人民银行等部门发布《网络小额贷款业务管理暂行办法（征求意见稿）》。《办法》包含7章，共43条。《办法》出台的目的是规范小额贷款公司网络小额贷款业务，防范网络小额贷款业务风险，表明了金融创新须在审慎监管下进行的理念，也反映出金融监管部门对强化反垄断、消费者权益保护的重视。《办法》

---

① 作者：余金馨，《中国金融政策报告》项目实习生、清华大学五道口金融学院博士。

明确监管主体,对网络小贷在经营过程中的风控体系、单户上限、信息披露等问题进行了详细规范,并划定了禁止跨省展业、借贷上限、联合贷款出资不低于30%的若干红线,是自2008年银监会23号文《关于小额贷款公司试点的指导意见》发布以来,为数不多的小贷行业监管政策。

虽然《办法》目前正在征求意见阶段,但新规的正式落地关系到业务整改、公司增资、组织架构调整、资质重新审批及过渡期起止时间等,将会对网络小额贷款行业格局和发展规则产生重大影响。其中,蚂蚁集团的主要利润引擎就来自两大网络小额贷款产品"花呗"和"借呗",主体分别为重庆市蚂蚁小微小额贷款有限公司和重庆市蚂蚁商诚小额贷款有限公司。11月2日,人民银行、银保监会、证监会、国家外汇管理局等四部门对蚂蚁集团实际控制人马云、董事长井贤栋、总裁胡晓明进行了监管约谈。12月26日,人民银行、银保监会、证监会、国家外汇管理局等金融管理部门再度联合约谈蚂蚁集团,督促指导蚂蚁集团按照市场化、法治化原则,落实金融监管、公平竞争和保护消费者合法权益等要求,规范金融业务经营与发展。人民银行副行长潘功胜就此答记者问,谈及此次约谈背景、约谈主要内容以及对金融科技监管的政策取向。他表示,未来金融科技监管的政策取向将遵循以下原则:一是坚决打破垄断;二是坚持所有金融活动必须依法依规纳入监管;三是坚持"两个毫不动摇",依法保护产权,弘扬企业家精神,激发市场主体活力和社会创造力,增强我国金融科技企业在全球的核心竞争力。

网贷本应是满足普惠金融诉求的创新产品,但硬币的另一面却是不合规发展所释放的系统风险。事实上,自2016年4月起,监管部门发布了一系列以互联网金融风险专项整治方案和网贷机构管理办法为主的行业监管和发展规则,助力网贷朝着健康化、规范化和可持续的道路发展。我们应看到,金融创新只有在审慎监管的框架和前提下进行,才能保持初心,服务好实体经济和人民群众。

## 二、股票市场发展政策[①]

### (一) 2020年股票市场概况

面对突如其来的新冠疫情带来的严峻考验,在党中央、国务院的统一领导、协调和部署下,监管部门始终坚持稳中求进的工作总基调,统筹推进疫情防控、深化市场改革和防范风险等多方面工作,坚持"建制度、不干预、零容忍"的思路,呵护了市场的平稳运行。面对疫情的冲击,监管部门稳定市场预期,努力实现正常开市,坚持"市场的事情交给市场自己解决"。在疫情的特殊时期,作出特殊安排,既体现出监管的温度和弹性,又落实了中央"六稳""六保"的方针。通过坚决推进改革,强化IPO和再融资的功能,有力地支持了实体经济的恢复与发展。年内新《证券法》正式实施,创业板注册制改革、新三板改革、退市制度健全等制度性革新有序推出,对外开放进一步加深,

---

① 作者:张玉龙,中信建投研究发展部策略首席分析师、《中国金融政策报告》项目(课题组)研究员。臧赢舜,中信建投研究发展部策略分析师。

投融资两端双向发力，股票市场也从危机走向了繁荣。

虽然2月新冠疫情的爆发给市场带来了一定冲击，但在人民银行、银保监会、证监会、外汇局等监管部门的金融政策支持下，股票市场在3月触底回升，整体进入牛市状态。全年来看，上证指数年涨幅13.87%，深成指数年涨幅38.73%，创业板年涨幅64.96%，科创50年涨幅39.30%。截至2020年末，沪深两地上市公司总市值79.72万亿元，较上年上升34.46%。

2020年申万一级行业中有21个行业录得正收益，整体赚钱效应较好，但行业间也出现一定分化。其中休闲服务板块涨幅为99.38%，电气设备板块涨幅为94.71%，食品饮料板块涨幅为84.97%，国防军工板块涨幅为57.98%，医药生物板块涨幅为51.10%，汽车板块涨幅为45.85%，电子板块涨幅为36.05%，整体涨幅居前。此外，仍有7个行业全年收益为负，其中房地产板块跌幅为10.85%，通信板块跌幅为8.33%，建筑装饰板块跌幅为7.92%，纺织服装板块跌幅为7.08%，银行板块跌幅为3.25%，采掘板块跌幅为1.34%，商业贸易板块跌幅为0.22%。2020年前半年市场最核心的影响因素就是疫情，医药板块也由此成为最强势的板块。半年以后，随着疫情被有效控制以及复工复产的持续推进，国民经济也逐渐复苏，休闲服务、汽车板块持续走强。随着十九届五中全会的临近，市场强化了对于电气设备和国防军工的追逐。

由于机构化的持续推进，市场出现了一定的"抱团现象"，以食品饮料为首的龙头公司被市场给予估值溢价。从板块上看，创业板市场估值持续走高。截至2020年末，沪深两市、沪深300、创业板、中证500、中证1000的滚动市盈率分别为21.08倍、19.30倍、53.13倍、25.17倍和32.11倍。

（二）2020年股票市场主要发展政策分析

1. 创业板注册制改革

2020年3月1日，新《证券法》开始正式施行。新《证券法》第九条规定明确提及注册制。新《证券法》开始实施同日，深交所表示，推进创业板改革并试点注册制。这是继科创板之后，另一个板块试点注册制，为市场整体向注册制过渡再向前迈出一步。

4月27日，中央全面深化改革委员会第十三次会议审议通过了《创业板改革并试点注册制总体实施方案》，正式拉开创业板注册制改革的大幕。方案明确改革后的创业板将定位于"深入贯彻创新驱动发展战略，适应发展更多依靠创新、创造、创意的大趋势"，主要服务成长型创新创业企业，支持传统产业与新技术、新产业、新业态、新模式深度融合。

6月12日，证监会主席易会满签署《创业板首次公开发行股票注册管理办法（试行）》《创业板上市公司证券发行注册管理办法（试行）》等4项文件，深交所亦发布实施《深圳证券交易所创业板股票上市规则》等相关业务规则及配套安排，共计8项业务规则及18项配套细则、指引和通知，涉及创业板发行上市审核、证券交易、持续监管等方面。创业板注册制主要文件基本出炉，配套规则进一步明晰。

创业板的注册制改革是一整套改革，对发行、退市、交易和投资者适当性管理等方面均进行了完善。科创板成功运行近一年，为创业板改革提供了足够的经验，创业板改革中部分制度借鉴了科创板的有效做法。

发行方面，审核方式由原规定中"保荐人向证监会申报，创业板发行审核委员会审核，证监会做出审核意见"改为"创业板上市委员会审核、证监会注册"。新股定价无市盈率价格限制，采用市场询价的方式确定发行价格。保荐机构跟投方面，创业板注册制对跟投机制进行了优化，不再强制保荐机构全面跟投，仅对未盈利、红筹架构、特殊投票权以及高价发行的四类公司采取强制性跟投。

竞价交易方面，本次改革延续了科创板关于涨跌幅的政策，新股不设涨跌幅天数，前5个交易日不设涨跌幅限制，放宽创业板股票竞价交易涨跌幅至20%。优化盘中临时停牌机制，设置30%、60%两档停牌指标，各停牌10分钟。增加连续竞价期间"价格笼子"，规定连续竞价阶段限价申报的买入申报价格不得高于买入基准价格的102%，卖出申报价格不得低于卖出基准价格的98%。同时，设置单笔申报数量上限，即限价申报单笔数量不超过10万股，市价申报单笔数量不超过5万股，保留现行创业板每笔最低申报数量为100股的制度安排。

盘后定价交易方面，引入盘后定价交易机制，在创业板股票竞价交易收盘后按照时间优先的原则，以当日收盘价对盘后定价买卖申报逐笔连续撮合，以满足投资者按照收盘价成交的交易需求。

投资者适当性管理方面，存量投资者继续参与交易，新申请开通创业板交易权限的个人投资者，权限开通前20个交易日证券账户及资金账户内的资产日均应不低于人民币10万元，并参与证券交易24个月以上。同时删除原规则中2日、5日冷静期要求。同时明确会员要对个人投资者是否符合门槛条件进行核查。明确普通投资者首次参与创业板交易的，应当以纸面或电子方式签署《风险揭示书》。

信息披露方面，构建符合创业板上市公司特点的持续监管规则体系，建立严格的信息披露规则体系并严格执行，提高信息披露的针对性和有效性。强化创新创业及未盈利企业的行业信息、经营风险、业绩波动等披露要求，取消强制业绩快报要求，放宽交易、关联交易事项披露标准并简化审议程序。

退市制度方面，创业板注册制改革简化退市程序，优化退市标准。丰富完善退市指标，增加"连续20个交易日市值低于5亿元"的市值类退市指标，以及上市公司"信息披露或者规范运作等方面存在重大缺陷"退市指标。对创业板存量公司可能出现的退市，设置过渡期，以利于平稳衔接。简化退市流程，取消暂停上市和恢复上市环节，交易类退市不再设置退市整理期。2020年7月10日，深交所发布关于创业板风险警示股票和退市整理期股票交易制度安排的通知，在《深圳证券交易所创业板交易特别规定》正式实施后，创业板风险警示股票涨跌幅限制比例为20%。12月31日，深交所对《深圳证券交易所创业板股票上市规则》进行了修订，优化退市规则，进一步完善市场化、常态化退出机制。

创业板的注册制改革总体沿袭了科创板试点注册制的制度安排。创业板注册制改革充分吸收了科创板试点注册制以信息披露为中心、增加制度包容性、明确并压实市场主体责任、加大处罚力度等成功做法，注册程序分为交易所审核和证监会注册两个环节，交易所主要通过向发行人提出审核问询、发行人回答问题方式开展审核工作，判断发行人是否符合发行条件、上市条件和信息披露要求。本次创业板注册制改革在体例架构、发行条件、信息披露要求、审核流程和监管处罚等主要方面与科创板的规则保持一致。

推进创业板改革并试点注册制，是深化资本市场改革、完善资本市场基础制度、提升资本市场功能的重要安排，是落实创新驱动发展战略、支持深圳建设中国特色社会主义先行示范区、助推粤港澳大湾区建设的重大举措。

2. 新三板改革

新三板改革是我国多层次资本市场建设的重要一环。2020年是新三板全面优化顶层设计和全面启动质效改革的一年。自年初以来，新三板各项改革政策接二连三推出，尤其在精选层的申购、审查以及公募基金入市等方面，证监会和全国中小企业股份转让系统有限责任公司（以下简称全国股转公司）不断完善相应的配套措施。

2020年1月3日，全国股转公司发布实施第二批改革有关业务规则共6件，其中包括《全国中小企业股份转让系统股票定向发行规则》、《全国中小企业股份转让系统挂牌公司信息披露规则》和《全国中小企业股份转让系统挂牌公司治理规则》3件基本业务规则。1月19日，全国股转公司发布实施第三批新三板全面深化改革有关业务规则，包括《股票向不特定合格投资者公开发行并在精选层挂牌规则（试行）》、《股票向不特定合格投资者公开发行保荐业务管理细则（试行）》和《全国中小企业股份转让系统发行与承销管理细则（试行）》共3件业务规则。2月28日，《全国中小企业股份转让系统精选层挂牌审查细则（试行）》、《全国中小企业股份转让系统挂牌委员会管理细则（试行）》和《全国中小企业股份转让系统股票向不特定合格投资者公开发行并在精选层挂牌与承销业务实施细则（试行）》出炉。这些政策对新三板企业定向发行、公开发行、承销保荐、信息披露、精选层审查等细节进行了明确规定，对新三板的发行规范建立了制度性规则。

多层次资本市场的关键在于市场层次的划分。对于新三板而言，分层与转板是核心，监管也对定期调层与转板等相关制度进行规范。2020年3月6日，证监会就《关于全国中小企业股份转让系统挂牌公司转板上市的指导意见》公开征求意见，对转入板块的范围、转板上市条件、程序、保荐要求、股份限售等事项作出原则性规定。具体来看重点有以下内容：第一，转入板块范围为科创板或创业板，上交所、深交所各选择一个板块作为试点。第二，为在新三板精选层连续挂牌一年以上的公司，且应当符合转入板块的首次公开发行并上市的条件。由于转板不涉及股票公开发行，转板无须经证监会核准或注册，只由交易所审核。第三，交易所可以聘请证券公司担任上市保荐人，进一步对挂牌公司转板上市的保荐要求和程序适当调整完善。第四，在股份限售安排上规定，计算股份限售期时，原则上可以扣除在精选层已经限售的时间。

此后，监管在新三板精选层开板前后又陆续出台了《全国中小企业股份转让系统非上市公众公司重大资产重组业务细则》、《全国中小企业股份转让系统挂牌公司股票停复牌业务实施细则》、《全国中小企业股份转让系统挂牌公司分层调整业务指南》、《全国中小企业股份转让系统表决权差异安排业务指南》、《非上市公众公司监管指引第6号——股权激励和员工持股计划的监管要求（试行）》、《全国中小企业股份转让系统股票挂牌业务操作指南》和《全国中小企业股份转让系统主办券商持续督导工作指引》等法规，对其他新三板涉及的业务方面进行了规定。2020年11月27日，深交所和上交所分别发布精选层向创业板和科创板转板上市办法（试行）公开征求意见稿，对精选层向创业板和科创板转板的条件进行了具体规定。精选层转板创业板/科创板要求：（1）在精选层连续挂牌一年以上，且近一年不存在应当调出精选层的情形；（2）符合创业板/科创板IPO的发行条件；（3）最近三年无证监会行政处罚及被立案调查且尚未有明确结论意见，或者最近十二个月未受到全国股转公司公开谴责；（4）股本总额不低于3000万元；（5）股东人数不少于1000人；（6）公众持股比例在25%以上（公司股本总额超过4亿元的，比例10%以上）；（7）转板公司应当符合《科创属性评价指引（试行）》定位。

此外，针对改善新三板的流动性的问题，监管正式引入公募基金。2020年1月3日，证监会公布《公开募集证券投资基金投资全国中小企业股份转让系统挂牌股票指引》并公开征求意见。该指引明确了公募基金管理人参与的要求、可参与投资的基金类型、新三板股票投资要求、流动性管理要求、估值、信息披露、风险揭示、投资者适当性管理、投资交易管控、存量基金监管安排等细节。

2020年全面改革以后，新三板整体完善了顶层设计，在上市、交易、重组等各方面均进行了改革。

市场方面，新三板形成了"基础层、创新层、精选层"的层级市场。挂牌满一年的创新层企业可公开发行；公开发行成功后的企业直接进入精选层；精选层企业符合《证券法》上市条件和交易所相关规定的情形下，可以直接向交易所申请转板上市。转板机制有利于拓宽上市渠道，更好发挥新三板市场承上启下的功能，促进多层次资本市场优势互补、错位发展，提升资本市场服务实体经济的能力。

发行制度方面，新三板引入向不特定合格投资者公开发行制度，允许挂牌公司向不特定合格投资者公开发行，配套实行保荐、承销制度；允许公开路演、询价，提高投融资对接效率，满足创新层、精选层企业高效融资的需求。与此同时，新三板现行的定向发行制度也将进一步完善，内容包括取消单次融资新增股东35人限制、允许小额融资实施自办发行等，以进一步提高融资效率、降低融资成本。

交易制度优化方面，新三板增加基础层、创新层集合竞价撮合频次，适度提高流动性水平，同时基础层公司和创新层公司可自行选择集合竞价或做市交易方式。为与公开发行后的股份流通需求相匹配，精选层将实行连续竞价交易机制。投资者门槛的界定上，新三板充分考虑不同市场层次挂牌公司的细分特征和风险情况，对精选层、创新层和基础层分别设置投资者准入标准。对于尚不符合投资者适当性标准的投资者，鼓励其通过公募基金等专业机构分享中小企业成长的"红利"。预计精选层投资者门槛将显著降低。

信息披露方面，全国股转公司表示，《全国中小企业股份转让系统挂牌公司信息披露规则》的修订基本原则是：对精选层挂牌公司的信息披露从严。对基础层挂牌公司的信息披露从简，促进提升挂牌公司信息披露质量。创新层挂牌公司的信息披露执行适中标准，重点是以分行业披露要求为切入点，提高信息披露的有效性和针对性；审计上要求执行关键事项审计准则，强化披露质量的外部保障。

### 3. QFII 和 RQFII 新规

2020 年 9 月 25 日中国人民银行、证监会和国家外汇管理局发布《合格境外机构投资者和人民币合格境外机构投资者证券期货投资管理办法》（以下简称《QFII、RQFII 办法》），并规定此办法于 11 月 1 日起开始实行。事实上，2019 年监管部门已经公布了相关文件的征求意见稿，一年多以后，外资证券期货投资管理办法正式落地。

根据中国证监会的说明，《QFII、RQFII 办法》及配套规则修订内容主要涉及三方面内容：（1）降低准入门槛，便利投资运作；（2）稳步有序扩大投资范围；（3）加强持续监管。

经历多次额度提升后，国家外汇管理局在 2019 年 9 月完全取消了 QFII 和 RQFII 投资额度限制，与此同时也取消了 RQFII 试点国家和地区限制。具备相应资格的境外机构投资者，只需进行登记即可自主汇入资金开展符合规定的证券投资。但从实际情况看，QFII、RQFII 投资并没有因为额度的上升而明显提高，没有触及额度上限。所以，造成 QFII、RQFII 流入较少的原因就与额度限制无关，而更多取决于流程中成本的相对较高。

此次，《QFII、RQFII 办法》放宽准入条件，简化申请文件，缩短审批时限，实施行政许可简易程序。《QFII、RQFII 办法》规定申请人通过托管人向证监会报送合格境外投资者资格申请文件，证监会自受理申请文件之日起 10 个工作日内给予批准或不批准的答复。此外，《QFII、RQFII 办法》取消委托中介机构数量限制，优化备案事项管理，减少数据报送要求。《QFII、RQFII 办法》取消了托管人数量限制，允许单家合格投资者委托 1 家以上境内托管人。合格境外投资者委托 2 个以上托管人的，应指定 1 个主报告人，负责代其统一办理资格申请、重大事项报告、主体信息登记等事项。

《QFII、RQFII 办法》同时扩大了投资范围。《QFII、RQFII 办法》新增允许 QFII、RQFII 投资新三板股票、私募投资基金、金融期货、商品期货、期权等，允许其参与债券回购、证券交易所融资融券、转融通证券出借交易。至此，合格境外机构投资者基本上可以拥有沪深交易所股票、新三板、期货等多种交易的投资品种，有助于其全方位参与境内多层次资本市场的投资，为其多种策略，特别是跨市场风险对冲策略提供更多工具，给予其更深程度参与中国金融市场投资的勇气。

《QFII、RQFII 办法》对加强持续监管能力，跨市场监管、跨境监管和穿透式监管能力提出更高要求。监管机构压实压严托管人、监管等各方面的责任要求，并对违反规定行为和惩戒措施进行了明确规定。

《QFII、RQFII办法》旨在放宽外资的流入，提升外资进入中国市场的热情。但外资的流入需要受到严格的监管。因为一方面外资的扩容，将会给市场带来更大的风险与挑战，使得境内受到外围市场和相关国家货币政策的影响加大，特别是在人民币汇率双向波动增强的背景下，资金运动的加强将带来资产价格波动的上升。另一方面，随着开放程度的加深，进入境内投资的主体也将会越发的丰富，监管的范围和难度也将逐步加大。

4. 取消证券公司外资股比例限制，外资机构渗透加深

2020年3月13日，证监会正式宣布自2020年4月1日起，取消证券公司外资股比例限制。此前，证监会宣布自2020年1月1日起，放开期货公司外资股比例限制，自2020年4月1日在全国范围内取消基金管理公司外资股比例限制。

总体来看，2020年4月1日是非常重要的一个时间节点，可以视为是中国金融机构对外开放的里程碑。4月起，证券公司、基金管理公司外资股比限制被取消，符合条件的境外投资者可根据法律法规、证监会有关规定和相关服务指南的要求，依法提交设立或变更公司实际控制人的申请。值得注意的是，证券公司的持股比例在4月放开是监管加速的结果。因为根据证监会之前的政策安排，证券公司原定取消外资股比限制的时点是在2020年12月1日。面对疫情的冲击，中国金融领域对外开放的步伐并没有放缓，反而进一步加速，无论是对外资证券投资资金的引入，还是对外资金融资本的引入都是如此。

目前，证券领域外资进入进展较好。其中，瑞银证券从合资券商转化为外资控股券商，这也是首家外资控股券商。2020年3月27日，证监会又批复了两家由参股转向控股的券商。摩根士丹利成为摩根士丹利华鑫证券有限公司的主要股东、控股股东，持股比例为51%；高盛集团成为高盛高华证券有限责任公司主要股东、控股股东，持股比例为51%。而摩根大通证券（中国）有限公司、野村东方国际证券有限公司则是证监会在2019年初批准新设立的券商，目前两家新设的外资控股券商均已开业。除了上述已经获批的外资控股券商外，还有外资正在申请，其中一家是由合资提升持股比例转换为控股的情形，即瑞信方正。新设券商方面，星展银行和大和证券两家已经向证监会递交了申请材料。在允许外资全资控股证券公司的背景下，部分海外的金融机构或许对独资控股的兴趣更高。如法国兴业银行境内业务的高层曾透露，此前已经找好设立控股券商的其他股东。所以，未来法国兴业银行有可能在国内成立一家独资券商。

除此之外，保险业也充分贯彻落实了党中央、国务院关于扩大金融业对外开放的决策部署，银保监会于2020年3月10日发布《关于修改〈中华人民共和国外资保险公司管理条例实施细则〉的决定》，进一步明确外国保险集团公司和境外金融机构投资外资保险公司的准入标准。此次修改删除了有关外资股比的限制性规定，外国保险公司或者外国保险集团公司作为外资保险公司股东，其持股比例可达100%。

事实上，自银保监会宣布实施取消合资寿险公司外资比例限制以来，外资机构已开

始行动。2020年5月，汇丰保险宣布将收购国民信托所持有的汇丰人寿50%股权，交易完成后，汇丰人寿将成为其在中国的全资控股子公司，公司内部已表决通过，目前尚待银保监会批准。6月，友邦保险"分改子"获批，其上海分公司改建为友邦人寿保险有限公司，成为中国首家获得设立批复的外资独资人身保险公司。

资管机构方面，外资也有进展。2020年8月28日，证监会公告显示，贝莱德基金管理有限公司核准成立，这也是首个外资公募基金。此外，路博迈、富达、范达集团、联博基金等外资也纷纷申请设立公募基金。银行理财子公司方面，外资也积极参与。摩根大通将增资入股招银理财，成为继东方汇理、贝莱德、施罗德后又一家瞄准理财子公司的全球资管巨头。

5. 提高上市公司质量

2020年10月5日，国务院发布《国务院关于进一步提高上市公司质量的意见》（以下简称《意见》）。此次《意见》共提出七点六个方面要求。其中第一点强调了上市公司质量改革对资本市场进一步发展的关键作用；第二点至第七点为具体规章，主要内容包括：提高上市公司治理水平，推动上市公司做优做强，健全上市公司退出机制，解决公司上市突出问题，提高上市公司及相关主体违法违规成本。

提高上市公司治理水平方面，《意见》要求应明确控股股东、实际控制人、董事、监事和管理高层的职责与法律责任，严格执行上市公司的内控制度，并提高内控体系的规范性和有效性。同时，上市公司应提升信息披露质量，相关监管机构应以投资者需求为导向，完善分行业信息披露标准，增强信息披露的针对性。

推动上市公司做优做强方面，《意见》旨在全面推行、分步实施证券发行注册制，加强对拟上市企业的培育和辅导，提升拟上市企业规范化水平，并鼓励和支持混合所有制改革试点企业上市，发挥股权投资机构在促进公司优化治理、创新创业、产业升级等方面的积极作用。同时，《意见》提出监管机构应促进市场化并购重组，支持境内上市公司发行股份购买境外优质资产，允许更多符合条件的外国投资者对境内上市公司进行战略投资，提升上市公司国际竞争力。相关机构应完善上市公司融资制度，引导上市公司兼顾发展需要和市场状况优化融资安排，完善上市公司再融资发行条件和公司股权激励及员工持股制度。

健全上市公司退出机制方面，《意见》强调要严格退市监管，简化退市程序，同时积极拓宽多元化退出渠道，完善并购重组和破产重整等制度。同时，有关地区和部门要综合施策，支持上市公司通过并购重组、破产重整等方式出清风险。

解决上市公司突出问题方面，《意见》强调要通过加强质押信息共享，严格执行分层次的质押信息披露制度，强化对金融机构、上市公司大股东及实际控制人的风险约束机制，建立多部门共同参与的上市公司股票质押风险处置机制来积极稳妥化解上市公司股票质押风险。同时相关监管机构应严肃处置资金占用、违规担保问题，强化应对重大突发事件政策支持。

提高上市公司及相关主体违法违规成本方面，《意见》规定司法机构应加大对欺诈发行、信息披露违法、操纵市场、内幕交易等违法违规行为的处罚力度，同时加重财务造假、资金占用等违法违规行为的行政、刑事法律责任，完善证券民事诉讼和赔偿制度。

形成提高上市公司质量的工作合力方面，《意见》提出证监会应加强全程审慎监管，推进科学监管、分类监管、专业监管、持续监管，提高上市公司监管有效性。同时各级政府和监管机构要强化上市公司的主体责任，督促中介机构归位尽责，并推进上市公司监管大数据平台建设，建立健全财政、税务、海关、金融、市场监管、行业监管、地方政府、司法机关等单位的信息共享机制。

整体来看，《意见》提出的关于公司治理、信息披露、提高违规成本、约束股票质押等举措有助于减少上市公司因信息不对称、管理不规范而带来的违约风险。同时健全的退市机制以及多部门的监管升级能够更有效地保证投资者的权益，减少投资者的违约损失，增加资本市场的吸引力。上市公司作为金融市场的重要一员，其质量的进一步提高有助于进一步防范系统性风险。此外，上市公司作为优质企业的代表，连接资本市场与实体经济，因此提高上市公司质量能够在增强资本市场的活力与竞争的基础上，同时带动下游非上市公司提质增效，为实体经济发展夯实基础。

6. 健全上市公司退市机制

2020年11月2日，中央全面深化改革委员会第十六次会议审议通过了《健全上市公司退市机制实施方案》和《关于依法从严打击证券违法活动的若干意见》。会议指出，"健全上市公司退市机制，依法从严打击证券违法活动，是全面深化资本市场改革的重要制度安排。要坚持市场化、法治化方向，完善退市标准，简化退市程序，拓宽多元退出渠道，严格退市监管，完善常态化退出机制"。

12月11日，证监会召开新闻发布会，会上表示，证监会认真贯彻落实党中央、国务院决策部署，从推进注册制改革的全局出发，全面梳理分析上市公司退市存在的突出问题，在认真总结科创板、创业板退市制度改革试点经验的基础上，针对当前退市中存在的问题，在六个方面进一步提出改革措施，即完善退市标准、简化退市程序、拓宽多元退出渠道、强化交易所退市实施的主体责任、强化退市监管力度、优化投资者保护机制，拟在全市场开展退市制度改革。

12月14日，沪深交易所就退市制度修订征求意见，12月31日，沪深两地交易所分别修订并正式印发《上海证券交易所股票上市规则（2020年12月修订）》、《深圳证券交易所股票上市规则》、《上海证券交易所科创板股票上市规则》、《深圳证券交易所创业板股票上市规则》等八项规则（以下合称退市新规正式稿），从发布之日起施行。这既表明了国家完善退市机制的决心，也说明了当下资本市场改革的紧迫性。

对比修订前的主板和创业板股票上市规则，本轮新规将退市准则单列成章，并吸取科创板的现行制度经验，新设了交易类、财务类、规范类和重大违法四类退市指标体系。同时针对科创板，本次修订也将其与主板进行了整合统一，包括对退市指标的修订增补以及缩短退市流程时间等。具体来看包括：（1）调整交易退市指标口径，包括新设总市值退市指标、将收盘价退市指标统一至 1 元和统一成交量指标;(2)交叉适用财务指标和中介机构意见,将审计意见与净资产、净利润和营业收入等其他财务类指标交叉适用,给予了成长股更大发展空间,也能更高效筛选出财务存在问题的标的;(3)完善信息披露制度,加大对披露不得当的处罚力度,包括新增对于无法按时有效披露、报告准确性长期得不到董事会确认的公司直接进行退市,有效保护投资者利益;(4)补充重大违法量化指标,在原规则的重大违法退市情形基础上,将财务造假量化后纳入其中。

除退市指标之外,新规正式稿的另一重点是全面修订了退市流程,包括了取消主板暂停和恢复上市环节、放开整理期涨跌幅限制以及缩短退市整理期和停牌时点。这一系列举措极大程度上减少了投资者在退市交易中的无效炒作时间,使得常态化的退市体制在短期内快速构建运行。

同时,对比 2020 年 12 月 14 日印发的征求意见稿,退市新规正式稿对于部分细节进行了修改,其中最重要的是针对财务造假量化指标的修订:(1)正式稿将财务造假退市的时间尺度从三年缩减到两年、比例尺度从 100% 降低至 50%,极大程度上缩减了 A 股上市公司虚增利润和营收、粉饰报表的空间,也降低了长期保壳的可操作性;(2)正式稿新增营业收入指标,形成了净利润、营业收入、利润总额和资产负债表四个指标共同监控的财务造假指标体系。此外,正式稿补充了对股东减持行为的规定,加大了退市过程中保护中小投资者利益的力度。

本次退市新规从指标、流程、交易规则等全角度对退市机制进行了完善。退市新规的落地将促成 A 股退市常态化,形成"宽进宽出"的市场格局,达到为上市公司全面提质的目的。退市机制常态化也有助于增强我国资本市场对投资者的吸引力,加速带动优质长期资金入市。在这一优胜劣汰的过程中,A 股市场对投资者的吸引力也会随之增强,在中长期能够加快各类长期资金入市步伐。退市机制的修改将增强资金向优质标的集中的趋势,为提高资本市场活力、推行主板注册制奠定良好基础。

7. 再融资新规

2020 年 2 月 14 日,中国证监会在充分征求公众意见后,对外公布《关于修改〈上市公司证券发行管理办法〉的决定》和《关于修改〈创业板上市公司证券发行管理暂行办法〉的决定》两份决定。此两份文件的征求意见稿的发布时间为 2019 年 11 月 8 日。与征求意见稿相比,决定主要的放宽条款均未发生变化,最主要变化在于提高了定增规模上限、宽泛了新老划断时点和限制关联方保底保收益三点上。

3 月 20 日,证监会对定增的战略投资者的标准进行了明确。根据《发行监管问答——关于上市公司非公开发行股票引入战略投资者有关事项的监管要求》,战略投资者的基本要求是"具有同行业或相关行业较强的重要战略性资源,与上市公司谋求双方协调互补的长期共同战略利益,愿意长期持有上市公司较大比例股份,愿意并且有能力认真履行相应职责,委派董事实际参与公司治理,提升上市公司治理水平,帮助上市公司显著提高公司质量和内在价值,具有良好诚信记录,最近三年未受到证监会行政处罚或被追究刑事责任的投资者"。

证监会要求满足以下两条之一：其一是"能够给上市公司带来国际国内领先的核心技术资源，显著增强上市公司的核心竞争力和创新能力，带动上市公司的产业技术升级，显著提升上市公司的盈利能力"；其二是"能够给上市公司带来国际国内领先的市场、渠道、品牌等战略性资源，大幅促进上市公司市场拓展，推动实现上市公司销售业绩大幅提升"。这意味着战略投资者与发行人在生产或经营上具有重要联系，必须在技术、市场、渠道、品牌领域能给发行人带来实质性的帮助，而不能单纯作为一个财务投资者。在信息披露上，需要穿透披露股权或投资者结构，严格对于战略投资者要求的执行。

总结来看，《上市公司证券发行管理办法》和《创业板上市公司证券发行管理暂行办法》的修订内容主要涉及针对放松创业板再融资公开或非公开发行条件和针对全部市场优化非公开发行制度改革两方面内容，总体原则是将再融资的标准放宽，提升资金方参与再融资愿望，鼓励企业通过再融资补充资金或进行资产重组。

对于创业板再融资改革的特殊规定方面，一是取消创业板上市公司公开发行证券最近一期末资产负债率高于45%的要求，二是取消创业板非公开发行股票连续2年盈利的条件，三是将创业板前次募集资金基本使用完毕，且使用进度和效果与披露情况基本一致从发行条件移至信息披露要求。

针对全部市场优化非公开发行制度改革方面，主要从发行定价机制、定增对象数量、锁定期和批文有效期四个方面进行放松，改革支持上市公司引入战略投资者和财务投资者。

发行定价机制上，一是将发行价不得低于定价基准日前20个交易日公司股票均价的9折改为8折，从而相对降低定增成本价，扩大投资者潜在的盈利空间，二是将提前确定发行对象且为战略投资者的定价基准日改为除本次非公开发行股票的发行期首日外还可以选择本次非公开发行股票的董事会决议公告日或股东大会决议公告日。

定增对象数量方面，将目前主板（中小板）上市公司、创业板上市公司非公开发行股票发行对象数量分别不超过10名和5名，统一调整为不超过35名。此举便于小额资金参与定向增发，一是降低了寻找资金的难度，二是也为小额资金参与定增扩大了可能性、降低了潜在成本。

锁定期方面，由现在的36个月和12个月分别缩短至18个月和6个月，且不适用减持规则的限制。创业板上市公司非公开发行股票的定价和锁定机制与主板（中小板）上市公司保持一致，从而使快速退出成为可能，使得投资者无论是参与借壳上市还是普通的定向增发的意愿都趋于增强。

延长批文有效期方面，将再融资批文有效期从6个月延长至12个月，与重大资产重组配套融资批文有效期匹配，且增加了发行选择期。

此外，针对新三板改革，《非上市公众公司监督管理办法》和《上市公司信息披露管理办法》修订的主要内容是引入向不特定合格投资者公开发行制度，放开挂牌公司定向发行35人限制，优化公开转让和发行的审核机制及差异化信息披露。

总体来看，再融资标准被放宽、融资规模扩大，降低了投资者参与的风险，扩大了潜在盈利空间，降低了资金参与门槛与成本，有利于提升资金方参与再融资愿望，增加企业寻找到资金的可能性，便于上市公司通过再融资补充资金。再融资规则的优化可以改善上市公司流动性，降低资产负债率，提升市场基本面质量。事实上，2020年的增发市场也更加活跃，全年募集家数为362家，高于2019年的251家，募集总金额为8341亿元，高于2019年的6888亿元。

8. 从严打击证券违法活动

2020年4月以来，国务院金融稳定发展委员会四次会议提及有关内容，中央高度重视打击资本市场违法犯罪行为。作为进一步提高上市公司质量的举措之一，提高上市公司及相关主体违法违规成本是其中的重要一项。国务院要求监管层加大执法力度，严格落实《证券法》等法律规定，加大对欺诈发行、信息披露违法、操纵市场、内幕交易等违法违规行为的处罚力度。

2020年11月2日，中央全面深化改革委员会第十六次会议审议通过了《健全上市公司退市机制实施方案》和《关于依法从严打击证券违法活动的若干意见》（以下简称《若干意见》）。会议指出，"健全上市公司退市机制，依法从严打击证券违法活动，是全面深化资本市场改革的重要制度安排"。其中对于打击证券违法活动，中央全面深化改革委员会提出要加快健全证券执法司法体制机制，加大对重大违法案件的查处惩治力度，夯实资本市场法治和诚信基础，加强跨境监管执法协作，推动构建良好市场秩序。执法必严，违法必究，针对证券领域的违法行为的打击将进一步加大力度，以维护注册制的建设成果。

实际上，监管层对于《若干意见》的贯彻执行很快。2020年12月29日，证监会首席律师焦津洪表示，证监会将立足资本市场新发展阶段实际，持续做好资本市场改革发展和法治建设各项工作。争取利用两年左右时间，在资本市场法律体系建设方面取得重要进展，推动完善具有中国特色的证券执法体制，显著提高证券违法犯罪成本，进一步畅通投资者权利救济渠道，明显改善资本市场秩序。这是对《若干意见》中"加快健全证券执法司法体制机制"的直接回应，预计后续监管层面的执法能力建设将持续推进。

从严打击证券违法活动与健全证券执法司法体制机制并行。2021年1月31日，中国证券业协会以抽签方式，确定对2021年1月30日前受理的20家科创板和创业板首发企业进行信息披露质量检查。截至2月24日，20家被抽检公司中，16家撤回材料终止审核，比例高达80%，体现出信息披露方面存在一定的问题。2021年2月26日，上交所就科创板首发企业信息披露质量现场检查情况对外表示，上交所将坚持"建制度、不干预、零容忍"，充分发挥现场检查、现场督导与审核问询的监管联动机制，严把上市"入口关"。对于现场检查进场前撤回的项目，审核中心正在对相关问题进行分析梳理，如发现存在涉嫌财务造假、虚假陈述等重大违法违规问题的，保荐人、发行人都要承担相应的责任，绝不能"一撤了之"。这样的表态表达了明确的监管态度，符合提高上市公司及相关主体违法违规成本的核心思路。

随着一线监管部门更多实操性指引的落地，以及现场督导、抽查等监管措施的强化,提高信息披露质量将成为发行人和中介机构的第一任务。注册制已经逐步试点,未来将向全市场铺开。但与全市场实行注册制相矛盾的是我国的保荐机构执业质量并不能安全适应注册制发展的要求。不少中介机构尚未真正具备与注册制相匹配的理念、组织和能力,这将影响注册制的行稳致远,给未来留下隐患。所以当前必须加大执法力度,采取针对性措施,对"带病闯关"严肃处理,维护资本市场的风清气正。

中央层面审议通过关于打击证券违法活动的专门文件,在我国资本市场历史上是第一次,这将有助于保护投资者合法权益,构建公平有序、诚信自律的资本市场良好生态。

9. 上市公司信息披露

信息披露是股票发行注册制改革的核心,信息披露监管是上市公司监管工作的重心,监管层必须高度重视上市公司信息披露制度建设。

2020年3月1日,新《证券法》正式施行,对信息披露作了专章规定。证监会在认真总结信息披露监管经验的基础上,在2020年7月24日对外公布《上市公司信息披露管理办法(修订稿)》(以下简称《管理办法》),向社会公开征求意见。

从内容上看,《管理办法》主要在三个方面进行了修订。

第一,完善了信息披露原则。《管理办法》新增了简明清晰、通俗易懂的原则要求,完善公平披露原则,同时明确自愿披露原则的相关要求,进一步鼓励自愿披露。同时,《管理办法》按照新证券法对临时报告事项进行了完善,如将"公司的实际控制人及其控制的其他企业从事与公司相同或者相似业务的情况发生较大变化"、"公司分配股利、增资的计划,公司股权结构的重要变化"等事项纳入临时报告;对于同时发行公司债券的上市公司,增加债券临时披露事项,明确披露要求。

第二,《管理办法》还进一步强调董监高等相关主体的责任。董监高是信息披露的重点对象。强化董事会在定期报告披露中的责任,明确要求定期报告内容应当经董事会审议通过;要求董事、监事和高级管理人员无法保证定期报告内容的真实性、准确性、完整性或者有异议的,应当在书面确认意见中发表意见并陈述理由,上市公司应当披露;同时进一步明确控股股东、实际控制人的配合义务。

第三,完善临时报告事项。《管理办法》对部分临时报告信息披露事项进行了细化、明确,在原有临时报告信息披露重大事件基础上扩大了事件范围,充分保证投资者的知情权。例如,将"重大的购置财产的决定"明确为"公司在一年内购买、出售重大资产超过公司资产总额百分之三十,或者公司营业用主要资产的抵押、质押、出售或者报废一次超过该资产的百分之三十"。再如,将"公司的实际控制人及其控制的其他企业从事与公司相同或者相似业务的情况发生较大变化""公司分配股利、增资的计划,公司股权结构的重要变化"纳入临时报告需披露的"重大事件"的范围。

除了对于证券发行人进行严格要求,提出完善上市公司信息披露事务管理外,《管理办法》也对服务机构提出明确要求。《管理办法》要求证券服务机构应当妥善保存客户委托文件、核查和验证资料、工作底稿等信息和资料,并且应配合证监会的监督管理,证券服务机构要确保其提供、报送或披露的资料、信息真实、准确、完整,不得有虚假记载、误导性陈述或者重大遗漏。压实发行人、证券服务机构各方面的责任，有利于从多方面约束发行人，保证信息披露的真实、及时，也为执法提供充分依据，有助于打击证券违法活动。

### （三）政策评价与展望

股票市场发展政策在2020年延续和深化了2019年以来整体的改革思路，始终坚持"建制度、不干预、零容忍"的基本理念，坚持系统观念，建设服务新发展格局的多层次资本市场。在实践中进行经验总结，在2019年成功设立科创板的基础上，进一步深化改革，成功地完成了创业板注册制改革。为了更好地服务实体经济，强化再融资市场功能，便利上市公司权益融资，助力企业做大做强。在对外开放方面，继续加快脚步，改革QFII和RQFII制度，取消证券、基金、期货等金融机构外资持股比例限制。在提高上市公司质量方面，规范公司治理和内部控制，提升信息披露质量，支持优质企业上市，健全退市机制，解决股票质押、资金占用、违规担保等风险问题，提高违法违规成本，以法制化、规范化，促进资本市场良性发展。

展望2021年，中国股票市场政策将科学合理保证IPO和再融资的常态化运行，通过完善金融期货工具，保证股票市场平衡发展。针对新发展格局，重点支持创新经济，完善科创属性评价标准。注册制改革继续完善发展，加快配套政策出台，压实中介机构责任，以"零容忍"的态度，打击证券违法活动，保护资本市场的改革成果，为全市场注册制推进创造条件。坚决打赢防范化解重大金融风险攻坚战持久战，密切关注流动性和杠杆水平，严防跨市场跨区域跨境的交叉性、输入性风险。

## 附表

**2020年中国股票市场主要发展政策一览**

| 日期 | 政策名称 | 发文单位 |
| --- | --- | --- |
| 1月13日 | 【第3号公告】非上市公众公司信息披露内容与格式准则第3号——定向发行说明书和发行情况报告书（2020年修订） | 证监会 |
| 1月13日 | 【第4号公告】非上市公众公司信息披露内容与格式准则第4号——定向发行申请文件（2020年修订） | 证监会 |
| 1月13日 | 【第5号公告】非上市公众公司信息披露内容与格式准则第9号——创新层挂牌公司年度报告 | 证监会 |
| 1月13日 | 【第6号公告】非上市公众公司信息披露内容与格式准则第10号——基础层挂牌公司年度报告 | 证监会 |
| 1月14日 | 【第7号公告】证券期货违法违规行为举报工作暂行规定 | 证监会 |
| 1月17日 | 【第8号公告】非上市公众公司信息披露内容与格式准则第11号——向不特定合格投资者公开发行股票说明书 | 证监会 |
| 1月17日 | 【第9号公告】非上市公众公司信息披露内容与格式准则第12号——向不特定合格投资者公开发行股票申请文件 | 证监会 |
| 2月14日 | 【第11号公告】关于修改《上市公司非公开发行股票实施细则》的决定 | 证监会 |

续表

| 日期 | 政策名称 | 发文单位 |
|---|---|---|
| 2月14日 | 【第12号公告】关于商业银行、保险机构参与中国金融期货交易所国债期货交易的公告 | 证监会、财政部、中国人民银行、银保监会 |
| 2月14日 | 【第163号令】关于修改《上市公司证券发行管理办法》的决定 | 证监会 |
| 2月14日 | 【第164号令】关于修改《创业板上市公司证券发行管理暂行办法》的决定 | 证监会 |
| 2月19日 | 【第13号公告】关于非上市公众公司行政许可事项的有关事宜 | 证监会 |
| 3月3日 | 【第18号公告】关于取消或调整证券公司部分行政审批项目等事项的公告 | 证监会 |
| 3月6日 | 【第17号公告】上市公司创业投资基金股东减持股份的特别规定 | 证监会 |
| 3月6日 | 关于发布《深圳证券交易所上市公司创业投资基金股东减持股份实施细则（2020年修订）》的通知 | 深交所 |
| 3月6日 | 关于发布《上海证券交易所上市公司创业投资基金股东减持股份实施细则（2020年修订）》的通知 | 上交所 |
| 3月13日 | 【第165号令】证券期货规章制定程序规定 | 证监会 |
| 3月13日 | 关于修订《上海证券交易所交易规则》的通知 | 上交所 |
| 3月13日 | 取消证券公司外资股比限制 | 证监会 |
| 3月20日 | 【第20号公告】关于修改部分证券期货规范性文件的决定 | 证监会 |
| 3月20日 | 【第21号公告】科创属性评价指引（试行） | 证监会 |
| 3月20日 | 【第166号令】关于修改部分证券期货规章的决定 | 证监会 |
| 3月27日 | 关于发布《上海证券交易所科创板企业发行上市申报及推荐暂行规定》的通知 | 上交所 |
| 4月7日 | 【第22号公告】关于做好当前上市公司等年度报告审计与披露工作有关事项的公告 | 证监会 |
| 4月17日 | 【第23号公告】公开募集证券投资基金投资全国中小企业股份转让系统挂牌股票指引 | 证监会 |
| 4月24日 | 关于金融支持粤港澳大湾区建设的意见 | 中国人民银行、银保监会、证监会、国家外汇管理局 |
| 4月27日 | 关于发布《深圳证券交易所创业板投资者适当性管理实施办法（2020年修订）》的通知 | 深交所 |
| 4月28日 | 【第25号公告】公开发行证券的公司信息披露编报规则第24号——注册制下创新试点红筹企业财务报告信息特别规定 | 证监会 |
| 4月30日 | 【第24号公告】关于废止《创业板市场投资者适当性管理暂行规定》的决定 | 证监会 |
| 4月30日 | 【第26号公告】关于创新试点红筹企业在境内上市相关安排的公告 | 证监会 |
| 5月29日 | 【第28号公告】关于修改《证券公司次级债管理规定》的决定 | 证监会 |
| 6月3日 | 【第29号公告】中国证监会关于全国中小企业股份转让系统挂牌公司转板上市的指导意见 | 证监会 |
| 6月12日 | 【第31号公告】公开发行证券的公司信息披露内容与格式准则第28号——创业板公司招股说明书（2020年修订） | 证监会 |

续表

| 日期 | 政策名称 | 发文单位 |
| --- | --- | --- |
| 6月12日 | 【第32号公告】公开发行证券的公司信息披露内容与格式准则第29号——首次公开发行股票并在创业板上市申请文件（2020年修订） | 证监会 |
| 6月12日 | 【第33号公告】公开发行证券的公司信息披露内容与格式准则第35号——创业板上市公司向不特定对象发行证券募集说明书（2020年修订） | 证监会 |
| 6月12日 | 【第34号公告】公开发行证券的公司信息披露内容与格式准则第36号——创业板上市公司向特定对象发行证券募集说明书和发行情况报告书（2020年修订） | 证监会 |
| 6月12日 | 【第35号公告】公开发行证券的公司信息披露内容与格式准则第37号——创业板上市公司发行证券申请文件（2020年修订） | 证监会 |
| 6月12日 | 【第36号公告】创业板首次公开发行证券发行与承销特别规定 | 证监会 |
| 6月12日 | 【第169号令】创业板上市公司持续监管办法（试行） | 证监会 |
| 6月12日 | 【第168号令】创业板上市公司证券发行注册管理办法（试行） | 证监会 |
| 6月12日 | 【第167号令】创业板首次公开发行股票注册管理办法（试行） | 证监会 |
| 6月12日 | 【第170号令】证券发行上市保荐业务管理办法 | 证监会 |
| 6月12日 | 关于发布《深圳市场首次公开发行股票网下发行实施细则（2020年修订）》的通知 | 深交所 |
| 6月12日 | 关于发布《深圳证券交易所行业咨询专家库工作规则》的通知 | 深交所 |
| 6月12日 | 关于发布《深圳证券交易所创业板上市委员会管理办法》的通知 | 深交所 |
| 6月12日 | 关于发布《深圳证券交易所创业板发行上市申请文件受理指引》的通知 | 深交所 |
| 6月12日 | 关于发布《深圳证券交易所创业板创新试点红筹企业财务报告信息披露指引》的通知 | 深交所 |
| 6月12日 | 关于发布《深圳证券交易所创业板企业发行上市申报及推荐暂行规定》的通知 | 深交所 |
| 6月12日 | 关于发布《深圳证券交易所创业板股票发行上市审核规则》的通知 | 深交所 |
| 6月12日 | 关于发布《深圳证券交易所创业板股票首次公开发行上市审核问答》的通知 | 深交所 |
| 6月12日 | 关于发布《深圳证券交易所创业板上市保荐书内容与格式指引》的通知 | 深交所 |
| 6月12日 | 关于发布《深圳证券交易所创业板上市公司证券发行上市审核问答》的通知 | 深交所 |
| 6月12日 | 关于发布《深圳证券交易所创业板上市公司重大资产重组审核规则》的通知 | 深交所 |
| 6月12日 | 关于发布《深圳证券交易所创业板上市公司证券发行上市审核规则》的通知 | 深交所 |
| 6月12日 | 关于发布《深圳证券交易所创业板上市公司证券发行与承销业务实施细则》的通知 | 深交所 |
| 6月12日 | 关于发布《深圳证券交易所创业板首次公开发行证券发行与承销业务实施细则》的通知 | 深交所 |
| 6月12日 | 关于发布《深圳证券交易所创业板上市公司规范运作指引（2020年修订）》及有关事项的通知 | 深交所 |
| 6月12日 | 关于发布《深圳证券交易所创业板股票上市规则（2020年修订）》的通知 | 深交所 |
| 6月12日 | 关于发布《深圳证券交易所创业板股票上市规则（2020年12月修订）》的通知 | 深交所 |

续表

| 日期 | 政策名称 | 发文单位 |
| --- | --- | --- |
| 6月12日 | 关于创业板股票涉及股票质押回购及约定购回交易有关事项的通知 | 深交所 |
| 6月12日 | 关于发布《深圳证券交易所 中国证券金融股份有限公司 中国证券登记结算有限责任公司创业板转融通证券出借和转融券业务特别规定》的通知 | 深交所 |
| 6月12日 | 关于发布《深圳证券交易所创业板交易特别规定》的通知 | 深交所 |
| 6月12日 | 关于发布《深圳证券交易所创业板股票异常交易实时监控细则（试行）》的通知 | 深交所 |
| 6月19日 | 关于做好创业板上市公司适用再融资简易程序相关工作的通知 | 深交所 |
| 6月19日 | 关于明确科创板股票异常波动认定所涉基准指数有关事项的通知 | 上交所 |
| 6月19日 | 关于修订上证综合指数编制方案的公告、关于发布上证科创板50成份指数的公告 | 上交所 |
| 7月3日 | 【第37号公告】公开发行证券的公司信息披露内容与格式准则第43号——科创板上市公司向不特定对象发行证券募集说明书 | 证监会 |
| 7月3日 | 【第38号公告】公开发行证券的公司信息披露内容与格式准则第44号——科创板上市公司向特定对象发行证券募集说明书和发行情况报告书 | 证监会 |
| 7月3日 | 【第39号公告】公开发行证券的公司信息披露内容与格式准则第45号——科创板上市公司发行证券申请文件 | 证监会 |
| 7月3日 | 【第171号令】科创板上市公司证券发行注册管理办法（试行） | 证监会 |
| 7月3日 | 关于发布《上海证券交易所科创板上市公司股东以向特定机构投资者询价转让和配售方式减持股份实施细则》的通知 | 上交所 |
| 7月3日 | 关于发布《上海证券交易所科创板上市公司证券发行承销实施细则》的通知 | 上交所 |
| 7月3日 | 关于做好2020年科创板上市公司适用再融资简易程序相关工作的通知 | 上交所 |
| 7月3日 | 关于发布《上海证券交易所科创板上市公司证券发行上市审核问答》的通知 | 上交所 |
| 7月3日 | 关于发布《上海证券交易所科创板上市公司证券发行上市审核规则》的通知 | 上交所 |
| 7月10日 | 【第42号公告】关于修改《证券公司分类监管规定》的决定 | 证监会 |
| 7月10日 | 【第43号公告】关于首次公开发行股票并上市公司招股说明书财务报告审计截止日后主要财务信息及经营状况信息披露指引（2020年修订） | 证监会 |
| 7月10日 | 【第172号令】证券投资基金托管业务管理办法 | 证监会 |
| 7月10日 | 【第173号令】关于修改《首次公开发行股票并上市管理办法》的决定 | 证监会 |
| 7月10日 | 【第174号令】关于修改《科创板首次公开发行股票注册管理办法（试行）》的决定 | 证监会 |
| 7月10日 | 关于创业板风险警示股票和退市整理期股票交易制度安排的通知 | 深交所 |
| 7月22日 | 【第46号公告】非上市公众公司监管指引第5号——精选层挂牌公司持续监管指引（试行） | 证监会 |
| 7月22日 | 【第47号公告】非上市公众公司信息披露内容与格式准则第13号——精选层挂牌公司年度报告 | 证监会 |
| 7月22日 | 【第48号公告】非上市公众公司信息披露内容与格式准则第14号——精选层挂牌公司中期报告 | 证监会 |

续表

| 日期 | 政策名称 | 发文单位 |
| --- | --- | --- |
| 7月22日 | 【第49号公告】非上市公众公司信息披露内容与格式准则第15号——创新层挂牌公司中期报告 | 证监会 |
| 7月22日 | 【第50号公告】非上市公众公司信息披露内容与格式准则第16号——基础层挂牌公司中期报告 | 证监会 |
| 7月22日 | 【第51号公告】非上市公众公司信息披露内容与格式准则第17号——精选层挂牌公司季度报告 | 证监会 |
| 7月24日 | 关于发布《深圳证券交易所上市公司股份协议转让业务办理指引(2020年修订)》的通知 | 深交所 |
| 7月24日 | 上市公司信息披露管理办法(修订稿) | 证监会 |
| 7月31日 | 【第53号公告】《上市公司重大资产重组管理办法》第二十八条、第四十五条的适用意见——证券期货法律适用意见第15号 | 证监会 |
| 8月6日 | 【第54号公告】公开募集基础设施证券投资基金指引(试行) | 证监会 |
| 8月21日 | 【第57号公告】非上市公众公司监管指引第6号——股权激励和员工持股计划的监管要求(试行) | 证监会 |
| 8月28日 | 【第58号公告】关于实施《公开募集证券投资基金销售机构监督管理办法》的规定 | 证监会 |
| 8月28日 | 【第175号令】公开募集证券投资基金销售机构监督管理办法 | 证监会 |
| 8月30日 | 关于发布《深圳证券交易所上市公司风险分类管理办法》的通知 | 深交所 |
| 9月11日 | 关于发布《上海证券交易所上市公司自律监管规则适用指引第1号——重大资产重组》的通知 | 上交所 |
| 9月11日 | 关于发布《上海证券交易所科创板上市公司自律监管规则适用指引第1号——规范运作》的通知 | 上交所 |
| 9月17日 | 【第62号公告】关于修改《关于加强上市证券公司监管的规定》的决定 | 证监会 |
| 9月25日 | 【第63号公告】关于实施《合格境外机构投资者和人民币合格境外机构投资者境内证券期货投资管理办法》有关问题的规定 | 证监会 |
| 9月25日 | 【第176号令】合格境外机构投资者和人民币合格境外机构投资者境内证券期货投资管理办法 | 证监会 |
| 9月25日 | 关于发布《上海证券交易所科创板上市公司自律监管规则适用指引第2号——自愿信息披露》的通知 | 上交所 |
| 9月25日 | 合格境外机构投资者和人民币合格境外机构投资者境内证券期货投资管理办法 | 国家外汇管理局 |
| 10月5日 | 国务院关于进一步提高上市公司质量的意见 | 国务院 |
| 10月16日 | 关于发布《上海证券交易所上市公司自律监管规则适用指引第2号——纪律处分实施标准》的通知 | 上交所 |
| 10月30日 | 关于发布《深圳证券交易所合格境外机构投资者和人民币合格境外机构投资者证券交易实施细则(2020年修订)》的通知 | 深交所 |

续表

| 日期 | 政策名称 | 发文单位 |
|---|---|---|
| 10月30日 | 【第66号公告】关于修改、废止部分证券期货制度文件的决定 | 证监会 |
| 10月30日 | 【第177号令】关于修改、废止部分证券期货规章的决定 | 证监会 |
| 11月2日 | 健全上市公司退市机制实施方案 | 中央全面深化改革委员会 |
| 11月24日 | 关于发布《上海证券交易所上市公司自律监管规则适用指引第3号——信息披露分类监管》的通知 | 上交所 |
| 12月4日 | 关于发布《上海证券交易所科创板上市委员会管理办法》的通知 | 上交所 |
| 12月4日 | 关于发布《上海证券交易所科创板股票上市审核规则（2020年修订）》的通知 | 上交所 |
| 12月4日 | 关于修改《深圳证券交易所证券投资基金交易和申购赎回实施细则》相关条款的通知 | 深交所 |
| 12月18日 | 关于发布《上海证券交易所上市公司自律监管规则适用指引第4号——向特定对象发行可转换公司债券》的通知 | 上交所 |
| 12月31日 | 【第178号令】可转换公司债券管理办法 | 证监会 |
| 12月31日 | 关于发布《上海证券交易所风险警示板股票交易管理办法（2020年12月修订）》的通知 | 上交所 |
| 12月31日 | 关于发布《上海证券交易所退市公司重新上市实施办法（2020年12月修订）》的通知 | 上交所 |
| 12月31日 | 关于发布《上海证券交易所科创板股票上市规则（2020年12月修订）》的通知 | 上交所 |
| 12月31日 | 关于发布《上海证券交易所股票上市规则（2020年12月修订）》的通知 | 上交所 |
| 12月31日 | 关于发布《深圳证券交易所上诉复核委员会工作细则（2020年修订）》的通知 | 深交所 |
| 12月31日 | 关于发布《深圳证券交易所自律监管措施和纪律处分实施办法（2020年修订）》的通知 | 深交所 |
| 12月31日 | 关于发布《深圳证券交易所自律监管听证程序细则（2020年修订）》的通知 | 深交所 |
| 12月31日 | 关于发布《深圳证券交易所股票上市规则（2020年修订）》的通知 | 深交所 |
| 12月31日 | 关于发布《深圳证券交易所上市委员会工作细则（2020年修订）》的通知 | 深交所 |
| 12月31日 | 关于发布《深圳证券交易所退市公司重新上市实施办法（2020年修订）》的通知 | 深交所 |
| 12月31日 | 关于发布《深圳证券交易所创业板股票上市规则（2020年12月修订）》的通知 | 深交所 |
| 12月31日 | 关于发布《深圳证券交易所交易规则（2020年12月修订）》的通知 | 深交所 |
| 12月31日 | 关于修改《深圳证券交易所融资融券交易实施细则》第6.1条、第6.2条的通知 | 深交所 |

## 专栏4

### 《创业板改革并试点注册制总体实施方案》审议通过,证监会出台系列规则[①]

2020年4月27日,中央全面深化改革委员会会议审议通过《创业板改革并试点注册制总体实施方案》,正式启动了创业板注册制改革。创业板注册制改革是注册制改革中承前启后的关键一环,它的落地意味着注册制正从科创板"试验田"迈向"深水区",从增量改革迈向存量改革。

同日,证监会就《创业板首次公开发行股票注册管理办法(试行)》《创业板上市公司证券发行注册管理办法(试行)》《创业板上市公司持续监管办法(试行)》草案和《证券发行上市保荐业务管理办法》修订草案向社会公开征求意见,搭建起创业板改革并试点注册制的整体制度框架。深交所同步就《创业板股票发行上市审核规则》等8项业务规则公开征求意见。

2009年10月,创业板开市,中国多层次资本市场迈出重要一步。11年来,创业板在发行、管理上不断规范和完善,但仍存在不良资产库存较多、管理制度与国际不接轨等问题,改革势在必行。2018年11月5日,科创板注册制试点启动,此后近两年的实践为创业板注册制改革提供了可以借鉴的成功经验。

2020年3月30日,中共中央、国务院发布《关于构建更加完善的要素市场化配置体制机制的意见》,明确表示要推进资本要素市场化配置,完善股票市场基础制度,制定出台完善股票市场基础制度的意见,完善主板、科创板、中小企业板、创业板和全国中小企业股份转让系统市场建设。新修订的《证券法》自2020年3月1日起施行,为深化注册制改革提供了坚实的法制保障。

本轮创业板试点注册制改革重点解决两个问题:一是在科创板的基础上,扩大注册制试点,为存量板块推行注册制积累经验;二是增强对创新创业企业的包容性,突出板块特色。改革将把握"一条主线"和"三个统筹"。"一条主线",即实施以信息披露为核心的股票发行注册制,提高透明度和真实性,由投资者自主进行价值判断,真正把选择权交给市场。"三个统筹"则是统筹创业板改革与多层次资本市场体系建设、统筹注册制试点与其他基础制度建设、统筹增量改革与存量改革。

2020年6月12日,证监会发布了《创业板首次公开发行股票注册管理办法(试行)》《创业板上市公司证券发行注册管理办法(试行)》《创业板上市公司持续监管办法(试行)》和《证券发行上市保荐业务管理办法》,自公布之日起施行。与此同时,证监会、深圳证券交易所、中国证券登记结算有限公司、中国证券业协会等发布了相关配套规则。

2020年8月18日,最高人民法院发布《关于为创业板改革并试点注册制提供司法保障的若干意见》(法发〔2020〕28号),从增强为创业板改革并试点注册制提供司法

---

[①] 作者:刘宇,《中国金融政策报告》项目实习生、清华大学五道口金融学院博士。

保障的自觉性、依法保障创业板改革并试点注册制顺利推进、依法提高市场主体违法违规成本、依法有效保护投资者合法权益等四方面提出了10条举措。

创业板注册制改革应严格落实新《证券法》对提高违法成本的要求，严防财务造假行为，切实提高上市公司质量。同时，要深入总结试点经验，研究制定全市场推广注册制实施方案，在科创板、创业板注册制试点的经验基础上，走好从创业板到全市场的"第三步"，推动构建差别化的资本市场体系，促进资本市场高质量健康发展。

## 专栏5

### 紧扣核心，多管齐下，进一步提高上市公司质量①

上市公司质量是资本市场可持续发展的主要基石。我国资本市场建立30年来，上市公司数量显著增长、质量持续提升，在促进国民经济发展中的作用日益凸显。但上市公司经营和治理不规范、发展质量不高等问题仍较突出，与建设现代化经济体系、推动经济高质量发展的要求还存在差距。同时，面对新冠肺炎疫情等外部因素影响，上市公司生产经营和高质量发展面临新的考验。

2020年10月5日，国务院发布《关于进一步提高上市公司质量的意见》（以下简称《意见》），提出6个方面共17项重点举措，对提高上市公司质量作出了全面系统的部署安排。

《意见》总体目标是使上市公司运作规范性明显提升，信息披露质量不断改善，突出问题得到有效解决，可持续发展能力和整体质量显著提高。《意见》体现了问题导向的改革方法，针对市场反映突出的退市不畅、股票质押风险、资金占用、违规担保等问题，作出了明确的部署。抓住了公司治理和信息披露这两个核心点，涵盖了上市公司在资本市场的整个生命周期，打通入口、畅通出口，支持上市公司依托资本市场发展壮大。

确保对《意见》的有效落实及上市公司质量的切实提升，第一还是要紧扣公司治理和信息披露两个核心关键。一方面要提高上市公司治理水平。要进一步规范公司治理和内部控制，加强对上市公司董监高、控股股东及实际控制人行为规范的指引。另一方面要进一步提升信息披露质量。要推动上市公司及其他信息披露义务人以投资者需求为导向，充分披露投资者作出价值判断和投资决策所必需的信息。同时也要充分发挥好中介机构作用，推动中介机构进一步归位尽责，强化资本市场看门人的作用，激发中介机构担当作为的内在动力。第二要从多个方面支持上市公司做优做强。持续推进战略新兴产业和制造业升级等企业库建设，通过精准服务和深度孵化培育支持优质企业上市，鼓励上市公司运用资本市场融资并购等综合功能强化主业、做优做强，并推动上市公司形成优势产业集群。第三是强化上市公司退出机制。支持上市公司通过企业合并、主动退

---

① 作者：徐克非，信达证券股份有限公司副总经理、《中国金融政策报告》项目（课题组）高级研究员。

市、破产重整等多元化渠道依法退出，并做好退市相关处置安排，进一步推动资本市场的优胜劣汰。第四是要推动机构投资者、中小投资者和媒体等发挥好外部监督作用，共同塑造良好外部生态。第五还要加大违法违规惩处力度。严厉打击财务造假、侵占上市公司资金、违规担保、内幕交易、操纵市场等违法违规行为。通过以上系列措施，推动上市公司高质量发展，助力构建中国资本市场发展新格局。

### 三、保险市场发展政策[①]

2020年是全面建成小康社会和"十三五"规划收官之年，也是脱贫攻坚决战决胜之年，在以习近平同志为核心的党中央坚强领导下，保险业努力克服新冠肺炎疫情冲击、稳妥应对各种风险挑战，提升服务实体经济质效，提高重大风险防范能力，继续保持稳健运行良好态势。

（一）2020年保险市场政策主要内容

1. 规范银行业保险业消费投诉处理工作，维护金融市场秩序

为规范银行业保险业消费投诉处理工作，保护消费者合法权益，中国银保监会于2020年1月14日印发《银行业保险业消费投诉处理管理办法》（以下简称《管理办法》）。

《管理办法》包含总则、组织管理、投诉处理、工作制度、监督管理、附则等六大部分，主要体现了以下特点。

一是明确消费投诉事项。《管理办法》明确界定消费投诉为消费者因购买银行、保险产品或者接受银行、保险相关服务与银行保险机构或者其从业人员产生纠纷，并向银行保险机构主张其民事权益的行为。

二是规定银行保险机构职责。《管理办法》明确银行保险机构是处理消费投诉的责任主体，按照依法合规、便捷高效、标本兼治和多元化解原则，对消费投诉事项进行属地管理，落实分级责任，充分考虑和尊重消费者的合理诉求，公平合法作出处理结论。

三是明确投诉处理程序。《管理办法》明确了银行保险机构处理消费投诉的受理渠道、受理范围、处理时限等程序要求。为最大化满足消费者合理诉求，结合投诉处理工作实际，鼓励提高投诉处理效率，对于事实清楚、争议情况简单的消费投诉，银行保险机构应当在15日内办理完毕并告知投诉人，情况复杂的可延长至30日；情况特别复杂或者有其他特殊原因的，经过必要审批程序后，办理期限再延长30日。加入了对于第三方机构合作业务投诉的处理要求，银行保险机构应当要求相关第三方机构配合处理消费投诉，对投诉事项进行核实，及时提供相关情况，促进消费投诉顺利解决。

四是完善投诉处理制度机制。为改变投诉处理"头痛医头脚痛医脚"的状况，《管理办法》要求银行保险机构建立健全溯源整改、责任追究制度。综合运用正向激励和负面约束手段，要求银行保险机构健全信息披露和考核评价制度。为避免利益冲突，要求

---

[①] 作者：中国保险行业协会课题组；统稿人：王未，中国保险行业协会人身险二部室主任。

银行保险机构建立投诉处理回避制度，指定与被投诉事项无直接利益人员处理投诉。

五是便民高效化解投诉。《管理办法》从强化机构主体责任角度，要求最大限度方便消费者投诉。简化受理程序，规定银行保险机构不得拒绝接受消费者合理投诉诉求，不得要求投诉人提供机构已经掌握或者通过查询内部信息档案可以获得的材料。为避免银行保险机构分支机构久拖不决、问题隐瞒不报等，规定了投诉核查程序，要求银行保险机构上级机构对下级机构投诉处理工作进行核查，并且在答复投诉处理意见时，应当告知消费者申请核查、调解、仲裁、诉讼等救济途径，充分保障消费者的申诉权利。为保护消费者合法权益，银行保险机构在投诉处理中应当核实投诉人身份，保护投诉人信息安全，发现消费投诉不是由投诉人或者其法定代理人、受托人提出的，银行保险机构可不予办理。

六是强化监管督查和对外披露。《管理办法》明确监管部门负责对银行保险机构消费投诉处理情况进行监督检查，定期通报披露转送银行保险机构的消费投诉情况。将银行保险机构投诉处理工作情况纳入消费者权益保护监管评价。强化监管措施，对于未按照《管理办法》规定处理消费投诉或者开展投诉处理管理工作的银行保险机构，依据《中华人民共和国银行业监督管理法》和《中华人民共和国保险法》，视情形可采取责令改正以及监督管理谈话、暂停相关业务、行政处罚等监管措施。

《管理办法》的制定实施将进一步推动银行保险机构树立以人民为中心的发展思想，提升消费者对银行保险机构投诉处理工作满意度。同时，也将有利于银保监会及其派出机构强化监管为民理念，维护金融市场秩序，为推进国家治理体系和治理能力现代化作出贡献。

2. 坚持市场化改革，强化市场监管，夯实意外险发展根基

近年来，意外险为提升全社会利用商业保险等市场化手段应对风险意识、增强全社会风险抵御能力作出了重要贡献，但由于市场基础薄、定价机制科学性不强、销售行为不规范等问题，意外险与现代保险服务业的要求不相适应。为建立意外险费率市场化形成机制，更好保护保险消费者合法权益，推动意外险市场高质量发展，中国银保监会办公厅于2020年1月17日印发《关于加快推进意外险改革的意见》（以下简称《意见》）。

《意见》分五个部分，第一部分为意外险改革的总体要求，包括指导思想、基本原则和主要目标；第二至第四部分为2020年及2021年的改革任务，包括推进市场化定价改革、强化市场行为监管和夯实发展根基；第五部分为有关工作要求。

《意见》重点突出2020年及2021年的改革任务，主要围绕推进市场化定价改革、强化市场行为监管、夯实发展根基等三个方面采取相关举措。

一是推进市场化定价改革。主要包括：健全意外险精算体系，进一步完善意外险定价假设规定，强化法定责任准备金监管，切实防范风险；建立产品价格回溯调整机制，逐步淘汰赔付率过低、渠道费用过高、定价明显不合理的产品；编制意外险发生率表，探索建立意外伤害发生率表动态修订机制。

二是强化市场行为监管。主要包括：针对搭售和捆绑销售、手续费畸高、财务业务

数据不真实等问题，组织开展意外险市场清理整顿；系统梳理意外险市场行为监管的政策规定，制定统一的意外险专项监管制度；建立健全信息披露机制，提高意外险市场透明度；建立健全意外险保单信息共享机制，研究制定"黑名单""灰名单"标准，加强风险预警。

三是夯实发展根基。主要包括：加快推进标准化建设，研究制定意外险风险等级和职业分类标准，完善保险业意外伤残评定标准，努力争取纳入国家标准体系中；探索制定意外险基本条目示范写法，推动产品条款标准化、简单化、通俗化；建立反保险欺诈长效协作机制。

《意见》对深化意外险市场改革、提高意外险服务经济社会发展能力、增强广大群众获得感具有重要意义。

3. 完善人身保险精算制度体系，加大风险保障类产品发展力度

2020年1月21日，中国银保监会印发了《普通型人身保险精算规定》（以下简称《规定》）。保险公司新开发的普通型人身保险产品须按《规定》要求执行。在《规定》印发前已审批或备案的普通型人身保险产品可继续销售，但应按要求提取责任准备金。

《规定》涉及适用范围、保险金额、保险费、现金价值和责任准备金五个方面的内容，重点体现了三个方面的产品监管导向。一是推动风险保障类产品发展，更好地保护保险消费者权益。《规定》调整了健康保险、意外伤害保险、定期寿险、终身寿险等风险保障类产品的现金价值参数，下调了年金保险、部分趸交保险产品定价的平均附加费用率上限，提升了年金保险等长期储蓄类产品的最低现金价值标准。这个调整，有助于推动降低产品价格，提升产品竞争力，更好地满足消费者的保险消费需求。二是整合和细化监管规定，完善产品精算监管体系。《规定》整合了对不同保险产品的风险保障要求，适用范围包括所有的普通型人寿保险、年金保险、健康保险和意外伤害保险，同时涵盖保险期限一年及以下的普通型人身保险，监管体系更加健全，监管政策更加清晰。结合产品特点，细化相关规定，通过差别设定参数，支持风险保障类产品发展。三是适应当前形势发展，填补监管制度空白。《规定》是继分红险和万能险精算规定之后的又一大单独的精算规定，与《分红保险精算规定》《万能保险精算规定》《投资连结保险精算规定》等共同构建涵盖各类产品形态的、基本健全完善的精算制度体系。

4. 强化人身保险法定责任准备金监管，完善非现场监测机制

2020年1月21日，中国银保监会印发了《关于强化人身保险精算监管有关事项的通知》（以下简称《通知》）。

《通知》重点围绕进一步强化法定责任准备金监管、规范分红险红利分配和利益演示机制、健全非现场监测机制等出台相关规定。一是进一步强化法定责任准备金监管。以责任准备金覆盖率为抓手，将其纳入非现场监测指标体系，并与产品监管等监管措施挂钩。二是规范分红险市场发展。修订完善了分红险利益演示的方法，明确了演示利率上限，并将红利分配比例统一为70%。三是完善非现场监测机制。对《中国保监会关于做好人身保险业有关数据报送工作的通知》中季度负债业务信息表中相关内容进行了调

整，新增责任准备金覆盖率、万能险账户基本情况、投连险账户基本情况等，加大负债业务监管力度。

《通知》进一步强化了法定责任准备金监管，完善了非现场监测机制，充分体现了审慎监管的核心原则，增强了监管政策的科学性、有效性，有助于引导人身保险业强化风险意识，守住不发生系统性风险的底线，有利于防范行业利差损风险，推动人身保险业长期健康发展。

5. 提高风险保障水平，增加长期资金供给，推动商业保险在社会服务领域进一步发挥积极作用

近年来，保险业认真贯彻落实习近平新时代中国特色社会主义思想，坚持以人民为中心的发展理念，持续深化供给侧结构性改革，积极参与多层次医疗、养老保障体系建设，探索在社会服务领域创新保障产品，加强对养老、健康等相关产业的长期资金支持，有力促进了社会服务领域发展。但总体来看，仍存在支撑作用不够充分、保障功能和资金支持力度有待提升等问题。为深化金融供给侧结构性改革，充分发挥商业保险在保障民生、促进消费和拉动内需等方面的重要作用，中国银保监会、国家发展改革委、教育部等13部门于2020年1月23日联合发布《关于促进社会服务领域商业保险发展的意见》（以下简称《意见》）。

《意见》明确，要促进社会服务领域商业保险发展，提高相关领域风险保障水平，增加长期资金供给，重点做好以下五个方面工作。

一是完善健康保险产品和服务。鼓励保险机构适应消费者需求，提供综合性健康保险产品和服务。力争到2025年，商业健康保险市场规模超过2万亿元。完善保险机构承办大病保险运行及监管机制。加快发展商业长期护理保险，推动健康保险与健康管理融合发展。

二是强化商业养老保险保障功能。积极发展多样化商业养老年金保险、个人账户式商业养老保险。在安全审慎的基础上，拓宽商业养老保险资金运用范围。力争到2025年，为参保人积累不低于6万亿元养老保险责任准备金。发挥保障功能，提升60岁及以上老年人保障水平。优化老年人住房反向抵押养老保险支持政策，完善公证赋予合同强制执行效力、公证机构担任遗产管理人等制度，促进养老服务产业发展。

三是大力发展教育、育幼、家政、文化、旅游、体育等领域商业保险，积极开发专属保险产品。鼓励地方政府及有关部门更多运用保险机制加强和改进社会治理。

四是支持保险资金投资健康、养老等社会服务领域。发挥保险资金期限长、稳定性强等优势，为社会服务领域提供更多长期股本融资，降低融资成本，更好地服务创新创业及民营、中小微企业发展。

五是完善保险市场体系。鼓励商业保险机构在风险可控前提下，适度提高定期寿险产品定价利率。强化保险市场行为监管，保护保险消费者合法权益。加快推进保险市场对外开放，完善配套政策。

《意见》的贯彻落实将在丰富产品供给、加大对外开放等方面，为社会服务领域商

业保险创造新的发展机遇。

**6. 推动简政放权改革、优化营商环境**

为推动简政放权改革、优化营商环境，中国银保监会于2020年2月4日印发《关于废止和修改部分规范性文件的通知》（以下简称《通知》）。

根据《通知》，对《关于印发〈信托投资公司信息披露管理暂行办法〉的通知》等11件规范性文件予以修改，同时对《关于指定披露保险信息报纸的通知》等6件规范性文件予以废止。

《通知》的发布将对落实公平竞争审查有关工作要求、进一步完善银行业保险业监管制度发挥重要作用。

**7. 重塑健康保障委托管理业务监管框架，满足人民群众多层次健康保障需求**

近年来，随着经济社会的发展和人民群众保险意识的提升，越来越多的企事业单位为员工提供基本医疗保障之外的健康保障服务，并委托给保险公司经办，健康保障委托管理为推进多层次多样化医疗保障体系建设作出了重要贡献。为加强对健康保障委托管理业务的监管，中国银保监会办公厅于2020年2月11日印发《关于进一步规范健康保障委托管理业务有关事项的通知》（以下简称《通知》）。

《通知》是对原保监会2008年印发的《关于健康保障委托管理业务有关事项的通知》的修订。本次修订重塑了健康保障委托管理业务监管框架，回归业务本源，补齐监管短板，防范潜在风险。

一是明确开展条件，充实委托内容。《通知》明确保险公司开展健康保障委托管理业务，应符合《健康保险管理办法》规定的经营健康保险的条件，并在开办地区设有分支机构或服务合作机构。同时规定可将疾病审核和费用支付、失能收入损失审核和费用支付、护理审核和费用支付、健康管理服务等纳入委托事项。

二是回归业务本源，取消产品备案。《通知》回归健康保障委托管理业务的实质，取消对该业务的产品备案管理，保险公司可以根据银保监会对健康保障委托管理业务的规定审慎开展业务，依法签订合同，享受权利、履行义务和承担责任。

三是取消委托投资功能，规范管理费用。《通知》要求保险公司不得将健康保障委托管理业务异化为理财业务，对委托资金提供各种形式的增值保证。要求保险公司收取的管理费用应覆盖委托管理业务的各项成本，也可以根据实际管理成本进行浮动，但浮动办法应在委托管理合同中列明。

四是加强业务监管，防范潜在风险。《通知》通过明确禁止性行为、加强保险公司主体责任、探索行业自律等措施强化对此项业务的监管。

《通知》的发布将引导行业依法合规开展健康保障委托管理业务，为确保健康保障委托管理业务各方当事人的合法权益、满足人民群众多层次多样化的健康保障需求起到积极作用。

**8. 进一步加强和改进财产保险公司产品监管，深化"放管服"改革**

2015年5月12日，国务院召开全国推进简政放权放管结合职能转变工作电视电话会议，首次提出了"放管服"改革的概念；2020年5月22日，国务院总理李克强在发布的2020年国务院政府工作报告中提出，"放管服"改革纵深推进。因此，为深化"放管服"改革，突出监管重点，统筹监管资源，提高监管效率，提升财产保险行业产品质量，中国银保监会于2020年2月19日发布了《关于进一步加强和改进财产保险公司产品监管有关问题的通知》（以下简称《通知》）。

此次调整，进一步提高了产品监管效率，强化了产品监管有效性，对原保监会印发的《关于实施〈财产保险公司保险条款和保险费率管理办法〉有关问题的通知》中财产保险公司产品审批备案范围进行调整，将使用示范产品的机动车辆商业保险、1年期以上信用保险和保证保险产品由审批改为备案，原属于备案类的产品仍采用备案管理。同时，银保监会将坚持放管结合、并重的原则，对备案产品持续强化监管。

为了充分发挥各银保监局贴近一线、熟悉市场的优势，形成上下联动监管合力，《通知》规定对财产保险公司产品实施分类监管和属地监管。一是使用示范产品的机动车辆商业保险、中央财政保费补贴型农业保险产品（以下简称"两类产品"）由银保监会负责备案并监管；二是其他产品均由相关银保监局负责备案并监管；三是银保监会将根据市场情况变化和产品监管工作需要，适时调整由银保监局负责备案并监管的产品范围。

《通知》的印发是银保监会简政放权、放管结合、优化服务的重要改革举措，是统筹监管资源、形成上下联动监管合力的重要政策措施，是规范财产保险公司产品管理、提升产品总体质量的重要工作规定，有利于进一步完善财产保险公司产品监管体系，激发产品创新的市场活力，更好地满足人民群众日益增长的保险需求，服务经济社会高质量发展。

9. 完善银行业保险业从业人员金融违法犯罪预防工作机制，加强公司治理和制度建设

为进一步完善银行业保险业从业人员金融违法犯罪预防工作机制，防控银行保险机构案件风险，促进银行业保险业健康发展，中国银保监会于2020年2月20日发布《关于预防银行业保险业从业人员金融违法犯罪的指导意见》（以下简称《指导意见》）。

《指导意见》一共由四部分组成，分别是：基本原则；预防重点领域金融违法犯罪；强化机构内控和行业自律机制建设；依法严惩，加强监管和联动协调。

《指导意见》提出四项基本原则：加强党的领导和党的建设；坚持健全长效机制与短期重点惩治并重；坚持内部管控、行业自律与外部监管三管齐下；坚持金融监管部门与监察机关、公安机关和司法机关联动协调，形成防范打击合力。同时列举重点预防违法犯罪行为的11个领域：信贷业务领域；同业业务领域；资产处置领域；资产管理业务领域；信用卡业务领域；现金管理领域；保险业务领域；第三方合作领域；金融市场领域；洗钱和恐怖融资相关领域；信息科技领域。并对强化机构内控和行业自律机制建设提出了6点要求：强化公司治理；强化制度流程控制；加强案件风险监测和排查；严肃责任追究；完善教育培训体系；强化行业性约束惩戒。对依法严惩，加强监管和联动

协调提出了 5 点建议：完善案防管理体系；加强检查与评估结果应用；严格依法惩处和问责；发挥联合惩戒警示作用；强化联动协调。

《指导意见》的发布有助于加强公司内部治理和制度建设，建立健全员工培训机制，争取从源头上遏制金融违法犯罪行为的发生，以保障保险资金的稳定，维护投资人、投保人的资金安全。

10. 统一保险资管产品监管标准，促进保险资管产品业务持续健康发展

为规范保险资产管理产品（以下简称保险资管产品）业务发展，统一保险资管产品监管标准，引导保险机构更好地服务实体经济，有效防范金融风险，2020 年 3 月 18 日，中国银保监会制定了《保险资产管理产品管理暂行办法》（以下简称《办法》）。

《办法》共八章六十六条，包括总则，产品当事人，产品发行、存续与终止，产品投资与管理，信息披露与报告，风险管理，监督管理以及附则。主要内容：一是明确产品定位和形式；二是明确产品发行机制；三是严格规范产品运作；四是压实产品发行人责任；五是强化产品服务机构职责；六是完善产品风险管理机制；七是落实穿透监管。

制定《办法》是贯彻落实《关于规范金融机构资产管理业务的指导意见》要求、完善我国资管业务监管体系的重要举措，有利于规范保险资管产品业务发展，拓宽保险资金等长期资金的配置空间和投资渠道；有利于统一保险资管产品监管规则，补齐监管短板，强化事中事后监管；有利于深化金融供给侧结构性改革，发挥保险资管产品优势，引导长期资金参与资本市场，支持基础设施项目建设，提升服务实体经济质效。

11. 鼓励长期医疗保险发展，保护消费者合法权益

近年来，健康保险快速发展，医疗保险作为健康保险的主要险种之一，也受到了消费者的热烈欢迎和市场的广泛关注。但从期限来看，绝大部分医疗保险为 1 年期业务，长期医疗保险产品较少，不能有效满足人民群众的长期健康保障需求。为丰富医疗保险产品供给，鼓励保险公司开发销售长期医疗保险产品，规范相关经营管理行为，中国银保监会办公厅于 2020 年 3 月 25 日发布了《关于长期医疗保险产品费率调整有关问题的通知》（以下简称《通知》）。

《通知》主要规范了以下内容：

一是明确费率可调的长期医疗保险产品范围。考虑到科学性和可操作性，目前仅限于采用自然费率定价的长期医疗保险，包括保险期间超过 1 年，或者保险期间虽不超过 1 年但含有保证续保条款的医疗保险产品。

二是明确费率调整的基本要求。保险公司应当制定费率调整办法，明确费率调整的触发条件、内部决策机制和工作流程。首次费率调整时间不早于产品上市销售之日起满 3 年，每次费率调整间隔不得短于 1 年。保险公司不得因单个被保险人身体状况的差异实行差别化费率调整政策。

三是明确产品条款及产品说明书相关内容。规定保险公司销售费率可调的长期医疗保险产品，应当向投保人提供产品说明书。产品条款和产品说明书应当对费率调整情况进行详细说明，包括费率调整具体触发条件、费率调整时间间隔、单次调整上限、调整

流程以及信息披露要求等。产品说明书还应当以案例形式演示本产品提供的保障,以及投保人可能面临的各年度费率调整情况。

四是明确费率调整的信息披露要求。规定保险公司应当在公司网站披露费率调整办法和相关产品信息,并对费率调整情况进行公示。对于每一次费率调整,保险公司应当以投保单中约定的方式通知投保人。

五是规范保险公司销售行为,明确对违规行为的监管措施。

《通知》解决了困扰医疗保险发展的制度障碍,明确传达了鼓励发展长期医疗保险的积极信号,将有利于深化人身保险供给侧结构性改革,有效解决因被保险人健康状况变化或者产品停售而无法续保的风险,更好地保障消费者权益。

12. 畅通产业链资金流,提升复工复产整体效应

新型冠状病毒肺炎疫情期间,银行业保险业认真贯彻落实党中央、国务院决策部署,立足金融服务实体经济高质量发展的功能定位,精准有力推进复工复产、复商复市,在防控疫情和支持经济社会发展方面发挥了关键作用。针对复工复产期间产业链上下游部分企业面临的现金流压力问题,中国银保监会办公厅于 2020 年 3 月 26 日发布《关于加强产业链协同复工复产金融服务的通知》(以下简称《通知》)。

《通知》包括以下六个方面内容。一是加大对产业链核心企业的金融支持力度。支持核心企业通过信贷、债券等方式融资后,以适当方式减少对上下游企业的资金占用,帮助产业链上下游中小微企业解决流动资金紧张等问题。二是优化产业链上下游企业金融服务。通过应收账款融资、订单融资、预付款融资、存货与仓单质押融资等方式加大对产业链上下游中小微企业的信贷支持。三是加强金融支持全球产业链协同发展。强化银行业金融机构金融支持"稳外贸"作用,增加外贸信贷投放,落实好中小微企业贷款临时性延期还本付息等政策。鼓励保险机构进一步拓宽短期出口信用保险覆盖面。四是提升产业链金融服务科技水平。通过线上线下相结合的方式,为企业提供方便快捷的供应链融资服务。鼓励大中型银行、政策性银行按照市场化、法治化原则加强与主要依靠互联网运营的银行的业务合作。五是完善银行业金融机构考核激励和风险控制。对产业链协同复工复产相关授信予以差别化安排,完善激励机制。明确核心企业准入标准,认真审核核心企业融资需求和贷款用途,严格审核供应链交易背景。六是加大保险和担保服务支持力度。在风险可控的前提下,鼓励保险机构和政策性担保机构为产业链上下游中小微企业获取融资提供增信措施,人身保险公司可适度延长保单质押贷款期限,提升贷款额度。

作为保险行业助力疫情防控大局的系列政策之一,《通知》在引导银行保险机构增强金融支持和服务、畅通产业链资金流、提升产业链协同复工复产整体效应等方面发挥了十分重要的作用。

13. 促进市场化债转股健康发展,规范金融资产投资公司资产管理业务

为促进市场化债转股健康发展,规范金融资产投资公司资产管理业务,依法保护投资者合法权益,按照《国务院关于积极稳妥降低企业杠杆率的意见》、《关于规范金融机

构资产管理业务的指导意见》、《金融资产投资公司管理办法（试行）》等相关规定，2020年4月16日，中国银保监会印发了《关于金融资产投资公司开展资产管理业务有关事项的通知》（以下简称《通知》）。

《通知》从总体要求、资金募集、投资运作、登记托管、信息披露与报送等方面明确金融资产投资公司开展资产管理业务的有关事项。根据《通知》，金融资产投资公司开展资产管理业务，是指其接受投资者委托，设立债转股投资计划并担任管理人，依照法律法规和债转股投资计划合同的约定，对受托的投资者财产进行投资和管理。债转股投资计划应当主要投资于市场化债转股资产，包括以实现市场化债转股为目的的债权、可转换债券、债转股专项债券、普通股、优先股、债转优先股等资产。

14. 加强信用保险和保证保险业务监管，促进信保业务持续健康发展

2017年7月，原保监会印发《信用保证保险业务监管暂行办法》（以下简称《暂行办法》），明确了业务发展边界和原则，整治了前期市场乱象行为，取得了一定成效。随着金融新业态的发展，为进一步加强信用保险和保证保险业务（以下简称"信保业务"）监管，规范经营行为，防范化解风险，保护保险消费者合法权益，促进信保业务持续健康发展，2020年5月8日，中国银保监会办公厅发布了《关于印发信用保险和保证保险业务监管办法的通知》（以下简称《通知》），对保险公司经营融资性信保业务作出要求。

《通知》的修订以风险为导向，围绕"差异化监管，高质量发展"的思路，始终坚持依法合规、小额分散、风险可控的经营原则，主要呈现以下三方面特点。一是聚焦重点业务，实施差异化监管。《通知》区分融资性和非融资性信保业务，重点聚焦高风险的融资性信保业务的监管，提高对融资性信保业务在经营资质、承保限额、基础建设等方面的监管要求。二是有收有放，兼顾监管与发展。一方面，《通知》通过压缩融资性信保业务的承保限额、扩大险种范围（即商业性出口信用保险）等方式，控制风险敞口，防范业务风险；另一方面，《通知》通过对融资性信保业务设置弹性限额的方式鼓励保险公司为普惠型小微企业提供融资增信支持、通过适度调整业务类型，支持保险公司在风险可控的前提下探索发展新业务领域。三是强化内控管理，促进高质量发展。《通知》通过要求保险公司提升自身管控能力，促进信保业务高质量发展，在内控管理方面进一步强化制度建设、系统建设、流动性管理、风险预警等，防范经营风险、流动性风险；在合作方管理方面，要求建立准入、评估、退出、消费者投诉等制度要求，降低合作的潜在风险。

《通知》的实施对防范信保业务风险、推动信保业务高质量发展等方面有着积极作用和深远意义。《通知》通过设置弹性的承保限额，促使保险公司调整当前业务结构，预计融资性信保业务中个人消费类业务占比有所降低，普惠型小微企业的业务占比有所提高。同时，《通知》对融资性信保业务予以重点监管，进一步明确了流动性管理、内部审计、合作方管理等内控管理要求，在存量风险逐步消化的同时，增量业务风险也将得到进一步控制。

15. 强管理、提素质、促转变、树形象,全面加强保险公司销售人员管理

2020年5月12日,中国银保监会发布《关于落实保险公司主体责任 加强保险销售人员管理的通知》(以下简称《通知》)。《通知》是在《保险法》及《保险代理人监管规定》、《保险经纪人监管规定》、《保险公估人监管规定》三部监管规章等法律法规框架下,紧密结合2019年在从业人员清核中发现的问题,紧扣保险机构管理责任这个关键点,对保险机构主体责任的条分细捋和明晰化。

《通知》共23条,分为全面提高认识、加强战略统筹、严格招录管理、严格培训管理、严格资质管理、严格从业管理、夯实基础管理、严格监管监督八个部分。确立了落实法律责任、管理责任的基本原则,提出了健全管理架构体系、杜绝销售人员"带病"入岗、持续提升销售人员职业素养、建设销售人员销售能力分级体系、建立销售人员队伍诚信体系、持续治理销售人员数据质量、依法严厉处罚和严肃责任追究等任务。

16. 切实加强保险专业中介机构从业人员管理

当前我国保险市场正在向高质量转型发展,保险消费需求正在升级深化,从业人员作为保险业的一方重要参与者,应当而且必须对其实施更加有力有效的管理,才能使之更加适应行业发展新要求和老百姓保险消费新需求。从业人员直接面对保险消费者从事保险销售、咨询等服务,其素质水平、诚信状况直接关系到保险消费者的切身利益,直接影响保险行业形象。2015年以来,保险从业人员快速增长,目前仅保险公司个人代理人就达900万人。面对如此庞大的人员队伍,落实保险机构管理主体责任、强化其管理意识、督促其完善制度机制至关重要。2019年中国银保监会部署开展了保险公司销售人员、保险专业中介机构从业人员执业登记清核工作。从清核情况看,从业人员素质参差不齐、大进大出等问题较为突出,其根源在于保险机构在从业人员管理的理念、架构、举措等方面存在缺失和偏差,没有切实肩负起主体管理责任。

为切实推动保险专业中介机构落实主体责任,从强管理、提素质、促转变、树形象等方面全面加强从业人员队伍管理,中国银保监会于2020年5月12日发布《关于切实加强保险专业中介机构从业人员管理的通知》(以下简称《通知》)。

《通知》是在《保险法》及《保险代理人监管规定》、《保险经纪人监管规定》、《保险公估人监管规定》三部监管规章等法律法规框架下,紧密结合2019年在从业人员清核中发现的问题,紧扣保险机构管理责任这个关键点,对保险机构主体责任的条分细捋和明晰化。

《通知》针对保险专业中介机构的特点和市场定位,从全面承担管理主体责任、加强统筹管理、严格招录管理、严格培训管理、建立销售能力分级体系、严格诚信管理、夯实基础管理、严格监管监督等方面进行了明确。

《通知》明确了销售能力分级的监管要求,支持保险行业自律组织发挥平台优势,推动销售人员销售能力分级工作,督促保险机构综合考察从业人员学历水平、从业年限、保险产品知识、诚信记录等情况,推进从业人员销售能力资质建设。

《通知》主旨是强调保险机构对保险销售服务等保险从业人员依法承担从业人员相应业务活动的法律责任,强调保险机构在法律责任前提下所产生的对这些从业人员的管

理主体责任，强调保险机构对这些从业人员的全过程、全环节管理要求。

17. 拓宽银行资本补充渠道，扩大保险资金运用空间

为贯彻落实国务院金融稳定发展委员会相关会议精神，进一步拓宽银行资本补充渠道，扩大保险资金运用空间，中国银保监会对《关于保险资金投资银行资本补充债券有关事项的通知》进行了修订，并于2020年5月20日制定了新一版《关于保险资金投资银行资本补充债券有关事项的通知》（以下简称《通知》）。

《通知》主要内容包括：一是放宽保险资金投资的资本补充债券发行人条件。取消发行人总资产不低于1万亿元，净资产不低于500亿元的要求；将发行人"核心一级资本充足率不低于8%，一级资本充足率不低于9%，资本充足率不低于11%"的要求调整为"资本充足率符合监管规定"；取消发行人外部信用等级AAA级的要求。二是取消可投债券的外部信用等级要求。取消可投资的二级资本债券的债项评级（AAA级）和无固定期限资本债券的债项评级（AA+级）要求。三是明确保险机构信用风险管理能力应当达到银保监会规定的标准，并且上季度末偿付能力充足率不得低于120%。四是要求保险机构按照发行人对资本补充债券权益工具或者债务工具的分类，相应确认为保险机构的权益类资产或者固定收益类资产，并纳入相应监管比例管理。

《通知》有利于丰富保险资产配置品种，拓宽保险资金配置空间；有利于扩大保险机构投资自主权，将投资价值和风险判断的权利更多交给保险机构；有利于支持中小银行多渠道补充资本，优化资本结构；有利于扩大资本补充债券投资者群体，完善市场化发行定价机制。同时，新版《通知》要求保险机构切实加强风险管理，审慎判断投资的效益与风险。保险机构应当强化风险自担意识，持续加强风险管理能力建设；应当跟踪监测投资风险，及时履行报告义务。

18. 明确农业保险业务经营条件，深化农业保险供给侧结构性改革

2019年5月29日，中央全面深化改革委员会第八次会议审议并原则同意《关于加快农业保险高质量发展的指导意见》，意见指出农业保险作为分散农业生产经营风险的重要手段，对推进现代农业发展、促进乡村产业振兴、改进农村社会治理、保障农民收益等具有重要作用。为贯彻落实《关于加快农业保险高质量发展的指导意见》精神，按照党中央、国务院关于"放管服"改革要求和对农业保险工作部署，进一步深化农业保险供给侧结构性改革，建立健全农业保险业务经营条件管理机制，中国银保监会2020年6月12日发布《关于进一步明确农业保险业务经营条件的通知》（以下简称《通知》）。

《通知》针对行业反映较为集中的农险市场准入问题，明确农业保险业务经营条件，强化动态监管，建立农险经营评估机制，畅通退出机制，建立完善的全流程的农险业务经营条件管理制度体系，深入推进农业保险供给侧结构性改革，促进农业保险市场平稳健康发展。

《通知》共计19条，主要内容有：一是明确农险业务经营条件。根据国务院2012年印发的《农业保险条例》（以下简称《条例》）的规定，《通知》从总公司和省级分公

司两个层面分别制定农险业务经营条件。凡符合经营条件的保险机构均可在本地开展农险业务，无须向监管机构提出经营资格申请。二是提高农险业务经营标准。2016年修订后的《条例》在取消农险市场准入审批的同时，仍然保留了保险机构经营农险业务应当具备相应条件，并规定要符合国务院保险监督管理机构规定的其他条件。《通知》从依法合规、风险管控能力、农险服务能力、信息化水平等方面进一步提高了农险经营标准。三是建立完善退出机制。为同步做好改革的协同配套工作，《通知》根据《条例》规定，明确规定建立农险经营的退出机制。此外，《通知》还建立了农险经营综合考评机制，对保险机构农险经营管理情况进行动态评估。

《通知》作为完善农业保险制度体系的重要制度安排，将进一步完善农业保险业务经营条件管理机制，优化农业保险机构布局，规范农业保险市场秩序，有利于促进农业保险持续健康发展，指导各地制定符合当地实际的细化规则，完善农业保险市场准入退出机制，推动农业保险更好地服务"三农"事业。同时，各保险公司将面临更多合规经营的监管，农业保险将进入一个新的高质量发展阶段，而高质量发展必然是更加合规的。

19. 规范互联网保险销售行为，维护消费者合法权益

当前，互联网与保险结合产生的互联网保险业务快速增长，碎片化、小额化的互联网保险广泛触达各类消费者，互联网保险侵害消费者合法权益的问题也呈爆发式增长。2019年，中国银保监会接到互联网保险消费投诉共1.99万件，同比增长88.59%，是2016年投诉量的7倍，销售误导和变相强制搭售等问题突出，严重影响消费者的获得感。

针对投诉暴露出的互联网保险领域突出问题，中国银保监会立足互联网新形式与消费新行为，于2020年6月22日发布《关于规范互联网保险销售行为可回溯管理的通知》（以下简称《通知》）。结合保险销售可回溯管理经验，以行为监管为抓手，规范互联网保险销售行为。

《通知》全文共26条，主要包括以下五方面内容：

一是明确互联网保险销售行为可回溯管理的定义和范围。明确互联网保险销售行为可回溯，是指保险机构通过销售页面管理和销售过程记录等方式，对在自营网络平台上销售保险产品的交易行为进行记录和保存，使其可供查验。管理范围是投保人为自然人的商业保险产品。

二是明确销售页面和销售页面管理的定义。对销售页面管理主体、互联网保险销售行为的边界和销售风险点管控作出要求。特别强调销售页面只能设置在保险机构自营网络平台，且需要与非销售页面进行分隔。对于重要条款内容，要求单独设置页面展示，且由投保人自主确认，保护消费者知情权。

三是对保险机构互联网销售过程管理作出要求。包括保护投保人自主选择权、明确保险机构实名验证职责、细化销售过程记录标准、制定信息收集原则等内容。对于收集、使用消费者个人信息，《通知》特别强调保险机构应遵循合法、正当、必要的原则，

并采取有效措施保护信息,保护消费者信息安全权。

四是明确可回溯内控管理。主要对可回溯资料内容、保管、安全防护及相关内控制度作出规定,要求保险机构建立全面、系统、规范的内部控制体系。特别强调互联网保险销售行为可回溯资料应当可以还原为可供查验的有效文件,销售页面应当可以还原为可供查验的有效图片或视频,以便调查检查使用。

五是明确对融合业务和自助终端业务的管理要求,以及相关法律责任和实施时间。

《通知》的发布有利于维护市场秩序、防范操作风险,进一步保障金融消费者知情权、自主选择权和公平交易权等基本权利。

20. 巩固乱象整治成果,打赢防范化解金融风险攻坚战

保险行业自 2017 年起连续开展整治市场乱象工作,已取得了明显成效,经营管理乱象得到有效遏制,重点领域突出风险得到有序化解,资金脱实向虚问题得到有力纠正,为当前金融更好支持实体经济发展奠定了良好基础。为进一步巩固拓展乱象整治成果,坚决打赢防范化解金融风险攻坚战,中国银保监会于 2020 年 6 月 23 日印发《关于开展银行业保险业市场乱象整治"回头看"工作的通知》(以下简称《通知》)。

《通知》要求,乱象整治"回头看"工作要按照"六稳"和"六保"要求,以党的政治建设为统领,以依法严查严处为导向,防止乱象反弹回潮,推动金融支持疫情防控和产业链协同复工复产等各项政策落到实处。通过持续集中整治,实现屡查屡犯的违法违规行为明显减少,银行保险机构内控合规长效机制建设明显进步,金融服务实体经济质效明显提升。

《通知》明确,对连续三年市场乱象整治工作进行"回头看"。一看主体责任是否落实到位,二看实体经济是否真正受益,三看整改措施是否严实有效,四看违法违规是否明显遏制,五看合规机制是否健全管用。要求全系统提高政治站位,深刻领会金融支持中小微企业对做好"六稳"工作、落实"六保"任务的重大意义,把握好治乱象、防风险与稳增长的有机统一。督促银行保险机构把普惠金融政策红利切实传导到民营小微企业,不断推动降低企业融资综合成本,依法严厉打击通过融资政策便利获得的贷款违规进行资金套利行为。持续深入开展宏观政策执行、股权与公司治理、业务经营、影子银行和交叉金融业务等领域违法违规问题排查,对打着"金融创新"幌子花式翻新的违规行为,依法严肃处理。

《通知》强调,各银行保险机构要大力推进根源性整改,做到深自查、真整改、严问责,建立健全全员管理制度,把治理金融乱象与培育稳健风险文化深度融合,有效提升依法合规经营和风险管理水平。各级监管机构对违反宏观调控政策、侵害金融消费者合法权益以及屡查屡犯等违规问题要加大查处力度,对因金融腐败和违法犯罪破坏市场秩序、造成重大损失甚至诱发风险事件的一律严惩不贷。

《通知》是对过去三年保险行业整治乱象工作的总结和巩固,标志着深化保险行业合规建设的进一步深化,将有力促进保险市场秩序建设、回归保障本源及持续高质量发展。

21. 加强资产负债管理,增强风险抵御能力

为支持保险资金参与国债期货交易,有效防范风险,根据《关于商业银行、保险机构参与中国金融期货交易所国债期货交易的公告》的精神,中国银保监会于2020年6月23日制定了《保险资金参与国债期货交易规定》,并同步修订了《保险资金参与金融衍生产品交易办法》和《保险资金参与股指期货交易规定》。

《保险资金参与国债期货交易规定》共17条,主要内容为:一是明确参与目的与期限,保险资金参与国债期货应以对冲风险为目的,不得用于投机目的。二是明确保险资金参与方式,保险资金应以资产组合形式参与并开立交易账户,实行账户、资产、交易、核算等的独立管理,严格进行风险隔离。三是规定卖出及买入合约限额,控制杠杆比例,强化流动性风险管理。四是强化操作、技术、合规风险管控。五是明确监督管理和报告有关事项。

《保险资金参与金融衍生产品交易办法》由原来的36条增加为37条。调整的内容包括:一是明确保险资金运用衍生品的目的,删除期限限制,具体期限根据衍生品种另行制定。二是强化资产负债管理和偿付能力导向,根据风险特征的差异,分别设定保险公司委托参与和自行参与的要求。三是新增保险资金参与衍生品交易的总杠杆率要求。四是严控内幕交易、操纵证券和利益输送等行为。

《保险资金参与股指期货交易规定》调整的内容包括:一是调整对冲期限、卖出及买入合约限额和流动性管理相关要求。二是明确合同权责约定,委托投资和发行资管产品应在合同或指引中列明交易目的、比例限制、估值方法、信息披露、风险控制、责任承担等事项。三是增加回溯报告,保险机构参与股指期货须每半年报告买入计划与实际执行的偏差。

《保险资金参与国债期货交易规定》的发布,进一步丰富了保险资金风险对冲工具,有利于保险公司加强资产负债管理,增强风险抵御能力。同时,《保险资金参与金融衍生产品交易办法》《保险资金参与股指期货交易规定》的修订,统一了监管口径,完善了保险资金参与金融衍生品交易的监管规制体系,有利于扩大保险机构的选择权,也有利于夯实保险机构履行全面风险管理的主体责任,强化风险意识,持续加强风险管理能力建设。

22. 做好融资担保公司非现场监管工作,规范市场经营行为

为全面、深入贯彻实施国务院《融资担保公司监督管理条例》,做好融资担保公司非现场监管工作,融资性担保业务监管部际联席会议制定了《融资担保公司非现场监管规程》(以下简称《规程》),于2020年7月14日由中国银保监会印发。

《规程》要求融资担保公司应当建立和落实非现场监管信息报送制度,按照监督管理部门的要求和时限报送非现场监管数据和非数据信息。对融资担保公司的非现场监管应当重点关注融资担保公司的外部经营环境变化、公司治理状况、内部控制状况、风险管理能力、担保业务情况、关联担保风险、资产质量状况、流动性指标和投资情况等。

《规程》指出融资担保公司出现重大风险、异常变动、突发事件等情况,监督管理

部门应当分析原因,及时处置融资担保公司风险,并按照有关重大风险事件报告制度的要求向本级人民政府、银保监会和中国人民银行报告。

《规程》提出监督管理部门可以根据融资担保公司风险严重程度确定相应的应对机制,依法采取提高信息报送频率、督促开展自查、要求充实风险管理力量、做出风险提示和通报、进行监管谈话、开展现场检查、责令其暂停部分业务、限制其自有资金运用的规模和方式、责令其停止新设分支机构等监管措施。

《规程》重点围绕融资担保公司非现场监管工作职责分工和非现场监管流程,在信息收集与核实、风险监测与评估、信息报送与使用、监管措施等方面作出了规定,完善了融资担保公司监管报表和指标解释,实现了监管指标统计与监管制度要求相统一,有利于监督融资担保公司的经营行为,促进监管制度要求的落实和执行,更好地支持普惠金融发展。

23. 提升资金运用自主决策空间,优化权益类资产配置监管

为进一步深化保险资金运用市场化改革,引导保险资金更好地服务实体经济,积极发挥保险机构作为资本市场重要机构投资者的作用,提升保险公司资金运用的自主决策空间,2020年7月17日,中国银保监会制定了《关于优化保险公司权益类资产配置监管有关事项的通知》(以下简称《通知》)。

《通知》共有12条,主要内容如下:一是设置差异化的权益类资产投资监管比例。二是强化对重点公司的监管。三是增加集中度风险监管指标。四是引导保险公司开展审慎投资和稳健投资。

《通知》的发布实施是贯彻落实党中央、国务院"六稳"要求的重要举措,对促进保险资金稳健投资和完善保险资金运用监管具有重要的积极意义,有利于进一步推进保险资金运用的市场化改革,拓宽保险资金投资的自主决策空间;有利于探索建立差异化的监管机制,提高保险资金运用监管工作的针对性、精准性和有效性,切实防范重点公司和重点品种风险;有利于引导保险公司开展价值投资、长期投资和审慎投资,为实体经济和资本市场提供更多资本性资金。

24. 充分发挥政府性融资担保机构作用,建立健全政府性融资担保体系

为充分发挥政府性融资担保机构作用,大幅拓展政府性融资担保覆盖面并明显降低费率,扎实做好"六稳"工作,全面落实"六保"任务,根据《国务院关于促进融资担保行业加快发展的意见》有关精神,按照《国务院办公厅关于有效发挥政府性融资担保基金作用切实支持小微企业和"三农"发展的指导意见》有关要求,中国银保监会等七部门于2020年8月5日发布了《关于做好政府性融资担保机构监管工作的通知》(以下简称《通知》)。

《通知》主要包含以下内容:

一是开展政府性融资担保机构确认工作。各地省级财政部门会同省级融资担保公司监督管理部门开展确认工作,建立政府性融资担保机构名单,并予以公布。二是要求政府性融资担保机构坚守准公共定位,弥补市场不足,聚焦支小支农主业,稳步提高小微

企业和"三农"融资担保在保余额占比。三是内外结合,促进提升政府性融资担保机构服务质效。政府性融资担保机构应当加强自身建设,改善内部管理、优化正向激励、创新担保产品、提高服务效能,推动建立"能担、愿担、敢担"的长效机制。在外部环境及政策方面,应当加强统筹协调,鼓励银行积极与政府性融资担保机构合作,落实风险分担机制,完善政府性融资担保机构绩效评价体系,落实支小支农贷款担保降费补贴政策。四是加强监管指导,监督管理部门应当统筹运用现场检查、非现场监管等手段对政府性融资担保机构支小支农业务规模、综合担保费率、放大倍数等指标加强监控分析,引导其聚焦支小支农主业,扩大担保规模,降低担保费率。

《通知》的印发实施是贯彻落实政府工作报告、建立健全政府性融资担保体系的重要举措。下一步,银保监会将持续完善相关监管规制,促进政府性融资担保机构聚焦支小支农主业,健康可持续发展。

### 25. 提升公司治理质效,构建中国特色银行业保险业公司治理机制

2020年8月17日,中国银保监会在监管系统内印发《健全银行业保险业公司治理三年行动方案(2020—2022年)》(以下简称《方案》)。制定出台《方案》是银保监会认真贯彻党中央、国务院关于完善金融机构公司治理一系列决策部署的重要举措,将全面提升公司治理监管的系统性、针对性和前瞻性,推动我国银行业保险业切实提升公司治理质效。

《方案》突出强调以习近平新时代中国特色社会主义思想为指导,坚持加强党的领导,坚持完善现代金融企业制度。明确要坚持问题导向、标本兼治、分类施策、统筹推进的原则,聚焦主要问题、弥补制度短板、强化差异化监管、注重工作整体性和协同性。力争通过三年努力,初步构建起中国特色银行业保险业公司治理机制。

《方案》共10个部分,涉及总体要求(包括指导思想、基本原则、总体目标)、党的领导与公司治理融合、公司治理评估、股东行为规范、董事会等治理主体履职、激励约束机制、利益相关者保护、外部市场约束、监管能力建设、组织保障等方面。《方案》围绕公司治理各个方面规划了一系列重点工作安排,是今后三年我国银行业保险业公司治理监管的行动指南。

《方案》借鉴国际先进经验,充分吸收了前期银保监会关于《二十国集团/经合组织公司治理原则》在我国银行业保险业实施情况的评价结果。对于评价发现的差距和不足之处,研究提出了针对性的改进措施。如完善大股东行为约束机制,进一步明确包括股权董事在内的所有董事都要公平对待全体股东,改进董事提名和选任机制,推动机构建立并严格执行高标准的职业道德准则等。

《方案》的发布和有效实施,是中国银保监会依法加强银行业保险业公司治理监管的重要举措,将全面提升公司治理监管的系统性、针对性和前瞻性,有力推动银行保险机构稳步提升公司治理质效,切实增强风险抵御能力和经营可持续性,为打赢防范化解重大风险攻坚战、全面建成小康社会提供有力支持。

26. 支持市场化法治化债转股业务

为贯彻落实中央经济工作会议精神和政府工作报告部署，提升保险资金服务实体经济质效，优化保险资产配置结构，支持市场化法治化债转股业务，2020年9月4日，中国银保监会制定了《关于保险资金投资债转股投资计划有关事项的通知》（以下简称《通知》）。

《通知》的主要内容包括：一是明确监管依据。保险资金投资债转股投资计划，纳入《关于保险资金投资有关金融产品的通知》管理。二是明确发行人条件。保险资金投资的债转股投资计划，其发行人应当公司治理良好、经营审慎稳健、具有良好的守法合规记录和较强的投资管理能力。三是明确投资范围。保险资金投资的债转股投资计划，投向市场化债转股资产原则上不低于净资产的60%，可投资的其他资产包括合同约定的存款（包括大额存单）、标准化债权类资产等银保监会认可的资产；债转股投资计划进行份额分级的，应当为优先级份额。四是按照穿透原则实施分类管理。保险资金投资的债转股投资计划，根据权益类资产的比例相应纳入权益类资产或其他金融资产投资比例管理。五是加强集中度监管。设置单一公司50%和集团合计80%的投资比例限制。

《通知》是落实供给侧结构性改革要求、推进保险资金与金融资产投资公司合作、促进市场化法治化债转股业务发展的重要举措，有利于支持金融资产投资公司债转股业务，进一步拓宽债转股资金来源；有利于丰富保险资金投资品种，发挥保险资金长期投资优势，更好地服务实体经济发展；有利于降低企业杠杆率，支持有较好发展前景的优质企业渡过难关，增强经济中长期发展韧性。

27. 提升保险行业健康管理服务质量和水平，丰富健康保险产品内涵

党的十九大报告、《关于促进社会服务领域商业保险发展的意见》等政策文件明确提出"为人民群众提供全方位全周期健康服务"，"推动健康保险与健康管理融合发展"。近年来，保险行业积极探索为客户提供健康管理服务，在丰富健康产品内涵、提升人民群众健康水平等方面发挥了积极作用，但保险行业开展的健康管理业务整体上仍处于初期发展阶段，尚未形成成熟的服务模式。为规范保险公司健康管理服务行为，进一步推动健康管理服务与健康保险业务融合发展，中国银保监会办公厅于2020年9月6日印发了《关于规范保险公司健康管理服务的通知》（以下简称《通知》）。

《通知》主要包括以下内容：

一是明确健康管理服务的概念和目的。《通知》对健康管理服务的概念、服务内容和实施目的进行界定，将保险公司健康管理服务分为健康体检、健康咨询、健康促进、疾病预防、慢病管理、就医服务、康复护理等七大类型，并提出保险公司开展健康管理服务是通过对客户健康危险因素的干预，预防疾病发生、控制疾病发展、促进疾病康复，通过降低疾病发生率、提升健康水平，进而降低医疗费用支出。

二是提出健康管理服务应遵循的原则和要求。《通知》明确保险公司开展健康管理服务应遵循科学性、合理性、安全性、有效性、客观性及符合伦理学要求等基本原则；同时提出保险公司开展健康管理服务要尊重客户的知情同意权、保护客户的隐私权，确

保相关数据和信息安全,并及时做好服务评价反馈和投诉处理等工作。

三是完善健康管理服务的运行规则。《通知》对保险公司组织管理、制度建设、从业人员、人才培养、信息系统,第三方服务机构的合作范围和资质条件、遴选考核、合作协议、服务监督、质量评价等方面要求进行了明确。此外,还对保险公司开展健康管理服务的信息披露内容、原则和途径提出了要求,切实保护消费者合法权益。

四是强化健康管理服务的监督管理。《通知》明确了保险公司开展健康管理服务的合规要求和内部问责机制,压实公司主体责任。对保险公司开展健康管理服务的信息报送、重大事故和突发群体事件应急处置与报告等提出了要求。此外,《通知》注重发挥保险行业协会自律组织作用,支持其探索建立保险公司间健康管理业务交流平台和健康管理服务机构评价体系,并牵头组织行业制定管理、技术、数据等相关标准。

在健康保险与健康管理融合发展已成为行业发展趋势、保险公司普遍把健康管理作为健康保险增长新动能的背景下,《通知》完善了健康管理服务监管制度,将在规范公司服务行为、提升服务质量和水平、更好地保护消费者合法权益等方面发挥积极作用。

28. 规范现场检查立项和实施程序,提升现场检查效率

为规范现场检查立项和实施程序,提升现场检查效率,中国银保监会于2020年9月6日印发了《中国银保监会现场检查立项和实施程序规定(试行)》(以下简称《试行规定》)。

《试行规定》依据2019年发布的《中国银保监会现场检查办法(试行)》(以下简称《试行办法》),就中国银保监会及其派出机构对监管对象开展现场检查中的立项和实施流程进行了规定,内容涉及检查立项、检查准备、检查实施、检查处理、检查档案整理等五大环节,在《试行办法》有关现场检查工作的严肃性、科学性和公平性的原则指导下,对各环节的工作流程、工作内容、组织架构、操作细则等问题提供了全面而详细的规定。《试行规定》同时废止了2007年发布的《中国银行业监督管理委员会现场检查规程》及2009年发布的《中国保险监督管理委员会现场检查工作规程》。

《试行规定》为《试行办法》提供了明确的落地方案,为提升中国银保监会现场检查的科学性、规范性和有效性创造了有力抓手,将更好地推动银行业和保险业做好防范金融风险、支持实体经济、维护金融安全稳定大局工作。

29. 贯彻落实"资管新规",进一步规范保险资产管理产品业务发展

为了贯彻落实《关于规范金融机构资产管理业务的指导意见》(以下简称"资管新规"),进一步规范保险资产管理产品业务发展,细化《保险资产管理产品管理暂行办法》(以下简称《产品办法》)相关规定,2020年9月7日,中国银保监会制定了《组合类保险资产管理产品实施细则》《债权投资计划实施细则》和《股权投资计划实施细则》等三个细则。

三个细则遵循以下原则:一是坚持严控风险的底线思维。二是坚持服务实体经济的导向。三是坚持深化"放管服"改革优化营商环境。四是坚持与大资管市场同类私募产品规则拉平。

《组合类保险资产管理产品实施细则》共18条，主要内容包括明确产品登记时限、细化产品投资范围、严格规范面向合格自然人销售行为、强化事中事后监管措施等。《债权投资计划实施细则》共18条，主要内容包括明确产品登记时限、统一基础设施和非基础设施类不动产债权投资计划的资质条件及业务管理要求、适当拓宽债权投资计划资金用途、完善信用增级等交易结构设计以及风险管理机制等。《股权投资计划实施细则》共17条，主要内容包括明确产品登记时限、适当拓展投资资产范围、设置产品投资比例要求、明确禁止行为以及强化信息披露要求等。

三个细则针对不同类别保险资产管理产品的特点，对"资管新规"和《产品办法》有关要求做了进一步细化，有利于对三类产品实施差异化监管，有利于促进保险资产管理产品业务规范健康发展，也有利于维护资产管理行业公平良性的竞争环境，更好地保护投资者合法权益。

30. 完善车险精算制度，防范非理性竞争行为

在车险综合改革即将启动、前端价格放开的情况下，为完善车险精算制度，防范非理性竞争行为，中国银保监会于2020年9月9日发布了《示范型商车险精算规定》（以下简称《精算规定》）。

《精算规定》主要从两个方面着手：

1. 建立费率回溯和产品纠偏机制，解决公司车险产品费率备案及后续执行过程中的不规范问题；

2. 明确保费不足准备金的评估标准，通过要求公司将亏损及时反映在财务报表和偿付能力指标中，倒逼公司理性经营。

《精算规定》分为7个部分：一是适用范围，明确适用于使用行业示范条款的商车险产品。二是保费构成，明确了保费厘定基本原则、保费计算公式及所使用的行业基准、附加费用率的标准等。三是费率回溯和产品纠偏，规定保险公司应建立费率回溯和产品纠偏机制，动态监测、分析费率精算假设与公司实际经营情况的偏离度，及时对商车险费率进行调整。四是保费不足准备金的评估，明确了保费充足性测试的计算公式和保费不足准备金的评估标准。五是总精算师的职责，要求总精算师应定期对定价假设合理性进行评估，若定价假设与实际经营结果发生重大偏差或保险公司出现定价不足等方面重大风险，总精算师应及时向监管机构报告。六是监管措施，为严肃车险市场纪律，明确监管部门可采取责令保险公司停止使用产品等监管措施。七是附则，明确文件废止等事项。

《精算规定》的发布完善了监管制度，优化了车险费率自主定价体系，配套的费率回溯和产品纠偏制度以及保费不足准备金制度有效防范化解了车险经营的风险，使车险费率价格与风险匹配更合理，为顺利推进车险综合改革提供了制度保障。同时，《精算规定》通过制度的形式，明确了经营主体在防范风险方面的主体责任，相关处罚规定更是传递了监管机关对违法违规"零容忍"，坚决防控风险的决心，贯彻了党中央以人民为中心的发展思想，深化供给侧结构性改革，更好地维护消费者权益，让市场在资源配

置中起决定性作用，进一步推动车险高质量发展。

31. 规范应对突发事件金融服务，维护银行业保险业安全稳健运行

为深入贯彻落实习近平新时代中国特色社会主义思想和党的十九届四中全会精神，落实习近平总书记针对新冠肺炎疫情应对工作提出的"抓紧补短板、堵漏洞、强弱项"，同时为了规范银行保险机构应对突发事件的经营活动和金融服务，保护客户的合法权利，增强监管工作的针对性，维护银行业保险业安全稳健运行，中国银保监会于2020年9月9日制定了《银行保险机构应对突发事件金融服务管理办法》（以下简称《办法》）。

《办法》贯彻支持实体经济和维护金融体系稳健相结合、提供便利金融服务和有效防范风险相结合、坚持审慎监管底线和灵活应对突发情况相结合的基本理念，坚持框架性、包容性和原则性的导向，为监管部门和银行保险机构应对突发事件提供全面指引，主要内容包括以下几个方面。

一是明确突发事件定义、应对基本原则和组织管理制度安排。《办法》明确了突发事件应对的组织管理制度，要求与业务连续性管理等制度有效结合，强调了职责分工、预案演练、协调配合、信息报告等基本要求。

二是既要求做好基本金融服务，又鼓励提供金融支持措施。《办法》规定银行保险机构应当在突发事件应对中保证金融服务的持续性；保险公司应当开发针对性的保险产品，增加业务供给，积极发挥保险的风险防范作用；进一步倡导和支持银行保险机构积极履行社会责任。

三是强调提供金融服务和金融支持的同时要守住风险底线。《办法》要求及时进行业务回溯和后评估，严格防范侵害客户合法权利的行为，加强舆情监测、管理和应对。

四是规定有针对性地调整监管方式和要求。《办法》要求保持监管工作连续性、有效性、灵活性，对银行保险机构突发事件应对机制、行动和效果加强指导和监督检查。

32. 规范保险公司资本保证金账户查询、冻结、扣划事宜

2020年9月11日，中国银保监会办公厅印发了《关于规范银行业金融机构协助有权机关办理保险公司资本保证金账户查询、冻结、扣划有关事宜的通知》（以下简称《通知》）。《通知》旨在进一步规范银行业金融机构协助有权机关办理保险公司资本保证金账户查询、冻结、扣划有关事宜，维护保险市场的平稳、健康发展。

《通知》共6条，明确了实施范围和资本保证金的定义。《通知》要求银行业金融机构应当建立保险公司资本保证金账户管理制度，妥善处理相关账户接受有权机关查询、冻结、扣划等事项；应与存款人核实账户资金性质，在存放期限内，不得同意存款人变更存款的性质、将存款本金转出本存款银行以及其他对本存款的处置要求。对于保险公司资本保证金账户，应在系统中进行特殊标识，并在相关网络查控平台、电子化专线信息传输系统等相关平台、系统中作出整体限制冻结、扣划设置。银行业金融机构接到有权机关对于保险公司资本保证金账户资金的查询、冻结、扣划指令时，应当按照法律法规规定，通过人工或系统等方式，向有权机关提示账户资金仅可用于清算时清偿债

务等特定用途，以及账户允许查询但不得冻结、扣划等安排。银行业金融机构遇到保险公司资本保证金账户因不当操作被有权机关冻结、扣划等重大异常情况时，应当及时向中国银保监会报告。

33. 规范监管数据安全管理工作，防范监管数据安全风险

为规范银保监会监管数据安全管理工作，提高监管数据安全保护能力，防范监管数据安全风险，中国银保监会于2020年9月23日发布了《中国银保监会监管数据安全管理办法（试行）》（以下简称《办法》）。

《办法》分为7章34条，分别对部门工作职责、监管数据的采集存储和处理、数据的委托和使用等方面进行了规定，同时规范了数据监督体系，切实加强了监管数据安全管理，防范监管数据安全风险；《办法》要求监管数据安全管理实行归口管理，统计信息部门负责统筹，业务部门发现重大安全风险事项48小时上报至归口管理部门；《办法》对监管数据采集、存储、加工处理和使用均提出明确而规范的要求，如数据脱敏等。此外，《办法》还规定了监管数据委托服务管理的准入要求。

近年来网络信息和数据安全在影响着人们的生活，个人信息与金融数据安全监管越发受到重视，金融行业做好金融数据合规工作刻不容缓。

34. 深入推进保险资金运用市场化改革，持续加强投资管理能力事中事后监管

为持续推进简政放权，推动优化营商环境，进一步深化保险资金运用市场化改革，根据《保险资金运用管理办法》及相关规定，2020年9月30日，中国银保监会制定了《关于优化保险机构投资管理能力监管有关事项的通知》（以下简称《通知》）。

《通知》由正文和7项附件构成，正文主要规定了保险机构投资管理能力自评估、管理和信息披露的基本要求，附件对各项投资管理能力的具体建设标准进行了细化要求。一方面，优化整合保险机构投资管理能力，细化能力建设标准要求。调整后，保险机构投资管理能力共有信用风险管理能力、股票投资管理能力、股权投资管理能力、不动产投资管理能力、衍生品运用管理能力、债权投资计划产品管理能力、股权投资计划产品管理能力等7类。另一方面，进一步深化"放管服"改革，取消投资管理能力备案管理，将保险机构投资管理能力管理方式调整为公司自评估、信息披露和持续监管相结合，对信息披露的内容、形式、方式、频次等进行了明确，并规定了违规情形和责任，全面压实保险机构主体责任。

《通知》的发布实施是银保监会贯彻落实党中央、国务院关于深化"放管服"改革，推动优化营商环境的重要举措，是对保险机构现有投资管理能力监管框架的优化完善，对于进一步推进保险资金运用市场化改革、提高保险机构自主投资决策效率意义重大，有利于推进保险机构持续、全面强化投资管理能力建设，有利于激发保险资金投资活力，更好地支持实体经济和资本市场发展。

35. 提升保险业在创新驱动发展战略、科技攻关能力建设方面的作用

为贯彻落实创新驱动发展战略，推进国务院及相关部委下发的《武汉城市圈科技金融改革创新专项方案》《关于印发中国（湖北）自由贸易试验区总体方案的通知》等文

件要求,中国银保监会及湖北省人民政府于2020年9月30日联合发布《关于印发东湖科技保险创新示范区总体方案的通知》(以下简称《通知》)。

《通知》明确了全面建设东湖科技保险创新示范区的六项任务:一是深化科技保险产品与服务的创新,二是创新保险资金投资科技产业的体制机制,三是创新科技保险市场组织体系,四是加大科技保险市场开发力度,五是打造具备示范效应的科技保险特色,六是夯实科技保险发展基础。

《通知》还提出,将从改革对科技保险业务的财政支持模式、建立对科技风险管理与保险机构的补贴与奖励政策、完善人才激励与培育政策三个方面提供政策支持,创新一批科技保险产品和服务,建立一套保险资金参与科技企业发展的机制,成立、引进一批保险机构和科技风险管理平台,聚集一批科技风险管理与保险的高端人才,建成完整的科技保险市场体系和运行机制,使科技保险成为科技创新风险管理的有效方式。

《通知》的发布将进一步鼓励保险行业充分发挥在提高创新能力和科技攻关能力方面的保障作用。

36. 助力安徽经济高质量发展,支持安徽参与长三角一体化发展

为支持安徽积极参与、融入长三角一体化发展,中国银保监会安徽监管局于2020年10月12日出台《关于扎实推进安徽银行业保险业一体化建设和支持加快融入长三角一体化发展的指导意见》(以下简称《指导意见》),明确在建立健全适应一体化发展的金融协同机制的基础上,着力加大对科技创新重点领域的金融支持,探索创新金融支持一体化发展路径。

《指导意见》侧重行业引领、引导、引向,重点突出"两个推动"。

一是推动安徽银行业保险业加快融入长三角一体化发展。建立健全适应一体化发展的金融协同机制,提升区域同城化金融服务水平,初步形成具有安徽特色的金融一体化发展经验,逐步建成多层次、广覆盖、有差异、高质量的一体化银行业保险业发展体系,稳步提升地区综合金融实力。

二是推动银行业保险业大力支持安徽融入长三角一体化发展。加强区域内金融资源优化配置和产业转型升级有效对接,力争实现安徽银行业主要指标增速快于全国,战略新兴产业、科技创新、先进制造业和绿色领域贷款显著增长,信贷在全国占比与GDP占比基本匹配,保费收入增速明显高于经济增速,逐步缩小与沪苏浙的差距,在构建新发展格局、加快建设美好安徽中体现银行业保险业的更大作为。

《指导意见》提出,坚持融合发展,着力提升银行业保险业一体化发展水平,在加快机构融入、加强资本补充、创新一体经营、推动信贷合作、完善同城服务等八个方面明确了发展方向。

《指导意见》的出台将引领推动银行业保险业助力安徽经济高质量发展、支持安徽参与长三角一体化发展。

37. 完善重大核事故保险风险分散机制,规范核保险巨灾责任准备金管理

自2018年1月1日起,我国正式施行《中华人民共和国核安全法》。我国核电快速

发展，已经成为全球第三大核电国家和最大在建市场。伴随着核电规模的快速扩大，核安全的重要性日趋凸显，党和政府高度重视核安全问题，将核安全视为国家安全的重要组成部分。

核保险是专门为涉核风险提供保险服务的特殊风险保险，是分散重大核事故风险的有效手段。根据2018年实施的《核安全法》，核保险是核安全保障的组成部分，现阶段我国核保险经营主要存在两个突出问题：一是保险公司赔付资金积累不足，核保险保费盈利转化成保险公司利润，未能有效积累。二是核保险按一年期短期业务管理不能准确反映核风险的"长尾风险"特征。2020年10月15日，为进一步完善重大核事故保险风险分散机制，规范核保险巨灾责任准备金管理，促进核保险持续稳健经营，更好地服务于我国核电事业发展，中国银保监会、财政部、生态环境部联合发布了《核保险巨灾责任准备金管理办法》（以下简称《办法》）。

《办法》共6章22条，对核保险巨灾责任准备金的适用范围、计提标准、使用条件、日常管理、监督处理五个方面的主要问题进行了规范。一是适用范围，为核设施或与核设施相关的核材料、放射性废物的运输过程提供财产损失、第三者损害赔偿等保障的保险业务，需纳入核保险巨灾责任准备金管理。二是计提标准，核保险巨灾准备金按核保险业务承保利润的75%计算，从年度净利润中计提。计提标准与国际水平基本一致。三是使用条件，在发生一次保险事故造成的核保险行业自留责任预估赔款超过3亿元人民币或等值外币，且核保险行业自留责任年度已报告赔付率超过150%时，可以使用核保险巨灾责任准备金。四是在日常管理方面，要求核保险巨灾准备金永久留存、资金运用收益纳入准备金管理。五是针对监督处理，对通过增加费用等方式减少承保利润、规避准备金计提等行为作出禁止性规定。

《办法》通过核保险巨灾责任准备金形成了核保险长期稳健经营的政策导向，产生积极影响。此举一出，保险公司逐步累积核保险巨灾责任准备金，应对核巨灾风险能力进一步加强；核保险经营管理更加规范、科学，进一步夯实核保险为核能风险提供长期、稳健保障的基础。与此同时，保险公司为守护核安全贡献行业经验，保险与核能的行业合作更紧密，跨行业核安全命运共同体的基础更加牢固，更好地服务实体经济发展。

38. 加快安徽省农业保险高质量发展

2019年5月29日，习近平总书记主持召开中央全面深化改革委员会第八次会议，审议通过《关于加快农业保险高质量发展的指导意见》，9月19日，财政部、农业农村部、银保监会、林草局印发文件，明确了农业保险高质量发展的指导思想、基本原则、主要目标、保障措施，并要求各省制订工作方案。为贯彻落实相关要求，2020年10月26日，安徽省财政厅、安徽省农业农村厅、中国银保监会安徽监管局等联合发布《关于印发〈安徽省加快农业保险高质量发展工作方案〉的通知》（以下简称《通知》）。

《通知》在有效提升农业保险服务能力、不断优化农业保险运行机制、持续加强农业保险基础设施建设等方面提出了一系列具体措施。《通知》提出到2022年，安徽省全省基本建成功能完善、运行规范、基础完备、保障合理,与农业农村现代化发展阶段相适应、与农户风险保障需求相契合,各级分工负责的多层次农业保险体系。《通知》中方案涉及共五个部分17条。第一部分为总体目标,明确了安徽省农业保险高质量发展的指导思想,提出了到2022年、2030年要完成的主要目标。第二部分为有效提升农业保险服务能力,包括扩大保险覆盖面、提高保险保障水平、拓宽保险产品供给、落实便民惠民举措等四个方面路径。第三部分为不断优化农业保险运行机制,包括明晰政府与市场边界、完善大灾风险分散机制、规范农业保险市场、鼓励开展"农业保险+"等四个方面要求。第四部分为持续加强农业保险基础设施建设,包括完善保险条款和费率拟订机制、建立信息共享机制、优化保险机构布局、完善风险防范机制等四个方面内容。第五部分为切实做好组织实施工作,包括加强组织领导、加大政策扶持、强化协同推进、优化发展环境、做好政策解读宣传等五个方面工作。

《通知》一是突出目标引领。提出将三大主粮作物保险覆盖率稳定在90%左右,超出中央目标20个百分点,保持领先地位。同时,方案增加了特色农产品保险占比目标。二是突出协同配合。按照四部委文件精神,结合安徽省实际,《通知》提出在省金融工作领导小组框架下,成立由省财政厅牵头,省农业农村厅、省林业局、省地方金融监管局、安徽银保监局、省气象局等参加的省农业保险工作小组,统筹规划、协同推进全省农业保险工作。三是突出政策供给。用足用活中央政策,提出完善蓄滞洪区农业保险政策措施;全面推开育肥猪保险,降低投保条件,提高保额;积极开展特色农产品保险,争取将大棚蔬菜、茶叶等优势品种纳入中央财政奖补试点范围;合理设定森林保险保额标准,降低费率;鼓励开展"农业保险+",构建适合"三农"发展的保险产品体系。四是突出市场监管与风险防范。建立健全农业保险保费补贴资金使用监控机制,加强对保险机构的日常监管。建立科学规范、适度竞争、合作共赢、平稳有序的农业保险经营机制和以服务能力为导向的保险机构招投标与动态考评制度。探索建立巨灾保险制度,强化保险机构防范化解风险主体责任,提升风险预警、识别、管控能力。

39. 夯实重大疾病保险发展基础,加强健康保险保障作用

在我国,重大疾病保险已有20多年发展历史,是保险业的一大重要险种。在原保监会指导下,中国保险行业协会与中国医师协会在2007年联合印发了《重大疾病保险疾病定义使用规范》,对保险中的重大疾病进行了规范定义,中国精算师协会又于2013年首次编制了《中国人身保险业重大疾病经验发生率表(2006—2010)》,为推动重大疾病保险发展发挥了重要作用。然而,随着经济社会的快速发展和医疗技术的不断革新,疾病谱及重疾发生率发生了较大变化,现有的疾病定义及发生率表已不能满足保险行业发展和消费者多元化需求的需要。为此,中国银保监会自2018年以来,指导行业开展相关修订工作。2020年,中国保险行业协会和中国医师协会合作修订完成《重大疾病保险的疾病定义使用规范(2020年修订版)》,中国精算师协会修订完成《中国人身保险业重大疾病经验发生率表(2020)》。在以上工作基础上,中国银保监会于2020年11月5日正式印发《关于使用〈中国人身保险业重大疾病经验发生率表(2020)〉有关事

项的通知》（以下简称《通知》）。

《通知》适用于包含重大疾病保险责任的长期人身保险产品，主要包含以下内容：

一是规定2020版重疾表为法定责任准备金评估基础的最低要求。《通知》要求保险公司在评估包含重大疾病保险责任的人身保险产品的法定责任准备金时，应以2020版重疾表作为重大疾病发生率评估基础的下限。为规范各张表格的使用，《通知》将适用范围内的产品类别按备案或审批时间、承保病种、销售区域等划分为2007版定义重疾险、2020版定义重疾险、2020版定义恶性肿瘤（重度）险和2020版定义粤港澳大湾区专属重疾险，分别规定重大疾病发生率评估下限的确定规则，列明不同情形应使用不同的表。

二是明确2020版重疾表对产品定价的参考作用。《通知》明确，保险公司在开发2020版定义重疾险、2020版定义粤港澳大湾区专属重疾险和2020版定义恶性肿瘤（重度）险时，可以将2020版重疾表作为重大疾病发生率的定价参考。

三是建立重大疾病经验发生率表动态修订机制。中国精算师协会根据重大疾病保险发展的需要，组织更新重大疾病经验发生率表。如新发生率表用于法定责任准备金评估，中国银保监会须重新认定相关内容，并就新发生率表出台配套监管规定，保险公司根据新发生率表及相应使用规范进行法定责任准备金评估。

为落实党中央、国务院关于粤港澳大湾区建设的战略部署，中国银保监会还配套制定了2020版定义粤港澳大湾区专属重疾险产品监管规则。

《通知》从保护消费者利益角度出发，将对夯实重大疾病保险发展基础、提升保险产品供给质量、更好地发挥健康保险对社会保障体系的补充作用产生积极影响。

40. 理顺保险代理人监管体系，加强代理人监管力度

保险代理人是指根据保险公司的委托，向保险公司收取佣金，在保险公司授权的范围内代为办理保险业务的机构或者个人，包括保险专业代理机构、保险兼业代理机构及个人保险代理人。截至目前，全国共有保险专业代理法人机构1776家，保险兼业代理机构3.2万家、网点22万个，个人保险代理人900万人，保险中介机构从业人员300万人。《保险法》对保险代理人的概念进行了明确的规定，但是在部门规章和规范性文件层面，有关要求散见在不同的文件之中，在一定程度上造成保险代理人法律关系不清、监管体系不明、管理标准不统一的问题。

为了解决上述问题，并巩固近年来乱象治理成果，落实保险中介市场改革中完善准入退出管理、鼓励推动变革创新、强化机构自我管控、加强监督管理等工作任务，2015年起，原中国保监会启动了相关制度的起草工作，将《保险专业代理机构监管规定》《保险销售从业人员监管办法》《保险兼业代理管理暂行办法》等文件进行修改整合，以期理顺法律关系，统一监管尺度，形成监管合力。2020年11月12日，中国银保监会正式印发了《保险代理人监管规定》（以下简称《规定》）。

《规定》共7章119条，把保险专业代理机构、保险兼业代理机构和个人保险代理人纳入同一部规章进行规范调整，建立了相对统一的基本监管标准和规则，涉及机构

多、人员广。

《规定》对保险专业代理机构的要求主要有以下方面：一是加强市场准入管理。强化对保险专业代理机构股东的审查，并对股东的出资能力作出要求。同时，在资本金托管、治理结构、内控制度以及商业模式等方面作出规定。二是加强分支机构管控。为切实防止内控管理薄弱、风险隐患大的保险专业代理公司滥设分支机构，列明了设立分支机构应当符合的具体条件，同时进一步强化保险专业代理法人机构的管控责任。三是理顺后置审批流程。要求保险专业代理公司取得许可证后，应及时在监管信息系统中登记相关信息；对于未取得许可证或者其许可证被注销的，应当及时办理相关事项变更登记，确保其名称中无"保险代理"字样。四是提升最低注册资本。把区域性保险专业代理机构最低注册资本调整为2000万元，有利于专业代理机构增强抵御风险能力，提升依法合规意识，促进长期稳健经营。对新设立的区域性代理公司，应严格按照新标准执行。

《规定》对缴纳职业责任保险、保证金相关要求进行了调整，对违规销售非保险金融产品、经营互联网保险业务的行为设定了相应罚则，加强日常合规管理。

《规定》对保险兼业代理机构的要求主要有以下方面：一是明确准入条件，规定了保险兼业代理机构业务准入的基本条件，明确了法人持有许可证、授权分支机构经营的模式，并对报告事项与信息披露、保险代理业务责任人等提出要求。二是完善退出机制，规定了保险兼业代理机构依法注销许可证的情形，以及业务退出流程。三是设置相应罚则，对保险兼业代理机构违法违规行为依法设定了规章权限范围内的罚则。

《规定》首次提出了"独立个人保险代理人"概念，表明市场发展趋势和监管引领方向。独立个人保险代理人相关制度将在实践的基础上发展并完善。《规定》明确了保险代理机构从业人员的概念，将保险代理机构中从事销售保险产品或者进行损失勘查、理赔等业务的人员纳入本规定，对其行为作出约束，并对违反规定的行为制定相应的罚则。

《规定》取消了许可证3年有效期的设置，是落实"放管服"要求，加强和改进保险监管的重要举措。许可证有效期的取消，将激发企业活力，支持优质公司加快发展。

41. 规范保险资金直接投资未上市企业股权行为，加大保险资金对各类企业的股权融资支持力度

为贯彻落实国务院常务会议精神，加大保险资金对实体经济股权融资的支持力度，提升社会直接融资比重，2020年11月12日，中国银保监会制定了《关于保险资金财务性股权投资有关事项的通知》（以下简称《通知》）。

《通知》共10条，核心内容是取消保险资金财务性股权投资的行业限制，通过"负面清单+正面引导"机制，提升保险资金服务实体经济能力。主要内容包括：一是明确财务性股权投资的概念，保险机构及其关联方对所投资企业不构成控制或共同控制的，即为财务性股权投资。二是取消财务性股权投资行业限于保险类企业、非保险类金融企业和与保险业务相关的养老、医疗等特定企业要求，允许保险机构自主选择投资行业范

围，扩大保险资金股权投资选择面。三是建立财务性股权投资负面清单，禁止保险资金投资存在十类情形的企业，同时鼓励保险资金开展市场化、法治化债转股项目。四是明确资金性质要求，允许保险机构运用自有资金和责任准备金开展财务性股权投资。五是加强风险控制，要求保险机构承担开展财务性股权投资的主体责任，完善股权投资管理制度，加强股权投资管理能力建设，审慎开展投资运作，不得利用股权投资开展内幕交易或利益输送。六是强化监督管理，规定保险机构开展财务性股权投资应当履行有关报告义务，违反规定开展投资的，中国银保监会将依法采取监管措施或给予相应行政处罚。

保险资金开展的股权投资在满足行业资产配置需要、分散投资风险的同时，为战略性新兴产业等现代产业体系发展提供了长期稳定资金，促进了产业整合和优化升级。

### 42. 规范互联网保险业务，有效防范风险

随着互联网等技术在保险行业的不断深入运用，互联网保险业务作为保险销售与服务的一种新形态，深刻影响了保险业态和保险监管。互联网保险业务在快速发展的同时也暴露出了一些问题和风险隐患，给行业和监管带来了挑战。

为规范互联网保险业务，有效防范风险，保护消费者合法权益，提升保险业服务实体经济和社会民生的水平，2020年12月7日，中国银保监会发布实施《互联网保险业务监管办法》（以下简称《办法》）。

《办法》共5章83条，具体包括总则、基本业务规则、特别业务规则、监督管理和附则。重点规范内容包括：一是厘清互联网保险业务本质，明确制度适用和衔接政策；二是规定互联网保险业务经营要求，强化持牌经营原则，定义持牌机构自营网络平台，规定持牌机构经营条件，明确非持牌机构禁止行为；三是规范互联网保险营销宣传，规定管理要求和业务行为标准；四是全流程规范互联网保险售后服务，改善消费体验；五是按经营主体分类监管，在规定"基本业务规则"的基础上，针对互联网保险公司、保险公司、保险中介机构、互联网企业代理保险业务，分别规定了"特别业务规则"；六是创新完善监管政策和制度措施，做好政策实施过渡安排。

《办法》贯彻了中央加强金融监管、防范金融风险的要求，有助于规范互联网保险业务、推动保险业供给侧改革、促进保险业高质量发展。

### 43. 积极应对人口老龄化，扩大长期护理保险制度试点

根据国家医保局、财政部《关于扩大长期护理保险制度试点的指导意见》（医保发〔2020〕37号），2020年12月15日，天津市人民政府办公厅印发《天津市长期护理保险制度试点实施方案》（以下简称《方案》）。

《方案》对参保范围、资金筹集、待遇支付、服务与结算等方面的基本政策做了明确规定。一是明确了参保对象。试点阶段，在天津市参加职工基本医疗保险参保人员同步参加长期护理保险，覆盖约610万人，其中，在职职工（含灵活就业人员）390万人，退休职工约220万人。下一步适时将参保对象扩大至城乡居民基本医疗保险参保人员，实现全覆盖。二是明确了参保缴费。单位和个人缴费标准原则上分别按照职工工资总

额、上年度本市职工平均工资的 0.16% 确定。试点阶段,单位缴费每人每年 120 元,个人缴费每人每年 120 元。其中,单位缴费从其缴纳的职工基本医疗保险费中按月划出,不增加单位负担;个人缴费从其缴纳的城镇职工大额医疗救助费中按月划出,不增加个人负担。三是明确了如何进行失能评定。《方案》实施后,将分批次启动失能评定受理和失能评定工作,失能评定每人每次 200 元。评定未通过的,6 个月后才可以重新申请。四是明确了可享受的报销待遇。参保人员发生符合规定的护理服务费用纳入长期护理保险基金支付范围。其中,入住定点护理机构护理床位接受规范的机构护理服务的,按照每人每天 70 元标准,由长期护理保险基金支付 70%,全年人均支付约 1.8 万元;接受定点护理机构规范的居家护理服务的,按照每人每月 2100 元标准,由长期护理保险基金支付 75%,全年人均支付约 1.9 万元。五是对定点护理机构、失能评定机构、护理服务人员、如何进行待遇结算以及如何进行经办管理等方面做了细致规定。

《方案》的出台和试点,将在解决重度失能人员长期护理保障问题、健全更加公平更可持续的社会保障体系、培育和规范养老服务市场、积极应对人口老龄化等方面发挥积极的作用。

### 44. 规范责任保险经营行为,保护责任保险活动当事人合法权益

随着发展环境的不断优化、功能作用的有效发挥,责任保险市场规模不断扩大,经营能力不断提高,服务经济社会和辅助社会治理作用逐步显现。然而,责任保险作用的发挥、市场的健康发展高度依赖于责任保险市场的规范程度。在责任保险发展过程中,出现了少量保险公司的部分产品承保了故意行为、罚金罚款、履约信用风险、确定损失、投机风险等风险或损失,跨越了责任保险与财产损失保险、保证保险、意外伤害保险等险种的界限,造成了不良的社会影响。2020 年 12 月 22 日,中国银保监会发布《责任保险业务监管办法》(以下简称《办法》),自 2021 年 1 月 1 日正式施行。

《办法》一方面严格责任保险承保范围,另一方面要求保险公司厘清责任保险与四类险种的关系,合理确定承保险种。《办法》共 5 章 35 条,主要内容有四大方面。

一是规范责任保险承保边界。针对责任保险边界不断扩大,一方面严格责任保险承保范围,明确责任保险应当承保被保险人给第三者造成损害依法应负的赔偿责任,不得承保故意行为、罚金罚款、履约信用风险、确定损失、投机风险等风险或损失,另一方面要求保险公司厘清责任保险与财产损失保险、保证保险、意外伤害保险等险种的关系,合理确定承保险种。

二是规范市场经营行为。针对当前不规范竞争行为,明确不得存在未按规定使用经批准或备案的条款费率、销售误导、不正当竞争、违规承诺等行为,不得以承保担保机构责任等形式实质承保融资性信用风险,不得以机动车辆保险以外的责任保险主险或附加险承保机动车第三者责任。

三是规范保险服务。明确保险公司提供保险服务,应当遵循合理性、必要性原则,以降低赔付风险为主要目的,不得随意扩大服务范围、服务内容。要求保险公司制定保险服务相关制度,严格按照会计准则进行账务处理,确保数据真实准确。

四是强化内控管理。进一步强化保险公司开展责任保险业务的业务管理、授权体系、队伍建设、业务核算、信息系统、数据统计、风险管控等方面的要求。

保险市场主体将严格落实《办法》，不断丰富责任保险产品，改进保险服务，提升保障水平，聚焦重大战略，服务实体经济，积极发挥责任保险在参与社会治理、化解矛盾纠纷、保障和改善民生中的积极作用。

45. 持续推动简政放权，提升监管效能

为贯彻落实党中央、国务院关于深化"放管服"改革、优化营商环境的决策部署，推进银行业保险业简政放权、优化服务，中国银保监会办公厅于2020年12月30日印发《关于深化银行业保险业"放管服"改革 优化营商环境的通知》（以下简称《通知》）。《通知》主要包含以下内容。

一是营造公开、公平、公正的市场准入环境。银保监会及其派出机构设定和实施行政许可，应遵循公开、公平、公正的原则，严格依照法定的权限、范围、条件和程序，依法平等对待各类市场主体，主动公布制定的有关行政许可规定。银保监会对上位法设定的行政许可事项作出具体规定时，严格控制行政许可实施范围。

二是持续推动银行业保险业监管简政放权。银保监会及其派出机构应在有效防范金融风险和保障金融安全的前提下，对于通过创新监管方式、优化监管资源配置等手段可以管住的事项，按照"成熟一批、取消或下放一批"的原则，积极探索取消或下放行政许可事项。对实行行政许可管理的事项，应按照减环节、减材料、减时限的要求，持续优化审批服务，提高审批效率，减轻市场主体负担。从2021年2月1日起，取消银行业保险业董事、监事（保险业）和高级管理人员任职资格考试。取消考试后，银保监会及其派出机构在任职资格核准工作中应通过审核申请材料、考察谈话等方式对拟任人是否具备履职基本条件进行审查；同时，通过现场检查、非现场监管等方式加强对银行保险机构董事、监事（保险业）和高级管理人员履职情况的监管。

三是进一步提升事中事后监管效能。对已取消或下放的行政许可事项，不得"一放了之""只放不管"，应加强风险评估，加大事中事后监管力度，确保"放得下、接得住、管得好"。要加强审批与监管的衔接，明确监管对象和范围，健全监管规则和标准，杜绝监管盲区和真空。对地方中小法人银行跨区域设立机构等事项，要加强事前沟通，探索行之有效的工作安排，强化上下联动和信息共享，形成工作合力，提升监管质效。要压实机构主体责任，加大对违法违规行为的查处力度，切实提高违法违规成本。此外，银保监会及其派出机构应当充分运用互联网、大数据等技术手段，推进"互联网+监管"和信用监管，提升监管效能。要强化银行保险机构数据治理，加强监管信息归集共享和关联整合，加强对风险的跟踪预警，提升监管精准化、智能化水平。

四是切实提高银行保险机构金融服务质效。银行保险机构要持续提升民营、小微企业金融服务质效，改善市场融资环境。银行机构在授信中不得设置不合理条件，不得对民营企业、中小企业设置歧视性要求。此外，银行保险机构要切实承担消费者权益保护工作的主体责任，加强消费者权益保护工作体制机制建设，维护金融消费者合法权益。加快建立消费者权益保护审查机制、完善消费者权益保护内部考核机制和信息披露机制,积极开展金融知识宣传教育,扎实做好消费投诉处理工作,提高金融消费者获得感。

(二)2020年保险市场发展政策效果

2020年,保险业经受住了新冠肺炎疫情冲击,积极应对,多渠道增强风险抵御能力,资产负债及业务稳步增长,服务实体经济质效持续提高,改革开放取得积极进展。

1. 保险市场运行总体情况

2020年度,保险业原保险保费收入45257.34亿元,同比增长6.13%,增速较前三季度下降1.03个百分点,较上年同期下降6.04个百分点(见图1)。赔款和给付支出13907.10亿元,同比增长7.86%,增速较前三季度提高1.72个百分点,较上年同期提高3.01个百分点。

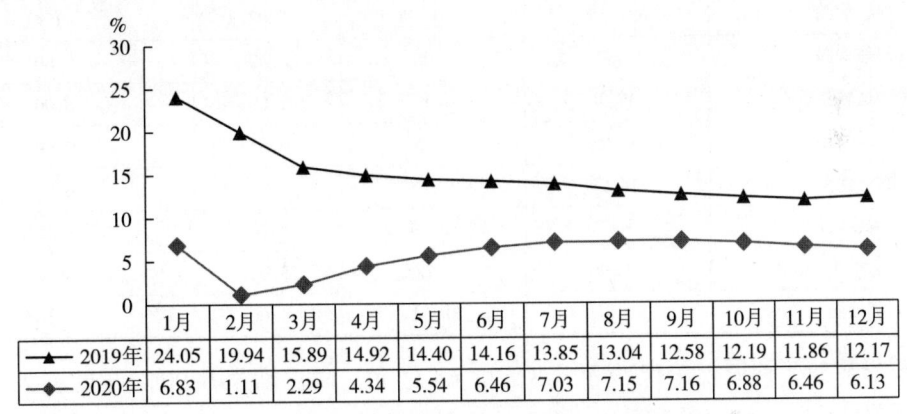

图1 2019—2020年各月累计保费收入增速

分业务看,产险业务原保险保费收入11928.58亿元,同比增长2.40%,增速较前三季度下降4.11个百分点,较上年同期下降5.77个百分点;赔款6954.79亿元,同比增长6.97%,增速较前三季度下降0.68个百分点,较上年同期下降3.28个百分点。寿险业务原保险保费收入23981.93亿元,同比增长5.40%,增速较前三季度提高0.56个百分点,较上年同期下降4.40个百分点;给付3715.11亿元,同比下降0.75%,降幅较前三季度缩窄2.65个百分点,较上年同期缩窄13.95个百分点。健康险业务原保险保费收入8172.71亿元,同比增长15.66%,增速较前三季度下降1.75个百分点,较上年同期下降14.04个百分点;赔款与给付2921.16亿元,同比增长24.23%,增速较前三季度提高4.63个百分点,较上年同期下降10.58个百分点。意外险业务原保险保费收入1174.11亿元,同比下降0.09%,降幅较前三季度缩窄1.43个百分点,上年同期增速为9.26%;赔款316.04亿元,同比增长6.17%,增速较前三季度提高0.40个百分点,较上年同期下降5.02个百分点。

分公司看,财产险公司实现原保险保费收入13583.69亿元,同比增长4.36%(见表1),增速较前三季度下降4.07个百分点,较上年同期下降6.36个百分点;赔款支出7880.42亿元,同比增长8.27%,增速较前三季度下降0.31个百分点,较上年同期下降

4.49 个百分点。

表1 财产险公司分险种原保险保费收入

| 险种 | 原保险保费收入（亿元） | 同比增长（％） | 占比（％） | 占比较上年同期增长（百分点） |
|---|---|---|---|---|
| 合计 | 13583.69 | 4.36 | 100.00 | — |
| 企业财产保险 | 490.26 | 5.64 | 3.61 | 0.04 |
| 家庭财产保险 | 90.79 | -0.47 | 0.67 | -0.03 |
| 机动车辆保险 | 8244.75 | 0.69 | 60.70 | -2.21 |
| 工程保险 | 138.41 | 17.45 | 1.02 | 0.11 |
| 责任保险 | 901.13 | 19.62 | 6.63 | 0.85 |
| 信用保险 | 204.88 | 2.46 | 1.51 | -0.03 |
| 保证保险 | 688.57 | -18.38 | 5.07 | -1.41 |
| 船舶保险 | 57.71 | 3.96 | 0.42 | 0.00 |
| 货物运输保险 | 135.96 | 4.49 | 1.00 | 0.00 |
| 特殊风险保险 | 72.16 | 4.75 | 0.53 | 0.00 |
| 农业保险 | 814.93 | 21.18 | 6.00 | 0.83 |
| 健康险 | 1114.21 | 32.60 | 8.20 | 1.75 |
| 意外险 | 540.90 | 2.72 | 3.98 | -0.06 |
| 其他险 | 89.02 | 38.91 | 0.66 | 0.16 |

人身险公司实现原保险保费收入31673.64亿元，同比增长6.90%（见表2），增速较前三季度提高0.25个百分点，较上年同期下降5.92个百分点；赔款与给付合计6026.59亿元，同比增长7.33%，增速较前三季度提高4.02个百分点，上年同期为下降3.89%。

表2 人身险公司分险种原保险保费收入

| 险种 | 原保险保费收入（亿元） | 同比增长（％） | 占比（％） | 占比较上年同期增长（百分点） |
|---|---|---|---|---|
| 合计 | 31673.64 | 6.90 | 100.00 | — |
| 寿险 | 23981.92 | 5.40 | 75.72 | -1.08 |
| 　—普通寿险 | 12545.94 | 19.79 | 39.61 | 4.26 |
| 　—分红寿险 | 11327.18 | -6.90 | 35.76 | -5.30 |
| 　—投资连结保险 | 4.33 | -1.57 | 0.01 | 0.00 |
| 　—万能保险 | 104.47 | -4.28 | 0.33 | -0.04 |
| 意外险 | 633.21 | -2.37 | 2.00 | -0.19 |
| 健康险 | 7058.50 | 13.38 | 22.29 | 1.27 |

保险金额8709.91万亿元，同比增长34.62%；新增保单件数526.34亿件，同比增长6.25%。产、寿险公司资产合计22.32万亿元，较年初增长15.95%。

## 2. 保险市场发展特点

（1）保险市场总体平稳，业务结构持续优化

①"车险综改"落地，产险公司降速提质

2020年财产险公司保费增长出现两个拐点，一是年初受疫情影响，收入增速明显回落，2月累计保费增速0.62%，为全年最低点，较上年同期下降13.07个百分点。3月开始增速回升，逐步回归常态，9月累计保费增速达到全年峰值，实现8.43%（见图2）。二是随着"车险综改"落地，9月以后保费增速有所放缓，但车险降价进一步惠及民生，全年财产险公司保费收入增长4.36%，较上年同期下降6.36个百分点。

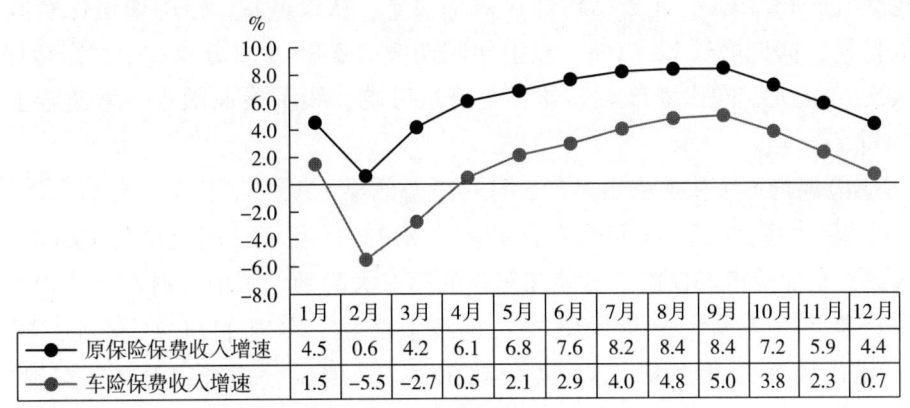

| | 1月 | 2月 | 3月 | 4月 | 5月 | 6月 | 7月 | 8月 | 9月 | 10月 | 11月 | 12月 |
|---|---|---|---|---|---|---|---|---|---|---|---|---|
| 原保险保费收入增速 | 4.5 | 0.6 | 4.2 | 6.1 | 6.8 | 7.6 | 8.2 | 8.4 | 8.4 | 7.2 | 5.9 | 4.4 |
| 车险保费收入增速 | 1.5 | -5.5 | -2.7 | 0.5 | 2.1 | 2.9 | 4.0 | 4.8 | 5.0 | 3.8 | 2.3 | 0.7 |

**图2　2020年财产险公司各月累计保费收入增速**

车险综合改革9月正式实施，车险业务总体实现"降价、增保、提质"。全年车险保费同比增长0.69%，较上年同期下降3.83个百分点，第四季度当季车险保费由上年同期增长5.96%转为下降10.43%。具体来看，10月、11月和12月当月车险保费同比下降6.50%、11.35%和12.62%，降幅逐渐扩大。虽然市场规模放缓，但车险业务保障进一步增加，更好地满足消费者的风险保障需求，车险全年提供风险保障323.80万亿元，同比增长28.32%，较上年同期提高8.87个百分点。

②非车业务快速发展，产险保障更加全面

财产险公司非车险保费保持较高增速，同比增长10.58%，其中健康保险、农业保险、责任保险和工程保险快速增长，增速分别实现32.60%、21.18%、19.62%和17.45%。其中短期健康险业务拉动行业增长2.10个百分点。全年非车险市场占比39.30%，较上年同期提高2.21个百分点。新公司深耕非车险业务，部分公司加快转型，84家产险公司中，非车险原保险保费收入占比高于20%的公司共32家，与2018年商业车险自主定价改革试点实施前相比，增加8家①。

③人身险公司价值业务提升，转型效果初显

年初受疫情影响，"开门红"计划较晚的人身险公司受到影响，全年人身险公司保费

---

① 包括2017年以后新成立的公司。

增速呈先增长后平稳的趋势,第一季度人身险公司保费逐步恢复,从4月开始保持平稳增长,增速保持在6%至7%,全年保费增速实现6.90%,较上年同期下降5.92个百分点。

2020年,人身险公司保费收入31673.64亿元,同比增长6.90%。从险种看,普通寿险是行业增长的主要动力,全年普通寿险实现保费收入12545.94亿元,同比增长19.79%,较上年同期提高4.96个百分点,普通寿险为行业增长提供6.99个百分点。从业务结构看,虽然全年受疫情影响,新单业务增长不及预期,全年新单业务保费收入12586.51亿元,同比下降2.08%,但近年行业坚持高质量发展路线,价值业务比例提高,行业风险抵御能力增强,续期保费拉动行业实现增长,全年续期保费收入19087.13亿元,同比增长13.79%,业务结构优化效果初显。从渠道看,银邮渠道保费收入实现10108.16亿元,同比增长12.61%,较上年同期增加0.86个百分点。个代渠道保费收入实现17965.96亿元,同比增长4.27%,受疫情影响,线下展业困难,增速较上年同期下降7.23个百分点。

④ 健康险保持持续快速稳定发展,社会效益凸显

健康险业务快速发展,全年实现保费收入8172.71亿元,同比增长15.66%,与车险体量接近,是保险市场仅次于寿险和车险的第三大险种。其中,财产险公司健康险业务近年保持高增长态势,全年保费收入突破千亿元,实现1114.21亿元,同比增长32.60%,增速从2017年至今,连续4年超30%。人身险公司健康险业务实现7058.50亿元,同比增长13.38%,依然保持较高增速,但较上年同期放缓14.22个百分点,其中短期健康险保费收入1719.05亿元,同比增长11.11%,较上年同期放缓19.65个百分点,长期健康险保费收入5339.45亿元,同比增长14.13%,较上年同期放缓12.46个百分点。2020年11月重疾险重定义后,人身险公司推出新旧条款交替日前购买,可择优理赔等服务,助推消费者获得更好的服务和公司实现2021年"开门红"双赢局面。

全年健康险提供风险保障1833.11万亿元,同比增长50.26%,赔款和给付支出2921.16亿元,同比增长24.23%,商业健康保险在服务健康中国、完善医保体系、支持健康产业等方面发挥了积极作用。

(2) 牢守风险底线,服务普惠金融

保险业运行稳健,偿付能力充足率保持在合理区间。第四季度末,178家保险公司平均综合偿付能力充足率为246.3%,平均核心偿付能力充足率为234.3%。

保险业发挥保障功能,全年提供风险保障8709.91万亿元,同比增长34.62%。其中,财产险公司提供7511.89万亿元,同比增长39.92%;人身险公司提供1198.02万亿元,同比增长8.79%。保险业切实服务普惠金融,助力三大攻坚战,全年提供农业风险保障4.13万亿元,同比增长8.57%,农险赔款支出592.52亿元,同比增长12.25%,提供责任保险赔款395.11亿元,同比增长15.64%,信用和保证保险赔款697.50亿元,同比增长42.31%。

(3) 推进对外开放进程,外资公司发展向好

保险业稳步扩大对外开放,2018年以来,首家外资独资保险控股公司安联(中国)

保险控股、外资独资寿险公司友邦人寿保险有限公司等先后获准设立。外资保险市场保持增长态势，2020年全年实现原保险保费收入3524.44亿元，同比增长12.43%，超中资保险公司6.80个百分点，其中外资人身险公司保费收入3176.72亿元，同比增长13.27%，外资产险公司保费收入347.72亿元，同比增长5.31%。外资保险公司市场占比7.79%，同比提高0.62个百分点。在北京和上海两地，外资保险公司市场份额均超过20%。

（4）大型险企总体稳定，中小公司存在差异

88家财产险公司中，48家险企增速超过财产险行业均值。91家人身险公司中，62家险企增速超过人身险行业均值（见表3）。

表3　　　　　　　　　2020年度保险公司保费增速分布区间

| 财产险公司 | | | | | |
| --- | --- | --- | --- | --- | --- |
| 增速区间 | 负增长 | 0~4.36% | 4.36%~60% | 60%~100% | 100%以上 | 新公司 |
| 公司数量 | 31家 | 8家 | 46家 | 2家 | 0家 | 1家 |
| 人身险公司 | | | | | |
| 增速区间 | 负增长 | 0~6.90% | 6.90%~60% | 60%~100% | 100%以上 | 其他公司 |
| 公司数量 | 15家 | 10家 | 47家 | 5家 | 10家 | 4家 |

注：1. 4.36%为财产险公司平均增速；新增大家财险无法计算增速。
2. 6.90%为人身险公司平均增速；4家无保险业务的养老险公司无法计算保费增速。

财产险"老三家"[①]稳定发展，全年实现原保费收入8645.90亿元，同比增长3.57%，行业占比63.65%，较上年同期下降0.49个百分点；中小财产险公司[②]原保险保费收入4937.79亿元，同比增长5.77%。在疫情冲击和"车险综改"双重影响下，中小财产险公司风险抵抗和转型能力各有不同，业务状况差异明显，保费正增长56家，其中增速较上年同期扩大的公司[③]有26家，保费负增长31家，其中降幅扩大的公司有28家[④]。

人身险"老七家"[⑤]公司实现保费收入18415.09亿元，同比增长3.33%，市场占比58.14%，较上年同期下降2.01个百分点；中小人身险公司[⑥]保费收入13258.55亿元，同比增长12.30%，保费正增长72家，其中增速较上年同期扩大的公司有28家，保费负增长15家，其中降幅扩大的公司有11家。

（5）财产险承保利润承压，人身险利润稳中有进

财产险公司业务承压，综合成本率为100.90%，同比增长0.92个百分点。其中信保业务和车险业务压力明显，一是受疫情影响，部分企业和个人还款能力下降，信用和

---

① "老三家"为人保财险、平安财险和太保产险。
② 除"老三家"以外的财产险公司。
③ 包括保费收入由负增长转为正增长的公司。
④ 包括保费收入由正增长转为负增长的公司。
⑤ "老七家"为国寿股份、平安人寿、太保寿险、新华人寿、太平人寿、泰康人寿和人保寿险。
⑥ 除"老七家"以外的人身险公司。

保证保险承保利润率分别为-22.52%和-15.05%。二是"车险综改"后，车险承保利润有所下降，实现承保利润79.57亿元，同比下降23.19%，承保利润率1.01%，较前三季度下降0.74个百分点。

人身险公司利润恢复平稳增长，预计利润总额实现2772.10亿元，同比增长15.68%，增速较前三季度提高11.54个百分点。同时，人身险公司持续经营能力提升，全年退保率为2.39%，同比下降2.58个百分点。

(6) 资金运用效率提升，投资收益显著增长

保险资金配置结构优化，截至2020年末，行业资金运用余额为21.68万亿元，较年初增长17.02%，其中债券占比最高，占比达36.59%，较年初提高2.03个百分点。保险业发挥长期稳定资金优势，投资能力进一步提升，在资本市场运行稳定和《保险资产管理产品管理暂行办法》等一系列政策出台的影响下，资金运用平均收益率实现5.41%，较上年同期提高0.47个百分点。

(三) 2021年保险市场发展展望

2021年保险业压力中有希望，挑战中有机遇。

一是政策有导向。《中华人民共和国国民经济和社会发展第十四个五年规划和2035年远景目标纲要》中134次提到"保障"，35次提到"保险"，对农业保险、科技保险、环责险、三支柱养老保险和长期护理保险等方面提出了明确的建议，提出了要稳妥推进保险等金融领域的对外开放。

二是新格局助推保险发展。加快形成以国内大循环为主体、国内国际双循环相互促进的新发展格局，发挥保险内需潜力，助力保险业发展。

三是数字化转型。疫情的反复对保险业传统线下展业造成压力，但行业加快数字化转型，拓宽线上渠道，提高经营效率和服务消费者能力。

四是全民健康意识提高。在健康中国战略的长期指引和疫情敲响的警钟下，全民健康意识进一步提高，对保险产品的需求增加。

五是业务转型加快。"车险综改"等深化行业改革的措施落地，加快行业高质量发展步伐，部分险企调头转型，虽然短期承压，但长期有利于险企走专业化、差异化路线，满足人民群众多层次的保险需求。

综上所述，预计2021年保险市场发展将继续保持总体稳定。

## 四、债券市场发展政策[①]

2020年，中国债券市场继续有效发展，发行规模大幅增长，市场交易活跃度不断提升，对外开放成果显著，产品创新、机制创新与规范管理持续加强，债券市场服务实体经济功能进一步提升。

(一) 市场发展概况

一是债券价格指数先升后降。中债总财富指数年初大幅上涨，4月末达到全年最高

---

① 作者：荣艺华，中国人民银行上海总部金融市场管理部副主任、《中国金融政策报告》项目（课题组）高级研究员。

点 202.1 点，随后逐步回落企稳，全年小幅上涨，指数从年初的 192.1 点上涨至年末的 198.0 点，上涨了 3.1%。上海清算所银行间信用债综合指数基本同步，呈现先升后降再回升的走势，从年初的 126.8 点上涨至年末的 131.0 点，涨幅达 3.3%。上证公司债指数总体呈上升走势，年初为 202.9 点，年末升至 211.5 点，增幅为 4.3%。

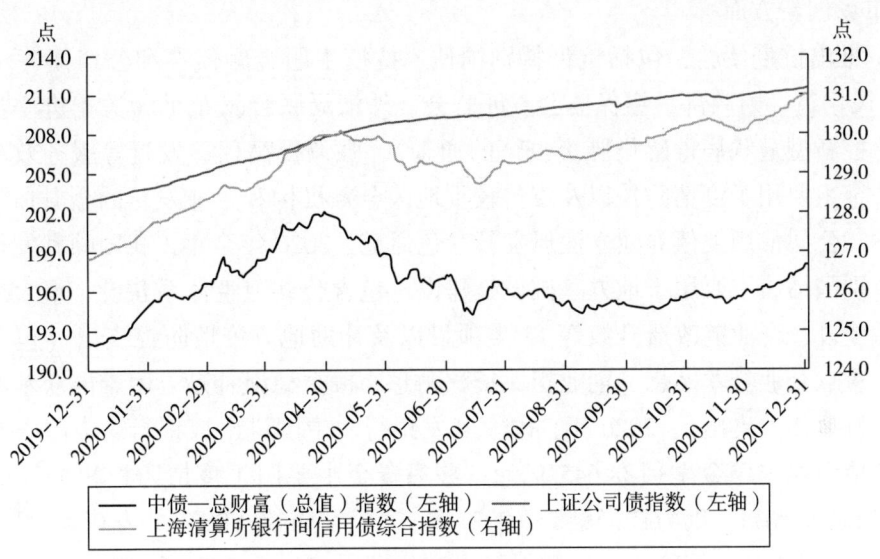

**图 1　2020 年债券价格指数**

（数据来源：中央国债登记结算有限责任公司、上海清算所、上海证券交易所）

二是债券发行大幅增长。2020 年，中国债券市场共发行各类债券 57.3 万亿元，较上年同比增长 26.5%，增速提高了 23.4 个百分点。其中，全国银行间债券市场发行 48.7 万亿元，同比增长 27.9%，占债券市场发行总量的 85.0%；交易所债券市场发行量为 8.6 万亿元，同比增长 18.2%，占债券市场发行总量的 15.0%。发行量前三大券种依次是同业存单、公司信用类债券和金融债券，发行量分别为 19.0 万亿元、12.9 万亿元和 9.3 万亿元。

三是交易量上升，但增速降低。2020 年，债券市场现券累计成交 253.0 万亿元，同比增长 16.5%，增速回落 22.1 个百分点。其中，银行间债券市场现券成交 232.8 万亿元，同比增长 11.5%，占全国银行间债券市场成交量的 92.0%；交易所债券市场现券累计成交 20.2 万亿元，同比增长 141.6%，占全国债券市场现券交易量的 8.0%。从银行间债券市场现券交易的券种结构看，排名前三的券种是政策性银行债、同业存单和国债，占比分别为 36.7%、20.1% 和 19.3%。

四是境外机构投资者持债规模显著增加。截至 2020 年末，共有 905 家境外机构投资者进入银行间债券市场，较上年增加了 109 家。境外机构持债量为 3.25 万亿元，较上年增加了 1.05 万亿元，增长了 47.7%，占银行间市场债券托管量的 3.2%。其中，持有国债 1.88 万亿元，净增持 5708 亿元，增长了 167%。

五是债券市场违约家数和债券只数下降，违约金额增加。2020 年，共有 54 家企业的 168 只债券发生违约，较上年分别减少了 15 家和 23 只；违约金额为 1356 亿元，增长了 7.1%。其中，民营企业债券违约 36 家，违约债券 84 只，违约规模 543.7 亿元，占比 43.5%；国有企业违约 11 家，违约债券 51 只，违约规模 566.5 亿元，占比 45.3%。

（二）出台的主要政策

1. 市场创新方面

（1）推出抗疫债券，包括抗疫特别国债、抗疫主题金融债券和公司债等。2020 年 1 月，人民银行、财政部、银保监会、证监会、外汇局联合发布了《关于进一步强化金融支持防控新型冠状病毒感染肺炎疫情的通知》，强调提高债券发行等服务效率，明确对募集资金主要用于疫情防控以及疫情较重地区金融机构和企业发行的金融债券、资产支持证券、公司信用类债券建立注册发行绿色通道。2020 年全年，我国顺利发行 1 万亿元抗疫特别国债，主要用于地方基础设施建设，包含公共卫生体系建设、重大疫情防控救治体系建设、产业链改造升级等 12 类项目以及补助地方疫情防控支出（包含减免房租补贴、重点企业贷款贴息、创业担保贷款贴息、援企稳岗补贴、困难群众基本生活补助和其他抗疫相关支出）。2020 年，国家开发银行、中国进出口银行、中国农业发展银行发行疫情防控主题金融债券 645 亿元，募集资金主要用于疫情防控相关领域信贷投放。"疫情防控 ABS"助力抗疫融资。2020 年，"疫情防控 ABS"共发行 44 只，规模合计 750 亿元，对支持疫情防控工作和保障生产经营平稳运行起到了积极作用。发行疫情防控公司债 110 只，共计 1078 亿元，帮助多家公司缓解疫情期间的流动性压力，对企业复工复产、经济复苏发挥了积极作用。

（2）推出脱贫攻坚相关专题债券。2020 年 4 月，国家开发银行面向银行间债券市场和商业银行柜台市场发行脱贫攻坚专题债券 110 亿元，主要用于向深度贫困地区发放重大基础设施、农村基础设施和产业扶贫等领域的扶贫贷款。发行扶贫专项公司债券 33 只，共计 196 亿元，发债企业所在贫困地区已覆盖贵州、四川、重庆、湖南、江西等全国十余省市。

（3）政策性金融债券推出多项创新。2020 年，中国农业发展银行先后合作推出脱贫攻坚、生态环保、抗洪救灾、西部大开发、疫情防控、消费扶贫等多种创新主题债券，发挥债券市场融资功能支持国家战略落地。国家开发银行多市场同时发行应对气候变化绿色金融债券，探索债券市场互联互通。中国进出口银行以弹性招标创新发行支持临港新片区主题债券，完善发行定价机制。

（4）绿色金融债券创新持续推进。2020 年 4 月中国农业发展银行发行"两山"生态环保主题金融债券，8 月建设银行发行的中资银行绿色债券首次在纳斯达克迪拜交易所上市，9 月中国银行在境外成功定价发行中资及全球商业机构首只双币种蓝色债券。

（5）推出补充中小银行资本专项债券。2020 年 12 月，广东省政府发行全国首单支持中小银行发展专项债券，此后多个省份成功发行专项债券，助力提升中小银行风险抵御能力和服务实体经济能力。另外，永续债发行主体拓展至中小银行，30 多家中小银行发行永续债，民营银行也发行了永续债。

（6）推出县城新型城镇化建设专项企业债。2020年8月，国家发展改革委办公厅印发《县城新型城镇化建设专项企业债券发行指引》，推出县城新型城镇化建设专项企业债券，旨在加快推进县城城镇化补短板强弱项工作，积极发挥企业债券融资在县城新型城镇化建设方面的积极作用。

2. 债券发行方面

（1）企业债和公司债发行全面实施注册制。2020年3月1日，新《证券法》正式实施。国家发展改革委明确企业债券发行由核准制改为注册制，证监会明确公司债券公开发行实行注册制，并均对债券发行条件、信息披露等作出相关要求。7月，中央国债登记结算有限责任公司（以下简称中央结算公司）配套发布《企业债券受理工作规则（试行）》，正式上线运行企业债券受理审核系统，并联合中国银行间市场交易商协会发布《企业债券审核工作规则（试行）》和《企业债券注册发行业务问答》。11月，上海证券交易所制定了《上海证券交易所公司债券发行上市审核规则适用指引第1号——申请文件及编制》和《上海证券交易所公司债券发行上市审核规则适用指引第2号——特定品种公司债券》，规范公司债券发行上市审核工作和特定品种公司债券发行上市申请相关业务。

（2）规范地方政府债券发行。2020年12月，财政部印发《关于印发〈地方政府债券发行管理办法〉的通知》，从发行额度和期限、信用评级、信息披露、债券发行和托管等方面，对地方债发行管理进行全面规范。《地方政府债券发行管理办法》明确，地方财政部门应当在国务院批准的分地区限额内发行地方政府债券；应当根据项目期限、融资成本、到期债务分布、投资者需求、债券市场状况等因素，合理确定债券期限结构；重申了此前地方债信息披露有关规定相关要求等。

（3）拓宽中小银行债券资本补充渠道。2020年5月，国务院金融稳定发展委员会出台《中小银行深化改革和补充资本工作方案》，强化债券市场对中小银行资本补充的支持。7月，国务院常务会议决定，在新增地方政府专项债限额中安排一定额度，允许地方政府依法依规通过多种方式，合理补充中小银行资本金。11月，财政部下达新增专项债券额度2000亿元，用于支持化解地方中小银行风险。

（4）完善非金融企业债务融资工具注册发行业务制度。2020年，中国银行间市场交易商协会修订发布《非金融企业债务融资工具公开发行注册工作规程》和《定向发行注册工作规程》等，完善分层分类机制安排，优化企业储架发行便利，整合注册工作流程；修订发布《非金融企业债务融资工具发行规范指引》、《非金融企业债务融资工具簿记建档发行工作规程》和《关于进一步加强债务融资工具发行业务规范有关事项的通知》，进一步强化发行定价市场化等规范性要求和优化簿记建档监督留痕机制，并且围绕严禁发行人自融、加强关联方认购披露和提升簿记操作规范等方面加强市场纪律约束。另外，修订发布了《定向债务融资工具专项机构投资人遴选细则》等来提升定向发行投资交易便利。

（5）健全中介机构尽职履责制度。2020年6月，中国银行间市场交易商协会修订发布《银行间债券市场非金融企业债务融资工具中介服务规则》，进一步完善主承销商团机制和加强中介机构尽职履责工作要求，同时新增受托管理人角色和强化存续期管理主体职责。12月，中国银行间市场交易商协会修订发布《非金融企业债务融资工具主承销商尽职调查指引》，进一步明确主承销商尽职调查职责。

（6）修订完善债务融资工具存续期管理制度。2020年12月，中国银行间市场交易商协会发布了《银行间债券市场非金融企业债务融资工具存续期管理工作规程》，整合了前期关于存续期管理的相关规范文件，进一步明晰了存续期管理机构的责任边界，同时进一步细化罚则条款，对存续期违规行为予以严肃惩戒。

3. 规范债券交易

（1）加强银行间债券市场交易行为管理。2020年以来，银行间债券市场加强交易的制度建设和纪律建设，全面修订债券交易、货币经纪、债券做市等交易自律规则，细化机构业务内控和行为规范要求，完善交易自律管理框架。同时加大债券交易违规查处力度，全年对银行、证券公司、基金公司、信托公司、期货公司等10余家机构进行现场调查，并对5家机构的交易违规行为进行自律处分。

（2）完善银行间债券市场现券做市制度。2020年12月，人民银行发布《完善银行间债券市场现券做市商管理有关事宜》（中国人民银行公告〔2020〕第21号），取消银行间债券市场双边报价商行政许可审批。

（3）商业银行参与交易所债券市场。2020年1月，上海证券交易所、深圳证券交易所分别联合中国证券登记结算有限责任公司发布了通知，将参与债券交易的银行范围由上市商业银行进一步扩大至政策性银行、国家开发银行、国有大型商业银行、股份制商业银行、城市商业银行、在华外资银行及境内上市的其他银行，明确符合条件的银行可申请债券交易参与人和结算参与人资格，并开设自有交易单元，以"直接入场、直接结算"模式直连入市或者通过券商"间接入场、券商结算"模式入市。

（4）全面修订自律处分规则体系。2020年8月，中国银行间市场交易商协会发布了《银行间债券市场自律处分规则》、《银行间债券市场自律处分会议工作规程》、《银行间债券市场违规事项自律调查和自律问询工作规程》和《银行间债券市场自律处分会议专家管理办法》，进一步优化自律处分程序、引入自律管理措施、提升总体惩戒标准，以及建立自律处分与行政处罚有序衔接机制等，以形成程序公正、规则透明、执法从严的自律处分制度安排。

4. 强化市场约束力

（1）统一公司信用类债券信息披露标准。2020年12月，人民银行、国家发展改革委、证监会联合发布《公司信用类债券信息披露管理办法》，以及配套文件《募集说明书编制要求》和《定期报告编制要求》，统一公司信用类债券信息披露标准，明确公司信用类债券信息披露的基础性和原则性要求，对公司信用类债券信息披露要件、内容、时点和频率等作了统一要求，规范公司信用类债券信息披露行为。

（2）加强地方政府债券信息披露管理。2020年1月，财政部发布《关于启用地方政府新增专项债券项目信息披露模板的通知》，规定自 2020 年 4 月 1 日起各地发行地方政府新增专项债券时，必须披露地方政府新增专项债券项目信息，并在债券存续期内按照模板格式披露存续期间相关信息。

（3）完善债务融资工具注册发行信息披露。2020 年 4 月，中国银行间市场交易商协会修订发布《非金融企业债务融资工具公开发行注册文件表格体系（2020 版）》和《非金融企业债务融资工具定向发行注册文件表格体系（2020 版）》，规范信息披露，提升信息披露的针对性和差异化，进一步发挥信息披露的风险揭示作用。9 月，推出《非金融企业债务融资工具募集说明书投资人保护机制示范文本》，为募集说明书中与投资人保护密切相关的内容提供了示范性表述，提升信息披露质量，切实保护投资人权益。

（4）强化信用评级行业自律管理。中国银行间市场交易商协会和中国证券业协会加强沟通协调，着力推动对信用评级机构的市场化评价标准的统一，完善以评级质量为核心的评价体系，强化对信用评级业务的监测调查力度，并对违规行为严格自律处分。

5. 债券市场互联互通

2020 年 7 月，人民银行、中国证监会联合发布《中国人民银行 中国证券监督管理委员会公告〔2020〕第 7 号》，推动银行间债券市场与交易所债券市场的电子交易平台和债券登记托管结算机构等基础设施机构互联互通。银行间债券市场债券登记托管结算机构之间、银行间和交易所债券市场债券登记托管结算机构之间应相互开立名义持有人账户，记载全部名义持有债券的余额。

6. 建立违约债券处置机制

（1）构建统一的公司信用类债券违约处置框架。2020 年 6 月，中国人民银行、国家发展改革委、证监会联合发布通知，构建统一的公司信用类债券违约处置制度框架，推动债券市场违约处置向市场化、法治化迈进。7 月，最高人民法院发布《全国法院审理债券纠纷案件座谈会纪要》，进一步畅通债券纠纷法治化救济渠道，提高司法救济效率，全面保障投资人的权利。11 月，国务院金融稳定发展委员会第四十三次会议研究规范债券市场发展、维护债券市场稳定工作，要求秉持"零容忍"态度，维护市场公平和秩序。12 月，中央经济工作会议召开，提出完善债券市场法制，打击逃废债等违法违规行为。

（2）积极推进非金融企业债务融资工具受托管理业务备案。中国银行间市场交易商协会在 2019 年底发布的《银行间债券市场非金融企业债务融资工具受托管理人业务指引（试行）》的基础上，推进市场开展受托管理业务。截至 2020 年末，已有 77 家机构完成受托管理业务备案工作，覆盖证券公司、信托公司、金融资产管理公司和律师事务所等多类机构。

（3）完善债券违约处置机制。2020 年 8 月，中央结算公司与上海清算所联合发布《全国银行间债券市场债券托管结算机构到期违约债券转让结算业务规则》，正式确立相关业务制度和机制，标志着银行间市场到期违约债券转让结算机制的建立。

（4）推出持有人名册定期推送服务。2020 年 6 月 30 日，上海清算所推出债券持有人名册定期推送服务。2019年，上海清算所推出债券持有人名册查询业务，拓展了查询主体和场景，明确了查询特定日期债券持有人名册的业务流程，为存续期管理、债券持有人会议和违约处置等提供了有力支持。债券持有人名册定期推送服务有助于进一步提升持有人名册查询效率、完善持有人名册服务体系，以及提升金融信息化服务能力。

7. 加大市场对外开放力度

（1）明确中国债券市场对外开放的整体性制度安排。2020年9月2日，人民银行、证监会、国家外汇管理局联合发布《关于境外机构投资者投资中国债券市场有关事宜的公告（征求意见稿）》，明确中国债券市场对外开放的整体性制度安排，统一准入管理，统一资金管理，与国际接轨，并深化跨部门监管合作。9月21日，人民银行、国家外汇管理局发布《境外机构投资者投资中国债券市场资金管理规定（征求意见稿）》，明确债券市场资金管理规则。

（2）合并QFII和RQFII制度。2020年9月，证监会、人民银行、国家外汇管理局联合发布《合格境外机构投资者和人民币合格境外机构投资者境内证券期货投资管理办法》，证监会同步出台配套规则，合并QFII、RQFII资格和制度规则，取消委托中介机构数量限制，稳步有序扩大投资范围，强化跨市场监管、跨境监管和穿透式监管，加大违规惩处力度。

（3）优化熊猫债发行制度。2020年12月，中国银行间市场交易商协会发布《外国政府类机构和国际开发机构债券业务指引（试行）》，优化外国政府类机构和国际开发机构在境内发行债券制度，明确了注册发行流程、信息披露和中介机构要求等方面的制度安排。同时发布的《境外非金融企业债务融资工具业务指引（2020版）》，在备案要求、注册文件提交和信息披露要求等方面进行了优化。

（4）允许外资银行参与地方政府债券承销。2020年1月，财政部发布公告，放开外商独资银行、中外合资银行、外国银行分行加入地方政府债券承销团的资格限制，按程序吸收外资银行加入承销团。

（5）进一步提高交易效率。2020年3月，上海清算所、中央结算公司向境外机构投资者推出循环结算和特殊结算周期服务（T+N），满足境外投资者多样化结算需求。9月，中国外汇交易中心实现交易双方无需提交申请即可线上自主选择达成T+N交易，进一步提高境外投资者交易结算效率。9月1日，全国银行间同业拆借中心开始试运行直投模式下直接交易服务，境外机构投资者可直接向境内做市机构发送报价请求并达成现券交易，还可使用交易分仓、一揽子交易等便利性功能，投资交易中国债券的效率进一步提升。9月15日，全国银行间同业拆借中心、上海清算所、中央结算公司联合公告，明确结算周期为T+1及以上的现券买卖交易时段延长至20：00。

（三）政策评估

1. 债券市场规模达117万亿元。在优化、规范债券发行机制的政策推动下，债券市场发行量显著增长，市场规模进一步增加。2020年全国债券市场共发行各类债券57.3万亿元，较上年增长26.5%，增速提高了23.4个百分点。年末，全国债券市场托管余额为117.0万亿元，同比增长18.1%，世界排名第二。

2. 全方位加大对实体经济的支持力度。2020年，公司信用类债券发行量继续以超过30%的增速增长，全年公司信用类债券发行总额为13.6万亿元，同比增长34.3%，有效地发挥了债券市场直接融资功能，在支持抗疫、企业复工复产、高新领域、先进制造业、绿色经济、民营经济、中小企业以及扶贫等领域发挥了重要作用，支持实体经济健康发展。

3. 交易活跃度上升。2020年，债券市场现券成交量在突破200万亿元的基础上继续增长，全年成交量为253.0万亿元，同比增长16.5%。银行间债券市场现券换手率为269%，同比上升50个百分点。交易活跃度高的前三大券种依次为政策性银行债、同业存单和记账式国债，换手率分别为539%、454%和288%。

4. 市场开放度继续大幅提高。在投资方面，2020年，有109家境外法人机构投资者进入银行间债券市场，境外机构交易活跃度进一步提升，全年现券成交量达9.16万亿元，同比增长72.5%。截至2020年末，共有905家境外机构主体进入银行间债券市场，境外机构在银行间市场的债券托管总量为3.25万亿元，同比增长47.9%，占银行间债券市场总托管量的3.2%。在中介服务方面，5月，惠誉博华信用评级有限公司完成了开展银行间债券市场B类信用评级业务的注册，这也是继标普信用评级（中国）有限公司之后第二家可在银行间债券市场开展信用评级业务的外资评级机构。10月，标普信用评级（中国）有限公司在证监会完成从事证券评级业务的备案，其执业范围从银行间债券市场扩大到交易所市场。在纳入国际债券指数方面，2月28日，摩根大通将9只中国政府债券纳入摩根大通旗舰全球新兴市场政府债券指数系列（GBI-EM），此次纳入的债券将达到该指数10%的权重上限。9月25日，富时罗素宣布拟将中国国债纳入富时世界国债指数（WGBI），至此全球三大债券指数已经或计划将中国债券纳入相关指数。

（四）展望

2021年是"十四五"规划开局之年，债券市场将根据党的十九大精神和中央经济工作会议决策部署，立足新时代，以新的发展理念，继续紧紧围绕服务实体经济、推动中国经济高质量发展主线，坚持市场化、法治化和国际化原则，进一步加强体制机制建设和产品创新，防范化解金融风险，深化金融改革，持续推动债券市场对外开放，进一步加大服务实体经济的能力和水平。

## 专栏6

**规范债券市场发展，维护债券市场稳定，促进资本市场健康可持续发展**[①]

近年来，我国债券市场发展势头良好，已成为我国金融市场体系中最为开放、最具

---

① 作者：杨超，中国银河证券研究院高级研究员，《中国金融政策报告》项目（课题组）研究员。

活力的部分，在提升直接融资比重、提高市场资源配置效率、服务实体经济方面发挥了重要作用。但是，同时也存在信用体系建设不完善、法律体系不完备等问题。2014年以来，信用债风险事件逐渐增多，债券市场信用违约备受关注。2020年11月10日，永煤集团因流动资金紧张，未能按期足额偿付"20永煤SCP003"本息，构成实质性违约。11月27日，证监会依法对永煤控股及希格玛会计师事务所立案调查。永煤集团违约使市场对政府的隐性支持再定价，市场高度关注未来城投债是否会打破刚兑信仰，引发资本市场持续波动。

11月21日，中共中央政治局委员、国务院副总理、国务院金融稳定发展委员会主任刘鹤主持召开国务院金融稳定发展委员会第四十三次会议，研究规范债券市场发展、维护债券市场稳定工作。会议指出，党中央、国务院高度重视资本市场健康可持续发展。我国债券市场改革开放不断深化，服务实体经济功能持续增强，市场整体稳健运行。近期违约个案有所增加，是周期性、体制性、行为性因素相互叠加的结果。要坚持稳中求进的工作总基调，按照市场化、法治化、国际化原则，处理好促发展与防风险的关系，推动债券市场持续健康发展。

会议要求，一是提高政治站位，切实履行责任。金融监管部门和地方政府要从大局出发，按照全面依法治国要求，坚决维护法制权威，落实监管责任和属地责任，督促各类市场主体严格履行主体责任，建立良好的地方金融生态和信用环境。二是秉持"零容忍"态度，维护市场公平和秩序。要依法严肃查处欺诈发行、虚假信息披露、恶意转移资产、挪用发行资金等各类违法违规行为，严厉处罚各种"逃废债"行为，保护投资人合法权益。三是加强行业自律和监督，强化市场约束机制。发债企业及其股东、金融机构、中介机构等各类市场主体必须严守法律法规和市场规则，坚持职业操守，勤勉尽责，诚实守信，切实防范道德风险。四是加强部门协调合作。健全风险预防、发现、预警、处置机制，加强风险隐患摸底排查，保持流动性合理充裕，牢牢守住不发生系统性风险的底线。五是继续深化改革。要深化债券市场改革，建立健全市场制度，完善市场结构，丰富产品服务；要深化国有企业改革，提升运行的质量和效率。

构筑有效监管和风险防控体系、维护债券市场稳定、促进资本市场健康可持续发展，对支持我国实体经济高效发展具有深远意义。随着我国金融改革的推进，直接融资将扮演更为重要的角色，债券市场将有力支持实体经济发展。一方面，加强立法，严格执法，提高惩处力度，对债券市场违法行为零容忍，严肃市场纪律。2020年12月，中央经济工作会议明确完善债券市场法制。12月24日，人民银行召开债券市场法制建设座谈会，表示下一步将与相关部门、学界、业界共同努力以债券市场法制建设中的问题为导向，推动完善债券市场法律体系，全面提升债券市场法治水平。这些政策动向均体现出国家和监管层高度重视债券市场的风险防范，也预示着未来债券市场的法制建设将加速推进。另一方面，在推进法制建设与有效监管的同时，应对债券市场中政府隐性担保、刚性兑付等问题进行全面研究，促进地方政府治理模式的完善，深化国企改革，从而优化市场产品结构，夯实债券市场信用基础，助力债券市场健康平稳发展。

## 五、证券投资基金市场发展政策①

### (一) 基金行业市场发展概述

2020年,全球新冠肺炎疫情持续蔓延,给世界经济带来剧烈冲击。我国疫情防控取得重大战略成果,在全球主要经济体中唯一实现经济正增长,金融供给侧结构性改革和对外开放进程深入推进,资产管理业基础环境不断改善,行业发展取得难能可贵的进展。

中国证券投资基金业协会统计数据显示,截至2020年末,基金管理公司及其子公司、证券公司、期货公司、私募基金管理机构资产管理业务总规模约为58.99万亿元②,较上年末增加6.76万亿元。其中,公募基金规模为19.89万亿元,证券公司及其子公司私募资产管理业务规模为8.55万亿元③,基金管理公司及其子公司私募资产管理业务规模为8.06万亿元,基金公司管理的养老金规模为3.36万亿元④,期货公司及其子公司私募资产管理业务规模约为2197亿元,私募基金规模为16.96万亿元,资产支持专项计划规模为2.11万亿元。

2020年以来,公募基金快速发展,结构进一步优化,资本市场买方功能及普惠金融积极作用进一步彰显。2019年10月,证监会开展公募基金投资顾问业务扩大试点工作。目前,已有18家机构取得基金投资顾问业务试点资格,15家机构正式展业。2020年全年,公募基金新发基金募资达3.16万亿元,达到历史年度募集顶峰。截至2020年末,公募基金管理了19.89万亿元基金资产,较上年末规模增长34.7%;居民持有占比53%,较上年末增加5个百分点,投资者覆盖面更广,普惠金融特性深入人心。产品结构进一步优化,权益类基金占比达32.3%,较上年末提高10.7个百分点,公募基金投资A股4.69万亿元,占两市流通总市值的7.3%,创2013年以来新高,在促进直接融资、服务实体经济等方面的作用进一步提升。基金公司管理养老金规模3.36万亿元,较上年末增长39.3%,服务养老资产配置效能进一步发挥。

证券期货经营机构私募资管业务结构继续优化,降杠杆、缩通道效果明显,行业机构主动管理能力提升。截至2020年末,私募资管业务规模为16.83万亿元,较上年末下降13.7%。通道业务规模持续下降,较资管新规发布前下降12.89万亿元,降幅69.7%。在中国证券投资基金业协会备案的资产证券化产品规模为2.11万亿元,较上年末增长28.2%,对盘活存量资产、提高资本运用效率具有重要作用。

私募基金稳健发展,为增加直接融资、促进创新资本形成作出了重要贡献。截至2020年末,在中国证券投资基金业协会登记的私募基金管理人为24561家,备案私募基金规模为16.96万亿元,较上年末规模增长20.4%。在协会备案的各类私募基金在投项

---

① 作者:蔡恒培,中国证券投资基金业协会投教与国际部(研究与统计专项小组)资深主办。
② 总规模中剔除了私募基金顾问管理类产品与私募资管计划重复部分。
③ 不含证券公司管理的养老金。
④ 此处养老金包括基金管理公司管理的社保基金、基本养老金、企业年金和职业年金,不包含境外养老金。

目 10.55 万个，在投本金 8.10 万亿元。其中，在投中小企业项目 6.80 万个，在投本金 2.20 万亿元；在投高新技术企业 4.01 万个，在投本金 1.68 万亿元。互联网等计算机运用、机械制造等工业资本品、原材料、医药生物、医疗器械与服务、半导体等产业升级及新经济代表领域成为私募基金布局重点，在投项目 6.67 万个，在投本金 3.51 万亿元。2020 年全年，私募基金投向境内未上市未挂牌企业股权的本金新增共 7020 亿元，相当于同期新增社会融资规模的 2.0%，为企业发展提供了宝贵的资本金，有力推动了供给侧结构性改革与创新增长。截至 2020 年末，科创板上市企业 215 家，中国证券投资基金业协会数据显示，上述科创板上市企业中，共有 176 家在成长过程中获得了私募股权、创投基金的资本支持，获投比例高达 81.9%。

（二）基金行业政策分析

2020 年以来，多层次资本市场建设和全面深化改革深入推进，资产管理行业制度体系及展业环境不断优化，发展空间不断拓展。作为直接融资体系的重要组成部分，以服务实体经济和大众理财为目标，监管部门坚持"建制度、不干预、零容忍"，引导行业回归本源。一方面，通过加强监管和制度约束，提高行业合规水平、加强风险防控，充分保护投资者合法权益；另一方面，通过制度供给和有效引导，促进行业稳步创新、丰富产品线、开拓业务布局，培育行业专业能力和国际竞争力水平，推动行业纵深发展。

1. 顶层设计不断完善，夯实行业法律根基

新《证券法》正式生效。2020 年 3 月 1 日，新《证券法》正式生效。新《证券法》施行以来，注册制改革稳步推进，投资者保护和信息披露进一步加强，证券违法成本提高、监管执法更加严格，进一步净化了资本市场环境。特别是新《证券法》明确，由国务院依照本法的原则规定资产管理产品发行、交易的管理办法，为国务院依法规范相关产品的发行、交易活动，提供了法律依据和保障。

资管新规过渡期延长。2020 年 7 月 31 日，为深入贯彻党中央、国务院关于统筹推进新冠肺炎疫情防控和经济社会发展工作的决策部署，经国务院同意，人民银行会同国家发展改革委、财政部、银保监会、证监会、外汇局等部门，审慎研究决定延长《关于规范金融机构资产管理业务的指导意见》过渡期至 2021 年底，同时建立健全激励约束机制，完善配套政策安排，平稳有序推进资管行业规范发展。过渡期适当延长，有利于推动资管存量业务整改平稳进行，缓解金融机构整改压力，为资管机构进一步提升新产品投研和创新能力、加强投资者教育和长期资金培育，提供更好的环境和条件。

鼓励机构投资者发挥买方作用、推动提升上市公司质量。2020 年 10 月 5 日，《国务院关于进一步提高上市公司质量的意见》发布，明确提出"建立董事会与投资者的良好沟通机制，健全机构投资者参与公司治理的渠道和方式"，"发挥股权投资机构在促进公司优化治理、创新创业、产业升级等方面的积极作用"，对发挥资产管理机构买方功能、促进机构投资者积极参与上市公司治理具有重要指导作用。

2. 强化监管、防范风险，加强投资者保护

规范公募基金投资新三板挂牌股票行为。2020 年 4 月 17 日，证监会发布《公开募

集证券投资基金投资全国中小企业股份转让系统挂牌股票指引》，明确管理人要求和可参与投资的基金类型，严格防控风险，提出加强流动性风险管理、做好信息披露、投资者适当性管理等要求，保护投资人合法权益。允许公募基金投资新三板精选层股票，有助于改善新三板投资者结构，提升市场交易活跃度，有利于拓展公募基金投资范围，帮助投资者分享优质创新创业型企业成长红利。

加强公募基金流动性风险管理。为进一步提升公募基金风险防控能力，更好地保护投资者合法权益，2020年7月10日，证监会发布《公开募集证券投资基金侧袋机制指引（试行）》。侧袋机制是指将基金投资组合中的特定资产从原有基金账户中分离至一个专门账户进行独立管理的机制，是流动性风险管理工具之一。侧袋机制的推出，有利于进一步丰富公募基金的流动性风险管理工具，缓解特定情形下因基金赎回引发的潜在系统性风险，也可防范先赎占优等行为，保障投资者合法权益。

完善基金托管及销售监管要求，优化行业生态。2020年7月10日，证监会和银保监会联合修订发布《证券投资基金托管业务管理办法》，允许外国银行在华分行申请基金托管业务资格，强化配套风险管控安排；结合监管实践完善监管要求，防范基金托管业务风险；持续推进简政放权，简化申请材料、优化审批程序，实行"先批后筹"；统一商业银行及其他金融机构的准入标准与监管要求。8月28日，证监会发布《公开募集证券投资基金销售机构监督管理办法》（以下简称《销售办法》）及其配套规则《关于实施〈公开募集证券投资基金销售机构监督管理办法〉的规定》、《公开募集证券投资基金宣传推介材料管理暂行规定》，强化基金销售活动的持牌准入要求，优化基金销售机构准入、退出机制，夯实业务规范与机构管控，完善独立基金销售机构监管。《销售办法》进一步完善基金销售行为规范、加强基金销售机构合规内控，对于强化投资者权益保护、优化基金市场生态、促进基金行业良性发展具有积极意义。

强化私募基金监管。为进一步加强私募基金监管，严厉打击各类违法违规行为，严控私募基金增量风险，稳妥化解存量风险，提升行业规范发展水平，保护投资者及相关当事人合法权益，2020年12月30日，证监会发布《关于加强私募投资基金监管的若干规定》，提出了私募基金管理人及从业人员等主体的"十不得"禁止性要求，通过重申和细化私募基金监管的底线要求，让私募行业真正回归"私募"和"投资"的本源，推动优胜劣汰的良性循环，促进行业规范可持续发展。

3. 全面改革开放深入推进，行业发展空间不断拓展

基础设施领域公募REITs试点正式起步。2020年4月30日，证监会、国家发展改革委联合发布《关于推进基础设施领域不动产投资信托基金（REITs）试点相关工作的通知》（以下简称《通知》），明确了基础设施REITs试点的基本原则、试点项目要求和试点工作安排。根据《通知》要求，中国证监会与国家发展改革委将加强合作，按照市场化、法治化原则，充分依托资本市场，积极支持符合国家政策导向的重点区域、重点行业的优质基础设施项目开展REITs试点。8月6日，证监会发布《公开募集基础设施证券投资基金指引（试行）》，明确了产品定义与运作模式、基金份额发售方式，明确基

金投资限制、关联交易管理、借款安排、基金扩募、信息披露等要求,推动基础设施REITs平稳落地。

资本市场对外开放进一步提升。2020年9月25日,证监会、中国人民银行、外汇局发布《合格境外机构投资者和人民币合格境外机构投资者境内证券期货投资管理办法》(以下简称《QFII、RQFII办法》),证监会同步发布配套规则《关于实施〈合格境外机构投资者和人民币合格境外机构投资者境内证券期货投资管理办法〉有关问题的规定》。《QFII、RQFII办法》及配套规则修改内容包括降低准入门槛,便利投资运作;扩大投资范围,新增允许QFII、RQFII投资私募投资基金、金融期货等;加强持续监管等。《QFII、RQFII办法》及配套规则有利于建立健全公开透明、操作便利、风险可控的QFII、RQFII制度,推进资本市场高水平双向开放。

4. 优化政策环境,有效引导行业服务实体经济

完善创业投资基金反向挂钩政策。为进一步完善创业投资基金退出渠道,畅通"投资—退出—再投资"良性循环,促进创业资本形成,2020年3月6日,证监会修订并发布《上市公司创业投资基金股东减持股份的特别规定》,简化反向挂钩政策适用标准,加大对专注于长期投资的基金的优惠力度,拓宽享受反向挂钩政策的适用主体,在中国证券投资基金业协会依法备案的私募股权投资基金参照适用。证监会对反向挂钩政策简化优化,有利于更好地发挥私募股权和创业投资对于支持中小企业、科创企业创业创新的作用,加大对实体经济的支持力度。

引导支持行业有效服务中小微企业。2020年5月26日,人民银行会同银保监会、国家发展改革委、工业和信息化部、财政部、市场监管总局、证监会、外汇局出台《关于进一步强化中小微企业金融服务的指导意见》(以下简称《意见》),明确提出"引导私募股权投资和创业投资投早投小",具体包括"修订《私募投资基金监督管理暂行办法》,强化对创业投资基金的差异化监管和自律……鼓励资管产品加大对创业投资的支持力度,并逐步提高股权投资类资管产品比例……"。《意见》对发展私募股权和创业投资基金、提高直接融资比重、精准服务实体经济发展具有重要意义。

5. 深化私募基金登记备案改革,行业现代化治理水平提升

私募基金产品备案"分道制+抽查制"改革试点。为进一步完善私募基金行业全流程动态信用管理机制,引导管理人更加重视专业诚信经营与信用积累,提升信用良好机构的备案效率,落实扶优限劣政策导向,自2020年2月7日起,中国证券投资基金业协会对持续合规运行、信用状况良好的私募基金管理人,试行采取"分道制+抽查制"方式办理私募基金产品备案。即符合条件的私募基金管理人提交私募基金备案申请后,将于次日在协会官网以公示该私募基金基本情况的方式完成该基金备案。协会将在该基金备案后抽查其合规情况。私募基金备案"分道制+抽查制"试点,是遵循私募基金事后备案工作规律的创新改革举措,行业信用运用机制由量变到质变,有利于激发私募基金管理人强化自身信用的内生动力,构建行业守信激励、失信约束机制,促进行业信义义务落地生根。

私募基金管理人登记清单及办理进度公开。为落实全面深化资本市场改革要求，进一步增强办理私募基金管理人登记申请工作的公开透明，便利申请机构事前准备申请材料，2020年2月28日，中国证券投资基金业协会发布《关于便利申请办理私募基金管理人登记相关事宜的通知》（以下简称《通知》）。《通知》按照不同类别私募基金管理人登记申请要求，公布了差异化的私募基金管理人申请登记材料清单，并向行业全流程公示申请机构办理登记进度，行业可通过协会官网"私募基金管理人登记办理流程公示"界面查询。此外，为加强社会监督，便利投资人及市场机构持续全面了解管理人展业情况，协会官网"私募基金管理人公示平台"增加私募基金管理人公示信息。登记清单和全流程公开，方便申请机构做好事前准备，有利于私募基金管理人登记工作有序、高效地开展以及申请登记工作的公开、透明，强化社会公众监督。

（三）行业发展展望

资产管理行业经过20余年的发展，已经成为现代金融体系的重要组成部分，是大众理财和实体经济资本形成的重要工具与载体。2021年是我国"十四五"规划开局之年，在高质量发展和构建国内国外双循环经济体系格局要求下，产业转型升级、培育国内经济增长新动能迫在眉睫。新的经济发展路径要求匹配新的资本支持方式，提高直接融资比重、优化融资结构、促进创新资本形成是重中之重，资产管理行业在其中发挥的作用不可替代。

资产管理行业的发展根植于实体经济与居民财富理财需求。我国实体经济率先走出新冠疫情的不利影响，成为全球唯一实现经济正增长的主要经济体，经济长期向好的趋势持续巩固，产业发展升级的势头强劲，资管行业有坚实的发展根基。我国人均国内生产总值已跨越1万美元关口，中等收入群体超过4亿人，强劲的理财需求为资产管理行业的发展提供了重要支撑。特别是资本市场以注册制为代表的全面深化改革、扩大更高水平双向开放的步伐加快，为行业发展提供了有利环境和广阔空间。行业应积极发挥专业价值、回归资管本源，提升专业能力和国际竞争力、坚持长期价值投资、大力发展权益类产品、提高直接融资比重，实现行业自身变革和长期健康发展。

**附表**

**2020年以来基金行业主要监管政策一览表**

| 日期 | 政策名称 | 发文单位 | 发文文号 |
| --- | --- | --- | --- |
| 2月28日 | 关于便利申请办理私募基金管理人登记相关事宜的通知 | 中国证券投资基金业协会 | — |
| 3月6日 | 上市公司创业投资基金股东减持股份的特别规定 | 证监会 | 证监会公告〔2020〕17号 |
| 4月1日 | 私募投资基金备案须知 | 中国证券投资基金业协会 | — |
| 4月17日 | 公开募集证券投资基金投资全国中小企业股份转让系统挂牌股票指引 | 证监会 | 证监会公告〔2020〕23号 |
| 4月30日 | 关于推进基础设施领域不动产投资信托基金（REITs）试点相关工作的通知 | 证监会、国家发展改革委 | 证监发〔2020〕40号 |

续表

| 日期 | 政策名称 | 发文单位 | 发文文号 |
|---|---|---|---|
| 5月26日 | 关于进一步强化中小微企业金融服务的指导意见 | 中国人民银行、银保监会、国家发展改革委、工业和信息化部、财政部、市场监管总局、证监会、外汇局 | 银发〔2020〕120号 |
| 7月10日 | 证券投资基金托管业务管理办法 | 证监会、银保监会 | 证监会令【第172号】 |
| 7月10日 | 公开募集证券投资基金侧袋机制指引（试行） | 证监会 | 证监会公告〔2020〕41号 |
| 8月6日 | 公开募集基础设施证券投资基金指引（试行） | 证监会 | 证监会公告〔2020〕54号 |
| 8月28日 | 公开募集证券投资基金销售机构监督管理办法 | 证监会 | 证监会令【第175号】 |
| 8月28日 | 关于实施《公开募集证券投资基金销售机构监督管理办法》的规定 | 证监会 | 证监会公告〔2020〕58号 |
| 8月28日 | 公开募集证券投资基金宣传推介材料管理暂行规定 | 证监会 | 证监会公告〔2020〕59号 |
| 9月25日 | 合格境外机构投资者和人民币合格境外机构投资者境内证券期货投资管理办法 | 证监会、中国人民银行、外汇局 | 证监会令【第176号】 |
| 9月25日 | 关于实施《合格境外机构投资者和人民币合格境外机构投资者境内证券期货投资管理办法》有关问题的规定 | 证监会 | 证监会公告〔2020〕63号 |
| 10月5日 | 国务院关于进一步提高上市公司质量的意见 | 国务院 | 国办发〔2019〕49号 |
| 12月30日 | 关于加强私募投资基金监管的若干规定 | 证监会 | 证监会公告〔2020〕71号 |

## 专栏7

### 我国不断加快推进资本市场对外开放，致力于发展更高水平的开放型经济[①]

2019年7月2日，国务院总理李克强在第十三届夏季达沃斯论坛开幕式上指出，"我们将深化金融等现代服务业开放举措，将原来规定的2021年取消证券、期货、寿险外资股比限制提前至2020年"。

2020年，我国资本市场对外开放的步伐不断加快。2020年1月1日，银保监会取消经营人身保险业务的合资保险公司的外资比例限制；3月13日，证监会公布4月1日起取消证券公司外资股比限制；5月7日，人民银行及外汇局公布《境外机构投资者境内证券期货投资资金管理规定》，取消境外机构投资者额度限制，取消投资收益汇出限制；9月2日，人民银行等三部门公布《关于境外机构投资者投资中国债券市场有关事宜的公告（征求意见稿）》，进一步便利境外机构投资者配置人民币债券资产；10月，中共

---

[①] 作者：解学成，中国银河证券研究院副院长（主持工作）、《中国金融政策报告》项目（课题组）高级研究员。

中央政治局委员、国务院副总理刘鹤，人民银行党委书记、银保监会主席郭树清，人民银行行长易纲，证监会主席易会满等领导相继发声持续推动金融业对外开放。

2020年，我国积极推进资本市场改革开放，树立良好营商环境。中国要向全世界表明在金融业、服务业领域开放步伐不会停，坚持扩大债券市场双向开放。中国人民银行多次表态，在这一过程中要保持人民币汇率合理均衡水平上的稳定，中国不会搞竞争性贬值，要进一步降低关税水平，扩大商品、服务进口，继续完善对外开放法律体系，《外商投资法》的配套法规加紧建立，不合时宜的该废就废，制度建设提前布局，2020年和外商投资法同步实施，为我国宏观经济结构性改革提供良好的营商环境，为深化供给侧结构性改革提前做好充分准备，为加速构建国内国际双循环相互促进的新发展格局提供良好的土壤环境。

2020年11月3日，《中共中央关于制定国民经济和社会发展第十四个五年规划和二〇三五年远景目标的建议》发布，翔实阐述了实行高水平对外开放，开拓合作共赢新局面的规划。该建议指出，构建与国际通行规则相衔接的制度体系和监管模式，健全外商投资准入前国民待遇加负面清单管理制度，进一步缩减外资准入负面清单，落实准入后国民待遇，促进内外资企业公平竞争；建立健全跨境服务贸易负面清单管理制度，健全技术贸易促进体系；稳妥推进银行、证券、保险、基金、期货等金融领域开放，深化境内外资本市场互联互通，健全合格境外投资者制度；稳慎推进人民币国际化，坚持市场驱动和企业自主选择，营造以人民币自由使用为基础的新型互利合作关系；完善出入境、海关、外汇、税收等环节管理服务。

我国不断加快推进资本市场对外开放，对发展更高水平的开放型经济具有深远意义。在经历全球贸易摩擦与突如其来的新冠疫情背景下，加快推进资本市场对外开放，以开放促改革，以改革促进更大的开放，充分发挥我国超大规模市场优势和内需潜力，形成资本市场高水平对外开放新格局，更好地推动国内国际经济双循环发展。资本市场开放是双向的开放。一方面，持续推进产品体系和资本市场制度对外开放，例如，进一步扩大沪深股通的投资范围和标的，持续加大商品期货市场开放力度，提升国际资金的投资便利性等；另一方面，支持境内经营机构走出去，监管层积极参与国际金融治理，加强与境外资本市场监管机构的沟通和政策协调，及时防范和化解跨境资本市场风险，不断提高开放环境下资本市场运行的活力和韧性。

**专栏8**

**从"扩、优、广、强"四字把握"科创金融十七条"政策要义**[①]

在我国，科技创新一直都具有十分重要的战略地位。2020年12月11日，中共中央政治局明确提出，要整体推进改革开放，强化国家战略科技力量。科创企业作为强化国

---

[①] 作者：刘勇，中关村互联网金融研究院院长、《中国金融政策报告》项目（课题组）高级研究员。

家战略科技力量的主体,在推动科技创新、提升科技动能等方面发挥着关键作用。在我国社会经济发展的新阶段,加快构建以国内大循环为主体、国内国际双循环相互促进的新发展格局,是贯穿"十四五"及未来较长时期发展的战略纲领。而推动金融供给侧结构性改革,是进一步扩展深化新发展格局的重要举措和抓手。金融供给侧结构性改革对于推动科技创新的战略意义,在于调动金融资源、优化资金配置,为科创企业更好地发挥自身战略价值提供充足的资本"弹药",为金融更好地服务实体经济优化范式。

北京市作为创新驱动发展的前沿阵地,依托科技、金融等区位优势,不断优化营商环境,科技创新企业集聚。在此背景下,2020年1月10日,北京市地方金融监督管理局等多部门联合制定《关于加大金融支持科创企业健康发展的若干措施》(后文简称"科创金融十七条"),作为深入贯彻落实中央经济工作会议精神、深化金融供给侧结构性改革、大力推进科创金融建设的重要举措。"科创金融十七条"共包括6大方面共17条措施,实质上是按照"扩、优、广、强"的思路,系统强化金融系统对科创企业的支撑力,全面提升不同类型机构服务科创企业的凝聚力,重点优化配置资金发挥科创金融影响力。"扩"是指扩增量,重点在于扩大信贷融资规模、加大资本市场支持力度,从点和面两个维度做好整个科创金融资本市场体量支撑;"优"是指优结构,关键在于优化融资担保体系,筑牢安全发展压舱石;"广"是指广联动,核心在于加强金融机构联动,以协同创新发展构建共享共赢机制;"强"是指强服务,着力点在于加强金融服务创新,优化政务服务环境,持续提升服务能力。"科创金融十七条"中提出的"三个15%""不低于150亿元"以及"增资30亿元"等量化指标,一方面明确政策支持的力度、范围和重点,精准施策,提出支持科创企业在京发展的要求;另一方面,以量化指标倒逼金融机构服务模式变革,加快新时代新动能构建,推动科创金融创新生态发展。因此,"科创金融十七条"的发布不仅是为金融服务科创企业提供政策支持,更是为金融供给侧结构性改革探索新思路。

## 六、货币市场发展政策[①]

2020年,面对新冠肺炎疫情带来的严重冲击,在稳健的货币政策背景下,货币市场运行总体平稳,利率中枢整体下行,市场规模进一步扩大,票据市场规范发展等政策出台,市场功能有效深化。

(一)同业拆借市场

1. 市场运行概况

2020年,同业拆借市场运行总体平稳,市场主体继续增加,交易规模稳中略降,利率中枢下行,交易结构仍以短期限品种为主。如图1所示,全年,同业拆借市场累计成交147.14万亿元,同比减少2.96%,日均成交量为5909.34亿元。同业拆借全年加权平均利率为1.64%,同比下行63个基点。全国银行间同业拆借市场成员共计2293家,

---

[①] 荣艺华,中国人民银行上海总部金融市场管理部副主任、《中国金融政策报告》项目(课题组)高级研究员。

较上年新增市场成员 26 家。

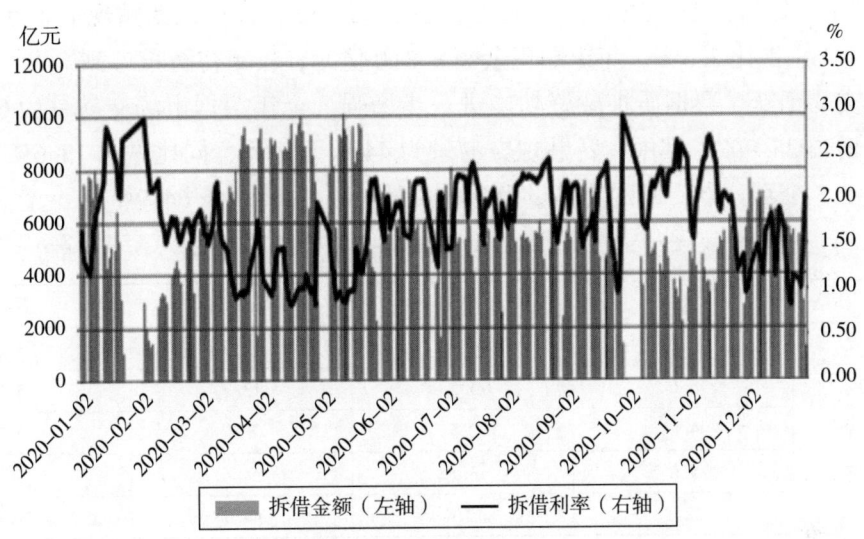

**图 1　2020 年全国银行间同业拆借市场成交情况**
（数据来源：中国外汇交易中心）

同业拆借市场利率中枢整体下行。2020 年，同业拆借加权平均利率较上年下行 63 个基点。年末，隔夜、7 天拆借加权成交利率分别收于 1.34% 和 2.55%，较年初分别下降了 16 个和 66 个基点。全年日加权成交利率极差为 207 个基点，较上年减少 3 个基点。

2020 年，同业拆借市场交易主体仍以银行类机构为主，占交易总量的 85.92%。从各类金融机构同业拆借市场资金流向看，大型商业银行、政策性银行、股份制银行是市场的主要资金融出方，证券公司、城商行和财务公司是主要的资金融入方。

2. 展望

2021 年，同业拆借市场将继续平稳有序运行，市场利率将继续围绕人民银行政策利率体系合理波动，市场主体规范运行有效强化，进一步突出同业拆借市场流动性调剂功能。

（二）票据市场

2020 年，票据市场制度建设稳步推进，制度性政策有序推出，票据资产流动性逐步改善，票据业务创新层出不穷，市场规模进一步扩大，票据市场充分发挥了政策传导、精准滴灌、支持实体的功能。

1. 市场运行情况

2020 年，票据业务继续稳健发展，各项业务指标均保持正增长，市场利率下行，支持实体经济成效显著。

票据承兑规模增加，银行汇票承兑稳中有升，商业汇票签发占比明显提高。2020 年，企业累计签发商业汇票 22.1 万亿元，同比增长 8.4%；年末商业汇票未到期金额为 14.1 万亿元，同比增长 10.7%。其中，全市场银行汇票承兑金额为 18.5 万亿元，同比增长 6.4%；商业汇票签发金额为 3.6 万亿元，同比增长 19.8%，市场占比为 16.4%。

票据贴现增长，银行汇票占比超过九成。全年票据贴现 13.4 万亿元，同比增长 7.7%。其中，银行汇票贴现 12.4 万亿元，占比 92.5%；商业汇票贴现 1.0 万亿元，同比增长 9.9%，占比 7.5%。年末贴现余额 8.8 万亿元，较年初增长 7.3%。

票据交易活跃，票据质押融资功能进一步增强。全年票据市场交易量为 64.1 万亿元，同比增长 25.9%。其中，转贴现交易量为 44.1 万亿元，同比增长 13.6%，增速较上年提高 1.5 个百分点；回购交易量为 20.0 万亿元，同比增长 64.9%。

表1　　　　　　　　　　　　2020 年票据市场规模　　　　　　　　单位：万亿元

| 季度 | 承兑 | 贴现 | 转贴现 | 回购 |
| --- | --- | --- | --- | --- |
| 第一季度 | 6.0 | 4.4 | 12.2 | 3.6 |
| 第二季度 | 5.6 | 3.5 | 13.3 | 5.7 |
| 第三季度 | 4.8 | 2.5 | 8.7 | 5.7 |
| 第四季度 | 5.6 | 3.1 | 9.9 | 5.0 |
| 合计 | 22.1 | 13.4 | 44.1 | 20.0 |

数据来源：上海票据交易所。

票据利率中枢总体下降。全年票据贴现加权平均利率为 2.98%，同比下降 47 个基点；转贴现加权平均利率为 2.71%，同比下降 60 个基点；质押式回购加权平均利率为 1.87%，同比下降 64 个基点。

再贴现力度进一步加大。全年人民银行共计三次增加了 1.8 万亿元再贷款、再贴现额度，支持抗疫保供、复工复产和中小微企业等实体经济发展。年末再贴现余额为 5784 亿元，较上年同期增长 22.7%。

2. 出台的主要政策

2020 年 2 月，中国人民银行发布《关于加大再贷款、再贴现支持力度促进有序复工复产的通知》（银发〔2020〕53 号），在前期已经设立 3000 亿元疫情防控专项再贷款的基础上，再增加再贷款再贴现专用额度 5000 亿元。同时下调支农、支小再贷款利率 0.25 个百分点至 2.5%。

4 月，中国人民银行杭州中心支行、上海分行、南京分行、合肥中心支行联合发布《长三角地区电子商业承兑汇票推广应用工作方案》（杭银发〔2020〕58 号），进一步推进电子商业承兑汇票在长三角地区的应用。

4 月，人民银行下发《关于增加再贷款再贴现额度支持中小银行加大涉农、小微企业和民营企业信贷投放的通知》，增加再贷款再贴现额度 1 万亿元。

5 月，银保监会等六部门联合下发《关于进一步规范信贷融资收费　降低企业融资综合成本的通知》（银保监发〔2020〕18 号），要求不得忽视企业实际需求将部分授信额度划为银行承兑汇票，或强制以银行承兑汇票等非现金形式替代信贷资金。

6 月，中国人民银行发布《标准化票据管理办法》（中国人民银行公告〔2020〕第 6 号），正式推出标准化票据，规范标准化票据融资机制，更好地服务中小企业融资和供应链金融发展。

6月，中国人民银行、银保监会、证监会、国家外汇管理局联合发布《标准化债权类资产认定规则》（中国人民银行　银保监会　证监会　国家外汇管理局公告〔2020〕第5号），明确标债资产与非标资产的界限、认定标准及监管安排。其中，标准化票据需申请认定通过之后才能成为标准化债权资产。

9月，人民银行等八部门联合发布《关于规范发展供应链金融　支持供应链产业链稳定循环和优化升级的意见》（银发〔2020〕226号），明确提出要加快实施商业汇票信息披露制度，提升应收账款标准化和透明度，支持供应链票据发展和标准化票据融资。

12月，中国人民银行发布《规范商业银行汇票信息披露》（中国人民银行公告〔2020〕第19号），明确商业承兑汇票信息披露有关事宜，以改善市场信用环境，促进商票更好发挥功能。

3. 政策效果分析

有力地支持了实体企业发展。2020年初以来，为有效应对新冠肺炎疫情对实体经济造成的冲击，人民银行分层次、分梯度地先后三次安排了共计1.8万亿元再贷款、再贴现额度，支持抗疫保供、复工复产和中小微企业等实体经济发展，切实解决了企业复工复产面临的债务偿还、资金周转和扩大融资等迫切问题。截至年末，再贴现余额为5784亿元，较上年同期增长22.7%，实现了资金的精准滴灌，支持了实体经济特别是民营及中小微企业的发展。

加强了市场机制建设。上海票据交易所于2020年1月16日上线试运行商业汇票信息披露平台，2月28日上线自主注册功能，商业汇票承兑机构可通过平台披露票据相关信息，平台按日披露承兑人承兑票据的信用情况，包括承兑发生额、承兑余额、累计逾期发生额、逾期余额，21家企业成为首批试点参与机构。年末，人民银行根据试点情况发布了商业承兑汇票信息披露有关事宜公告，建立商业承兑汇票信息披露制度，有效提高了市场透明度。

降低了企业融资成本。为持续加大减费让利力度，缓解企业融资难融资贵问题，银保监会等六部门联合下发《关于进一步规范信贷融资收费　降低企业融资综合成本的通知》，以融资各环节为主线，以是否提高融资综合成本为标准，同时考虑信贷资金供给侧和需求侧，对信贷、助贷、增信和考核环节收费行为及收费管理作了规范，强化了内部管控、外部监督与激励的作用，并明确了跨部门监督合力和正向激励机制。票据方面，针对贷存挂钩和强制捆绑搭售等问题，要求"不得忽视企业实际需求将部分授信额度划为银行承兑汇票，或强制以银行承兑汇票等非现金形式替代信贷资金"，切实服务企业真实融资需求。

营造良好发展氛围。八部门联合发布的《关于规范发展供应链金融　支持供应链产业链稳定循环和优化升级的意见》，首次界定了供应链金融的内涵，明确了供应链金融的发展目标，提出提升应收账款标准化和透明度，支持供应链票据发展和标准化票据融资的政策举措，对票据市场规范创新、提高供应链产业链运行效率、支持供应链产业链稳定升级和国家战略布局有很好的指导和推动作用。《长三角地区电子商业承兑汇票推广应用工作方案》就提升市场效率、共享市场信息、健全信用体系、支持产品创新、加大再贴现支持、强化约束机制等方面提出了10条具体措施，明确提出了推进"票付通"业务应用、推动"贴现通"业务试点、开展应收账款票据化试点。《标准化票据管理办法》的推出，将票据市场与债券市场联通，发挥债券市场的专业定价能力和投资能力，提高票据交易的规范性。

票据产品创新层出不穷。截至2020年末，标准化票据成功创设57只，金额为61.18亿元，已完成兑付31只，兑付金额为32.26亿元，未出现兑付失败的情况。4月24日供应链票据平台上线运行，提高了票据的支付流通能力，为应收账款票据化提供了新的思路和渠道，首日共有17家企业签发供应链票据17笔合计104.42万元，2家企业背书流转供应链票据3笔合计5.1万元。6月18日，首批供应链票据贴现业务成功落地，9家企业通过供应链票据贴现融资10笔合计506.81万元，贴现利率为2.85%~3.8%，贴现票据全部为商业承兑汇票。上线"贴现通""票付通"，截至2020年末，累计有7819家企业通过"贴现通"获得票据经纪服务，28165笔票据合计469.8亿元达成贴现意向，促进了票据创新业务的健康发展，更好服务了民营企业和中小企业的贴现融资需求，票据市场服务实体经济的质量和效率进一步提升。

4. 展望

2021年是"十四五"的开局之年，在构建双循环新发展格局及金融业深化改革开放的大背景下，中国票据市场将继续完善制度体系、健全基础设施、创新体制机制、推进透明度建设、加快科技赋能，更加有效支持供应链产业链，为促进实体经济高质量发展发挥更好的作用。

## 专栏9

### 国务院批复《深化北京市新一轮服务业扩大开放综合试点建设国家服务业扩大开放综合示范区工作方案》[①]

2020年8月28日，国务院正式批复了北京市人民政府和商务部共同上报的《深化北京市新一轮服务业扩大开放综合试点建设国家服务业扩大开放综合示范区工作方案》（以下简称方案）。方案旨在贯彻落实党中央、国务院关于深化北京市新一轮服务业扩大开放综合试点的重大决策部署，促进服务业高质量发展。

党中央、国务院高度重视服务业、金融业扩大开放。2020年9月4日，习近平总书记在中国国际服务业贸易交易会全球服务贸易峰会上发表重要讲话，提出北京应在开放中国服务业进程中发挥引领作用，支持北京打造国家服务业扩大开放综合示范区，以探索更多可推广的经验。其中，推进金融服务领域扩大开放更是服务业开放发展的重要牵引，这一点也体现在2021年的政府工作报告和"十四五"规划纲要中。

---

① 作者：张宸，中国信达资产管理股份有限公司研究部宏观形势与金融风险首席研究员，《中国金融政策报告》项目（课题组）研究员。

北京市委、市政府大力推动服务业、金融业高质量发展。2021年2月22日，北京市委书记蔡奇就推动金融业高质量发展开展调研，并召开北京市金融工作座谈会。他强调，要深入贯彻习近平总书记对北京改革发展的重要指示精神，立足高质量发展新阶段、贯彻新发展理念、构建新发展格局，积极培育发展与大国首都地位相匹配的现代金融业，在金融改革发展上走在全国前列。蔡奇从金融基础设施建设、加强多层次资本市场建设、提高金融服务实体经济水平等三个方面对北京金融业深化改革和扩大开放作出了战略部署，从抓住"两区"建设机遇、进一步扩大金融开放、加强国家金融管理中心建设等三个方面提出了具体要求。

"十四五"规划纲要多次提及金融要为服务业发展提供要素支持，推动金融业、服务业扩大开放。第十章第三节深化服务领域改革开放，提出要完善支持服务业发展的政策体系，创新适应服务新业态新模式和产业融合发展需要的金融政策，深入推进服务业综合改革试点和扩大开放。第十三章第二节提高国际双向投资水平，要求完善境外生产服务网络和流通体系，加快金融服务业国际化发展。第四十一章第三节深化经贸投资务实合作，提出建立健全"一带一路"金融合作网络，推动金融基础设施互联互通，支持多边和各国金融机构共同参与投融资。

批复充分肯定了北京市首都城市战略定位，要求在风险可控前提下，通过对服务业深化改革、扩大开放，为全国提供示范经验。批复要求北京市坚持深化市场化改革，扩大高水平开放，对标国际先进贸易投资规则，吸收借鉴国际成熟经验，推动由商品和要素流动型开放向规则等制度型开放转变，为服务业高质量发展营造良好制度环境，在扩大服务业对外开放、建设更高水平开放型经济新体制方面取得更多可复制可推广的经验，为全国服务业开放发展、创新发展提供示范引领，为推动全方位对外开放作出更大贡献。

方案共分为四个部分，内容涵盖北京市新一轮服务业扩大开放综合试点的总体要求、发展目标、主要任务与措施和组织实施等方面内容。明确了首都城市战略定位，提出了努力探索服务业开放发展的新业态、新模式、新路径，打造国家服务业扩大开放综合示范区的总体要求。

发展目标方面，方案以2025年和2030年为时间节点，用两个五年的时间，分阶段对制度建设和开放体系建设提出了具体要求。到2025年，要求基本健全以贸易便利、投资便利为重点的服务业扩大开放政策制度体系。到2030年，实现贸易自由便利、投资自由便利、资金跨境流动便利、人才从业便利、运输往来便利和数据安全有序流动，基本建成与国际高标准经贸规则相衔接的服务业开放体系。

主要任务方面，方案围绕打造科技服务、数字经济与贸易、金融服务等9大服务业重点行业领域，推动服务业扩大开放在中关村国家自主创新示范区、金融街、国家文化与金融合作示范区等7个重点区域示范发展。要求形成投资贸易、财税、产业链供应链协同等6个方面制度创新，优化资金、数据、人才、土地等4类要素供给等维度，提出了聚焦科技创新、服务业开放、数字经济和数字贸易等26方面开放创新政策措施。

金融服务领域扩大开放仍是重中之重。在方案全部120余项政策中，涉及金融服务的有29项，占比近1/4，尤其在进一步放宽外资准入限制、资金跨境流动更加便利等方面有较多政策突破。

方案的出台，为北京市服务业、金融业对外开放提供了良好的制度支撑，有利于进一步改善外资参与中国服务业、金融业发展的营商环境；有利于为我国建设更高水平开放型经济新体制探索路径、提供示范，使中国服务业、金融业的改革开放能够在新时代行稳致远。

## 七、信托与财富管理市场发展政策①

### （一）2020年主要政策内容

2020年，信托与财富管理市场发展政策成果斐然，堪称重磅政策年份。

**1.《关于推动银行业和保险业高质量发展的指导意见》**

2019年12月30日，中国银行保险监督管理委员会发布《关于推动银行业和保险业高质量发展的指导意见》（银保监发〔2019〕52号）（以下简称《指导意见》）。

随着我国经济由高速增长阶段转向高质量发展阶段，金融供给与需求之间不平衡不适应的矛盾日益凸显，银行业和保险业高质量发展面临多重挑战。为深入贯彻落实党中央的决策部署，推动银行业和保险业高质量发展，更好地服务现代化经济体系建设，中国银保监会正式发布《指导意见》。作为重要的纲领性文件，《指导意见》展望2025年，从推动形成多层次、广覆盖、有差异的银行保险机构体系，完善服务实体经济和人民群众生活需要的金融产品体系，精准有效防范化解银行保险体系各类风险，建立健全中国特色现代金融企业制度，实现更高水平的对外开放、加强金融监管和廉洁金融建设等方面提出了体系化目标要求。

《指导意见》不仅就银行业总体提出了目标要求，还专门就信托业提出了两个直接目标。

（1）在机构体系构建上，要求信托公司回归"受人之托、代人理财"的职能定位，积极发展服务信托、财富管理信托、慈善信托等本源业务。

（2）在风险防范化解上，要求逐步清理压缩不合规的表外理财非标资产投资、表内特定目的载体投资、同业理财等业务规模，严控银信类通道业务。

**2.《信托公司股权管理暂行办法》**

2020年1月20日，中国银保监会发布《信托公司股权管理暂行办法》（以下简称《暂行办法》），自2020年3月1日起施行。

《暂行办法》包括总则、信托公司股东责任、信托公司职责、监督管理、法律责任、附则6章，共78条。《暂行办法》充分参考了《商业银行股权管理暂行办法》中关于股东穿透监管、股东分类管理等制度设计，明确了信托公司股东、信托公司、监管部门三

---

① 作者：李青云，天津民晟资产管理有限公司总裁、《中国金融政策报告》项目（课题组）高级研究员。

方在股权管理不同阶段的职责。具体上,《暂行办法》主要内容有以下几方面。

(1) 关于股东责任

在这一部分,《暂行办法》对股东资质、股权取得、股权持有和股权退出等环节作出了明确规定。

① 股东资质。《暂行办法》要求"经国务院银行业监督管理机构或其派出机构审查批准,境内非金融机构、境内金融机构、境外金融机构和国务院银行业监督管理机构认可的其他投资人可以成为信托公司股东"。对于不同类型的机构,《暂行办法》又从经营水平、资产规模等方面进一步明确了要求。与此同时,《暂行办法》对担任信托公司主要股东禁止性条款也做了明确规定。

② 股权取得。《暂行办法》规定,"投资人可以通过出资设立信托公司、认购信托公司新增资本、以协议或竞价等途径取得信托公司其他股东所持股权等方式入股信托公司"。对于信托公司主要股东,应当按照向上穿透的原则"逐层说明其股权结构直至实际控制人、最终受益人,以及与其他股东的关联关系或者一致行动关系"。

③ 股权持有。《暂行办法》就信托公司的公司治理、交叉持股、兼职任职、风险隔离等方面提出常态化规范的同时,还特别加强了对信托公司股东信息披露方面的要求:股东出现"可能影响股东资质条件变化或导致所持信托公司股权发生变化的情况",必须在15日内书面通知信托公司。

④ 股权退出。《暂行办法》对股权退出设定了时限要求:"信托公司股东自取得股权之日起五年内不得转让所持有的股权。"但持股不足5%的股东不受此项限制。

(2) 关于公司职责

在这一部分,《暂行办法》从变更期间、股权事务管理、股东行为管理等角度提出明确要求。

① 变更期间。《暂行办法》要求,在"信托公司变更股权或调整股权结构、合并、分立以及其他涉及信托公司股权发生变化"期间,信托公司必须保障公司治理有效,严防出现内部人控制。

② 股权事务管理。《暂行办法》就日常股权管理提出多项规定,并要求信托公司"建立和完善股权管理制度,做好股权信息登记、关联交易管理和信息披露等工作"。同时,《暂行办法》还要求信托公司建立股权托管制度,原则上应将股权集中托管。此外,《暂行办法》还专门就责任人作了规定:"信托公司董事长是处理信托公司股权事务的第一责任人。董事会秘书协助董事长工作,是处理股权事务的直接责任人。"

③ 股东行为管理。《暂行办法》在股东资质审查、关联交易管理、公司治理机制等方面提出规范要求。尤其提出信托公司应当加强对股东资质的审查,"对主要股东及其控股股东、实际控制人、关联方、一致行动人、最终受益人等相关信息进行核实,并掌握其变动情况,就主要股东对信托公司经营管理的影响进行判断"。

(3) 关于监督管理。《暂行办法》显著加强了对信托公司股权管理的监督管理,在监管内容、监管措施和监管手段等方面都做了详尽规定。特别地,《暂行办法》对穿透监管进行了专门强调,要求"加强对信托公司股东的穿透监管,加强对主要股东及其控股股东、实际控制人、关联方、一致行动人及最终受益人的审查、识别和认定"。

3.《关于开展银行业保险业市场乱象整治"回头看"工作的通知》

2020年6月23日,中国银保监会发布《关于开展银行业保险业市场乱象整治"回头看"工作的通知》(银保监发〔2020〕27号,以下简称《工作通知》)。

《工作通知》对信托公司专门提出了如下工作要求。

(1)宏观政策执行

《工作通知》主要对房地产类信托提出重点关注,要求对房地产开发项目贷款规范性、土地储备贷款或流动资金贷款、房地产关联贷款、资金违规流入房地产市场、向地方政府融资平台提供融资、地方政府及其所属部门担保等方面进行重点核查。

(2)公司治理

《工作通知》对公司治理方面的关注较为细致,要求从股东资质、股东出资、股东信息、股东违规质押股权、间接转让股权、滥用股东权利或不履行股东义务、关联交易、公司章程、任职资格、关键岗位空缺、关联方识别更新、关联交易控制委员会运作、激励约束机制等诸多方面进行自查整改。

(3)影子银行和交叉金融业务

影子银行和交叉金融业务与信托行业关联度较大,《工作通知》要求对非标资金池业务清理、滚动发行、变相新增非标资金池、不良资产承接、穿透管理等方面进行核查。

(4)融资类信托业务

《工作通知》对融资类信托业务的核查重点主要有尽职调查、贷后管理、资产减值准备计提、压缩计划等。

(5)非金融子公司管理

《工作通知》对非金融子公司管理高度关注,要求对非金融子公司设立、非金融子公司清理、类信托或监管套利、通道业务、非标资金池业务、关联交易、组织架构等方面进行自查整改。

(6)经营管理

《工作通知》在经营管理方面的关注重点是互联网引流和第三方推介、"双录"制度、违规承诺保本保收益、隐性担保、信息披露、风险资产转移等。

(7)创新业务

创新业务也受到了《工作通知》的关注,《工作通知》要求对"明股实债"、收(受)益权或其他伪创新、受益权流转、多层嵌套业务、创新业务资格等方面进行自查整改。

4.《标准化债权类资产认定规则》

2020年7月3日,中国人民银行会同中国银保监会、中国证监会、国家外汇管理局发布了《标准化债权类资产认定规则》(以下简称《认定规则》)。

根据 2018 年资管新规中的"标准化债权类资产的具体认定规则由中国人民银行会同金融监督管理部门另行制定"要求，人民银行会同银保监会、证监会、国家外汇管理局制定了《认定规则》，明确标债资产和非标准化债权类资产（以下简称"非标资产"）的界限、认定标准及监管安排，引导市场规范发展。

《认定规则》为债权类资产提供了标债资产认定路径，有助于提升债券市场的包容性。对于已明确为标债资产的各类债权类资产，无须进行标债资产认定；对于新增的其他各类债权类资产，可按相关程序进行认定；对于通过认定的标债资产，资管产品可将其用于置换存量非标资产。

《认定规则》对广受关注的"非非标"资产进行了确认，明确认定银行业信贷资产登记流转中心、北京金融资产交易所、上海保险交易所等交易场所的"非非标"为非标，但保留其申请成为标债资产的权利。

5.《关于信托公司风险资产处置相关工作的通知》

2020 年 7 月 17 日，中国银保监会发布了《关于信托公司风险资产处置相关工作的通知》（以下简称《处置通知》）。

《处置通知》主要包含三方面的内容：（1）要求信托公司加大表内外风险资产的处置和化解工作；（2）对压降信托通道业务提出明确要求；（3）要求信托公司压降违法违规严重、投向不合规的融资类信托业务。

《处置通知》进一步明确了需要压降的重点领域：一是金融机构借助信托通道开展监管套利、规避政策限制的融资类业务；二是信托公司偏离受托人定位，将自身作为"信用中介"，风险实质由信托公司承担，违法违规开展融资类业务。

6.《优化资管新规过渡期安排　引导资管业务平稳转型》

2020 年 7 月 31 日，中国人民银行发布了公告《优化资管新规过渡期安排　引导资管业务平稳转型》（以下简称《过渡期公告》）。

《过渡期公告》的核心内容是根据现实情况变化，对资管新规过渡期进行调整。由于新冠疫情对经济金融带来显著冲击，《过渡期公告》明确："为平稳推动资管新规实施和资管业务规范转型，经国务院同意，人民银行会同国家发展改革委、财政部、银保监会、证监会、国家外汇管理局等部门审慎研究决定，资管新规过渡期延长至 2021 年底。"

《过渡期公告》同时指出："过渡期延长不涉及资管新规相关监管标准的变动和调整。"

7.《关于开展新一轮房地产信托业务专项排查的通知》

2020 年 10 月 30 日，中国银保监会信托监管部下发《关于开展新一轮房地产信托业务专项排查的通知》（以下简称《排查通知》）。

《排查通知》显然与房企"三道红线"政策一脉相承。《排查通知》要求各银保监局切实履行属地监管责任，保持对房地产信托高压监管态势不放松，提前谋划风险防控工作，严厉查处违法违规行为，健全房地产信托监管长效机制。具体排查内容有以下几方面。

（1）排查房地产信托业务的持续合规监管情况。主要对信托公司违规开展房地产信托贷款、信托公司通过不当"创新"等变相形式突破监管要求、为各类资金违规流入房地产市场提供通道便利等情况进行排查。

（2）排查房地产信托业务风险防范化解情况。主要包括以下几个方面：对房地产信托业务逐笔排查，对风险缓释措施进行分析，摸清风险底数；全面排查信托公司对房企集团（含其关联方）的信托融资集中度情况，评估集中度风险；制定和执行风险应对预案情况。

（3）落实房地产信托业务的整改问责情况。针对信托公司房地产信托合规与风险问题，总结 2020 年以来（含本次专项排查工作）的整改情况和追责问责情况。

8. 《中国银保监会信托公司行政许可事项实施办法》

2020 年 11 月 16 日，中国银保监会发布《中国银保监会信托公司行政许可事项实施办法》（银保监会令〔2020〕12 号，以下简称《许可办法》），自 2021 年 1 月 1 日起施行。

《许可办法》包括总则、机构设立、机构变更、机构终止、调整业务范围和增加业务品种、董事和高级管理人员任职资格、附则 7 章，共 76 条。《许可办法》是《中国银监会信托公司行政许可事项实施办法》基础上的修订版本，并且与《信托公司股权管理暂行办法》形成有机衔接。此次发布的《许可办法》的修订内容主要体现在股东资格、机构变更、业务资格、董事和高管任职资格等四个方面。

（1）关于股东资格

① 信托公司法人机构设立。《许可办法》明确要求"股东管理、股东的权利义务等相关内容应按规定纳入信托公司章程"，同时对信托公司法人机构的"公司治理结构""投资者保护机制"提出具体要求。

② 境内非金融机构作为股东。《许可办法》对拟取得信托公司控股权的非金融机构设置了相应要求，且新增内容均与《信托公司股权管理暂行办法》保持一致。关于入股信托公司的数量，也要求符合《信托公司股权管理暂行办法》的规定，即"同一投资人及其关联方、一致行动人参股信托公司的数量不得超过 2 家，或控股信托公司的数量不得超过 1 家"。

③ 境内金融机构作为股东。《许可办法》延续老版本的主要内容，但对境内金融机构作为信托公司出资人提出了新要求："如取得控股权，应最近 3 个会计年度连续盈利。"

④ 境外金融机构作为股东。《许可办法》删除了"最近 1 个会计年度末总资产原则上不少于 10 亿美元"的要求，与金融业对外开放的政策导向相一致。其他新修订要求则与境内非金融机构的要求一致。

（2）关于机构变更

《许可办法》对信托公司经营过程中可能的变更事项提出了规范，主要涉及事项有变更名称、变更股权或调整股权结构、变更注册资本、变更住所、修改公司章程、分立或合并等。

特别地,《许可办法》在这一部分的新修订内容充分显现了简化流程的意图,如:信托公司上市应向银保监会派出机构申请;信托公司实际位置未变化、临时变更住所6个月以内不需申请变更住所;信托公司因行政区划调整、股东名称变更等原因引起公司章程内容变更的不需申请修改章程。

(3) 关于业务资格

《许可办法》对信托公司的业务资格范围进行了确认,主要有企业年金基金管理业务资格、特定目的信托受托机构资格、受托境外理财业务资格、股指期货交易等衍生产品交易业务资格、以固有资产从事股权投资业务资格。其中以固有资产从事股权投资业务资格属于新增内容。具体而言,《许可办法》的新修订内容主要体现在以下部分。

① 特定目的信托受托机构资格。《许可办法》删除了 "完成重新登记3年以上" "监管评级良好" 2项,相比之前适当放宽了条件。同时,《许可办法》还取消了资产支持证券发行前报告的要求,进一步简化了业务流程。

② 以固有资产从事股权投资业务资格。《许可办法》新增了这一业务资格,基本条件与特定目的信托受托机构资格基本一致。与其他业务资格不同的是,信托公司开展此类业务时应当及时向监管机构提供报告,报告内容主要有 "项目基本情况及可行性分析、投资运用范围和方案、项目面临主要风险及风险管理说明、股权投资项目管理团队及人员" 等。

具体到业务开展,《许可办法》又设定了多项操作要求,如不得投资于关联方、不得控制被投资企业、持有股权不得超过5年、投资总额不超过净资产的20%等。

(4) 关于任职资格

《许可办法》要求董事和高管人员任职须经任职资格许可,其中董事人员主要包括 "信托公司董事长、副董事长、独立董事、其他董事会成员以及董事会秘书",高管人员则在传统范围的基础上新增了风险总监(首席风险官)。

《许可办法》在任职程序上明确 "信托公司申请核准董事和高级管理人员任职资格,应当向银保监分局或所在地银保监局提交申请",但对董事长、总经理则提出了更严格的要求——信托公司董事长、总经理(首席执行官、总裁)的任职资格许可应征求银保监会意见。

(二) 2020年政策效果评估

1. 收紧货币循环、稳定宏观杠杆

2020年信托相关政策,关于约束融资/地产信托业务的内容占据了主要篇幅,典型如《工作通知》、《处置通知》和《排查通知》等。从宏观审慎角度考虑,约束融资/地产信托业务规模会对货币创造循环形成一定影响,从长期看将有助于化解货币规模与资金成本双高这一系统性难题。信托相关政策的这一价值,要从大额实物商品需求与货币需求的相关性入手,并结合货币创造机制加以理解。

过去20年来,我国广义货币$M_2$增速一直保持大幅超越GDP增速的态势,并在2019年达到了200万亿元人民币的水平,远超GDP规模。横向比较显示,我国$M_2$/GDP

比值相比其他主要经济体的情况也明显偏高。但从另一角度看，在广义货币规模明显偏高的同时，我国市场利率水平也一直居高不下，民间借贷利率尤甚。市场利率高意味着资金成本高，也就是通常说的融资贵。在广义货币增速远高于 GDP 增速的前提下，却同时存在资金成本高企的情况，这显然不符合货币超发的传统定义。货币供应量偏大的前提下仍然融资难，意味着收缩货币供应势必造成资金成本的进一步抬升，这导致货币政策取向经常陷入两难。

按照经典货币创造理论，货币创造是基础货币与存款准备金率的协同结果，信用货币通过"存款—贷款"循环而不断派生。需要注意的是，发起并推动这一循环的是贷款行为，而非存款行为。只有旺盛而持续的贷款需求，才能推动货币创造循环持续进行。进一步地，信贷需求与重资产产能需求高度相关，背后则是地产、基建与耐用消费品。因此，经济体通常在地产、基建需求的高速释放阶段形成强烈信贷需求，从而推动货币规模扩大。需要注意的是，信贷需求得以实现的重要前提是价值匹配的抵押品，而这一点会在地产价格上升后得到解决，并形成正反馈循环。在以地产、基建为核心需求的阶段，释放出的资金必然以地产、基建领域为核心流入方向，继而导致其他行业出现融资难的情况，随之融资贵。

这样的需求结构，还会从货币流通速度角度进一步强化这一难题。依据费雪方程式可知，货币流通速度与货币供应量成反比，货币流通速度越慢，对货币供应量的需求就越大。在以基建、地产、汽车等为核心的需求结构下，交易频率自然较低，货币流通速度则处于慢速时期。有关我国货币流通速度的研究表明，过去 20 年我国货币流通速度一直处于稳步下降的态势。与我国相比，主要发达经济体的地产、基建需求早已走过高峰步入平稳，在缺少新增信贷需求支撑的情况下，即使是宽松政策也难以导致货币规模大幅上升。显然，需求结构上的实质性差异，是主要发达经济体 $M_2$/GDP 比率显著小于我国的基础性原因。

多项数据表明，我国实物需求的主升浪已近尾声，我们不能再放任"地产价格—信贷扩张"的货币供应正反馈进一步加强。尽管信托业务不是标准的银行业务，却是银行业务的影子，能够配合银行变相扩大信贷。随着银行表内业务监管的不断加强，通过信托方式扩大表外业务或变相发放贷款的规模不断扩大，信托业早已成为资产规模仅次于银行的第二大金融子行业。"地产价格—信贷扩张"的循环不可能永续进行，必然会以某种方式结束。为防止地产"灰犀牛"出现，我们应当对货币扩张循环加以主动抑制。相形之下，通过抑制信贷扩张端形成对货币创造效率的收紧，显然是一项稳妥举措。因而，2020 年对融资、地产信托业务的坚决抑制政策，势必有利于收紧货币供应的副闸门，从而有助于货币规模与资金成本双高这一难题稳步化解。

2. 深化风险防范、促进回归本源

根据《中国影子银行报告》，信托业务中的资金信托和信托贷款属于典型影子银行业务。基于影子银行往往是风险源头的特点，加大对影子银行业务的风险防控显然是防范风险的重中之重。一般来说，信用状况与流动性水平出现持续不利变化是导致金融资产风险的根本原因。目前,我国正处于经济增速换挡的关键阶段,经济运行状态正从传统的供需循环向新兴供需循环转化。从产业结构角度看,重资产行业占比将在一定期限内稳步降低,由此必然出现渐进的系统性调整:需求、产能、融资规模和杠杆水平。

在此背景下,部分企业主体信用状况和阶段性流动性水平出现不利变化的可能性不容忽视,而影子银行业务的风险水平显然更高一些。因此,当前时期是防范金融风险的重要阶段,尤其要严防地产"灰犀牛"之类的重大风险。融资类信托尤其是地产信托,作为典型的影子银行业务,在信托业务规模中长期占据核心地位,从防风险的角度来说不能继续坐视融资、地产信托业务占比居高不下。因此,2020年的多项政策在防范金融风险方面具有极强针对性。

另一方面,上述政策还具有鲜明的促使信托业务回归本源的效果。信托作为"受人之托、代人理财"的专业资产管理机构,理应将重点放在资产管理、财富管理等更符合本源属性的业务类型上。但在信贷需求旺盛的背景下,融资、地产信托业务明显具有更高的性价比,抑制了信托行业发展本源业务的积极性。只有在严格压降融资、地产信托业务的约束下,信托行业才会更关注本源业务。

3. 完善制度环境、防范治理风险

我国信托行业历史上曾经出现过多次大规模整顿,这是其他金融子行业中较为少见的情况。导致信托行业屡次陷入整顿的原因复杂多样,典型有业务属性的复杂性、金融市场发展不充分、经营能力有短板等。但不可否认的是,信托公司在公司治理方面存在的不足,也是导致信托行业发展屡屡出现问题的重要因素之一,甚至是决定性因素。公司治理存在瑕疵,其不利影响必然会逐渐传导至具体经营活动中,并对日常业务形成长期不利影响,甚至导致业务风险持续累积。历史上,由于公司治理机制运行不畅而出现的信托公司风险事件并不罕见,有的甚至形成了较大社会影响。因此,如何从制度上推动督促信托公司深入完善公司治理机制,对于信托行业发展具有重大意义。

2020年,银保监会发布/修订了关于股权管理的《暂行办法》和关于行政许可的《实施办法》,在完善信托公司治理机制方面形成了较为系统的制度环境,将极大促进信托公司对公司治理机制进行系统性规范。在公司治理机制运行良好的前提下,信托公司在发展战略、经营管理、合规风控等重大事项上的规范性水平有望显著提升,必将有助于防范治理风险的发生和累积。

(三) 2021年政策展望

1. 压降通道业务规模

受人口结构影响,以大额实物商品为核心的消费者数量正处于见顶回落的状态,传统行业的需求侧也将随之出现调整。在新旧需求调整过程中,债务杠杆与资本结构的调整也将随之展开。总体而言,资本结构将呈现债务融资比重收缩、股本融资比重提高的长期趋势。以此为背景,无论从适应变化还是从风险防范角度出发,都应该对债务融资规模加以优化。对于具有典型"影子银行"特征的通道类业务,则更应保持审慎姿态。因此,稳妥压降通道类信托业务规模,仍将是新一年的政策关注重点。

## 2. 推动创新业务发展

随着社会财富状况的不断深化发展,财富管理需求正日益成为社会关注焦点。信托作为一种典型的财产管理机制,其制度需求或者适应性恰恰与财富保有水平高度相关。无论以投资规划为主的财富增值需求还是以财产安全为主的财富保护需求和以继承安排为主的财富传承需求,近年来已经呈现快速增长势头。在传统业务逐步进入收缩期的前提下,应当加快推动信托创新业务的发展,典型如服务信托与慈善信托等。

## 3. 鼓励非标资产转标

资管新规过渡期延长一年至2021年底,信托产品要力争在年底前完成相应的标准化改造。因此,现有大量信托产品仍然存在非标转标的巨大压力。为稳妥有效保障这一目标实现,可以考虑出台一定的鼓励措施,一方面促使信托公司在产品规划和业务能力等方面实现优化或者提升,另一方面促使信托公司与其他金融子行业形成全面有效合作,以便保障非标转标任务的顺利完成。

## 附表

**中国信托与财富管理市场发展主要政策**

| 日期 | 文件名称 | 发布单位 |
| --- | --- | --- |
| 2019年12月30日 | 关于推动银行业和保险业高质量发展的指导意见(银保监发〔2019〕52号) | 中国银保监会 |
| 2020年1月20日 | 信托公司股权管理暂行办法 | 中国银保监会 |
| 2020年6月23日 | 关于开展银行业保险业市场乱象整治"回头看"工作的通知(银保监发〔2020〕27号) | 中国银保监会 |
| 2020年7月3日 | 标准化债权类资产认定规则 | 中国人民银行、中国银保监会、中国证监会、国家外汇管理局 |
| 2020年7月17日 | 关于信托公司风险资产处置相关工作的通知 | 中国银保监会 |
| 2020年7月31日 | 优化资管新规过渡期安排 引导资管业务平稳转型 | 中国人民银行 |
| 2020年10月30日 | 关于开展新一轮房地产信托业务专项排查的通知 | 中国银保监会 |
| 2020年11月16日 | 中国银保监会信托公司行政许可事项实施办法(银保监会令〔2020〕12号) | 中国银保监会 |

# 专栏10

## 放大国际金融中心辐射支撑功能打造金融与实体经济双翼起飞的高质量发展新格局[①]
### ——点评《关于进一步加快推进上海国际金融中心建设和金融支持长三角一体化发展的意见》

上海国际金融中心建设是一项国家战略。在党中央、国务院的重视和支持下,上海

---

① 由《中国金融政策报告》项目高级研究员撰稿。

国际金融中心建设已取得重大进展和显著成效。但"以国内大循环为主体、国内国际双循环相互促进"的新发展格局对于上海国际金融中心建设提出了新要求。金融业既面临自身改革开放提升国际化的诉求，聚焦"国际化"在参与跨境业务、国际金融秩序和规则制定、资本项下自由兑换及人民币国际化方面下功夫，又需要反哺实体经济，在服务投资贸易自由化、产业链创新链和价值链国际化布局及长三角区域一体化方面发力，形成金融与实体经济良性互动、相互支持的同步高质量发展新格局。

在防控疫情的大背景下，国家出台《关于进一步加快推进上海国际金融中心建设和金融支持长三角一体化发展的意见》（以下简称《意见》）不仅是为了支持上海和支持金融业的发展，更是要向全世界彰显中国持续扩大开放和加快金融改革的信心与决心。贯彻落实的支撑点是临港新片区与长三角一体化，尤其是临港新片区要聚焦全方位扩大开放。《意见》提出总体要求为服务实体经济高质量发展，深化金融体制机制改革，防范系统性金融风险。在具体措施上，《意见》指出：要积极推进临港新片区金融先行先试，包括支持临港新片区发展具有国际竞争力的重点产业，促进投资贸易自由化便利化；在更高水平上加快上海金融业对外开放，包括扩大金融业高水平开放，促进人民币金融资产配置和风险管理中心建设，建设与国际接轨的优质金融营商环境；金融支持长三角一体化发展，包括推动金融机构跨区域协作，提升金融配套服务水平，建立健全长三角金融政策协调和信息共享机制。

此后，为促进《意见》的细化落实，人民银行上海总部等12个部门于4月发布《关于在长三角生态绿色一体化发展示范区深化落实金融支持政策推进先行先试的若干举措》，围绕推进同城化金融服务、试点跨区域联合授信、支持设立一体化金融机构等方面提出16条具体举措。临港新片区管委会会同人民银行上海总部、银保监会上海监管局、证监会上海监管局、上海市金融工作局于5月8日共同发布《全面推进中国（上海）自由贸易试验区临港新片区金融开放与创新发展的若干措施》，提出50条关于新片区金融业发展的具体规划。

在各部门的齐心推动下，《意见》的落实取得实质性进展。金融机构加速集聚，特别是一批创新型、功能性的标志性项目落户上海。友邦人寿保险有限公司正式开业，成为内地首家外资独资人身保险公司。首家外资控股理财公司汇华理财获批开业，全国第二家外资控股理财公司贝莱德建信理财公司获批筹建。中信银行理财子公司获批开业，广发银行、浦发银行理财子公司获批筹建。交通银行在自贸区临港新片区内注册成立科技子公司交银金融科技有限公司。银保监会上海监管局印发出台《上海自贸试验区（含新片区）保险分支机构设立、迁址、撤销备案管理办法》，将保险支公司及以下分支机构在上海自贸试验区（含新片区）内的设立、营业场所变更和撤销管理，由审批改为备案，深入推动"放管服"改革，进一步增强市场活力。

**（一）政策构成及特点**

《意见》聚焦提升上海国际金融中心的金融创新能力和全球影响力，有三方面亮点：一是对标国际最高标准，体现高质量发展要求。《意见》紧紧围绕建设"具有国际影响力和竞争力的特殊经济功能区",探索更加灵活的金融政策体系、监管模式和管理体制,推动上海国际金融中心在更大范围、更宽领域、更深层次的高水平开放发展。二是推动人民币金融资产配置和风险管理中心建设。《意见》在上海前期改革开放实践的基础上,通过进一步深化跨境人民币业务创新、开展人民币贸易融资资产跨境转让、发展人民币利率期权等试点,鼓励和吸引更多的境外投资者在上海国际金融中心配置人民币资产。三是注重加强金融改革开放过程中的风险防控。《意见》高度重视金融法治环境建设,加强金融监管协调,完善风险防控体系,把维护金融稳定作为牢牢守住的底线。

《意见》背后的一大主线是推进人民币国际化,另一大主线则是与更多国际规则进行对接,强调了金融基础设施的国际化,对上海金融中心的进一步国际化非常重要。

### (二) 政策展望

上海国际金融中心建设已取得重大进展和显著成效,但若要引领亚洲辐射全球,仍需要多方面的坚实支撑。一是建成充分开放的金融市场体系和金融机构体系。完善金融市场层次并提高金融市场的流动性、定价能力和资源配置效率,推进各类金融机构加速聚集并发展更高能级的总部经济。二是打造国际领先的金融基础设施体系和金融科技体系,积极建设国际先进水平的支付、登记、结算、清算、托管等金融基础设施。三是完善与国际对接的金融法治监管体系和现代化金融系统风险防范体系,在提升金融法治水平、增强金融监管能力的基础上,推动上海自贸试验区临港新片区在法制与监管上的先行先试。四是形成高度国际化的营商环境和一流人才队伍,完善法律服务、国际化城市管理服务、社会信用、中介服务体系建设,进一步完善金融人才政策。

## 八、金融衍生品市场发展政策[①]

### (一) 相关热点政策效应

1. 场内金融衍生品市场

(1) 商业银行参与国债期货业务

2020年2月21日,经国务院同意,证监会、财政部、人民银行、银保监会发布联合公告,允许商业银行、保险机构在依法合规、风险可控、商业可持续的前提下,分批推进参与中国金融期货交易所(以下简称中金所)国债期货交易。商业银行参与国债期货市场,对于完善我国金融市场体系、提升金融机构风险管理能力、健全国债收益率曲线具有重要意义。

(2) 发布商业银行参与国债期货业务试点相关通知,修订会员管理办法等实施细则和期货公司会员资格管理业务指引

2020年3月1日,中金所发布《关于商业银行参与国债期货业务试点有关事项的通知》,修订并发布《中国金融期货交易所会员管理办法》等12个实施细则和《中国金融期货交易所期货公司会员资格管理业务指引》。修订后的实施细则和业务指引于2020年

---

[①] 作者:王勤淮,中国外汇交易中心研究部总经理、《中国金融政策报告》项目(课题组)高级研究员。

3月9日起正式实施。此次规则修订主要包括在现有会员体系中增加"非期货公司会员"主体，完善会员管理制度，优化国债期货合约持仓限额制度，规范期货公司会员资格管理业务，切实满足市场发展的需要。

（3）修订并发布《〈中国金融期货交易所异常交易管理办法〉国债期货有关监管标准及处理程序》和《中国金融期货交易所国债期货信息发布指引》

2020年4月8日，中金所修订并发布《〈中国金融期货交易所异常交易管理办法〉国债期货有关监管标准及处理程序》和《中国金融期货交易所国债期货信息发布指引》（以下简称《国债期货信息发布指引》）。上述规则于2020年4月9日起正式实施，《国债期货信息发布指引》第四条第（二）项自2020年9月14日起正式实施。此次规则修订包括明确非期货公司结算会员信息披露安排、在规则条款中增加非期货公司会员主体等内容。优化信息披露规定有助于保护非期货公司会员的商业秘密，促进国债期货市场发展。

（4）修订并发布国债期货合约及合约交易细则等实施细则

2020年6月12日，中金所修订并发布国债期货合约及其相关实施细则。为配合商业银行开展国债期货业务试点整体工作，此次修订将国债期货开盘时间推迟15分钟，此举对于促进国债期货市场健康发展和平稳运行具有重要意义。调整后，国债期货开盘时间与交易所债券市场和股指期货开盘时间一致。

（5）进一步优化沪深300股指期权交易限额

2020年6月22日，中金所对沪深300股指期权交易限额进行调整。根据稳中求进的工作总基调，遵循新产品循序渐进的发展规律，中金所在有效防范市场风险的基础上，对沪深300股指期权交易限额进行进一步调整。此次调整有利于进一步提升市场运行质量，优化投资者结构，完善市场生态，促进市场功能有效发挥。

（6）发布《关于合格境外机构投资者和人民币合格境外机构投资者参与股指期货交易有关事项的通知》

2020年10月30日，中金所发布《关于合格境外机构投资者和人民币合格境外机构投资者参与股指期货交易有关事项的通知》（以下简称《通知》），旨在贯彻落实2020年9月25日中国证监会、中国人民银行、国家外汇管理局联合发布的《合格境外机构投资者和人民币合格境外机构投资者境内证券期货投资管理办法》，以及中国证监会发布的《关于实施〈合格境外机构投资者和人民币合格境外机构投资者境内证券期货投资管理办法〉有关问题的规定》，并做好相关政策的衔接工作。《通知》进一步明确了合格境外投资者可参与交易的金融期货品种和交易方式，确保了合格境外投资者参与股指期货交易的有序衔接。

（7）修订做市商管理办法

2020年11月6日，中金所发布修订后的《中国金融期货交易所做市商管理办法》，增加了交易所可以对做市商实施分级管理的有关规定。此次修订做市商管理相关制度，实施做市商分级管理，既有利于完善相关业务规则，也有助于激发做市商活力。

（8）修订结算细则

2020年12月11日，中金所发布修订后的《中国金融期货交易所结算细则》及《中国金融期货交易所国债作为保证金业务操作指引》。上述规则于12月14日起正式实施。新修订的结算细则和业务操作指引正式实施后，国债担保品将可通过中央国债登记结算有限责任公司担保品处置平台，以拍卖、协议折价、变卖等方式处置。此举将提升国债担保品处置效率，增强交易所快速、有效处置结算会员违约风险事件的能力。

（9）修订风险控制管理办法

2020年12月24日，中金所发布修订后的《中国金融期货交易所风险控制管理办法》（以下简称《办法》），对期货交易过程中的异常情况以及交易所可采取的紧急措施进行了细化和完善。《办法》于2020年12月25日正式实施。《办法》的实施将为期货市场结算风险隔离提供更为完备的规则支持，有利于交易所快速处理计算机系统故障等异常情况，保障市场正常有序运行。

2. 场外金融衍生品市场

（1）推出利率期权，完善银行间市场产品序列

2020年3月，中国外汇交易中心（以下简称交易中心）推出并试运行挂钩贷款市场报价利率（LPR）的利率期权产品，进一步丰富了银行间利率衍生品市场产品序列。基于银行间衍生品市场管理框架，交易中心制定了利率期权交易规则，为市场的稳健运行奠定了制度基础。同时，交易中心优化交易服务，提供利率期权产品全生命周期服务，自主研发利率期权交易系统功能，为机构提供了期权交易一站式服务，包括报价成交、模型定价、行权交割、风险管理、盯市估值、交割金额代理计算等，覆盖期权业务生命周期的全部环节。另外，交易中心建立了利率期权双边报价制度，组织有能力、有意愿的机构通过交易系统对标准期权合约每日进行报价，并根据机构日终报价形成市场首个完整的LPR利率期权的波动率曲面，为市场提供流动性和定价基准。

（2）标准债券远期合约持续优化，交易活跃度提高

2020年3月，交易中心进一步完善标准债券远期市场现金结算机制，将每个品种的季月（季月是指3月、6月、9月、12月）合约数量缩减至2个，且可交割券在合约上市之初即确认，合约上市期间内不再切换；并组织报价机构通过交易系统向市场提供标准债券远期的双边报价。自标准债券远期推出以来，交易中心不断完善交易机制，丰富交易品种，市场活跃度持续提高。10月，交易中心推出农发债标准债券远期合约，对于标债远期策略的丰富和提升农发债二级流动性都有重要意义。2020年，标准债券远期市场累计成交4532.3亿元，同比增长3.8%。

（3）外汇市场衍生品新增参考利率，接轨新国际基准

为保证境内外币利率市场与国际新基准利率平稳衔接，交易中心密切跟踪基准利率改革进展，于2020年4月20日推出挂钩新外币浮动利率相关产品的交易服务。在交易品种货币掉期、外币利率互换中的外币端增加美元担保隔夜融资利率（SOFR）、境内美元同业拆放参考利率（CIROR）、英镑隔夜指数平均值（SONIA）、欧元短期利率（ES-

TER）及东京隔夜平均利率（TONAR）等新的外币浮动基准利率，市场对新的基准利率接受度高，报价较活跃。挂钩 SOFR 的美元利率互换交易和人民币对美元货币掉期交易、挂钩 CIROR 的美元利率互换交易、挂钩 SOFR 和 SONIA 的英镑对美元货币掉期、挂钩隔夜 SOFR 和 CIROR 隔夜的美元基差交易陆续在交易系统中达成，为市场参与机构管理外币利率风险提供了有力支撑。

（4）完善衍生品市场交易机制

2020 年 5 月，交易中心上线新一代本币交易系统衍生品模块，X-Swap 匿名点击系统功能进一步优化，新增聚合行情、隐含订单等功能，继续提升撮合效率和性能，提高交易效率，目前市场占比稳步保持在 60% 以上，成为市场成员利率风险管理的重要工具。2020 年 12 月，交易中心推出利率互换询价（RFQ）交易机制，支持同时向多家机构发送请求报价并获取回复及成交，进一步提升价格发现效率。利率衍生品系统功能、交易机制持续优化。2020 年，交易中心全面提升接口服务，新增对话报价、交谈、成交功能，实现 X-Swap 交易接口覆盖各品种授信、订单、行情全流程。接口交易显著提高了衍生品交易自动化程度，目前 X-Swap 上接口订单（API）量占比近 80%。

（5）推出银企交易服务平台

2020 年 11 月 2 日，交易中心上线银企交易服务平台（以下简称银企平台），进一步支持实体经济发展，满足企业外币资金交易和风险管理需求。银企平台通过独立于银行间交易的专用模块为银行对客结售汇业务提供线上电子化平台。银企平台的推出是交易中心在监管部门的指导下，顺应金融供给侧结构性改革和落实金融服务实体经济要求的重要举措。银企平台为银行和实体企业之间的外汇交易提供安全、高效和低成本的服务，一方面能够提高实体企业询价的时效性和价格透明度，另一方面可以保障交易的合规性和数据安全。交易中心在业务筹备期间，配合监管部门与多家做市机构及重点企业对平台交易方式、相关制度安排等内容进行了充分研讨。银企平台将境内电子化外汇交易平台的内涵由银行间拓展至对客业务，优化了银行间外汇市场的分层结构，进一步完善了人民币汇率形成机制。

（6）支持基准利率体系建设，推动基准利率运用

2020 年 11 月 11 日，为落实人民银行关于"进一步培育以 DR（存款类机构间利率债抵押的回购利率）为代表的银行间基准利率体系"的要求，交易中心推出挂钩 FDR001 的利率互换产品。FDR001 利率互换既可以扩大 DR 应用范围，提高其市场认可度和影响力，还有利于为发行挂钩 DR 的浮息债提供配套支持，满足 DR 浮息债发行人和投资方管理利率风险的需要，便利市场主体开展利率风险管理和对冲，并为基准利率体系建设提供有利条件。

（二）金融衍生品市场发展展望

一是进一步丰富金融市场产品，发挥市场功能。在利率衍生品市场，要进一步丰富利率衍生产品，发挥衍生品交易对基准利率的支撑作用。发展银行间利率衍生品市场对基准利率建设有以下几方面的重要意义：一是能扩大货币市场基准利率的应用范围，提

升货币市场基准利率的影响力;二是通过衍生品价格能验证基准利率的有效性,同时通过衍生品交易能使市场各类价格保持一个比较合理的均衡关系;三是随着央行向价格型为主的调控框架转型,利率衍生品的价格发现功能将进一步增强。

二是加强金融衍生品市场监管和风险防范,维护市场安全平稳运行。要继续依法依规加强金融衍生品市场监管和风险防范,切实履行监管职责,强化监管效能,不断提高运行保障水平,维护金融衍生品市场安全平稳运行;加强市场风险监测与交易行为监管,积极完善监管制度;加强金融衍生品立法工作,促进金融衍生品市场健康有序发展。

## 附表

**2020年金融衍生品市场新出相关政策法规、制度公告**

| 日期 | 主要内容 | 颁布机构 |
| --- | --- | --- |
| 1月22日 | 关于落实完善银行间债券市场境外机构投资者外汇风险管理有关安排的公告（中汇交公告〔2020〕7号） | 中国外汇交易中心 |
| 2月14日 | 关于免除湖北省市场成员相关业务费用的通知（中汇交发〔2020〕42号） | 中国外汇交易中心 全国银行间同业拆借中心 |
| 2月14日 | 关于发布债券估值手册、利率互换估值手册的通知 | 中国外汇交易中心 |
| 2月28日 | 关于进一步完善标准债券远期市场现金结算机制的通知（中汇交发〔2020〕52号） | 全国银行间同业拆借中心 |
| 2月28日 | 关于利率期权业务试运行上线的通知（中汇交发〔2020〕51号） | 全国银行间同业拆借中心 |
| 3月1日 | 关于商业银行参与国债期货业务试点有关事项的通知 | 中国金融期货交易所 |
| 3月1日 | 关于修订《中国金融期货交易所会员管理办法》《中国金融期货交易所交易细则》等业务规则的通知 | 中国金融期货交易所 |
| 3月12日 | 关于调整本币衍生品市场数据接口相关服务的通知（中汇交发〔2020〕64号） | 全国银行间同业拆借中心 |
| 3月13日 | 关于向市场成员提供利率期权估值相关服务的通知 | 中国外汇交易中心 |
| 3月23日 | 关于在银行间外币对市场推出即期撮合业务的通知（中汇交发〔2020〕75号） | 中国外汇交易中心 |
| 4月8日 | 关于修订《〈中国金融期货交易所异常交易管理办法〉国债期货有关监管标准及处理程序》《中国金融期货交易所国债期货信息发布指引》的通知 | 中国金融期货交易所 |
| 4月15日 | 关于银行间外汇市场货币掉期等交易品种新增外币浮动利率类型的通知（中汇交发〔2020〕103号） | 中国外汇交易中心 |
| 4月27日 | 关于银行间市场本币交易平台回购及衍生品（一期）功能上线的通知（中汇交发〔2020〕111号） | 全国银行间同业拆借中心 |
| 5月27日 | 关于在银行间外汇市场推出主经纪业务的通知（中汇交发〔2020〕143号） | 中国外汇交易中心 |
| 6月3日 | 关于在银行间外币对市场推出掉期撮合业务的通知（中汇交发〔2020〕150号） | 中国外汇交易中心 |

续表

| 日期 | 主要内容 | 颁布机构 |
|---|---|---|
| 6月12日 | 关于修订《2年期国债期货合约》等合约及实施细则的通知 | 中国金融期货交易所 |
| 6月12日 | 关于推出外币对即远掉交易确认服务的通知（中汇交发〔2020〕161号） | 中国外汇交易中心 |
| 6月15日 | 关于在银行间外汇期权市场推出报价接口服务的通知 | 中国外汇交易中心 |
| 6月18日 | 关于调整沪深300股指期权交易限额有关事项的通知 | 中国金融期货交易所 |
| 9月24日 | 关于落实完善债券通渠道资金汇兑和外汇风险管理有关安排的公告（中汇交公告〔2020〕45号） | 中国外汇交易中心 |
| 10月15日 | 关于新一代本币交易平台现券匿名询价（X-Bargain）和衍生品（二期）等功能上线的通知（中汇交发〔2020〕286号） | 全国银行间同业拆借中心 |
| 10月20日 | 中国外汇交易中心推出银企交易服务平台 | 中国外汇交易中心 |
| 10月30日 | 关于合格境外机构投资者和人民币合格境外机构投资者参与股指期货交易有关事项的通知（中金所发〔2020〕20号） | 中国金融期货交易所 |
| 11月6日 | 关于修订《中国金融期货交易所做市商管理办法》的通知（中金所发〔2020〕21号） | 中国金融期货交易所 |
| 11月11日 | 关于推出FDR001利率互换交易服务有关事项的通知 | 全国银行间同业拆借中心 |
| 12月11日 | 关于修订《中国金融期货交易所结算细则》等业务规则的通知（中金所发〔2020〕32号） | 中国金融期货交易所 |
| 12月24日 | 关于修订《中国金融期货交易所风险控制管理办法》的通知（中金所发〔2020〕36号） | 中国金融期货交易所 |

资料来源：课题组整理。

## 专栏11

### 打造粤港澳高质量跨境金融服务合作示范区[①]

2020年4月，人民银行、银保监会、证监会、国家外汇管理局四部门联合发布《关于金融支持粤港澳大湾区建设的意见》（以下简称《意见》）。这既是对此前中共中央、国务院印发的《粤港澳大湾区发展规划纲要》金融部分的细化，也是《关于进一步加快推进上海国际金融中心建设和金融支持长三角一体化发展的意见》的姊妹篇。《意见》的内容可预期、可实现，明确粤港澳大湾区作为我国金融开放窗口，有利于加强跨境合作，强化三地优势互补互助，彰显国家支持粤港澳大湾区打造为世界级城市群的决心。

粤港澳大湾区是中国实体经济发展的主引擎之一，也有扎实的金融业发展基础。一是地区生产总值占比高，跨境贸易规模领先。2020年粤港澳大湾区地区生产总值总量约

---

[①] 作者：赵湘怀，光大证券企划与经营管理部总经理、《中国金融政策报告》项目（课题组）研究员；刘思达，光大证券企划与经营管理部经理；刘甲，光大证券企划与经营管理部团队负责人。

11.59万亿元，全国占比11%。其中，深圳地区生产总值达到2.7万亿元，广州地区生产总值达到2.5万亿元，香港地区生产总值达到2.4万亿元。2020年，以粤港澳为依托的广东省进出口总值为7.08万亿元，全国占比22%。二是人口基数和人均收入较高，消费潜力巨大。2020年初，粤港澳大湾区总人口超7000万，人均地区生产总值约为全国平均水平的2.3倍。三是金融行业活跃，市场体量居前。截至2020年末，粤港澳大湾区共有2319家上市公司（包括A股、港股、美股），其中，A股上市公司608家，总市值为15.66万亿元，占A股总市值的20%。

《意见》就粤港澳大湾区高质量跨境金融服务和多中心体系的构建提出了五条基本原则以及五大项26条具体措施，概括起来如下。

第一，促进跨境贸易和投融资便利化。一是有利于推进贸易支付便利化，企业结汇灵活度得以增强，跨境金融交易成本有望降低。《意见》提出完善贸易新业态外汇管理，推进资本项目便利化改革，探索建立与粤港澳大湾区发展相适应的账户管理体系。二是有利于提升粤港澳大湾区企业投融资自主性，满足初创型、创新型、科技型企业融资需求。《意见》提出支持银行开展跨境贷款业务，开展私募股权投资基金跨境投资试点等。

第二，扩大金融业对外开放。一是有利于"走出去"，促进境内金融机构境外展业。《意见》提出试点证券期货经营机构跨境业务。二是有利于"引进来"，吸引境外金融机构拓展境内业务。《意见》提出积极支持港澳银行等金融机构拓展在粤港澳大湾区内地的发展空间。三是有利于为粤港澳大湾区居民提供丰富的理财产品和廉价的金融服务，增强区域财富管理行业活力。《意见》提出支持商业银行在粤港澳大湾区内地发起设立不设外资持股比例上限的金融资产投资公司和理财公司，支持粤港澳保险机构合作开发跨境医疗保险等更多创新产品，建立跨境理财通机制等。

第三，推进粤港澳资金融通渠道多元化。一是明确通过金融开放打造开放型经济的导向，增加本外币兑换和跨境流通使用便利度的制度安排，致力于构建跨境资产配置双向互联互通的基础设施。《意见》提出支持港澳发展离岸人民币业务，推动人民币在粤港澳大湾区跨境便利流通和兑换。二是促进粤港澳三地金融行业打造新业态，实现差异化发展。《意见》提出支持香港打造粤港澳大湾区绿色金融中心，建设成为葡语国家人民币清算中心，支持港澳发展特色金融产业等。

第四，进一步提升粤港澳大湾区金融服务创新水平。粤港澳大湾区的核心战略定位之一是建设成"具有全球影响力的国际科技创新中心"，经过多年积淀，大湾区产业优势和技术优势突出，科技龙头包括腾讯、华为及其孵化企业等，平安集团、招商银行等金融企业的科技发展水平也均处于行业前列，为金融引领科技发展提供基础。《意见》明确加强科技创新金融服务，支持内地银行加强与外部创投机构合作，积极探索多样化的金融支持科技发展业务模式，提升粤港澳大湾区金融服务创新水平和金融科技载体建设等。

第五，切实防范跨境金融风险。一方面，随着粤港澳三地金融合作不断加强，跨境金融创新产品持续丰富，跨境资金流动日趋频繁，金融风险的积累对跨境金融监管提出更高要求。另一方面，粤港澳金融监管尚未形成统一框架，需强化三地金融监管机构的沟通交流及协调合作，建立健全跨境金融风险管理长效机制。《意见》提出加强粤港澳金融监管合作，建立和完善金融风险预警、防范和化解体系，加强粤港澳金融消费权益保护等。

## 九、商品期货市场发展政策①

(一) 2020年商品期货市场政策主要内容

1. 助力国家扶贫攻坚战

2020年是我国全面建成小康社会目标实现之年，是全面打赢脱贫攻坚战收官之年，期货市场通过"保险+期货"模式为贫困地区天然橡胶、玉米、大豆、鸡蛋、苹果、棉花、白糖、红枣等品种提供了价格保障，助力国家扶贫攻坚战。2020年1月2日，中央一号文件《中共中央 国务院关于抓好"三农"领域重点工作 确保如期实现全面小康的意见》提出优化"保险+期货"试点模式，这是自2016年以来，中央一号文件连续五年提出支持"保险+期货"模式的发展，在多种多样的期货扶贫中，"保险+期货"逐渐成为期货行业精准扶贫的重要抓手，为打好脱贫攻坚战、促进农民增收、助力乡村振兴以及服务实体经济发挥了重要作用。同时，继2019年中央一号文件之后，2020年中央一号文件再次提出"继续推进农产品期货期权品种上市"，在推出苹果、红枣等具有扶贫特色的农产品期货品种外，其他如生猪、花生、干辣椒、马铃薯等农产品期货品种也被交易所提上上市日程。

2. 服务粤港澳大湾区和国家"一带一路"建设

2020年4月，中国人民银行、中国银保监会、中国证监会、国家外汇管理局《关于金融支持粤港澳大湾区建设的意见》明确提出：依托广州绿色金融改革创新试验区，建立完善粤港澳大湾区绿色金融合作工作机制。充分发挥广州碳排放交易所的平台功能，搭建粤港澳大湾区环境权益交易与金融服务平台。开展碳排放交易外汇试点，允许通过粤港澳大湾区内地碳排放权交易中心有限公司资格审查的境外投资者（境外机构及个人），以外汇或人民币参与粤港澳大湾区内地碳排放权交易。研究设立广州期货交易所。7月28日，广东省地方金融监管局等《关于贯彻落实金融支持粤港澳大湾区建设意见的实施方案》提出，制定广州期货交易所筹备及运营保障机制，继续研究上市品种，建设粤港澳大湾区重要金融基础设施平台。9月，广州市地方金融监督管理局在《关于贯彻落实金融支持粤港澳大湾区建设意见的行动方案》中指出，推动广州期货交易所落地，积极推动广州期货交易所在穗落户政策兑现落实，配合国家有关部委做好交易所落地及交易品种研究储备，全力推动广州期货交易所等机构的筹建工作。2020年10月，证监会宣布广州期货交易所筹备组成立，广州期货交易所的挂牌进入倒计时阶段。广州期货交易所立足服务实体经济，服务绿色发展，秉持创新型、市场化、国际化的发展定位，对完善我国资本市场体系、助力粤港澳大湾区和国家"一带一路"建设、服务经济高质

---

① 作者：甘正在，国元期货有限公司副总经理、《中国金融政策报告》项目（课题组）高级研究员。

量发展具有重要意义。

**3. 加大商品期货期权产品供给**

2020年中国证监会和三家商品期货交易所以市场为导向，为更好满足实体经济的避险需求，推出了一系列期货期权新品种，其中包括液化石油气、低硫燃料油、短纤期货、国际铜期货4个商品期货和菜籽粕、液化石油气、线型低密度聚乙烯、动力煤、聚丙烯、聚氯乙烯、铝、锌期权8个商品期权。其中，液化石油气、低硫燃料油等品种的上市，加速了以油、煤、气为代表的国内能源期货市场体系建设。纺织、化工领域相关衍生品，有利于完善产业风险工具体系和增强板块"集聚效应"，推动产业优化整合和加速升级。分交易所来看，上海期货交易所上市了4个品种，包括低硫燃料油、国际铜期货和铝、锌期权；郑州商品交易所上市了3个品种，包括短纤期货和菜籽粕、动力煤期权；大连商品交易所上市了5个品种，包括液化石油气期货和液化石油气、聚丙烯、聚氯乙烯、线型低密度聚乙烯期权。目前，我国期货市场上市品种数量达到90个，其中商品期货品种62个、期权品种22个。

**4. 加速完善现有规则制度**

2020年，为规范期货公司的互联网开户行为，保护客户合法权益，中国期货业协会3月4日发布《期货公司互联网开户规则》（2020年修订），为期货行业的线上服务水平提供规范指引。为实现期货市场结算风险隔离提供规则支持，三家商品期货交易所分别就风险控制管理办法进行修订，对期货交易过程中的异常情形及可采取的紧急措施进行了细化和完善。持续深化合约连续活跃工作，全面推广做市机制，全年新增32个期货期权做市品种，已实施做市制度的期货期权品种总数达到65个。做市品种的流动性和活跃合约连续性显著提升。2020年三家商品期货交易所开展国债作为保证金业务，将国债作为保证金业务不仅有利于扩大保证金业务的担保品范围，同时有效降低了期货交易资金成本，提高了市场流动性。修订完善现有品种合约规则，优化交割库布局，科学调整品种交易保证金，降低交割成本，激发现有期货品种活力。

**5. 场外衍生品市场初见成效**

伴随着风险管理业务的快速发展，场外衍生品市场建设初见成效。三家商品期货交易所仓单交易、基差贸易、商品互换等场外期现结合业务平台相继上线，对场内工具形成有益补充，形成期货与现货、场内与场外、线上与线下的互联互通，进一步促进了衍生品市场的发展，有效拓展了服务实体经济的空间。大连商品交易所场外业务板块先后推出豆油等6个品种的标准仓单交易和铁矿石、合成树脂品种的非标仓单交易业务，有效建立了煤焦矿和化工品两个品种圈，成功推出2家商品现货行情，场外市场轮廓初显。郑州商品交易所综合业务平台仓单交易客户参与度和市场规模不断增长，场外市场服务实体经济功能逐步显现。上海期货交易所标准仓单交易平台，通过推出标准仓单交易，盘活仓单存量，满足实体企业的个性化交割需求。期货保证金监控中心牵头建设的场外衍生品交易报告库获得了金融稳定理事会（FSB）的认证，成为我国首个正式获得FSB认证的报告库，将对我国场外衍生品市场的稳定发展起到重要作用。

6. 扩大期货市场对外开放

一是扩大特定品种范围。大力推进现有商品期货品种国际化，继续扩大特定开放品种范围。2020年11月19日，国际铜合约在上海国际能源交易中心正式上市，作为中国期货市场上首个以"双合约"模式实现国际化的期货品种，国际铜合约对进一步促进国内外铜产业链和供应链深度融合具有重要意义。随着低硫燃料油期货及棕榈油期货先后对境外投资者开放，我国对外开放期货品种已达到7个。在现有对外开放品种中，铁矿石期货已吸引21个国家和地区的约270家境外客户参与交易，成为全球交易量最大的铁矿石衍生品。精对苯二甲酸、天然橡胶和20号胶期货等品种已经成为行业标杆性的价格基准。二是支持交易所优化交割机制，探索特定品种境外提货机制。推动解决每日盈亏强制换汇问题、商品期货保税交割免征增值税问题。通过跨境商品期货交易所交易基金（ETF）、结算价授权、推出结算价交易指令等方式，对外开放的形式更加多元。三是推动期货公司高水平双向开放，加快推进外商独资或控股期货公司。2020年6月，首家外资全资控股期货公司成立；9月25日，证监会允许合格境外机构投资者（QFII）、人民币合格境外机构投资者（RQFII）投资期货期权，境外资金参与交易将增加市场的深度和活跃度，扩大我国资本市场的国际影响力。

（二）2020年期货市场政策效果

1. 期货市场成交量创历史新高

2020年中国期货市场高速发展，成交量创历史新高，连续两年大幅增长。2020年，中国期货市场成交61.53亿手，成交额437.53万亿元，同比分别增长55.29%和50.56%。全球农产品、金属和能源三类品种的成交量排名中，中国期货品种包揽农产品前10名、金属前4名，能源也有4个品种排入前10位。中国期货市场成交量占全球期货市场总成交量的13.2%，较2019年占比11.5%提升了1.7个百分点。分交易所来看，上海期货交易所成交21.29亿手合152.80万亿元，同比分别增长47.04%和35.80%，市场占比分别为34.60%和34.92%。郑州商品交易所成交17.01亿手合60.09万亿元，同比分别增长55.74%和51.97%，市场占比分别为27.65%和13.73%。大连商品交易所成交22.07亿手合109.20万亿元，同比分别增长62.83%和58.43%，市场占比分别为35.88%和24.96%。2020年，期货市场资金量和成交持仓量均创历史新高，中国商品期货市场的国际地位进一步提升。

2. 期货行业服务脱贫攻坚战见成效

期货市场充分发挥风险管理功能，将精准扶贫、服务"三农"与服务实体经济相结合起来，全力以赴服务国家脱贫攻坚战略。截至2020年12月31日，123家期货经营机构与242个国家级贫困县（乡、村）签署了455份结对帮扶协议，行业累计投入扶贫资金达6.11亿元。期货经营机构通过"保险+期货"模式为贫困地区累计开展项目622个，覆盖天然橡胶、玉米、大豆、鸡蛋、苹果、棉花、白糖、红枣等品种，为农户提供了价格保障，承保货值约188.26亿元；帮助29家贫困地区企业成为期货交易所交割仓库，推动贫困地区产业转型升级，带动当地物流产业发展。为贫困地区实体机构或个人提供合作套保、点价、场外期权等风险管理服务方案119个，名义本金约10.94亿元。期货行业通过实践，在促进农民增收、助力乡村振兴以及服务实体经济发挥了积极作用。

（三）2021年商品期货市场政策展望

1. 期货品种供给继续增加

2021年期货市场将进一步加大品种供给，丰富商品期货期权体系。郑州商品交易所在花生已经上市的基础上，将有序推进对苯二甲、瓶片、钢坯、烧碱、鸡肉、葵花籽、马铃薯等品种研发工作。大连商品交易所在2021年1月8日上市我国第一个活体期货品种——生猪期货后，将继续加快推进干辣椒期货上市，开展乙醇、果葡糖浆、原木等储备品种上市的可行性研究。上海期货交易所将重点打造上海原油、上海铜、上海胶国际化品种，推动氧化铝、铬铁、合成橡胶等期货产品上市，抓紧研究上市成品油、天然气等期货产品。在商品期货期权方面，将根据实体经济发展需求，逐步实现已上市期货品种的期权全覆盖，并加大对商品指数期货、航运指数期货、电力指数期货等指数类期货的研究开发力度。

2. 运行机制将不断完善

2021年期货市场将不断丰富交易指令，研究推出大宗交易，探索结算价交易机制；进一步扩大做市商制度试点范围，持续改善合约连续性，提升产业客户的套保效率。在降低市场交易成本方面，优化担保品管理，研究推出组合保证金，提高市场资金使用效率。在提高市场流动性方面，逐步推出更多品种、不同类型的期货ETF产品。

3. 广州期货交易所成立

2021年1月22日，证监会宣布，经国务院同意，证监会正式批准设立广州期货交易所。2月5日，广州期货交易所已完成工商注册登记，注册资本为30亿元人民币，注册地点是广州市南沙区。目前交易所股东构成包括证监会管理的四家期货交易所，广东国资企业、民营企业和境外企业，共引入8名股东，将成为我国第一家混合所有制的交易所。从股东构成及股比情况来看，上海期货交易所、郑州商品交易所、大连商品交易所、中国金融期货交易所股份有限公司、中国平安保险（集团）股份有限公司的持股比例均为15%，广东珠江投资控股集团有限公司和广州金融控股集团有限公司的持股比例均为9%，香港交易及结算所有限公司的持股比例为7%。引入境外资本及民营资本，在贯彻粤港澳经济融合发展理念的同时，将有利于交易所在经营理念、人才招聘、企业管理等多方面进行市场化探索。碳排放权期货、大宗商品指数和电力指数等品种将成为广州期货交易所上市备选品种。

4. 期货法立法进程加快

期货法是期货市场的基本大法，将从法律层面对我国期货市场的改革开放做好顶层设计，明确各参与主体的法律地位，明确期货市场基础法律关系、民事权利义务和法律责任；明确对场外市场的监管；对市场准入、投资者保护和对外开放等作出明确规定，为期货市场对外开放以及跨境监管提供法制保障。根据2021年全国人民代表大会常务委员会工作报告，期货法已列入2021年立法工作计划，表明制定期货法的时机已经成熟,期货法的立法进程将加快。

## 附表

**2020年中国商品期货市场主要政策**

| 日期 | 政策名称 | 发文单位 |
|---|---|---|
| 1月2日 | 中共中央 国务院关于抓好"三农"领域重点工作 确保如期实现全面小康的意见 | 中共中央、国务院 |
| 1月2日 | 关于发布《郑州商品交易所仓单交易业务指引》和《郑州商品交易所基差贸易业务指引》修订案的公告 | 郑州商品交易所 |
| 3月4日 | 期货公司互联网开户规则(2020年修订) | 中国期货业协会 |
| 3月19日 | 关于同意大连商品交易所开展液化石油气期货及期权交易的批复 | 中国证监会 |
| 3月25日 | 关于发布《郑州商品交易所投资者教育专项工作管理办法》的公告 | 中国证监会 |
| 3月30日 | 大连商品交易所期货交割注册品牌工作办法 | 大连商品交易所 |
| 4月9日 | 关于发布《郑州商品交易所期货交易细则》修订案的公告 | 郑州商品交易所 |
| 4月24日 | 关于金融支持粤港澳大湾区建设的意见 | 中国人民银行、中国银保监会、中国证监会、国家外汇管理局 |
| 5月7日 | 大连商品交易所期权交易管理办法 | 大连商品交易所 |
| 5月15日 | 大连商品交易所标准仓单交易管理办法(试行) | 大连商品交易所 |
| 5月28日 | 关于同意上海国际能源交易中心开展低硫燃料油期货交易的批复 | 上海期货交易所 |
| 6月12日 | 关于同意大连商品交易所开展聚丙烯、聚氯乙烯、线型低密度聚乙烯期权交易的批复 | 中国证监会 |
| 6月12日 | 关于同意郑州商品交易所开展动力煤期权交易的批复 | 中国证监会 |
| 6月12日 | 关于同意上海期货交易所开展铝、锌期权交易的批复 | 中国证监会 |
| 6月22日 | 关于发布动力煤期权合约的公告 | 郑州商品交易所 |
| 7月28日 | 关于贯彻落实金融支持粤港澳大湾区建设意见的实施方案 | 广东省地方金融监管局等 |
| 8月7日 | 大连商品交易所指定交割仓库资格管理工作办法 | 大连商品交易所 |
| 9月11日 | 关于贯彻落实金融支持粤港澳大湾区建设意见的行动方案 | 广州市地方金融监督管理局 |
| 9月24日 | 关于开展国债作为保证金业务有关事项的通知 | 上海期货交易所 |
| 9月25日 | 合格境外机构投资者和人民币合格境外机构投资者境内证券期货投资管理办法 | 中国证监会、中国人民银行、国家外汇管理局 |
| 9月28日 | 关于发布《郑州商品交易所期权交易管理办法》修订案的公告 | 郑州商品交易所 |
| 9月28日 | 关于发布《郑州商品交易所做市商管理办法》修订案的公告 | 郑州商品交易所 |
| 9月28日 | 关于发布短纤期货合约及相关业务规则修订案的公告 | 郑州商品交易所 |
| 12月7日 | 关于发布《上海期货交易所风险控制管理办法》修订版的公告 | 上海期货交易所 |
| 12月8日 | 大连商品交易所非标仓单业务管理办法(试行) | 大连商品交易所 |
| 12月8日 | 大连商品交易所场外会员管理办法(试行) | 大连商品交易所 |
| 12月31日 | 大连商品交易所生猪期货合约 | 大连商品交易所 |

专栏 12

## 设立北京金融法院，加大金融司法保护力度①

金融是国家重要的核心竞争力，金融安全是国家安全的重要组成部分。北京作为监管机构集聚的金融中枢，是事实上的国家金融管理中心，肩负着维护国家金融安全与促进金融业健康发展的使命。法治是金融安全与金融发展的根本保障，金融司法对于推进金融治理体系和治理能力现代化具有非常重要的现实意义。2021年1月22日第十三届全国人民代表大会常务委员会第二十五次会议通过了《关于设立北京金融法院的决定》，确定由北京金融法院对金融案件进行集中管辖，这有利于实施国家金融战略，维护金融安全，健全金融审判体系，加大金融司法保护力度，为国家的现代化建设营造良好的金融法治环境。

### 一、政策出台的背景

近年来，习近平总书记在讲话中多次强调金融和金融安全的重要性，我国多项重要战略部署文件也明确了服务实体经济、防控金融风险、深化金融改革三大主要任务，明确提出设立金融公诉和审判机构。北京作为国家金融管理中心，是重要金融基础设施和大型国有金融机构总部所在地，金融司法审判工作具有坚实的基础，较好的审判队伍人才以及足够的案件数量支撑。在这样的条件下，结合北京独特的功能定位和特点，设立北京金融法院，是贯彻落实中央重大战略部署的必然要求，对于保障国家金融战略实施、服务金融工作三项重大任务、完善金融审判体系、防范化解系统性金融风险、为国家经济社会持续健康发展提供有力司法保障具有重要意义。

### 二、政策构成和特点

北京金融法院兼顾民商事案件与行政诉讼案件，具体而言，专门管辖北京市内应由中级人民法院管辖的金融民商事案件和涉金融行政案件。北京金融法院的案件管辖范围包括三类一审案件，分别是由北京市中级人民法院管辖的第一审金融民商事案件、以金融监管机构为被告的第一审涉金融行政案件和以住所地在北京市的金融基础设施机构为被告或者第三人、与其履行职责相关的第一审金融民商事案件和涉金融行政案件。这实际上意味着重大金融民商事一审案件、以金融监管机构为被告的一审案件，以及以金融基础设施机构为被告或者第三人的一审民事和行政案件都将经由北京金融法院介入确定统一的司法裁判尺度。此外，北京市基层人民法院第一审金融民商事案件和涉金融行政案件判决、裁定的上诉、抗诉案件以及再审案件，依照法律规定应由北京金融法院执行的案件，以及最高人民法院确定由其管辖的其他金融案件，也由北京金融法院统一负责。

在管理方面，北京金融法院审判庭的设置，由最高人民法院根据金融案件的类型和数量决定。在监督方面，北京金融法院依法定程序设立后，对北京市人民代表大会常务委员会负责并报告工作，受最高人民法院和北京市高级人民法院监督，并依法接受人民

---

① 作者：史广龙，腾讯金融研究院副秘书长、《中国金融政策报告》项目（课题组）研究员。本文不代表所在机构观点。

检察院法律监督。在法官任免方面，北京金融法院副院长、审判委员会委员、庭长、副庭长、审判员由北京金融法院院长提请北京市人民代表大会常务委员会任免。

### 三、政策展望

北京金融法院是继 2018 年设立上海金融法院后，我国第二家专门的金融司法机构，是司法审判系统全面贯彻落实习近平同志法治思想的新举措。设立北京金融法院将有助于增强国家金融监管机构、国家金融基础设施和北京金融司法机关在共同化解金融风险领域、推动金融业健康发展方面的对话与协同，有助于进一步提升北京的金融法治环境，提高中国在制定金融交易规则与审判金融纠纷案件中的国际话语权和国际影响力。

## 十、外汇市场发展政策①

### （一）政策列表

**2020 年中国外汇市场主要政策**

| 日期 | 发文单位 | 政策文件名称 | 文件号 |
| --- | --- | --- | --- |
| 1月13日 | 国家外汇管理局 | 关于完善银行间债券市场境外机构投资者外汇风险管理有关问题的通知 | 汇发〔2020〕2号 |
| 2月13日 | 国家外汇管理局 | 关于修订《个人本外币兑换特许业务试点管理办法》的通知 | 汇发〔2020〕6号 |
| 2月13日 | 全国银行间同业拆借中心 | 全国银行间同业拆借中心银行间市场到期违约债券转让规则 | 中汇交发〔2020〕39号 |
| 2月28日 | 全国银行间同业拆借中心 | 关于利率期权业务试运行上线的通知 | 中汇交发〔2020〕51号 |
| 2月28日 | 全国银行间同业拆借中心 | 关于进一步完善标准债券远期市场现金结算机制的通知 | 中汇交发〔2020〕52号 |
| 3月11日 | 中国人民银行、国家外汇管理局 | 关于调整全口径跨境融资宏观审慎调节参数的通知 | 银发〔2020〕64号 |
| 4月10日 | 国家外汇管理局 | 关于优化外汇管理支持涉外业务发展的通知 | 汇发〔2020〕8号 |
| 4月24日 | 中国人民银行、中国银保监会、中国证监会、国家外汇管理局 | 关于金融支持粤港澳大湾区建设的意见 | 银发〔2020〕95号 |
| 5月7日 | 中国人民银行、国家外汇管理局 | 境外机构投资者境内证券期货投资资金管理规定 | 中国人民银行 国家外汇管理局公告〔2020〕第2号 |
| 5月9日 | 国家外汇管理局 | 关于印发《银行外汇业务合规与审慎经营评估内容及评分标准（2020年）》的通知 | 汇综发〔2020〕35号 |
| 5月20日 | 国家外汇管理局 | 关于支持贸易新业态发展的通知 | 汇发〔2020〕11号 |

---

① 作者：尚昕昕，国家外汇管理局外汇研究中心研究员。

续表

| 日期 | 发文单位 | 政策文件名称 | 文件号 |
|---|---|---|---|
| 5月26日 | 中国人民银行、中国银保监会、国家发展改革委、工业和信息化部、财政部、市场监管总局、中国证监会、国家外汇管理局 | 关于进一步强化中小微企业金融服务的指导意见 | 银发〔2020〕120号 |
| 8月28日 | 国家外汇管理局 | 关于印发《经常项目外汇业务指引（2020年版）》的通知 | 汇发〔2020〕14号 |
| 9月18日 | 国家外汇管理局 | 关于印发《对外金融资产负债及交易统计业务指引（2020年版）》的通知 | 汇综发〔2020〕71号 |
| 9月25日 | 中国证监会、中国人民银行、国家外汇管理局 | 合格境外机构投资者和人民币合格境外机构投资者境内证券期货投资管理办法 | 证监会令〔第176号〕 |
| 10月22日 | 全国银行间同业拆借中心、银行间市场清算所股份有限公司 | 关于推出农发债标准债券远期业务的通知 | 中汇交发〔2020〕302号 |
| 12月14日 | 国家外汇管理局 | 对外金融资产负债及交易统计核查规则（2020年版） | 汇综发〔2020〕94号 |

（二）政策效果

1月13日，国家外汇管理局发布了《关于完善银行间债券市场境外机构投资者外汇风险管理有关问题的通知》（汇发〔2020〕2号），确定于2月1日起进一步便利银行间债券市场境外机构投资者使用外汇衍生品管理外汇风险。

2月13日，国家外汇管理局发布了《关于修订〈个人本外币兑换特许业务试点管理办法〉的通知》（汇发〔2020〕6号），促进个人本外币兑换特许业务合规、健康发展。

2月13日，全国银行间同业拆借中心发布了《全国银行间同业拆借中心银行间市场到期违约债券转让规则》（中汇交发〔2020〕39号），规范银行间市场到期违约债券转让行为，保护投资者合法权益，提供到期违约债券转让报价成交、市场监测、行情信息等服务。

2月28日，全国银行间同业拆借中心发布了《关于利率期权业务试运行上线的通知》（中汇交发〔2020〕51号），确定于2020年3月23日起试运行利率期权交易及相关服务，业务运行前两年暂免利率期权的交易手续费。

2月28日，全国银行间同业拆借中心发布了《关于进一步完善标准债券远期市场现金结算机制的通知》（中汇交发〔2020〕52号），确定于3月18日起正式对标准债券远期交易结算机制进行优化，提升标准债券远期市场流动性，促进债券远期市场发展。

3月11日，中国人民银行、国家外汇管理局联合发布了《关于调整全口径跨境融资宏观审慎调节参数的通知》（银发〔2020〕64号），决定将《中国人民银行关于全口径跨境融资宏观审慎管理有关事宜的通知》（银发〔2017〕9号）中的宏观审慎调节参数由1上调至1.25。

4月10日，国家外汇管理局发布了《关于优化外汇管理 支持涉外业务发展的通知》（汇发〔2020〕8号），确定于6月1日起进一步优化外汇业务管理，完善外汇服务方式，提升跨境贸易投资便利化水平。

4月24日，中国人民银行、中国银保监会、中国证监会、国家外汇管理局联合发布《关于金融支持粤港澳大湾区建设的意见》（银发〔2020〕95号），进一步推进金融开放创新，深化内地与港澳金融合作，加大金融支持粤港澳大湾区建设力度，提升粤港澳大湾区在国家经济发展和对外开放中的支持引领作用。

5月7日，中国人民银行、国家外汇管理局联合发布了《境外机构投资者境内证券期货投资资金管理规定》（中国人民银行 国家外汇管理局公告〔2020〕第2号）。

5月9日，国家外汇管理局发布了《关于印发〈银行外汇业务合规与审慎经营评估内容及评分标准（2020年）〉的通知》（汇综发〔2020〕35号），自该通知下发之日起，《银行外汇业务合规与审慎经营评估内容及评分标准（2019年）》（汇发〔2019〕15号附表）废止。

5月20日，国家外汇管理局发布了《关于支持贸易新业态发展的通知》（汇发〔2020〕11号），旨在促进外贸提质增效，加快跨境电子商务等贸易新业态发展，提高贸易外汇收支便利化水平。

5月26日，中国人民银行、银保监会、国家发展改革委、工业和信息化部、财政部、市场监管总局、证监会、国家外汇管理局联合发布《关于进一步强化中小微企业金融服务的指导意见》（银发〔2020〕120号），旨在疏通内外部传导机制，促进中小微企业融资规模明显增长、融资结构更加优化，实现"增量、降价、提质、扩面"，推动加快恢复正常生产生活秩序，支持实体经济高质量发展。

8月28日，国家外汇管理局发布《关于印发〈经常项目外汇业务指引（2020年版）〉的通知》（汇发〔2020〕14号），全面整合了相关法规，形成《经常项目外汇业务指引（2020年版）》，并废止前期指引中部分规定，确定了于自发布之日起施行。

9月18日，国家外汇管理局发布了《关于印发〈对外金融资产负债及交易统计业务指引（2020年版）〉的通知》（汇综发〔2020〕71号），为指导申报主体更准确地理解具体报送要求，根据《国际收支统计申报办法》（中华人民共和国国务院令第642号）和《对外金融资产负债及交易统计制度》（汇发〔2018〕24号印发），修订形成《对外金融资产负债及交易统计业务指引（2020年版）》。

9月25日，中国证监会、中国人民银行、国家外汇管理局联合发布了《合格境外机构投资者和人民币合格境外机构投资者境内证券期货投资管理办法》（证监会令〔第176号〕），确定于2020年11月1日起施行。

10月22日，全国银行间同业拆借中心和银行间市场清算所股份有限公司联合发布了《关于推出农发债标准债券远期业务的通知》（中汇交发〔2020〕302号），确定于10月29日推出农发债标准债券远期业务。

12月14日，国家外汇管理局发布了《对外金融资产负债及交易统计核查规则

(2020年版)》(汇综发〔2020〕94号),新增了关于上下期余额衔接的多维度校验规则、关于名称要素项及相应所属部门和所属国家/地区要素项间一致性的校验规则等内容。

(三)外汇市场发展展望

2021年是"十四五"规划的开局之年。外汇管理部门要坚持以习近平新时代中国特色社会主义思想为指导,全面贯彻党的十九大和十九届二中、三中、四中、五中全会精神,认真落实中央经济工作会议部署,增强"四个意识"、坚定"四个自信"、做到"两个维护",坚持稳中求进的工作总基调,立足新发展阶段、贯彻新发展理念、构建新发展格局,继续做好"六稳"工作、落实"六保"任务,更好统筹发展和安全,强化机遇意识、风险意识,以深化外汇领域改革开放激发新发展活力,改革完善与新发展格局下更高水平开放型经济新体制相适应的外汇管理体制机制,微观上着力提升贸易投资自由化便利化水平,宏观上有效维护国家经济金融安全,以优异成绩庆祝建党100周年。

2021年外汇管理重点工作有以下几个方面。一是防范跨境资本异常流动风险。加强外汇形势监测评估,密切关注疫情等外部冲击影响,引导金融机构和企业坚持风险中性原则,打击外汇投机行为,加强市场预期管理和宏观审慎管理,避免外汇市场无序波动。二是深化外汇领域改革开放。以金融市场双向开放为重点,稳妥有序推进资本项目开放。完善境外机构境内发行股票、债券资金管理,推进私募股权投资基金跨境投资试点,改革外债登记管理,促进跨境投融资便利化。扩大贸易外汇收支便利化试点,促进贸易新业态发展。建设开放多元、功能健全的外汇市场,支持金融机构推出更多适应市场需求的外汇衍生品。三是完善外汇市场"宏观审慎+微观监管"两位一体管理框架。以加强宏观审慎为核心改善跨境资本流动管理,以转变监管方式为核心完善外汇市场微观监管。完善以风险评估为导向的分类管理信用体系建设。加强非现场监管能力建设。以"零容忍"态度严厉打击地下钱庄、跨境赌博等外汇领域违法违规活动,维护外汇市场健康秩序。四是完善中国特色外汇储备经营管理。坚持市场化原则,前瞻性地做好战略配置,动态优化投资组合。保障外汇储备资产安全、流动和保值增值。五是夯实外汇管理基础工作。深入研究"十四五"时期外汇管理改革思路,推进"数字外管"和"安全外管"建设,完善国际收支统计体系,做好常态化疫情防控工作。

**专栏13**

**自由贸易的胜利——RCEP成功签署**[①]

2020年11月15日,涵盖15个成员国的《区域全面经济伙伴关系协定》(RCEP)在RCEP第四次领导人会议期间签署,这意味着世界上人口数量最多、成员结构最多

---

[①] 张燕生,信达证券股份有限公司研发中心首席研究员、《中国金融政策报告》项目(课题组)研究员。

元、发展潜力最大的自贸区正式诞生。

RCEP 由东盟十国（印度尼西亚、马来西亚、菲律宾、泰国、新加坡、文莱、柬埔寨、老挝、缅甸、越南）于 2012 年发起，邀请中国、日本、韩国、澳大利亚、新西兰、印度 6 个对话伙伴国参加，是以发展中经济体为中心的区域自贸协定。谈判于 2012 年 11 月正式启动，其间经过 3 次领导人会议、19 次部长级会议、28 轮正式谈判；2019 年 11 月 4 日，第三次《区域全面经济伙伴关系协定》领导人会议发表联合声明，宣布 15 个 RCEP 成员国已经结束全部 20 个章节的文本谈判以及实质上所有的市场准入问题的谈判，将启动法律文本审核工作，以便在 2020 年签署协定。

RCEP 协定包括 20 个章节：初始条款和一般定义，货物贸易，原产地规则，海关程序和贸易便利化，卫生和植物卫生措施，标准、技术法规和合格评定程序，贸易救济，服务贸易，自然人临时流动，投资，知识产权，电子商务，竞争，中小企业，经济技术合作，政府采购，一般条款和例外，机构条款，争端解决，最终条款章节。其中，知识产权、电子商务等多项举措承诺水平超过世界贸易组织（WTO），是地区国家以实际行动维护多边贸易体制、建设开放型世界经济的重要一步。

国务院总理李克强 2020 年 11 月 15 日出席第四次区域全面经济伙伴关系协定（RCEP）领导人会议时表示，"这不仅仅是东亚区域合作极具标志性意义的成果，更是多边主义和自由贸易的胜利，必将为促进地区的发展繁荣增添新动能，为世界经济实现恢复性增长贡献新力量"。中国商务部副部长兼国际贸易谈判副代表王受文对 RCEP 的签署表示，"RCEP 不仅是目前全球最大的自贸协定，而且是一个全面、现代、高质量和互惠的自贸协定"。

RCEP 的签署对地区和全球而言，有利于整合东亚地区的资源，促进区域经济融合发展，推动世界自由贸易进程。在近年以美国为首的逆全球化倒车背景下，RCEP 的签署是全球自由贸易的胜利。

我国拥有制造业的比较优势，因此在全球的贸易分歧中往往是被附加关税、增加成本的一方。然而也并非所有的商品都如此，特别是资源品。我国目前对 RCEP 发起国的部分商品也有额外的关税政策。RCEP 的签署对其中任何一方都是权利与义务并存的，共同推进自由贸易的进程。

我国的经济高速发展带动国民收入不断提高，在制造业中的人力成本优势在减小。东南亚国家的工业化进程也在加速，承接了部分低端制造业的转移。RCEP 的签署有利于东南亚国家在此类制造业上更好地打开市场。而我国提高经济发展质量、实现产业结构升级不仅是我国人民的需要，也是我国制造业必须要完成的任务。

## 十一、黄金市场发展政策[①]

2020 年，中国黄金市场在积极抗击疫情和稳步开展业务的同时，持续推进制度体系

---

① 作者：罗江，上海黄金交易所研究发展部副总经理、《中国金融政策报告》项目（课题组）研究员。

建设，市场基础设施不断完善，市场运行平稳有序，交易规模持续扩大，市场服务功能进一步提升。上海黄金交易所（以下简称上金所）市场运行平稳有序，清算、交割安全顺畅，总交易规模持续增长。上海期货交易所（以下简称上期所）黄金期货交易量保持增长。黄金市场在我国金融基础设施中的作用进一步提升。

（一）黄金市场发展概况

2020年初，新冠肺炎疫情扩散冲击全球经济，股票与商品市场普遍下跌，市场流动性短缺波及贵金属市场，国际现货黄金价格最低下探至1451.13美元/盎司。3月，美联储连续推出开放式量化宽松政策缓解全球流动性恐慌，低实际利率和通胀预期推升现货黄金价格大幅反弹。8月上旬，国际现货黄金价格最高触及2075.14美元/盎司，国内现货黄金价格最高触及449.00元/克，均创历史新高。第四季度，受新冠肺炎疫苗研发取得积极进展、市场不确定性下降等因素影响，黄金价格高位回调整理。年末，国际现货黄金价格收于1897.53美元/盎司，比2019年末上涨380.35美元/盎司，涨幅25.07%。上金所黄金Au9999合约年初开盘价341.95元/克，全年最高价449.00元/克，最低价327.60元/克，振幅35.62%，年末收盘价390.00元/克，同比上涨14.44%。

2020年，上金所成交金额43.32万亿元（双边），同比增长50.66%，其中黄金成交量5.87万吨。上金所国际板成交金额8.26万亿元，同比增长125.24%，其中黄金成交量8028.83吨。上期所黄金期货成交41.44万亿元（双边），同比增长38.16%，累计成交量10.48万吨。

截至2020年底，上金所会员总数达280家。其中，普通会员共计156家，包括金融类会员31家，综合类会员125家；特别会员共计124家，包括外资金融类会员7家，国际会员89家和券商、信托、中小银行等机构类的特别会员28家。主板代理机构客户11850户，通过国际会员代理的国际客户87户，个人客户1046.83万户。

（二）行业市场发展政策

2020年，黄金市场认真贯彻执行人民银行有关黄金市场的各项政策，保险资产管理产品投资黄金政策放开；黄金市场金融基础设施进一步完善；反洗钱机制不断健全；市场风险管理制度升级；多举措抗击疫情承担社会责任；稳步推进产品创新，完善交易机制。年内，黄金市场政策体系得到进一步完善。

1. 保险资产管理公司投资黄金政策放开

2020年9月7日，中国银保监会下发了《组合类保险资产管理产品实施细则》（银保监办发〔2020〕85号），允许保险资产管理公司投资黄金。继信托公司、证券公司和基金公司等金融机构参与黄金市场后，保险资产管理公司投资黄金，标志着中国黄金市场已充分与其他金融市场互联互通。保险资管公司等大型机构投资者投资黄金可以满足资产配置的需求，同时成为黄金市场合格金融机构参与者，对促进市场持续、稳健、积极发展具有重大意义。

2. 完善黄金市场金融基础设施

2020年，黄金市场金融基础设施进一步完善。人民银行1月正式认证上金所成为合格中央对手，同月上金所接入人民银行大额支付系统。中国黄金市场交易报告库一阶段系统于10月上线运行，场内业务数据报送工作顺利启动。

上金所贯彻落实人民银行办公厅文件《关于黄金资产管理业务有关事项的通知》（银办发〔2018〕215号）和《金融机构互联网黄金业务管理暂行办法》（银办发〔2018〕221号），黄金资产管理业务的登记托管工作有序开展，逐步步入正轨。

3. 修改《黄金及黄金制品进出口管理办法》

2020年4月，人民银行、海关总署根据《中国人民银行法》、《海关法》和《国务院对确需保留的行政审批项目设定行政许可的决定》等法律法规，对《黄金及黄金制品进出口管理办法》（人民银行 海关总署令〔2015〕第1号发布）作出修改，发布《黄金及黄金制品进出口管理办法》（人民银行 海关总署令〔2020〕第3号），规范黄金及黄金制品进出口行为，加强黄金及黄金制品进出口管理，进一步推进"放管服"改革，减证便民。此次修改将第十条第一款第七项修改为"银行业金融机构还应当提供内部黄金业务风险控制制度有关材料"；将第十条第一款第八项修改为"黄金矿产的生产企业还应当提交省级环保部门出具的污染物排放许可证件和年度达标检测报告复印件、商务部门有关境外投资批复文件复印件、银行汇出汇款证明书复印件，境外国家或者地区开采黄金有关证明，企业近3年的纳税记录，申请出口黄金的还应当提交在国务院批准的黄金现货交易所的登记证明"。

4. 健全反洗钱机制

上金所根据人民银行《会员反洗钱、反恐怖融资和反逃税自律指引》和《上海黄金交易所会员反洗钱和反恐怖融资工作实施办法（试行）》，履行自身反洗钱义务，积极推进贵金属行业反洗钱制度体系不断完善。上金所积极协助监管机构履职，持续跟进并落实反洗钱金融行动特别工作组（FATF）国际互评估整改工作，参与撰写《贵金属行业洗钱风险评估报告》，加强内部制度建设，印发《会员身份识别工作指引》，做好会员身份持续识别，组织会员填写《2020年度尽职调查问卷》并开展会员信息重新登记工作。贵金属行业反洗钱制度体系逐步建立。

5. 夯实市场风险管理制度

为更好落实党中央金融防风险重任，上金所2020年6月增设了风险管理部，加强交易风险管理，规范交易行为，维护交易当事人的合法权益，维护市场交易秩序，保障市场稳定运行，完善市场风险管理制度。上金所于11月发布《上海黄金交易所全面风险管理规定》，明确了交易风险管理原则、领导监督部门、防风险资源管理方式等，并对保证金制度、涨跌停板制度、延期补偿费制度与超期费制度、限仓制度、交易限额制度、大户报告制度、强行平仓制度以及风险警示制度与异常交易监控制度做了明确具体规定。

6. 抗击疫情，承担社会责任

新冠肺炎疫情发生后，上金所关怀疫区会员，减免湖北地区会员单位2020年度年会费、席位使用费、交易手续费、仓储费、出入库费等费用，降低疫区会员及相关机构运行成本。

上金所积极承担社会责任，2020年7月发布首版《社会责任报告》，11月与中国黄金协会、世界黄金协会共同发布《中国黄金行业防疫抗疫社会责任报告》。

**7. 推进产品创新，完善交易机制**

上金所积极推进创新发展，丰富完善业务体系，2020年内实现3只传统黄金交易所交易基金（ETF）上市及首批4只"上海金"ETF上市，并推动保险资金通过投资黄金ETF参与黄金市场。场外产品创新持续推进，履约担保型询价产品实现技术上线，研究挂钩"上海银"询价衍生产品，推动多边询价产品创新储备。

**（三）政策评价与展望**

持续推出的市场制度为黄金市场创新发展、防范风险和进一步开放提供了有力保障，取得了良好效果。

保险资产管理公司投资黄金方案完成。2020年3月开始，在人民银行指导下，上金所与保险资产管理协会、世界黄金协会、中国人寿资产管理公司、中国人保资产管理公司等金融机构成立了保险资金投资黄金课题组，克服疫情困难，经过不懈努力，8月完成了一系列研究报告和黄金投资产品设计方案，获得银保监会肯定。9月，银保监会印发《保险资产管理产品管理暂行办法》三个细则，进一步规范保险资产管理产品业务发展。根据《组合类保险资产管理产品实施细则》，中国人保资产管理有限公司投资黄金指数的组合类资产管理产品"人保资产安心创优黄金驱动资产管理产品"方案完成。该产品是"资管新规"及《保险资产管理产品管理暂行办法》相关规定下，保险资管行业首只尝试推出的投资黄金资产的保险资管产品。

黄金市场金融基础设施进一步完善。上金所成为合格中央对手方后，金融基础设施进一步完善。上金所在人民银行的指导下，积极研究推动黄金市场金融标准化工作；完成四代系统整体实施方案，推动两地三中建设，保障系统安全稳定运行；增加询价市场夜盘交易时间，调整后询价业务整体交易时段达10.5小时，上线了询价线上经纪与协商功能。上金所第三代清算系统、上金所国际板系统分别荣获2019年度银行科技发展奖二等奖、三等奖。"上海金"金锭标准成功入选上海市首批"上海标准"。根据《上海黄金交易所黄金资产管理业务登记托管实施细则》，上金所2020年全年黄金资产管理业务登记托管系统已完成533只资管产品的登记托管。

反洗钱工作初见成效。上金所推动会员履行反洗钱义务，明确制度要求，将反洗钱要求融入会员资格审查，要求会员全面建立反洗钱内控制度、配备相应岗位人员并自觉履行反洗钱义务，通过会员资格重新登记、调研座谈等方式引导会员建立合格的反洗钱工作体系。上金所助力监管机构深入了解贵金属市场业务模式及风险现状，前期工作受到反洗钱部际联席会议表彰。上金所落实"三反"义务和投资者保护责任，开展会员反洗钱尽职调查，向中国反洗钱监测分析中心成功报送4份可疑交易报告，反洗钱工作获得人民银行表彰。

市场风险管理体系逐步健全。上金所增设风控部并发布《上海黄金交易所全面风险管理规定》，使市场风险管理水平明显提高。受国际政治经济形势、新冠疫情等影响，贵金属市场价格波动剧烈，投资交易风险加大。在贵金属市场出现极端行情冲击下，上金所依据风险防控制度有效应对市场波动，采取应对措施，多次调整延期合约涨跌停板及保证金比例，适时约谈会员进行窗口指导，实时统计个人客户风险信息，及时发布风险提示，妥善处置极端行情和违约事件，维护市场稳定运行。上金所优化会员管理，严格防范场外风险，依规加大违法违规行为处罚力度，严肃处理深圳黄金资讯、武汉金凰和江西壹牛等违规违法会员，引入公开警示和市场禁入举措。优化会员资格全周期管理，建立事前准入严格审核、事中实时风险监测、事后限期整改与处罚的制度机制，设立会员入市辅导期，启动会员资格重新登记工作，约谈、警告并清退多家不合格机构。

黄金市场积极承担社会责任。2020年，在人民银行领导下，上金所有效保障疫情防控，稳步开展业务，有效降低交易成本，保障疫情地区市场正常运行。《中国黄金行业防疫抗疫社会责任报告》被"中国企业社会责任报告评级专家委员会"评为五星级的行业社会责任报告。

展望未来，黄金市场进入新发展阶段，需要坚持新发展理念，统筹推进风险防控和业务发展，应对各项挑战，推动高质量发展。黄金市场持续稳健发展的制度基础正在不断夯实，市场政策将以实现《中华人民共和国国民经济和社会发展第十四个五年规划和2035年远景目标纲要》需要为导向，推动构建黄金市场国内大循环的中心节点和国内国际双循环战略，增强黄金市场服务实体经济能力，建设国际一流的综合性黄金市场。

## 专栏 14

**中欧投资协议与碳中和共同推动实现中国与欧洲共同、长期、绿色发展的战略**[①]

《中欧全面投资协议》（EU – China Comprehensive Agreement on Investment，CAI）旨在为中欧投资关系建立一个统一的法律框架，取代中国和欧盟26个成员国之间的现有双边投资条约。

《中欧全面投资协议》经历7年35轮谈判，于2020年底达成一致，将有力拉动后疫情时期世界经济复苏，促进中国与欧盟成员国，以及全球贸易与投资的自由化和便利化，加快绿色发展和推动多边合作，为构建开放型世界经济作出中欧两大市场的重要贡献。

《中欧全面投资协议》核心内容包括：(1)保证相互投资获得保护，尊重知识产权，确保补贴透明性；(2)改善双方市场准入条件；(3)确保投资环境和监管程序清晰、公平和透明；(4)改善劳工标准，支持可持续发展。

2018年以来，在美国单方面的贸易保护主义压力之下，中国和欧盟面临的国际贸易环境都变得更加严峻；过去5年中国与欧盟之间的直接投资金额合计在1000亿美元左

---

① 作者：郭荆璞，国金证券研究院副所长，《中国金融政策报告》项目（课题组）研究员。

右，仅相当于双边贸易额的2%~3%，投资规模扩张乏力；贸易保护与疫情带来的特定领域安全担忧，对双边投资都产生持续的压力。

为了应对新冠疫情带给全世界的巨大冲击，也为了更长远的绿色和可持续发展，中欧双方在谈判中集中精力解决双方在公平竞争和市场准入方面的分歧，特别是中国在碳中和方面提出与欧洲趋同的2060年碳中和目标，大大加速了中欧投资协议的谈判进程。

《中欧全面投资协议》将推动中国与欧盟之间的直接投资规模增长，双方承诺相互开放部分制造业和服务业领域的投资。在市场准入方面，《中欧全面投资协议》采取的是准入前国民待遇加负面清单的模式，是中方首次在包括服务业和非服务业在内的所有行业以负面清单的形式作出了开放的承诺。《中欧全面投资协议》落地将推动欧洲资本在中国的金融、建筑、海运和航空相关辅助服务等领域的投资，以中国的稳定回报资产吸引低廉的全球资金，降低国内融资成本，扩大资金来源，增加中国的金融系统稳定性。

欧盟国家同样希望引起中国对欧洲先进制造业和服务业领域的兴趣，特别是吸引中国具有技术和先发优势的绿色能源以及数字化领域的成功企业到欧洲投资。此举有利于中国企业寻找更加广阔的投资机会和市场，获得全球化、弱周期的回报，同时学习欧洲企业在相应领域的经验，促进中国国民生产总值（GNP）的增长。

根据克林伯格等学者的研究，美国的外交政策存在约50年的内敛—外扩周期，2015—2035年，美国的外交政策有转向内敛和孤立主义的可能性。这段时间给予中国稳定与欧盟之间的双边关系，加强双方的经济贸易联系，进而在全球治理和长远发展方面求同存异，深化合作，建立更广泛的全球影响力的战略机遇。

中国政府在2020年8月宣布了2060年达到碳中和的长远目标，体现了大国责任，与欧盟国家追求绿色发展的理念趋同。碳中和与《中欧全面投资协议》将一同勾勒出中国与欧洲之间良性互动、积极作为、深化合作的图景，携手育新机、开新局，实现中国与欧洲国家共同发展、绿色发展的战略。

# 主要金融监管政策

## 一、中国人民银行主要监管政策[①]

（一）2020年人民银行主要监管政策梳理

一是持续构建要素完备的宏观审慎政策框架。建立逆周期资本缓冲机制。分步实施宏观审慎压力测试，完善系统性风险监测、评估和预警体系。建立健全跨境资金流动宏观审慎管理框架。统筹监管系统重要性金融机构和金融控股公司。

二是金融风险攻坚战取得重要阶段性成果。及时调整不同阶段金融风险处置的重点和优先序。牵头协调银保监会、证监会顺利接管"明天系"旗下9家核心金融机构，妥善应对债券市场违约风险。有效遏制系统性金融风险上升势头，金融脱实向虚、盲目扩张的情况得到根本扭转。

三是加强国际金融合作，有序扩大金融业高水平对外开放。加强疫情下国际宏观政策协调。积极参与多边危机防范救助。参与制定G20缓债倡议并全面落实相关国家缓债申请，推动国际货币基金组织开展特别提款权（SDR）普遍分配，支持低收入国家应对疫情冲击。全面参与《区域全面经济伙伴关系协定》（RCEP）关于金融业的谈判，首次将新金融服务、金融信息转移纳入自贸协定规则。继续主动推进国际绿色金融合作。

四是金融改革取得新进展。建立国务院金融稳定发展委员会（以下简称金融委）办公室地方协调机制。推动出台两批26条金融改革开放措施。深入推进外汇、区域金融领域的改革开放。试点深入推进。公司信用类债券违约处置与信息披露规则逐步统一，债券市场基础设施互联互通持续推进。做实存款保险公司和存款保险机构职能。开发性政策性金融机构业务分类管理持续推进。积极推进资管业务过渡期整改。

五是金融服务和管理呈现新亮点。根据疫情防控需要，及时开通金融服务"绿色通道"。推动履行统筹金融业重要立法职责。支付监管与服务水平进一步提升。人民币现金管理及数字人民币试点工作稳步推进。国库服务质量持续提升。征信体系规划总体完成。反洗钱监管取得积极成效，风险评估和执法检查"双支柱"监管机制基本建立，反洗钱调查和监测分析成效显著，顺利完成金融行动特别工作组（FATF）主席国履职，

---

[①] 作者：朱小川，上海市法学会金融法研究会、《中国金融政策报告》项目（课题组）研究员。本部分主要参考中国人民银行网站内容，人民银行货币政策梳理详见前面章节。

互评估整改工作取得积极进展。持续整治侵害消费者金融信息安全行为。

（二）2020年人民银行主要监管政策评价

2020年，人民银行以习近平新时代中国特色社会主义思想为指导，坚持党中央对金融工作的集中统一领导，践行以人民为中心的发展思想，坚决贯彻落实党中央、国务院决策部署，在金融委统筹指挥下，全力支持稳企业保就业，持续打好防范化解重大金融风险攻坚战，进一步深化金融改革开放，认真履行金融委办公室职责，重大监管政策在出台前及时向社会公开征集意见，降低了监管政策不周全因素，稳定了监管政策的社会预期，取得了较好的社会效果。

有待加强和完善的监管工作包括更好发挥金融业重要立法的统筹职责，推动形成更为完善的金融业规范体系。进一步增加监管透明度，提升监管效能。在《统筹监管金融基础设施工作方案》的基础上，形成可操作的监管办法。加强对金融科技的理解和监管，充分利用科技促进监管，也通过监管规范金融科技发展等。

（三）未来人民银行监管政策展望

2021年，人民银行将持续以习近平新时代中国特色社会主义思想为指导，坚持党对金融工作的全面领导，进一步加强政治建设和法治央行建设。积极从政治角度观察和思考经济金融问题，把人民利益放到最高位置，提升金融管理的水平。深入贯彻习近平法治思想，依靠法治方式深化改革、推动发展、化解矛盾、维护稳定，积极推动金融领域的立法修法，提高违法成本，澄清灰色地带，阳光执法透明办案。

一是落实碳达峰碳中和重大决策部署，完善绿色金融政策框架和激励机制。做好政策设计和规划，引导金融资源向绿色发展领域倾斜，增强金融体系管理气候变化相关风险的能力，推动建设碳排放权交易市场，为排碳合理定价。逐步健全绿色金融标准体系，明确金融机构监管和信息披露要求，建立政策激励约束体系，完善绿色金融产品和市场体系，持续推进绿色金融国际合作。

二是加快完善宏观审慎政策框架，将主要金融活动、金融机构、金融市场和金融基础设施纳入宏观审慎管理。加强系统性金融风险监测评估，分步推动建立宏观审慎压力测试体系。加快建立健全跨境资本流动等重点领域宏观审慎管理框架。完善金融控股公司监管制度体系。

三是持续防范化解金融风险。加强风险排查，做好风险应对。完善风险防范处置长效机制，压实金融机构和股东主体责任、地方政府属地责任、金融监管部门监管责任和最后贷款人责任。完善存款保险制度建设和机构设置。加强互联网平台公司金融活动的审慎监管。坚决落实党中央、国务院关于强化反垄断和防止资本无序扩张、统筹金融发展与金融安全的决策部署，抓紧补齐监管制度短板。强化支付领域监管，个人征信业务必须持牌经营，严禁金融产品过度营销，诱导过度负债，严肃查处侵害金融消费者合法权益的违法违规行为。确保金融创新在审慎监管前提下发展，普惠金融服务质量和竞争力稳中有升。

四是深度参与全球金融治理，严密防控外部金融风险，稳步扩大金融双向开放。妥善应对低收入国家债务问题。进一步扩大金融业高水平开放，推动全面实施准入前国民待遇加负面清单管理制度。深度参与全球金融治理，切实维护多边主义。

五是稳慎推进人民币国际化。着眼于服务实体经济，顺势而为，促进贸易投资便利化。完善人民币使用相关政策制度。继续推动金融市场高质量双向开放。促进本外币、离岸在岸市场的良性协调发展。

六是深化金融市场和金融机构改革。牵头制定债券市场发展规划，推动完善债券市场法制，促进基础设施互联互通。健全多渠道债券违约处置机制。推动完善债券市场统一执法框架，加大对债券市场逃废债、欺诈发行等违法违规行为的查处力度。落实房地产长效机制，实施好房地产金融审慎管理制度，完善金融支持住房租赁政策体系。引导大型银行下沉服务重心，推动中小银行完善公司治理，聚焦主责主业。

七是持续改进外汇管理和服务。稳妥有序推进资本项目开放。支持企业合理审慎运用外汇衍生品管理汇率风险。加快完善外汇市场"宏观审慎＋微观监管"两位一体管理框架。以"零容忍"态度严厉打击外汇领域违法违规行为。集约高效做好外汇储备经营管理，维护外汇储备规模基本稳定。

八是提升金融服务和管理水平。统筹推进金融法治体系建设。进一步提升人民银行研究工作影响力。扎实做好"十四五"国家规划纲要金融重点内容与金融业"十四五"规划的研究编制工作。扎实推进金融业综合统计。深入推进支付行业治理现代化。提升金融科技应用和管理水平。稳妥开展数字人民币试点测试。深化征信在数字金融和经济治理中的应用。构建反洗钱工作新发展格局，认真研究制定国家反洗钱发展战略，积极推进《反洗钱法》修订工作进程，加强反洗钱协调机制建设，提升反洗钱监管质量和成效，发挥反洗钱调查和监测分析优势，参与国际反洗钱治理，稳步推进FATF互评估后续整改。

## 附表

**2020年中国人民银行的主要监管政策**

| 日期 | 政策名称 | 发文单位 | 文件号 |
| --- | --- | --- | --- |
| 1月31日 | 关于进一步强化金融支持防控新型冠状病毒感染肺炎疫情的通知 | 中国人民银行、财政部、银保监会、证监会、国家外汇管理局 | 银发〔2020〕29号 |
| 2月7日 | 关于打赢疫情防控阻击战 强化疫情防控重点保障企业资金支持的紧急通知 | 财政部、国家发展改革委、工业和信息化部、人民银行、审计署 | 财金〔2020〕5号 |
| 2月14日 | 关于进一步加快推进上海国际金融中心建设和金融支持长三角一体化发展的意见 | 中国人民银行、银保监会、证监会、国家外汇管理局、上海市人民政府 | 银发〔2020〕46号 |
| 3月1日 | 关于对中小微企业贷款实施临时性延期还本付息的通知 | 银保监会、中国人民银行、国家发展改革委、工业和信息化部、财政部 | 银保监发〔2020〕6号 |
| 3月5日 | 统筹监管金融基础设施工作方案 | 中国人民银行、国家发展改革委、财政部、银保监会、证监会、国家外汇管理局 | — |

续表

| 日期 | 政策名称 | 发文单位 | 文件号 |
|---|---|---|---|
| 3月20日 | 中国人民银行行政许可实施办法 | 中国人民银行 | 中国人民银行令〔2020〕第1号 |
| 4月16日 | 修改《黄金及黄金制品进出口管理办法》 | 中国人民银行、海关总署 | 中国人民银行海关总署令〔2020〕第3号 |
| 4月24日 | 关于金融支持粤港澳大湾区建设的意见 | 中国人民银行、银保监会、证监会、国家外汇管理局 | 银发〔2020〕95号 |
| 4月29日 | 关于修改《教育储蓄管理办法》等规章的决定 | 中国人民银行 | 中国人民银行令〔2020〕第2号 |
| 5月26日 | 关于进一步强化中小微企业金融服务的指导意见 | 中国人民银行、银保监会、国家发展改革委、工业和信息化部、财政部、市场监管总局、证监会、国家外汇管理局 | 银发〔2020〕120号 |
| 6月1日 | 关于进一步对中小微企业贷款实施阶段性延期还本付息的通知 | 中国人民银行、银保监会、财政部、发展改革委、工业和信息化部 | 银发〔2020〕122号 |
| 6月1日 | 关于加大小微企业信用贷款支持力度的通知 | 中国人民银行、银保监会、财政部、国家发展改革委、工业和信息化部 | 银发〔2020〕123号 |
| 6月2日 | 修订《非金融机构支付服务管理办法实施细则》等5件规范性文件 | 中国人民银行 | 中国人民银行公告〔2020〕第3号 |
| 6月15日 | 关于公司信用类债券违约处置有关事宜的通知 | 中国人民银行、国家发展改革委、证监会 | — |
| 6月24日 | 标准化票据管理办法 | 中国人民银行 | 中国人民银行公告〔2020〕第6号 |
| 6月24日 | 标准化债权类资产认定规则 | 中国人民银行、银保监会、证监会、国家外汇管理局 | 中国人民银行中国银保监会中国证监会国家外汇管理局公告〔2020〕第5号 |
| 6月29日 | 关于在粤港澳大湾区开展"跨境理财通"业务试点的联合公告 | 中国人民银行、香港金融管理局、澳门金融管理局 | — |
| 7月19日 | 银行间债券市场与交易所债券市场相关基础设施机构开展互联互通合作有关事宜 | 中国人民银行、证监会 | 中国人民银行中国证监会公告〔2020〕第7号 |
| 7月23日 | 关于印发《普通纪念币普制币发行管理暂行规定》的通知 | 中国人民银行 | 银发〔2020〕173号 |

续表

| 日期 | 政策名称 | 发文单位 | 文件号 |
|---|---|---|---|
| 9月11日 | 金融控股公司监督管理试行办法 | 中国人民银行 | 中国人民银行令〔2020〕第4号 |
| 9月14日 | 人民银行会同有关部门印发两省三市普惠金融改革试验区总体方案 | 中国人民银行 | — |
| 9月15日 | 中国人民银行金融消费者权益保护实施办法 | 中国人民银行 | 中国人民银行令〔2020〕第5号 |
| 9月18日 | 关于规范发展供应链金融 支持供应链产业链稳定循环和优化升级的意见 | 中国人民银行、工业和信息化部、司法部、商务部、国资委、市场监管总局、银保监会、国家外汇管理局 | 银发〔2020〕226号 |
| 9月30日 | 关于建立逆周期资本缓冲机制的通知 | 中国人民银行、银保监会 | — |
| 10月26日 | 关于规范代收业务的通知 | 中国人民银行 | 银发〔2020〕248号 |
| 11月12日 | 修改"证照分离"改革涉及的规范性文件 | 中国人民银行 | 中国人民银行公告〔2020〕第15号 |
| 11月18日 | 中国人民银行关于印发假币收缴、鉴定业务专用凭证印章等样式有关事项的通知 | 中国人民银行 | 银发〔2020〕281号 |
| 12月2日 | 关于印发《系统重要性银行评估办法》的通知 | 中国人民银行、银保监会 | 银发〔2020〕289号 |
| 12月9日 | 规范人民币现金收付行为有关事项的公告 | 中国人民银行 | 中国人民银行公告〔2020〕第18号 |
| 12月18日 | 规范商业承兑汇票信息披露 | 中国人民银行 | 中国人民银行公告〔2020〕第19号 |
| 12月23日 | 完善银行间债券市场现券做市商管理有关事宜 | 中国人民银行 | 中国人民银行公告〔2020〕第21号 |
| 12月25日 | 公司信用类债券信息披露管理办法 | 中国人民银行、国家发展改革委、证监会 | 中国人民银行 国家发展改革委 中国证监会公告〔2020〕第22号 |
| 12月28日 | 关于建立银行业金融机构房地产贷款集中度管理制度的通知 | 中国人民银行、银保监会 | 银发〔2020〕322号 |
| 12月31日 | 关于进一步优化跨境人民币政策 支持稳外贸稳外资的通知 | 中国人民银行、国家发展改革委、商务部、国资委、银保监会、国家外汇管理局 | 银发〔2020〕330号 |
| 12月31日 | 就生产设备、原材料、半成品、产品等四类动产抵押登记的有关过渡安排公告 | 中国人民银行、国家市场监管总局 | 中国人民银行 国家市场监督管理总局公告〔2020〕第23号 |

资料来源：中国人民银行官网。发布日期以文件落款时间为准；如没有落款日期，则以官网发布的日期为准。

专栏 15

### 搭建监管框架，促进良性循环①

2020年9月11日，国务院发布《关于实施金融控股公司准入管理的决定》（以下简称《准入决定》）。同日人民银行印发《金融控股公司监督管理试行办法》（以下简称《金控办法》）。11月2日，人民银行就《金融控股公司董事、监事、高级管理人员任职备案管理暂行规定（征求意见稿）》（以下简称《暂行规定》）公开征求意见。

金融控股公司，也即"金控公司"，是在金融创新和市场竞争加剧的背景下，金融业综合经营，通过集团下各业务子公司协同提供一站式金融综合服务的集团公司。金控公司通过拓展业务链、展开多元化经营、实现产融结合，获得了综合服务能力强、业务成本低和利润来源多样化等竞争优势。

由于分业监管模式下的监管真空，无论是金融机构控股还是非金融机构控股，都形成了公司股权结构不清晰、组织架构不合理、集团内部存在大额关联交易风险、盲目追求大而全、风险管理不完善和业务协同水平较差等问题。甚至还有少数股东干预金融机构经营，利用关联交易隐蔽输送利益，套取金融机构资金，形成了巨大的金融风险。

2017年第五次全国金融工作会议后，按照党中央、国务院的决策部署，人民银行会同司法部等相关部门着手开始对金融控股公司实施准入管理和持续监管。《准入决定》、《金控办法》和《暂行规定》的先后出台，标志着对金融控股公司的监督管理正式展开。

《准入决定》分为三部分。一是对金融控股公司实施准入管理，对金融控股公司的主体范围和设立标准作出界定。二是明确设立金融控股公司的条件和程序。三是对时间节点等其他事项作出规定。

《金控办法》细化了《准入决定》中金融控股公司准入的条件和程序，进一步明确人民银行对金融控股公司实施监管，金融管理部门依法按照金融监管职责分工对金融控股公司所控股金融机构实施监管。《金控办法》对股东资质条件、资金来源和运用、资本充足性要求、股权结构、公司治理、关联交易、风险管理体系和风险"防火墙"制度等关键环节提出了监管要求。

《暂行规定》明确了金融控股公司董监高的监管主体，设定金控公司董监高的任职条件，加强任职管理，规定备案流程和材料，加强事中、事后监管，明确管理手段。

《准入决定》、《金控办法》和《暂行规定》将金融控股公司整体纳入监管，在金融业总体分业经营为主的原则下，从制度上隔离实业板块与金融板块，有利于防范风险交叉传染，更好地满足全社会多元化、综合化、便捷化的金融服务需求，有利于进一步促进经济金融良性循环。

然而，为了完全实现规范整合行业乱象，遏制盲目扩张，必须进一步制定相关监管细则，厘清股权结构，强化公司内部管理，从而突出金控主业，建立协同机制。未来，

---

① 作者：童浩翔，《中国金融政策报告》项目助理研究员，供职于中国建设银行金融市场部。

需更加强调整体监管,以防范化解系统性风险为核心,明确金融控股公司资本充足率、公司治理等审慎监管标准,降低金融控股公司风险的复杂性、传染性和集中性,推动金融控股公司健康有序发展。

## 二、中国银行业主要监管政策[①]

(一) 2020年中国银行业监管政策主要内容

一是做好疫情防控相关金融服务,有力支持国民经济复苏。

第一,指导银行做好金融服务,确保疫情期间金融秩序不乱、服务不断。2020年面对突如其来的新冠肺炎疫情的冲击,银行业监管部门统筹做好疫情防控和经济社会发展金融服务工作,不断满足工商企业和人民群众金融需求。1月31日人民银行和银行业监管部门等五部门联合印发《关于进一步强化金融支持防控新型冠状病毒感染肺炎疫情的通知》,加大对疫情防控相关领域的信贷支持力度,为受疫情影响较大的地区、行业和企业提供差异化优惠的金融服务。2月1日人民银行和银行业监管部门等四部门联合发布《关于做好春节假期后金融服务工作的通知》,强调切实做好支持疫情防控所必需的金融服务,以及人民群众生活必需的金融需求,确保金融市场平稳有序运行。3月26日银行业监管部门出台《关于加强产业链协同复工复产金融服务的通知》,加大产业链核心企业金融支持力度,优化产业链上下游企业金融服务,推动产业链协同复工复产,着力提升金融服务质效。

第二,强化普惠金融支持力度,提高金融服务实体经济水平。2020年银行业监管部门协调推进普惠金融发展各项工作,引导银行做好小微等普惠金融重点领域和薄弱环节的服务。3月1日银行业监管部门等五部门联合发布《关于对中小微企业贷款实施临时性延期还本付息的通知》,要求银行业金融机构对中小微企业贷款实施一定期限的临时性延期还本付息安排,并为湖北地区配备专项信贷规模,实施内部资金转移定价优惠。3月10日银行业监管部门印发《关于优化银行业金融机构分支机构变更营业场所事项的通知》,支持和鼓励银行业金融机构持续优化分支机构网点布局,增加对金融服务薄弱地区的金融服务供给,扩大普惠金融覆盖面。5月26日人民银行和银行业监管部门等八部门联合印发《关于进一步强化中小微企业金融服务的指导意见》,要求银行业金融机构落实中小微企业复工复产信贷支持政策,开展商业银行中小微企业金融服务能力提升工程,优化商业银行监管政策外部激励和完善金融企业绩效评价制度。6月1日人民银行和银行业监管部门等五部门发布《关于加大小微企业信用贷款支持力度的通知》,各银行业金融机构要增加对小微企业的信贷资源配置,支持更多小微企业获得免抵押担保的纯信用贷款支持;同日,人民银行和银行业监管部门等五部门联合印发《关于进一步对中小微企业贷款实施阶段性延期还本付息的通知》,缓解企业尤其是中小微企业年内还本付息资金压力,进一步对符合条件的贷款实施阶段性延期还本付息,同时对地方法

---

[①] 作者:周金飞,浦发银行战略发展与执行部高级分析师。

人银行办理延期还本普惠小微贷款给予适当奖励。6月29日银行业监管部门制定并印发《商业银行小微企业金融服务监管评价办法（试行）》，从评价体系、评价机制、评价流程及评价结果运用等方面全面科学评价商业银行小微企业金融服务工作开展情况和成效，督促和激励商业银行提升服务小微企业的质效。8月5日银行业监管部门等七部门发布《关于做好政府性融资担保机构监管工作的通知》，要求政府性融资担保机构坚守准公共定位，弥补市场不足，聚焦支小支农主业，稳步提高小微企业和"三农"融资担保在保余额占比，支持小微企业及"三农"发展。

第三，支持供应链产业链发展，降低企业综合融资成本。2020年银行业监管部门推动银行业金融机构持续加大减费让利力度，规范发展供应链金融，缓解企业融资难融资贵问题。5月18日银行业监管部门等六部门联合发布《关于进一步规范信贷融资收费降低企业融资综合成本的通知》，从信贷环节、助贷环节、增信环节及考核环节四个方面规范信贷融资收费与管理，维护企业知情权、自主选择权和公平交易权，降低企业融资综合成本。9月18日人民银行和银行业监管部门等八部门发布《关于规范发展供应链金融 支持供应链产业链稳定循环和优化升级的意见》，明确供应链金融的内涵和发展方向，推动供应链金融规范、发展和创新，加强供应链金融配套基础设施建设，完善供应链金融政策支持体系，防范供应链金融风险，严格对供应链金融的监管约束。

二是聚焦重点领域风险管控，保障金融市场健康平稳发展。

第一，建立健全重点领域规章制度，弥补监管制度短板。2020年银行业监管部门把弥补监管制度短板作为一项重要任务持续推进，不断夯实银行业高质量发展的制度保障。2月20日银行业监管部门印发《关于预防银行业保险业从业人员金融违法犯罪的指导意见》，明确预防银行业金融违法犯罪案件的基本原则，重点强化预防银行业重点领域的金融违法犯罪案防要求，进一步强调银行业金融机构公司治理等方面的内控和行业自律机制作用。5月26日银行业监管部门发布《关于印发融资租赁公司监督管理暂行办法的通知》，明确融资租赁公司的业务范围、融资渠道、租赁物范围及禁止业务，明确规定融资租赁公司的监管指标，整改空壳、失联和违法违规经营的企业，明确监管分工。6月30日银行业监管部门发布《关于印发金融租赁公司监管评级办法（试行）的通知》，从评级要素和评级方法、评级操作流程、分类监管等方面，全面评估金融租赁公司的经营管理与风险状况，合理配置监管资源，促进金融租赁公司持续健康发展。7月12日银行业监管部门发布《商业银行互联网贷款管理暂行办法》，从风险管理体系、风险数据和风险模型管理、信息科技风险管理及贷款合作管理等方面规范商业银行互联网贷款业务经营行为，推进商业银行互联网贷款业务健康发展。7月14日银行业监管部门发布《关于印发融资担保公司非现场监管规程的通知》，围绕融资担保公司非现场监管工作职责分工和非现场监管流程，在信息收集与核实、风险监测与评估、信息报送与使用、监管措施等方面作出了规定，完善融资担保公司监管报表和指标解释，监督融资担保公司的经营行为。9月7日银行业监管部门发布《关于加强小额贷款公司监督管理的通知》，从业务经营、经营管理、行业秩序和支持力度四个方面加强对小额贷款公司的监督管理,促进小额贷款公司行业规范健康发展。11月2日人民银行和银保监会起草《网络小额贷款业务管理暂行办法(征求意见稿)》,从业务准入、业务范围和基本规则、经营管理、监督管理及法律责任等方面加以明确说明,保障小额贷款公司及客户的合法权益。12月30日银行业监管部门发布《关于印发消费金融公司监管评级办法(试行)的通知》,明确从公司治理与内控、资本管理、风险管理、专业服务质量及信息科技管理等方面监管评级消费金融公司,评级要素由定量和定性两类评级指标组成。

第二,整治金融市场乱象,保障金融消费者合法权益。2020年银行业监管部门继续整治金融市场乱象,切实保护广大金融消费者合法权益,督促市场经营主体严格依法合规开展金融活动。1月14日银行业监管部门出台《银行业保险业消费投诉处理管理办法》,明确银行业金融机构处理消费投诉的受理渠道、受理范围、处理时限等程序要求,要求银行业金融机构建立健全溯源整改、责任追究制度及投诉处理回避制度,并规定银行业金融机构不得拒绝接受消费者合理投诉诉求。5月8日银行业监管部门印发《关于加强典当行监督管理的通知》,从完善准入管理、依法合规经营、压实监管责任、整顿行业秩序及优化营商环境五个方面指导各地加强典当行业事前、事中和事后监管,促进典当行业规范发展。10月26日人民银行发布《中国人民银行关于规范代收业务的通知》,从付款人授权与付款人开户机构管理、收款人与代收机构管理、代收业务适用场景及清算机构业务规范等方面进行明确,保障当事人合法权益。12月9日人民银行发布《规范人民币现金收付行为有关事项的公告》,从现金收付主体规范、现金收付服务主体规范及现金收付生态规范等方面加以明确,保障公众使用现金的权益。12月30日银行业监管部门起草《金融机构反洗钱和反恐怖融资监督管理办法(修订草案征求意见稿)》,从金融机构反洗钱内部控制和风险管理、反洗钱监督管理及法律责任等方面进行阐述明确。

第三,稳妥推进重点领域风险处置,守住不发生系统性风险的底线。2020年是打好防范化解金融风险攻坚战收官之年,银行业监管部门持续有序处置问题金融机构,有效缓解重点领域风险。7月3日人民银行会同银行业监管部门等联合发布《标准化债权类资产认定规则》,明确标准化债权类资产与非标准化债权类资产的清晰界定,并明确标准化债权类资产认定路径,引导新增债权类资产向债券等标准化债权类资产规范转型。9月9日银行业监管部门发布《银行保险机构应对突发事件金融服务管理办法》,明确突发事件定义、应对基本原则和组织管理制度安排,既要求做好基本金融服务,又鼓励提供金融支持措施,强调提供金融服务和金融支持的同时要守住风险底线,规定有针对性地调整监管方式和要求。9月30日人民银行和银行业监管部门联合发布《关于建立逆周期资本缓冲机制的通知》,明确我国逆周期资本缓冲的计提方式、覆盖范围及评估机制,并将综合考虑宏观经济金融形势、杠杆率水平、银行体系稳健性等因素,定期评估和调整逆周期资本缓冲要求,防范系统性金融风险。

三是深化金融业改革和对外开放,推动银行业高质量发展。

第一,深化金融供给侧结构性改革,推动银行业高质量发展。2020年银行业监管部门多渠道全面深化金融供给侧结构性改革,加大重点领域和薄弱环节的金融服务体系建设。3月5日人民银行和银行业监管部门等六部门联合印发《统筹监管金融基础设施工作方案》，加强对我国金融基础设施的统筹监管与建设规划，包括金融资产登记托管系统、清算结算系统、交易设施、交易报告库、重要支付系统、基础征信系统等六类设施及其运营机构。12月28日人民银行和银行业监管部门联合发布《关于建立银行业金融机构房地产贷款集中度管理制度的通知》，明确房地产贷款集中度管理制度的机构覆盖范围、管理要求及调整机制，综合考虑银行业金融机构的资产规模、机构类型等因素，分档设置房地产贷款余额占比和个人住房贷款余额占比两个上限，对超过上限的机构设置过渡期，并建立区域差别化调节机制。12月30日银行业监管部门发布《关于深化银行业保险业"放管服"改革 优化营商环境的通知》，营造公开、公平、公正的银行业市场准入环境，持续推动银行业监管简政放权，进一步提升事中、事后监管效能，切实提高银行业金融机构服务质效。12月31日人民银行和银行业监管部门等六部门联合发布《关于进一步优化跨境人民币政策 支持稳外贸稳外资的通知》，涵盖围绕实体经济需求推动更高水平贸易投资人民币结算便利化、进一步简化跨境人民币结算流程、优化跨境人民币投融资管理、便利个人经常项下人民币跨境收付、便利境外机构人民币银行结算账户使用等五个方面内容。

第二，支持国家重大区域发展战略，深化金融业对外开放。2020年银行业监管部门联合其他部门引导银行业金融机构围绕国家重大区域发展战略，推进区域金融业对外开放。2月14日人民银行和银行业监管部门等四部门及上海市人民政府联合发布《关于进一步加快推进上海国际金融中心建设和金融支持长三角一体化发展的意见》，推进临港新片区金融先行先试，加快上海金融业对外开放，从金融机构跨省市协作等三方面支持长三角一体化发展，高标准对接国际规则，建设优质金融环境。4月24日人民银行和银行业监管部门等四部门发布《关于金融支持粤港澳大湾区建设的意见》，聚焦促进粤港澳大湾区跨境贸易和投资便利化，扩大金融业对外开放，促进金融市场和金融基础设施互联互通，提升粤港澳大湾区金融服务创新水平，切实防范跨境金融风险。

四是完善金融业监管方式与制度，提高金融监管有效性及针对性。

第一，持续优化金融业监管方式，提高金融监管有效性。2020年银行业监管部门不断完善金融业监管规则，督促银行业金融机构合规健康发展。5月22日银行业监管部门发布《关于印发银行保险机构涉刑案件管理办法（试行）的通知》，明确案件定义分类和信息报送、案件风险事件定义和信息报送、案件处置及案件监督管理，进一步规范和加强银行机构涉刑案件管理工作，提出要依法、及时、稳妥处置案件。6月23日银行业监管部门发布《关于开展银行业保险业市场乱象整治"回头看"工作的通知》，主要内容包括看主体责任是否落实到位，看实体经济是否真正受益，看整改措施是否严实有效，看违法违规是否明显遏制以及看合规机制是否健全管用。8月17日银行业监管部门发布《关于印发健全银行业保险业公司治理三年行动方案（2020—2022年）的通知》，从推动党的领导与公司治理有机融合、开展公司治理全面评估、规范股东行为、提升董事会等治理主体的履职质效、健全激励约束机制、加强利益相关者权益保护等方面深化银行业公司治理改革,加强公司治理监管。

第二,制定差异化监管政策,提升金融监管针对性。2020年银行业监管部门不断完善差异化监管政策,推动银行业金融机构高质量发展。9月30日人民银行会同银行业监管部门起草《全球系统重要性银行总损失吸收能力管理办法(征求意见稿)》,明确总损失吸收能力规则的基本原则、外部总损失吸收能力的风险加权比率和杠杆比率的计算方法及达标要求,同时还明确外部总损失吸收能力的构成和外部总损失吸收能力的扣除项。12月2日人民银行和银行业监管部门联合发布《系统重要性银行评估办法》,从评估目的、评估方法及评估流程三个方面建立系统重要性银行评估与识别机制,根据名单对系统重要性银行进行差异化监管,完善我国系统重要性金融机构监管框架。12月18日人民银行发布《规范商业承兑汇票信息披露》,完善市场化约束机制,规范金融机构办理商业承兑汇票行为,保障持票人合法权益。

(二)2020年中国银行业监管政策效果

一是支持国民经济迅速从停滞下滑恢复到正常发展。新冠肺炎疫情暴发后,银行业监管部门坚持人民至上生命至上,制定一系列政策措施,紧急提供专项信贷5.3万亿元,全力支持打赢疫情防控总体战、阻击战。截至2020年末,人民币贷款比年初增加19.6万亿元,累计对6.6万亿元贷款实施延期还本付息,发放应急贷款242.7亿元,全年实现向实体经济让利1.5万亿元目标,有力支持复工复产和"六稳""六保"。全年新增制造业贷款2.2万亿元,超过前5年总和。新增民营企业贷款5.7万亿元,比上年多增1.5万亿元。全国普惠型小微企业贷款余额15.3万亿元,增速超过30%,其中5家大型银行增长54.8%。

二是高风险金融机构和重点领域风险得到有序处置。银行业风险从快速发散转为逐步收敛,一批重大问题隐患"精准拆弹",牢牢守住了不发生系统性风险的底线。银行业监管部门持续做好包商银行风险处置,依法接管"明天系"6家保险、信托机构,安邦集团结束接管。稳妥推进高风险中小银行、信托机构风险处置,全年处置银行业不良资产3.02万亿元,2017年至2020年处置不良贷款超过之前12年总和。有序拆解高风险影子银行业务,房地产贷款增速8年来首次低于各项贷款增速,全国实际运营的P2P网贷机构全部归零,探索金融反垄断治理机制。配合地方党委政府化解大型企业集团债务风险,处置一批重大非法集资案件。

三是银行业改革开放取得积极进展。银行业监管部门持之以恒推进完善银行业金融机构公司治理,深化党的领导和公司治理有机融合,严格规范股权管理,强化董监高等治理主体履职监督。印发中小银行深化改革和补充资本工作方案,积极推动发行2000亿元地方政府专项债补充中小银行资本,全面部署推进城商行、农信社改革化险工作。稳步扩大金融对外开放,推动更多对外开放措施落地,积极审核外资机构市场准入申请。自2018年以来,共批准外资银行和保险公司来华设立近100家各类机构。目前,我国商业银行体系不断优化,市场竞争充分,四家大型商业银行经营效率已接近国际先进水平,在劳动生产率、成本收入比、盈利能力、科技创新等方面实现赶超。

四是强监督强监管的良好氛围基本形成。银行业监管部门坚定不移加强党风廉政建设和金融反腐败斗争，强化监督执纪，一批官商勾结、利益输送、违法侵占的腐败分子被绳之以法。严格执行公私分开、履职回避和监管问责，2020年银保监系统共纪律处分164人。加快补齐监管短板，堵塞制度漏洞，2020年完成61项监管规章制度建设。重拳治理乱象，保持案件处罚问责高压态势，2020年处罚违法违规银行保险机构3178家次，处罚责任人员4554人次，罚没金额合计22.8亿元。推动金融纠纷多元化解，清退、赔付消费者177亿元，切实保护金融消费者合法权益。

面对当前复杂的国内外经济金融形势，银行业监管还有待进一步完善。主要表现在：金融有效服务实体经济的体制机制还需加快构建；现代金融监管体系还有待完善；高风险影子银行业务还需持续整治；反垄断和防止资本无序扩张还需持续强化；银行业金融机构公司治理还需持续加强；金融法治化水平还需进一步提高；监管科技还需大力发展，监管效能还需持续提升。

（三）2021年中国银行业监管政策展望

2021年是全面建设社会主义现代化国家新征程开启之年，也是"十四五"开局之年。银行业监管部门重点将立足新发展阶段，贯彻新发展理念，构建新发展格局，持续深化金融供给侧结构性改革，着力提升服务实体经济质效，深入推进改革开放，切实防范化解金融风险，全力维护经济金融安全和社会政治稳定。

第一，为构建新发展格局提供有力支持，进一步提升金融服务整体效能。2021年银行业监管部门将全力支持构建新发展格局，积极探索促进科技创新的各种金融服务，持续促进扩大内需，推动巩固拓展脱贫攻坚成果与乡村振兴有效衔接。积极发展绿色信贷和绿色信托，加强外贸领域综合金融服务，稳步推进银行业高水平对外开放。同时，银行业监管部门还将保持对经济恢复的必要支持力度，强化对中小微企业的金融支持，持续加大首贷、续贷、信用贷款、中长期贷款投放力度。加强民生领域金融支持，保护金融消费者合法权益。

第二，防范化解金融风险，大力规范整治重点业务。2021年银行业监管部门将努力保持宏观杠杆率基本稳定，严格落实房地产贷款集中度管理制度和重点房地产企业融资管理规定，并将继续做好不良资产处置，加快推动高风险机构处置，完善重大案件风险和重大风险事件处置机制，加大对非法金融以及"无照驾驶"的打击力度，积极防范外部风险冲击。同时，银行业监管部门还将持续整治影子银行，对高风险影子银行业务的新形式新变种露头就打，对理财存量资产处置不力的机构加大监管力度，深入整治金融市场乱象，大力整治名实不符金融产品。

第三，加强对互联网平台金融活动监管，持续深化金融供给侧结构性改革。2021年银行业监管部门将依法对金融活动全面纳入监管，对同类业务、同类主体一视同仁，加强对银行业金融机构与互联网平台合作开展金融活动的监管，坚决遏制垄断和不正当竞争行为，防止资本在金融领域的无序扩张和野蛮生长。同时，银行业监管部门还将持续改革优化银行业金融机构体系，支持中小银行多渠道补充资本金，继续推动发行地方政府专项债补充资本,推动大型银行向中小银行输出风控工具和技术,有序推进村镇银行改革化险和兼并重组。

第四,持续提升公司治理和内控管理水平,加强监管能力建设。2021年,银行业监管部门将落实股东承诺制,加强股东穿透审查,依法规范大股东行为,持续清理违法违规股东,建立重大违法违规股东常态化公开披露机制,加强关联交易监管制度建设和系统建设,提升董事监事履职能力,完善董事会监事会运行规则,大力倡导合规文化建设。同时,银行业监管部门还将提高严格执法能力,对重大风险和重大案件,做到执法必严、过罚相当,提高全流程监管能力,强化事前预警和早期介入,强化事中干预,完善事后风险处置机制,提高协同监管能力和科技运用能力。

## 附表

**2020年中国银行业主要监管政策**

| 日期 | 政策名称 | 发文单位 |
| --- | --- | --- |
| 1月14日 | 银行业保险业消费投诉处理管理办法 | 银保监会 |
| 1月31日 | 关于进一步强化金融支持防控新型冠状病毒感染肺炎疫情的通知 | 人民银行、财政部、银保监会、证监会、外汇局 |
| 2月1日 | 关于做好春节假期后金融服务工作的通知 | 人民银行、银保监会、证监会、外汇局 |
| 2月14日 | 关于进一步加快推进上海国际金融中心建设和金融支持长三角一体化发展的意见 | 人民银行、银保监会、证监会、外汇局、上海市人民政府 |
| 2月20日 | 关于预防银行业保险业从业人员金融违法犯罪的指导意见 | 银保监会 |
| 3月1日 | 关于对中小微企业贷款实施临时性延期还本付息的通知 | 银保监会、人民银行、发展改革委、工业和信息化部、财政部 |
| 3月5日 | 统筹监管金融基础设施工作方案 | 人民银行、发展改革委、财政部、银保监会、证监会、外汇局 |
| 3月10日 | 关于优化银行业金融机构分支机构变更营业场所事项的通知 | 银保监会 |
| 3月26日 | 关于加强产业链协同复工复产金融服务的通知 | 银保监会 |
| 4月24日 | 关于金融支持粤港澳大湾区建设的意见 | 人民银行、银保监会、证监会、外汇局 |
| 5月8日 | 关于加强典当行监督管理的通知 | 银保监会 |
| 5月18日 | 关于进一步规范信贷融资收费 降低企业融资综合成本的通知 | 银保监会、工业和信息化部、发展改革委、财政部、人民银行、市场监管总局 |
| 5月22日 | 关于印发银行保险机构涉刑案件管理办法(试行)的通知 | 银保监会 |
| 5月26日 | 关于进一步强化中小微企业金融服务的指导意见 | 人民银行、银保监会、发展改革委、工业和信息化部、财政部、市场监管总局、证监会、外汇局 |
| 5月26日 | 关于印发融资租赁公司监督管理暂行办法的通知 | 银保监会 |

续表

| 日期 | 政策名称 | 发文单位 |
|---|---|---|
| 6月1日 | 关于加大小微企业信用贷款支持力度的通知 | 人民银行、银保监会、财政部、发展改革委、工业和信息化部 |
| 6月1日 | 关于进一步对中小微企业贷款实施阶段性延期还本付息的通知 | 人民银行、银保监会、财政部、发展改革委、工业和信息化部 |
| 6月23日 | 关于开展银行业保险业市场乱象整治"回头看"工作的通知 | 银保监会 |
| 6月29日 | 关于印发商业银行小微企业金融服务监管评价办法（试行）的通知 | 银保监会 |
| 6月30日 | 关于印发金融租赁公司监管评级办法（试行）的通知 | 银保监会 |
| 7月3日 | 标准化债权类资产认定规则 | 人民银行、银保监会、证监会、外汇局 |
| 7月12日 | 商业银行互联网贷款管理暂行办法 | 银保监会 |
| 7月14日 | 关于印发融资担保公司非现场监管规程的通知 | 银保监会 |
| 8月5日 | 关于做好政府性融资担保机构监管工作的通知 | 银保监会、发展改革委、工业和信息化部、财政部、农业农村部、商务部、人民银行 |
| 8月17日 | 关于印发健全银行业保险业公司治理三年行动方案（2020—2022年）的通知 | 银保监会 |
| 9月7日 | 关于加强小额贷款公司监督管理的通知 | 银保监会 |
| 9月9日 | 银行保险机构应对突发事件金融服务管理办法 | 银保监会 |
| 9月18日 | 关于规范发展供应链金融 支持供应链产业链稳定循环和优化升级的意见 | 人民银行、工业和信息化部、司法部、商务部、国资委、市场监管总局、银保监会、外汇局 |
| 9月30日 | 全球系统重要性银行总损失吸收能力管理办法（征求意见稿） | 人民银行、银保监会 |
| 9月30日 | 关于建立逆周期资本缓冲机制的通知 | 人民银行、银保监会 |
| 10月26日 | 关于规范代收业务的通知 | 人民银行 |
| 11月2日 | 网络小额贷款业务管理暂行办法（征求意见稿） | 人民银行、银保监会 |
| 12月2日 | 系统重要性银行评估办法 | 人民银行、银保监会 |
| 12月9日 | 规范人民币现金收付行为有关事项的公告 | 人民银行 |
| 12月18日 | 规范商业承兑汇票信息披露 | 人民银行 |
| 12月28日 | 关于建立银行业金融机构房地产贷款集中度管理制度的通知 | 人民银行、银保监会 |
| 12月30日 | 关于印发消费金融公司监管评级办法（试行）的通知 | 银保监会 |
| 12月30日 | 关于深化银行业保险业"放管服"改革 优化营商环境的通知 | 银保监会 |
| 12月30日 | 金融机构反洗钱和反恐怖融资监督管理办法（修订草案征求意见稿） | 人民银行 |
| 12月31日 | 关于进一步优化跨境人民币政策 支持稳外贸稳外资的通知 | 人民银行、发展改革委、商务部、国资委、银保监会、外汇局 |

专栏 16

### 精准施策，金融抗"疫"政策"组合拳"成效显著[①]

2020年初，突如其来的新冠肺炎疫情，无论是对中国还是对全世界都产生了巨大的冲击，使原本处于衰退进程中的全球经济更是雪上加霜。多项数据表明，2020年全球经济的衰退程度超过2008年全球金融危机，且仅次于1929年大萧条。

新冠肺炎疫情暴发后，党中央、国务院高度重视并有效推进疫情防控和经济发展，及时采取多项举措，精准施策，不仅在较短时间内成功地控制住了疫情蔓延，而且不失时机努力地推进复工复产，使我国成为2020年全球唯一实现经济正增长的主要经济体。

新冠肺炎疫情暴发以来，金融系统认真贯彻落实党中央、国务院决策部署，多个部门围绕受疫情冲击较大的领域、行业、企业和居民，精准而高效地制定和实施了一系列金融政策，支持各地疫情防控，确保金融服务畅通，助力生产生活恢复，稳住经济基本盘，形成了金融抗"疫"的中国最佳实践。

自2020年1月26日以来，人民银行、银保监会、证监会、外汇局等部门积极主动并及时精准地制定和实施了多项金融宏观调控政策，综合运用货币、利率、信贷、投资等多种政策工具，向企业减息让利，降低企业融资成本，拓宽企业融资渠道，保持流动性合理充裕，为疫情防控和经济恢复提供了有力的金融支撑。主要举措包括：一是保持流动性合理充裕，通过专项再贷款等手段，支持金融机构加大信贷支持力度。二是通过中央财政安排贴息资金，降低企业融资成本。三是合理调度金融资源，保障人民群众日常金融服务。四是通过延期还本付息、增加信用贷款、拓宽融资渠道、降低贷款利率等多种方式，进一步提高对中小微企业的金融支持力度，确保中小微企业得到"精准滴灌"。五是保障金融基础设施安全，维护金融市场平稳有序运行。

上述金融抗"疫"政策"组合拳"的精准有效实施，显著地降低了疫情对各领域、各行业、广大企业和广大居民的负面冲击，有力地推动了保供稳价、复工复产和经济恢复，不仅是打赢疫情防控阻击战的重要支撑，而且是推动经济社会恢复的关键因素。在此次疫情大考中，我国金融系统探索出了行之有效的金融抗"疫"的中国模式，这既是我国集中力量办大事的制度优势在金融系统中的具体体现，也是我国金融政策部门可以迅速调配金融资源的能力所在。实践表明，我国金融系统不仅可以确保金融"大动脉"不会因为遭受疫情冲击而发生"中梗阻"，而且还可以很好地处理疫情防控与经济恢复之间的关系，用合理的代价取得最大的成效。

尽管我国疫情防控取得了巨大成功，经济增长也已经恢复常态，但是，需要引起高度重视的是，疫情仍在全球蔓延，世界形势依然严峻，国内疫情防控仍有薄弱环节，经济恢复基础尚不牢固，消费和投资增长乏力，中小微企业困难重重，防范金融风险任务依然艰巨。这意味着，在疫情防控常态化的背景下，精准有效地实施金融宏观调控政

---

[①] 作者：张伟，清华大学国家金融研究院副院长。

策，助力经济恢复和增长，依然任重道远。

### 三、中国证券业主要监管政策[①]

(一) 2020 年证券业监管政策主要内容

1. 逐步推进以全面注册制为核心的基础制度改革

创业板改革并试点注册制。2020 年 6 月 12 日，证监会发布了《创业板首次公开发行股票注册管理办法（试行）》（以下简称《创业板首发办法》）、《创业板上市公司证券发行注册管理办法（试行）》（以下简称《创业板再融资办法》）、《创业板上市公司持续监管办法（试行）》（以下简称《创业板持续监管办法》）和《证券发行上市保荐业务管理办法》（以下简称《保荐办法》）。与此同时，证监会、深圳证券交易所（以下简称深交所）、中国证券登记结算有限责任公司（以下简称中国结算）、中国证券业协会等发布了相关配套规则。

修改完善后的《创业板首发办法》共 7 章 75 条。主要内容包括：一是精简优化创业板首次公开发行股票的条件，将发行条件中可以由投资者判断的事项转化为更加严格的信息披露要求，强调按照重大性原则把握企业的法律合规性和财务规范性问题。二是对注册程序作出制度安排，实现受理和审核全流程电子化和全流程公开，减轻企业负担，提高审核透明度。三是强化信息披露要求，严格落实发行人等相关主体在信息披露方面的责任，制定针对创业板企业特点的差异化信息披露规则。四是明确市场化发行承销的基本规则，并规定定价方式、投资者报价要求、最高报价剔除比例等事项应同时遵守深交所相关规定。五是强化监督管理和法律责任，加大对发行人、中介机构等市场主体违法违规行为的追责力度。

修改完善后的《创业板再融资办法》共 7 章 93 条。主要内容包括：一是明确适用范围，上市公司发行股票、可转换公司债券、存托凭证等证券品种适用《创业板再融资办法》。二是精简优化发行条件，区分向不特定对象发行和向特定对象发行，差异化设置各类证券品种的再融资条件。三是明确发行上市审核和注册程序，深交所审核期限为 2 个月，证监会注册期限为 15 个工作日。同时，针对"小额快速"融资设置简易程序。四是强化信息披露要求，要求有针对性地披露业务模式、公司治理、发展战略等信息，充分揭示可能对公司核心竞争力、经营稳定性以及未来发展产生重大不利影响的风险因素。五是对发行承销作出特别规定，就发行价格、定价基准日、锁定期，以及可转债的转股期限、转股价格、交易方式等作出专门安排。六是强化监督管理和法律责任，加大对上市公司、中介机构等市场主体违法违规行为的追责力度。

修改完善后的《创业板持续监管办法》共 35 条。主要内容包括：一是明确适用原则，创业板公司应遵守上市公司持续监管的一般规定，但《创业板持续监管办法》另有

---

[①] 作者：蒋健蓉，申万宏源研究所副所长、首席研究员，《中国金融政策报告》项目（课题组）高级研究员；谢云霞，申万宏源研究所资深高级研究员。

规定的除外。二是明确公司治理相关要求，并针对存在特别表决权股份的公司作出专门安排。三是建立具有针对性的信息披露制度，强化行业定位和风险因素的披露，突出控股股东、实际控制人等关键少数的信息披露责任。四是明确股份减持要求，适当延长未盈利企业控股股东、实际控制人、董监高的持股锁定期。五是完善重大资产重组制度，明确创业板上市公司并购重组涉及发行股票的实行注册制，并规定重组标的资产要求等。六是调整股权激励制度，扩展可以成为激励对象的人员范围，放宽限制性股票的价格限制，并进一步简化限制性股票的授予程序。

本次《保荐办法》修订的主要内容有：一是与新《证券法》保持协调衔接，调整审核程序相关条款，完善保荐代表人管理。二是落实创业板注册制改革要求，明确发行人及其控股股东、实际控制人配合保荐工作的相关要求，细化中介机构执业要求，督促中介机构各尽其责、合力把关，提高保荐业务质量。三是强化保荐机构内部控制要求，将保荐业务纳入公司整体合规管理和全面风险管理范围，推动行业自发形成合规发展、履职尽责的内生动力和自我约束力。四是加大问责力度，丰富监管措施类型，提高违法违规成本。

此外，为做好创业板改革并试点注册制具体实施工作，证监会配套制定、修订了《创业板首次公开发行证券发行与承销特别规定》《公开发行证券的公司信息披露内容与格式准则第 28 号——创业板公司招股说明书》等 6 部规范性文件，与《创业板首发办法》《创业板再融资办法》一并发布。深交所制定、修订了业务规则，主要涉及上市条件、审核标准、股份减持制度、持续督导等方面。中国证券业协会制定了有关创业板发行承销的自律规则。中国结算制定、修订了登记结算、转融通等方面的业务规则。

科创板再融资办法出台，进一步完善科创板试点注册制的重大决策部署。按照《证券法》和《关于在上海证券交易所设立科创板并试点注册制的实施意见》，2020 年 7 月 3 日，证监会发布《科创板上市公司证券发行注册管理办法（试行）》（以下简称《科创板再融资办法》）。修改完善后的《科创板再融资办法》共 7 章、93 条，主要包括以下内容：一是明确适用范围，上市公司发行股票、可转换公司债券、存托凭证等证券品种的，适用《科创板再融资办法》。二是精简优化发行条件。区分向不特定对象发行和向特定对象发行，差异化设置各类证券品种的再融资条件。三是明确发行上市审核和注册程序。上交所审核期限为两个月，证监会注册期限为十五个工作日。同时，针对"小额快速"融资设置简易程序。四是强化信息披露要求，要求有针对性地披露行业特点、业务模式、公司治理等内容，充分披露科研水平、科研人员、科研资金投入等信息。五是对发行承销作出特别规定，就发行价格、定价基准日、锁定期，以及可转债的转股期限、转股价格、交易方式等作出专门安排。六是强化监督管理和法律责任，加大对上市公司、中介机构等市场主体违法违规行为的追责力度。

为推动新三板各项改革措施平稳落地，完善新三板改革配套细则。2020 年 1 月 13 日，证监会对《非上市公众公司信息披露内容与格式准则第 3 号——定向发行说明书和发行情况报告书》《非上市公众公司信息披露内容与格式准则第 4 号——定向发行申请文件》(以下统称定向发行格式准则)进行修订，同时制定《非上市公众公司信息披露内容与格式准则第9号——创新层挂牌公司年度报告》和《非上市公众公司信息披露内容与格式准则第10号——基础层挂牌公司年度报告》(以下统称创新层、基础层年报格式准则)。1月17日，证监会发布了《非上市公众公司信息披露内容与格式准则第11号——向不特定合格投资者公开发行股票说明书》《非上市公众公司信息披露内容与格式准则第12号——向不特定合格投资者公开发行股票申请文件》(以下统称公开发行格式准则)。

本次修订定向发行格式准则，主要依据《非上市公众公司监督管理办法》，调整了以下几方面内容：一是统一定向发行的要求，将信息披露及申报文件要求的适用范围扩大至全体公众公司；二是完善信息披露内容，明确了发行股份购买资产等方面的披露要求，细化了募集资金用途等披露要求；三是督促中介机构勤勉尽责，补充了对中介机构发表意见的要求；四是继续推进简政放权，明确挂牌公司申请定向发行需要履行行政许可的，由全国中小企业股份转让系统有限责任公司（以下简称全国股转公司）先行出具自律监管意见，作为申请行政许可的必备文件。

本次制定创新层、基础层年报格式准则，主要依据《非上市公众公司信息披露管理办法》，细化创新层、基础层挂牌公司的年度报告披露要求。一是明确创新层、基础层年报的差异化披露要求，同时对披露内容进行适当简化。二是借鉴科创板改革成果，以投资者需求为核心，提升年报信息披露的可读性、有用性。三是从中小企业特点出发，强化对创新层、基础层公司经营业绩影响较大的风险因素的披露。

本次发布公开发行格式准则，主要依据《非上市公众公司监督管理办法》，规范了以下几方面内容：一是提出公开发行信息披露的总体要求，明确发行人及中介机构相关各方的主体责任；二是明确公开发行说明书的披露内容和章节设置要求，要求发行人重点披露业务与技术、公司治理、财务会计信息和募集资金运用等方面信息；三是规定公开发行申请文件的制作和报送要求，并列明申请文件目录。

新三板转板机制建立。2020年6月3日，为规范转板上市行为，统筹协调不同上市路径的制度规则，做好监管衔接，证监会发布《关于全国中小企业股份转让系统挂牌公司转板上市的指导意见》(以下简称《指导意见》)。建立转板上市机制是落实党中央、国务院决策部署的重要举措，有助于丰富挂牌公司上市路径，打通中小企业成长壮大的上升通道，加强多层次资本市场的有机联系，增强金融服务实体经济能力。《指导意见》主要内容包括三个方面。一是基本原则。建立转板上市机制将坚持市场导向、统筹兼顾、试点先行、防控风险的原则。二是主要制度安排。对转入板块的范围、转板上市条件、程序、保荐要求、股份限售等事项作出原则性规定。三是监管安排。明确证券交易所、全国股转公司、中介机构等有关各方的责任。对转板上市中的违法违规行为，依法依规严肃查处。上交所、深交所、全国股转公司、中国结算等将依据《指导意见》制定或修订业务规则，进一步明确细化各项具体制度安排。

进一步完善新三板披露制度。2020年7月22日，按照证监会党委关于深化新三板改革工作的统一部署,证监会发布《非上市公众公司监管指引第 5 号——精选层挂牌公司持续监管指引(试行)》(以下简称《监管指引》)及五项挂牌公司定期报告格式准则。制定《监管指引》,主要有三个方面的目的:一是从新三板市场实际情况出发,建立适合精选层公司特点的持续监管制度;二是以行政规范性文件的形式对精选层公司的监管要求进行强化,为加强精选层公司行政监管、结合市场分层实施分类监管奠定制度基础;三是借鉴上市公司监管经验,针对精选层公司构建证监会、派出机构和全国股转公司"三点一线"的工作机制,提高监管效能。本次制定的五项挂牌公司定期报告格式准则,包括精选层年度报告、中期报告及季度报告格式准则,创新层、基础层中报格式准则。制定过程中坚持以下原则:一是精选层、创新层、基础层三个层次之间的披露要求呈梯度化,依次降低;二是注重层次内部规则衔接,中期报告披露要求低于年度报告,高于季度报告;三是以现有新三板监管规则为基础,借鉴上市公司制度理念,充分体现挂牌公司特点。

规范新三板实施股权激励和员工持股计划。2020 年 8 月 21 日,为深化新三板改革,支持鼓励民营经济、中小企业创新发展,进一步发挥新三板市场服务实体经济的功能,证监会发布了《非上市公众公司监管指引第 6 号——股权激励和员工持股计划的监管要求(试行)》(以下简称《监管指引》)。《监管指引》坚持市场化、法治化原则,扩大公司自主决策空间,丰富员工持股计划形式,强化市场约束机制,发挥主办券商督导作用,明确了适应新三板市场实践和挂牌公司特点的股权激励和员工持股计划监管规则。《监管指引》分三个部分:第一部分规定了股权激励的对象、激励方式、定价方式、股票来源、条件、必备内容和各方权利义务安排,对绩效考核指标、分期行权、信息披露以及实施程序等进行规定。其中,股权激励的方式主要是限制性股票和股票期权,股票来源主要为发行新股、回购股票和股东赠与。第二部分规定了员工持股计划的资金和股票来源、持股形式、管理方式和信息披露要求。其中按管理方式分为委托管理型和自我管理型两类,委托管理型应备案为金融产品且持股 12 个月以上,自我管理型需"闭环运行"至少 36 个月,两类员工持股计划在参与发行时均视为一名股东,无需穿透或还原。第三部分附则主要规定禁止利用股权激励和员工持股计划进行内幕交易等违法违规活动。

再融资迎来政策暖春,上市公司再融资大幅松绑。为深化金融供给侧结构性改革,完善再融资市场化约束机制,增强资本市场服务实体经济的能力,助力上市公司抗击疫情、恢复生产,2020 年 2 月 14 日证监会发布《关于修改〈上市公司证券发行管理办法〉的决定》《关于修改〈创业板上市公司证券发行管理暂行办法〉的决定》《关于修改〈上市公司非公开发行股票实施细则〉的决定》。此次再融资制度部分条款调整的内容主要包括:一是精简发行条件,拓宽创业板再融资服务覆盖面。取消创业板公开发行证券最近一期末资产负债率高于 45% 的条件;取消创业板非公开发行股票连续 2 年盈利的条件;将创业板前次募集资金基本使用完毕,且使用进度和效果与披露情况基本一致由发行条件调整为信息披露要求。二是优化非公开制度安排,支持上市公司引入战略投资者。上市公司董事会决议提前确定全部发行对象且为战略投资者的，定价基准日可以为关于本次非公开发行股票的董事会决议公告日、股东大会决议公告日或者发行期首日；调整非公开发行股票定价和锁定机制，将发行价格由不得低于定价基准日前20个交易日公司股票均价的9折改为8折；将锁定期由36个月和12个月分别缩短至18个月和6个月，且不适用减持规则的相关限制；将主板（中小板）、创业板非公开发行股票发行对象数量由分别不超过10名和5名，统一调整为不超过35名。三是适当延长批文有效期，方便上市公司选择发行窗口。将再融资批文有效期从6个月延长至12个月。

2. 全方位改善投资生态，提升投资功能

（1）提高上市公司质量

六维度提升上市公司质量。2020年10月9日，国务院发布《关于进一步提高上市公司质量的意见》，从以下六个方面做出了要求和指示：一是提高上市公司治理水平，二是推动上市公司做优做强，三是健全上市公司退出机制，四是解决上市公司突出问题，五是提高上市公司及相关主体违法违规成本，六是形成提高上市公司质量的工作合力。为贯彻落实国务院《关于进一步提高上市公司质量的意见》提高上市公司治理水平的有关要求，中国证监会特别开展了上市公司治理专项行动。此次专项行动拟通过强化公司治理内生动力、完善公司治理制度规则、构建公司治理良好生态等方式，进一步健全各司其职、各负其责、协调运作、有效制衡的上市公司治理结构，夯实上市公司高质量发展的基础。上市公司对公司治理问题进行自查是此次专项行动的一项重要内容。上市公司在自查过程中遇到问题和困难，可及时与辖区证监局进行沟通，确保工作顺利进行。2020年12月31日，上海证券交易所（以下简称上交所）发布《上海证券交易所风险警示板股票交易管理办法（2020年12月修订）》的通知，进一步完善退市标准，简化退市程序，加大退市监管力度，保护投资者权益，这是继2020年5月后当年的第二次修订。为进一步完善市场化、常态化退市机制，更好发挥资本市场功能，保护投资者权益，上交所还对《上海证券交易所退市公司重新上市实施办法（2018年8月修订）》（上证发〔2018〕99号）进行了修订。

（2）规范股东及投资者行为

规范科创板上市公司股东以向特定机构投资者询价转让和配售方式减持股份的行为，保护投资者合法权益。根据《关于在上海证券交易所设立科创板并试点注册制的实施意见》《科创板上市公司持续监管办法（试行）》《上海证券交易所科创板股票上市规则》等规定，上交所制定了《上海证券交易所科创板上市公司股东以向特定机构投资者询价转让和配售方式减持股份实施细则》，自2020年7月22日起施行。

明确科创板上市公司可转债转股环节的投资者适当性管理要求。2020年12月4日，上交所发布《关于科创板上市公司向不特定对象发行的可转换公司债券转股环节投资者适当性管理相关事项的通知》，明确科创板非定向发行可转债转股环节的投资者适当性管理要求，按照科创板股票的投资者适当性管理要求执行。符合科创板股票投资者适当性管理要求的投资者，方可参与科创板非定向发行可转债的转股。

（3）培育中长期资金和机构投资者

允许公募基金投资新三板精选层股票，改善新三板投资者结构。2020年4月17日，中国证监会发布《公开募集证券投资基金投资全国中小企业股份转让系统挂牌股票指引》（以下简称《指引》）。《指引》主要作出如下安排：一是明确管理人要求和可参与投资的基金类型。要求基金管理人应具备相应投研能力，配备充足的投研人员。可参与投资的基金类型为股票基金、混合基金及中国证监会认定的其他基金。二是严格防控风险。规定基金的投资范围仅限于精选层股票。要求基金管理人在机构内控、产品设计、投资限制、申赎管理、流动性风险管理工具、估值披露等方面加强流动性风险管理，采用公允估值方法估值并依照证监会规定在法定情形下启用侧袋机制。要求基金管理人严格做好信息披露及风险揭示，切实做好投资者适当性管理。要求存量公募基金履行法定程序后，方可投资精选层股票。

完善创业投资基金反向挂钩政策，引导投长、投早、投中小、投科技。2020年3月6日，证监会修订并发布《上市公司创业投资基金股东减持股份的特别规定》（以下简称《特别规定》），上交所、深交所同步修订实施细则，3月31日正式实施。为进一步完善创业投资基金退出渠道，畅通"投资—退出—再投资"良性循环，促进创业资本形成，更好发挥创业投资对于支持中小企业、科创企业创业创新的作用，通过私募股权和创投基金助力疫情防控，加大对实体经济的支持力度，证监会对反向挂钩政策作了修订完善。一是简化反向挂钩政策适用标准。明确创业投资基金项目投资时满足"早期企业""中小企业""高新技术企业"三个条件之一即可享受反向挂钩政策，并删除基金层面"对早期中小企业和高新技术企业的合计投资金额占比50%以上"的要求。二是为激活大宗交易方式下受让方的交易动力，通过同步修订证券交易所实施细则，完善大宗交易环节反向挂钩政策，取消减持受让方锁定期限制。三是加大对专注于长期投资的基金的优惠力度，允许投资期限在五年以上的创业投资基金锁定期满后减持比例不受限制。四是合理调整期限计算方式，投资期限截至点由"发行申请材料受理日"修改为"发行人首次公开发行日"。五是拓宽享受反向挂钩政策的适用主体，在中国证券投资基金业协会依法备案的私募股权投资基金参照适用。

（4）丰富投资品种完善产品体系

基础设施领域不动产投资信托基金（REITs）试点工作开启并推进。为贯彻落实党中央、国务院关于防风险、去杠杆、稳投资、补短板的决策部署，积极支持国家重大战略实施，深化金融供给侧结构性改革，强化资本市场服务实体经济能力，进一步创新投融资机制，有效盘活存量资产，促进基础设施高质量发展，2020年4月24日，中国证监会和国家发展改革委发布《关于推进基础设施领域不动产投资信托基金（REITs）试点相关工作的通知》。基础设施REITs试点工作安排如下：①试点初期，由符合条件的取得公募基金管理资格的证券公司或基金管理公司，依法依规设立公开募集基础设施证券投资基金，经中国证监会注册后，公开发售基金份额募集资金，通过购买同一实际控制人所属的管理人设立发行的基础设施资产支持证券,完成对标的基础设施的收购,开展基础设施 REITs 业务。公开募集基础设施证券投资基金符合《证券法》《证券投资基金法》规定的,可以申请在证券交易所上市交易。②各省级发展改革委主要从项目是否符合国家重大战略、宏观调控政策、产业政策、固定资产投资管理法规制度,以及鼓励回收资金用于基础设施补短板领域等方面出具专项意见。各省级发展改革委要加强指导,推动盘活存量资产,促进回收资金用于基础设施补短板项目建设,形成投资良性循环。在省级发展改革委出具专项意见基础上,国家发展改革委将符合条件的项目推荐至中国证监会,由中国证监会、沪深证券交易所依法依规,并遵循市场化原则,独立履行注册、审查程序,自主决策。中国证监会各派出机构、沪深证券交易所与省级发展改革委加强协作,做好项目遴选与推荐工作。③中国证监会制定公开募集基础设施证券投资基金相关规则,对基金管理人等参与主体履职要求、产品注册、份额发售、投资运作、信息披露等进行规范。沪深证券交易所比照公开发行证券相关要求建立基础设施资产支持证券发行审查制度。中国证监会各派出机构、沪深证券交易所、中国证券业协会、中国证券投资基金业协会等有关单位要抓紧建立基础设施资产支持证券受理、审核、备案、信息披露和持续监管的工作机制,做好投资者教育和市场培育,参照公开发行证券相关要求强化对基础设施资产支持证券发行等环节相关参与主体的监督管理,压实中介机构责任,落实各项监管要求。此外,2020 年 8 月 6 日,证监会正式发布相关配套细则,即《公开募集基础设施证券投资基金指引(试行)》(以下简称《指引》)。《指引》共 51 条,主要包括以下内容:一是明确产品定义与运作模式。公开募集基础设施证券投资基金(简称基础设施基金)属于上市交易的封闭式公募基金,应具备以下条件:80%以上基金资产投资于基础设施资产支持证券,通过资产支持证券和项目公司等特殊目的载体取得基础设施项目完全所有权或经营权利;基金管理人主动运营管理基础设施项目以获取稳定现金流,并将 90%以上合并后基金年度可供分配金额按要求分配给投资者。二是压实机构主体责任,严控基础设施项目质量。强化基金管理人与托管人的专业胜任要求和诚实守信、谨慎勤勉的受托职责。聚焦优质基础设施资产,严把项目质量关。发挥外部管理机构、会计师事务所、评估机构等专业作用。三是明确基金份额发售方式,采取网下询价的方式确定基金份额认购价格,公众投资者以询价确定的认购价格参与基金份额认购。四是规范基金投资运作,加强风险管控,夯实投资者保护机制。明确基金投资限制、关联交易管理、借款安排、基金扩募、信息披露等要求,全面落实"以信息披露为中心",确保投资者充分知情权。五是明确证监会监督管理和相关自律组织管理职责,强化违规行为约束。

(5) 扩大国债期货市场参与主体

完善国债期货市场主体结构,允许商业银行、保险机构参与中国金融期货交易所国债期货交易。为进一步完善市场主体结构,经国务院同意,中国证监会、财政部、中国人民银行、中国银保监会发布《关于商业银行、保险机构参与中国金融期货交易所国债期货交易的公告》,明确符合条件的商业银行可以风险管理为目的,试点参与中国金融期货交易所国债期货交易；具备投资管理能力的保险机构可以风险管理为目的，参与中国金融期货交易所国债期货交易；商业银行、保险机构应在依法合规、风险可控、商业可持续的前提下，参与国债期货交易；参与国债期货交易的商业银行、保险机构，应建立完善的全面风险管理和内部控制制度及业务处理系统，具备专业的管理团队和规范的业务操作流程，防范和控制交易风险；中国证监会、财政部、中国人民银行、中国银保监会发挥跨部委协调机制作用，加强监管合作和信息共享，分批推进商业银行和保险机构参与国债期货市场交易，促进国债期货市场健康发展。

### 3. 加强中介机构审慎监管

进一步增强证券公司风控指标体系的有效性和适应性，推动证券行业持续稳健发展。2020年1月23日，证监会发布了《证券公司风险控制指标计算标准规定》（以下简称《计算标准》），于2020年6月1日正式施行。2016年6月16日，证监会发布了《证券公司风险控制指标管理办法》（以下简称《风控办法》）及配套风控指标计算标准，完善了以净资本和流动性为核心的证券公司风控指标体系。三年多来的实践表明，现行风控指标体系有效提升了证券公司风险管理水平，切实增强了行业抵御系统性风险的能力。同时，随着资本市场和证券行业的发展变化，有必要进一步完善证券公司风控指标体系，特别是部分新业务的计算标准，以适应新形势下风险管理和行业发展的需要。为此，2019年下半年以来，证监会起草了《计算标准》，并于2019年8月9日至9月9日向社会公开征求意见。《计算标准》遵循"框架不变、风险导向、局部完善、宽严相济"的原则，根据不同业务、产品的风险特征进行差异化调整，完善指标体系的科学性和完备性，进一步提升对证券公司资本配置的导向作用。与现行风控指标体系相比，调整完善的内容主要有以下五方面。一是鼓励价值投资，引入长期增量资金。对证券公司投资政策性金融债、指数基金、成分股等适度"松绑"，推动资本市场引入长期增量资金。二是有针对性地强化资本约束，防范突出风险点。重点规制股票质押、私募资产管理、私募基金托管和代销服务等高风险业务，并对高杠杆、高集中度资管产品、第一大股东高比例质押、履约保障比例较低等特定情形，进一步优化了计算标准。三是结合市场发展实践，提升指标体系完备性。结合"资管新规"以及近年来相继推出的沪伦通、科创板、信用衍生品、股指期权等新业务，明确风控指标计算标准，实现对证券公司业务和风险的全覆盖。四是满足差异化发展需求，择优释放资本空间。结合证券公司分类评价结果，将"连续三年A类AA级及以上的证券公司"的风险资本准备调整系数由0.7降至0.5，进一步提升优质券商的资本使用效率。与征求意见稿相比，《计算标准》从三个方面作了适度放宽：一是为引导行业防范股票质押业务增量风险、稳妥化解存量风险，对该业务的信用风险计算标准设置了"新老划断"的安排；二是优化了信用债券投资的计算标准，将AA级信用债券的市场风险计算比例由50%降至15%，将BBB级信用债券的计算比例由80%降至50%，并适当放宽上述信用债券的流动性指标计算标准，有利于行业在风险可控的前提下进一步支持各类企业特别是民营企业债券融资；三是为满足母子证券公司风险管理的合理需求，允许证券公司为其投行、资管等证券业务子公司提供的流动性担保承诺,计入子公司可用流动性资产转移。此外,为便于平稳有序过渡,《计算标准》设置了一定的过渡期,于2020年6月1日正式施行。

支持证券公司充实资本,增强风险抵御能力。2020年5月26日,证监会发布《关于修改〈证券公司次级债管理规定〉的决定》。此次《证券公司次级债管理规定》修改,主要包括以下内容:一是允许证券公司公开发行次级债券。二是为证券公司发行减记债等其他债券品种预留空间。三是统一法规适用。将规定中机构投资者定义统一至《证券期货投资者适当性管理办法》要求,将次级债券销售相关要求按照《公司债券发行与交易管理办法》进行调整。四是增加《国务院办公厅关于贯彻实施修订后的证券法有关工作的通知》《公司债券发行与交易管理办法》等作为上位法依据。

有效实施证券公司审慎监管,促进证券公司的业务活动与其治理结构、内部控制、合规管理、风险管理等情况相适应,实现持续规范发展。2020年7月10日,证监会发布了《关于修改〈证券公司分类监管规定〉的决定》。本次修改维持分类监管制度总体框架不变,适应证券行业发展状况和审慎监管需要,重点优化分类评价指标体系,集中解决实践中遇到的突出问题。主要修改内容包括:一是进一步强化合规、审慎经营导向。为更加准确反映证券公司的合规风控状况,完善对证券公司及其相关人员被采取行政监管措施、自律管理措施的扣分规则,明确对公司治理与内部控制严重失效等情形予以调降分类级别的依据,完善证券公司风险管理能力评价指标和标准。优化风险管理能力加分指标,促进证券公司强化资本约束,提高全面风险管理的有效性,切实实现风险管理全覆盖。二是进一步适应专业化、差异化发展需要。适应证券行业发展变化,从投资银行、资产管理、机构客户服务及交易、财富管理、盈利能力、信息技术投入等方面,优化调整业务发展状况评价指标,体现监管支持证券公司突出主业、做优做强,差异化、特色化发展的导向。修改后的《证券公司分类监管规定》再次强调,分类评价结果主要供证监会及其派出机构使用。证监会按照审慎监管、分类监管原则,对不同类别证券公司规定不同的风控指标标准和风险资本准备计算比例,进行针对性监管资源配置。证券公司不得将分类结果用于广告、宣传、营销等商业目的。

4. 推动资本市场高水平对外开放

完善合格境外机构投资者(QFII)、人民币合格境外机构投资者(RQFII)制度,推动外资享有国民待遇。2020年9月25日,经国务院批准,中国证监会、中国人民银行、国家外汇管理局发布《合格境外机构投资者和人民币合格境外机构投资者境内证券期货投资管理办法》(以下简称《QFII、RQFII办法》),中国证监会同步发布配套规则《关于实施〈合格境外机构投资者和人民币合格境外机构投资者境内证券期货投资管理办法〉有关问题的规定》。《QFII、RQFII办法》及配套规则自2020年11月1日起施行。《QFII、RQFII办法》及配套规则修订内容主要涉及以下方面:一是降低准入门槛,便利投资运作。将QFII、RQFII资格和制度规则合二为一,放宽准入条件,简化申请文件,缩短审批时限,实施行政许可简易程序;取消委托中介机构数量限制,优化备案事项管理,减少数据报送要求。二是稳步有序扩大投资范围。新增允许QFII、RQFII投资全国中小企业股份转让系统挂牌证券、私募投资基金、金融期货、商品期货、期权等，允许参与债券回购、证券交易所融资融券、转融通证券出借交易。QFII、RQFII 可参与金融衍生品等的具体交易品种和交易方式，将本着稳妥有序的原则逐步开放，由中国证监会商中国人民银行、国家外汇管理局同意后公布。三是加强持续监管。加强跨市场监管、跨境监管和穿透式监管，强化违规惩处，细化具体违规情形适用的监管措施等。随后不久，上交所正式发布了《上海证券交易所证券交易规则适用指引第 1 号——合格境外机构投资者和人民币合格境外机构投资者》（以下简称《指引》）；深交所发布了新修订的《深圳证券交易所合格境外机构投资者和人民币合格境外机构投资者证券交易实施细则》（以下简称《细则》）。总体来看，修订后的 QFII、RQFII 细则、指引，大致呈现以下变化。一是扩大投资范围。允许合格境外投资者投资存托凭证、股票期权、政府支持债券等，允许参与债券回购、融资融券、转融通证券出借交易。二是将外资持股初始披露比例从 26% 下调至 24%，其主要是由于近年来随着 A 股纳入 MSCI、富时罗素等国际重要指数，境外投资者投资 A 股的热情和信心不断增强。在与境外投资者和金融机构交流的过程中，不少投资者和机构提出，希望可以及时了解外资对上市公司整体持股水平，以便有更充分的时间作出反应。

5. 进一步防范和化解金融风险

资管新规过渡期延长一年。2020 年 7 月 31 日，为平稳推动资管新规实施和资管业务规范转型，经国务院同意，人民银行会同发展改革委、财政部、银保监会、证监会、外汇局等部门审慎研究决定将资管新规过渡期延长一年至 2021 年底，这是疫情突发背景下有力的应对举措。

促进可转债市场规范发展，避免可转债被过分炒作。2020 年 12 月 31 日，为落实新《证券法》的规定，完善可转换公司债券（以下简称可转债）各项制度，防范风险，保护投资者合法权益，证监会近日发布《可转换公司债券管理办法》（以下简称《管理办法》）。《管理办法》共 23 条，涵盖交易转让、信息披露、转股、赎回、回售、受托管理、监管处罚、规则衔接等内容。一是关于交易制度。要求证券交易场所根据可转债的风险和特点，完善现行交易规则，防范和抑制过度投机，同时要根据正股所属板块的投资者适当性要求，制定相应的投资者适当性管理规则；明确强制赎回条款触发前后发行人的信息披露要求；明确证券交易场所的风险监测职责等。二是关于信息披露。以《证券法》第 80 条、第 81 条关于信息披露的规定为基础，结合可转债的特点以及交易所实际监管经验，对临时披露重大事件进行了完善。三是关于转股价格。按照兼顾发行人、股东与可转债持有人权益的原则，结合现行再融资办法，对上市公司发行可转债转股价格的确定、修正及调整进行了完善。四是关于受托管理制度。依照《证券法》第 92 条规定建立可转债受托管理制度，明确受托管理人职责要求等。五是关于监管处罚。对于违反《管理办法》规定的行为，证监会将采取相关监管措施；依法应予行政处罚的，依照有关规定进行处罚；情节严重的，对有关责任人员采取证券市场禁入措施；涉嫌犯罪的，依法移送司法机关追究刑事责任。六是关于规则衔接。《管理办法》不改变可转债现有发行规则，同时为上市公司向特定对象发行可转债购买资产预留一定的制度空间。七是关于新老划断。《管理办法》施行日及施行日以后发行申请被受理的可转债适用本办法，但是本办法有关交易规则、投资者适当性、信息披露、赎回回售等交易环节的要求，一体适用于已经发行和尚未发行的可转债。

进一步提升公募基金风险防控能力，更好地保护投资者合法权益。借鉴境外市场成熟经验，2020年7月10日，证监会发布《公开募集证券投资基金侧袋机制指引（试行）》（以下简称《指引》）。修改完善后的《指引》共17条，一是明确侧袋机制是在符合法定条件下将难以合理估值的风险资产从基金组合资产中分离出来进行处置清算，确保剩余基金资产正常运作的机制。二是规定了侧袋机制的启用条件、实施程序和主要实施环节的操作要求。三是压实基金管理人的风险管控主体责任，着力规范费用收取、信息披露等投资运作环节及相关内部控制，并明确托管人和会计师事务所职责，形成管理人内部约束、公众监督、外部专业机构制衡的机制。侧袋机制的推出，有利于进一步丰富公募基金的流动性风险管理工具，缓解特定情形下因基金赎回引发的潜在系统性风险，也可防范先赎占优等行为，保障投资者合法权益。下一步，证监会将按照《指引》以及相关法律法规的要求，督促基金管理人练好内功、筑牢防线，持续提升公募基金风险管控能力，并及时总结实践经验，不断完善优化监管制度。

统筹加强私募基金监管和促进行业规范可持续发展。私募基金行业在快速发展同时，也伴随着各种乱象，包括公开或者变相公开募集资金、规避合格投资者要求、不履行登记备案义务、错综复杂的集团化运作、资金池运作、利益输送、自融自担等，甚至出现侵占、挪用基金财产，非法集资等严重侵害投资者利益的违法违规行为，行业风险逐步显现，近年来以阜兴系、金诚系等为代表的典型风险事件对行业声誉和良性生态产生重大负面影响。2020年12月30日，证监会发布《关于加强私募投资基金监管的若干规定》（以下简称《规定》）。《规定》共14条，形成了私募基金管理人及从业人员等主体的"十不得"禁止性要求。主要内容如下：一是规范私募基金管理人名称、经营范围，并实行新老划断。二是优化对集团化私募基金管理人监管，实现扶优限劣。三是重申私募基金应当向合格投资者非公开募集。四是明确私募基金财产投资要求。五是强化私募基金管理人及从业人员等主体规范要求，规范开展关联交易。六是明确法律责任和过渡期安排。

完善和统一基金托管行业监管制度。2020年7月10日，中国证监会和中国银保监会联合发布《证券投资基金托管业务管理办法》（以下简称《托管办法》）。《托管办法》自2020年5月9日至6月23日向社会公开征求意见。同时，证监会和银保监会通过征求相关部委意见、召开座谈会、视频调研等多种形式听取了各方面的意见。《托管办法》修订内容主要涉及以下几个方面：一是按照国家金融业对外开放的统一安排，允许外国银行在华分行申请证券投资基金（以下简称基金）托管业务资格，净资产等财务指标可按境外总行计算，并明确境外总行应承担的责任，强化配套风险管控安排。执行中，外国银行在华子行一体适用。二是结合监管实践完善监管要求，适当调整基金托管人净资产准入标准,强化基金托管业务集中统一管理,完善基金托管人持续合规要求,进一步丰富行政监管措施,强化实施有效监管。三是持续推进简政放权,简化申请材料,优化审批程序,实行"先批后筹"。四是统一商业银行及其他金融机构的准入标准与监管要求,将非银行金融机构开展基金托管业务有关规定整合并入《托管办法》。《托管办法》出台后,证监会相应更新基金托管资格相关行政许可事项的服务指南,包括外国银行在华分行在内符合条件的金融机构均可依法报送相关申请。证监会将会同银保监会加强对基金托管人及基金托管业务的日常监管,持续强化执法力度,惩处违法违规行为,切实保护投资者合法权益。

优化公募基金销售监管制度,进一步完善基金销售行为规范、加强基金销售机构合规内控,强化投资者权益保护,优化基金市场生态,促进基金行业良性发展。2020年8月28日,证监会发布《公开募集证券投资基金销售机构监督管理办法》(以下简称《销售办法》)及配套规则,自2020年10月1日起施行。本次《销售办法》及配套规则修订主要涉及以下内容:一是强化基金销售活动的持牌准入要求,厘清基金销售机构及相关基金服务机构职责边界。明晰基金销售业务内涵外延,厘清基金销售机构与互联网平台合作的业务边界和底线要求,支持基金管理人、基金销售机构规范利用互联网平台拓展客户。二是优化基金销售机构准入、退出机制,着力构建进退有序、良性发展的基金销售行业生态。调整优化资格注册程序,实行"先批后筹";整合各类金融机构注册条件,进一步完善独立基金销售机构及其股东准入要求;引入基金销售业务许可证有效期延续制度,强化停止业务、吊销牌照等制度安排。三是夯实业务规范与机构管控,推动构建以投资者利益为核心的体制机制。突出强调基金销售行为的底线要求,细化完善投资者保护与服务安排;推动基金销售机构构建以投资者利益为核心、促进长期理性投资的考核体系;强化私募基金销售业务规范;增设"内部控制与风险管理"专章,要求各类基金销售机构健全与基金销售业务相匹配的内部制度。四是完善独立基金销售机构监管,促进独立基金销售机构专业合规稳健发展。完善对独立基金销售机构股权管理与内部治理的要求,强调展业独立性,并在合规风控、分支机构管理、展业范围等方面提出针对性要求。

(二)2020年证券业监管政策效果

2020年,资本市场发展稳中有进,各项监管政策效果逐步体现。

首先,资本市场服务实体经济能力显著增强。2020年首发IPO公司数为396家,募集总金额为4699.63亿元,分别同比增长95.07%与85.57%,有力地支持了实体经济恢复发展;2020年再融资公司数达到380家,总金额达到8854.34亿元,分别同比增长46.15%、26.10%。

其次,股票市场保持健康发展。一是股票市场容量稳步扩大,2020年末上市公司总计达到4154家,较上年末增长9.98%;二是股票市场预期正面,市值显著增长,2020年末总市值为79.7万亿元,同比增长34.46%;三是股票市场退出机制不断完善,2020年退市公司有20家,退市数量较上年同期上升了66.67%,监管力度不断加强。

再次,国债期货市场活跃度增强。2020年以单边计算的国债期货交割金额为209.0亿元,同比增长128.7%。

最后,资本市场法治化建设不断向前发展。2020年证监会共办理案件740件。其中,新启动调查353件(含立案调查282件);办理重大案件84件,同比增长34%;全年向公安机关移送及通报案件线索116件,同比增长一倍。

(三)2021年证券业监管政策展望

当今世界正经历百年未有之大变局,当前和今后一个时期,我国发展仍然处于重要战略机遇期。综观国内,我国经济已经进入高质量发展的新时代,以国内大循环为主体、国内国际双循环相互促进的新发展格局正在加快形成。资本市场作为经济活动的枢纽,联结和主导着经济新阶段的转型,在这个新时代中将肩负更加重要的历史使命,是我国经济和金融体制改革的新方位。

2021年1月28日,2021年证监会系统工作会议在京召开,会上研究部署了2021年资本市场改革发展稳定重点任务:一是把党的领导优势和资本市场发展规律有机结合,二是扎实推进全面深化资本市场改革,三是保持复杂环境下资本市场稳健发展势头,四是全面落实"零容忍"的执法理念和打击行动,五是坚决打赢防范化解重大金融风险攻坚战持久战,六是加快推进科技和业务的深度融合。具体来看,以下政策发布已箭在弦上,2021年有望出台。

1. 注册制有望全面铺开,配套制度持续完善

注册制有望全面铺开。在科创板、创业板已经推行注册制的基础上,2021年政府工作报告再度提出"稳步推进注册制改革",距离注册制的全面铺开或为时不远。从2019年的"设立科创板并试点注册制"到2020年的"改革创业板并试点注册制",再到2021年的"稳步推进注册制改革",这已经是连续第三年将"注册制"写进政府工作报告里。随着实行全面注册制的时机逐步成熟,资本市场改革有望继续深入,其中离不开注册制配套制度的进一步完善。

投资者关系管理有望进一步增强。强化投资者关系管理是提高上市公司质量的重要举措,也是投资者保护的重要内容。2005年7月,证监会发布了《上市公司与投资者关系工作指引(2005)》(以下简称《指引(2005)》),作为上市公司开展投资者关系管理工作的基本行为指南。实施以来,在指导上市公司开展投资者关系管理、推进上市公司规范运作、保护投资者合法权益等方面发挥了积极作用。近年来,资本市场全面深化改革的不断推进、证券市场基础制度的不断完善,对上市公司加强投资者关系管理提出了新的要求;上市公司投资者关系管理实践积累了新做法新经验,同时也出现了一些新情况新问题;资本市场双向开放背景下投资者关系管理需要与境外市场进一步接轨;互联网的发展也为投资者关系管理带来新的改变。因此有必要梳理总结近年来上市公司具体实践,对《指引(2005)》进行修订和完善,这也是贯彻落实好新《证券法》的重要举措。2021年2月5日,中国证监会对《指引(2005)》进行了修订,形成了《上市公司投资者关系管理指引(征求意见稿)》。

上市公司信息披露管理有望进一步增强。为落实2020年3月1日起施行的新《证券法》，持续加强信息披露监管，2020年7月24日，证监会就《上市公司信息披露管理办法（修订稿）》（征求意见稿）对外公开征求意见。《上市公司信息披露管理办法（修订稿）》（征求意见稿）主要修改以下内容：一是完善信息披露原则规定。新增了简明清晰、通俗易懂的原则要求，完善公平披露原则，同时明确自愿披露原则的相关要求，进一步鼓励自愿披露。二是完善临时报告事项。按照新《证券法》对临时报告事项进行了完善，如将"公司的实际控制人及其控制的其他企业从事与公司相同或者相似业务的情况发生较大变化""公司分配股利、增资的计划，公司股权结构的重要变化"等事项纳入临时报告；对于同时发行公司债券的上市公司，增加债券临时披露事项，明确披露要求。三是进一步强调董监高等相关主体的责任。强化董事会在定期报告披露中的责任，明确要求定期报告内容应当经董事会审议通过；要求董事、监事和高级管理人员无法保证定期报告内容的真实性、准确性、完整性或者有异议的，应当在书面确认意见中发表意见并陈述理由，上市公司应当披露；同时进一步明确控股股东、实际控制人的配合义务。此外，此次修订按照新《证券法》的相关规定，对指定媒体披露要求、会计师事务所的相关表述、法律责任等相关条文进行了调整，同时配合注册制对发行文件披露要求进行了完善，借鉴了科创板非交易时段信息披露的相关规定。

2. 培育机构投资者或再迈阔步

（1）资管新规配套细则有望查漏补缺持续完善

证券公司资管公募业务持牌放开。2020年7月31日，证监会就《公开募集证券投资基金管理人监督管理办法（征求意见稿）》（以下简称《管理人办法》）及相关配套规则公开征求意见。为增强公募基金行业服务实体经济能力，支持行业机构做优做强，创造良好的行业发展生态，证监会对《证券投资基金管理公司管理办法》进行修订，且更名为《公开募集证券投资基金管理人监督管理办法》。一，《管理人办法》第二条清晰地界定了公募基金管理人的构成，经核准取得公募基金管理人资格的证券公司资管子公司是公募基金管理人中的第一大类。二，优化公募牌照制度，适当放宽"一参一控"限制。《管理人办法》允许同一主体同时控制1家基金公司和1家公募持牌机构。同一主体或者受同一主体控制的不同主体控制的其他公募基金管理人数量不得超过1家，参股基金管理公司的数量不得超过2家，其中控制基金管理公司的数量不得超过1家，同时在公司治理等方面拉平公募持牌机构与基金公司的监管安排。

进一步规范证券期货经营机构私募资产管理业务。为有效防控金融风险，更好发挥资产管理业务促进资本形成、深化直接融资、服务实体经济的功能，2020年10月23日，中国证监会拟对《证券期货经营机构私募资产管理业务管理办法》《证券期货经营机构私募资产管理计划运作管理规定》进行修改，并起草和对外发布征求意见稿。修改的主要内容包括以下几方面。

一是进一步完善私募资管计划负债杠杆（总资产/净资产）的比例限制，加强逆回购风险管理。要求资管计划设定合理的负债比例上限，保持充足的现金或者其他高流动性金融资产偿还到期债务;明确对高比例投资单一资产、高杠杆产品的相关规范;要求集合资管计划合理分散逆回购交易的到期日、交易对手及回购证券的集中度,并按照穿透原则强化交易对手管理,健全质押品管理制度。

二是结合私募股权投资基金投资运作特征,优化相关制度安排。主要包括:豁免私募股权投资基金适用"同一证券期货经营机构管理的全部集合资产管理计划投资于同一资产的资金不得超过该资产的25%"的限制;完善分期缴付、开放参与等制度安排,满足私募股权投资基金等分期、分步投资的需要;与现行关于创业投资基金、政府产业投资基金的特殊规定做好衔接;对通过特殊目的载体间接投资未上市企业股权留出空间;放宽管理人自有资金参与比例限制,进一步满足管理人跟投的实际需要。

三是适当放宽期货经营机构相关投资限制。允许最近两期分类评价均为A类AA级的期货公司及其子公司设立投资标准仓单、场外衍生品等非标资产的资管产品,选取头部期货公司进行试点,充分发挥期货经营机构专业优势,提升服务能力与专业水平,满足实体企业风险管理需求。

四是对照新《证券法》,将相关条款中"具有证券相关业务资格的会计师事务所"的表述修改为"符合《证券法》规定的会计师事务所";落实简政放权要求,进一步精简有关备案、报告事项,切实解决多头报送的问题。

五是对照资管新规过渡期延长工作安排,将资管细则过渡期同步延长至2021年底。

(2)证券基金投资咨询业务或迎全面规范

投资咨询业务是基础性的资本市场中介服务,在消除资本市场信息不对称、促进中介机构专业化分工、加强投资者教育等方面,有积极作用。同时,由于市场快速发展和内外部环境变化,投资咨询业务发展中也暴露出一些突出问题,有必要根据行业发展情况,制定统一的部门规章,对投资咨询业务进行全面规范,以保障行业长期规范发展。为了规范证券基金投资咨询业务(以下简称投资咨询业务),保护投资者及相关当事人的合法权益,维护资本市场秩序,2020年4月17日,证监会就《证券基金投资咨询业务管理办法》(以下简称《管理办法》)公开征求意见。《管理办法》主要内容包括:一是明确业务类型和内涵,将《证券法》《证券、期货投资咨询管理暂行办法》规定的证券投资咨询业务、《证券投资基金法》规定的基金投资顾问业务整合为证券基金投资咨询业务,并具体划分为证券投资顾问业务、基金投资顾问业务、发布证券研究报告业务等类别;二是分类作出准入安排,明确从事证券基金投资咨询业务应依法经中国证监会核准或者注册,并依据上位法的规定,明确了具体准入要求和申请审批程序;三是加强合规内控要求,要求投资咨询机构健全合规管理、内部控制和风险管理;四是建立以机构为主体提供服务的业务组织方式,全面提升服务质量;五是完善人员管理和行为规范要求,严格从业人员和高管人员资质管理,要求投资咨询机构及从业人员诚实守信、勤勉尽责;六是健全退出机制,强化事后监管等。

3. 资本市场法律、监管体系建设进一步完善

监管措施的实施规则有望进一步优化。2020年3月27日,为进一步规范监督管理

措施的实施程序，充分发挥监督管理措施防范市场风险、维护市场秩序的作用，证监会在《证券期货市场监督管理措施实施办法（试行）》（以下简称2008年试行办法）基础上，结合新《证券法》有关规定，起草了《证券期货市场监督管理措施实施办法》（以下简称《实施办法》），并向社会公开征求意见。《实施办法》共31条，主要内容包括：一是明确监督管理措施的种类和设定，经梳理现有制度规则，列明16种常见的监督管理措施类型，并以"法律、行政法规、规章规定的其他监督管理措施"作为兜底，为后续出现新的监管措施类型预留空间。同时，为提高依法行政水平，加强自我规范，明确证监会规章以外的规范性文件不得设定监管措施。二是明确监管措施的适用，规定监管措施可以单独适用，也可以合并适用。三是明确实施监督管理措施的通用程序，实施监管措施应当有充分的证据、依据，采取部分监督管理措施的，应当履行事先告知程序，并可以通报相关单位。四是明确各类监管措施的具体实施程序，包括实施步骤、方式、矫正目标、时限等内容。五是明确作出监督管理措施决定的要求，实施机构应当及时作出监管措施，违法行为在二年内未被发现的，不再采取监管措施。明确监督管理措施决定书的内容、公开要求、送达程序等。

规范执法行为，促进严格、规范、公正、文明执法，防范执法风险。2020年7月17日，证监会在《行政处罚法》基础上，结合新《证券法》有关规定，就《证券期货违法行为行政处罚办法》（以下简称《处罚办法》）公开征求意见。《处罚办法》共39条，主要内容包括：一是明确立案调查条件和调查权限。《处罚办法》规定证监会及其派出机构发现涉嫌违反证券期货法律、法规和规章，符合相关条件的，经批准后应当立案调查。同时，为保障行政处罚工作依法顺利开展，结合新《证券法》，进一步明确细化了证监会及其派出机构执法权限和措施，以及不配合调查的情形及后果。二是规范调查取证行为。调查取证的规范性直接关系案件处理结果，是行政处罚的关键。《处罚办法》结合相关法律规定和执法实践，对取证要求、调查措施作了进一步明确。三是优化查审流程。探索多样化、差异化的查审模式，分类分层予以不同处理，提升案件查处效率。四是明确行刑衔接程序。结合执法实际，明确"直接刑事移送""先处罚后刑事移送""处罚、刑事移送并行"等三种模式，加强证券行政执法与刑事司法的有机衔接。五是落实执法公示和执法全过程记录制度，规定对执法全过程进行记录，行政处罚决定按照政府信息公开的规定予以公开。六是加强对当事人的权利保障和对执法人员的监督。

4. 继续深化资本市场高水平对外开放

继续推动债券市场对外开放。为了进一步加强中国债券市场对外开放的系统性、整体性、协同性，同步推进相关市场规则逐步统一，2020年9月2日，人民银行与证监会、国家外汇管理局共同起草了《关于境外机构投资者投资中国债券市场有关事宜的公告（征求意见稿）》，旨在明确中国债券市场对外开放的整体性制度安排，进一步便利境外机构投资者配置人民币债券资产。2020年9月21日，为推动中国债券市场整体开放，中国人民银行、国家外汇管理局起草了《境外机构投资者投资中国债券市场资金管理规定（征求意见稿）》，统一债券市场资金管理规则，进一步便利境外机构投资者投资中国债券市场。

## 附表

**2020 年中国证券业主要监管政策一览表**

| 日期 | 政策文件名称 | 发文单位 |
| --- | --- | --- |
| 2月14日 | 关于修改《上市公司证券发行管理办法》的决定 | 证监会 |
| 2月14日 | 关于修改《创业板上市公司证券发行管理暂行办法》的决定 | 证监会 |
| 3月6日 | 上市公司创业投资基金股东减持股份的特别规定 | 证监会 |
| 3月13日 | 证券期货规章制定程序规定 | 证监会 |
| 3月20日 | 关于修改部分证券期货规章的决定 | 证监会 |
| 4月17日 | 公开募集证券投资基金投资全国中小企业股份转让系统挂牌股票指引 | 证监会 |
| 6月12日 | 创业板首次公开发行股票注册管理办法（试行） | 证监会 |
| 6月12日 | 创业板上市公司证券发行注册管理办法（试行） | 证监会 |
| 6月12日 | 创业板上市公司持续监管办法（试行） | 证监会 |
| 6月12日 | 证券发行上市保荐业务管理办法 | 证监会 |
| 7月3日 | 科创板上市公司证券发行注册管理办法（试行） | 证监会 |
| 7月10日 | 证券投资基金托管业务管理办法 | 证监会、银保监会 |
| 7月10日 | 关于修改《首次公开发行股票并上市管理办法》的决定 | 证监会 |
| 7月10日 | 关于修改《科创板首次公开发行股票注册管理办法（试行）》的决定 | 证监会 |
| 7月10日 | 公开募集证券投资基金侧袋机制指引（试行） | 证监会 |
| 8月6日 | 公开募集基础设施证券投资基金指引（试行） | 证监会 |
| 8月28日 | 公开募集证券投资基金销售机构监督管理办法 | 证监会 |
| 9月25日 | 合格境外机构投资者和人民币合格境外机构投资者境内证券期货投资管理办法 | 证监会、人民银行、国家外汇管理局 |
| 10月30日 | 关于修改、废止部分证券期货规章的决定 | 证监会 |
| 12月10日 | 关于开展上市公司治理专项行动的公告 | 证监会 |
| 12月31日 | 可转换公司债券管理办法 | 证监会 |

## 专栏17

### 退市新规落地，强化市场约束[①]

2020年12月31日，沪深证券交易所发布了修订后的退市规则。退市新规的落地，进一步增强了我国上市公司退市制度的严肃性、规范性和可操作性，必将对我国资本市场的长期健康发展产生深远的影响。

1999年《证券法》初步确立退市制度框架以来，证监会先后进行了4次退市制度改革，建立了与市场发展阶段相适应的、相对完整的退市规则体系。但与成熟市场相

---

① 作者：杜书明，中国银河证券研究院副院长兼研究部总经理、《中国金融政策报告》项目（课题组）高级研究员。

比，我国资本市场退市不系统、不坚决、不彻底等问题仍然比较突出，年均退市率仍然偏低。

2019年12月28日，十三届全国人大常委会第十五次会议全体会议审议通过了新修订的《证券法》，修订后的《证券法》于2020年3月1日起施行。新《证券法》取消了对退市的具体要求，将退市标准交由交易所制定，为简化退市流程、强化退市制度的实施落地打开了充足的操作空间。10月5日，国务院印发《关于进一步提高上市公司质量的意见》，将健全上市公司退出机制作为一项重要任务，要求完善退市标准，简化退市程序，加大退市监管力度。11月2日，中央全面深化改革委员会审议通过《健全上市公司退市机制实施方案》，再次明确强调健全上市公司退市机制安排是全面深化资本市场改革的重要制度安排。11月3日公布的《中共中央关于制定国民经济和社会发展第十四个五年规划和二〇三五年远景目标的建议》中也明确提出了"建立常态化退市机制"。12月14日，沪深交易所发布退市配套规则征求意见稿。12月31日，沪深交易所正式发布新修订的《上海证券交易所股票上市规则》《深圳证券交易所股票上市规则》以及《上海证券交易所科创板股票上市规则》《深圳证券交易所创业板股票上市规则》等多项配套规则，退市新规正式落地。

退市新规加强与注册制改革的协同，吸收科创板、创业板退市改革试点经验，广泛借鉴了成熟市场的经验，对过去退市政策中的漏洞进行了有针对性的改进，对交易类退市、财务类退市、规范类退市和重大违法类强制退市的退市标准和退市程序进行了详细的规定，大大提高了退市的规范性和可操作性。在全部板块取消单一连续亏损退市指标，制定扣非净利润与1亿元营业收入组合财务指标，明确营业收入应当扣除与主营业务无关的业务收入和不具备商业实质的收入；进一步缩短退市流程，将财务类退市指标的退市流程缩短至两年；在保留"面值退市"等交易类退市标准的基础上，设置"3亿元市值"标准；增加信息披露及规范运作存在重大缺陷且拒不改正的标准；增加重大违法退市细化认定情形；设立风险警示板，优化相应交易安排等。同时，取消了暂停上市、恢复上市环节，优化退市整理期等，提高退市效率。

上市公司退市制度是资本市场的一项基础性制度，完善和优化退市规则，严格执行退市制度，使上市公司"有进有出"，将有助于加快垃圾公司、僵尸公司的出清，长期看，将有利于净化市场环境，强化资本市场约束，促进新陈代谢，进一步发挥资本市场资源优化配置功能。

### 四、中国保险业主要监管政策[①]

（一）2020年中国保险业主要监管政策分析

2020年，银保监会进一步加强金融监管、防范金融风险，聚焦重点领域风险管控，

---

[①] 作者：谈亮，德勤中国中国战略客户与市场主管合伙人、《中国金融政策报告》项目（课题组）高级研究员；徐倩倩，德勤中国金融服务高级经理。

牢牢守住风险底线。相关制度涵盖保险公司偿付能力管理、银行保险机构涉刑案件管理、互联网保险业务监管、公司治理监管等。同时，进一步深化保险改革和对外开放，深化保险资金运用、车险综合改革、意外险改革等，推进商业养老保险改革发展和健康保险稳步成长，推动高质量发展。相关制度涵盖保险机构业务改革、落实对外开放举措等。全年主要监管政策如下。

1. 强化金融科技监管，引导新型业态健康合规发展

金融行业数字化的快速发展，带来了网络安全、市场垄断、数据权属不清、消费者权益保护等方面的问题，影响市场公平和金融稳定。2020年下半年，针对金融科技的监管全面趋严，监管部门陆续在互联网保险、互联网存贷款、反垄断、金融控股集团、金融消费者权益保护等方面出台了新规。金融科技趋同传统金融业务，已全面纳入了监管体系，聚焦于强化约束资本无序扩张，维护公平竞争和金融市场秩序。

在保险领域，互联网与保险的融合速度加快，问题也在逐步显现，如非法经营、营销噱头、销售误导风险等。监管部门陆续出台了新规，规范互联网保险业务，促使其健康发展。

一是严格市场准入。12月7日，银保监会发布《互联网保险业务监管办法》（银保监会令2020年第13号），厘清互联网保险业务本质，规定互联网保险业务经营要求，强化持牌经营原则，强调"互联网保险业务应由依法设立的保险机构开展，其他机构和个人不得开展互联网保险业务"；定义持牌机构自营网络平台，规定持牌机构经营条件，明确非持牌机构禁止行为，包括但不限于"提供保险产品咨询服务，比较保险产品、保费试算、报价比价，为投保人设计投保方案，代办投保手续，代收保费"。销售宣传、技术支持等属于保险机构的主体责任，实质性和核心职能不再允许外包，进一步压实保险机构主体责任。

二是规范营销宣传。银保监会消费者权益保护局于2020年10月28日发布了《关于防范金融直播营销有关风险的提示》（2020年第5号风险提示），提醒社会公众防范直播营销中可能隐藏的销售误导等风险，也再次强调了"各金融机构应当落实金融营销宣传行为的主体责任，切实规范本机构及合作方的金融营销宣传行为"，体现了规范业务行为、营造健康、合规的互联网保险营销环境的要求。同时，《互联网保险业务监管办法》中强化了持牌机构管理责任，规定保险机构应为互联网保险营销宣传建立一系列管理制度，开展营销宣传信息审核、监测、检查，并承担合规主体责任；关于从业人员营销宣传，明确要求从业人员应在保险机构授权范围内开展互联网营销宣传，营销宣传内容应由所属保险机构统一制作等；关于营销宣传内容，也规定应遵循清晰准确、通俗易懂、符合社会公序良俗的原则，并与保险合同条款保持一致等。

三是加强互联网消费者权益保护。首先，强调充分保障消费者的知情权、自主选择权和公平交易权。如银保监会6月22日发布的《关于规范互联网保险销售行为可回溯管理的通知》（银保监发〔2020〕26号），明确规定销售页面应对保险产品进行充分说明，披露信息准确、完整；充分尊重消费者意愿，由投保人自主确认已阅读后，进入投

保流程，确保投保行为是消费者本人的真实意思表示；并设置单独页面向投保人展示说明免除保险人责任等重要条款等。其次，细化互联网保险销售行为可回溯的要求。上述两个监管规定（银保监发〔2020〕26号和银保监会令2020年第13号），均强调需实现"销售和服务等主要行为信息不可篡改并全流程可回溯"，明确互联网保险销售环节、页面内容和互动方式，严格管控互联网保险销售页面管理和销售过程记录，确保销售行为可还原，有效遏制销售误导，保护消费者合法权益。另外，规范客户信息保护。《互联网保险业务监管办法》要求保险机构建立客户信息保护制度，构建覆盖全生命周期的客户信息保护体系，防范信息泄露。

2. 细化监管重点业务领域，推动行业高质量发展

随着金融新业态的发展，非车业务增速迅猛。业务风险发生了变化，金融风险的聚集、交叉、传染也变得越来越复杂，野蛮生长的后遗症随之而来。5月8日银保监会发布的《信用保险和保证保险业务监管办法》（银保监办发〔2020〕39号），从经营规则、内控管理、监督管理等方面对信用保证保险业务提出明确要求。一是重点聚焦高风险的融资性信保业务的监管，区分融资性和非融资性信保业务，提高对融资性信保业务在经营资质、承保限额、基础建设等方面的监管要求。二是有收有放，兼顾监管与发展。一方面，压缩融资性信保业务的承保限额，扩大险种范围（即商业性出口信用保险）等，控制风险敞口。另一方面，设置弹性限额，鼓励保险公司为普惠型小微企业提供融资增信支持。通过适度调整业务类型，支持在风险可控的前提下探索发展新业务领域。三是强化内控管理，促进高质量发展。要求保险公司提升自身管控能力，进一步强化制度建设、系统建设、流动性管理、风险预警等。

另一方面，9月14日发布的《融资性信保业务保前管理操作指引》和《融资性信保业务保后管理操作指引》（银保监办发〔2020〕90号），针对融资性信保业务的保前风险管理和保后监测管理两大环节，细化要求建立标准化操作规范。一是细化了操作要求。《融资性信保业务保前管理操作指引》在销售管理、核保管理、承保管理、合作方管理、产品管理、系统和信息管理等方面作了细化要求；《融资性信保业务保后管理操作指引》在保后监控、逾期催收、理赔处理、代位追偿、投诉处理等方面作了细化要求。二是针对当前存在的突出问题建立操作标准。明确了销售管理的操作标准，如"在销售过程中充分做好投保提示，提示内容包括但不限于保证保险的功能和属性、产品的关键信息、违约后的债务追偿、人民银行征信系统信息上传"等；明确了核保和系统功能要求，如"保险公司要根据核保规则与流程要求，在系统中建立核保模块管理和反欺诈审核规则"等；强化合作方要求和过程管理，如"保险公司要制定销售、资金方、催收追偿等合作方管理制度，至少要明确合作方准入标准、评估体系和退出机制"等。

另外，银保监会于12月22日发布《责任保险业务监管办法》（银保监办发〔2020〕117号），作为国内首个责任险监管办法，该办法从承保边界、经营行为、保险服务、内控管理等方面进行规范。一方面，强调保险公司应当厘清责任保险与财产损失保险、保证保险、意外伤害保险等险种的关系，合理确定承保险种，规范保险服务，强化内控管

理等。另一方面，规范保险责任，通过负面清单形式，明确不得承保的风险或损失，并突出强调"不得以承保担保机构责任等形式实质承保融资性信用风险"，"不得通过责任保险承保履约信用风险或损失"等。

总体来看，这些关于非车业务的"整修"规定，有利于防范化解业务风险，回归保障本源，发挥增信属性，推动业务高质量发展，在普惠金融进程中发挥更大的作用。

3. 积极推进保险资金运用"放管服"改革，持续加强对保险资产负债管理硬约束

2020年，监管部门围绕保险资金运用出台了一系列的监管政策，进一步推进保险资金运用市场化改革，增强保险资金运用效率和监管效能，持续重风控、调结构，保障保险资金的安全，更好地服务实体经济发展。

一是深入推进"放管服"改革。9月4日银保监会发布的《关于保险资金投资债转股投资计划有关事项的通知》（银保监办发〔2020〕82号）明确，保险资金可以投资金融资产投资公司设立的债转股投资计划，体现了提升服务实体经济质效，优化保险资产配置结构的方向。9月7日，银保监会发布了《组合类保险资产管理产品实施细则》、《债权投资计划实施细则》和《股权投资计划实施细则》（银保监办发〔2020〕85号）等三个细则，明确三类产品的登记机制、投资范围、风险管理和监督管理等要求。推进简政放权，改革保险资产管理产品登记机制，提高三类产品的登记效率；完善了债权投资计划资金投向和信用增级要求，拓展了股权投资计划的投资范围，扩大社会有效投资。11月12日发布《关于保险资金财务性股权投资有关事项的通知》（银保监发〔2020〕54号），明确提出"保险资金开展财务性股权投资，可在符合安全性、流动性和收益性条件下，综合考虑偿付能力、风险偏好、投资预算、资产负债等因素，依法依规自主选择投资企业的行业范围"，取消财务性股权投资行业限于保险类企业、非保险类金融企业和与保险业务相关的养老、医疗等特定企业要求，允许保险机构自主选择投资行业范围；通过"负面清单＋正面引导"机制，拓宽保险资金投资的自主决策空间，提升保险资金服务实体经济能力。

二是推行保险机构投资管理能力的备案改革，着力加强事中事后监管。银保监会9月30日发布了《关于优化保险机构投资管理能力监管有关事项的通知》（银保监发〔2020〕45号），细化了保险机构投资管理能力建设标准要求。调整后，保险机构投资管理能力共有七类，包括信用风险管理能力、股票投资管理能力、股权投资管理能力、不动产投资管理能力、衍生品运用管理能力、债权投资计划产品管理能力、股权投资计划产品管理能力。能力标准主要在保险机构的组织结构设计、专业团队构成、制度体系建设、投资运作机制、风险控制体系、信息系统建设等方面做了详细的规定，并针对不同投资管理能力提出了差异化要求；取消投资管理能力备案管理，将保险机构投资管理能力管理方式调整为公司自评估、信息披露和持续监管相结合。这将进一步提升保险机构自主投资决策效率和投资主动性，形成保险机构、自律组织与监管机构各司其职、彼此支撑的监管体系，既实现了市场化改革，有利于激发保险资金投资活力；又通过调动保险机构自身合规意识与自律组织的监督管理，有机地增加了监管维度、频度与覆盖

度，全面压实了保险机构主体责任。

三是在有效控制风险的前提下，对保险公司权益类资产配置实施差异化监管。银保监会于7月17日印发《关于优化保险公司权益类资产配置监管有关事项的通知》（银保监办发〔2020〕63号），支持投资能力强的公司增加权益投资。根据保险公司偿付能力充足率、资产负债管理能力及风险状况等指标，明确八档权益类资产监管比例，权益类资产投资余额最高可占到上季末总资产的45%；强化对重点公司的监管，明确规定"保险公司上季末综合偿付能力充足率不足100%时，应当立即停止新增权益类资产投资"；以及当存在"上季末责任准备金覆盖率不足100%的人身险公司、最近一年资金运用出现重大风险事件、资产负债管理能力较弱且匹配状况较差、最近三年因重大违法违规行为受到银保监会处罚、具有重大风险隐患或被银保监会列为重点监管对象"等情形之一的，权益类资产监管比例不得超过15%。通过分类监管和适度提高投资比例，引导保险公司开展价值投资、长期投资和审慎投资，推动权益投资回归服务保险保障业务的本源。

4. 健全统一保险销售人员和销售渠道管理的监管框架体系

当前，保险业正在向高质量转型发展，消费者的保险需求更加多元化、复杂化，从业人员（保险销售人员、保险专业中介机构从业人员、保险代理人等）的能力水平须与消费者的保险需求以及保险产品的复杂程度相适应，因此，需要对从业人员实施更加精细化的管理。2020年，监管部门密集发布了相关监管政策，以建立销售人员管理制度体系，突出保险机构主体责任；并巩固近年来乱象治理成果，转变保险营销发展模式，深化保险中介市场改革。

一是加强保险销售人员和保险专业中介机构从业人员管理。从业人员直接面对保险消费者从事保险销售、咨询等服务，其素质水平、诚信状况直接关系到保险消费者的切身利益。银保监会于5月12日发布了《关于落实保险公司主体责任加强保险销售人员管理的通知》（银保监办发〔2020〕41号），从健全管理架构体系、杜绝销售人员"带病"入岗、持续提升销售人员职业素养、建设销售人员销售能力分级体系、建立销售人员队伍诚信体系、依法严厉处罚等方面对加强保险销售人员管理提出了要求。同日银保监会还发布了《关于切实加强保险专业中介机构从业人员管理的通知》（银保监办发〔2020〕42号），针对保险专业中介机构的特点和市场定位，从全面承担管理主体责任、加强统筹管理、严格招录管理、建立销售能力分级体系、严格诚信管理和监管等方面提出了明确要求。两个通知均明确了销售能力分级的监管要求，围绕从业人员管理过程链条中的主要环节，以及从入职到离职过程中的关键环节进行细化规定。

二是完善保险中介监管制度体系。银保监会于11月12日发布的《保险代理人监管规定》（银保监会令2020年第11号），把保险专业代理机构、保险兼业代理机构和个人保险代理人纳入规范调整，建立了相对统一的基本监管标准和规则。首先，对保险专业代理机构明确要求，主要包括：强化对保险专业代理机构股东的审查，并对股东的出资能力作出要求。同时，在资本金托管、治理结构、内控制度以及商业模式等方面作出规定，加强市场准入管理；加强分支机构管控，列明了设立分支机构应当符合的具体条件，同时进一步强化法人机构的管控责任；理顺后置审批流程。要求保险专业代理公司取得许可证后，应及时在监管信息系统中登记相关信息；提升最低注册资本，把区域性保险专业代理机构最低注册资本调整为2000万元等。其次，对保险兼业代理机构明确要求，主要包括：明确准入条件，以及法人持有许可证、授权分支机构经营的模式；完善退出机制，规定了保险兼业代理机构依法注销许可证的情形以及业务退出流程等。另外，首次提出了"独立个人保险代理人"概念，明确了保险代理机构从业人员的概念，将保险代理机构中从事销售保险产品或者进行损失勘查、理赔等业务的人员纳入规定，对其行为作出约束，并对违反规定的行为制定相应的罚则。

同时，银保监会于12月23日发布了《关于发展独立个人保险代理人有关事项的通知》（银保监办发〔2020〕118号），作为《保险代理人监管规定》的配套性文件，该通知对"建立独立个人保险代理人制度"内容进行了细化补充，从独立个人保险代理人定位、条件标准、行为规范、选拔机制、公司管理、监督管理等方面提出具体的要求。还明确了独立个人保险代理人不隶属团队、自主独立开展保险销售的本质特征，严格规定人员基本条件及选拔机制，着力规范人员从业行为，强调保险公司管控责任及监管部门监管责任。另外规定保险专业代理、保险经纪机构及其从业人员可参照执行独立个人保险代理人政策。

5. 持续完善保险机构公司治理机制，推动保险业切实提升公司治理质效

良好的公司治理是保险机构长期稳健运行的前提和基础。7月3日《经济日报》刊发中国人民银行党委书记、银保监会主席郭树清文章《完善公司治理是金融企业改革的重中之重》，提出要从多方面推动完善公司治理机制，涉及压实金融企业自身的主体责任，管理部门要把公司治理作为基础性的监管要求，要把加强党的领导和党的建设落到实处，依法清理规范金融企业股权关系，充分发挥市场、中介机构和各方面利益相关者的监督作用等。随后，银保监会副主席梁涛于7月15日在《中国金融》杂志发表《奋力构建中国特色银行保险业公司治理机制》指出，加强董事会建设是下一步健全银行保险业公司治理的重点。另外，股东股权和关联交易方面的问题是近年来中小银行保险机构乱象丛生的根源；良好的外部市场约束和利益相关者权益保护机制是中国特色银行保险业公司治理的重要组成部分。同时，银保监会官网于7月23日刊发银保监会副主席曹宇署名文章《优化体制机制建设，强化投资者保护，全面提升银行保险资管机构公司治理水平》，文章指出要推进完善符合我国资产管理行业特点的公司治理机制。应以保护投资者利益为核心，不断提高董事会履职效能；强化信息披露，提升运营管理的透明度；强化关联交易管理，严格防范利益输送；完善监管制度体系，强化监督管理等。

近年来，银保监会高度重视公司治理监管工作，不断完善监管制度体系，持续推进股东股权乱象整治，已经建立了全国统一的银行保险机构投资人股权管理不良记录，并于2020年7月首次向社会公开一批严重违法违规股东，此后又于12月公开第二批重大违法违规股东，把强化公司治理作为转变银行业保险业体制机制的重要着力点。

8月17日，银保监会在监管系统内印发了《健全银行业保险业公司治理三年行动方案（2020—2022年）》（银保监发〔2020〕40号，以下简称《方案》）。《方案》内容体现了问题导向、标本兼治、分类施策、统筹推进的原则。一是紧紧盯住当前银行业保险业公司治理存在的主要问题，提出针对性的改进措施；二是既着力于及时化解存量风险，又立足于构建健全公司治理的长效机制；三是在具体监管措施上充分考虑了不同类型机构公司治理的差异性；四是坚持系统论的思想，注重完善公司治理各环节的整体性和协同性。最终目标，就是落实《二十国集团/经合组织公司治理原则》，构建起中国特色银行业保险业公司治理机制。

《方案》共十个部分，涉及总体要求（包括指导思想、基本原则、总体目标）、党的领导与公司治理融合、公司治理评估、股东行为规范、董事会等治理主体履职、激励约束机制、利益相关者保护、外部市场约束、监管能力建设、组织保障等方面，是2020—2022年保险业公司治理监管的行动指南。其中，将推动党的领导与公司治理有机融合放在首要位置，提出要将党的领导融入公司治理进一步制度化、规范化、程序化，持续探索完善党的领导与公司治理有机融合的方式和路径，推动国有机构党组织切实发挥把方向、管大局、保落实的作用。另外，借鉴国际先进经验，《方案》充分吸收了前期银保监会关于《二十国集团/经合组织公司治理原则》在我国银行业保险业实施情况的评价结果。对于评价发现的差距和不足之处，研究提出了针对性的改进措施。如完善大股东行为约束机制，进一步明确包括股权董事在内的所有董事都要公平对待全体股东，改进董事提名和选任机制，推动机构建立并严格执行高标准的职业道德准则等。

6. 包括保险业在内的金控集团风险管理进入全口径监管时代

2020年是保险偿付能力监管体系二期工程紧锣密鼓研究、论证和测试阶段，因此保险偿付能力监管体系二期工程的正式发文尚未颁布。但是，监管对加强金融监管，防范金融风险，聚焦重点风险管控，牢牢守住风险底线的要求更加严格。9月11日人民银行发布《金融控股公司监督管理试行办法》（中国人民银行令〔2020〕第4号），对包括保险在内的金融控股公司，要求建立与其组织架构、业务规模、复杂程度和声誉影响相适应的全面风险管理体系；应当对纳入并表管理范围内所控股机构的公司治理、资本和杠杆率等进行全面持续管控，有效识别、计量、监测和控制金融控股集团的总体风险状况，包括信用风险、市场风险、流动性风险、操作风险、声誉风险、战略风险、信息科技风险以及集中度等其他风险。并且，应当建立与服务实体经济相适应的集团风险偏好体系，确定风险管理目标，确定各类风险的风险容忍度和风险限额，建立超限额处置机制等。该办法明确，对金控集团的资本、行为及风险进行全面、持续、穿透监管，防范金融风险跨行业、跨市场传递。

(二) 2021年保险监管政策展望

2021年1月，银保监会召开了2021年中国银保监会工作会议。会议以习近平新时代中国特色社会主义思想为指导，全面贯彻党的十九大和十九届二中、三中、四中、五中全会以及中央经济工作会议精神，回顾2020年主要工作，分析当前经济金融形势，部署2021年重点工作任务。

根据会议精神，2021年度保险业监管政策将很可能在以下方面有所强化和突破。一是为构建新发展格局提供有力支持。如推动巩固拓展脱贫攻坚成果与乡村振兴有效衔接，积极发展绿色保险，稳步推进保险业高水平对外开放等。二是进一步提升金融服务整体效能。如加强民生领域金融支持，推动发展养老、健康、责任、巨灾等保险，保护消费者合法权益等。三是毫不松懈防范化解金融风险。如完善重大案件风险和重大风险事件处置机制，加大对非法金融以及"无照驾驶"的打击力度，积极防范外部风险冲击等。四是大力规范整治重点业务。如深入整治保险市场乱象，大力整治名实不符金融产品等。五是切实加强对互联网平台金融活动的监管。如加强对保险机构与互联网平台合作开展金融活动的监管等。六是持续深化金融供给侧结构性改革。如持续改革优化保险机构体系，规范发展第三支柱养老保险。巩固车险改革，持续深化意外险和健康险改革，推进保险资金运用市场化改革和保险营销体制转型变革。七是持续提升公司治理和内控管理水平。如落实股东承诺制。加强股东穿透审查，依法规范大股东行为，持续清理违法违规股东，建立重大违法违规股东常态化公开披露机制；加强关联交易监管制度建设和系统建设。提升董事监事履职能力，完善董事会监事会运行规则。大力倡导合规文化建设。八是加强监管能力建设。如提高严格执法能力和全流程监管能力，强化事前预警和早期介入，强化事中干预，完善事后风险处置机制等。

2021年是"十四五"开局之年，银保监会以实现银行业保险业高质量发展的新突破、促进国民经济加快构建新发展格局为重心。新年伊始，银保监会密集出台了一系列监管政策或其征求意见稿。

一是持续提升公司治理水平。如《银行保险机构公司治理准则（征求意见稿）》，将作为保险业公司治理的纲领性制度；《银行保险机构董事监事履职评价办法（试行，征求意见稿）》，规范银行保险机构董事监事履职行为及评价。准则及评价办法的出台，是落实上述三年行动方案的具体措施，意味着对公司治理的监管升级。根据银保监会的规划，2021年重点研究完善公司治理监管横向和纵向协作机制，进一步促进公司治理监管权责清晰、协同高效和运行规范。继续加强制度建设，细化银行保险机构股权监管办法，优化董事会运作规则，完善信息披露、薪酬考核等方面的监管规制。

二是强化风险防控及内控管理水平。如修订并发布了《保险公司偿付能力管理规定》征求意见稿，对"偿二代"现行规则进行了全面修订，形成了"偿二代"二期工程20项监管规则修订稿（征求意见稿）和修订说明，目前在业内征求意见，预计将在2021年6月底或7月初发布。结合"偿二代"二期工程建设，监管明确偿付能力监管的三支柱框架，提高了保险偿付能力监管体系的风险针对性和风险覆盖面，从定性与定量的角度更加科学有效地反映出保险行业的风险变化情况，从而引导企业作出针对性的改进和管理，优化产品结构，调整投资策略等，提高险企自身的风险管理水平和风险抵御能力，进而保障保险行业的长期稳定发展。另外，银保监会还出台了《银行保险机构声誉风险管理办法（试行）》，明确了保险机构声誉风险管理全流程体系、常态化建设等重要内容,将推动机构更加重视消费者体验,努力提升服务意识和服务能力。

三是进一步推进"简政放权、放管结合、优化服务"。保险监管主体职责改革再进一步,行业监管逐步下沉,从功能监管到机构监管,保险公司监管正与银行接轨。2021年1月,银保监会发布的《人身保险公司监管主体职责改革方案》对银保监会、银保监局的监管职责进行了明确分工。其中,银保监会统筹整体监管政策;银保监会、银保监局分别承担直接监管公司和属地监管公司的行政许可事项、日常监管职责。再加上2020年7月发布的《财产保险公司、再保险公司监管主体职责改革方案》,保险业正式进入属地监管时代。

四是将大力规范整治重点业务,如与互联网平台合作开展对金融活动的监管,加大对非法金融、非法集资的打击力度,发布《防范和处置非法集资条例》;巩固车险改革,持续深化意外险和健康险改革,如发布《关于规范短期健康保险业务有关问题的通知》等,重点聚焦行业短期业务发展存在的突出问题,促进保险行业高质量发展。

五是落实深化金融供给侧结构性改革,主要包括在保险市场准入和市场退出方面的制度建设有所推进,车险改革向纵深推进,保险营销体制改革,特别是个人独立代理人制度向前稳步推进;借助金融科技加快数字化转型;进一步推动金融服务业双向开放等。

## 附表

**2020年中国保险业主要监管政策**

| 日期 | 政策文件名称 | 发文单位 | 文件号 |
| --- | --- | --- | --- |
| 1月3日 | 中国银保监会规范性文件管理办法 | 中国银保监会 | 中国银保监会令(2020年第1号) |
| 1月14日 | 中国银保监会信访工作办法 | 中国银保监会 | 中国银保监会令(2020年第2号) |
| 1月14日 | 银行业保险业消费投诉处理管理办法 | 中国银保监会 | 中国银保监会令(2020年第3号) |
| 1月17日 | 关于加快推进意外险改革的意见 | 中国银保监会 | 银保监办发〔2020〕4号 |
| 1月21日 | 关于强化人身保险精算监管有关事项的通知 | 中国银保监会 | 银保监办发〔2020〕6号 |
| 1月21日 | 关于印发普通型人身保险精算规定的通知 | 中国银保监会 | 银保监办发〔2020〕7号 |
| 1月23日 | 关于促进社会服务领域商业保险发展的意见 | 中国银保监会、国家发展改革委、教育部、民政部、司法部、财政部、人力资源和社会保障部、自然资源部、住房城乡和建设部、商务部、卫生健康委、税务总局、医保局 | 银保监发〔2020〕4号 |
| 1月31日 | 关于进一步强化金融支持防控新型冠状病毒感染肺炎疫情的通知 | 中国人民银行、财政部、银保监会、证监会、外汇局 | 银发〔2020〕29号 |

续表

| 日期 | 政策文件名称 | 发文单位 | 文件号 |
|---|---|---|---|
| 2月1日 | 关于做好春节假期后金融服务工作的通知 | 中国人民银行、银保监会、证监会、外汇局 | 银发〔2020〕30号 |
| 2月4日 | 关于废止和修改部分规范性文件的通知 | 中国银保监会 | 银保监发〔2020〕5号 |
| 2月7日 | 关于推广人身保险电子化回访工作的通知 | 中国银保监会 | — |
| 2月11日 | 关于进一步规范健康保障委托管理业务有关事项的通知 | 中国银保监会 | 银保监办发〔2020〕13号 |
| 2月14日 | 关于进一步加快推进上海国际金融中心建设和金融支持长三角一体化发展的意见 | 中国人民银行、银保监会、证监会、外汇局、上海市人民政府 | 银发〔2020〕46号 |
| 2月14日 | 关于商业银行、保险机构参与中国金融期货交易所国债期货交易的公告 | 中国证监会、财政部、人民银行、中国银保监会 | 证监会公告〔2020〕12号 |
| 2月19日 | 关于进一步加强和改进财产保险公司产品监管有关问题的通知 | 中国银保监会 | 银保监办发〔2020〕17号 |
| 2月20日 | 关于预防银行业保险业从业人员金融违法犯罪的指导意见 | 中国银保监会 | 银保监办发〔2020〕18号 |
| 3月18日 | 保险资产管理产品管理暂行办法 | 中国银保监会 | 中国银保监会令（2020年第5号） |
| 3月25日 | 关于长期医疗保险产品费率调整有关问题的通知 | 中国银保监会 | 银保监办发〔2020〕27号 |
| 3月26日 | 关于加强产业链协同复工复产金融服务的通知 | 中国银保监会 | 银保监办发〔2020〕28号 |
| 4月9日 | 关于做好2020年银行业保险业服务"三农"领域重点工作的通知 | 中国银保监会 | 银保监办发〔2020〕31号 |
| 4月16日 | 关于金融资产投资公司开展资产管理业务有关事项的通知 | 中国银保监会 | 银保监发〔2020〕12号 |
| 4月24日 | 关于金融支持粤港澳大湾区建设的意见 | 中国人民银行、银保监会、证监会、外汇局 | 银发〔2020〕95号 |
| 5月8日 | 关于印发信用保险和保证保险业务监管办法的通知 | 中国银保监会 | 银保监办发〔2020〕39号 |
| 5月12日 | 关于落实保险公司主体责任加强保险销售人员管理的通知 | 中国银保监会 | 银保监办发〔2020〕41号 |
| 5月12日 | 关于切实加强保险专业中介机构从业人员管理的通知 | 中国银保监会 | 银保监办发〔2020〕42号 |
| 5月18日 | 关于进一步规范信贷融资收费 降低企业融资综合成本的通知 | 中国银保监会、工业和信息化部、国家发展改革委、财政部、人民银行、市场监管总局 | 银保监发〔2020〕18号 |

续表

| 日期 | 政策文件名称 | 发文单位 | 文件号 |
|---|---|---|---|
| 5月20日 | 关于保险资金投资银行资本补充债券有关事项的通知 | 中国银保监会 | 银保监发〔2020〕17号 |
| 5月22日 | 关于印发银行保险机构涉刑案件管理办法（试行）的通知 | 中国银保监会 | 银保监发〔2020〕20号 |
| 5月24日 | 中国银保监会行政许可实施程序规定 | 中国银保监会 | 中国银保监会令（2020年第7号） |
| 5月26日 | 关于进一步强化中小微企业金融服务的指导意见 | 中国人民银行、银保监会、发展改革委、工业和信息化部、财政部、市场监管总局、证监会、外汇局 | 银发〔2020〕120号 |
| 6月1日 | 关于进一步明确农业保险业务经营条件的通知 | 中国银保监会 | 银保监办发〔2020〕51号 |
| 6月15日 | 中国银保监会行政处罚办法 | 中国银保监会 | 中国银保监会令（2020年第8号） |
| 6月22日 | 关于规范互联网保险销售行为可回溯管理的通知 | 中国银保监会 | 银保监发〔2020〕26号 |
| 6月23日 | 关于开展银行业保险业市场乱象整治"回头看"工作的通知 | 中国银保监会 | 银保监发〔2020〕27号 |
| 6月23日 | 关于印发保险资金参与金融衍生产品交易办法等三个文件的通知 | 中国银保监会 | 银保监办发〔2020〕59号 |
| 7月16日 | 关于印发财产保险公司、再保险公司监管主体职责改革方案的通知 | 中国银保监会 | — |
| 7月17日 | 关于优化保险公司权益类资产配置监管有关事项的通知 | 中国银保监会 | 银保监办发〔2020〕63号 |
| 7月22日 | 关于印发推动财产保险业高质量发展三年行动方案（2020—2022年）的通知 | 中国银保监会 | 银保监办发〔2020〕68号 |
| 8月17日 | 关于印发健全银行业保险业公司治理三年行动方案（2020—2022年）的通知 | 中国银保监会 | 银保监发〔2020〕40号 |
| 9月2日 | 关于印发实施车险综合改革指导意见的通知 | 中国银保监会 | — |
| 9月4日 | 关于保险资金投资债转股投资计划有关事项的通知 | 中国银保监会 | 银保监办发〔2020〕82号 |
| 9月6日 | 关于规范保险公司健康管理服务的通知 | 中国银保监会 | 银保监办发〔2020〕83号 |
| 9月6日 | 关于印发银保监会现场检查立项和实施程序规定（试行）的通知 | 中国银保监会 | 银保监办发〔2020〕84号 |
| 9月7日 | 关于印发组合类保险资产管理产品实施细则等三个文件的通知 | 中国银保监会 | 银保监办发〔2020〕85号 |
| 9月9日 | 关于印发示范型商车险精算规定的通知 | 中国银保监会 | 银保监发〔2020〕42号 |

续表

| 日期 | 政策文件名称 | 发文单位 | 文件号 |
| --- | --- | --- | --- |
| 9月9日 | 银行保险机构应对突发事件金融服务管理办法 | 中国银保监会 | 中国银保监会令（2020年第10号） |
| 9月9日 | 关于调整交强险责任限额和费率浮动系数的公告 | 中国银保监会 | — |
| 9月11日 | 关于规范银行业金融机构协助有权机关办理保险公司资本保证金账户查询、冻结、扣划有关事宜的通知 | 中国银保监会 | 银保监办发〔2020〕91号 |
| 9月11日 | 金融控股公司监督管理试行办法 | 中国人民银行 | 中国人民银行令〔2020〕第4号 |
| 9月14日 | 关于印发融资性信保业务保前管理和保后管理操作指引的通知 | 中国银保监会 | 银保监办发〔2020〕90号 |
| 9月23日 | 关于印发监管数据安全管理办法（试行）的通知 | 中国银保监会 | 银保监发〔2020〕43号 |
| 9月30日 | 关于优化保险机构投资管理能力监管有关事项的通知 | 中国银保监会 | 银保监发〔2020〕45号 |
| 10月15日 | 关于印发核保险巨灾责任准备金管理办法的通知 | 中国银保监会、财政部、生态环境部 | 银保监发〔2020〕47号 |
| 11月5日 | 关于使用《中国人身保险业重大疾病经验发生率表（2020）》有关事项的通知 | 中国银保监会 | 银保监发〔2020〕51号 |
| 11月12日 | 关于保险资金财务性股权投资有关事项的通知 | 中国银保监会 | 银保监发〔2020〕54号 |
| 11月12日 | 保险代理人监管规定 | 中国银保监会 | 中国银保监会令（2020年第11号） |
| 12月7日 | 互联网保险业务监管办法 | 中国银保监会 | 中国银保监会令（2020年第13号） |
| 12月22日 | 关于印发责任保险业务监管办法的通知 | 中国银保监会 | 银保监办发〔2020〕117号 |
| 12月22日 | 关于发展独立个人保险代理人有关事项的通知 | 中国银保监会 | 银保监办发〔2020〕118号 |
| 12月30日 | 关于深化银行业保险业"放管服"改革 优化营商环境的通知 | 中国银保监会 | 银保监办发〔2020〕129号 |
| 12月30日 | 金融机构反洗钱和反恐怖融资监督管理办法（修订草案征求意见稿） | 中国人民银行 | — |

专栏 18

## 多地出台地方金融监督管理条例①

习近平总书记在第五次全国金融工作会议中强调,要加强金融监管协调、补齐监管短板,地方政府要在坚持金融管理主要是中央事权的前提下,按照中央统一规则,强化属地风险处置责任。2020年1月16日,中国人民银行召开金融法治工作电视电话会议,会议明确加快推进地方金融监督管理条例等立法是全年重点工作。2020年,上海、浙江、广西、内蒙古、厦门、江西、北京、贵州等地地方金融监督管理条例密集出台。综合来看,各地地方金融监督管理条例在条例定位、监管对象、监管手段、监管机制和职能协调方面呈现出以下特征。

1. 从条例定位来看,各地金融监督管理条例是地方金融监管工作的"基本法"。条例对地方金融组织作出基础性制度安排,明确地方金融组织范围,发布行为规范,授权监管手段,为今后配套文件的制修订提供依据。作为省级地方性法规,条例改善了地方金融组织的监管依据多为部门规章和规范性文件,以及地方金融监管法律法规依据不足的现状。

2. 从监管对象来看,各地金融监督管理条例关注了新兴金融业态。监管对象基本覆盖了"7+4"类机构——"7"是指小额贷款公司、融资担保公司、区域性股权市场、典当行、融资租赁公司、商业保理公司、地方资产管理公司,"4"是指区域内投资公司、开展信用互助的农民专业合作社、社会众筹机构和地方各类交易所。

3. 从监管手段来看,多地金融监督管理条例创新了监管模式。上海、广西、厦门等地赋予地方金融监管部门进行现场检查、查封、扣押以及采取监管谈话、出示风险预警函、通报批评、责令改正等措施的权力。上海还明确地方金融监管部门应当建立地方金融组织的信用档案,归集地方金融组织及其从业人员的信用信息,公布严重失信主体名单。江西指出地方金融监管部门应当利用大数据、云计算等现代金融科技手段,对地方金融组织业务活动及其风险状况进行分析、评价和监督管理。

4. 从监管机制来看,多地金融监督管理条例结合了地方金融发展特点。《上海市地方金融监督管理条例》提及要完善长江三角洲区域金融监管合作机制,建立健全风险监测预警和监管执法联动机制,强化信息共享和协同处置,推动金融服务长江三角洲区域高质量一体化发展。《浙江省地方金融条例》指出将支持云计算、大数据、人工智能、区块链等新兴科技在金融服务和金融监督管理领域的运用,推动金融科技产品、服务和商业模式的合规创新。此外还将民间融资服务企业也纳入监管范围内。《厦门经济特区地方金融条例》鼓励中国(福建)自由贸易试验区厦门片区、两岸区域性金融中心片区等在地方金融领域的体制机制、政策措施、对台交流等方面先行先试,推动地方金融业务、监管互动机制创新。

---

① 作者:刘学庆,上海保险交易所执行委员会委员兼法律合规部总经理。本文内容不代表作者任职单位观点。

5. 从职能协调的角度来看，多地金融监督管理条例既强调了中央与地方之间的"央地联动"，又强调了地方各层级、各部门之间的"监管联动"。上海、浙江、北京等地均明确加强与国务院金融稳定发展委员会办公室地方协调机制在金融监管、风险处置、信息共享和消费者权益保护等方面的协作。浙江、江西等地构建了省、设区的市、县（市、区）三级地方金融监管工作部门的体制安排，将地方金融组织监督管理的工作职责层层压实。上海、广西、内蒙古等地规范了地方金融监督管理部门、公安机关、市场监管部门、网信、通信管理部门、人民法院、人民检察院和其他相关行业主管部门的职责分工与风险处置流程。

多地出台地方金融监督管理条例，有助于补齐监管短板，避免监管空白，增强金融监管协调的权威性、有效性，强化金融监管的专业性、统一性、穿透性，做到在创新发展中提高监管能力，在监管中推动稳健发展，形成金融发展和监管的强大合力。

# CHINA FINANCIAL POLICY REPORT

## 2021

Chief Editor: Wu Xiaoling  Lu Lei
Executive Editor: He Haifeng

# Editorial Board

**Chief Editor:** Wu Xiaoling   Lu Lei

**Executive Editor:** He Haifeng

**Advisors:**

| | | |
|---|---|---|
| Xing Wei | Zhu Min | Ruan Lu |
| Li Yang | He Yanchun | Zhang Xiaojing |
| Lu Lei | Chen Gongyan | Fan Wenzhong |
| Zhao Hong | Hong Lei | Nie Weixun |
| Tu Guangshao | Xie Dong | Pan Guangwei |
| Huo Xuewen | Richard N. Cooper | Hal S. Scott |

# Foreword

*The China Financial Policy Report 2021* was jointly prepared by the National Institute of Financial Research (NIFR) of Tsinghua University and the Institute of Financial Policy (IFP) of the Chinese Academy of Social Sciences (CASS). As the first comprehensive annual financial policy report in China, it was established in 2011 with the mission and principle of "communicating China's financial policies with the world." Over the past decade, we have upheld and adhered to this stance, comprehensively and accurately reflected the major themes and policy dynamics in China's financial policies annually, strived to paint a true picture of China's financial development, and contribute the positive energy of China's financial policies to the world. Our efforts have been confirmed and recognized by the financial industry, which, in turn, has increased our confidence and sense of responsibility.

2020 was an unusual year. Faced with the complicated international situation, the difficult and onerous tasks of domestic reform, development, and stability, especially the severe impact of the COVID-19 pandemic, China achieved remarkable results in COVID-19 prevention and control, as well as economic and social development. According to the preliminary calculations of the National Bureau of Statistics of China, the annual GDP in 2020 will be RMB 101.6 trillion, an increase of 2.3% year-on-year (YOY); the annual GDP per capita will be RMB 72,447, up 2.0% YOY. From the economic perspective, facing shocks of a severity rarely seen before and based on what we had done to ensure stability on six key fronts, we carried out the task of maintaining security in six key areas. Improving quarter by quarter, China's economy gradually returned to normalcy and became the world's only major economy to achieve growth. We attained complete victories in the fight against poverty and in building a moderately prosperous society in all respects. From the financial perspective, China maintained its prudent monetary policy. While resolutely innovating financial services for COVID-19 prevention and control and fully safeguarding enterprises and ensuring employment, we continued to prevent and defuse financial risks. We orderly resolved the risks concerning high-risk financial institutions and key fields. We deepened financial opening up and innovation. The capital market, which generally maintained a steady momentum of development, enacted a number of landmark reforms such as the GEM, IPO registration system, NEEQ reform, as well as finetuning the delisting mechanism. In 2020, the 13th Five-Year Plan was accomplished in its entirety. The research team of *China Financial Policy Report* and Xinhua Finance jointly selected "Top Ten Financial Policies of 2020", which comprised top 10 global financial policies, top 10 financial policies in China, and top 10 regional and local financial policies within China. This inclusive list covers domestic and foreign financial policies that have positively influenced economic and financial development, financial market development, and the deepening of financial reforms.

As the first year of the 14th Five-Year Plan, 2021 marks China's commencement of a new journey to build a modern socialist country. This year also sees the centenary of the CPC. Therefore, we have set the following objectives: consolidate and expand the achievements made during the COVID-19 pandemic as well as economic and social development; ensure better coordination in pursuing development and upholding security; ensure stability on six key fronts and maintain security in six key areas; systematically implement targeted macro policies; keep major economic indicators within an appropriate range; continue to expand domestic demand; strengthen science and technology to provide strategic support for development; pursue opening up with higher standards; and maintain social harmony and stability. These efforts will empower a great start in the 14th Five-Year Plan period and commemorate the centenary of the CPC with outstanding achievements in development. This puts forward new requirements for financial policy in 2021. We will keep our prudent monetary policy flexible, targeted, and at a reasonable and appropriate level. We will improve the green financial policy framework and incentive mechanism, and further enhance the overall effectiveness of financial services, accelerate the improvement of the macro-prudential policy framework, strengthen the supervision of financial activities on online platforms, vigorously regulate key businesses, promote the comprehensive deepening of the capital market reform and opening-up in solid steps, maintain the momentum of steady development of the capital market in a complex environment, promote the internationalization of the renminbi in a prudent manner, and continuously upgrade foreign exchange management and services.

Maintaining its previous framework, the *China Financial Policy Report 2021* is divided into two major modules: thematic report and dynamic reports. The former, entitled "A New Chapter Amid Great Change — Toward a New Phase of China Financial Policy", reviews the practice of financial policy in response to sudden change and looks forward into the future of China's finance that is opening a new chapter of high-quality development. Moreover, we included two feature articles on financial policies in 2020: "An Analysis of Fiscal and Monetary Policy Coordination from the Perspective of Traditional and Modern Monetary Theory Divergence" and "Scientific & Technological Innovation and Economic & Financial Transformation in the Post-Pandemic Era."

For the 2020 dynamic reports, we reviewed and analyzed monetary policies, exchange rate and balance of payments, the development of banking, the stock market, the bond market, the securities fund market, the money market, the trust and wealth management market, the financial derivatives market, the commodity and futures market, the foreign exchange market, and the gold market. Apart from the major regulatory policies of the People's Bank of China and of China's banking, securities, and insurance industries, the reports also include evaluations on policy effects and outlooks.

In addition, we compiled 18 articles to reflect the trending issues of China's financial policies, including articles on financial reform and development, financial opening-up, financial markets, regional and local finance, and financial innovations such as fintech.

In order to comprehensively and timely reflect the latest developments and dynamic changes

# Foreword

in China's financial policies, *Financial Policy Information*, a derivative of the *China Financial Policy Report*, was officially introduced to weekly newspapers and monthly magazines in 2019. We will continue to compile policy information and evaluate policy effects to improve laws and regulations and promote the rule of law in our country, expanding the global influence of *China's Financial Policy Report*.

The *China Financial Policy Report 2021* is a result of collective research. The team mainly comprises professionals from financial management, financial institutions, universities, and academic institutions (although their views do not represent those of their respective organizations). The report was revised and edited by Wu Xiaoling, Lu Lei, and He Haifeng. Authors included Wu Xiaoling, Lu Lei, He Haifeng, Zhang Anyuan, Ma Yun, Zhang Yulong, Zang Yingshun, Li Peijia, He Xiaobei, Shen Yi, Ma Qiang, Zhao Qingming, Zhao Xianghuai, Liang Chaoyi, Ren Xiaoxun, Zhou Kunping, Zhao Yarui, Yu Jinxin, Liu Yu, Xu Kefei, Wang Wei, Rong Yihua, Yang Chao, Cai Hengpei, Xie Xuecheng, Liu Yong, Zhang Chen, Li Qingyun, Wang Qinhuai, Li Sida, Liu Jia, Gan Zhengzai, Shi Guanglong, Shang Xinxin, Zhang Yansheng, Luo Jiang, Guo Jingpu, Zhu Xiaochuan, Tong Haoxiang, Zhou Jinfei, Zhang Wei, Jiang Jianrong, Xie Yunxia, Du Shuming, Tan Liang, Xu Qianqian, Liu Xueqing. Ding Yuxi and Yu Yue edited and proofread the English manuscript. The interns of the *China Financial Policy Report* collected and compiled information such as financial policies of 2020. We are grateful to Director Wang Xiaoduan and Editor Zhang Juxiang of the China Financial Publishing House for their conscientious and prudent attitude toward work.

We, as always, look forward to criticism and advice from our readers.

**Director of the Institute of Financial Policy,**
**Chinese Academy of Social Sciences**
**He Haifeng (Foreword Author)**
**May 10, 2021**

# Top 10 Global Financial Policies of 2020

| Serial number | Policy Name | Date of Release | Issuing/Developing agency |
|---|---|---|---|
| 1 | Federal Reserve announces "unlimited" quantitative easing | March 23 | Federal Reserve |
| 2 | RCEP, the world's largest FTA, successfully signed | November 15 | RCEP member countries (10 ASEAN countries, and China, Japan, Korea, Australia, and New Zealand) |
| 3 | The World Bank and the International Monetary Fund (IMF) announce to provide up to USD 12 billion and 50 billion to respond to COVID-19, and World Health Organization (WHO) provides approximately USD 675 million to launch a strategic preparedness and response programme for the COVID-19 | March 3-4, February 5 | World Bank, IMF, WHO |
| 4 | Bank for International Settlements (BIS) and seven of the world's largest central banks release the report "Central Bank Digital Currencies" | October 4 | BIS, Federal Reserve, European Central Bank (ECB), Bank of Japan, Bank of England, Bank of Canada, Swiss National Bank, and Riksbank |
| 5 | ECB adopts a package of measures to counter the impact of the COVID-19 outbreak | March 12 | European Central Bank |
| 6 | IMF releases Global Financial Stability Report on the possibility of economic recovery | October | International Monetary Fund |
| 7 | World Trade Organization partners with 6 multilateral development banks to support trade finance | July 6 | World Trade Organization, International Finance Corporation, European Bank for Reconstruction and Development, Asian Development Bank, African Development Bank, International Islamic Trade Finance Corporation, and Inter-American Development Bank |
| 8 | Biden's nomination of ex-Federal Reserve chair Janet Yellen as his nominee for treasury secretary would make history | November 30 | The United States government |
| 9 | Trump signs new round of spending bills to address the worsening COVID-19 pandemic | December 27 | The United States government |
| 10 | China-EU investment agreement negotiations completed | December 30 | China, EU |

# Top 10 Financial Policies in China of 2020

| Serial number | Policy Name | Date of Release | Development/Issuing Agency |
|---|---|---|---|
| 1 | "Guidance Readings on the Proposal of the CPC Central Committee on Formulating the Fourteenth Five-Year Plan for National Economic and Social Development and the Long-Term Goals for the Year 2035" published a signed article by governors of the PBC, CBIRC, and CSRC | December 3 | CPC Central Committee |
| 2 | The "Overall Implementation Plan for the Growth Enterprise Market Reform and Registration System Pilot" approved and the China Securities Regulatory Commission issued series of regulations | April 27 | Central Commission for Comprehensively Deepening Reform, China Securities Regulatory Commission |
| 3 | The opening-up of the capital market has been accelerated, with the original provision of removing the restrictions on foreign shareholding in securities, futures, and life insurance in 2021 being brought forward to 2020 | Since January 1 | State Council, People's Bank of China, China Banking and Insurance Regulatory Commission (CBIRC), and China Securities Regulatory Commission |
| 4 | Opinions Concerning Further Raising the Quality of Listed Companies | October 5 | State Council |
| 5 | A number of government departments have introduced a series of financial policies and special policies to combat the pandemic | February 9, June 1 | Ministry of Finance, NDRC, MIIT, PBC, National Audit Office, CBIRC, CSRS, SAFE, and State Administration for Market Regulation |
| 6 | The "Decision on the Implementation of Financial Holding Company Admission Management", "Trial Measures on Supervision and Administration of Financial Holding Companies", and "Interim Provisions on the Administration of Filing of Directors, Supervisors and Senior Managers of Financial Holding Companies (Exposure Draft)" were released, bringing financial holding companies into formal regulation | September 11, September 11, November 2 | State Council, PBC |

# Top 10 Financial Policies of 2020

Continued

| Serial number | Policy Name | Date of Release | Development/Issuing Agency |
|---|---|---|---|
| 7 | The Law of the People's Republic of China on Commercial Banks (Draft Revised Law) and the Law of the People's Republic of China on the People's Bank of China (Revised Draft for Comments) were promulgated | October 16, October 23 | People's Bank of China |
| 8 | The 43rd meeting of the Financial Stability and Development Committee under the State Council was held to study the work of regulating the development of the bond market and maintaining its stability | November 21 | Financial Stability and Development Committee under the State Council |
| 9 | Interim Measures for the Management of Network Microfinance Business (Exposure Draft) | November 2 | China Banking and Insurance Regulatory Commission (CBIRC) and the People's Bank of China (PBC) |
| 10 | Shanghai and Shenzhen release new delisting rules to promote delisting reform | December 14, December 31 | Shanghai Stock Exchange, Shenzhen Stock Exchange |

## Top 10 Regional and Local Financial Policies of 2020

| Serial number | Policy Name | Date of Release | Development/Issuing Agency |
|---|---|---|---|
| 1 | Opinions on Financial Support for the Development of the Guangdong-Hong Kong-Macao Greater Bay Area | April 24 | PBC, CBIRC, CSRC, and SAFE |
| 2 | Opinions on Further Accelerating the Development of Shanghai as an International Financial Center and Providing Financial Support for the Integrated Development of the Yangtze River Delta | February 14 | PBC, CBIRC, CSRC, SAFE, and Shanghai Municipal People's Government |
| 3 | China's fintech innovation regulatory pilot achieves full implementation | All year round | People's Bank of China |
| 4 | Approval of the State Council on the Work Program for Deepening the New Round of Integrated Pilot of Expanding Opening-up of the Service Industry in Beijing and Building a National Comprehensive Demonstration Area of Expanding Opening-up of the Service Industry | August 28 | State Council |

Continued

| Serial number | Policy Name | Date of Release | Development/Issuing Agency |
|---|---|---|---|
| 5 | Digital Currency Electronic Payment pilot lands in multiple cities | April 17 | Digital Currency Research Institute of the People's Bank of China |
| 6 | Planning Outline for the Construction of Chengdu-Chongqing Economic Circle is officially issued | November 18 | The CPC Central Committee and the State Council |
| 7 | Several Measures on Increasing Financial Support for the Healthy Development of Science and Technology Innovation Enterprises | January 10 | Beijing Local Financial Supervision Administration, Business Administration Department of the People's Bank of China, Beijing Supervision Bureau of the China Banking and Insurance Regulatory Commission, Beijing Supervision Bureau of the China Securities Regulatory Commission |
| 8 | Various local departments have jointly issued action plans to further upgrade and strengthen a series of measures such as financial support for epidemic prevention and control and economic and social development in the previous period | July | People's Bank of China Beijing Business Administration Department and other departments<br>PBC Shanghai Head Office and other departments<br>People's Bank of China Tianjin Branch<br>People's Bank of China Chongqing Business Administration Department and other departments |
| 9 | Several local authorities rolled out financial supervision and administration regulations | All year round | Standing Committee of Shanghai Municipal People's Congress<br>Standing Committee of Zhejiang Municipal People's Congress<br>Standing Committee of the People's Congress of Inner Mongolia Autonomous Region<br>Standing Committee of the People's Congress of Guangxi Zhuang Autonomous Region<br>Standing Committee of Jiangxi Municipal People's Congress |
| 10 | Programme on the Establishment of the Beijing Financial Court | December 30 | Central Commission for Comprehensively Deepening Reform |

# Contents

## Part One   Thematic Report and Feature Articles

**Thematic Report: A New Chapter Amid Great Change—Toward a New Phase of China Financial Policy** ·································································································································· 3
  I. Introduction ································································································································· 3
  II. Financial policy practice in response to sudden change ························································· 5
  III. Opening a new chapter with high-quality development ······················································ 11
  IV. Conclusion ······························································································································ 17

**Feature Article 1: An Analysis of Fiscal and Monetary Policy Coordination from the Perspective of Traditional and Modern Monetary Theory Divergence** ···················································· 19

**Feature Article 2: Scientific & Technological Innovation and Economic & Financial Transformation in the Post-Pandemic Era** ········································································· 23

## Part Two   Chinese Financial Policies in 2020

**Macro Financial Policies** ················································································································ 31
  I. Monetary Policy ······················································································································· 31
  II. Exchange Rate and Balance of Payments Policies ······························································· 45

**Major Development Policies for the Financial Market** ······························································· 59
  I. Development Policies in the Banking Market ······································································· 59
  II. Stock Market Development Policies ······················································································ 81
  III. Development Policies for the Insurance Market ······························································· 112
  IV. Bond Market Development Policy ······················································································ 165
  V. Policies for the Development of the Securities Investment Fund Market ······················· 177

Ⅵ. Development Policy of the Money Market ········ 189
Ⅶ. Trust and Wealth Management Market Development Policy ········ 197
Ⅷ. Financial Derivatives Market Development Policies ········ 212
Ⅸ. Development Policies for the Commodity Futures Market ········ 222
Ⅹ. Foreign Exchange Market Development Policies ········ 232
Ⅺ. Development of Gold Market Policies ········ 239

**Major Financial Regulatory Policies** ········ 247
  Ⅰ. Major Regulatory Policies of the People's Bank of China (PBC) ········ 247
  Ⅱ. Major Regulatory Policies in China's Banking Sector ········ 256
  Ⅲ. Major Regulatory Policies for China's Securities Industry ········ 272
  Ⅳ. Major Regulatory Policies in China's Insurance Industry ········ 301

# Part One

Thematic Report and Feature Articles

# THEMATIC REPORT:

## A New Chapter Amid Great Change
### —Toward a New Phase of China Financial Policy

### I. Introduction

2020 was an extraordinary year. Weathering the COVID-19 pandemic and trade disputes, China's financial industry embarked on a path of new opportunities. It coordinated pandemic prevention and control with economic and social development, and satisfactorily completed a number of financial reforms in the 13th Five-Year Plan, laying a solid foundation for the 14th Five-Year Plan and high-quality development.

**(I) During the 13th Five-Year Plan period, financial reform made significant progress**

During the 13th Five-Year Plan period, "stability" was the general theme for China's financial industry, while reform and innovation acted as the driving force. Supply-side structural reform in the financial sector was deepened and great efforts were made to address short-term challenges and long-term contradictions. Various financial reform tasks stipulated in the 13th Five-Year Plan were successfully completed. The overall strength of the financial industry steadily increased. Financial risks were broadly contained. Actively and positively responding to the impact of COVID-19, the financial sector played a definitive role in the high-quality development of the real economy.

The regulatory two-pillar structure of "monetary policy plus macroprudential policy" was continuously improved. China took the lead worldwide in establishing a two-pillar regulatory framework of "monetary policy plus macroprudential policy" to better achieve monetary and financial stability. Monetary policy has gradually been forming a price-based control framework, actively cultivating a DR-based benchmark interest rate system for the money market, constructing interest rate channels to guide the operations of the Money Market Rate, and initiating reform of the loan prime rate (LPR). The macroprudential management system is improved, with stronger integrated supervision over systemically important financial institutions, financial holding companies, and financial infrastructure. Financial institutions received guidance in boosting support to weak links in the economy.

The banking industry reached new levels of comprehensive strength and competitiveness. From the end of 2015 to the end of 2020, the total asset size of the banking industry grew from RMB

199.34 trillion to RMB 319.74 trillion, with a compound annual growth rate of 9.9%. Optimization of the credit structure continued apace. In 2020, inclusive loans from financial institutions to micro and small businesses reached RMB 15.1 trillion, while comparable loans from large commercial banks consecutively expanded by more than 30% for several years. By the end of 2020, the number of banking institutions in China had exceeded 4,500, signaling the gradual maturity of the country's multi-level commercial banking system.

Reform of the capital market drove steady market development. Overcoming various predicaments including the pandemic, China's capital market maintained normal operations and market capacity continued to expand. By the end of 2020, the total market value of the stock market stood at approximately RMB 80 trillion and the bond custody balance was approximately RMB 114 trillion, each ranking second in the world. A number of landmark reforms were enacted in 2020 to steadily refine the multi-level capital market system. These include the GEM reform, IPO registration system pilot, NEEQ reform, and adjustments for the delisting mechanism. Efforts to open up gained momentum as well, with improved interconnection mechanisms and significantly more participation on the part of global investors. At the end of 2020, foreign investors (including institutions and individuals) held a total of RMB 8.98 trillion in domestic RMB financial assets, marking an increase of RMB 5.38 trillion over the end of 2015 and a growth rate of more than 150%.

Decisive victories were secured in the war against financial risks. China continued to optimize its financial regulatory framework, gradually forming a structure of "One Committee, One Bank, Two Commissions and One Administration" — referring to the Financial Stability and Development Committee under the State Council, PBC, CBIRC and CSRC, and the State Administration of Foreign Exchange, respectively — with responsibility being shared by local divisions. Thus, a modern financial regulatory system took shape. Financial irregularities continued to be met with effective rectifying measures, and the development of financial institutions became increasingly unified. Compared with its historical peak, the scale of shadow banking receded by approximately RMB 20 trillion. P2P platforms were dispelled. Financial holding companies gradually standardized their operations. The disposal of non-performing bank assets was actively accelerated. Non-performing loan ratio for commercial banks sank to 1.84% in 2020; this was the first time it had declined in recent years.

**(II) In 2020, China's financial industry successfully responded to the pandemic and other external uncertainties**

The COVID-19 pandemic, superimposed on economic and trade frictions, has complicated the circumstances for the financial industry. The world is undergoing profound changes that have not been witnessed in a hundred years. Global economic growth has stalled, with protectionism and geopolitical risks on the rise. In particular, the COVID-19 pandemic, having infected more than 150 million people worldwide, poses far-reaching consequences for the global economy and finance. The economic repercussions will extend into the medium and long-term — not only in terms of demand, but also for the supply side, affecting both volume and structure. As the core of the modern economy, the financial industry will continue to be impacted as well. From the perspective of the real economy, despite accelerated vaccine rollouts from major world powers, there remains a high degree of uncertainty for global economic recovery as weak fundamentals imperil financial stability. On the other hand, the overreliance on pandemic-induced monetary easing has pressured major economies to keep monetary policy expansionary. The risk of a global financial asset bubble is looming, which poses a policy constraint hazard on economic stability. The pandemic has only exacerbated the debt burden for the global economy, and global finance has become even more vulnerable with the rising global leverage ratio. According to the International Finance Association (IIF), the COVID-19 pandemic increased global debt by USD 24 trillion in 2020 compared with 2019, accumulating to a record of USD 281 trillion. Meanwhile, global debt-to-GDP ratio surged by 35 percentage points over 2019 to 355%, which is well past the 10–15 percentage-point hike during the 2008 global financial crisis.

Financial policies have helped China cope with the effects of the pandemic in a timely and effective manner. In addressing the COVID-19 outbreak and worldwide transmission, the CPC Central Committee and the State Council acted decisively with comprehensive plans to coordinate pandemic prevention and control with economic and social development. Financial departments moved quickly, implementing multiple measures and a series of financial support policies. In addition to providing direct financing support for pandemic prevention and control, they prioritized stable growth, employment protection, and people's livelihoods through meeting macro-level needs. Various financial factors were leveraged to serve the real economy. New micro-direct financing tools were created to support enterprises — especially micro, small, and medium-sized enterprises (MSMEs) — to tide over difficult times. With guidance, the financial system applied RMB 1.5 trillion to benefit the real economy, providing crucial financial support for enterprises to resume work and production, and making China the only major economy in the world to achieve positive growth in 2020.

## II. Financial policy practice in response to sudden change

At the beginning of the COVID-19 outbreak, the CPC Central Committee and State Council acted decisively, deploying sweeping strategies to coordinate pandemic prevention and control with economic and social development. In April 2020, they underlined security in six areas - employment, people's basic livelihood, market players, food and energy security, stable industrial and supply chains, and government operations at the grassroot level. Compared with stability on six fronts previously, security in six areas further emphasized bottom-line thinking. Under the unified leadership of the Finance Committee of the State Council, financial departments adopted a series of financial policies — macro and micro, short-term and long-term — to achieve stability on six fronts and security in six areas. Other than providing direct financing support for pandemic prevention and control, the Finance Committee also effectively activated the role of financial factors in serving the real economy. Through the creation of micro-direct financing tools, enterprises — especially MSMEs — received enough support to overcome their difficulties. In addition, total contribution of the financial industry to the real economy reached RMB 1.5 trillion. Enterprises also utilized monetary and financial macro-counter-cyclical policy tools to ensure employment, people's livelihoods, and steady growth. At the same time, the relationship between development and security, between reform and stability, should be balanced to avoid an over-inundation of strong stimulus measures. The focus should be on the three-year battle to prevent and resolve financial risks, on the accurate handling of risk events in key areas, and on maintaining the bottom line of zero systemic financial risks.

### (I) Multiple measures were taken to directly support the financing of pandemic prevention and control

Following the initial outbreak of COVID-19, financial regulators acted swiftly to support pandemic prevention and control through the issuance of a number of policies supporting the financing of pandemic-fighting enterprises. These funds were not only crucial in supplying key materials and safeguarding people's livelihoods during China's outbreak, they also provided new impetus for enterprises to resume work and production.

Financial policies guaranteed the easy cross-border movement of pandemic supplies. Ever since the earliest stages of the pandemic, China's foreign trade has been beleaguered by recurring outbreaks both domestically and overseas. Financial supervisory departments implemented list-system management and launched green channels for key enterprises engaged in businesses of important medical and life-supporting supplies. They established a green channel for foreign exchange policy, relaxed previous documentation requirements for the income settlement and payments of capital projects involved in pandemic response, and further facilitated and satisfied the needs of cross-border financing related to pandemic prevention and control. For enterprises in dire need of cross-border financing, restrictions on borrowing foreign debt were lifted and online handling was enabled. Financing arrangements and support were strengthened for import and export enterprises, and green channels were opened for the import of vital medical products and essential supplies.

Financial support for pandemic-fighting areas increased. During the outbreak, the PBC supplied financial institutions with low-cost funds through a special refinancing project totaling RMB 300 billion. In the hardest-hit areas, national commercial banks and local commercial banks offered preferential credit support to key enterprises involved in the production, transport, and sales of crucial medical supplies and necessities. At the same time, by better matching services among financial institutions and hospitals, medical research units, and companies, and by providing sufficient credit resources, the government worked to meet the reasonable financing needs of organizations and enterprises in health care and pandemic prevention, medical supply manufacturing and procurement, public health infrastructure construction, and so on.

Financial infrastructure services were established to guarantee financial channels for pandemic-fighting. At the beginning of the pandemic-fighting campaign, the PBC, together with the CBIRC, CSRC, SAFE, and other financial regulatory authorities, acted decisively to strengthen the service guarantee capacity of financial market infrastructure — in terms of operation mechanisms, staffing, office space, system operation and maintenance, technical support, etc. — to ensure the normal operation of issuance, trading, clearing and settlement, and other businesses, putting as much of the processes online as possible. Emergency plans were formulated for quick and efficient responses to unexpected events. Various market institutions and financial infrastructures cooperated closely to keep the smooth connection and running of business systems.

**Table 1  National financing policies to support pandemic-fighting enterprises**

| Date | Policy Title | Issuing Department | Policy |
|---|---|---|---|
| February 14 | The Notice on Further Improving Financial Services for Epidemic Prevention and Control | China Banking and Insurance Regulatory Commission (CBIRC) | Funding support should particularly go to key health and medical fields such as therapeutic drug manufacture, vaccine research and development, and related enterprises manufacturing important supplies or providing transportation and logistics. Funding costs should be reduced through the proper implementation of central government policies and optimization of internal processes. Favorable interest rates and quality financial services should be provided to support enterprises' resumption and expansion of production. Insurance institutions are encouraged to provide accident, health, pension, medical, and other preferential insurance services to frontline pandemic staff in accordance with their own circumstances. |
| February 9 | Notice on the Response to the COVID-19 to Help Small and Medium-sized Enterprises to Resume Work and Production and Tide over the Difficulties | Ministry of Industry and Information Technology of People's Republic of China (MIIT) | The Notice stipulates advancing the implementation of national fiscal support policies for key enterprises engaged in pandemic prevention and control. Meanwhile, it encourages local governments to launch their own preferential fiscal policies to support SMEs in addition to the central government's loan interest subsidies. |
| February 1 | Notice on Strengthening Financial Services for the Prevention and Control of the COVID-19 | MOF | For newly-added key enterprises that were engaged in pandemic prevention and control in 2020, in addition to the preferential interest rates offered by financial institutions through the PBC's special refinancing project, the central fiscal authority offered a 50% discount on its refinancing interest rate. The discount period is not to exceed one year and the discount funds are to be allocated from special funds for the development of inclusive finance. |

Continued

| Date | Policy Title | Issuing Department | Policy |
|---|---|---|---|
| January 31 | Circular on Further Strengthening Financial Support for COVID-19 Epidemic Prevention and Control | The People's Bank of China (PBC), Ministry of Finance of People's Republic of China (MOF), China Banking and Insurance Regulatory Commission (CBIRC), China Securities Regulatory Commission (CSRC), and State Administration of Foreign Exchange (SAFE) | It implements a list system for enterprises engaged in pandemic prevention and control fields as well as key enterprises producing important daily necessities. The PBC provided financial institutions with low-cost funds through special refinancing, supported their offering credit with preferential interest rates to listed enterprises, and assisted development banks and policy banks to increase financial support to any abovementioned enterprises experiencing difficulties in market-based financing. |

Sources: CBIRC, PBC, MOF, China Securities.

**(II) Focus was on "steady growth" in the real economy and the strengthening of counter-cyclical financial regulation**

Since 2020, the COVID-19 pandemic has severely impacted China's social and economic development. GDP fell by 6.8% year-on-year (YOY) in Q1 alone. China's financial regulatory authorities moved quickly to step up the counter-cyclical regulation and control of monetary and financial policy. They endeavored to maintain stability while achieving progress, formulate more precise policies, optimize structure, and bring profits to market entities, all for the stable recovery of national economic operations. As a result, China was the only major economy in the world to achieve positive economic growth in 2020.

Monetary and credit policies were promptly applied to create a suitable monetary and financial environment. In 2020, financial regulatory authorities utilized financial tools such as reserve requirement ratio (RRR) cuts, medium-term lending facilities (MLF), refinancing, and rediscounts, introducing more than RMB 9 trillion in monetary support overall. By the end of 2020, M2 had increased by 10.1% YOY, and the scale of social financing multiplied by 13.3% YOY — each maintaining reasonable growth. Forward guidance on MLFs and open market operations led the bid-winning rates to drop by 30 basis points, simultaneously driving down the market interest rate and the one-year LPR. Comprehensive financing costs for enterprises dropped significantly in 2020, with the weighted average interest rate of corporate loans down to 4.61% in December — 0.51 percentage point lower than the same period the previous year and a new low since statistics have been recorded.

Precise, innovative financial structure policy stabilized enterprises and safeguarded employment. In light of both the pandemic and economic development needs, three batches of refinancing and rediscount policies were introduced at different levels and gradients, amounting to

RMB 1.8 trillion in total. On June 1, 2020, the PBC created two monetary policy tools to directly reach the real economy — namely, the "Support Tool for Loan Extension for Inclusive Small and Micro Enterprises" and the "Support Plan for Inclusive Small and Micro Enterprise Credit Loans", which aimed to improve the system of structural monetary policy tools and strengthen financial support for corporate stability and employment security. The overall credit structure continued to be optimized throughout the remainder of the year. By the end of 2020, inclusive small and micro-loans had increased by 30.3% YOY and medium-to-long-term manufacturing loans had increased by 35.2% YOY.

Key reforms were deepened in the financial sector, including ones on the formation mechanisms of interest and exchange rates. Effectively facilitating monetary policy transmission, key reforms realized the pricing benchmark conversion of the floating interest rate for loans in accordance with the principles of marketization and the rule of law, encouraging banks to incorporate LPR into their funds transfer pricing (FTP) system, resolutely breaking the implicit lower limit on loan interest rates, demonstrably raising the efficiency of interest rate transmission, guiding a greater allocation of financial resources to private micro and small enterprises and lowering real interest rates for loans. Reform of exchange rate marketization pressed forward, with improvements to the formation mechanism for the renminbi exchange rate, enhanced exchange rate flexibility, newly activated interbank foreign exchange market transactions, lower costs of exchange for microeconomic agents, and the overall liberalization and facilitation of China's foreign trade and investment.

High-level financial openness in services and investment was promoted through further liberalization and facilitation. Financial regulatory departments stuck closely to the policy of "stabilizing the fundamentals of foreign trade and foreign investment", cooperating with other macro-control departments to introduce a series of financial policies to stabilize foreign trade. A package of foreign exchange facilitation policies was issued in order to support the development of foreign-related businesses, assist the development of new trade formats such as cross-border e-commerce and raise the level of cross-border trade investment and financing facility. The financial capacities of China Export & Credit Insurance Corporation and the Export-Import Bank of China were fully utilized — along with the full product line of export credit insurance and special financing services — to provide export enterprises with comprehensive financial support. Policy-based financial synergy was also leveraged to help companies cope with the risks of new market development, order cancellations, shipment rejections, payments, and other risks, effectively alleviating export financing difficulties to help enterprises expand their businesses, guarantee orders, and secure the market.

**(III) Capital market development was actively reformed**

In 2020, the capital market coordinated planning to meet the needs of reform and development amid pandemic prevention and control, emphasized the role of endogenous market structures, promoted investment and financing-side reforms in an all-round manner, stabilized market expectations by deepening reforms, and maintained the capital market's overall momentum of steady development.

In 2020, China's capital market reform accelerated quite noticeably. 2020 saw the successful implementation of the GEM reform and the IPO registration system pilot. A number of landmark reform measures were launched successively, including the GEM and NEEQ reforms. In addition, regulatory measures were effectively implemented, such as improvements to the delisting mechanism and to the quality of listed companies. All in all, significant progress was made in the country's capital market reform.

The capital market's rule of law and ecological environment showed continuous improvement as well. Banks and other financial institutions received guidance to adopt a comprehensive credit approach in order to support listed companies with sound production and operation fundamentals and ample space for development. Commercial banks were encouraged to establish financial management subsidiaries, expand their institutional investor base, and attract high-quality funds into the market. In response to the impact of COVID-19, new asset management regulations were quickly fine-tuned and pre-adjusted to appropriately extend the transition period from existing businesses to their rectification, thus lessening the pandemic's impact on the financial system and completing the standardized improvement of existing asset management in a steady and orderly manner.

Qualified insurance companies received support for their capital market investments. Insurance companies with strong solvency and good asset/liability matching capabilities were given more investment autonomy to improve their investment in equity assets and give full play to insurance funds' long-term and value investment advantages. This initiative helped increase the proportion of equity investment to promote the long-term, stable and healthy development of the capital market.

### (IV) Financial risks were systematically and resolutely resolved, financial institutions' capacities for risk prevention enhanced

Supplementary capital helped offset the impact of the pandemic for small and medium-sized banks. The July 2020 executive meeting of the State Council first proposed that a certain amount should be allocated within the new special limits on local government debts, that local governments may explore reasonable options for replenishing the capital of small and medium-sized banks by such lawful means as, for example, convertible bonds subscription. At the same time, supplementary capital allocation prioritized those marbet-viable small and medium-sized banks so as to promote various reform and transformation mechanisms. This not only enhances small and medium-sized banks' ability to serve MSMEs, but also helps improve their governance and internal control, further deepening their own reform.

The plan to dispose of high-risk small and medium-sized financial institutions was successfully implemented. To overcome the pandemic's adverse effects on the financial environment, the disposal of high-risk small and medium-sized financial institutions advanced in 2020, achieving notable progress and important milestones. The reform and restructuring of key financial institutions, such as Hengfeng Bank and the Bank of Jinzhou, progressed according to plan, while the bankruptcy liquidation of Baoshang Bank was conducted in a steady and orderly manner. The effective disposal of high-risk financial institutions ensures the smooth operation of the financial system during this critical and sensitive time, firmly holding the bottom line of zero systematic risk.

China's capital market is now stronger and more resilient to risks. The capital market withstood the impact of the pandemic and other external risk events, maintaining normal operation. Liquidity risks associated with listed companies' share pledges have been effectively prevented and resolved by applying the concept of "controlling increments and eliminating stock." Substantial results have been achieved in this regard, while risks in key areas such as bond defaults and private equity funds have generally been minimized.

**(V) The two new foci of high-quality financial development have been seized**

By the major strategic decision of focusing on green finance, China is assuming its responsibility according to the inherent requirements of sustainable development and the building of a community with a shared future for mankind. At the general debate of the 75th United Nations General Assembly in 2020, President Xi Jinping announced that China would strive to achieve peak carbon dioxide emissions by 2030 and carbon neutrality by 2060. The same year, the fifth plenary session of the 19th CPC Central Committee and the Central Economic Work Conference called for accelerated green and low-carbon development to make fair progress toward carbon peak and carbon neutrality. From 2020 onward, the financial sector has gradually improved its standard system for green finance, regulatory and information disclosure requirements, policy incentives, product and market systems and international cooperation through financial resource allocation, risk management and carbon price discovery. By the third quarter of 2020, China's balance of green loans in domestic and foreign currencies had exceeded RMB 11 trillion, ranking first in the world.

Focus on innovation support. President Xi Jinping has argued that for China to rejuvenate and strengthen, it must strive to become the world's major science center and innovation highland through the vigorous development of science and technology. Scientific and technological innovation, however, requires the support of a high-quality financial system. Unblocking financing channels for domestic listing of technology enterprises enhances both the "hard technology" characteristics of the Science and Technology Innovation Board and the GEM market's capacity to serve growth-oriented innovation and entrepreneurship; it also encourages the development of angel investment and venture capital and better utilize the roles of venture capital guidance funds and private equity funds. Financial institutions are encouraged to develop technological financial products such as intellectual property pledge financing and sci-tech insurance while carrying out pilot projects for loan risk compensation as a way to transform scientific and technological achievements.

## III. Opening a new chapter with high-quality development

2020, marking the successful conclusion of the 13th Five-Year Plan period, was a key year for determining financial reform and development objectives for the 14th Five-Year Plan. Invaluable experience in financial policy practice during the 13th Five-Year Plan period inculcated bottom-line thinking and facilitated the active recognition and initiation of changes, scientific responses to change, ability to nurture opportunities amid crisis and turn the tide amid volatile situations. Practices during the 13th Five-Year Plan period promoted the high-quality development theme. Based on deepened supply-side structural reform, with reform and innovation as the fundamental driving forces, the financial industry responded to various internal and external risks and challenges through high-quality development, thus contributing financial strength for the construction of a new development pattern.

### (I) Modernizing China's financial governance system and capacity

The "14th Five-Year Plan for National Economic and Social Development of the People's Republic of China" and the "Proposals for 14th Five-Year Plan and 2035 Long-Range Objectives" state the necessity of improving macroeconomic governance — with national development planning as the strategic orientation, fiscal and monetary policy as the main instruments, close coordination among employment, industry, investment, consumption, environmental protection, and regional policy, and with optimized objectives, a reasonable division of labor and efficient synergy to provide a foundation of compliance for improving the macroeconomic and financial governance system. To this end, efforts should focus on the following reform tasks:

Maintaining the continuity, stability, and sustainability of macro-financial policy. So long as the pandemic is not fully under control worldwide, the primary objective of the macro-financial policy is protecting employment and market entities. The modern central bank system and currency control mechanisms should continue to be improved. We should maintain policy continuity, stability, and sustainability, strengthen economic governance, and push forward cross-cyclical policy design. An aggregate balance, economic structural optimization, and a balance between internal and external dynamics should all be promoted. We must uphold the principle of stability. Actions should be moderate and reasonable; there should be no sharp turn; monetary policy should be prudent; the renminbi exchange rate must be kept at a reasonable equilibrium and stable and healthy economic operations should be promoted. Prices should be kept at relatively stable levels, with special attention paid to commodity price trends. In the medium to long term, the focus should be on improving the framework of modern monetary policy, improving the mechanism for money supply regulation, improving the central bank's long-term mechanism for regulating liquidity, capital, and interest rate constraints on money creation, and maintaining growth rates in the money supply and social financing scale to basically match the growth rate of nominal GDP reflecting potential output. With the deepening of market-oriented interest rate reform as the effective means, we shall unblock the channels for monetary policy transmission, improve the central bank's policy interest rate system with the open market operations rate serving as the short-term policy interest rate and the MLF rate as the medium-term policy interest rate, deepen the reform of the LPR and eradicate the hidden lower limit on loan interest rates.

Continuously optimized coordination between fiscal and monetary policies. In order to achieve currency stability, the central bank needs to keep a healthy and sustainable balance sheet through regulating the banking system's currency creation process in alignment with market conditions. Systematic implementation of independent financial budget management is thus necessary for the central bank to prevent the monetization of fiscal deficits and to build a "firewall" between the two "purses" of finance and the central bank. At the same time, the central bank's balance sheet must be kept from taking on corporate credit risk, which would ultimately affect the credit of the renminbi. To further clarify the division of labor between fiscal and monetary policy, fiscal policy should focus on its particular advantages of optimizing economic structure while carrying out counter-cyclical aggregate control, whereas monetary policy should focus on guiding the optimal allocation of financial resources while creating a suitable monetary and financial environment. Each policy type putting its specialized strengths into play will fully demonstrate the advantages of our national system.

**(II) Building institutional mechanisms to provide the real economy with effective financial support**

Serving the real economy is the bounden duty of finance. President Xi Jinping has stressed the need for finance to serve the real economy and thereby meet the needs of economic development, social development, and the people. During the 14th Five-Year Plan period, deepened supply-side structural reform in the financial sector must apply the new concept of development, strengthen the functionality of financial services, pinpoint the foci of financial services, and fully instantiate service to the real economy and to people's lives in both purpose and positioning.

Comprehensive capacity improvement for financial service entities. Efforts aim to bolster financial support, stabilize enterprises and guarantee employment. Support shall be increased for inclusive finance, and continue to be increased for private businesses, small and micro companies, agriculture, rural areas, farmers, and other sectors to achieve inclusive growth. Financing shall be promoted for micro and small businesses to achieve "increases in volume, decreases in price and expansions in scope"; medium-to-long-term loan support will be increased to the manufacturing industry; market expectations should be stabilized and a policy of deferred principal and interest repayment put in place to support inclusive micro and small business loans and inclusive small and micro credit loans. Every effort should be made to assist targeted poverty alleviation at the closing stage. Basic financial services in poverty-stricken areas will be consolidated and their quality improved, helping impoverished counties rid themselves of such designation. Investment in rural revitalization resources will continue to grow. The rural property rights system will be further optimized, financial services reformed, the collective economy developed and expanded, and the mortgage loan business for the management rights of rural contracted land promoted.

Increasing support to key links in national economy-building. We should stick to the strategic focus of expanding domestic demand and focus on ensuring smooth circulation in all links of production, distribution, circulation, and consumption. We will continue to help unclog the internal circulation system in accordance with the internal requirements of industrial, regional, and urban-rural coordination. In line with the trend of restructuring global industrial and value chains, we will increase support for high-end manufacturing and new infrastructure. Better consumer financial services shall be provided from both the supply and demand sides to help form a strong domestic market. Green finance will be vigorously developed to gradually improve the green financial system in five aspects: perfecting the system of green financial standards, perfecting information disclosure requirements for the supervision of financial institutions, constructing a system of policy incentives and restraints, continuously improving the market system and products of green finance, and strengthening international cooperation in green finance.

Deepening regional financial reform to promote openness and innovation in the industry. In accordance with the decisions and arrangements of the CPC Central Committee and State Council, we will push regional financial reform to a deeper level, focusing on supply-side structural reforms while exploring and cultivating new competitive advantages. Incremental, focused, and targeted efforts shall be made to further promote pilot reforms for financial openness and innovation, green finance, rural finance, and inclusive financing in free trade zones (FTZs). We will promote coordinated regional development and strengthen support for national regional-development strategies — such as for the Beijing-Tianjin-Hebei region, the Yangtze River Delta, the Guangdong-Hong Kong-Macao Greater Bay Area, the Hainan Free Trade Zone, and the Chengdu-Chongqing Economic Circle. We shall, in a timely manner, review and summarize experience gained from various regions' pilot reforms to get a rational hold on the layout of newly-added pilot areas. We will bring regional financial reform to a new level, improving the overall capacity of financial service reform, opening up, and economic development.

### (III) Accelerating the establishment of a modern financial system to befit the status of a financial power

In accordance with the principles of marketization, internationalization, and the rule of law, we shall raise the modern financial system to a higher level of adaptability, competitiveness, and inclusivity.

Promoting the healthy development of a multi-level capital market system. The positioning of multi-level capital markets should be scientifically grasped to improve differentiated institutional arrangements and smooth out transfer mechanisms, ultimately forming a market system characterized by staggered development, complementary functions, and organic links. We shall continue to promote innovations in key institutions and provide diversified financing services for various enterprises with multi-level capital market systems. The Science and Technology Innovation Board shall operate with integrity, for which we will research and launch institutional innovations, related products and tools and support the development and growth of more "hard technology" enterprises through the use of the capital market. Learning from international best practices, we will continually summarize the experience of the pilot registration system for the Science and Technology Innovation Board and the GEM, steadily implementing a registration system centered on information disclosure across the entire market. Commercial banks will be encouraged to set up financial management subsidiaries, while qualified insurance companies will be supported for investments in the capital market. The ranks of institutional investors shall be strengthened and high-quality funds guided into the market. The innovation and development of the bond market will be advanced, the registration system for bond issuance improved. The interbank bond market will see more interconnection and intercommunication with exchange infrastructure.

The vigorous development of green finance. The "Green Financial Performance Evaluation Scheme for Deposit Financial Institutions in Banking" will be studied and revised to better facilitate the active exploration of higher-accuracy, lower-cost methods for qualified financial institutions to support green, low-carbon projects. We will actively participate in the construction of a system of standards for green finance, explore both national and industry-level standards and promote the overall development of green financial standards. The comprehensive and standardized development of the carbon financial market will be promoted to enhance the authority and transaction efficiency of carbon market pricing. The construction of digital infrastructure for green finance will be strengthened; asymmetry in environmental/climatic information between the supply and demand sides of funds shall be minimized, the problem of green identification resolved, and a basis provided for precise policy implementation.

Orderly promotion of high-level opening up in the financial industry. The international and domestic markets and their respective resources will fully utilized, to continuously improve the quality and efficiency of financial services in the real economy. We will promote the orderly two-way opening up of the financial industry, improve the relevant institutional arrangements of the Shanghai-Hong Kong Stock Connect, Shenzhen-Hong Kong Stock Connect and Bond Connect, and strengthen the connection between China's financial market and investors overseas. Global transaction and pricing capacities will be refined for the Chinese market and Chinese assets in order to improve the competitiveness of China's financial system in the international arena. Meanwhile, innovation will be boosted in cross-border financial businesses to improve the global competitiveness and service capabilities of Chinese-funded financial institutions, and raise the level of financial services for Chinese-funded enterprises going global.

### (IV) Properly guarding the bottom line of zero systematic risk

The overall principle of national security must be upheld, bottom-line thinking stressed, relations between development and security integrated, solid trenches put in place for financial security, and the interests of national security and development duly safeguarded.

Strengthening the centralized and unified leadership of finance. The function of overall coordination of the Financial Stability and Development Committee under the State Council should be fully utilized as a means to further improve the system of financial supervision in accordance with national conditions. Focusing on the need to safeguard national security and development interests, we will strengthen our ability to supervise central financial authorities, continue to improve the system of modern financial supervision, make up for shortcomings within the system, improve the regulatory framework for full risk coverage and improve levels of marketization, the rule of law, internationalization and transparency in financial supervision. Local financial supervision systems shall be optimized, local financial institutions supported and guided to focus on their main businesses, to adhere to their positioning of serving local, micro and small businesses as well as urban and rural residents, and to promote a balanced structure of regional financial supply and demand. Adhering to the principle of local management, financial regulatory departments should strengthen their guidance of local governments, collaborate, and build synergy together. At the same time, local governments' main obligations in local financial institutions' capital management and risk disposal should be brought into full play, with a "zero tolerance" attitude toward legal and regulatory violations.

Building a mechanism for efficient and timely financial risk disposal. We shall strengthen counter-cyclical and cross-market financial macroprudential management. We shall likewise strengthen the cooperation between macro and micro-prudential supervision, and formulate and improve financial risk monitoring, identification, early warning, and disposal systems that are cross-market, cross-format, or cross-region. A mechanism of countercyclical capital buffer has been established; a preliminary regulatory framework has been established for financial holding companies; a regulatory framework has been improved for systemically important financial institutions. Risk identification shall be strengthened to realize the early discovery, early intervention, and early prevention of risks. Emergency management and disposal plans will be improved for sudden risk emergence, as will market-based mechanisms for risk disposal and relief. The means of exit will be optimized to allow financial institutions with well-controlled risks but poorly run operations to go bankrupt and liquidate.

Improving financial systems' micro-governance and supervision systems. Financial regulatory departments should tighten the supervision of shareholders and actual controllers of financial institutions, risk concentration, connected transactions, data authenticity, and so on, enhance capital adequacy, strengthen supervision and inspection, and toughen market constraints, filling in systemic shortcomings and regulatory loopholes and improving the efficiency of supervision to achieve full supervision coverage. To improve accountability, dereliction of duty and other acts of financial regulatory misconduct must be seriously investigated and penalized. Local financial institutions must improve their corporate governance, strengthen risk management and prudent operations and refrain from excessive expansions or sped-up development. The professional ethics of financial practitioners must be improved. There needs to be a clear behavioral bottom line and higher costs for legal violations. In particular, the behavior of high-level officials need to be restricted.

Maintaining a fair, efficient, and transparent financial ecological environment. The financial industry must be encouraged to fulfill its social responsibilities; inclusive and green finance must be strengthened; virtual and speculative arbitrage must be prevented. While supporting financial innovation, we should strictly guard against monopolies, maintain market order and promote fair competition. A sound behavioral supervisory system should be established with the protection of financial consumers' rights and interests at its core. Meanwhile, ex-ante, in-process, and ex-post supervision mechanisms should be improved to better protect the rights and interests of consumers and investors in finance. To earnestly safeguard the security of personal property and social stability, illegal fundraising, illegal deposits, and financial fraud must be resolutely quashed, with crackdowns on all manner of investment and financing activities that violate regulations by means of disguise.

Actively participating in the construction of an international financial governance system. We will build systems for overseas interest protection and early warning and risk prevention, establish a mechanism for national financial security review, optimize review systems for foreign investment in terms of national security and anti-monopoly, build a "safety dam" for financial risk prevention, and equip liberalization with a proper "safety valve".

### (V) Expanding supervision capacity for financial technology

With the ongoing rapid development of financial technology (fintech), we should maintain a positive and prudent attitude by encouraging innovation while holding fast to the bottom line. As we value risk management, we should also promote tech-empowered finance. In order to effectively address new problems and threats, there should be a dynamic balance and optimal combination between fintech development and the accumulated risk prevention.

Actively and steadily developing financial technology. More extensive research should be conducted on new technologies such as big data, cloud computing, artificial intelligence, blockchain, and the mobile internet. The digital transformation of financial institutions shall be accelerated. IT infrastructure in banking must be reshaped, while ecological and enterprise value chains re-identified and built. In addition, fintech should be used to reduce operating costs. Multiple measures should be taken to promote the orderly and healthy development of fintech in the capital market, to conduct pilot fintech innovation projects in the capital market, to actively explore the application of blockchain in the capital market, to construct a chain of capital market supervision, and to improve capital market's quality and efficiency in serving the real economy.

Creating a prudent and inclusive regulatory environment. Financial technology has not changed the risk attributes of finance. We should uphold the principle of "same business, same supervision", put substance above form, implement penetrating supervision, maintain a general consistency in business rules and standards and the orientation of regulatory policy, and resolutely prevent regulatory arbitrage. We should increase penalties for monopolistic behavior, use legislation to better protect data and information, improve the fintech regulatory framework, and prevent regulatory arbitrage and the cross-contagion of risks. In a market environment of equitable supervision, equal access, and fair competition, we will promote a balance among the rational expansion of capital, sustained innovation vitality, and the protection of public rights, such that science and technology may be used for good.

### IV. Conclusion

As President Xi Jinping pointed out, the world is now experiencing a profound change not seen in the past century, and the COVID-19 pandemic has only accelerated this great change. The practical experience of financial policy in 2020 definitively affirms the positive role played by high-quality development in China's financial industry during the 13th Five-Year Plan period, notably evident in the financial industry's effective support of the real economy in response to the pandemic and against internal and external risks. Policy in 2020 laid a solid foundation for the higher-quality development of the financial industry.

Looking ahead to the 14th Five-Year Plan period, financial policy will base around the new stage of development, implementing new development concepts, and better serving the new development pattern. The formulation and implementation of various financial policies will continue to follow the theme of high-quality development. Basing on supply-side structural reforms, with reform and innovation as the fundamental driving force, policies will comprehensively enhance the ability of finance in serving the real economy. In terms of macro-policy, we must continuously improve the system of macro-economic governance, improve the modern monetary policy framework, and optimize coordination between fiscal and monetary policy. In terms of systems and mechanisms, we will increase support for key areas and key links in the national economy, promote the reform and opening up of regional finance, and maintain the bottom line of zero systematic risk. In terms of innovation and development, efforts should go toward building a modern financial system, improving the multi-level capital market system, vigorously developing green finance, and promoting the orderly, high-level opening up of the financial industry. In terms of regulatory policy, fintech should be actively and steadily developed and a prudent and inclusive regulatory environment established; full play should be given to the positive role of finance in resource allocation, price discovery, and risk dispersion; financial development and financial security should be properly coordinated.

Finance is one of China's core competencies. It is therefore essential that the nature and laws of finance are accurately grasped, that we learn from beneficial foreign experiences, approach finance in accordance to China's actual conditions, follow a path of financial development with Chinese characteristics and promote the high-quality development of the financial industry during the 14th Five-Year Plan period.

# Feature Article 1:

## An Analysis of Fiscal and Monetary Policy Coordination from the Perspective of Traditional and Modern Monetary Theory Divergence[①]

### First, modern monetary theory's divergence from traditional monetary theory

The modern monetary theory started out as a peripheral idea. However, many countries' implementation of quantitative easing monetary policy in recent years has not led to inflation; and many countries' fiscal debt ceiling has been repeatedly hit due to the increasing financial constraints resulting from the financial crisis and/or the COVID-19 pandemic. This has caused some controversy around the issue of fiscal debt, such that the monetization of debt has drawn more attention. Now some have begun to approach the relationship between fiscal and monetary policy from new perspectives. Amid the increasing uncertainty of global economic recovery and the complexity of geopolitics, all economies are faced with the challenge of restructuring or structurally adjusting international industrial chains. Meanwhile, the integration of the traditional economy and the new economy, represented by information technology, is deepening.

We need to pay attention to the influence of modern monetary theory and digital currency on traditional monetary theory and economic practice, and focus on the coordination between monetary policy and fiscal policy and its implementation. The modern monetary theory considers currency as a voucher of government debt, where the government's right to taxation determines the status of legal tender. The public receives money out of the need to pay taxes; and taxes drive the issuance and circulation of money. Government debt is a means of regulating interest rates. Under a system of independent sovereign currency, as long as the government does not promise to convert foreign currency or gold at a fixed exchange rate, then the government's fiscal deficits are unlimited and the government cannot go bankrupt. This is because the government can repay its debts by issuing currency and recover excess currency by raising taxes or borrowing (i.e., raising debt). Here lies the biggest divergence from traditional monetary theory, which believes that money is created

---

[①] Author: Wu Xiaoling, Chairwoman of PBC School of Finance (PBCSF) at Tsinghua University, former Deputy Governor of the People's Bank of China.

out of the need to trade (thus there are multiple kinds of currency), but ultimately it is the power of the government and its taxation power that will determine what can become legal tender. Actually, at this point, traditional and modern monetary theories have something in common. But regarding the origin of money, a currency is traditionally considered as a medium, one among many currency types. The modern monetary theory focuses, particularly, on finance. It argues that money originates in fiscal taxation and legal jurisdiction. It thus focuses entirely on fiscal policy, hardly considering monetary policy at all, and introduces the concept of "functional finance".

Functional finance means that if the level of domestic revenue and the proportion of tax revenue are each too low, the government has to increase spending. Unemployment offers the best example of this point. The emergence of unemployment means that government spending is too low. If a country's interest rates are too high, the government will need to spend more money and provide more base money to lower interest rates. Abba Lerner, the founder of functional finance, rejected the concept of sound finance. Lerner argued that the correct deficit ratio is that of full employment, and the correct debt ratio is that consistent with the interest rate target, where overall fiscal policy is determined using the level of market interest rates and the level of employment.

### Second, the role of central banks in structural adjustment

Not long ago, everyone was discussing what the monetization of fiscal deficits meant. Most were thinking that such monetization only referred to a central bank buying fiscal bonds in the primary market. Secondary-market buying seemed not to count. But in fact, regardless of whether it is in the primary or secondary market, any purchase of fiscal bonds counts as the monetization of fiscal deficits. Under a credit-money system, legal tender is a debt that never needs to be repaid. On this point, traditional monetary banking and modern monetary theory are in agreement. Moreover, the modern monetary theory does not deny the central banking system. It also believes that even if the currency is directly created by the treasury and through payments, it has to go through the central bank payment system. Therefore, in that respect, monetization of fiscal deficits is really the same issue as the creation of credit money or legal tender.

The question then becomes who will lead the use of the central bank's assets, since spending is all conducted through the central bank's balance sheet. The modern monetary theory also does not believe that the government should directly issue money for purchases. The government spends through the central bank and the payment order is issued depending on the initiative of the treasury: the treasury could borrow RMB 100 billion from the central bank, and then the treasury has RMB 100 billion to spend; or it could issue RMB-100-billion government bonds, which will be bought by the central bank and used in the form of debt certificates. At this time, if the central bank's assets and liabilities are mainly gold and bonds of the treasury, the initiative for the use of money creation is in the hands of the treasury. Although the central bank has some regulatory power in terms of quantity and interest rates when buying on the secondary market, the initiative all lies with the treasury because it is the treasury that spends this money. If the central bank has re-lending in its balance sheet structure, that re-lending means that the central bank gives loans directly to commercial banks, and the commercial banks can use base money to create other currencies. Here, the central bank has the decision-making power. Central banks expand their assets independently and the initiative to issue currency lies with them.

Western countries originally followed a fiscal approach; but after the financial crisis, their central banks bought the assets of non-financial institutions directly through a number of quantitative easing monetary policies. These are actually structural adjustments. China's central bank has always adopted a structural adjustment approach, and our textbooks state that monetary policy governs the aggregate while fiscal policy governs the structure. But if you look at the nature of money creation, central banks have room to adjust the structure of their balance sheets, or they have great power of initiative. In fact, central banks can guide certain adjustments in market structure through the use of their own assets. In the past, the People's Bank of China (PBC) often said that this was a phased task, but now it does not necessarily seem to be so, but rather an exploratory comparison — whether it is more efficient for the treasury to dispose of money directly or more efficient and binding through the central bank channel. I do not find that China's fiscal budget system is particularly well developed, and the line between necessary economic spending and basic public spending is not very clear. There are some aspects involving economic development where guidance through the central bank's base money may be the better choice.

### Third, focusing on budget quality rather than the budget deficit

Under a credit-money system, a sovereign entity can technically issue unlimited currency, but there is an economic limitation in the form of the inflation rate. If inflation is high, people's lives will be heavily impacted. However, the modern monetary theory assumes that sovereign currency government deficits under a floating exchange rate can be unlimited — provided that there is an effective budget for public objectives and a budget guaranteeing full employment — with special emphasis on budgetary issues. Because budgets are the financial mechanism of money creation, having an effective budget for public objectives that guarantees full employment is a necessity. It is not government solvency that constrains government spending, but rather the unintended effects it has, such as resource outflows from more efficient sectors and moral hazards from overprotection. A national budget will provide effective project management and evaluation mechanisms to ensure that budgeting is used for public purposes. We have been trying to establish an assessment of fiscal performance, but so far, China lacks a sound assessment tool.

Governments are very worried about fiscal deficits. When the EU was founded, its members set a deficit rate of 3 percent and a debt ratio of 60 percent. However, there now seems to be a mismatch in the EU's monetary and fiscal policies. This is most evident and severe in countries with significant debt problems. In 2008, the EU did not issue EU debt to assist the four southern European countries suffering from debt problems. During the COVID-19 pandemic in 2020, EUR 750 billion of recovery funds were issued, of which EUR 390 billion were non-repayable bailout funds and the rest were low-interest loans. EU leaders also agreed on a budget of EUR 1.074 trillion for the next seven years, which they will have to use to solve the economic problems Europe now faces. Japan has no foreign debts, only local debts, so its deficit and debt rate are very high; the deficit rate is basically around 6 percent; the debt rate has been more than 200 percent, but there has been no large impact on the financial markets.

As for China, the deficit in the budget is under control, with the government using 3 percent and 60 percent limits to constrain it. I actually see this as a constraint on the public. Three percent and 60 percent are not natural limits that must absolutely be kept. If we have to keep these limits and disregard scientific fiscal budgeting's role in stimulating the economy, what we bring about will be behavioral distortion. China's current published deficit ratio is 3.6 percent, but the issuances of special central and local government bonds are contrary to the original intent of special CGBs and LGBs. Special CGBs and LGBs must have the ability to recover the principal and pay interest, but local governments are short of spending on current projects, not short of money for construction. Issuing such debt will either result in the money not being used at all or being used in disguise. Disguise means using money as a substitute for some loans from commercial banks, and since special bonds have lower interest rates than policy loans and commercial bank loans, they exert a crowding-out effect. China's rigid adherence to a 3 percent deficit rate and the issuance of more than RMB 2 trillion of additional special CGBs and LGBs has ultimately left us with a distorted result. It would be better if we just accept a 6.1 percent deficit ratio and use deficit and debt to solve the problems we need to solve. Now China has proposed to "maintain security in the six areas", but the money is not enough. Local governments are not short of money for construction, but for daily expenses. The deficit and debt rates under the credit-money system are not fixed for a country. It is important to actually remain true to our original aspiration and spend money well, growing the economy for the better of the people.

# Feature Article 2:

## Scientific & Technological Innovation and Economic & Financial Transformation in the Post-Pandemic Era[①]

**Key Point:** With the implementation of macro policies to cover basic needs during the COVID-19 pandemic outbreak, emerging drivers of technological innovation, and the long-term process of digitalization, internal economic restructuring is an inevitability; this fact has led to a series of economic and economic policy considerations.

The outbreak of COVID-19 in 2020 became a major event. It has already brought profound changes to the global political and economic landscape. Its aggregate economic impact is comparable to that of the Great Depression of the 1930s — in terms of both supply and demand sides. It has also had an unprecedented effect on human society's methods of production and communication and economic and trade activities worldwide. The COVID-19 pandemic has also induced a structural shock to the long-term business cycle. This will accelerate the effective use of new knowledge and technology worldwide and make digital development an important factor driving economic recovery, transforming communication, and promoting theoretical development in the post-epidemic period, and will profoundly affect international political and economic relations, becoming a catalyst for changes unseen in a century.

### I. Original models and new forces propel post-pandemic economics and finance

Since the beginning of 2020, the COVID-19 pandemic— a true "black swan" event — has continued to disturb global economic and social development. In response, major economies have basically taken two necessary measures. The first is short-term policy response — managing economic downturn and systemic financial risks caused by the pandemic's shocks through necessary policy instruments. The second is a long-term structural adjustment — working to fully or partially address the root causes of pandemic-related disruptions while minimizing the probability of similar disruptions evolving into crises and developing new modes of production and factor organization. Over the most recent period, the long-term structural adjustment paradigm has been a commitment

---

[①] Author: Lu Lei, Deputy Administrator of the State Administration of Foreign Exchange (SAFE).

to fossil fuel alternatives in the fight against climate change. Therefore, to judge post-pandemic economic and financial performance, it is necessary to study both the effects of short-term response policies (their costs and efficacy) as well as the effects of long-term structural adjustment following the pandemic.

In the short term, policy and expectation adjustments have effectively driven economic rebound. The pandemic brought a heavy brunt to both the supply and demand sides of economic operation, but as fiscal and monetary policies have been implemented, citizens and enterprises each came to understand the characteristics of the virus and effectively adjusted their expectations and investment decisions. The result is varying degrees of rebound. According to the April 2021 forecast of the International Monetary Fund (IMF), the global economy's growth rate was -3.3 percent in 2020 and is expected to increase to 6 percent in 2021. These figures are up 1.1 and 0.8 percentage points, respectively, from the previous forecast issued in October 2020. In terms of actual performance, the real GDP of the US contracted by 3.5 percent year-on-year (YOY) in 2020, and the first quarter of 2021 showed a rapid quarter-on-quarter (QOQ) annualized growth rate of 6.4 percent. Meanwhile, the EU's real GDP contracted by 6.6 percent YOY in 2020 and narrowed to 1.8 percent YOY in the first quarter of 2021. China's economic performance has been most impressive. It was the only major economy to achieve positive growth in 2020, and its GDP saw a 18.3 percent YOY growth in the first quarter of 2021. However, there are also costs to the recovery, such as rising macro leverage and compressed space for macro policies. Following 2008, the world's major economies have once again entered an era of comprehensive quantitative easing. Central banks in more than 40 countries and regions around the world have cut interest rates since 2020. Among these, the Federal Reserve has implemented an average inflation targeting system and announced an open-ended quantitative easing policy to expand the size of money market liquidity facilities, and bought unlimited bonds and mortgage securities (MBS) on demand. A series of policies from various countries have ushered in a global period of "abundant money and low interest". Major financial markets rebounded quickly after a steep downswing, as open market financial transactions were less affected by the movement of people and easily influenced by market expectations and sentiment.

Historically, major shocks are often followed by leaps in technological progress. After the spread of the bubonic plague across 14th-century Europe, the continent saw the birth of modern medicine and physiology, followed by the cultural and artistic Renaissance, and later, the Industrial Revolution. In the early 20th century, the Spanish flu pandemic claimed a death toll of 20 to 50 million worldwide. At the same time, it spawned the rapid development of bacteriology, pandemic prevention, and pharmaceutical R&D, promoting the deep integration of physics, chemistry, and life medicine. It also gave rise to a large number of scientific and technological innovations that would greatly affect human society, such as the discovery of antibiotics and the use of X-rays for medical diagnosis. Those achievements have protected human health and also contributed to social and economic prosperity. It is the same case with scientific and technological innovation amid the COVID-19 pandemic. As of November 2020, there were 48 vaccines undergoing clinical testing, including lipid nanoparticle-based mRNA vaccines, DNA vaccines, adjuvant protein vaccines, inactivated virus vaccines, and non-replicating viral vector vaccines. There were also 164 drugs in clinical testing. It is expected that the virus and its effects will be contained within the space of socio-economic tolerance. Gradual economic and financial recovery has thus been supported by both traditional policy and emerging scientific research.

## II. Factor revolution: digitalization constitutes a major conversion of factors in the post-pandemic period

What are the defining traits of the post-pandemic period? There is sufficient evidence to tell us that digitalization is one of the period's irreversible trends.

Before the pandemic, the digital economy expanded rapidly to occupy up to 40 percent of the global economy. As shown in "A New Vision of the Global Digital Economy (2020)", published by the China Academy of Information and Communications Technology (CAICT) in October 2020, the global digital economy reached USD 31.8 trillion in 2019, accounting for 41.5 percent of global GDP, up 5.4 percent YOY and 3.1 percentage points higher than the rate of nominal GDP growth over the same period. In 2019, the size of China's digital economy reached RMB 35.8 trillion, accounting for 36.2 percent of domestic GDP, up 15.6 percent YOY and 7.9 percentage points higher than the rate of GDP growth over the same period. The Hurun Research Institute's Hurun Global Unicorn List 2020 indicates that, among the 586 unicorn enterprises worldwide, 89 are e-commerce companies; 63 are AI and financial technology companies; 53 are software service companies; 33 are sharing economy companies; 28 are health technology companies, and 20 are big data companies. All in all, companies involved in the digital economy account for half of the total.

The global spread of the pandemic is accelerating the development of the digital economy. The outbreak of the pandemic in early 2020 disrupted social contact. As a result, many companies were forced to move their business online. Digital operations became a critical means for companies to maintain business. In September 2020, Forbes reported on research data from Twilio Consulting showing that 97 percent of companies said that the pandemic had accelerated their digital transformation. The report also estimated that the pandemic had advanced the process of global digitalization by at least five to seven years.

There are growing signs that data has become a new factor of production. As with traditional factors of production, data's quality and quantity improvements can, in turn, improve the quality and quantity of digital economy products. Data has become one of the independent variables of the production function. From labor and land to productive capital and data, the factors of humans' production activities are becoming more ethereal and less competitive, while economies of scale, network effects, and economies of scope generated by the factors of production are becoming stronger. For example, the development of digital finance can enable finance to better serve the real economy. Models based on big data and AI in asset and risk management have been implemented in various financial institutions, and advanced management technologies based on big data and block chain are being explored and improved within China's financial regulatory departments.

## III. Theory and policy considerations for structural adjustment

With the implementation of macro policies to cover basic needs during the pandemic outbreak, emerging drivers of technological innovation, and the long-term process of digitalization, internal economic restructuring is an inevitability; this fact has led to a series of economic and economic policy considerations.

The first is the exploration of monetary theory and macro policy from a macroeconomic perspective. In 2021 — and for years to come — the process of monetary "anchor hunting" will continue, with real interest rates as the key indicator. On the one hand, how and at what point to implement monetary policy normalization are issues that national macroeconomic regulatory authorities should carefully consider. There are two possibilities here: an active withdrawal of policies under the normalization of employment indicators, or a passive withdrawal driven by high debt ratios and systemic financial risks. On the other hand, when combined with the above analysis of digitalization, once digitalization reaches a certain level of popularization within government, corporate, and financial sectors, the transmission path of liquidity delivery will probably change. For example, monetary policy authorities may achieve precise and efficient digital-based monetary injection to resolve the issue of ineffective monetary policy transmission mechanisms. At that time, the problems of unlimited easing and financial risks will probably be solved. Another more theoretically challenging issue is the restructuring of monetary theory, including the introduction of digital M0 in combination with smart contracts, which could potentially lead to the zeroing of any unnecessary liquidity reserves. The earlier Keynesian theory of money demand being based on transactional, speculative, or prudential motives is then likely to be rewritten. The questions "what is monetary equilibrium" and "how to achieve monetary equilibrium" will become a major direction for future research.

The second is approaching the future of digital integration in economics and finance from the perspective of microeconomics. From the perspective of welfare economics, digital technology innovation and its deep integration with economic and social activities, at the levels of both private and public goods, may constitute a tool for increasing social welfare. In terms of private goods, humans in the future will rely on digital technology innovations for more accurate decision-making on clothing, food, housing, transportation, medical care, retirement, and savings purchases simply because they will have better abilities to obtain and process information. At the same time, enterprises will be better able to provide customized services because of their ability to process personal information (as long as authorization is obtained and privacy protected). The popularization of digital currencies will reduce the demand for cash reserves among the subjects of social and economic activities, but it will increase the demand for yield, thus realizing the yield of traditional cash reserves. In terms of public goods, the government will be able to provide public goods more accurately and efficiently by applying social big data in a scientific, reasonable, and legal manner, whether in macro adjustments or monetary and fiscal policy decisions. For example, based on big social and economic data, research can produce more accurate judgments of the macroeconomic situation and precise predictions of economic inflection points, social emergencies, etc. This will help decision-makers formulate scientific, forward-oriented policies and regulate the operations of society and the economy more stably and efficiently. From the perspective of microeconomics, special attention needs to be paid to the pricing of the digital economy and digital finance. For example, does differentiated customization imply different products? If the products are fundamentally the same, does a difference in price difference mean complete price discrimination, or is it the leftward shift of the supply curve due to information's cost-reduction effect? The former implies the disappearance of consumer surplus, while the latter implies welfare. This is also an academic issue in need of study.

The third is investigating problems in data ecology from the perspective of regulation. The monopolistic growth of large platform companies, use of big data to set different consumer prices for the same product or service, leaks of personal information, and other problems demand that regulatory and legislative authorities keep up with the times, continuously building and improving institutional mechanisms and the framework of the legal system. There need to be increased penalties for monopolistic behavior; legislation must be passed to better protect data and information; the fintech regulatory framework must be strengthened; regulatory arbitrage and the cross-contagion of risks must be prevented. The present digitalization of the economy and society faces many challenges in common, but we are confident of great innovations to come in the theory and practice of digital regulation.

# Part Two

## Chinese Financial Policies in 2020

## Macro Financial Policies

### I. Monetary Policy[1]

The COVID-19 epidemic in 2020 has had an enormous impact on the global economy. Countries have substantially cut interest rate and implemented various other unconventional monetary policies to save their economies and maintain the stability of their financial markets. The People's Bank of China (PBC) also reacted with policy measures such as cuts to the required reserve ratio (RRR) and reverse repo rate for open market operations, and introduced a number of anti-epidemic credit policies including re-lending, re-discount and innovative monetary policies to directly stimulate the real economy. In general, the PBC played a flexible and precise role in the trickle-down of monetary policies on the basis of reserving space for monetary policy. This activity was important for the strong recovery of China's economy in the second half of the year. The pace of global economic recovery in 2021 is still highly uncertain, and other major countries' monetary and fiscal policies may have spillover effects on China. As a result, monetary policy formulation in 2021 faces a more complex internal and external environment.

#### (I) Main Content of 2020 Monetary Policies

**1. Open Market Operations**

(1) Open Market Operations

On March 30, 2020, the PBC lowered the seven-day reverse repo rate for open market operations from 2.40% to 2.20%, which remained unchanged throughout the rest of the year. By the end of 2020, the PBC had conducted reverse repo operations totaling RMB 15.04 trillion, double that of 2019. Among that total, seven-day operations came to RMB 11.59 trillion, likewise double that of 2019 (RMB 5.21 trillion).

(2) Central Bank Bills Swap (CBS)

Since 2020, the PBC has conducted 12 CBS operations, with a stable, once-per-month frequency. Cumulative operation volume was RMB 61 billion, with respective quarterly totals of RMB 16 billion, RMB 15 billion, RMB 15 billion and RMB 15 billion. Tenor was three months and the rate was 0.10%. CBS operation has helped improve the secondary-market liquidity of bank-issued perpetual bonds, and helped supporting banks — especially small and mid-sized banks — replenish capital through the issuance of perpetual bonds, thereby enhancing the capacity

---

[1] Authors: He Xiaobei, Head of Macro Finance, Center for Finance and Development, National Institute of Finance, Tsinghua University, and project fellow of Program for China's Financial Policy Report. Shen Yi, Research Fellow, Center for Finance and Development, National Institute of Finance, Tsinghua University.

of financial services to the real economy.

### 2. Medium-term Lending Facility (MLF) & Standing Lending Facility (SLF)

(1) Medium-term Lending Facility (MLF)

On February 17, 2020, the PBC lowered the MLF one-year interest rate by 10 basis points to 3.15% from 3.25%, then, on April 15, by 20 basis points to 2.95%. The PBC conducted RMB 5.15 trillion in MLF operations over 2020 (an approximate 40% increase over 2019), all of which had a one-year term. The closing balance for MLFs came to RMB 5.15 trillion, up RMB 1.46 trillion over the beginning of the year.

(2) Standing Lending Facility (SLF)

On April 10, 2020, the PBC lowered SLF interest rates by 30 basis points for each tenor — to 3.05% for overnight, 3.20% for seven-day, and 3.55% for one-month. Cumulative first-quarter SLF operations came to RMB 102.7 billion, while cumulative SLF operations for the whole year came to RMB 186.2 billion, with an ending balance of RMB 19.8 billion.

### 3. Required Reserve Ratio & Excess Reserve Ratio

(1) Required Reserve Ratio (RRR)

In 2020, the PBC lowered the RRR three times —including an across-the-board RRR reduction, a targeted RRR cut for inclusive finance, and a targeted RRR reduction. Specifically, on January 6, 2020, the PBC lowered the RRR for financial institutions (excluding financial companies, financial leasing companies, and auto financing companies) by 0.5 percentage points, releasing more than RMB 800 billion in long-term funds. On March 6, 2020, the PBC conducted a targeted reduction in RRR for inclusive finance. Based on institutions' performance according to 2019 annual assessments, RRR was lowered by 0.5 or 1.5 percentage points, releasing RMB 400 billion in long-term funds and an additional RMB 150 billion for the issuance of inclusive financial loans. On April 3, 2020, the PBC announced cuts of one percentage point to RRR for rural credit cooperatives, rural commercial banks, rural cooperative banks, village banks, and urban commercial banks operating exclusively within the provincial administrative region. On April 15 and May 15, RRR was reduced by 0.5 percentage point respectively, releasing approximately RMB 400 billion total in long-term funds. These three RRR cuts released a cumulative RMB 1.75 trillion in long-term funds.

(2) Rate on Excess Reserves (ERR)

As the lower limit of the interest rate corridor, the ERR has been maintained at 0.72 % since November 2008. After the PBC's 2020 first-quarter release of liquidity, the pledged repo rate (DR007) of deposit-taking institutions dropped to 1.13% at one point in March. In order to open space for market interest rates to descend, and to encourage bank lending and excess reserve reductions, the PBC has lowered the ERR of financial institutions in the PBC from 0.72% to 0.35% since April 7, 2020. This constitutes the first reduction in ERR since the 2008 financial crisis.

### 4. Monetary and Credit Policies in Response to COVID-19

(1) Central Bank Re-lending and Re-discount

In order to support the anti-epidemic provisions, the PBC arranged special central bank re-lending program of RMB 300 billion during January 31 of Spring Festival 2020 as a way to support key areas and enterprises in epidemic prevention and control. On February 26, the amount was increased by RMB 500 billion to support enterprises' orderly return to work and production, while the central bank re-lending rate for rural, small, and micro-businesses was reduced by 0.25 percentage point to 2.5%. On April 20, re-lending and re-discount programs were increased by RMB 1 trillion to further support economic recovery. All in all, RMB 1.8 trillion was issued.

By the end of June 2020, a total of RMB 300 billion had been issued in special central bank lending, and relevant banks had been supported to release preferential loans (totaling RMB 283.4 billion) to 7,597 national and local key enterprises at a weighted average interest rate of 2.49%, and enterprises' actual financing interest rates were approximately 1.25% after a 50% financial discount. Central bank re-lending and re-discount programs totaling RMB 500 billion had been completed, and locally incorporated banks had been supported to release RMB 498.3 billion in prime-based loans to 590,000 enterprises, with a weighted average interest rate of 4.22%. By the end of December 2020, a total of RMB 1 trillion inclusive central bank re-lending and re-discount programs had been issued, and locally incorporated banks had been guided to support 1.58 million enterprises, with a weighted average interest rate of 4.67%.

Special credit policies for epidemic prevention and control or the return to work and production also included the phased deferment of loans. On March 1, the China Banking and Insurance Regulatory Commission (CBIRC), the PBC, and other five regulatory authorities jointly issued the "Notice on Extending the Policy of Phased Deferment of Loan Principal and Interest Repayments for Micro-, Small and Medium-sized Enterprises", which encouraged micro-, small and mid-sized enterprises (MSMEs) experiencing difficulties to apply for the phased deferment of principal and interest payments.

(2) Monetary Policy Instruments Enabling Direct Support for the Real Economy

In order to support the development of small and mid-sized enterprises, the PBC launched two monetary policy instruments in direct support of the real economy on June 1, 2020: one supporting deferred payments on micro- and small businesses' (MSBs) inclusive loans, the other a support plan for inclusive MSB credit loans. These two innovative monetary policy instruments have improved the structural monetary policy instruments system and strengthened financial support for stabilizing enterprises and ensuring employment.

The support instrument for deferring inclusive MSB loan repayment supplies RMB 40 billion in funds. The PBC provides banks with incentives equivalent to one percent of the principal of inclusive MSB loans under deferred repayment. It does so by interest rate swap agreements signed between special-purpose vehicles (SPVs) and locally incorporated banks. By the end of 2020, banking financial institutions nationwide had deferred RMB 7.3 trillion total in loan principal and interest repayments. The support instrument for deferring the repayment of inclusive MSB loans operates on a monthly basis, supporting the deferred principal of the inclusive MSB loans totaling RMB 873.7 billion, with a weighted average extension period of 12.8 months, which alleviates MSBs' pressure to repay principal and interest in stages.

To address challenges arising from MSBs' lack of collateral guarantees, the PBC launched a support plan for inclusive MSB credit loans, through which RMB 400 billion of funds was to be provided. The PBC would provide favorable funding support for locally incorporated banks through credit loan support plan agreements signed between SPVs and banks. The support plan for inclusive MSB credit loans operates quarterly, supporting the issuance of credit loans for MSBs from March through December to total RMB 480.8 billion, substantively addressing the difficulties MSBs face in raising funds. In 2020, banking financial institutions issued inclusive MSB credit loans totaling RMB 3.9 trillion, up RMB 1.6 trillion over the previous year.

### 5. Structural Monetary Policy

**(1) Pledged Supplementary Lending (PSL)**

In 2020, the PBC issued RMB 20.2 billion in PSL, down 92% year on year (YOY). By the end of 2020, the closing PSL balance was RMB 3.235 trillion, down RMB 322.4 billion YOY. In the first half of the year, the PBC recovered a total of RMB 28.3 billion in PSL from policy and development banks, including RMB 48.5 billion in the second quarter.

**(2) Targeted Medium-term Lending Facility (TMLF)**

The PBC first launched TMLF for the first time in 2019. Its goal was to encourage banks to increase the credit supply to private enterprises and SMEs and to reduce their financing costs via a market-oriented approach. In January and April 2020, the PBC conducted TMLF operations totaling RMB 240.5 billion and RMB 56.1 billion, respectively. The tenor was one year and the rate was 2.95%. The year-end TMLF balance was RMB 296.6 billion, while TMLF for the whole year amounted to RMB 526 billion, of which RMB 400 billion was continued in the form of MLF.

**(3) Inclusive Finance**

2020 was the year that China was to achieve its goal of building a moderately prosperous society by eliminating poverty in all respects. Aiming for "targeted poverty alleviation", we actively used such tools as central bank lending, central bank discounts, and pledged supplementary lending to support agriculture and MSBs. We also guided financial institutions to increase their support of MSBs, private enterprises, "agriculture, rural areas and farmers", poverty alleviation, and other key areas or weak links in the national economy.

Starting from July 1, 2020, the central bank lending interest rate for supporting agriculture and central bank loans and discounts for supporting MSBs were lowered by 25 basis points. After the adjustment, three-month, six-month, and one-year interest rates for central bank lending to support agriculture and MSBs were 1.95%, 2.15% and 2.25% respectively, while the central bank discount rate was 2%. Over the respective quarters of 2020, special central bank lending for poverty alleviation amounted to RMB 6.3 billion, RMB 8 billion, RMB 7.2 billion and RMB 7.9 billion respectively, with a balance of RMB 37 billion at the end of the year. At the end of 2020, central bank lending to support agriculture had a balance of RMB 457.2 billion, while that for supporting MSBs was RMB 975.6 billion; central bank lending for poverty alleviation had a balance of RMB 215.3 billion; and central bank discounts had a balance of RMB 578.4 billion.

In 2020, the Report on the Work of the Government instituted a requirement that "the growth rate of inclusive loans for micro and small enterprises (MSEs) in large commercial banks should be higher than 40%." By the end of 2020, the balance of inclusive loans for MSEs was RMB 15.1 trillion, with an increase of 7.2 percentage points and 30.3% YOY, over the end of 2019. MSE entities had been supported with 3.228 million, a YOY increase of 19.4%. In 2020, inclusive loans for MSEs increased RMB 3.5 trillion, for RMB 1.4 trillion of YOY growth.

### 6. Market-oriented Interest Rate Reform

Since 2020, the PBC has continuously promoted loan prime rate (LPR) reform. Since January 1, 2020, new loans have no longer been priced in reference to benchmark loan rates. From March to August 2020, the conversion of outstanding floating-rate loans' pricing benchmark was successfully completed according to the principles of marketization and legalization. By the end of August, the conversion rate of outstanding floating-rate loans' pricing benchmarks reached 92.4 %. Embedding LPR into the funds transfer pricing (FTP) system constitutes a key step in breaking benchmark loan rates' implicit lower limit and in the implementation of market-oriented interest rate pricing.

LPR effectively realizes the transition of interest rates. On February 17, 2020, the PBC lowered the MLF interest rate by 10 basis points, while the one-year and five-year LPR released on February 20 were each cut by five basis points — to 4.05% and 3.75%, respectively. Since the one-year MLF was reduced by 20 basis points on April 15, one- and five-year LPR prices have dropped by another 20 and 10 basis points respectively, to 3.85 and 4.65 percent.

### 7. Money Market Rate & Credit Market Rate

(1) Money Market Rate

In 2020, the money market rate exhibited a U-shaped annual trend. With first and second-quarter reductions in the policy rate and RRR, market liquidity gradually became sufficient, the money market rate reaching its lowest level for the whole year within the second quarter. As more monetary policies were introduced that directly stimulated the real economy, the PBC declined to cut interest rates or RRR in the second half of the year, such that money market rates rose steadily in the third and fourth quarters. The average seven-day pledged repo rate (DR007) of deposit institutions in the interbank market were 2.11%, 1.66%, 2.15% and 2.16% respectively over each quarter. The average seven-day pledged repo rate (R007) over the four quarters were 2.49%, 1.86%, 2.50% and 2.84% respectively. R007 reached approximately 4.0% at the end of December. The Shanghai Interbank Offered Rate (Shibor) in each quarter was 1.60%, 1.33%, 1.82% and 1.60% respectively.

(2) Weighted Average Interest Rate of Loans

Monetary policy has been effectively transmitted to the real economy. In the fourth quarter of 2019, the weighted average interest rate of loans was 5.44%. This figure dropped to 5.08% in the first quarter of 2020, then remained relatively stable throughout the year. In the fourth quarter of 2020, it hit 5.03%, its lowest value since 2009. The weighted average interest rate of loans at the end of 2020 had fallen by 53 percentage points as compared to the end of 2019.

### 8. PBC Digital Currency

Digital RMB is steadily advancing. In 2016, the PBC defined the issuance of digital currency as a strategic goal and launched the prototype research and development of a digital bill trading platform based on blockchain and digital currency. Then in 2017, the PBC established the Institute of Digital currency. In 2020, the PBC launched closed tests in Shenzhen, Suzhou, Xiong'an, Chengdu, and for the 2022 Winter Olympics.

## (II) Monetary Policy and Macro-prudential Policy for Preventing Financial Risks

On October 23, 2020, the PBC issued a notice to solicit public opinions on the "Law of the People's Republic of China on the PBC (Revised Draft for Comments)". This revision was the first legislative work done on the law in the 17 years since 2003. It filled institutional gaps in macroprudential policy, legally established the "dual-pillar regulatory framework of monetary policy and macro-prudential policy", and clarified the responsibilities of the PBC in formulating and implementing macroprudential policies.

### 1. Macroprudential Assessment (MPA)

Since 2020, macroprudential assessment (MPA) has continued to effectively optimize the credit structure and promote financial supply-side structural reform. First, it has increased the assessment weight of financing for MSEs, private enterprises, and the manufacturing industry; it has set up a temporary assessment index for "central bank lending application", guided financial institutions to increase support in key areas and weak links of the national economy; and it has ensured that new financing focuses on going to MSMEs and the manufacturing industry. Second, it has improved relevant assessments of LPR applications. Since August 20, statistics on loan interest rate fluctuations in reference to the benchmark interest rate have been replaced by statistics on points' increase/decrease on the basis of LPR. Unleashing the potential of LPR reform to lower lending rates could encourage banks to accelerate the conversion of pricing benchmarks for outstanding floating-rate loans and significantly reduce enterprises' comprehensive financing costs.

### 2. Concentrated Management of Real Estate Loans

In order to prevent systemic financial risks caused by an excessive rise in housing prices, the PBC and CBIRC jointly issued the "Notice on Establishing the Concentration Management of Real Estate Loans in Banking Financial Institutions" on December 31, 2020. This notice was meant to control the proportion of real estate loans. It set an upper limit on large state-owned banks' proportion of real estate loans at 40%, while mid-sized banks, small banks and non-county rural commercial banks, and county rural commercial banks and village banks' limits were respectively set at 27.5%, 22.5%, 17.5% and 12.5%, with a transitional period of more than two years.

### 3. New Mechanism of Countercyclical Capital Buffer

In order to enhance banks' anti-risk capacity during economic fluctuations, the PBC and CBIRC jointly issued the *Notice on Establishing Mechanism of Countercyclical Capital Buffer* (YF [2020] No. 233) in September 2020. This notice clearly established a mechanism for countercyclical capital buffer and set the initial countercyclical capital buffer ratio of banking financial institutions to zero. In the future, the PBC and CBIRC will reevaluate and adjust the countercyclical capital buffer ratio, both in due course and in comprehensive consideration of such factors as macroeconomic and financial conditions, the level of leverage ratio, the soundness of the banking sector, and the performance of systemic financial risks.

**4. Promoting the Regulated Development of Financial Holding Companies**

In order to prevent enterprises from blindly expanding into the financial sector and thus accumulating risks, the State Council issued the *Decision on Implementing Access Management of Financial Holding Companies* (GF [2020] No.12, hereinafter referred to as the "Decision") and the PBC released *Trial Measures on Regulation of Financial Holding Companies* (PBC Order [2020] No. 4, hereinafter referred to as the "Measures") in September 2020. The Decision and the Measures provide for comprehensive, ongoing, and penetrative access and supervision over financial holding companies formed by the investment holdings of non-financial enterprises based on consolidated management, and the regulation of financial holding companies' business behavior. The Decision and the Measures will continue to be implemented according to the general principle of separate operations models, which is conducive to the sustained and healthy development of financial holding companies and prevention of cross-sector risk contagion, fostering a virtuous cycle between the economy and the financial sector.

**5. Adjusted Macroprudential Management of Cross-border Financing**

On March 12, 2020, the PBC and State Administration of Foreign Exchange (SAFE) issued a notice. In order to further expand the use of foreign capital, facilitate cross-border financing by domestic institutions, and reduce financing costs of the real economy, the PBC and SAFE decided to increase the macroprudential adjustment parameter in the *Notice of the PBC on Macro-prudential Management of Full-scale Cross-border Financing* (YF [2017] No.9) from 1 to 1.25 in accordance with the current situation of macroeconomic and international balance of payments, which is conducive to the expansion of domestic institutions' cross-border financing.

With the appreciation of RMB in the second half of the year, enterprises' foreign currency financing grew rapidly, while the balance of foreign debt increased as well. To guard against corresponding risks, the PBC and SAFE decided to lower the macroprudential adjustment parameter for cross-border financing of financial institutions from 1.25 to 1 on December 14.

### (III) Exchange Rate and Financial Market Reform

**1. Exchange Rate Setting Mechanism**

In 2020, the United States and other developed countries launched unprecedented policies for monetary easing, while China maintained a regular monetary policy range, with the RMB gradually appreciating against the U.S. dollar from a mid-year low of 7.1 to 6.5 at the end of the year. Throughout the year, flexibility increased in the RMB exchange rate, while market expectations remained stable, cross-border capital flows stayed in order, and the performance of the foreign exchange market was smooth. The PBC therefore decided to cut the foreign exchange risk reserve ratio for forward foreign exchange sales from 20% to 0, effective from October 12, 2020. This is to keep the RMB exchange rate basically stable at a level of adaptive equilibrium.

**2. Offshore RMB Market**

In 2020, the PBC continued to issue central bank bills in Hong Kong on a regular basis.

Throughout the year, 12 terms of RMB-denominated central bank bills were issued, totaling RMB 155 billion. Respective quarter issuances were RMB 40 billion, RMB 40 billion, RMB 40 billion and RMB 35 billion; these included three varieties of terms — three-month, six-month, and one-year. The normalized issuance of RMB-denominated central bank bills in Hong Kong helps enrich RMB products in the offshore market, enhance activity therein, and promote the internationalization of the Renminbi. In 2020, the issuance of offshore RMB-denominated bills (excluding Hong Kong RMB-denominated central bank bills) exceeded RMB 130 billion, an increase of 30% compared to 2019.

**3. Currency Swap Agreement**

In 2020, the PBC successively signed bilateral currency swap agreements with 13 countries or regions (Egypt, Laos, Switzerland, Pakistan, Chile, Mongolia, Argentina, New Zealand, Hungary, South Korea, Iceland, Russia, and Hong Kong SAR), and expanded the scale of currency swapping with four of them (Pakistan, Chile, South Korea, and Hong Kong SAR).

**(IV) Effect and Evaluation of Monetary Policy Implementation in 2020**

The outbreak of COVID-19 in 2020 plunged the world into major public health and economic crises. Economies around the world have launched massive bail-out measures. In the United States, the Federal Reserve lowered interest rates by 150 basis points in a single cut and launched a number of emergency liquidity support measures to stabilize financial markets.

Faced with the complex domestic and international economic situations and ongoing uncertainty from the pandemic, China's monetary policies have steadily progressed while reserving space for policy. In addition to launching a number of anti-epidemic credit and innovative monetary policies, the PBC lowered the seven-day reverse repo rate for open market operations by 20 basis points and MLF interest rates by 30 basis points throughout the year, generating an overall decrease in market interest rates. By the end of December 2020, ordinary loans' weighted average interest rate had fallen 40 basis points from the end of 2019 to 5.03%, the lowest in a decade.

The effects of monetary policy adjustment have been felt in the real economy. In 2020, the total amount of aggregate financing to the real economy (AFRE) increased by RMB 34.86 trillion, with YOY growth of 13.3% and an increase of RMB 9.28 trillion over the previous year. In March 2020, AFRE reached 5.184 billion yuan, a record high for a single month. New RMB loans increased by RMB 20.03 trillion throughout the year, with a YOY increase of RMB 3.15 trillion. In 2020, the balance of broad money supply (M2) was RMB 218.68 trillion, with an average YOY growth rate of 10.33%.

With the growth of the scale of credit, the structure of credit continued to be optimized, with loans for MSEs and medium to long-term loans for manufacturing growing rapidly. At the end of 2020, enterprise (institution) loans had increased by RMB 12.2 trillion from the beginning of the year, with YOY growth of RMB 2.7 trillion. The growth rate for medium to long-term loans in the manufacturing industry was 35.2%, rising for 14 consecutive months. The balance of inclusive loans for MSBs exhibited a YOY increase of 30.3%.

Positive measures taken by the PBC to respond to the impact of the epidemic were remarkably effective. After falling to -6.8% in the first quarter of 2020, GDP gradually recovered to reach 2.3% for the year, which was significantly higher than market expectations, and made China the only major to experience positive growth over the same period. Inflation in 2020 was largely affected by the rise of pork prices but remained in a moderate range throughout the year. The consumer price index (CPI) gradually declined after peaking in early 2020, for a 2.51% YOY increase.

As the volatility of international financial markets increased, the RMB exchange rate remained stable at a level of adaptive equilibrium. Meanwhile, improvements in the flexibility of the exchange rate acted as an automatic stabilizer in balancing internal and external economies. At the end of 2020, China's RMB exchange rate index, the China Foreign Exchange Trade System (CFETS), was 94.84, showing a 3.78% appreciation over the end of the previous year.

**(V) Monetary Policy Outlook in 2021**

The prospect of global economic recovery in 2021 depends to a large extent on the speeds of production and application of COVID-19 vaccines. Major developed countries have introduced truly unprecedented monetary and fiscal stimulus policies. With the gradual lifting of quarantines, rebounds in consumption and investment are likely to drive up inflation in developed countries. The Federal Reserve's announcement of average-inflation targeting means that it will allow inflation to exceed the target inflation rate for a period of time without tightening monetary policy. However, major countries' monetary and fiscal policies will have certain spillover effects on China, so it is necessary to guard against the financial risks brought on by large-scale capital flows. A more flexible exchange rate will help absorb external shocks.

Domestic financial risks are also accumulating during China's post-epidemic period. 2020 anti-epidemic credit policy increased China's macro leverage ratio (the proportion of real economy debt to GDP) from 246% at the end of 2019 to 271% in the third quarter of 2020, growing by 25 percentage points, which was the fastest increase since 2010. As economic recovery accelerated in the fourth quarter, the macro leverage ratio remained stable, falling slightly to 270% at the end of 2020.

Looking ahead to 2021, as long as China's economy maintains steady growth, the goal of "stable leverage" is relatively easy to achieve, meaning that a significant shift in monetary policy is not necessary. Therefore, monetary policy is not expected to make a "sharp U-turn" in 2021. Because of the base level, nominal GDP growth in 2021 will have a significantly higher rate than normal, so matching of M2 and AFRE growth with "potential" growth will be more conducive to maintaining a prudent monetary policy.

The market-oriented reform of interest rate will also be deepened in 2021. During the anti-epidemic period, the PBC introduced a number of innovative monetary policies, but it still did everything it could to promote the transformation of monetary policy from a quantitative framework to a price framework. The PBC clearly stated, for example, that "the first thing to look at is whether the policy interest rate changes — mainly, whether the central bank's seven-day reverse repo rates for open market operations change — rather than the amount of open market operations." At the same time, the benchmark deposit interest rate will continue to play a role as "ballast". The PBC will strengthen self-regulation management of deposit interest rates, reduce non-standard deposit innovative products, and thereby maintain order in deposit market competition.

In 2020, General Secretary Xi Jinping announced that China would achieve "carbon neutrality" by 2060. Given this goal, one of the PBC's key tasks in the coming period is to improve the green finance policy framework, establish relevant mechanisms for incentive and restraint, and use structural monetary policy instruments to guide financial institutions to support green and low-carbon development in accordance with the principles of marketization.

## Appendix

### China's Monetary Policy Milestones in 2020

| Released on | Content |
| --- | --- |
| January 6 | The PBC lowered RRR for financial institutions (excluding financial companies, financial leasing companies, and auto financing companies) by 0.5 percentage point. |
| | The PBC and Bank of Lao P.D.R. signed a bilateral agreement on local currency cooperation, allowing direct settlement under all current and capital account items that have been liberalized between the two countries. |
| January 31 | The PBC issued the "Notice on Issuing Special Central Bank Lending to Support Prevention and Control of Novel Coronavirus Pneumonia" (YF [2020] No.28), which provided a total of RMB 300 billion in low-cost special central bank loans to major national banks and some locally incorporated banks in 10 key provinces (or provincial-level municipalities), such as Hubei, to support epidemic prevention and maintain supply. |
| February 10 | The PBC and the Central Bank of Egypt renewed a bilateral local currency swap agreement totaling RMB 18 billion / EGP 41 billion. |
| February 26 | The PBC issued the "Notice on Increasing Support of Central Bank Lending/Discounts to Promote Orderly Work and Production Resumption" (YF [2020] No. 53), which increased the special quota for central bank lending and discounts by RMB 500 billion. It also cut the central bank lending rate for agriculture and MSBs by 25 basis points to 2.5%, thereby providing low-cost and inclusive financial support for enterprises' orderly return to work and production. |
| March 16 | The PBC implemented targeted cuts to the RRR of inclusive finance, granting 0.5 or 1.5 percentage points of preferential RRR to banks meeting certain criteria in the assessment of the ratio of loans in inclusive finance, and reducing RRR by an additional percentage point for joint-stock commercial banks that received 0.5 percentage point of preferential RRR in the assessment. |
| April 3 | The PBC announced RRR cuts for rural credit cooperatives, rural commercial banks, rural cooperative banks, village banks, and urban commercial banks operating exclusively in the provincial administrative region by 1 percentage point, which were implemented on April 15 and May 15 respectively. The PBC has reduced their financial institutions' ERR from 0.72% to 0.35% since April 7, 2020. |
| May 20 | The PBC and Bank of Lao P.D.R signed a bilateral local currency swap agreement totaling RMB 6 billion / LAK 7.6 trillion. |

Continued

| Released on | Content |
|---|---|
| June 1 | The PBC issued the "Notice on Support Instrument for Deferring the Repayment of Inclusive MSB Loans" (YF [2020] No.124), and launched a support instrument for deferring the repayment of inclusive MSB loans. |
| | The PBC issued the "Notice on Support Plan for Inclusive MSB Credit Loans" (YF [2020] No.125) and launched a support plan for inclusive MSB credit loans. |
| June 29 | The PBC decided to cut the central bank lending and discount rates starting from July 1, 2020. Among these, the interest rates on central bank loans in support of agriculture and MSBs were lowered by 0.25 percentage point. After the adjustment, the corresponding lending interest rates for three-month, six-month and one-year loans were 1.95%, 2.15%, and 2.25% respectively. The central bank discount rate was reduced by 0.25 percentage point to 2%. And the central bank lending rate for financial stability was reduced by 0.5 percentage point. After the adjustment, the central bank lending rate for financial stability was 1.75%, and the central bank lending rate for financial stability (during deferment) was 3.77%. |
| July 31 | The PBC and State Bank of Pakistan renewed a bilateral local currency swap agreement, its size expanding to RMB 30 billion / PKR 720 billion. |
| | The PBC and Central Bank of Chile renewed a bilateral local currency swap agreement, the amount increasing to RMB 50 billion / CLP 5.6 trillion. |
| | The PBC and Central Bank of Mongolia renewed a bilateral local currency swap agreement of RMB 15 billion / MNT 6 trillion. |
| August 6 | The PBC and Central Bank of Argentina renewed a bilateral local currency swap agreement of RMB 70 billion / ARS 730 billion and signed a supplementary bilateral local currency swap agreement of RMB 60 billion. |
| August 22 | The PBC and the Reserve Bank of New Zealand renewed a bilateral local currency swap agreement of RMB 25 billion. |
| September 13 | The PBC issued the Trial Measures on Regulation of Financial Holding Companies (PBC Order [2020] No. 4). |
| September 17 | The PBC and Hungarian National Bank signed a supplementary bilateral local currency swap agreement of RMB 40 billion. |
| September 25 | The China Securities Regulatory Commission (CSRC), PBC, and SAFE jointly issued the "Measures for the Administration of Domestic Securities and Futures Investment by Qualified Foreign Institutional Investors and RMB Qualified Foreign Institutional Investors" (CSRC & PBC & SAFE Decree No. 176). |
| September 30 | The PBC and CBIRC jointly issued the "Notice on Establishing Mechanism of Countercyclical Capital Buffer" (YF [2020] No. 233). |
| | The PBC and Bank Indonesia signed the "Memorandum of Understanding for the Establishment of a Framework for Cooperation to Promote the Settlement of Current Account Transactions and Direct Investment in Local Currencies" to promote the use of local currencies for trade and direct investment settlement. |
| | The PBC and CBIRC jointly issued the "Notice on Establishing Mechanism of Countercyclical Capital Buffer" (YF [2020] No. 233). |
| October 10 | The PBC decided to lower the foreign exchange risk reserve ratio for forward foreign exchange sales from 20% to 0, effective October 12, 2020. |

Continued

| Released on | Content |
|---|---|
| October 11 | The PBC and Bank of Korea extended a bilateral currency swap agreement, increasing the amount to RMB 400 billion / KRW 70 trillion. |
| October 19 | The PBC and Central Bank of Iceland renewed a bilateral currency swap agreement of RMB 3.5 billion / ISK 70 billion. |
| October 27 | Based on their own judgments of economic fundamentals and market conditions, some RMB-USD central parity quotation banks have successively taken initiatives to fade out the countercyclical factors in the RMB-USD central parity quotation model. |
| November 23 | The PBC and Bank of Russia renewed a bilateral currency swap agreement of RMB 150 billion / RUB 1.75 trillion. |
| November 23 | The PBC and Hong Kong Monetary Authority renewed a bilateral currency swap agreement, its size expanding to RMB 500 billion / HKD 590 billion. |
| December 3 | The PBC and CBIRC jointly issued the "Evaluation Method of Systemically Important Banks" (YF [2020] No. 289) and established an evaluation framework for systemically important banks in China. |
| December 11 | In order to further improve the macroprudential management of full-scope cross-border financing and guide financial institutions to adjust their forex asset and liability structure in a market-based manner, the PBC and SAFE decided to lower the macroprudential adjustment parameter for financial institutions' cross-border financing from 1.25 to 1. |
| December 31 | The PBC and CBIRC jointly issued the Notice on Establishing the "Concentration Management of Real Estate Loans in Banking Financial Institutions". |
| December 31 | The PBC, CBIRC, the Ministry of Finance, National Development and Reform Commission, and the Ministry of Industry and Information Technology jointly issued the "Notice on Continuously Extending the Policy of Deferment of Loan Principal and Interest Repayments and Credit Loan Support for Micro and Small Enterprises in Inclusive Finance" (YF [2020] No. 324) and extended the policy of loan principal/interest deferment repayment and credit loan support for MSEs until March 21, 2021. |
| December 31 | The PBC decided that starting January 1, 2021, credit card overdraft interest rates would be determined through independent consultation between the card issuer and the cardholder, and management of upper and lower limits for credit card overdraft interest rates would be abolished. |

Source: http://www.pbc.gov.cn/zhengcehuobisi/125207/125227/125963/4190884/index.html.

## Article 1

Strengthening macro-prudential supervision and modernizing financial governance[1]

On October 23, 2020, the People's Bank of China (PBOC) published the *Law of the People's Republic of China on the People's Bank of China* (Draft Amendment for Comments), after the *Law of the People's Republic of China on Commercial Banks* (Revision of the Proposed Draft) published on

---

[1] Author: Ma Qiang, Executive Vice President of Shanghai Banking Association, and senior project fellow of Program for China's Financial Policy Report.

October 16. The Two Laws' new drafts were released for one-month public comment period. Drawing on good practices established in China and the best practices of the international community, the amendments strengthens macro-financial prudential supervision and systemic financial risk prevention, clarifies the positioning of the financial system as "serving the real economy", emphasize the authority and responsibility of the PBOC in maintaining national financial stability and preventing systemic financial risks, thus demonstrating China's thought on the rule of law as well as its determination to modernize and globalize financial governance.

Since the founding of the People's Republic of China and the beginning of Reform and Opening up, the first major financial law enacted was the *People's Bank of China Law* in March 1995. This marks the first major amendment to the Law in 17 years, the next most recent previous revision being the 2003 amendment. The *Law of the People's Republic of China on Commercial Banks* passed and implemented in 1995 was later amended in 2003 and 2015 respectively; its 2020 "Draft" thus constitutes the third amendment. It should be especially noted that the amendment to the *Law of the People's Republic of China on the People's Bank of China* is a "rectification", which is "comprehensive" and "principled" and seeks to improve top-level design for the financial rule of law, while the amendment of the *Law of the People's Republic of China on Commercial Banks* is a "revision", which is an "innovative" adjustment and "practical" supplement, focused on enhancing capital discipline capacity, corporate governance, and financial services for the real economy.

The *Law of the People's Republic of China on the People's Bank of China* (Revised Draft for Comments) consists of nine chapters and 73 articles in total. First, the amendment clarifies PBOC's responsibility to formulate and implement macro-prudential policies as well as the financial system's positioning of "serving the real economy". Second, the amendment expands the PBOC's powers from 13 to 19 items. The newly added powers include that to formulate and implement macro-prudential policies, to prepare major draft laws and regulations for the financial industry, and to organize and implement national financial security reviews. Third, the amendment aims to build a two-pillar regulatory framework of monetary and macro-prudential policy. It focuses on strengthening counter-cyclical regulation and penetrating supervision to form a sound macro-prudential policy toolbox. Fourth, the amendment stresses "coordinating three aspects"—namely, the supervision of systemically important financial institutions, supervision of financial holding companies, and supervision of important financial infrastructure. Fifth, the amendment aims to strengthen responsibility for maintaining financial stability and dealing with systemic financial risks. Sixth, the amendment aims to improve RMB management regulations, justifying digital currencies and warning of virtual currency's risks. Seventh, it seeks to improve the central bank governance and supervision system, which includes maintaining an open and transparent financial budget system and not providing loans to local governments. Eighth, the amendment aims to improve the PBOC's capacity to perform its duties and increase penalties for financial violations.

The *Law of the People's Republic of China on Commercial Banks* (Revision of the Proposed Draft) consists of 11 chapters and 127 articles in total. The revised version adds two new chapters and 32 articles total, which is compiled into four new or existing chapters. They cover corporate governance, capital and risk management, customer legal rights' protection, risk management, and market exit. As for this amendment's focus and intent, the first is to optimize the category of the commercial banks. It clarifies the legal status of village banks and reserves legal space for the emergence of new commercial banks in the future. Second, it establishes classified access and a differentiated regulatory mechanism. It seeks to improve market access conditions for commercial banks and strengthen shareholder supervision. Third, it seeks to improve the corporate governance of commercial banks based on good practices established in China and best practices in the international community. The fourth objective is strengthening capital management; the amendment aims to implement Basel III's capital regulatory requirements, establish the principle of capital constraint, and clarify requirements for macro-prudential management and risk regulation. The fifth is to improve the scope of business and rules of operation, highlighting financial services to the real economy. It also clarifies regional commercial banks' localization requirements. The sixth is to strengthen behaviour management and regulate the protection of customer's legal rights. A new chapter is also added with specific provisions on commercial banks' marketing, information disclosure, risk classification and appropriateness management, protection of personal information, fee management, and other customer protection specifications. The seventh is to improve risk disposal and the mechanism for the market exit. It intends to establish risk ratings and early warning, early correction, restructuring, take-over, bankruptcy, and other mechanisms for orderly disposal and exit in accordance with international rules and China's experience in banking industry disposal. It will also standardize disposal procedures, regulate disposal conditions, and improve the division of functions. The eighth objective is to increase violation penalties.

The PBC and commercial banks are widely known as the pillars of China's modern financial system. As a national strategic endeavour to deepen financial supply-side reform, the amendment to the *Law of the People's Republic of China on the People's Bank of China* aims to improve the modern central banking system, strengthen macro-prudential management and systemic financial risk prevention while enhancing the authority and responsibilities of the People's Bank of China. At this stage, commercial banks are the key players in China's financial system. The revision of the *Law of the People's Republic of China on Commercial Banks* has fully examined the banking industry's diversified, specialized, and international development trends in recent years and therefore reflects a policy orientation of differentiated risk supervision.

## II. Exchange Rate and Balance of Payments Policies[①]

2020 was an extraordinary year. Facing the serious impact of COVID-19 and a complex international situation, the People's Bank of China and the State Administration of Foreign Exchange (SAFE) resolutely implemented the decisions of the Party Central Committee and the State Council. While proactively responding to the epidemic, they worked to serve the real economy, promote reform and opening up, mitigate and eliminate risks, and ensure stability on the "six fronts" (keep employment, the financial sector, foreign trade, foreign and domestic investments, and expectations stable) and to maintain security in the "six areas" (ensure security in the six areas of employment, basic living needs, operations of market entities, food and energy security, stable industrial and supply chains, and the normal functioning of primary-level governments), thereby maintaining the smooth operation of the foreign exchange market and basic stability of the balance of payments.

### (I) Overview of RMB exchange rate and China's balance of payments in 2020

**1. The RMB appreciated slightly against a basket of currencies, in both nominal and real effective rate terms**

At end-2020, the CFETS RMB exchange rate index stood at 94.84, 3.78% higher than the end of the previous year. With reference to the SDR currency basket, the RMB exchange rate index stood at 94.23, up 2.64% relative to the previous year end. The RMB exchange rate index based on the Bank for International Settlements (BIS) currency basket stood at 98.68, 3.78% higher than the end of the previous year.

The BIS had projected that the RMB's nominal and real effective exchange rates would appreciate 4.05% and 3.33%, respectively, from end-2019 to end-2020. Between the reform of the RMB exchange rate formation mechanism in 2005, and end-2020, the RMB's nominal effective exchange rate had appreciated by 37.67%, and its real effective exchange rate had appreciated by 51.32%.

**2. RMB depreciated then strengthened against USD, showing increasing resilience**

The RMB exchange rate first depreciated then strengthened over 2020 as a whole, with the onshore and offshore RMB spot rates closing the year at RMB 6.5398/USD and RMB 6.5030/USD, respectively, representing appreciations of 6.62% and 7.05% relative to the previous year. The difference between the highest and lowest onshore RMB spot exchange rates during the year was 6,617 basis points, resulting in a 9.67% trading range, 2.21 percentage points wider than the previous year, and narrower than the 10.19% and 14.61% ranges in which the Yen and the euro, respectively, traded against the USD, during the same period. In 2020, the annualized volatility of the RMB against the USD stood at 4.5%, up slightly on the previous year's 4.0%.

During early 2020, the RMB continued a strengthening trend against the USD that had begun in the fourth quarter of the previous year, reaching as high as RMB 6.85/USD at one

---

[①] Author: Zhao Qingming, former Vice President of CFFEX Institute for Financial Derivatives.

point. After that, the RMB/dollar exchange rate began to weaken, breaking above 7 under the combined pressure of the rapid spread of the epidemic and the USD's rise on international foreign exchange markets. On May 27, the spot RMB rate in the onshore market fell to the annual low of RMB 7.1765/USD. Since then, as China's economic recovery has accelerated, and the USD has weakened on international markets, the RMB has returned to below 7 against the USD, and appreciated further. By end-2020, the RMB had risen to near 6.52 per dollar, its highest level for two-and-a-half years.

In 2020, the median exchange rate of the RMB against the USD ranged from a high of RMB 6.5236 to a low of RMB 7.1316, with 2020's 243 trading days comprising 140 appreciation and 103 depreciation days. The RMB's largest one-day appreciation was 1.00% (670 basis points) and the largest one-day depreciation was 0.76% (530 basis points). At end-2020, the RMB's central parity rate against the USD had appreciated 6.92% compared to end-2019. Between the reform of the RMB exchange rate formation mechanism in 2005 and end-2020, the RMB's central parity rate against the US dollar had appreciated 26.84%.

### 3. RMB exchange rate trends against other major international currencies diverged

At end-2020, the RMB's central parity rates against the euro, pound and yen were RMB 8.0250 per EUR, RMB 8.8903 per GBP and RMB 6.3236 per 100 JPY, respectively, representing a depreciation of 2.61%, appreciation of 2.92% and appreciation of 1.34% relative to end-2019.

Between the reform of the RMB exchange rate formation mechanism in 2005 and end-2020, the RMB had appreciated 24.79% against the euro and 15.53% against the Japanese yen.

### 4. The balance of payments continued to remain in sound balance without significant intervention, while foreign debts maintained steady growth

In 2020, China's current account surplus was USD 298.9 billion, equivalent to 2.0% to GDP during that year, representing an increase compared to 1.2% the previous year. Within this, there was a surplus of USD 533.8 billion on goods trade, an increase of USD 108.5 billion over the previous year, and a services trade deficit of USD 145.3 billion, representing a narrowing of USD 115.8 billion over the previous year. The sharp narrowing of the services trade deficit mainly reflected restrictions on cross-border travel resulting from the epidemic, which led to a sharp decline in the travel balance deficit, which, at USD 116.2 billion in 2020, narrowed by USD 102.6 billion relative to the previous year. In the capital and financial account, the surplus on foreign direct investment was USD 103.4 billion and reserve assets increased by USD 28 billion.

At end-2020, the balance of foreign exchange reserves was USD 3,216.522 billion, representing an increase of USD 108.598 billion compared with the previous year-end.

Foreign debt continued to grow steadily, while foreign debt risks remained generally controllable. As of end-December 2020, China's total foreign debt balance was USD 2, 400.8 billion, an increase of USD 343.5 billion from end-2019. Of this, the short-term external debt balance was USD 1, 316.4 billion. An increase of USD 110.9 billion from the previous year end, this accounted for 55% of the external debt balance, down 2 percentage points from end-2019.

## 5. Rapid cross-border RMB business growth, normalization of RMB PBC bill issuance in Hong Kong

In 2020, cross-border RMB receipts and payments totaled RMB 28.4 trillion, up 44% year-on-year, a growth rate 21 percentage points faster than the previous year's. Of this, receipts totaled RMB 14.1 trillion and payments totaled RMB 14.3 trillion, for a net outflow of RMB 0.2 trillion, compared with a net inflow of RMB 0.3 trillion in the previous year. The receipts-to-payments ratio was 1:1.01, compared with 1:0.97 in the previous year, indicating a closer balance between in and outflows. The total amount of cross-border RMB receipts and payments on the current account was RMB 6.8 trillion, up 13% year-on-year, of which RMB 4.8 trillion was in respect of goods trade and RMB 2 trillion was for services trade and other current account items. Capital account receipts and payments totaled RMB 21.6 trillion, up 59% year-on-year.

In 2020, the People's Bank of China made a total of 12 issues of RMB 155 billion PBC bills in Hong Kong, the same number as in the previous year, but with an RMB 5 billion increase in the amount issued. The regular issuance of RMB PBC bills in Hong Kong not only enriches the RMB investment products and liquidity management tools available to the Hong Kong market, but is also driving domestic and foreign market participants issuance of RMB bonds, and engagement in RMB business innovation in the offshore market, enhancing the RMB offshore market's activity and promoting its sustainable and healthy development. The issuance of offshore RMB bonds other than Hong Kong PBC bills exceeded RMB 130 billion in 2020, a 30% increase over 2019. Bank of China (Hong Kong) launched the Hong Kong PBC Bills Repo Business Market-making Mechanism on January 27, 2021, which will enhance the liquidity of the Hong Kong PBC bill secondary market.

## 6. Foreign exchange market transaction volume increased slightly year-on-year, number of participants continued to increase

In 2020, direct RMB transactions in the interbank foreign exchange market were fairly active, while liquidity remained stable, reducing microeconomic agents' exchange costs and promoting bilateral trade and investment. In 2020, the total value of RMB foreign exchange spot transactions was USD 8.4 trillion, up 5.6% year-on-year, while the total value of RMB foreign exchange swaps was USD 16.3 trillion, down 0.2% year-on-year. Of the latter, the total value of overnight USD swaps was USD 9.5 trillion, accounting for 58.3% of the total, while the total value of RMB foreign exchange forward transactions was USD 104.4 billion, up 37.4% year-on-year. Cumulative "foreign currency pair" turnover amounted to USD 810.9 billion, up 70.5% year-on-year, with the most traded product, the EUR/USD pair, accounting for 57.2% of the market.

The range of foreign exchange market participants continued to expand. At end-2020, 735 spot market members were active in the interbank foreign exchange market, an increase of 24 over the previous year end, with 266, 259, 213 and 163 members in the forward, foreign exchange swap, currency swap and options markets, respectively, all higher than the previous year-end. There were 30 market makers in the spot market and 27 market makers in the forward swap market, both unchanged from the previous year-end.

**7. Value of RMB under currency swap agreements used by foreign monetary authorities increased significantly**

Currency swaps have played a positive role in promoting bilateral trade and investment. At end-2020, under bilateral currency swap agreements signed between the People's Bank of China and overseas monetary authorities, the balance of RMB in use by overseas monetary authorities reached RMB 50.032 billion, an increase of RMB 17.110 billion or 51.97% compared with the previous year-end; the balance of foreign currency used by the People's Bank of China was equivalent to USD 516 million, a decrease of USD 1.738 billion compared with the previous year-end.

**(II) Analysis of major exchange rate and balance of payments policies in 2020**

**1. Promotion of market-oriented exchange rate reform continued, basic RMB exchange rate stability at reasonable equilibrium level continued**

In 2020, the People's Bank of China and the State Administration of Foreign Exchange continued to promote market-oriented exchange rate reform, and continued to improve the managed float exchange rate system based on market supply and demand adjusted by reference to a basket of currencies, to maintain the flexibility of the RMB exchange rate, allowing the exchange rate to play its role in regulating the macro-economy and automatically stabilizing the balance of payments. At the same time, the authorities focused on expectations guidance in order to maintain the basic stability of the RMB exchange rate at a reasonable equilibrium level.

In the second half of 2020, as China's macroeconomic recovery accelerated, market expectations began to stabilize. As cross-border capital flowed in an orderly manner, the foreign exchange market operated smoothly, with supply and demand in balance. As such, the People's Bank of China decided to lower the foreign exchange risk reserve ratio for forward foreign exchange sales from 20% to 0%, effective October 12, 2020. On October 27, 2020, the Secretariat of China's Foreign Exchange Market Self-Discipline Mechanism announced that some banks quoting the RMB/USD Central Parity Rate, had, based on their judgment of economic fundamentals and market conditions, chosen to phase out the "counter-cyclical factor" included in their RMB/USD central parity price models.

**2. During the adverse economic impact of the epidemic, several foreign exchange management measures were rapidly implemented, facilitating trade and investment and promoting macroeconomic recovery**

Firstly, in order to guarantee the timely arrival of epidemic prevention materials and donations of funds, business processes related to purchase and payment in foreign exchange were simplified. From January 27, 2020 to the end of the second quarter, China handled 14,000 foreign exchange transactions, with total value of USD 4.9 billion, through a "green channel" for goods trade. Secondly, ex-ante documentation requirements for settlement and payment of income for capital projects related to epidemic prevention and control were relaxed for a period. From January 27 to March 27, 2020, a total of 4, 895 capital project income facilitation payments, amounting to approximately USD 900 million, were processed nationwide. Thirdly, cross-border financing related to epidemic prevention and control was facilitated. For enterprises that really needed financing, foreign debt limits could be canceled and foreign debt registration applied for online. From January 27 to March 27, 2020, 742 online foreign debt contracts were registered, totaling USD 37 billion in value.

Furthermore, in order to promote enterprises' resumption of work and production, to facilitate cross-border financing for domestic institutions and reduce the real economy's financing costs, on March 12, 2020, based on the macroeconomic and balance of payments conditions prevailing at the time, the People's Bank of China and the State Administration of Foreign Exchange issued the *Notice on Adjustment of the Macroprudential Regulatory Parameters for Full-scale Cross-border Financing* (YF [2020] No. 64), raising the full-scale cross-border financing macroprudential adjustment parameter from 1 to 1.25. After this policy adjustment, the risk-weighted balance ceiling for cross-border financing was raised, facilitating the full use by domestic institutions, especially SMEs and private enterprises, of international and domestic resources and markets, permitting fund raising via multiple channels, alleviating difficulties related to financing and financing costs, promoting enterprises' resumption of work and production, and serving the development of the real economy. By the fourth quarter of 2020, as China's economy largely recovered to pre-epidemic levels, the above policies were phased out for macro-prudential management purposes. On December 11, 2020, the People's Bank of China and the State Administration of Foreign Exchange decided to lower the macro-prudential adjustment parameter for cross-border financing of financial institutions from 1.25 to 1. On January 7, 2021, the People's Bank of China and the State Administration of Foreign Exchange decided to lower the macro-prudential adjustment parameter for cross-border financing of enterprises from 1.25 to 1.

### 3. Enhancement of the level of trade balance facilitation continued

Firstly, the expansion of pilot areas of trade foreign exchange balance facilitation was continued. By end-September 2020, these pilots had been expanded to cover 56 pilot banks and 374 enterprises in 19 regions across China. Secondly, innovative development of new forms of trade was promoted. On May 20, 2020, the State Administration of Foreign Exchange (SAFE) issued the *Notice on Support for Development of New Forms of Trade* (HF [2020] No. 11), in order to optimize fund collections and payments for foreign trade integrated service enterprises and cross-border e-commerce, with the aim of accelerating the development of new forms of trade such as cross-border e-commerce. Thirdly current account foreign exchange regulations were streamlined and optimized. In August 2020, the State Administration of Foreign Exchange (SAFE) issued the *Notice on Issuance of Guidelines on Foreign Exchange Current Account Operations (2020 Edition)* (HF [2020] No. 14), integrating guidelines for handling foreign exchange current account business to significantly streamline these regulations and prune redundant provisions, repealing 29 regulations. Fourthly, facilitation of foreign exchange payments for the services trade continued. On November 1, 2020, the State Administration of Foreign Exchange (SAFE) launched a trial of the nationwide online verification function for tax filing of service trade payment information, promoting the electronic tax filing of service trade payments.

### 4. Innovation in individual foreign exchange service regulation was promoted

On February 19, 2020, in order to promote the compliance and orderly development of individual domestic and foreign currency exchange franchise businesses, the State Administration of Foreign Exchange (SAFE) issued the *Notice on Revision of the Pilot Management Measures for Individual Domestic and Foreign Currency Exchange Franchise Services* (HF [2020] No. 6), whose main contents included the following. Firstly, improvements in the environment for foreigners' use of foreign exchange, and promotion of pilot facilitation of domestic small consumption for foreign individuals and of foreign exchange for foreign talents' remuneration. Secondly, foreign exchange for Chinese individuals "Going Out" (investing overseas) and expansion of pilot online processing of foreign exchange purchases and payments within the annual facilitation quota, for study abroad, were further facilitated. And finally, foreign exchange settlement for the salaries of foreign-based employees of Chinese enterprises was facilitated.

### 5. Expansion of financial sector's two-way opening continued

Firstly, limits on foreign investors' percentage holdings in Chinese financial institutions were relaxed. The China Securities Regulatory Commission abolished the foreign equity ratio restriction on futures companies nationwide from January 1, 2020, and on securities and fund management companies nationwide from April 1.

Secondly, the two-way opening of the financial market was expanded with the abolition of restrictions on the investment quota for Qualified Foreign Institutional Investors (QFII) and Renminbi Qualified Foreign Institutional Investors (RQFII), simplifying the management of domestic securities and futures investment funds, while the issuance of quotas for Qualified Domestic Institutional Investors (QDII) was normalized. In May 2020, the People's Bank of China (PBC) and the State Administration of Foreign Exchange (SAFE) issued the *Regulations on the Administration of Funds for Domestic Securities and Futures Investments by Foreign Institutional Investors* (PBC SAFE Announcement [2020] No. 2), abolishing the quota restrictions on foreign institutional investors, and clarifying and simplifying the requirements concerning the administration of funds by foreign institutional investors on behalf of domestic securities and futures investment funds, further facilitating the participation of foreign investors in China's financial markets.

Thirdly, the opening up of the bond market was promoted. In March 2020, the People's Bank of China instructed relevant financial infrastructure providers to optimize transaction settlement arrangements and introduce cyclical trade settlement services, with flexible settlement cycles in the interbank bond market meeting the varied needs of foreign institutional investors, further facilitating their operations. In September 2020, the People's Bank of China, China Securities Regulatory Commission, and State Administration of Foreign Exchange jointly drafted the *Announcement on Matters Concerning Foreign Institutional Investors' Investments in China's Bond Market (Draft for Comment)*, clarifying overall institutional arrangements for the opening of China's bond market, and further facilitating foreign institutional investors' solicitation of market opinions concerning RMB bond asset allocation arrangements. In September 2020, FTSE Russell announced the inclusion of Chinese government bonds in the FTSE World Government Bond Index (WGBI) from October 2021. So far, all three major global bond index providers have included, or plan to include, Chinese bonds in their relevant indices, fully reflecting the confidence of international investors in the long-term healthy development of China's economy, and in the continued expansion and opening up of Chinese finance.

Fourthly the foreign debt facilitation pilot, supporting high-tech enterprises' cross-border financing, was expanded. Zhongguancun Science Park's Foreign Debt Facilitation pilot was expanded to Shanghai, Hubei, Guangdong, Shenzhen, and other regions, allowing eligible hi-tech enterprises to borrow specified amounts of foreign debt on their own accounts.

**6. Supervision of the foreign exchange market was strengthened to maintain order in the foreign exchange market**

In the context of regular epidemic prevention and control, a proper balance has been struck between epidemic prevention and control and mitigation and elimination of financial risks. Sustained efforts have been made to prevent and eliminate major financial risks in the foreign exchange field, to further improve the foreign exchange markets' micro and macro-prudential supervision management framework, to strengthen the monitoring and analysis of risks associated with cross-border capital flows, and to intensify enforcement against illegal financial activities such as underground bankers, cross-border gambling and online foreign exchange speculation, in order to ensure stability on the "six fronts" and maintain security in the "six areas". In 2020, 2,440 cases of foreign exchange violations were investigated and dealt with, and fines totaling RMB 940 million levied. Strict foreign exchange enforcement, serious punishment of violations, and publicity regarding typical cases have functioned as a deterrent, permitting maintenance of healthy order in the foreign exchange market.

**(III) Policy outlook for the next phase**

Major exchange rate and balance of payments-related tasks remaining for the People's Bank of China and the State Administration of Foreign Exchange include:

Firstly, deepening the market-oriented reform of the RMB exchange rate. The managed float exchange rate system based on market supply and demand should be improved, and adjusted based on a basket of currencies. The flexibility of the RMB exchange rate should be maintained, with the exchange rate playing a role in regulating the macro-economy and automatically stabilizing the balance of payments. Market expectations should be stabilized, enterprises and financial institutions should be guided to adopt the concept of "risk neutrality", and the basic stability of the RMB exchange rate should be maintained at a reasonable equilibrium level.

Secondly, the internationalization of the RMB should be prudently promoted. With a focus on serving the real economy and following the trend of promotion of trade and investment facilitation, policy systems related to usage of the RMB should be improved, and the promotion of the high-quality, two-way opening of financial markets, and of the healthy, coordinated development of local and foreign currency and offshore-onshore markets, should be continued.

Thirdly, measures to prevent abnormal cross-border capital flow risks should continue. The monitoring and assessment of the foreign exchange situation should be strengthened, paying close attention to the impact of the epidemic and other external shocks, and financial institutions and enterprises guided to adhere to the principle of risk neutrality. Foreign exchange speculation should be tackled, and market expectations management and macro-prudential management strengthened, in order to prevent disorderly foreign exchange market fluctuations.

Fourthly, the reform and opening up of the foreign exchange field should be deepened, with an emphasis on the two-way opening up of financial markets and promotion of the steady, orderly, opening up of capital projects. The management of domestic issuance of stocks and bonds by foreign institutions should be improved, pilot cross-border investment in private equity funds promoted, and the management of foreign debt registration reformed, in order to facilitate cross-border investment and financing. Pilot foreign exchange trade balance facilitation should be expanded, and the development of new forms of trade promoted. An open, diversified, functional foreign exchange market should be constructed, and the launching of further foreign exchange derivatives fulfilling market needs supported, as should be the reasonable and prudent use by enterprises of foreign exchange derivatives for exchange rate risk management purposes.

Fifthly, the foreign exchange market's micro- and macro-prudential supervision management framework should be improved. Management of cross-border capital flows should be improved through focusing on strengthening macro-prudential supervision, as should the micro-regulation of the foreign exchange market through a transformation of supervision methods. An improved risk assessment-oriented classification-based credit-risk management system should be constructed. Off-site supervision capacity building should be strengthened. A "zero tolerance" attitude should be maintained towards illegal activities in the field of foreign exchange, such as underground bankers and cross-border gambling, in order to maintain healthy order in the foreign exchange market.

Sixthly, the management of foreign exchange reserves with Chinese characteristics should be improved. Foreign exchange reserves should be managed in a skillful, intensive and efficient manner, while maintaining basic stability in their scale. Market-oriented principles should be adhered to, with forward-looking strategic allocation and dynamic optimization of the investment portfolio maintained. The safety and liquidity of the foreign exchange reserve assets should be safeguarded, preserving or increase their value.

Seventh, a solid foundation for foreign exchange management should be laid. Efforts should be made to study the ideas of the "14th Five-Year Plan" concerning reform of foreign exchange management, to promote "digital foreign exchange management" and "safe foreign exchange management", to improve the balance of payments statistics system, and to conscientiously implement regular epidemic prevention and control.

# Appendix
## Summary of Major Exchange Rate and Balance of Payments Policies, 2020

| Released on | Major Policies | Main Content |
| --- | --- | --- |
| January 13 | State Administration of Foreign Exchange's Notice on Issues Related to Improving Foreign Exchange Risk Management for Foreign Institutional Investors in the Interbank Bond Market (HF [2020] No. 2) | Further facilitates foreign exchange risk management for foreign institutional investors in interbank bond market. |
| February 13 | State Administration of Foreign Exchange's Notice on Revisions to Pilot Management Measures Concerning Domestic and Foreign Currency Exchange Franchise Services for Individuals (HF [2020] No. 6) | Improves the relevant management policies facilitating individual domestic and foreign currency exchange, on basis of maintaining existing licensing scope of individual domestic and foreign currency exchange services and unchanged principles for management of individual settlement and sale of foreign exchange. |
| February 14 | Opinions on Further Accelerating the Construction of Shanghai International Financial Center and Offering Financial Support for the Integrated Development of the Yangtze River Delta (YF [2020] No. 46) issued by People's Bank of China, China Banking and Insurance Regulatory Commission, China Securities Regulatory Commission, State Administration of Foreign Exchange, and Shanghai Municipal People's Government | Series of new initiatives supporting construction of Shanghai International Financial Center. |
| March 11 | The People's Bank of China and the State Administration of Foreign Exchange's Notice on Adjustment of Macroprudential Regulatory Parameters for Full-Scale Cross-Border Financing (YF [2020] No. 64) | Increased macro-prudential regulatory parameter for full-scale cross-border financing from 1 to 1.25 to reduce financing costs for real economy and expand utilization of foreign investment. |
| March 19 | State Administration of Foreign Exchange extends foreign debt facilitation pilot to support cross-border financing by high-tech enterprises | Expands scope of pilot foreign debt facilitation policy to Shanghai (Pilot Free Trade Zone), Hubei (Pilot Free Trade Zone and Wuhan East Lake High-tech Development Zone), Guangdong and Shenzhen (Guangdong-Hong Kong-Macao Greater Bay Area), and other provinces and cities. Improves level of foreign debt facilitation in Zhongguancun Science City, Haidian Park, and Beijing. |
| April 10 | State Administration of Foreign Exchange's Notice on Optimizing Foreign Exchange Management to Support Development of Foreign-related Services (HF [2020] No. 8) | Simplifies foreign exchange business processes, improves foreign exchange business services, enhances level of cross-border trade and investment facilitation, and actively supports enterprises' resumption of operation and production. |

Continued

| Released on | Major Policies | Main Content |
| --- | --- | --- |
| April 24 | Opinions on Financial Support for the Construction of the Guangdong-Hong Kong-Macao Greater Bay Area (YF [2020] No. 95) issued by People's Bank of China, China Banking and Insurance Regulatory Commission (CBIRC), China Securities Regulatory Commission (CSRC), and State Administration of Foreign Exchange (SAFE) | Facilitates cross-border trade, investment and financing in Guangdong-Hong Kong-Macao Greater Bay Area; enhances convenience of domestic and foreign currency exchange, cross-border circulation and use, etc. |
| May 7 | Regulations on Administration of Foreign Institutional Investors' Domestic Securities and Futures Investment Funds (PBC SAFE Announcement [2020] No. 2) | Clarifies and simplifies capital management requirements for foreign institutional investors' investments in domestic securities and futures to further facilitate foreign investors' participation in China's financial markets. |
| May 20 | State Administration of Foreign Exchange's Notice on Support for Development of New Forms of Trade (HF [2020] No. 11) | Improves foreign exchange policy for new forms of trade, supporting their development. |
| June 29 | People's Bank of China, the Hong Kong Monetary Authority, and the Monetary Authority of Macao's Joint Announcement on Launch of the Cross-Border Wealth Management Connection Pilot Scheme in Guangdong-Hong Kong-Macao Greater Bay Area | Launched the Cross-Border Wealth Management Connection Pilot Scheme in Guangdong-Hong Kong-Macao Greater Bay Area. |
| August 28 | State Administration of Foreign Exchange (SAFE)'s Notice on Issuance of Guidelines on Foreign Exchange Current Account Operations (2020 Edition) (HF [2020] No. 14) | Integrated guidelines for current account handling of foreign exchange services, streamlining some related business processes and materials. Repealed 29 regulations. |
| September 2 | People's Bank of China, China Securities Regulatory Commission, and State Administration of Foreign Exchange's Announcement on Matters Relating to Foreign Institutional Investors' Investments in China's Bond Market (Draft for Comments) | Bolsters systemic, holistic and synergistic opening of China's bond market to outside world, facilitating allocation to RMB bond assets by foreign institutional investors. |
| September 18 | General Affairs Department of the State Administration of Foreign Exchange Notice of Issuance of Business Guidelines on Foreign Financial Assets, Liabilities and Transactions Statistics (2020 Edition) (HZF [2020] No. 71) | Further improved statistical declaration of foreign financial assets, liabilities and transactions, facilitating reporting entities' more accurate understanding of specific reporting requirements. |
| September 21 | People's Bank of China and State Administration of Foreign Exchange notice on Regulations on Capital Management of Foreign Institutional Investors' Investments in China's Bond Market (Draft for Comments) | Promotes overall opening of China's bond market, unifies fund management for foreign institutional investors investing in China's bond market, further facilitating investment transactions. |

Continued

| Released on | Major Policies | Main Content |
|---|---|---|
| September 22 | State Administration of Foreign Exchange's Notice on Issuance of Implementation Rules for Balance of Payments Statistical Declarations through Banks (HF [2020] No. 16) | Further standardizes balance of payments statistics declarations for foreign-related payments and receipts via domestic banks. |
| October 10 | People's Bank of China decision to lower foreign exchange risk reserve ratio for forward foreign exchange sales to 0% | People's Bank of China lowered foreign exchange risk reserve ratio for forward foreign exchange sales from 20% to 0%, starting October 12, 2020. |
| October 29 | State Administration of Foreign Exchange Notice on Issuance of Regulations on Management of Foreign and Domestic Receipts and Payments Vouchers for Domestic Banks (HF [2020] No. 17) | Clarifies domestic banks' management requirements concerning documents for foreign and domestic payment and receipts. |
| November 30 | General Affairs Department of the State Administration of Foreign Exchange Notice on Issuance of State Administration of Foreign Exchange Management Regulations on Information Systems Code Standards (HZF [2020] No. 91) | Regulates foreign exchange information systems code standardization. |
| December 11 | People's Bank of China and State Administration of Foreign Exchange adjusted macro-prudential adjustment parameters for cross-border financing | Macro-prudential adjustment parameter for cross-border financing for financial institutions lowered from 1.25 to 1, reversing March 12 policy adjustment. |
| December 14 | State Administration of Foreign Exchange Notice on issuance of Foreign Financial Assets, Liabilities and Transactions Statistics Verification Rules (2020 Edition) (HZF [2020] No. 94) | Improves accuracy of foreign financial assets, liabilities and transactions statistics. |

Sources: Public information from People's Bank of China and State Administration of Foreign Exchange websites.

## Article 2

Guidance reading published for the Proposals of the Fourteenth Five-Year Plan: PBOC, CBIRC and CSRC leaders explain the direction of financial system reform[1]

On November 3, 2020, the fifth plenary session of the 19th Central Committee of the Communist Party of China adopted and released the *Proposals of the Central Committee of the Communist Party of China on Formulating the Fourteenth Five-Year Plan for National Economic and Social Development and the Long-term Goals for 2035* (the "Proposals"). The subsequently published guidance reading on the

---

[1] Author: Zhao Xianghuai, General Manager of the Planning and Operation Management Department at Everbright Securities; and project fellow of Program for China's Financial Policy Report; Liang Chaoyi, Senior Manager of the Planning and Operation Management Department at Everbright Securities;

Ren Xiaoxun, Senior Manager of the Planning and Operation Management Department at Everbright Securities.

Proposals consists of articles by key leaders at the People's Bank of China (PBOC), the China Banking and Insurance Regulatory Commission (CBIRC), and the China Securities Regulatory Commission (CSRC) interpreting key plans and objectives of the "Proposals" for finance.

## I. Build a modern central banking system

In his signed article "Building a Modern Central Banking System", PBOC Governor Yi Gang stresses the importance of the titular task to the national governance system's modernization and capacity-building as well as for promoting quality development and coping with challenges in the evolution of the international central banking system. The goal, he says, is to build a central banking institutional mechanism that supports financial and currency stability, full employment, and the international balance of payments. Such an institutional mechanism should manage the money supply well, provide high-quality financial infrastructure services, prevent and control systemic financial risks, manage external spillover effects, and promote the formation of a fair and rational international financial governance system.

## II. Improve the modern system of financial supervision

Guo Shuqing, Secretary of the Party Committee of the PBOC and Chairman of the CBIRC, contributed the signed article "Improving the Modern Financial Supervision System". Here Guo points to the history of financial regulation (both in China and abroad) to demonstrate that the monetary economy must not deviate from the real economy and that returns are always in proportion to risks. He argues that sustained efforts should be made to continue building the rule of law and an environment of integrity, to manage the boundaries of financial innovation and the money supply, to resolutely suppress the real estate bubble, and to focus on corporate governance as the key task. We must diligently learn from the above lessons and experience, have a correct understanding of the current financial situation, and take targeted measures appropriate to the circumstances. We must continue to improve risk prevention, early warning, disposal and accountability systems, and an effective, modern system of financial supervision that is consistent in authority and responsibility, comprehensive coverage and comprehensive coordination.

## III. Increase the proportion of direct financing

In his signed article "Increasing the Proportion of Direct Financing" CSRC Chairman Yi Huiman says that increasing the proportion of direct financing is key to efforts to deepen financial supply-side structural reform. It will also build a new development pattern more quickly and with higher quality, efficiency, equitability, sustainability and safety of development. Yi stressed the need to strengthen overall planning by taking a larger perspective of the overall economic and financial situation. The synergy between market players, regulators, macro-management departments, news media, and other parties should be brought into play as we strive to promote the coordinated development of direct and indirect financing, improve direct financing's support system, and build a sound market ecology conducive to a higher proportion of direct financing.

The three leaders' signed articles generally interpret the Proposal's key financial development goals and plans from the perspectives of indirect and direct financing, respectively, and in a forward-looking manner. First, the articles clarify the meaning of "building a modern central banking system": It means improving the money supply adjustment mechanism, maintaining policy continuity and sustainability, and steering the economy onto a path of stable, sound development. It also entails establishing a modern financial institution system and promoting the bidirectional liberalization of finance. Second, the articles propose that finance should support the development of the real economy: A registration system should be fully implemented for stock issuance, financial enterprises should be guided to surrender a portion of their profits to facilitate more stable and lower-cost financing for SMEs. Improvements must be made or fostered for the multi-level capital market system with Chinese characteristics, listed companies' quality, and direct financing's support system. Third, the three articles stress the building a market-oriented, legalized, and international modern financial system. They point the way to a sound market system, the protection of investors' rights and interests, and guarantees for the development of the real economy.

Table  Content summary of the articles written by leaders of PBOC, CBIRC, and CSRC

| Signed article and its author | Interpretation of the Proposals' plans and objectives | Major initiatives and tasks |
|---|---|---|
| "Building a Modern Central Banking System" Yi Gang | Build a modern central banking system, improve the money supply regulation mechanism, steadily promote the development of digital currency, and improve the market-based interest rate formation and transmission mechanism. Promote the bidirectional liberalization of finance. | 1. Improve the money supply regulation mechanism. 2. Build an institutional mechanism providing effective financial support to the real economy. 3. Establish a modern financial institution system. 4. Promote the bidirectional liberalization of finance. 5. Improve systems for financial risk prevention, early warning, disposal, and accountability. |
| "Improving the Modern Financial Supervision System" Guo Shuqing | Improve the modern financial supervision system, improve the transparency of financial supervision and the rule of law, improve the deposit insurance system, improve systems for financial risk prevention, early warning, disposal and accountability, and enforce zero tolerance for illegal and irregular behavior. Build an institutional mechanism providing effective financial support to the real economy, enhance financial technology and strengthen financial inclusion. Deepen the reform of state-owned commercial banks, support the sustainable and healthy development of small and mid-size banks and rural credit cooperatives, and reform and optimize policy finance. | 1. Comprehensively strengthen the centralized and unified leadership of the Party on financial work. 2. Break new ground in economic and social development. 3. Establish an efficient regulatory mechanism for coordination and communication in decision-making to improve the transparency of financial supervision and the rule of law. Ensure sound macro-prudential, micro-prudential and behavioral supervision. 4. Build an authoritative and efficient institutional arrangement for risk disposal. Strengthen financial infrastructure to support supervision. 5. Actively participate in reshaping the international framework for financial governance. 6. Cultivate a loyal, responsible and clean regulatory leadership. |

Continued

| Signed article and its author | Interpretation of the Proposals' plans and objectives | Major initiatives and tasks |
| --- | --- | --- |
| "Increasing the Proportion of Direct Financing" Yi Huiman | Fully implement a registration system for stock issuance, establish a normalized delisting mechanism, increase the proportion of direct financing, build an institutional mechanism providing effective financial support to the real economy, and enhance financial inclusion. | 1. Fully implement a registration system for stock issuance, promote the coordinated development of direct and indirect financing, and broaden access to direct financing. 2. Improve the multi-level capital market system with Chinese characteristics, expand direct financing's inclusiveness, and build a sound market ecology conducive to a higher proportion of direct financing. 3. Encourage listed companies to heighten quality, solidify the foundation of direct financing, and improve direct financing's support system. 4. Promote the innovative development of the bond market and enrich direct financing tools. Accelerate the development of private equity funds and highlight the strategic role of innovative capital. 5. Vigorously promote long-term funds' market entry to enrich the sources of direct financing. |

# Major Development Policies for the Financial Market

## I. Development Policies in the Banking Market[①]

### (I) Major Policies for the Development of China's Banking Market in 2020

In 2020, in light of the severe and complex domestic and international situation — especially the serious impact of the COVID-19 pandemic — the banking market focused on improving the quality and effectiveness of financial services in serving the real economy, ensuring stability on the "six fronts" (keep employment, the financial sector, foreign trade, foreign and domestic investments, and expectations stable) and maintaining security in the "six areas" (ensure security in the six areas of employment, basic living needs, operations of market entities, food and energy security, stable industrial and supply chains, and the normal functioning of primary-level governments) to help enterprises tide over difficult times. Although the domestic economy is gradually recovering, the epidemic continues to spread all over the world, which makes the business environment at home and abroad both more complex and more volatile. The "prevention of financial risks and resolutely winning the battle of financial risk prevention and resolution" remain focal points in regulatory work.

**1. We fought against the COVID-19 pandemic and fully supported the recovery and development of both economy and society.**

First, full efforts were made to improve financial services for epidemic prevention and control. Following the outbreak of COVID-19, the Central Committee of the CPC issued a series of crucial plans to coordinate epidemic prevention and control as well as economic and social development in accordance with the epidemic situation. Regulators and other departments have likewise issued a series of policies guiding the banking industry to support the return to work and production and to promote stable economic development. On January 26, the China Banking and Insurance Regulatory Commission (CBIRC) put forth the *Notice on Strengthening Financial Services of the Banking and Insurance Industry and Cooperating on Epidemic Prevention and Control* (YBJBF [2020] No.10). This notice provides specific measures in five aspects — namely, implementing epidemic prevention and control work in banks and insurance institutions, guaranteeing smooth financial services, opening green access to financial services, strengthening financial support for epidemic prevention and control, and offering special financial services to enterprises in distress. On January

---

[①] Authors: Zhou Kunping, Senior Expert from Development Research Department at Bank of Communications, and senior project fellow of Program for China's Financial Policy Report; Zhao Yarui, Senior Researcher from Development Research Department at Bank of Communications.

29, the CBIRC issued the *Notice on Mobilizing Party Organizations and Party Members and Cadres at All Levels of the System to Actively Engage in Epidemic Prevention and Control* (YBJF [2020] No.3), instructing banks and insurance institutions to fully cooperate in financial services. On January 31, the People's Bank of China (PBC), together with the Ministry of Finance of the People's Republic of China (MOF), CBIRC, and other departments issued the *Notice on Further Strengthening Financial Support for Epidemic Prevention and Control* (YF [2020] No.29). This notice emphasized reinforcing support for monetary credit, the proper scheduling of financial resources, guaranteeing financial services, and maintaining the smooth and orderly operation of financial market — which were important measures taken by the financial system to implement decisions of the Party Central Committee and the State Council. On February 1, the PBC, together with the CBIRC and two other ministries and commissions, issued the *Ensuring Quality Financial Services after the Spring Festival Holiday* (YF [2020] No.30). It highlighted epidemic prevention and control in the financial sector and financial services after the Spring Festival holiday to ensure the smooth and orderly operation of the financial market.

On February 7, the MOF, PBC, and other departments issued the *Notice on Matters Relating to the Issuance of Bonds by Financial Institutions during Epidemic Prevention and Control* (YSC [2020] No.5) and the *Urgent Notice on Epidemic Prevention and Control and Strengthening Financial Support for Key Enterprises Engaged in Epidemic Prevention and Control* (CJ [2020] No.5). These notices instructed financial institutions to support epidemic prevention and control and strengthened financial support for key enterprises engaged in said work. On February 14, the CBIRC issued the *Notice on Further Improving Financial Services for Epidemic Prevention and Control* (YBJBF [2020] No.15). It pointed out that efforts should be diverted across multiple areas, such as financial services, science and technology applications, and the improvement of mechanisms, so as to promote banks and insurance institutions' improvement of financial services for epidemic prevention and control. On March 26, the CBIRC issued the *Notice on Strengthening Financial Services for Coordinated Resumption of Work and Production across the Industrial Chain* (YBJBF [2020] No.28). In view of cash flow pressures faced by some enterprises upstream and downstream in the industrial chain following the resumption of work and production, this notice put forth specific measures guiding banking and insurance institutions to enhance financial support and services, facilitate the capital flow within the industrial chain, and improve the overall effect of coordinated returns to work and production throughout the industrial chain. On May 18, the CBIRC, together with the Ministry of Industry and Information Technology of the People's Republic of China (MIIT) and four other ministries and commissions, jointly issued the *Notice on Further Regulating Credit Financing Charges and Reducing Comprehensive Financing Cost of Enterprises* (YBJF [2020] No.18). This document further regulated credit financing fees and management in various aspects, safeguarding enterprises' right to know as well as the right to independent choice and fair trade, while reducing the comprehensive costs of corporate financing. On August 5, the CBIRC and six other departments issued the *Notice on the Supervision over Governmental Financing Guarantee Agencies* (YBJF [2020] No.39). This notice focused on establishing and improving the governmental financing guarantee system, promoting the functioning of governmental financing guarantee agencies, ensuring stability on *six fronts, and maintaining security in six areas*. On September 9, the CBIRC issued *Financial Services Management Measures for Banking and Insurance Institutions in Response to Emergencies* (CBIRC Order [2020] No.10). It promoted further implementation of what General Secretary Xi Jinping had stressed in response to COVID-19 — that is, the "need to strengthen areas of weakness and close the loopholes" exposed by the current epidemic. On September 18, the PBC, together with the MIIT and six other ministries and commissions, jointly issued *Opinions on Standardizing the Development of Supply Chain Finance to Support the Stable Cycle and Optimization of Supply Chain and Industrial Chain* (YF [2020] No.226). The opinions proposes that financial support be offered to safeguard enterprises and ensure employment, that accurate services be offered to keep supply and industrial chains integrated and stable, and that overall operational efficiency be improved to promote a virtuous economic cycle and optimize layout.

Second, financial support was strengthened for micro- and small enterprises. Since the COVID-19 outbreak has substantially impacted micro- and small enterprises, the relevant finance departments introduced a series of policies and measures for such enterprises, scaling up support for micro- and small private enterprises in distress. On March 1, the CBIRC and four other ministries and commissions jointly issued the *Notice on Extending the Policy of Provisional Deferred Repayment of Loan Principal and Interest for Micro, Small and Medium-Sized Enterprises* (YBJF [2020] No.6). The notice emphasized assisting micro-, small and medium-sized enterprises possessing good prospects but whose normal operations were temporarily affected by the epidemic, thereby further relieving difficulties for micro-, small and medium-sized enterprises, promoting the orderly resumption of work and production, and improving the relevance and effectiveness of financial services. On April 7, the State Taxation Administration (STA) and the CBIRC jointly issued the *Notice on Strengthening 'Banking-Taxation Interaction' to Help Micro and Small-sized Enterprises Resume Work and Production* (SZBF [2020] No.10). In view of the urgent capital needs of micro- and small enterprises during the epidemic period, the notice required that loans be made more accessible to through the conversion of tax credits into financing, allowing them to overcome difficulties and return to work and production. On May 26 and June 1, the PBC, together with the CBIRC and other ministries and commissions, issued the *Guidance on Further Strengthening Financial Services for Micro, Small and Medium-sized Enterprises* (YF [2020] No.120), the *Notice on Further Implementation of Phased Deferment of Capital and Interest Repayment for Micro, Small and Medium-sized Enterprises* (YF [2020] No.122), and the *Notice on Increasing Credit Support for Micro, Small and Medium-sized Enterprises* (YF [2020] No.123), which collectively aimed to promote the obvious growth of financing scale and more optimal financing structures for micro-, small and medium-sized enterprises (including individual entrepreneurs and small or micro-business owners, but excluding local government financing platforms), to accelerate the return to normal production and life, and to support the high-quality development of the real economy. On June 29, the CBIRC released a notice on the *Provisional Rules on Supervisory Assessment of Commercial Banks' Financial Services for Micro and Small Enterprises* (*Trial*). It aimed to ensure stability on "six fronts" and maintain security in "six areas", to effectively use supervisory tools to lead and encourage commercial banks to comprehensively improve financial services for micro- and small enterprises as a way to alleviate their financing difficulties and lower financing costs.

Generally, since the outbreak of COVID-19, regulators were quick to introduce a number of financial support policies and measures, putting forward clear requirements for banks and insurance institutions to support epidemic prevention and control and strengthen financial services. Through a series of actions — including improving policy support, providing differentiated preferential financial credit support, effectively reducing financing costs, and improving the efficiency and level of financial services — the CBIRC worked to improve financial support, significantly advancing epidemic prevention and control as well as economic and social development.

**2. Promoted stable development of the real economy with accurate and effective policies.**

First, special efforts were made to improve support in inclusiveness, "agriculture, rural areas and farmers" and other weak areas. 2020 is the final year of the "Development Plan for China's Financial Inclusion 2016–2020", as well as a year of victory for the decisive elimination of poverty. What's more, in the face of the unexpected COVID-19 outbreak, regulatory authorities have introduced a number of policies to support inclusive finance and help the banking industry achieve a complete victory in the fight against poverty. On March 10, in order to promote banking institutions' improvements to the structure and efficiency of financial services, and expansion of inclusive finance coverage, the CBIRC issued the *Notice on Optimizing the Change of Business Premises of the Branches of Banking Institutions* (YBJBF [2020] No. 25). On the same day, the CBIRC issued the *Notice on Further Increasing the Efforts of Banking and Insurance Sector in Poverty Alleviation in 'Three Districts and Three Autonomous Prefectures* (YBJBF [2020] No.24). The Notice made arrangements for advance poverty alleviation work under the banking and insurance sector in the deeply poverty-stricken *Three Districts and Three Autonomous Prefectures*. On April 9, the CBIRC issued the *Notice on Banking and Insurance Sectors Better Serving Key Work Priorities in Agriculture, Rural Areas and Farmers in 2020* (YBJBF [2020] No.31). This notice dictated that efforts should be made to support the three rural sectors (agriculture, rural areas, and farmers), to compensate for weaknesses, and to increase credit support for the three rural areas' key areas, strengthening rural areas' prevention and control for financial risks so as to achieve poverty alleviation and a generally well-off society as scheduled. On June 24, the CBIRC, together with the MOF and two other ministries and commissions, jointly issued the *Notice on Related Polices for the Further Improvement of Microfinance for Poverty Reduction* (YBJF [2020] No.28). Within, it is emphasized that microfinance should take full advantage of to promote high-quality poverty alleviation.

Second, continuous efforts were made to enhance policy support for regional economic strategy. In light of the new development paradigm featuring dual circulation, in which domestic and overseas markets reinforce each other, with the domestic market as the mainstay, regulators have introduced a number of policies to promote banking institutions' strengthened support in major strategic areas. On February 14, the People's Bank of China, CBIRC and other departments jointly issued the *Opinions on Further Accelerating the Building of Shanghai into an International*

*Financial Hub and Financially Supporting the Integrated Development of the Yangtze River Delta* (YF [2020] No.46). It puts forward 30 specific measures in terms of stepping up financial support for the construction of the Lin-gang Special Area in China (Shanghai) Pilot Free Trade Zone (Lin-gang Special Area), and driving the higher-level opening up of the Yangtze River Delta as well as financial support for said area's integrated development. This does not only promote the building of Shanghai into an International Financial Hub and the integrated development of the Yangtze River Delta, it is also of great strategic significance for leading China's high-quality development and accelerating the construction of a modern economic system. On April 24, the PBC, CBIRC and two other ministries and commissions jointly issued the *Opinions on Providing Financial Support for the Development of Guangdong-Hong Kong-Macao Greater Bay Area* (YF [2020] No.95). It puts forward 26 specific measures covering five main aspects. These include promotion of cross-border trade facilitation, investment and financing in the Guangdong-Hong Kong-Macao Greater Bay Area (GBA), expansion of the financial sector's opening up to the outside world, promotion of financial markets and infrastructures' connectivity, enhancement of the GBA's financial services innovation level, and effective prevention of cross-border financial risks. These measures aimed to further enhance the leading role of the GBA to support national economic development and opening up to the outside world. On June 29, the PBC, Hong Kong Monetary Authority and Monetary Authority of Macao issued the *Joint Announcement on the Launch of "the Cross-Boundary Wealth Management Connect Pilot Scheme" in the Greater Bay Area*. This notice aimed to facilitate cross-border investment by individual residents in the Guangdong-Hong Kong-Macao Greater Bay Area.

**3. Multiple measures were adopted to prevent and mitigate risks in high-risk financial institutions and key areas.**

While fully supporting the recovery of economic and social development, regulators took various measures to tackle existing risks and prevent incremental risks.

First, risk resolution was promoted in an orderly way within small and medium-sized banks. In 2020, regulators steadily promoted risk resolution in high-risk small and medium-sized banks as well as other financial institutions. On May 23, the PBC and the CBIRC issued the *Announcement on Extending Baoshang Bank Takeover* to strengthen its risk resolution work with the Baoshang Bank. On December 30, the CBIRC issued the *Notice on Further Promoting the Reform and Restructuring of Township and Village Banks to Resolve Risks* (YBJBF [2020] No.124). This notice further stresses the main initiating bank's responsibility in risk resolution, promotes the reform and restructuring of township and village banks, supports township and village banks' capital replenishment, and further strengthens efforts in risk resolution.

Second, the CBIRC strengthened credit risk prevention and resolution. Affected by the epidemic, non-performing assets were gradually and increasingly exposed, which in turn increased their pressure. In this case, regulators worked with commercial banks to broaden disposal channels for non-performing assets and increase disposal efforts. On June 15, the PBC, National Development and Reform Commission (NDRC) and China Securities Regulatory Commission (CSRC) jointly issued the *Notice on Matters Relating to the Disposal of Defaulted Corporate Credit Bonds*. This aimed to establish a sound mechanism for the resolution of bond defaults, improve the efficiency of default risk resolution, and effectively prevent and resolve bond market risks. On September 7, the CBIRC issued the *Notice on Strengthening the Supervision of Micro-credit Companies* (YBJBF [2020] No.86). This notice aimed to regulate the business operations of micro-credit companies and prevent or mitigate related risks. On December 18, the PBC and CBIRC jointly issued the *Notice on the Establishment of Real Estate Loan Concentration Management System for Banking Institutions* (YF [2020] No.322). The real estate loan concentration management system for banking institutions was meant to enhance the banking institutions' ability to withstand fluctuations in the real estate market, prevent potential systemic financial risks arising from excessive concentrations of real estate loans within the financial system, and improve the soundness of banking institutions.

Third, the CBIRC improved banks' prudent macro-. regulators prevented and managed possible risks and hazards in banking and financial institutions in a timely manner. On March 5, the PBC, NDRC and four other ministries and commissions jointly issued the *Work Plan for Coordinated Supervision over Financial Infrastructures*, which emphasized strengthening financial infrastructures, enhancing prudent macro-management, and improving services for the real economy as well as financial risk prevention and control abilities. On September 30, the PBC and CBIRC issued the *Notice on Establishing Countercyclical Capital Buffer Mechanism*. This notice specified countercyclical capital buffer's methods of provision and mechanisms for coverage and evaluation in China. It helped promote the sound operation of banking institutions and enhance macroprudential policy countercyclical adjustments, which provide a cushion for the negative impact of procyclical fluctuations and the unexpected shock of financial risks so as to safeguard the stable operation of China's financial system. On December 3, the People's Bank of China and CBIRC issued the *Assessment Measures of Domestic Systematically Important Banks* (YF [2020] No.289), which aimed to further improve the regulatory framework of China's systemically important financial institutions and establish a mechanism for the assessment and identification of systemically important banks domestically.

**4. CBIRC strengthened standardized operations and assisted the sound operation of the banking sector.**

On January 14, 2020, the CBIRC released the *Rules on Complaints Administration of Banking and Insurance Consumers*, which focused on effectively safeguarding the legitimate rights and interests of banking and insurance consumers, and further regulating the handling of consumer complaints against banking and insurance institutions. On February 20, the CBIRC issued the *Guidance on the Prevention of Financial Crime by Employees in the Banking and Insurance Industry*. The guidance aimed to improve the mechanism for preventing financial crime by employees within the banking and insurance industry, to prevent risks within banking and insurance institutions, and to promote the healthy development of the banking and insurance industry. On May 22, the CBIRC issued the *Notice on the Issuance of Measures for the Management of Criminal Cases Involving Banking and Insurance Institutions (Trial)* (YBJF [2020] No.20), which further standardized and strengthened the management of criminal cases involving banking and insurance institutions, established a working mechanism with clear responsibilities and orderly coordination, and allowed for the legal, timely, and reliable handling of cases. On June 15, the CBIRC issued the *Rules of CBIRC on Administrative Penalties* (CBIRC General Office [2020] No.8), which aimed to unify and standardize administrative penalty procedures within the banking and insurance sectors after the institutional reform, raise the costs for misconducts and violations in the financial industry, rectify financial market disorder, and prevent and mitigate financial risks. On June 23, the CBIRC issued the *Notice on the Rectification of Malpractice, Misconduct and Noncompliance in the Banking and Insurance Industry* (YBJF [2020] No.27), which further consolidated and expanded upon the results of disorder and misconduct rectification and promoted financial risk prevention and mitigation. On July 14, the CBIRC issued the *Report on Outstanding Issues of Shadow Banking and Cross-sector Financial Business in Recent Years* to detached offices and banking and insurance institutions at all levels within the system. The report unveiled outstanding issues — specifically, shadow banking and cross-sector financial business — which were found during recent years' supervision and inspection of relevant institutions. The report also put forward requirements for standardization and rectification, which aimed to further consolidate and deepen the results of the rectification targeting shadow banking and cross-sector financial business. On July 17, the CBIRC issued the *Construction Plan of National Illegal Fund Raising Monitoring and Early Warning System* (2020–2022), which aimed to build a monitoring and early warning system characterized by close online/offline integration and the interconnection of the central government platform with local platforms. The construction plan emphasized strengthening technological empowerment and enhancing early warning as a means to prevent disorderly expansion and the barbaric growth of illegal fund-raising and to effectively protect the safety of individuals' property. On December 30, the PBC compiled and drafted the *Supervision and Administrative Measures on Anti-money Laundering and Counter-terrorist Financing by Banking Institutions* (Revised Draft for Comments), which aimed to effectively prevent and resolve financial risks, improve the effectiveness of anti-money laundering supervision, and enhance the anti-money laundering work of financial institutions. On December 30, the CBIRC issued the *Notice on Deepening the Reform of the Banking and Insurance Industry* (*streamlining the government, delegating power and improving government services*) *to Optimize the Business Environment* (YBJBF [2020] No.129), which was meant to effectively streamline administration and delegate power to the lower levels in the banking and insurance industry, as well as to optimize services, stimulate market vitality, and promote continuous improvement of the business environment.

**5. CBIRC accelerated the repair of weak links in the system and advanced business transformation and upgrading.**

In 2020, regulators continued to focus on fixing weak links, closing loopholes, and overcoming weaknesses in the system to guide the upgrading and transformation of business operations among financial institutions. On February 14, the CSRC, MOF and two other ministries and commissions jointly issued the *Announcement on the Participation in Sovereign Bond Futures Trading on the China Financial Futures Exchange by Commercial Banks and Insurance Institutions* (CSRC Announcement [2020] No.12), which aimed to diversify treasury bond futures investors and promote the healthy and orderly development of the market. On May 20, the CBIRC released the *Notice on Issues Concerning Insurance Fund Investment in Bank Capital Replenishment Bonds* (YBJF [2020] No.17), which further expanded channels for bank capital replenishment. On June 5, the PBC issued the *Announcement on Standardizing Information Disclosure of Commercial Bills of Exchange* (*Draft for Comments*), which emphasized strengthening the construction of the credit system for commercial bills of exchange as well as establishing and improving the mechanism for market-based restraint in order to protect holders' legitimate rights and interests. On June 24, the PBC issued the *Measures for Standardized Administration of Notes* (PBC Announcement [2020] No.6). The measures put forward a standardized financing mechanism for notes as a way to better serve SMEs and supply chain financing. On July 3, the PBC, CBIRC and two other ministries and commissions jointly issued the *Rules for Standardized Identification of Creditor's Assets* (PBC, CBIRC, CSRC and SAFE Announcement [2020] No.5), which aimed to regulate investments in financial institutions' asset management products, strengthen investor protections, promote the healthy development of direct financing, and effectively prevent and control financial risks. On July 31, regulators clarified that they would "appropriately extend case management during the transition period" of the New Regulations on Asset Management (extended from 2020 to 2021), which aimed to further ease pressures from rectification within financial institutions and promote the smooth rectification of existing asset management. On September 15, the PBC issued the *Implementation Measures for the Protection of the Rights and Interests of Financial Consumers* (PBC Order [2020] No.5), which aimed to regulate the conduct of financial institutions in providing financial products and services, maintain a fair and just market environment, and promote the healthy and stable operation of the financial market. On December 18, the PBC issued the *Announcement on Matters Relating to Information Disclosure of Commercial Acceptances* (PBC Announcement [2020] No.19), which aimed to further strengthen the credit system's construction of commercial acceptances and improve the mechanism for market-based constraints. On December 19, the PBC issued the *Announcement on Matters Relating to the Regulation of RMB Cash Receipt and Payment* (PBC Announcement [2020] No.18), which aimed to further popularize standards and regulations on cash receipts and payments and build a harmonious cash circulation environment with diversified methods of payment. On December 25, the CBIRC issued the *Interim Measures on Wealth Management Product Sales by Wealth Management Subsidiaries of Commercial Banks* (*Draft for Comments*), which aimed to help regulate wealth management products sales by banks' wealth management subsidiaries, to protect investors' legitimate rights and interests, and to promote the healthy development of the wealth management business. The same day, the PBC, NDRC and CSRC jointly issued the *Measures for the Administration of Information Disclosure of Corporate Credit Bond* (PBC, NDRC and CSRC Announcement [2020] No.22), which aimed to improve corporate credit bonds' information disclosure system and promote the sustained and sound development of China's bond market. On December 31, the PBC, NDRC and other departments jointly issued the *Notice on Further Optimizing Cross-border RMB Policy to Support Stabilizing Foreign Trade and Foreign Investment* (YF [2020] No. 330), which further promoted the implementation of decisions and plans made by the Party Central Committee and the State Council to ensure stability on "six fronts" and maintain security in "six areas", propelled the new development paradigm featuring dual circulation, in which domestic and overseas markets reinforce each other, with the domestic market as the mainstay, and took advantage of the cross-border RMB business to serve the real economy and facilitate trade and investment.

**6. Banking sector's digital transformation was accelerated and the orderly development of FinTech was advanced.**

In recent years, Alibaba, Tencent and other large internet technology companies have experienced rapid development. Such companies continue to penetrate the financial sector, which brings certain potential risks. Since 2020, regulators have repeatedly and publicly indicated the need for top-level FinTech regulation design and the banking industry's accelerated digital transformation. On May 9, the CBIRC issued the *Provisional Rules on Internet Loans of Commercial Banks* (*Draft for Comments*), and the official document was issued on July 12, further regulating internet loans offered by commercial banks and promoting the stable and healthy development of the internet loan business. On October 21, in order to support the oversight of FinTech innovation, the PBC released three specifications on FinTech innovation — namely, "Application Testing Specification for FinTech Innovation", "Security General Specification for FinTech Innovation" and "Risk Monitoring Specification for FinTech Innovation". On October 26, the PBC issued the *Notice on Regulating Collection Business* (YF [2020] No.248), which aimed to regulate the collection business, protect interested parties' legitimate rights and interests, and prevent risks in the payment business. On November 2, the CBIRC and PBC publicly solicited comments on the "Interim Measures for the Management of Network Microfinance Business (Draft for Comments)", which aimed to regulate microfinance companies' network micro-financing business and prevent risks in the network microfinance business.

**7. Corporate governance of banking institutions was enhanced and the restraint mechanism was improved.**

In 2020, regulatory work continued to focus on improving corporate governance and achieving sound scientific development. On July 4, the list of shareholders with severe violations in banking and insurance institutions was made public for the first time on the official website of the CBIRC. On August 17, the CBIRC released the *Three-Year Action Plan for Sound Corporate Governance in the Banking and Insurance Industry* (2020–2022) (YBJF [2020] No.40), which aimed to further strengthen the Party's leadership in China's banking and insurance industry, draw on advanced international experience, and effectively improve the quality and effectiveness of corporate governance. On September 11, the State Council issued the *Decisions on Implementing Access Management of Financial Holding Companies* (GF [2020] No.12). On the same day, the People's Bank of China (PBC) issued the *Trial Measures for the Supervision and Administration of Financial Holding Companies* (PBC Order [2020] No.4). The documents put forward regulatory requirements for key aspects of corporate governance and aimed to effectively strengthen the supervision and management of non-financial enterprises, natural persons, and other subjects holding or effectively controlling financial institutions and regulating the conduct of financial holding companies. On October 16, the PBC issued the *Notice on Public Opinion Solicitation for The Law of the People's Republic of China on Commercial Banks (Revised Draft)*. The notice established a new chapter on the corporate governance of commercial banks and improved the restraint mechanism. On November 2, the PBC issued the Notice on Public Opinion Solicitation for the *Interim Provisions on the Management of Directors, Supervisors and Senior Managers of Financial Holding Companies (Draft for Comments)*, which aimed to regulate the operation of financial holding companies and prevent operational risks.

**8. The level of opening up was enhanced and continuous efforts were made to deepen reform and opening up in the financial sector.**

Since 2020, China has stepped up the opening up of the financial sector. On May 7, the PBC and SAFE formulated the *Regulations on the Management of Overseas Institutional Investors' Investment in China's Securities and Futures Market*, which aimed to regulate the management of foreign institutional investors' securities and futures investments in China. On May 27, the Office of Financial Stability and Development Committee under the State Council issued 11 measures on financial reform, including on the opening up of the financial sector. On September 21, the PBC and SAFE drafted the *Circular on the Administrative Provisions on Funds Used by Foreign Institutional Investors for Investment in China's Bond Market (Draft for Comment)*, which promoted the overall opening up of China's bond market, unified fund management for foreign institutional investors investing in China's bond market, and facilitated investment transactions. On December 31, in order to implement the decision of the Party Central Committee and the State Council on expanding the opening up of the financial industry, and to clarify entry standards for foreign-funded insurance groups and financial institutions, the CBIRC decided to amend certain articles in the *Implementation Rules of the Regulations of the People's Republic of China on Foreign-funded Insurance Companies*.

### (II) Market Development Policy Effects on China's Banking Industry in 2020

**1. 2020 witnessed remarkable achievements in various aspects of market development policy for the banking industry.**

2020 was the final year for establishing a generally well-off society and also the last year of the "13th Five-Year Plan". Multiple policies at the central and local levels were put into practice. Influenced and driven by a number of policies, the banking market generally operated soundly, indicators remaining within a reasonable range. In general, China's banking industry has exhibited positive changes, which are detailed below.

First, the scale of assets grew steadily and the decline in profits slowed. In 2020, under the impact of the COVID-19 pandemic, monetary policy counter-cyclical adjustment continued to improve and the scale of banking industry assets grew steadily. As of the end of 2020's fourth quarter (Q4), the total renminbi and foreign currency assets of China's banking institutions at home and abroad reached RMB 319.7 trillion, a year-on-year (YOY) increase of 10.1%. Among these, the assets of large commercial banks registered RMB 128.4 trillion, accounting for 40.2% of the total, for a 10% YOY increase. Meanwhile, the assets of joint-stock commercial banks reached RMB 57.8 trillion, accounting for 18.1% of the total and an increase of 11.7% YOY. As a result of the pandemic, commercial banks' net profit growth rate exhibited on a downward trend. In the second half of the year, as the epidemic came under control in China, the decline in net profit growth slowed. In 2020, commercial banks accumulated a net profit of RMB 1.94 trillion, a YOY decrease of 2.7%, and in Q4 the decline narrowed by 5.6 percentage points compared with the previous three quarters.

Second, credit risks were further eased and asset quality remained basically stable. In 2020, commercial banks' internal and external business environments became more complex and volatile. The pandemic accelerated economic downturn, leading to a rise in the banking sectors' non-performing loans. Overall credit risk remained at a manageable level, however, due to multiple factors such as the general improvement of the domestic economy and the introduction of a number of policies to mitigate credit risk. As of the end of 2020 Q4, the outstanding balance of commercial banks' performing loans came to RMB 144 trillion, among which, the balance of loans listed as "normal" (performing) was RMB 140 trillion and the balance of specially mentioned loans was RMB 3.8 trillion; the outstanding balance of commercial banks' NPLs was RMB 2.7 trillion, down by RMB 133.6 billion compared to the previous quarter. The NPL ratio of commercial banks was 1.84%, a decrease of 0.12 percentage points compared to the previous quarter.

Third, the capacity for risk offsetting was relatively sufficient. Despite the pandemic's impact, commercial banks' net profit growth and asset quality continued to feel pressure, but commercial banks supplemented RMB 1.34 trillion in capital by issuing preferred shares, perpetual bonds, secondary capital bonds, and other tools. The banking industry withdrew RMB 1.9 trillion for new provisions, an increase of RMB 113.9 billion compared to the same period last year. At the end of the year, commercial banks' balance of loan loss provisions reached RMB 5 trillion, a decrease by RMB 116.4 billion compared to the previous quarter. The provision coverage ratio was 184.5%, up by 4.58 percentage points compared to the end of last quarter. The loan provision ratio was 3.39%, down by 0.14 percentage point compared to the end of last quarter. Commercial banks continued to exhibit strong resilience to risks. As of the end of 2020 Q4, the core tier 1 capital adequacy ratio (CAR) of commercial banks (excluding branches of foreign banks) was 10.72%, up by 0.28 percentage point compared to the end of last quarter; tier 1 CAR was 12.04%, up by 0.36 percentage point and CAR was 14.7%, up by 0.29 percentage point compared to the end of last quarter.

In 2020, in the face of the severe and complex domestic and international situations — especially considering the effects of COVID-19 — banking institutions strictly implemented the decisions and plans of the Party Central Committee, the State Council and the Financial Stability and Development Committee under the State Council. Such implementation achieved significant results in a number of aspects, including support of the real economy, improvement of the quality and effectiveness of financial services, and the deepening of reform and development.

First, efforts went into improving financial services for epidemic prevention and control. The banking and insurance industry improved financial services for financial institutions during the outbreak in China. The amount of special emergency credit offered in 2020 came to RMB 5.3 trillion. Everything was did to support the fight against COVID-19 in Wuhan and the rest of Hubei. Banking and financial institutions offered a total of RMB 6.6 trillion for the deferred repayment of loan principal and interest to micro-, small and medium-sized enterprises as well as foreign trade enterprises, and granted RMB 24.27 billion in emergency loans.

Second, continuous improvements were made in the quality and effectiveness of services for the real economy. In 2020, Renminbi loans increased by RMB 19.6 trillion, a YOY increase of RMB 2.8 trillion. Loans to private enterprises and the manufacturing industry increased by RMB 5.7 trillion and RMB 2.2 trillion, respectively. Loans to inclusive micro- and small enterprises, scientific research and technology services, and information technology services increased by a respective 30.9%, 20.1%, and 14.9%, year-on-year.

Third, effective measures were taken to mitigate risks in key areas. In 2020, risk resolution work targeting small and medium-sized banks and financial institutions, such as Baoshang Bank, was steadily advanced. Credit risk continued to be resolved. Altogether and throughout the year, RMB 3.02 trillion worth of non-performing assets in the banking sector were disposed of. The high-risk shadow banking business was cut back in an orderly manner. For the first time in eight consecutive years, growth of real estate loans was lower than that of all other loans. The CBIRC worked with local party committees and governments to resolve large corporations' debt risks.

Fourth, solid steps were taken in the reform and opening-up of the banking industry. Since 2020, the reform of the banking industry has been progressively deepened. The CBIRC actively promoted the issuance of RMB 200 billion worth of local government special bonds to replenish the capital of small and medium-sized banks. Institutional reform was continuously advanced for banks and insurance companies. And a three-year action plan was enacted for improving corporate governance. Multiple opening up measures were finalized and implemented.

**2. There is still room for improvement in certain areas of banking market development policies.**

In 2020, under the promotion of a number of regulatory policies and measures, the banking industry generally operated smoothly. Positive results were achieved in operational reform. But there are still some areas in need of further regulatory policy.

First, financial risk prevention remains a daunting task. Since 2020, risks to small and medium-sized banks have been resolved in an orderly manner. Credit risks and shadow banking risks have been contained to some extent. However, the international economic and financial situation remain serious and complex, with many uncertainties due to the changes in the pandemic and both domestic and foreign external environments. Our country's foundation for achieving national economic recovery needs to be consolidated further. China is still under great pressure to stay vigilant, guarding against imported cases of COVID-19 alongside international economic and financial risks. The rise of non-performing loans and other credit risks may be revealed in a later period. Regional financial risks still exist as well. In the future, special attention should be given to these areas.

Second, banking financial institutions' corporate governance mechanism still needs refinement.

Under the industry's supervision and continuous efforts over the past year, corporate governance construction and reform targeting China's banking institutions have achieved positive results, but there remain some areas in need of improvement. The problems are as follows: some banking institutions lack transparency in their shareholding structures; proxy shareholding and invisible shareholders — as well as offside and misplaced shareholder behavior — remain prominent; some major shareholders directly interfere with institutional operations, manipulating the board of directors or senior management team behind the scenes, transferring interests through illegal related-party transactions, or wantonly encroaching on institutional interests; the operation of the board of directors is not standardized; some non-executive directors are either unable, afraid, or unwilling to perform their duties; a few directors have major deficiencies in independence and professionalism; information disclosure is not standardized; stakeholder rights and interests are not sufficiently protected, including those of financial consumers.

Third, internet finance supervision on internet finance needs to be improved. Restricted by a number of policies introduced in the early period, internet loan risks have undergone fundamental improvements. However, in general, a long-term mechanism for existing internet loan risk resolution and internet loan risk supervision has yet to be established. The normal monitoring and supervision of Internet financial activities needs to be strengthened. The malicious evasion of debts and illegal private financial activities still exist in society.

### (III) Policy Prospects and Suggestions for the Development of China's Banking Market in 2021

2021 marks the commencement of a new journey to build a modern socialist country as well as the start of the "14th Five-Year Plan". The CBIRC and its local offices should adhere to the spirit of the Central Economic Work Conference and its key tasks for 2021. They should implement new development concepts on building a new development pattern and deepen supply-side structural reform in the financial sector. Efforts should also be made to enhance the effective serving of the real economy, further advance reform and opening up, and prevent and resolve financial risks. It is recommended that future regulatory policies focus on improvement in the following areas.

First, substantial support should be provided for the establishment of a new development pattern and to enhance the overall effectiveness of financial services. The Fifth Plenary Session of the 19th CPC Central Committee clearly asserted that China should accelerate the construction of a new development paradigm featuring dual circulation, in which domestic and overseas markets reinforce each other, with the domestic market as the mainstay. Related major work arrangements have also been made. In the future, the focus of regulatory work should be on fully supporting the development of domestic and international dual circulation, actively exploring various financial services that promote technological innovation, and maintaining the expansion of domestic demands while steadily promoting the banking and insurance industries' high-level opening up to the outside world. In the post-epidemic period, it is important to enhance support for economic recovery as well as the overall effectiveness of financial services, especially when it comes to strengthening financial support for micro-, small and medium-sized enterprises, people's livelihoods, and other areas.

Second, the CBIRC should continue to prevent and resolve financial risks and strengthen financial supervision in certain areas. In 2021, the prevention and resolution of financial risks will remain a top priority for supervision. It's recommended that in the future, regulatory policies focus on the continued close monitoring of risk prevention and resolution for high-risk institutions — including high-risk urban commercial banks and rural financial institutions — as well as the implementation of a real estate loan concentration management system and management regulations on the financing of key real estate enterprises, and the resolution of non-performing assets. At the same time, attention to the prevention of external risk shocks is recommended, and online platforms' financial activities should be put under effectively strengthened supervision, to which end the supervision of banking and insurance institutions' financial activities in cooperation with online platforms should be tightened. Finally, monopolies and unfair competition should be resolutely curtailed.

Third, the CBIRC should continue to deepen supply-side structural reform in finance and improve corporate governance and internal control management. Based on the current positive results of commercial banks' reform of institutional mechanisms, it is recommended that regulatory policies and initiatives in 2021 focus on: further reforming and optimizing the system of banking and insurance institutions; supporting small and medium-sized banks to replenish capital; promoting village banks to resolve risks by means of reform and merger and acquisition; encouraging large banks to provide risk control tools and techniques to small and medium-sized banks, and so on. At the same time, efforts should be made to further compel banking and insurance industries to improve corporate governance and internal control. There should be a code launched for banking and insurance institutions' corporate governance, as well as regulations on the conduct of major shareholders, regulatory rules and systems for related-party transactions, and the performance evaluation of directors and supervisors. Commercial banks' trusteeship mechanism should be improved, as should shareholders' mid- to long-term disciplinary disposal mechanisms. Corporate governance supervision should undergo continuous assessment, improve its information system, improve the application of information technology in supervision, and so on.

## Appendix

### Key Development Policies in China's Banking Market in 2020

| Released on | Major Policies | Released by |
| --- | --- | --- |
| January 14 | Rules on Handling Reports on Illegal Acts of Banking and Insurance Institutions (CBIRC Order (2019 No.8)) | China Banking and Insurance Regulatory Commission (CBIRC) |
| January 14 | Rules on Complaints Administration of Banking and Insurance Consumers (CBIRC Order (2020 No.3)) | China Banking and Insurance Regulatory Commission (CBIRC) |

Continued

| Released on | Major Policies | Released by |
|---|---|---|
| January 26 | Notice on Strengthening Financial Services of the Banking and Insurance Industry and Cooperating on Epidemic Prevention and Control (YBJBF [2020] No.10) | China Banking and Insurance Regulatory Commission (CBIRC) |
| January 29 | Notice on Mobilizing Party Organizations and Party Members and Cadres at All Levels of the System to Actively Engage in Epidemic Prevention and Control (YBJDBF [2020] No.3) | China Banking and Insurance Regulatory Commission (CBIRC) |
| January 31 | Circular on Further Strengthening Financial Support for Epidemic Prevention and Control (YF [2020] No.29) | The People's Bank of China (PBC), Ministry of Finance of People's Republic of China (MOF), China Banking and Insurance Regulatory Commission (CBIRC), China Securities Regulatory Commission (CSRC) and State Administration of Foreign Exchange |
| February 1 | Ensuring Quality Financial Services after the Spring Festival Holiday (YF [2020] No.30) | The People's Bank of China (PBC), China Banking and Insurance Regulatory Commission (CBIRC), China Securities Regulatory Commission (CSRC) and State Administration of Foreign Exchange (SAFE) |
| February 7 | Notice on Matters Relating to the Issuance of Bonds by Financial Institutions during Epidemic Prevention and Control (YSC [2020] No.5) | People's Bank of China |
| February 7 | Urgent Notice on Epidemic Prevention and Control and Strengthening Financial Support for Key Enterprises Engaged in Epidemic Prevention and Control (CJ [2020] No.5) | Ministry of Finance of People's Republic of China (MOF), National Development and Reform Commission (NDRC), Ministry of Industry and Information Technology of People's Republic of China (MIIT), the People's Bank of China (PBC) and National Audit Office of the People's Republic of China |
| February 14 | The Notice on Further Improving Financial Services for Epidemic Prevention and Control (YBJBF [2020] No.15) | China Banking and Insurance Regulatory Commission (CBIRC) |
| February 14 | Opinions on Further Accelerating the Building of Shanghai into an International Financial Hub and Financially Supporting the Integrated Development of the Yangtze River Delta (YF [2020] No.46) | The People's Bank of China (PBC), China Banking and Insurance Regulatory Commission (CBIRC), China Securities Regulatory Commission (CSRC), State Administration of Foreign Exchange and Shanghai Municipal People's Government |
| February 14 | The Announcement on the Participation in Sovereign Bond Futures Trading on the China Financial Futures Exchange by Commercial Banks and Insurance Institutions (CSRC Announcement [2020] No.12) | China Securities Regulatory Commission (CSRC), Ministry of Finance of People's Republic of China (MOF), the People's Bank of China (PBC) and China Banking and Insurance Regulatory Commission (CBIRC) |

Continued

| Released on | Major Policies | Released by |
| --- | --- | --- |
| February 14 | Notice on Public Opinion Solicitation for the "Measures for Standardized Administration of Notes (Draft for Comment)" | People's Bank of China |
| February 20 | Guidance on the Prevention of Financial Crime by Employees in the Banking and Insurance Industry | China Banking and Insurance Regulatory Commission (CBIRC) |
| March 1 | Notice on Extending the Policy of Provisional Deferred Repayment of Loan Principal and Interest for Micro, Small and Medium-Sized Enterprises (YBJF [2020] No.6) | China Banking and Insurance Regulatory Commission (CBIRC), the People's Bank of China (PBC), National Development and Reform Commission (NDRC), Ministry of Industry and Information Technology of People's Republic of China (MIIT) and Ministry of Finance of People's Republic of China (MOF) |
| March 5 | Work Plan for Coordinated Supervision over Financial Infrastructures | The People's Bank of China (PBC), National Development and Reform Commission (NDRC), Ministry of Finance of People's Republic of China (MOF), China Banking and Insurance Regulatory Commission (CBIRC), China Securities Regulatory Commission (CSRC) and State Administration of Foreign Exchange (SAFE) |
| March 10 | Notice on Optimizing the Change of Business Premises of the Branches of Banking Institutions (YBJBF [2020] No. 25) | China Banking and Insurance Regulatory Commission (CBIRC) |
| March 10 | Notice on Further Increasing the Efforts of Banking and Insurance Sector in Poverty Alleviation in "Three Districts and Three Autonomous Prefectures" (YBJBF [2020] No.24) | China Banking and Insurance Regulatory Commission (CBIRC) |
| March 18 | Interim Rules on Insurance Asset Management Products (CBIRC Order [2020] No.5) | China Banking and Insurance Regulatory Commission (CBIRC) |
| March 26 | Notice on Strengthening Financial Services for Coordinated Resumption of Work and Production across the Industrial Chain (YBJBF [2020] No.28) | China Banking and Insurance Regulatory Commission (CBIRC) |
| April 7 | Notice on Strengthening "Banking-Taxation Interaction" to Help Micro and Small-sized Enterprises Resume Work and Production (SZBF [2020] No.10) | State Taxation Administration, China Banking and Insurance Regulatory Commission (CBIRC) |
| April 9 | The Provisional Rules on Supervisory Assessment of Commercial Banks' Financial Services for Micro and Small Enterprises (Draft for Comments) | China Banking and Insurance Regulatory Commission (CBIRC) |

Continued

| Released on | Major Policies | Released by |
|---|---|---|
| April 9 | Notice on Banking and Insurance Sectors Better Serving Key Work Priorities in Agriculture, Rural Areas and Farmers in 2020 (YBJBF [2020] No.31) | China Banking and Insurance Regulatory Commission (CBIRC) |
| April 24 | Opinions on Providing Financial Support for the Development of Guangdong-Hong Kong-Macao Greater Bay Area (YF [2020] No.95) | The People's Bank of China (PBC), China Banking and Insurance Regulatory Commission (CBIRC), China Securities Regulatory Commission (CSRC) and State Administration of Foreign Exchange (SAFE) |
| May 7 | Regulations on the Management of Overseas Institutional Investors' Investment in China's Securities and Futures Market (PBC, SAFE Announcement [2020] No.2) | The People's Bank of China (PBC) and State Administration of Foreign Exchange (SAFE) |
| May 9 | Provisional Rules on Internet Loans of Commercial Banks (Draft for Comments) | China Banking and Insurance Regulatory Commission (CBIRC) |
| May 18 | Notice on Further Regulating Credit Financing Charges and Reducing Comprehensive Financing Cost of Enterprises (YBJF [2020] No.18) | China Banking and Insurance Regulatory Commission (CBIRC), Ministry of Industry and Information Technology of People's Republic of China (MIIT), National Development and Reform Commission (NDRC), Ministry of Finance of People's Republic of China (MOF), the People's Bank of China (PBC) and State Administration for Market Regulation (SAMR). |
| May 20 | Notice on Issues Concerning Insurance Fund Investment in Bank Capital Replenishment Bonds (YBJF [2020] No.17) | China Banking and Insurance Regulatory Commission (CBIRC) |
| May 22 | Notice on the Issuance of Measures for the Management of Criminal Cases Involving Banking and Insurance Institutions (Trial) (YBJF [2020] No.20) | China Banking and Insurance Regulatory Commission (CBIRC) |
| May 23 | Announcement on Extending Baoshang Bank Takeover | China Banking and Insurance Regulatory Commission (CBIRC) |
| May 26 | Guidance on Further Strengthening the Financial Services for Micro, Small and Medium-sized Enterprises (YF [2020] No.120) | The People's Bank of China (PBC), China Banking and Insurance Regulatory Commission (CBIRC), National Development and Reform Commission (NDRC), Ministry of Industry and Information Technology of People's Republic of China (MIIT), Ministry of Finance of People's Republic of China (MOF), State Administration for Market Regulation (SAMR), China Securities Regulatory Commission (CSRC) and State Administration of Foreign Exchange (SAFE) |

Continued

| Released on | Major Policies | Released by |
|---|---|---|
| June 1 | Notice on Further Implementation of Phased Deferment of Capital and Interest Repayment for Micro, Small and Medium-sized Enterprises (YF [2020] No.122) | The People's Bank of China (PBC), China Banking and Insurance Regulatory Commission (CBIRC), Ministry of Finance of People's Republic of China (MOF), National Development and Reform Commission (NDRC), Ministry of Industry and Information Technology of People's Republic of China (MIIT) |
| June 1 | Notice on Increasing Support on Credit Loans for Micro and Small-sized Enterprises (YF [2020] No.123) | The People's Bank of China (PBC), China Banking and Insurance Regulatory Commission (CBIRC), Ministry of Finance of People's Republic of China (MOF), National Development and Reform Commission (NDRC), Ministry of Industry and Information Technology of People's Republic of China (MIIT) |
| June 5 | Notice on Public Opinion Solicitation for the "Announcement on Standardizing Information Disclosure of Commercial Bills of Exchange (Draft for Comments)" | People's Bank of China |
| June 15 | Rules of CBIRC on Administrative Penalties (CBIRC Order [2020] No.8) | China Banking and Insurance Regulatory Commission (CBIRC) |
| June 15 | Notice on Matters Relating to the Disposal of Defaulted Corporate Credit Bonds | The People's Bank of China (PBC), National Development and Reform Commission (NDRC) and China Securities Regulatory Commission (CSRC) |
| June 23 | Notice on the Rectification of Malpractice, Misconduct and Noncompliance in the Banking and Insurance Industry (YBJF [2020] No.27) | China Banking and Insurance Regulatory Commission (CBIRC) |
| June 24 | Measures for Standardized Administration of Notes (PBC Announcement [2020] No.6) | People's Bank of China |
| June 24 | Notice on Related Polices for the Further Improvement of Microfinance for Poverty Reduction (YBJF [2020] No.28) | China Banking and Insurance Regulatory Commission (CBIRC), Ministry of Finance of People's Republic of China (MOF), The People's Bank of China (PBC) and State Council Leading Group Office of Poverty Alleviation and Development |
| June 29 | Notice on the Issuance of Supervisory Evaluation Measures on Financial Services of Commercial Banks for Micro and Small-sized Enterprises (Trial) | China Banking and Insurance Regulatory Commission (CBIRC) |
| June 29 | Joint Announcement on the Launch of 'the Cross-Boundary Wealth Management Connect Pilot Scheme' in the Greater Bay Area | The People's Bank of China (PBC), Hong Kong Monetary Authority and Monetary Authority of Macao |

Continued

| Released on | Major Policies | Released by |
|---|---|---|
| July 3 | Rules for Standardized Identification of Creditor's Assets (PBC, CBIRC, CSRC and SAFE Announcement [2020] No.5) | The People's Bank of China (PBC), China Banking and Insurance Regulatory Commission (CBIRC), China Securities Regulatory Commission (CSRC) and State Administration of Foreign Exchange (SAFE) |
| July 12 | Provisional Rules on Internet Loans of Commercial Banks (CBIRC Order [2020] No.9) | China Banking and Insurance Regulatory Commission (CBIRC) |
| July 14 | Report on Outstanding Issues of Shadow Banking and Cross-sector Financial Business in Recent Years | China Banking and Insurance Regulatory Commission (CBIRC) |
| July 17 | Construction Plan of National Illegal Fund Raising Monitoring and Early Warning System (2020–2022) | China Banking and Insurance Regulatory Commission (CBIRC) |
| August 5 | Notice on the Supervision over Governmental Financing Guarantee Agencies (YBJF [2020] No.39) | China Banking and Insurance Regulatory Commission (CBIRC), National Development and Reform Commission (NDRC), Ministry of Industry and Information Technology of People's Republic of China (MIIT), Ministry of Finance of People's Republic of China (MOF), Ministry of Agriculture and Rural Affairs of the People's Republic of China, Ministry of Commerce of the People's Republic of China and the People's Bank of China (PBCPBC) |
| August 17 | Notice on the Three-Year Action Plan for Sound Corporate Governance in the Banking and Insurance Industry (2020–2022) (YBJF [2020] No.40) | China Banking and Insurance Regulatory Commission (CBIRC) |
| September 7 | Notice on Strengthening the Supervision of Micro-credit Companies (YBJF [2020] No.86) | China Banking and Insurance Regulatory Commission (CBIRC) |
| September 9 | Financial Services Management Measures for Banking and insurance institutions in Response to Emergencies (CBIRC Order [2020] No.10) | China Banking and Insurance Regulatory Commission (CBIRC) |
| September 11 | Decision on Implementing Access Management of Financial Holding Companies (GF [2020] No.12) | State Council |
| September 11 | Trial Measures for the Supervision and Administration of Financial Holding Companies (PBC Order [2020] No.4) | People's Bank of China |
| September 15 | Implementation Measures for the Protection of the Rights and Interests of Financial Consumers (PBC Order [2020] No.5) | People's Bank of China |

Continued

| Released on | Major Policies | Released by |
|---|---|---|
| September 18 | Opinions on Standardizing the Development of Supply Chain Finance to Support the Stable Cycle and Optimization of Supply Chain and Industrial Chain (YF [2020] No.226). | The People's Bank of China (PBC), Ministry of Industry and Information Technology of People's Republic of China (MIIT), Ministry of Justice of the People's Republic of China, Ministry of Commerce of the People's Republic of China, State-owned Assets Supervision and Administration Commission of the State Council, State Administration for Market Regulation (SAMR), China Banking and Insurance Regulatory Commission (CBIRC) and State Administration of Foreign Exchange (SAFE) |
| September 21 | Notice on Public Opinion Solicitation for "Circular on the Administrative Provisions on Funds Used by Foreign Institutional Investors for Investment in China's Bond Market (Draft for Comment)" | The People's Bank of China (PBC) and State Administration of Foreign Exchange (SAFE) |
| September 30 | Notice on Establishing Countercyclical Capital Buffer Mechanism | The People's Bank of China (PBC) and China Banking and Insurance Regulatory Commission (CBIRC) |
| October 16 | Notice on Public Opinion Solicitation for the "Law of the People's Republic of China on Commercial Banks" (Revised Draft) | People's Bank of China |
| October 26 | Notice on Regulating Collection Business (YF [2020] No. 248) | People's Bank of China |
| November 2 | Notice on Public Opinion Solicitation for "Interim Provisions on the Management of Directors, Supervisors and Senior Managers of Financial Holding Companies" (Draft for Comments) | People's Bank of China |
| November 2 | Risk Monitoring Specification for FinTech Innovation (JR/T 0120—2020) | People's Bank of China |
| November 12 | Notice on Public Opinion Solicitation for the "Interim Measures for the Management of Network Microfinance Business (Draft for Comments) | China Banking and Insurance Regulatory Commission (CBIRC) and the People's Bank of China (PBC) |
| December 3 | Assessment Measures of Domestic Systematically Important Banks (YF [2020] No.289) | The People's Bank of China (PBC) and China Banking and Insurance Regulatory Commission (CBIRC) |
| December 18 | Announcement on Matters Relating to Information Disclosure of Commercial Acceptances (PBC Announcement [2020] No.19) | People's Bank of China |

Part Two — Chinese Financial Policies in 2020

Continued

| Released on | Major Policies | Released by |
|---|---|---|
| December 18 | Notice on the Establishment of Real Estate Loan Concentration Management System for Banking Institutions (YF [2020] No.322) | The People's Bank of China (PBC) and China Banking and Insurance Regulatory Commission (CBIRC) |
| December 19 | Announcement on Matters Relating to the Regulation of RMB Cash Receipt and Payment (PBC Announcement [2020] No.18) | People's Bank of China |
| December 23 | Matters Relating to Improving the Management of Market Makers for Spot Securities in the Inter-bank Bond Market (PBC Announcement [2020] No.21) | People's Bank of China |
| December 25 | The Measures for the Administration of Information Disclosure of Corporate Credit Bond (PBC, NDRC and CSRC Announcement [2020] No.22) | The People's Bank of China (PBC), National Development and Reform Commission (NDRC) and China Securities Regulatory Commission (CSRC) |
| December 25 | Notice on Public Opinions Solicitation for the "Interim Measures on Wealth Management Product Sales by Wealth Management Subsidiaries of Commercial Banks (Draft for Comments)" | China Banking and Insurance Regulatory Commission (CBIRC) |
| December 30 | Notice on Deepening the Reform of the Banking and Insurance Industry (Streamlining the Government, Delegating Power and Improving Government Services) and Optimizing Business Environment (YBJBF [2020] No.129) | China Banking and Insurance Regulatory Commission (CBIRC) |
| December 30 | Supervision and Administrative Measures on Anti-money Laundering and Counter-terrorist Financing by Banking Institutions (Revised Draft for Comments) | People's Bank of China |
| December 30 | Notice on Further Promoting the Reform and Restructuring of Township and Village Banks to Resolve Risks (YBJBF [2020] No.124) | China Banking and Insurance Regulatory Commission (CBIRC) |
| December 31 | Notice of CBIRC on Public Opinion Solicitation for "Decision on 'Amending the Implementation Rules of the Regulations of the People's Republic of China on Foreign-funded Insurance Companies'" (Draft for Comments) | China Banking and Insurance Regulatory Commission (CBIRC) |
| December 31 | Notice on Further Optimizing the Cross-border RMB Policy to Support Stabilizing Foreign Trade and Foreign Investment (YF [2020] No.330) | The People's Bank of China (PBC), National Development and Reform Commission (NDRC), Ministry of Commerce of the People's Republic of China, State-owned Assets Supervision and Administration Commission of the State Council, China Banking and Insurance Regulatory Commission (CBIRC) and State Administration of Foreign Exchange (SAFE) |

## Article 3

### Commentary on the Interim Measures for the Management of Network Microfinance Business (Draft for Comments)[1]

On November 2, 2020, the China Banking and Insurance Regulatory Commission (CBIRC), together with the People's Bank of China (PBC) and other departments, issued the *Interim Measures for the Management of Network Microfinance Business (Draft for Comments)*. The *Interim Measures* consists of seven chapters and 43 articles in total. It is issued to regulate microfinance companies' network microfinance business and prevent corresponding business risks, reflecting that financial innovation must be carried out under prudential supervision and emphasizing the importance with which financial regulators view the strengthening of anti-trust and consumer protections. The *Interim Measures* defines regulatory subjects and provides detailed specifications on the risk control system, single-account ceiling, information disclosure, and other issues in the operation of network microfinance; it also draws a number of red lines for the development of inter-provincial business, lending caps, and joint loan contribution of no less than 30%. It is one of the few regulatory policies to be released for the small loan industry since the *Guidance on Pilot Microfinance Companies* (YJH [2008] No.23).

Although the *Interim Measures* is currently in the stage of comment solicitation, its formal implementation will have implications for business rectification, increase in corporate capital, organizational restructuring, qualification re-approval, and the timing (start and end) of the transition period; it will have a significant impact on the landscape and development rules of the network microfinance industry. The main profit of Ant Group comes from its two major online microfinance products, "Ant Credit Pay" and "Ant Cash Now", which belong to Chongqing Ant Small Microfinance Co., Ltd. and Chongqing Ant Mall Microfinance Co., Ltd., respectively. On November 2, the People's Bank of China, the China Banking and Insurance Regulatory Commission, the China Securities Regulatory Commission (CSRC), and the State Administration of Foreign Exchange (SAFE) conducted a regulatory interview with Ant Group's de facto controller Jack Ma, Chairman Eric Jing and President Simon Hu. On December 26, the PBC, CBIRC, CSRC, SAFE, and other financial authorities jointly re-interviewed Ant Group, urging and guiding Ant Group to ensure financial regulation and fair competition, to protect consumers' legitimate rights and interests in accordance with the principles of marketization and the rule of law, and to regulate the operation and development of financial business. Pan Gongsheng, Deputy Governor of the People's Bank of China, has spoken about the background and main contents of the interview and the policy orientation of fintech regulation. He said in the future, fintech regulation policy orientation of fintech would adhere to the following principles: first, the firm breaking down

---

[1] Author: Yu Jinxin, intern of the project "Report on China's Financial Policy", doctor of PBC School of Finance (PBCSF), Tsinghua University.

of monopolies; second, insistence upon the regulation of all financial activities in accordance with the law; third, an unswerving commitment to consolidation and development of the public sector as well as support for and development of the non-public sector, the protection of property rights in accordance with the law, promotion of the entrepreneurial spirit, stimulation of the vitality of market players and social creativity, and improvement of China's fintech enterprises in terms of global competitiveness.

Online lending is meant to be an innovative product serving the demands of financial inclusion, but the other side of the coin is systemic risk lying in non-compliant development. In fact, since April 2016, regulators have issued a series of industry regulations and development rules particularly focusing on a special rectification plan for internet financial risks and the management methods of online lending institutions. These efforts are aimed at guiding online lending down a healthier, more standardized, and more sustainable path. We will find that financial innovation can only be carried out under the framework and precondition of prudential regulation. This is how we have remained true to our original intention and served the real economy and the people well.

## II. Stock Market Development Policies[①]

### (I) Overview of the stock market in 2020

Facing severe challenges imposed by the sudden outbreak of the COVID-19 pandemic, regulators remained committed to the basic principle of progress amid stable performance, adopted a holistic approach to pandemic response, continued to deepen reform and opening up and forestalled risks under the unified leadership, coordination, and planning of the Party Central Committee and the State Council. They have thereby maintained market stability by a focus on institution building, nonintervention, and zero tolerance. Amid the effects of COVID-19, regulators endeavored to stabilize market expectations and keep the stock market operating normally, bearing the principle of "letting the market settle market issues" in mind. Arrangements regulators made during this special time show the warmth and flexibility of regulation while mirroring the central government's efforts to ensure "stability on the six fronts and security in the six areas". Overall, regulators have advanced reform and strengthened IPO and refinancing as ways to support the recovery and development of the real economy. The year 2020 witnessed the systemic adoption of institutional reforms like the implementation of the revised Securities Law of the People's Republic of China, the GEM registration system reform, the National Equities Exchange and Quotations

---

[①] Author: Zhang Yulong, Chief Strategy Analyst with the Research and Development Department of China Securities, project fellow of Program for China's Financial Policy Report; Zang Yingshun, Strategy Analyst with the Research and Development Department of China Securities.

reform, improvement of the delisting system, further opening up, and concerted efforts in both investment and financing amid the implementation of the new Securities Law. As a result of these efforts, the stock market emerged from crisis to gain strength.

While the outbreak of COVID-19 in February 2020 took a certain toll on the stock market, financial policies unveiled by the China Banking and Insurance Regulatory Commission (CBIRC), the China Securities Regulatory Commission (CSRC), and the State Administration of Foreign Exchange (SAFE) allowed the stock market to bottom out in March 2020 and grow into a bull market on the whole. In 2020, the SSE Composite Index, SZSE Component Index, GEM, and STAR Market 50 Index scaled up by 13.87%, 38.73%, 64.96%, and 39.30%, respectively. By the end of 2020, companies listed on the SSE and SZSE amounted to RMB 79.72 trillion in market value, up 34.46% year-on-year (YOY).

Also in 2020, 21 of the SWS primary industries registered positive returns for an overall good earnings effect. Yet, disparities are found between different industries. The boards with higher growth rates included recreational service (99.38%), electronic equipment (94.71%), food & beverage (84.97%), war & national defense (57.98%), biomedicine (51.10%), automotive, (45.85%) and electronics (36.05%). In contrast, seven boards registered negative returns, including real estate (-10.85%), communications (-8.33%), interior decoration (-7.92%), textiles & garments (-7.08%), banking (-3.25%), mining (-1.34%), and trade (-0.22%). The COVID-19 pandemic was the most crucial factor in the first half of 2020, making biomedicine the star sector. In the second half of the year, effective control over the pandemic and the return to work and production allowed the national economy to recover gradually and the recreational service and automotive sectors to grow strong. With the advent of the 5th plenary session of the 19th Central Committee of the CPC, market entities increasingly focused on the electronic equipment and war & national defense sectors.

Due to continued institutionalization, the stock market saw certain "clustering" phenomena. As such, leading companies — especially those in food & beverage — were overvalued. Of the various boards, the GEM market valuation kept growing. By the end of 2020, the PE-TTMs of the SSE and SZSE, CSI 300, GEM, CSI 500, and CSI 1000 were at 21.08, 19.30, 53.13, 25.17, and 32.11, respectively.

### (II) Analysis of stock market development policies in 2020

**1. GEM registration system reform**

On March 1, 2020, a new *Securities Law of the People's Republic of China* was formally implemented. Article 9 of the new Securities Law deals with the registration system explicitly. The same day when the new Securities Law went into effect, the SZSE announced its decision to advance the GEM reform and implement the pilot registration system. Identifying GEM as the next board to follow the SSE STAR Market in the pilot registration system represented a new step in the larger process of market transition.

On April 27, 2020, the *Overall Implementation Plan for the Reform of the GEM and the Pilot*

*Adoption of a Registration-based IPO System* was adopted upon deliberation at the 13th meeting of the Central Commission of Comprehensively Deepening Reform, opening the stage for application of the registration system reform on the GEM. According to the plan, the GEM board will prioritize the growth of innovative businesses and startups, new industries, the ongoing integration of traditional industries with new technologies, new forms of business, and new models, "thoroughly implementing the innovation-driven development strategy and following the general trend of relying more on innovation, creation, and creativity".

On June 12, 2020, Yi Huiman, Chairman of CSRC, signed the *Measures for the Administration of Registration of IPO Stocks on the GEM (Trial)*, *Measures for the Administration of Registration of Securities Offering by Companies Quoted on the GEM (Trial)* and two other documents. The SZSE made arrangements in support, issuing rules such as *Rules Governing the Listing of Shares on the GEM Market of Shenzhen Stock Exchange* — eight business rules and 18 supporting rules, guidelines, and notices in total, which cover the offering and listing of stocks, securities trading, and continuous supervision on the GEM. These developments signify that major documents for the GEM registration system reform are basically issued, along with documents for their clarification and supporting rules.

Comprising a complete set of measures, the GEM registration system reform spans improvements in the offering, delisting, trading, and investor suitability management. The successful operation of the SSE STAR Market over nearly one year lent ample best practices for the reform. In fact, some of the systems for this reform were devised specifically according to the best practices of the SSE STAR Market.

In terms of offerings, the review model was modified from "the sponsor applies to the CSRC, which gives an opinion after the GEM Issuance Examination Committee has examined the submitted documents" to "the GEM Listing Committee examines submitted documents, and the CSRC conducts registration procedures". The GEM board also lifts the P/E ratio restriction on new shares. That means a new share's issuing price is determined through the solicitation of bids. In terms of follow-up investment, the GEM registration system provides an improved mechanism by which follow-up investments are only compulsory for unprofitable companies, red chip firms, companies with special voting rights, or companies offering high issue prices — not for all sponsors.

In terms of auction trading, the reform follows the example of the SSE STAR Market policy on price gains and falls: no days of gain or fall are defined for a new share, and no restriction on gain or fall is imposed on a new share in the first five trading days. In addition, the range of gain/fall in price for auction trading on the GEM is widened to 20%. To improve the intraday temporary suspension mechanism, two thresholds (30% and 60%) are defined for 10-minute suspension. A "price cage" is added to the continuous auction. Accordingly, the limit order buying price offered in the stage of the continuous auction should not exceed 102% of the benchmark buying price, and the limit order selling price offered should be below 98% of the benchmark selling price. At the same time, ceilings are defined for shares reported per limit order (100,000 shares) or market order (50,000 shares). Still, the GEM retains the current floor on shares reported per limit or market order (100 shares).

The reform introduces a mechanism for after-hours transactions. Once auction trading has closed on the GEM, after-hours deals are reported one at a time and matched continuously in chronological sequence at the closing price for the day. This mechanism fulfills investors' demands for making trades at the closing price.

In terms of investor suitability management, an established stock investor who intends to get involved in subsequent trading or an individual investor who applies for trading authority on the GEM should maintain the daily average assets within his/her securities or capital account at no less than RMB 100,000 in the 20 trading days before an authorization is to be granted, and should participate in securities trading for more than 24 months. Meanwhile, the reform removes the two-day and five-day cooling-off periods. Beyond that, the GEM requires its members to examine whether individual investors meet the access criteria. An ordinary investor should sign the "Risk Disclosure Statement" (on paper or electronically) for initial participation in trading on the GEM.

In terms of information disclosure, the GEM has a system of rules for continuous supervision reflecting the characteristics of its listed companies, as well as a rigorous system of rules for information disclosure. Strict enforcement of the two systems improves the relevancy and effectiveness of the market's information disclosure. Disclosure requirements for industrial information, operational risks, and performance fluctuations are tightened for innovative businesses, startups, and unprofitable companies. The GEM has also removed mandatory requirements for performance reporting, relaxed disclosure standards for transactions and related-party transactions, and simplified review procedures.

In terms of the delisting system, the GEM reform simplifies the delisting procedure, improves delisting standards, and adds more delisting indicators such as "market value below RMB 500 million for 20 consecutive trading days", and "major defects are found in information disclosure or standardized operation". To smooth the transition process, companies facing potential delisting on the GEM are given a defined transition period. As a way to simplify the delisting procedure, the GEM canceled the links of listing suspension and resumption along with the delisting preparation period for transaction-based delisting. On July 10, 2020, the "Notice by the Shenzhen Stock Exchange of the Arrangements for the Trading Rules for Stocks under Risk Alert and Stocks during the Delisting Preparation Period on the GEM" was issued by the SSE. The "Special Provisions of the Shenzhen Stock Exchange Concerning Trading on the GEM", enacted the same year, defines the GEM's risk alert point for price gain/fall as 20%. On December 31, 2020, the SZSE published the "Rules Governing the Listing of Shares on the GEM Market of Shenzhen Stock Exchange (2020 Revision)" to improve delisting rules and thereby foster a normalized, market-based delisting mechanism.

Overall, the GEM registration system reform follows up on institutional arrangements made during the SSE STAR Market's registration system trial. It leverages the best practices of the pilot regarding information disclosure, inclusive systems, well-defined market entity responsibilities, and severe punishments. There are two links in its registration procedure: registration with the SZSE, and registration with the CSRC. In the course of the review, the SZSE addresses inquiries to the issuer, and the issuer gives answers. This is how the stock exchange determines whether the issuer meets the requirements for offering, listing, and information disclosure. This reform is also consistent with the SSE STAR Market's rules on major matters such as regulatory frameworks, issuing conditions, information disclosure requirements, review procedures, and regulatory penalties.

Advancing GEM reform and pilot of the registration system is an important step in deepening reform, improving basic systems, and upgrading functions of the capital market. It also constitutes a major step in establishing an innovation-driven development strategy, in Shenzhen's drive to become a pioneering demonstration area of socialism with Chinese characteristics, and in the overall development of the Guangdong-Hong Kong-Macao Greater Bay Area.

**2. National Equities Exchange and Quotations reform**

The National Equities Exchange and Quotations (NEEQ) reform is an important part of China's plan for a multi-layer capital market. The year 2020 witnessed optimization of the NEEQ's top-level design and introduction of comprehensive quality and efficiency reforms. Starting at the beginning of the year, various NEEQ reform measures were unveiled in succession, especially emphasizing the three areas of selection layer subscription, review, and publicly offered funds' market access. Meanwhile, the CSRC and NEEQ Co., Ltd. continued to improve supporting measures.

On January 3, 2020, NEEQ published a second batch (six documents) of reform-related business rules, including three basic business rules: *Rules of the National Equities Exchange and Quotations System for the Private Placement of Shares*, *Rules for Information Disclosure by Companies Quoted on the National Equities Exchange and Quotations System*, and *Rules for the Governance of Companies Quoted on the National Equities Exchange and Quotations System*. On January 19, 2020, NEEQ published the third batch of (three) business rules for deepening overall reform: the *Rules of the National Equities Exchange and Quotations System for the Public Offering of Stocks to Unspecific Qualified Investors and Quotation on the Selection Layer (Trial)*, *Detailed Rules of the National Equities Exchange and Quotations System for the Administration of the Sponsorship Business for the Public Offering of Stocks to Unspecific Qualified Investors (Trial)*, and *Detailed Rules of the National Equities Exchange and Quotations System for the Administration of the Public Offering and Underwriting of Stocks to Unspecific Qualified Investors (Trial)*. An additional release on February 28, 2020, included the *Detailed Rules of the National Equities Exchange and Quotations System for the Examination before Quotation on the Selection Layer*, *Detailed Rules for the Administration of the Quotation Committee of the National Equities Exchange and Quotations System*, and the *Detailed Implementation Rules of the National Equities Exchange and Quotations System for the Public Offering of Stocks to Unspecific Qualified Investors* and *Quotation on the Selection Layer and Underwriting Business (Trial)*. These policies clearly stipulate details for the private placement of shares by companies quoted on the NEEQ, public offerings, underwriting sponsorship, information disclosure, and selection layer review, providing institutional rules for offerings on the NEEQ.

The division of market layers is the defining feature of a multi-layer capital market. Layering and transfer to other boards lie at the heart of the NEEQ. Regulators thus standardized the systems for regular layer adjustment and transfer. On March 6, 2020, the CSRC solicited public opinions on the *Guiding Opinions of the China Securities Regulatory Commission on Transfer to Another Board for Listing by Companies Quoted on the National Equities Exchange and Quotations System*, which sets the principles for selection of a destination board, conditions and steps for transfer, requirements for sponsorship, and restrictions on share trading. The key points of the document are as follows: First, both the SSE STAR Market and the GEM may serve as the destination board. The SSE and SZSE should select one of them as a pilot. Second, a company to be transferred to another board must have been listed on the NEEQ's selection layer for more than one year and meet the conditions for IPO and listing on the destination board. Transfer to another board does not need the approval of the CSRC, or to register with the CSRC, as there is no public offering of shares involved. The only required review is conducted by the stock exchange. Third, a stock exchange may engage a securities company as the sponsor and has the power to adjust or improve requirements and steps for transferring to another board. Fourth, when calculating the restriction period for share trading, the duration of restriction on the selection layer may in principle be deducted.

Then, directly preceding and following the opening of the NEEQ's selection layer, regulators issued such regulations as *Detailed Rules for the Significant Asset Restructurings of Unlisted Public Companies on the National Equities Exchange and Quotations System*, *Detailed Rules for the Suspension and Resumption of Trading of Stocks by Companies Quoted on the National Equities Exchange and Quotations System*, Guidelines for the Layer Adjustment by Companies Quoted on the National Equities Exchange and Quotations System, *Guidelines for Voting Right Difference Arrangement Business on the National Equities Exchange and Quotations System*, *Guidelines for the Supervision of Unlisted Public Companies No. 6 – Supervisory Requirements for Equity Incentive and Employee Stock Option Plans (Trial)*, *Operating Guidelines of the National Equities Exchange and Quotations System for Stock Exchanges*, and *Guidelines of the National Equities Exchange and Quotations System for the Continuous Supervision of Sponsoring Brokers*. These provide for other business matters related to the new third board. On November 27, 2020, the SZSE and SSE respectively issued drafts to solicit public opinions on the *Measures for Transfer to the GEM or the SSE STAR Market from the Selection Layer (Trial)*, which stipulates conditions for transfer from the selection layer to the GEM or the SSE STAR Market. A company to be transferred to the GEM or SSE STAR Market from the selection layer needs to meet the following criteria: (1) The company has been listed on the selection layer for more than one year, and has not been involved in any situations under which it should have moved out of the selection layer over the past year; (2) The company meets the conditions for IPO on the destination market (GEM or SSE STAR); (3) The company has not received any administrative sanctions from the CSRC, is not registered with the CSRC as a respondent to any investigation without clear conclusion or comment, and has not been publicly condemned by NEEQ over the past 12 months; (4) The company has a total share capital of at least RMB 30 million; (5) The company has at least 1,000 shareholders; (6) The public shareholding ratio of the company is at least 25% (or, if the total share capital exceeds RMB 400 million, the ratio is over 10%); (7) The transfer conforms to the aims of the *Guidelines for the Evaluation of Science and*

*Technology Innovation Attributes (Trial).*

In addition, regulators introduced publicly offered funds as a way to improve the liquidity of the NEEQ. On January 3, 2020, the CSRC published and solicited public opinions on the *Guidelines on Publicly Offered Securities Investment Funds Investing in Stocks Quoted on the National Equities Exchange and Quotations System.* The document clarifies requirements for managers of publicly offered funds when investing in stocks quoted on NEEQ and on the types of publicly offered funds they may invest in, as well as requirements for investing in NEEQ stocks, for liquidity management, valuation, information disclosure, risk disclosure, investor suitability management, investment trading control, and arrangements for the supervision of existing funds.

Since the adoption of its overall reform in 2020, the NEEQ has widely improved its top-level design — in listing, trading, and restructuring.

Market-wise, the NEEQ forms a hierarchical market comprised of a basic layer, innovation layer, and selection layer. Within this structure, companies that have been listed on the innovation layer are eligible for public offerings; companies are directly included in the selection layer after making a successful public offering; companies on the selection layer meeting the listing conditions of the Securities Law and relevant provisions of the stock exchange may directly apply to the exchange for transfer to another board. The transfer mechanism provides wider listing access and makes fuller use of the NEEQ's role as "a connecting link". It enables market players to leverage different advantages according to different development scenarios, which improves the hierarchical capital market's positioning to serve the real economy.

In terms of the offering system, the NEEQ introduces a system for the public offering of stocks to unspecified qualified investors, allowing companies quoted on the NEEQ to publicly offer stocks to unspecified qualified investors with the support of sponsorship and underwriting systems. This also makes partnering more efficient in investment and financing by allowing roadshows and bid solicitation. This is how it meets innovation and selection layer companies' demands for efficient financing. At the same time, the NEEQ will improve its current private offering system through such steps as canceling the lower limit on new shareholders (35) per financing operation and allowing self-offerings for small-scale financing. In so doing, it improves financing efficiency and lowers financing costs.

Regarding optimization of the trading system, the NEEQ increases matching frequency for aggregate auctions on the basic and innovation layers in an effort to scale up the liquidity as appropriate. Meanwhile, companies listed on the basic or innovation layer may choose between aggregate auction and market-making per their own accord. The selection layer establishes a mechanism for continuous auction trading to meet demands for share circulation following public offerings.

Regarding investor thresholds, investor access criteria are defined differently for the selection layer, innovation layer, and basic layer according to their respectively listed companies' specific characteristics and risks. Investors falling short of investor suitability standards are encouraged to share the "dividends" of small and medium-sized enterprises' growth through professional institutions like public funds. A drastic lowering of the investment threshold for the selection layer is expected.

In terms of information disclosure, the basic principles announced by NEEQ in the revision of the *Rules for Information Disclosure by Companies Quoted on the National Equities Exchange and Quotations System* are as follows: tightening information disclosure requirements for companies listed on the selection layer, simplifying information disclosure procedures for companies listed on the basic layer, and promoting improvements in information disclosure for all listed companies. There are now moderate standards for information disclosure for companies quoted on the innovation layer. These emphasize improving the relevancy and effectiveness of information disclosure through industry-specific requirements. As for audits, the audit of key matters is standardized to more effectively strengthen external guarantees of quality.

### 3. New regulations on QFII and RQFII

On September 25, 2020, the People's Bank of China (PBC), CSRC, and SAFE published the *Administrative Measures for Securities and Futures Investment Made in China by Qualified Foreign Institutional Investors and RMB Qualified Foreign Institutional Investors*. The "QFII & RQFII Measures" took effect on November 1, 2020. In fact, the regulatory authorities had requested opinions on related documents back in 2019. Over a year later, the administrative measures for securities and futures investments by foreign investors were finally put in place.

As stated by the CSRC, the aim of the QFII & RQFII Measures and related rules and revisions are: (1) to facilitate investment operations by deregulating access; (2) to steadily and systematically expand the scope of investment; (3) to strengthen continuous supervision.

Following multiple quota increases, in September 2019 the SAFE fully lifted investment quota restrictions designed for QFIIs and RQFIIs, as well as restrictions on source countries and regions for RQFII pilot. As such, registration is the only requirement before eligible QFIIs can remit funds to China and independently engage in the specified securities investment. However, despite the lifted restrictions, dramatic increases in QFII and RQFII investments or approaching the quota ceiling have yet to be seen. This pins the blame for fewer investments made by QFIIs and RQFIIs on the higher cost of procedures, rather than the quota restrictions themselves.

The QFII & RQFII Measures expands access, reduces required application documents, and shortens the timeframe for approval. It also simplifies the procedure for administrative licensing. According to the measures, if an applicant submits QFII status application documents to the CSRC through a custodian, the CSRC should respond with approval or disapproval within 10 trading days of the date the documents were accepted. The QFII & RQFII Measures additionally lifts restrictions on the number of agencies, optimizes oversight of filing, and reduces the requirements for data submission. Similarly, it lifts the restriction on the number of custodians, allowing a single QFII to have more than one. However, if a QFII has more than two custodians, one of them should be appointed as the principal reporter, responsible for handling qualification applications, reporting major events, registering investor information, and other duties.

Another effect of the QFII & RQFII Measures is the expansion of the scope of investment.

Added QFII and RQFII investors are newly allowed to invest in stocks on the NEEQ, as well as private investment funds, financial futures, commodity futures, and options. Also, said investors are allowed to participate in bond repurchase, stock exchange securities margin trading, and securities lending in margin financing loans. With these steps, QFIIs may basically hold a variety of investment product types — stocks listed on the SSE or SZSE, stocks quoted on the NEEQ, futures, and so on.

This allows QFIIs to fully participate in China's multi-level capital market investment and opens up more tools that they may implement different strategies, especially the strategy of cross-market risk hedging. With this support, QFIIs will have the courage to continue investing in China's financial market.

On the other hand, the QFII & RQFII Measures imposes more stringent requirements for regulators' continuous supervision, cross-market supervision, cross-border supervision, and penetrating supervision. Regulators have therefore clarified custodian and supervision responsibilities and requirements, with express provisions on violations and disciplinary measures.

The QFII & RQFII Measures seeks to expand access for foreign investors and kindle their enthusiasm for participation in China's financial market. That said, the inflow of foreign capital must be strictly regulated. For one thing, expanding foreign investor access means greater risks and challenges for China's financial market; such expansion may expose domestic players to the risks of other countries' peripheral markets and monetary policies. Especially in the context of increasing bi-directional volatility in the RMB exchange rate, the movement of funds only tends to exacerbate fluctuations in asset prices. For another, with the deepening of opening-up, more (and more varied) varied foreign investors are entering China, such that the scope and range of supervision must expand in response.

**4. Lifting the restriction on the security company foreign ownership ratio deepens the penetration of foreign-funded entities**

On March 13, 2020, the CRSC formally announced that the restriction on securities company shares' foreign ownership ratio would be lifted on April 1, 2020. Prior to this, the CRSC had announced that the restriction on futures company shares' foreign ownership ratio would be lifted on January 1, 2020, and that on fund management company shares would be lifted nationwide on April 1, 2020.

In this sense, April 1, 2020 can be seen as a milestone in the opening up of Chinese financial institutions. With both securities and fund management companies released from the restriction on their foreign ownership ratios in April 2020, now any eligible foreign investor may submit an application for the appointing or changing of its actual controller in accordance with the relevant laws and regulations, CSRC provisions, and service guidelines. Worth noting is that relaxation on foreign ownership for securities companies in April 2020 as a result of regulators' expediting the matter. The original date was set to December 1, 2020, according to the CSRC's previous policy releases. The effects of the COVID-19 pandemic have not slowed down, which has only accelerated the opening up of China's financial market. This trend is quite obvious with the introduction of both foreign securities investment funds and foreign financial capital.

The securities sector is currently experiencing good progress in the introduction of foreign capital. For example, UBS Securities have been transformed from a joint-venture securities trader into a foreign-owned securities trader — the first-ever foreign-owned securities trader in China. On March 27, 2020, the CSRC approved two similar conversions: Morgan Stanley became a principal shareholder and the controlling shareholder of Morgan Stanley Huaxin Securities, with a shareholding ratio of 51%; Goldman Sachs became a principal shareholder and the controlling shareholder of Goldman Sachs Gaohua Securities Co. Ltd., also with a shareholding ratio of 51%. J.P. Morgan Securities (China) Company Limited and Nomura Orient International Securities are two securities traders founded in early 2019 with the approval of the CSRC. The two foreign-owned securities traders are now both in operation. In addition to these approved foreign-owned securities traders, other applications are underway. Of the applicants, Credit Suisse Founder is applying for its own conversion from a joint venture to a foreign-owned securities trader by increasing its foreign investor's shareholding ratio. Regarding new securities traders, the Development Bank of Singapore and Daiwa Securities have submitted applications to the CRSC to establish new securities traders. Now that foreign investors are allowed to fully control a securities company in China, some overseas financial institutions may be gaining interest in sole proprietorship-based control. For example, Société Générale (SocGen) executives in charge of its China business disclosed that the company has worked with other shareholders to jointly found a foreign-owned securities trader in the country. Thus it is reasonable to expect that SocGen will found a solely foreign-invested securities trader in China in the future.

Beyond this, the insurance sector has effectively implemented the decisions and plans of the Party Central Committee and State Council for expanding the opening up of the financial industry. On March 10, 2020, the CBIRC released the *Decision of the China Banking and Insurance Regulatory Commission to Amend the Detailed Rules for the Implementation of the Regulation of the People's Republic of China on the Administration of Foreign-Funded Insurance Companies* to further clarify the access criteria for investments made by foreign insurance groups and overseas financial institutions in foreign-funded insurance companies. Through this amendment, the CBIRC removed restrictive provisions on foreign ownership ratios — now the foreign ownership ratio of a foreign insurance company or group, as a shareholder of a foreign-funded insurance company, may be up to 100%.

Indeed, since the CBIRC lifted the restriction on the foreign ownership ratio for joint-venture life insurance companies, foreign entities have been making moves. In May 2020, HSBC Insurance announced that it would purchase a 50% stake in HSBC Life held by National Trust, thereby making HSBC Life a wholly-owned subsidiary of HSBC Insurance based in China. The move, already internally approved, is awaiting approval by the CBIRC. In June 2020, American International Assurance (AIA) was approved for its "subsidiary change" — converting its Shanghai branch into the subsidiary Asia Life Insurance Co., Ltd. Its approval signified the first-ever solely foreign-invested life insurance company approved for incorporation within China.

Foreign investors have also made progress incorporating fund management organizations.

On August 28, 2020, the CSRC announced its approval of BlackRock Fund Management Co., Ltd., the first-ever foreign-funded public offering fund in China. Neuberger Berman, Fidelity, Van Eck, and Alliance Bernstein have also applied to set up public offering funds in China. Another field that foreign investors are getting involved in is the financial subsidiaries of banks. JPMorgan Chase will inject more capital into CMB Wealth Management, meaning that the global fund management magnate will be following in the footsteps of Amundi, BlackRock, and Schroders, who have also turned their gaze to the financial subsidiaries of banks.

### 5. Improving the quality of listed companies

On October 9, 2020, the State Council published the *Opinions Concerning Further Raising the Quality of Listed Companies* (hereafter referred to as the "Opinions"). The Opinions makes seven main points through six different requirements. The first point stresses the importance of listed companies' quality improvement to the continued development of the capital market, while points 2–7 are specific rules. These focus on: improving listed companies' governance, pushing listed companies to be stronger and better, improving the delisting mechanism, resolving outstanding problems that hinder listing, and raising the cost of violations by listed companies and related entities.

According to the Opinions' provisions on improving internal governance, a listed company should clarify the duties and legal responsibilities of its controlling shareholders, its actual controller, directors, supervisors, and executives, and should strictly implement the corresponding internal governance regulations to ensure its control systems are standardized and effective. The listed companies also need to improve the quality of information disclosure. To this end, regulators should improve the standards and relevancy of industry-based information disclosure to better align with investors' needs.

In order to promote listed companies' high quality and strength, the Opinions aims to introduce and gradually implement a nationwide registration system for securities offerings and to further standardize listed companies by offering more fostering and guidance. In the meantime, the document encourages companies covered by the pilot program of mixed-ownership reform to go public and tries to harness the positive role of equity investment organizations for improved governance, innovation, business start-up, and industrial upgrading. Beyond that, the Opinions stipulates that regulators should push for market-oriented mergers and acquisitions, support domestic listed companies purchase high-quality overseas assets by issuing shares, allow more eligible foreign investors to make strategic investments in domestic listed companies, and make invested companies more competitive on the global stage. Competent authorities need to improve the listed company financing system, steer listed companies to optimize financial arrangements according to both their own development needs and the conditions of the market, and improve the conditions for listed companies' refinancing-oriented offerings as well as for stock option incentives and employee stock ownership systems.

In terms of improving the delisting mechanism, the Opinions stresses that delisting must be strictly regulated and the delisting procedures streamlined. In this regard, regulators should offer more diversified delisting paths, and improve the systems for mergers and acquisitions, restructuring, bankruptcy, and rehabilitation. At the same time, regions and government departments are expected to carry out policies in coordination to support listed companies in minimizing risks through mergers and acquisitions, restructuring, bankruptcy, and rehabilitation.

As for the resolution of outstanding problems that hinder listing, the Opinions stresses that pledge information sharing should be strengthened to strictly implement the hierarchical system of pledge information disclosure. Regulators are required to tighten risk control on financial institutions and listed companies' majority shareholders and actual controllers and to develop a multi-department mechanism to minimize risks for listed companies' stock pledging to actively and steadily defuse the risks posed thereby. Meanwhile, regulators should take harsher steps in response to embezzlement and illegal guarantees while providing more policy support for the handling of major emergencies.

As for raising the cost of violations by listed companies and related entities, the Opinions stipulates that judicial authorities should impose heavier penalties for such violations as deceptive offerings, illegal information disclosure, market manipulation, and insider trading, and should assign greater administrative and criminal responsibility for financial falsification and embezzlement. Efforts should also be made to improve securities-related civil action and compensation systems.

To complement efforts to improve listed companies' quality, the Opinions says that the CSRC needs to be more prudent throughout the entire process of supervision, advancing scientific, category-appropriate, professional, and continuous supervision to make the regulation of listed companies more effective. At the same time, government bodies and regulators at all levels should strengthen the responsibilities entrusted to listed companies as market entities, urge intermediary agencies to perform their mandatory duties, advance the construction of big data platforms for listed company supervision, and develop a mechanism for information sharing among fiscal, tax, customs, financial, market regulation, industrial regulation, and juridical authorities as well as local governments.

Overall, the Opinions' provisions in regard to corporate governance, information disclosure, violation costs, and stock pledging restrictions can help reduce the risk of default entailed by information asymmetry and the non-standard management of listed companies. Furthermore, improving the delisting mechanism and upgrading regulation across various government departments will better protect investors' rights and interests, reduce their losses from default, and thus make the capital market more attractive. As listed companies are an important component of the financial market, improving their quality is conducive to the prevention of systemic risks. Last but not least, because listed companies connect the capital market and real economy as the representatives of high-quality enterprises, better-quality listed companies will, in turn, make the capital market more vibrant and competitive while driving non-listed companies upstream and downstream to improve their quality and efficiency, consolidating a foundation for the development of the real economy.

### 6. Improving the delisting mechanism

On November 2, 2020, the *Implementation Plan for a Sound Delisting Mechanism of Listed*

*Companies* and *Several Opinions on Lawfully Cracking Down Hard on Securities-related Violations* was passed upon deliberation at the 16th meeting of the Central Commission of Comprehensively Deepening Reform. As stated at that meeting, "improving the delisting mechanism for listed companies and cracking down on securities violations in accordance with the law are important institutional arrangements for the comprehensive deepening of the capital market reform. Sticking to the path of marketization under the guidance of the rule of law, the delisting standards should be improved, procedures simplified, channels multiplied, supervision tightened, and mechanisms standardized".

At a press conference held on December 11, 2020, the CSRC stated that it would earnestly implement the decisions and plans of the Party Central Committee and State Council, fully analyze outstanding problems hindering delisting and keep in mind the bigger schematic of registration system reform. Building on experience gained from delisting system pilot programs on the SSE STAR Market and the GEM, the CSRC proposed six additional further measures in response to existing delisting problems. The measures are as follows: improving delisting standards; simplifying delisting procedures; offering more diversified delisting paths; tightening responsibilities for delisting from a stock exchange; increasing efforts in delisting supervision; and improving investor protection mechanisms. With these measures in place, the commission will be ready to introduce delisting system reform throughout the capital market.

On December 14, 2020, the SZSE and SSE solicited public opinions on the revision of the delisting system. Then on December 31, 2020, they officially issued the revised versions of eight rules (hereafter collectively referred to as the *New Delisting Regulations Official Draft*) including the *Rules Governing the Listing of Stocks on Shanghai Stock Exchange, Rules Governing the Listing of Shares on Shenzhen Stock Exchange, Rules Governing the Listing of Stocks on the Science and Technology Innovation Board of Shanghai Stock Exchange and Rules Governing the Listing of Shares on the GEM Market of Shenzhen Stock Exchange*. The New Delisting Regulations Official Draft took effect on the same date. This action demonstrates the Chinese government's resolve to improve the delisting mechanism and the urgency of capital market reform.

Unlike the former rules governing the listing of stocks on the mainboard and the GEM, the New Delisting Regulations Official Draft divides delisting rules by chapter, establishing four categories in the delisting index (transaction, financial, normative, and major violation indicators) based on experience gained from existing systems of the SSE STAR Market. In particular, the revision integrates the SSE STAR Market with the mainboard by the revision or addition of delisting indicators and shortens the timeframe for delisting procedures. Specifically, it: (1) adjusts the standard of trading delisting indicators, including the establishment of a new total market value delisting indicator, unifying the closing price delisting indicator to RMB 1 and unifying transaction volume indicators; (2) cross-applies financial indicators with intermediaries' opinions and audit opinions with other financial indicators such as net assets, net profit, and operating income, giving more room to growth stocks and screening for financial problems more efficiently; (3) improves the information disclosure system, increasing penalties for improper disclosure and adding a new rule for the direct delisting of companies that are unable to disclose on time or for whom the accuracy of reports is unconfirmed by the board of directors for a long period in order to protect investors' interests; (4) supplements quantitative indicators for major violations based on the original rules regarding delisting for major violations, adding and quantifying an indicator for financial fraud.

In addition to the delisting indicators, another key component in the New Delisting Regulations Official Draft is a comprehensive revision of the delisting process. The revision abolishes the suspension and resumption of listing on the mainboard, abolishes the gain/fall limit in the finishing period, and shortens both the delisting consolidation period and suspension point. This series of initiatives greatly reduces the time investors will spend on ineffective speculation in delisting transactions, allowing for the prompt and rapid building of a normalized delisting system.

Additionally diverging from the exposure drafts issued on December 14, 2020, the New Delisting Regulations Official Draft revises certain details; most important among these is the revision of quantitative indicators for financial fraud: (1) The official draft reduces the time scale for delisting due to financial fraud from three years to two years and the ratio scale from 100% to 50%, significantly shrinking the window of opportunity for A-share listed companies to inflate profits and revenues or whitewash their statements, and reducing the operability of long-term shell preservation; (2) The official draft adds new operating income indicators, forming a financial fraud indicator system featuring the joint monitoring of net profit, operating income, total profit, and balance sheet. The official draft also supplements regulations on shareholders' share reductions to better protect the interests of small and medium-sized investors in the process of delisting.

All in all, the new rules improve the delisting mechanism across the board — in terms of indicators, processes, and trading rules. The launch of the new delisting rules will continue the normalization of A-share delisting to form a market pattern of "loosened restrictions on entry and exit" and improve the overall quality of listed companies. The normalization of the delisting mechanism will also enhance the appeal of China's capital market to investors and accelerate the entry of high-quality long-term capital into the market. Through "survival of the fittest" activity, the A-share market will become increasingly attractive to investors. In the mid-to-long term, the pace of entry for all types of long-term capital will quicken. The revision of the delisting mechanism will direct the flow of capital to high-quality targets and lay a good foundation for the capital market's improved vitality and implementation of the registration system for the mainboard.

### 7. New refinancing regulations

On February 14, 2020, after fully gathering public opinions, the CSRC announced the *Decision on Amending the Measures for the Administration of Securities Issuance by Listed Companies* and the *Decision on Amending the Interim Measures for the Administration of Securities Issuance by Listed Companies on the Growth Enterprise Market*. The two documents' exposure drafts had been released on November 8, 2019. The main relaxation clauses of the Decisions remain unchanged from the exposure drafts. The most notable changes are a raised ceiling for the scale of the private placement, widening of the time point for old and new cut-offs, and restriction on related parties to guarantee income.

On March 20, 2020, the CSRC clarified the private placement criteria for strategic investors. According to the *Q&As about Issuance Supervision-Supervisory Requirements on Matters Relating to the Introduction of Strategic Investors in Non-Public Offerings of Shares by Listed Companies*, strategic investors are basically "investors who have strong and important strategic resources in the same industry or related industries, seek long-term common strategic interests with the listed company through coordination and complementary development, are willing to hold a large proportion of shares in the listed company for a long period of time, are willing and able to conscientiously perform the corresponding duties, assign directors to actually participate in corporate governance, improve the governance of the listed company, help significantly improve the quality and intrinsic value of the listed company, have a good integrity record, and have not been administratively punished or held criminally liable by the China Securities Regulatory Commission in the last three years".

The CSRC should meet one of the following two requirements: first, "bring international and domestic leading core technologies to the listed company, significantly enhance the core competitiveness and innovation ability of the listed company, drive industrial technology upgrades in the listed company, and significantly improve the profitability of the listed company"; second, "bring international or domestic leading market, channel, brand and other strategic resources to the listed company, and significantly promote the listed company's market expansion and sales performance". This means that a strategic investor should have significant production or operational ties with the issuer and must be able to provide the issuer with substantial assistance in the form of technology, marketing, or channels and branding, rather than simply as a financial investor. In terms of information disclosure, it is necessary to thoroughly disclose the equity or investor structure and strictly enforce the requirements for strategic investors.

To sum up, the revisions of the two abovementioned documents mainly involve the relaxation of public or non-public offering conditions for GEM refinancing and optimization of the entire market's non-public offering system reform. The overall principles are relaxing the criteria for refinancing, stoking investors' desire to participate in refinancing, and encouraging companies to supplement their capital or restructure their assets through refinancing.

In terms of special provisions for GEM refinancing reform — first of all, lifting of the requirement for GEM-listed companies' publicly offered securities' asset-liability ratio at the end of the most recent period (that it must be higher than 45%); second is the removal of the two consecutive years of profitability for the non-public offering of shares requirement; third is inclusion of the issuance condition "funds raised in previous GEM fundraising are basically used, and the progress and effect of said use should be basically consistent with disclosure" in information disclosure requirements.

Regarding the market-wide optimization of the non-public offering system reform, the terms of issuance pricing, the number of private placement targets, the lock-up period, and the validity of approval are all relaxed in order to support listed companies' introduction of strategic and financial investors.

In terms of the pricing mechanism, first, the issue price is changed from no less than 10% to 20% of the average price of the company's shares for the 20 trading days prior to the pricing benchmark date, thereby lowering the incremental cost price of the private placement and expanding investors' potential profit margin. Second, in addition to the first day of the offering period for non-public offerings, the pricing benchmark date for strategic investors may also be set to the corresponding stock's announcement date (by the resolution of the board of directors or the resolution of the general meeting of shareholders), with issuance targets identified in advance.

Regarding the number of private placement targets, companies listed on the mainboard (SMEs board) and the GEM used to not be permitted to exceed a current issuance of 10 and 5 non-public stocks, respectively; the revisions adjust these figures to no more than 35 each. This facilitates the participation of small capital in private placement — on the one hand, reducing the difficulty involved in fundraising, on the other hand, increasing the potential benefits and lowering the potential costs for small capital to participate in the private placement.

The lock-up periods are shortened from the previous 36 and 12 months to 18 months and 6 months, respectively, and the restrictions on reducing holding-shares do not apply. The pricing and lock-up mechanisms for non-public offerings of GEM-listed companies' shares are consistent with those for listed companies on the mainboard (SMEs board), enabling rapid exit and increasing investors' willingness to participate in either shell listings or ordinary private placement.

The validity period for refinancing approval is extended from 6 months to 12 months to match the supporting financing approval validity period for major asset restructuring; the issuance option period is also extended.

In response to the NEEQ reform, the main revision content in the "Measures for the Supervision and Administration of Unlisted Public Companies and the Measures for the Administration of Information Disclosure by Listed Companies" is as follows: introduction of a public offering system to unspecified qualified investors, removal of the 35-person limit on targeted offerings by listed companies, and optimization of the review mechanism and differentiated information disclosure for public transfers and offerings.

In general, refinancing criteria are loosened and the scale of financing is expanded. This effectively reduces investors' risk of participation, widens the potential profit margin, and lowers the threshold and cost of capital participation. This in turn will cultivate investors' desire to participate in refinancing, make it easier for enterprises to access capital, and facilitate listed companies' capital replenishment through refinancing. Optimization of refinancing rules can improve listed companies' liquidity, reduce their asset-liability ratios and enhance the quality of market fundamentals. In fact, the Secondary Public Offering (SPO) market became more active in 2020, with 362 companies raising funds for the year — up from 251 in 2019 — for a total of RMB 834.1 billion raised, up from 2019's total of RMB 688.8 billion.

### 8. Cracking down on illegal securities behavior

Since April 2020, the Financial Stability and Development Committee of the State Council have addressed illegal securities activities on four separate occasions. The central government attaches great importance to cracking down on crimes in the capital market. Raising the cost of listed companies and related entities' violations is an important measure for improving the quality of listed companies. The State Council has dictated regulators to step up enforcement, strictly implement the Securities Law and other legal provisions, and increase penalties for fraudulent issuance, information disclosure violations, market manipulation, insider trading, and other unlawful acts.

On November 2, 2020, the *Implementation Plan for a Sound Delisting Mechanism of Listed Companies* and *Several Opinions on Lawfully Cracking Down Hard on Securities-related Violations* was passed upon deliberation at the 16th meeting of the Central Commission of Comprehensively Deepening Reform. "Improving listed companies' delisting mechanism and cracking down on illegal securities activities in accordance with the law are important institutional arrangements for comprehensively deepening the capital market reform," noted the meeting. Among those two, when it comes to cracking down on illegal securities activities, the central committee for deepening overall reform proposed accelerating improvements to the judicial mechanism for securities law enforcement, strengthening the investigation and punishment of major illegal cases, solidifying the foundation of the rule of law and the integrity of the capital market, enhancing cross-border supervision and law enforcement collaboration, and promoting the building of a sound market order. Law enforcement must be strict and violations must be punished. The crackdown on illegal acts in the securities sector will be further intensified to safeguard the achievements of the registration system.

In fact, the regulatory authorities have been very quick to implement the *Several Opinions*. On December 29, 2020, Jiao Jinhong, Chief-Lawyer of the CSRC, said that the CSRC will base its efforts on the realities of the capital market at the new stage, and make sustained efforts to reform and develop the capital market and do good work in the legal building. The CSRC hopes to make significant progress in the building of the legal system of the capital market in about two years, improve the securities enforcement system with Chinese characteristics, significantly increase the cost of securities violations, smooth the channels for investor rights relief, and significantly improve the order of the capital market. This is a direct response to the Several Opinions' requirement to "accelerate improvements to the judicial mechanism for securities law enforcement". It is expected that law enforcement capacity-building at the regulatory level will only continue.

Strictly cracking down on illegal securities activities and improving the relevant judicial mechanism will work hand in hand. On January 31, 2021, the Securities Association of China announced inspections of information disclosure quality for 20 companies quoted on the STAR Market and the GEM market prior to January 30, 2021, determined by lottery. As of February 24, of the 20 randomly selected companies, 16 had withdrawn their materials and effectively terminated the review — in other words, 80% of them. This shows that certain problems currently exist in information disclosure. On February 26, 2021, the SSE commented regarding the recent on-site inspection of information disclosure quality for companies listed on the STAR Market, saying that it would adopt an approach of "institution building, nonintervention, and zero tolerance", make full use of on-site inspection, on-site supervision and audit and inquiry as regulation mechanisms, and strictly control the "entry gate" of listing. For projects withdrawn prior to the on-site inspection, the audit center has been analyzing and sorting the relevant problems. If it finds suspected cases of financial fraud, false statements, or other major violations of the law, the corresponding sponsor and issuer will have to bear responsibility accordingly. The SSE demonstrates a clear stance on regulation is in line with the core idea of raising the costs of violations by listed companies and related entities.

As frontline regulators put more practical guidelines in place and successfully strengthen supervisory measures such as on-site supervision and spot checks, improving the quality of information disclosure will become the next priority for issuers and intermediaries. The registration system has been gradually piloted and will be rolled out to the whole market in the future. However, in conflict with the market-wide implementation of the registration system is the fact that many of China's sponsor institutions cannot meet the development demands of the registration system in terms of quality of practice. Many intermediaries lack the concepts, organization, and ability needed to match the registration system, which will affect the stability of the registration system and leave hidden dangers for the future. Therefore, the current law enforcement efforts must be strengthened, and targeted measures shall be taken to seriously deal with relevant problems in listing, to maintain a sound order of the capital market.

This is the first time in the history of China's capital market that the central authority has adopted a special document addressing illegal securities behavior. This key move will help protect investors' legitimate rights and interests and build a fair, orderly, honest, and self-disciplined capital market ecosystem.

### 9. Listed companies' information disclosure

Information disclosure lies at the heart of the registration-based initial public offering (IPO) system reform, and information disclosure supervision is the focus of supervision over listed companies. Therefore, regulators must pay great attention to the construction of listed companies' information disclosure systems.

On March 1, 2020, the new Securities Law came into effect, with a special new chapter on information disclosure. Through summarizing the experience of previous information disclosure supervision, the CSRC released the *Measures for the Administration of Information Disclosure by Listed Companies* (*Revised Draft*) for public opinions on July 24, 2020.

The "Measures" features revisions in the following three aspects:

First, improvement to the principle of information disclosure. The Measures adds new requirements for concise, clear, and understandable information disclosure, improves the principle of fair disclosure, and clarifies relevant requirements for voluntary disclosure in order to encourage it. Provisions regarding matters of interim reports are improved in accordance with the new Securities Law. For example, the Measures includes such provisional report items as: "major changes to the situation where the company's actual controller and other enterprises under its control are engaged in the same or similar business as the company" and "changes in the company's dividend distribution, capital increase plan, or shareholding structure". For listed companies simultaneously issuing corporate bonds, interim bond disclosure is required, for which the requirements are clarified.

Second, the Measures further emphasizes the responsibilities of relevant subjects such as directors, supervisors, and other senior management. Directors, supervisors, and other senior executives are the key targets of information disclosure. The Measures strengthens the responsibility of the board of directors in the disclosure of periodic reports, clearly stipulates that the content of periodic reports is to be considered and approved by the board of directors. It requires that when directors, supervisors, and other senior management cannot guarantee the truthfulness, accuracy, or completeness of periodic reports' content, or if they disagree, they shall express their opinions and state their reasons in a written confirmation opinion to be disclosed by the listed company. It also clarifies the obligations of controlling shareholders and actual controllers in the cooperation.

Third, improvement to matters regarding the interim report. The Measures details certain information disclosure items for the interim report, expands the scope of events based on the major event disclosure of the original interim report, and fully ensures investors' right to know. For example, "major property acquisition decisions" are defined as "a company's purchase or sale of major assets in excess of 30% of the company's total assets within one year, or the mortgage, pledge, sale, or scrapping of the company's major assets for business purposes in excess of 30% of such assets at one time". Also included within the scope of "major events" to be disclosed in the interim report are "major changes to the situation where the company's actual controller and other enterprises under its control are engaged in the same or similar business as the company" and "changes in the company's dividend distribution, capital increase plan, or shareholding structure".

In addition to the strict requirements for issuers of securities and initiatives to improve the management of information disclosure by listed companies, the Measures also sets clear requirements for service providers. It requires securities service providers to keep and properly maintain information and materials such as customer entrustment documents, verification and validation materials, and working papers. Service providers must cooperate with the CSRC in supervision and administration and ensure that all materials and information they provide, report or disclose are truthful, accurate, and complete, without any false records, misleading statements, or major omissions. It clarifies the responsibilities of issuers and securities service providers in a number of aspects, which will help restrain various behavior among issuers and ensure the honesty and timeliness of information disclosure. Its clarification will also provide a sufficient basis for law enforcement and help crackdown on illegal securities activities.

### (III) Policy evaluation and outlook

Stock market development policy in 2020 continued and deepened the overall reform concepts in place since 2019. Its basic concepts continued to be "institution building, nonintervention, and zero tolerance". It stressed the concept of systems, aiming to build a multi-level capital market equipped to serve the new pattern of development. The experience can be summarized by practice. The successful establishment of the STAR Market in 2019, and its completion of the GEM registration system reform successfully deepened overall reform. The overarching goals are to better serve the real economy, strengthen the role of the refinancing market, facilitate equity financing for listed companies and help them grow bigger and stronger. Efforts have been continuous in accelerating opening up, reforming the QFII and RQFII systems, and removing restrictions on the proportion of foreign ownership in financial institutions such as securities, funds, and futures. In terms of improving the quality of listed companies, efforts focus on regulating corporate governance and internal control, improving the quality of information disclosure, supporting the listing of high-quality enterprises, enhancing the delisting mechanism, resolving issues of stock pledges, capital appropriation, illegal guarantees, and other risks, and raising the cost of violations to promote the sound development of the capital market through legalization and standardization.

Looking ahead to 2021, China's stock market policy will ensure the normal operation of listed companies and refinancing as well as the balanced development of the stock market by improving financial futures instruments. Considering the new development pattern, major support will go to the innovation-driven economy, and evaluation criteria will be improved for science and innovation attributes. Efforts will go into improving the registration system reform, issuing supporting policies more quickly, clarifying the responsibility of intermediaries, cracking down on illegal securities behavior via a "zero tolerance" approach, and protecting the gains of capital market reform to create a favorable environment for market-wide implementation of the registration system. The movement to prevent and resolve major financial risks will forge ahead with new strength. Liquidity and leverage levels will receive special attention, as will the prevention of cross-market, cross-regional, and cross-border imported risks.

## Appendix

### Key Development Policies in China's Stock Market in 2020

| Release Date | Policy Name | Issuing Units |
|---|---|---|
| January 13 | [Announcement No. 3] Guideline on the Content and Format of Information Disclosure by Unlisted Public Companies No. 3 — Prospectus for Directed Offerings and Report on the Status of Offerings (Revised in 2020) | CSRC |
| January 13 | [Announcement No. 4] Guideline on the Content and Format of Information Disclosure by Unlisted Public Companies No. 4 — Application Documents for Directed Offerings (Revised in 2020) | CSRC |
| January 13 | [Announcement No. 5] Guideline on the Content and Format of Information Disclosure by Unlisted Public Companies No. 9 — Annual Report of Innovative Tier Listed Companies | CSRC |
| January 13 | [Announcement No. 6] Guideline on the Content and Format of Information Disclosure by Unlisted Public Companies No. 10 — Annual Report of Basic Tier Listed Companies | CSRC |
| January 14 | [Announcement No. 7] Interim Provisions on Reporting Securities and Futures Violations | CSRC |

Continued

| Release Date | Policy Name | Issuing Units |
|---|---|---|
| January 17 | [Announcement No. 8] Guideline on the Content and Format of Information Disclosure by Unlisted Public Companies No. 11 — Prospectus for Public Offering of Shares to Unspecified Qualified Investors | CSRC |
| January 17 | [Announcement No. 9] Guideline on the Content and Format of Information Disclosure by Unlisted Public Companies No. 12 — Application for Public Offering of Shares to Unspecified Qualified Investors | CSRC |
| February 14 | [Announcement No. 11] Decision on Amending the Rules for the Implementation of Non-public Offering of Shares by Listed Companies | CSRC |
| February 14 | [Announcement No. 12] The Announcement on the Participation of Commercial Banks and Insurance Institutions in Government Bond Futures Trading on the China Financial Futures Exchange issued by the China Securities Regulatory Commission, the Ministry of Finance, the People's Bank of China, and China Banking and Insurance Regulatory Commission | CSRC |
| February 14 | [Order No. 163] Decision on Amending the Measures for the Administration of Securities Issuance by Listed Companies | CSRC |
| February 14 | [Order No. 164] Decision on Amending the Interim Measures for the Administration of Securities Issuance by Listed Companies on the Growth Enterprise Market | CSRC |
| February 19 | [Announcement No. 13] Matters Related to Administrative Licensing of Non-listed Public Companies | CSRC |
| March 3 | [Announcement No. 18] Announcement on the Cancellation or Adjustment of Some Administrative Approval Items of Securities Companies and Other Matters | CSRC |
| March 6 | [Announcement No. 17] Special Provisions for Shareholders of Listed Venture Capital Funds to Reduce Shareholdings | CSRC |
| March 6 | Notice on Issuance of Implementation Rules for Shareholding Reduction by Shareholders of Venture Capital Funds Listed on Shenzhen Stock Exchange (Revised in 2020) | SZSE |
| March 6 | Notice on Issuance of Implementation Rules for Shareholding Reduction by Shareholders of Venture Capital Funds Listed on Shanghai Stock Exchange (Revised in 2020) | SSE |
| March 13 | [Order No. 165] Provisions for the Formulation of Securities and Futures Regulations | CSRC |
| March 13 | Notice of Amendment to the Trading Rules of the Shanghai Stock Exchange | SSE |
| March 13 | Eliminating the Restriction on the Foreign Shareholding Ratio of Securities Companies | CSRC |
| March 20 | [Announcement No. 20] Decision on Amending Some Normative Documents on Securities and Futures | CSRC |

Continued

| Release Date | Policy Name | Issuing Units |
| --- | --- | --- |
| March 20 | [Announcement No. 21] Guidelines for Evaluating the Attributes of Science and Innovation (Trail) | CSRC |
| March 20 | [Order No. 166] Decision on Amending Some Securities and Futures Regulations | CSRC |
| March 27 | Notice on Issuing the Interim Regulations for Reporting and Recommending the Issuance and Listing of Enterprises on the STAR Market of Shanghai Stock Exchange | SSE |
| April 7 | [Announcement No. 22] Announcement on Matters Relating to the Audit and Disclosure of Annual Reports of Current Listed Companies | CSRC |
| April 17 | [Announcement No. 23] Guidelines for Publicly Raised Securities Investment Funds to Invest in Listed Stocks on the NEEQ System | CSRC |
| April 24 | Opinions on Financial Support for the Building of the Guangdong-Hong Kong-Macao Greater Bay Area | PBOC, CBIRC, CSRC, SAFE |
| April 27 | Notice on the Issuance of the Implementation Measures of the Shenzhen Stock Exchange GEM Investor Appropriateness Administration (Revised in 2020) | SZSE |
| April 28 | [Announcement No. 25] Rules for the Preparation of Information Disclosure by Companies Issuing Public Securities No. 24 — Special Provisions on Financial Reporting Information for Innovative Pilot Red Chip Enterprises under the Registration System | CSRC |
| April 30 | [Announcement No. 24] Decision on the Abolition of the Interim Provisions on the Administration of the Appropriateness of Investors in the GEM Market | CSRC |
| April 30 | [Announcement No. 26] Announcement on the Arrangements Relating to the Domestic Listing of Innovative Pilot Red Chip Enterprises | CSRC |
| May 29 | [Announcement No. 28] Decision on Amending the Regulations on the Administration of Subordinated Debt of Securities Firms | CSRC |
| June 3 | [Announcement No. 29] China Securities Regulatory Commission's Guidance on the Transfer and Listing of Companies Listed on the NEEQ | CSRC |
| June 12 | [Announcement No. 31] Guideline on the Content and Format of Information Disclosure by Companies Issuing Public Securities No. 28 — Prospectus for GEM Companies (Revised in 2020) | CSRC |
| June 12 | [Announcement No. 32] Guideline on the Content and Format of Information Disclosure by Companies Issuing Public Securities No. 29 — Application Documents for IPO of Shares and Listing on GEM (Revised in 2020) | CSRC |
| June 12 | [Announcement No. 33] Guideline on the Content and Format of Information Disclosure by Companies Issuing Public Securities No. 35 — Prospectus for the Issuance of Securities to Unspecified Objects by Listed Companies on GEM (Revised in 2020) | CSRC |

*Continued*

| Release Date | Policy Name | Issuing Units |
|---|---|---|
| June 12 | [Announcement No. 34] Guideline on the Content and Format of Information Disclosure by Companies Issuing Public Securities No. 36 — Prospectus and Report on Issuance of Securities to Specified Persons by Listed Companies on GEM | CSRC |
| June 12 | [Announcement No. 35] Guideline on the Content and Format of Information Disclosure by Companies Issuing Public Securities No. 37 — Application Documents for Issuance of Securities by Listed Companies on GEM (Revised in 2020) | CSRC |
| June 12 | [Announcement No. 36] Special Provisions on Offering and Underwriting of the Securities of IPO on the GEM | CSRC |
| June 12 | [Order No. 169] Measures for Continuous Supervision of Listed Companies on GEM (Trial) | CSRC |
| June 12 | [Order No. 168] Measures for the Administration of Registration of Securities Offering by Companies Quoted on the GEM (Trial) | CSRC |
| June 12 | [Order No. 167] Measures for the Administration of Registration of IPO Stocks on the GEM (Trial) | CSRC |
| June 12 | [Order No. 170] Administration Measures for Securities Issuance and Listing Sponsorship | CSRC |
| June 12 | Notice on the Issuance of the Implementation Rules for the Off-line Offering of Shares in the Shenzhen Market (Revised in 2020) | SZSE |
| June 12 | Notice on the Issuance of the Rules of Work of the Industry Consulting Expert Pool of Shenzhen Stock Exchange | SZSE |
| June 12 | Notice on the Issuance of the Measures for the Administration of the GEM Listing Committee of the Shenzhen Stock Exchange | SZSE |
| June 12 | Notice on the Issuance of the Guidelines for Acceptance of Application Documents for Listing on the GEM of the Shenzhen Stock Exchange | SZSE |
| June 12 | Notice on the Issuance of the Guidelines on Financial Report Disclosure for Innovative Pilot Red Chip Enterprises on the Shenzhen Stock Exchange | SZSE |
| June 12 | Notice on the Issuance of the Interim Regulations for Reporting and Recommending the Issuance and Listing of Enterprises on the GEM of the Shenzhen Stock Exchange | SZSE |
| June 12 | Notice on the Issuance of the Rules for Reviewing the Listing of Stocks on the GEM of the Shenzhen Stock Exchange | SZSE |
| June 12 | Notice on the Issuance of Q&As on the Review of the IPO of Stocks on the GEM of the Shenzhen Stock Exchange | SZSE |
| June 12 | Notice on the Issuance of the Guidelines on the Content and Format of the Sponsorship Letter for Listing on the GEM of the Shenzhen Stock Exchange | SZSE |
| June 12 | Notice on the Issuance of Q&As on the Review of the Listing of Securities Issued by Companies Listed on the GEM of the Shenzhen Stock Exchange | SZSE |

Continued

| Release Date | Policy Name | Issuing Units |
|---|---|---|
| June 12 | Notice on the Issuance of the Rules for the Review of Material Assets Reorganization of Listed Companies on the GEM of the Shenzhen Stock Exchange | SZSE |
| June 12 | Notice on the Issuance of the Rules for Reviewing the Listing of Securities Issued by Companies Listed on the GEM of the Shenzhen Stock Exchange | SZSE |
| June 12 | Notice on the Issuance of the Implementation Rules on Issuing and Underwriting Business for Securities Listed on the GEM of the Shenzhen Stock Exchange | SZSE |
| June 12 | Notice on the Issuance of the Implementation Rules on Issuing and Underwriting Business for the IPO of Securities Listed on the GEM of the Shenzhen Stock Exchange | SZSE |
| June 12 | Notice on the Issuance of the Guidelines for the Regulation of the Operation of Listed Companies on the GEM of the Shenzhen Stock Exchange (Revised in 2020) and Related Matters | SZSE |
| June 12 | Notice on the Issuance of the Rules Governing the Listing of Shares on the GEM Market of Shenzhen Stock Exchange (Revised in 2020) | SZSE |
| June 12 | Notice on the Issuance of the Rules Governing the Listing of Shares on the GEM Market of Shenzhen Stock Exchange (Revised in December 2020) | SZSE |
| June 12 | Notice on Matters Relating to the Pledge Repurchase and Agreed Repurchase Transactions in respect of GEM Stocks | SZSE |
| June 12 | Notice on the Issuance of the Special Provisions on Securities Lending and Securities Transfer on GEM of the Shenzhen Stock Exchange, China Securities Finance Corporation Limited, and China Securities Depository and Clearing Corporation Limited | SZSE |
| June 12 | Notice on the Issuance of the Special Provisions of the Shenzhen Stock Exchange Concerning Trading on the GEM | SZSE |
| June 12 | Notice on the Issuance of the Rules for Real-Time Monitoring of Abnormal Stock Transactions on the GEM of the Shenzhen Stock Exchange (Trial) | SZSE |
| June 19 | Notice on the Work Relating to the Application of Simplified Refinancing Procedures for GEM Listed Companies | SZSE |
| June 19 | Notice on Matters Relating to the Clarification of the Benchmark Indexes Involved in the Determination of Abnormal Stock Fluctuations on the STAR Market | SSE |
| June 19 | Announcement on the Revision of the Compilation Scheme of the SSE Composite Index, Announcement on the Release of the SSE STAR Market 50 Component Index | SSE |
| July 3 | [Announcement No. 37] Guideline on the Content and Format of Information Disclosure by Companies Issuing Public Securities No. 43 — Prospectus for the Issuance of Securities to Unspecified Objects by Listed Companies on the STAR Market | CSRC |

Continued

| Release Date | Policy Name | Issuing Units |
|---|---|---|
| July 3 | [Announcement No. 38] Guideline on the Content and Format of Information Disclosure by Companies Issuing Public Securities No. 44 — Prospectus and Report on Issuance of Securities to Specified Objects by Listed Companies on the STAR Market | CSRC |
| July 3 | [Announcement No. 39] Guideline on the Content and Format of Information Disclosure by Companies Issuing Public Securities No. 45 — Application Documents for Issuance of Securities by Listed Companies on the STAR Market | CSRC |
| July 3 | [Order No. 171] Administrative Measures for the Registration of Securities Issuance by Listed Companies on the STAR Market (Trial) | CSRC |
| July 3 | Notice on Issuance of Implementation Rules on Shareholding Reduction by Shareholders of Companies Listed on the STAR Market of the Shanghai Securities Exchange through Quotation Transfer and Placement to Specific Institutional Investors | SSE |
| July 3 | Notice on the Issuance of the Implementation Rules for Underwriting the Securities Issued by Companies Listed on the STAR Market of the Shanghai Securities Exchange | SSE |
| July 3 | Notice on the Work Related to the Application of Simplified Refinancing Procedures for Listed Companies on the STAR Market in 2020 | SSE |
| July 3 | Notice on the Issuance of Q&As on Reviewing the Listing of Securities Issued by Listed Companies on the STAR Market of the Shanghai Securities Exchange | SSE |
| July 3 | Notice on the Issuance of the Rules on Reviewing the Listing of Securities Issued by Listed Companies on the STAR Market of the Shanghai Securities Exchange | SSE |
| July 10 | [Announcement No. 42] Decision on Amending the Regulations on the Classified Supervision of Securities Firms | CSRC |
| July 10 | [Announcement No. 43] Guidelines on Disclosure of Key Financial Information and Operating Conditions after the Cut-off Date for the Audit of Financial Reports in IPOs and Prospectuses of Listed Companies (Revised in 2020) | CSRC |
| July 10 | [Order No. 172] Measures for the Administration of Custody Business of Securities Investment Funds | CSRC |
| July 10 | [Order No. 173] Decision on Amending the Measures for the Administration of IPO and Listing of Stocks | CSRC |
| July 10 | [Order No. 174] Decision on Amending the Measures for the Administration of Registration of IPO of Shares on the STAR Market (Trial) | CSRC |
| July 10 | Notice on the Arrangement of Trading System for Risk Warning Stocks and Delisting Stocks on GEM | SZSE |

Continued

| Release Date | Policy Name | Issuing Units |
|---|---|---|
| July 22 | [Announcement No. 46] Guidelines for Supervision of Non-listed Public Companies No. 5 — Guidelines for Ongoing Supervision of Listed Companies on Selected Tiers (Trial) | CSRC |
| July 22 | [Announcement No. 47] Guideline on the Content and Format of Information Disclosure by Unlisted Public Companies No. 13 — Annual Report of Listed Companies on Selected Tiers | CSRC |
| July 22 | [Announcement No. 48] Guideline on the Content and Format of Information Disclosure by Unlisted Public Companies No. 14 — Interim Report of Listed Companies on Selected Tiers | CSRC |
| July 22 | [Announcement No. 49] Guideline on the Content and Format of Information Disclosure by Unlisted Public Companies No. 15 — Interim Report of Innovative Tier Listed Companies | CSRC |
| July 22 | [Announcement No. 50] Guideline on the Content and Format of Information Disclosure by Unlisted Public Companies No. 16 — Interim Report of Basic Tier Listed Companies | CSRC |
| July 22 | [Announcement No. 51] Guideline on the Content and Format of Information Disclosure by Unlisted Public Companies No. 17 — Quarterly Report of Listed Companies on Selected Tiers | CSRC |
| July 24 | Notice on the Issuance of the Guidelines for Handling the Business of Agreed Transfer of Shares of Listed Companies on the Shenzhen Stock Exchange (Revised in 2020) | SZSE |
| July 24 | Measures for the Administration of Information Disclosure by Listed Companies (Revised Draft) | CSRC |
| July 31 | [Announcement No. 53] Opinions on the Application of Article 28 and Article 45 of the Administration Measures for the Reorganization of Major Assets of Listed Companies — Opinion on the Application of Securities and Futures Law No. 15 | CSRC |
| August 7 | [Announcement No. 54] Guidelines for Publicly Raised Infrastructure Securities Investment Fund (Trial) | CSRC |
| August 21 | [Announcement No. 57] Guidelines for Supervision of Non-listed Public Companies No. 6 — Supervisory Requirements for Share Incentives and Employee Stock Ownership Plans (Trial) | CSRC |
| August 28 | [Announcement No. 58] Decision on the Implementation of the Measures for the Supervision and Administration of Sales Institutions of Publicly Raised Securities Investment Funds | CSRC |
| August 28 | [Order No. 175] Measures for the Supervision and Administration of Sales Institutions of Publicly Raised Securities Investment Funds | CSRC |
| August 30 | Notice on the Issuance of the Measures for the Administration of Risk Classification of Listed Companies on Shenzhen Stock Exchange | SZSE |
| September 11 | Notice on the Issuance of the Guideline No. 1 on the Application of Self-Regulatory Rules for Listed Companies on Shanghai Stock Exchange — Major Asset Reorganization | SSE |

Continued

| Release Date | Policy Name | Issuing Units |
|---|---|---|
| September 11 | Notice on the Issuance of the Guideline No. 1 on the Application of Self-regulatory Rules for Listed Companies on the STAR Market of Shanghai Stock Exchange — Regulation of Operations | SSE |
| September 17 | [Announcement No. 62] Decision on Amending the Regulations on Strengthening the Supervision of Listed Securities Companies | CSRC |
| September 25 | [Announcement No. 63] Regulation on Issues Related to the Implementation of the Administrative Measures for the Investment in Securities and Futures in China of Qualified Foreign Institutional Investors and Qualified Foreign Institutional Investors of Renminbi | CSRC |
| September 25 | [Order No. 176] Administrative Measures for the Investment in Securities and Futures in China of Qualified Foreign Institutional Investors and Qualified Foreign Institutional Investors of Renminbi | CSRC |
| September 25 | Notice on the Issuance of the Guideline No. 2 on the Application of Self-Regulatory Rules for Listed Companies on the STAR Market of the Shanghai Stock Exchange — Voluntary Information Disclosure | SSE |
| September 25 | Administrative Measures for the Investment in Securities and Futures in China of Qualified Foreign Institutional Investors and Qualified Foreign Institutional Investors of Renminbi | State Administration of Foreign Exchange |
| October 5 | The State Council's Opinions Concerning Further Raising the Quality of Listed Companies | The State Council |
| October 16 | Notice on the Issuance of the Guideline No. 2 on the Application of Self-Regulatory Rules for Listed Companies on Shanghai Stock Exchange — Criteria for the Implementation of Disciplinary Punishment | SSE |
| October 30 | Notice on the Issuance of the Implementation Rules for Securities Trading by Qualified Foreign Institutional Investors and RMB Qualified Foreign Institutional Investors of Shenzhen Stock Exchange (Revised in 2020) | SZSE |
| October 30 | [Announcement No. 66] Decision on Amending and Repealing Some Documents of Securities and Futures System | CSRC |
| October 30 | [Order No. 177] Decision on Amending and Repealing Some Securities and Futures Regulations | CSRC |
| November 2 | Implementation Plan for a Sound Delisting Mechanism of Listed Companies | Central Commission for Comprehensively Deepening Reform |
| November 24 | Notice on the Issuance of the Guideline No. 3 on the Application of Self-Regulatory Rules for Listed Companies on Shanghai Stock Exchange — Information Disclosure Classification Regulation | SSE |
| December 4 | Notice on the Issuance of the Administration Measures of the Listing Committee of the STAR Market of the Shanghai Stock Exchange | SSE |

Continued

| Release Date | Policy Name | Issuing Units |
|---|---|---|
| December 4 | Notice on the Issuance of the Rules on Reviewing the Listing of Stocks on the STAR Market of the Shanghai Securities Exchange (Revised in 2020) | SSE |
| December 4 | Notice on Amending Relevant Provisions of the Implementation Rules on Securities Investment Fund Trading and Subscription and Redemption of the Shenzhen Stock Exchange | SZSE |
| December 18 | Notice on the Issuance of the Guideline No. 4 on the Application of Self-Regulatory Rules for Listed Companies on the Shanghai Stock Exchange — Issuance of Convertible Corporate Bonds to Specific Targets | SSE |
| December 31 | [Order No. 178] Management Measures of Convertible Corporate Bonds | CSRC |
| December 31 | Notice on the Issuance of the Shanghai Stock Exchange Risk Warning Board Stock Trading Management Measures (Revised in December 2020) | SSE |
| December 31 | Notice on the Issuance of the Implementation Measures for the Relisting of Delisted Companies on the Shanghai Stock Exchange (Revised in December 2020) | SSE |
| December 31 | Notice on the Issuance of the Rules for the Listing of Stocks on the STAR Market of the Shanghai Stock Exchange (Revised in December 2020) | SSE |
| December 31 | Notice on the Issuance of the Rules for the Listing of Stocks on the Shanghai Stock Exchange (Revised in December 2020) | SSE |
| December 31 | Notice on the Issuance of the Rules of Work of the Appellate Review Committee of the Shenzhen Stock Exchange (Revised in 2020) | SZSE |
| December 31 | Notice on the Issuance of the Measures for the Implementation of Self-regulatory Measures and Disciplinary Punishment of Shenzhen Stock Exchange (Revised in 2020) | SZSE |
| December 31 | Notice on the Issuance of the Rules on Self-regulatory Hearing Procedures of the Shenzhen Stock Exchange (Revised in 2020) | SZSE |
| December 31 | Notice on the Issuance of the Rules for the Listing of Stocks on the Shenzhen Stock Exchange (Revised in 2020) | SZSE |
| December 31 | Notice on the Issuance of Work Rules of the Listing Committee of the Shenzhen Stock Exchange (Revised in 2020) | SZSE |
| December 31 | Notice on the Issuance of the Implementation Measures for the Relisting of Delisted Companies on the Shanghai Stock Exchange (Revised in 2020) | SZSE |
| December 31 | Notice on the Issuance of the Rules Governing the Listing of Shares on the GEM Market of Shenzhen Stock Exchange (Revised in December 2020) | SZSE |
| December 31 | Notice on the Issuance of the Shenzhen Stock Exchange Trading Rules (Revised in December 2020) | SZSE |
| December 31 | Notice on Amending Article 6.1 and Article 6.2 of the Implementation Rules for Securities Margin Trading of the Shenzhen Stock Exchange | SZSE |

# Article 4

## Overall Implementation Plan for the Growth Enterprise Market Reform and Registration System Pilot Approved, China Securities Regulatory Commission Issues Series of Regulations[①]

On April 27, 2020, the Central Committee's Meeting for Comprehensively Deepening Reform adopted the *Overall Implementation Plan for the Growth Enterprise Market Reform and Registration System Pilot*, and the Growth Enterprise Market (GEM) registration system was officially launched. The reform is a key part of the registration system reform; its launch marks the registration system's progression from the "testing field" of the Science and Technology Innovation Board to the "deep water zone", and from "incremental reform" to "stock reform".

On the same day, the China Securities Regulatory Commission (CSRC) solicited public opinions for drafts of the *Administration Measures for the Registration of IPO of Shares on GEM (Trial)*, the *Administration Measures for the Registration of Securities Issuance by Listed Companies on GEM (Trial)*, the *Measures for Continuous Supervision of Listed Companies on GEM (Trial)*, and the *Administration Measures for Securities Issuance and Listing Sponsorship*. The drafts are aimed at building an overall institutional framework for the reform of the growth enterprise market and to pilot the registration system. At the same time, the Shenzhen Stock Exchange solicited opinions on eight business rules, including the *GEM Stock Issuance and Listing Approval Rules*.

The GEM opened in October 2009, marking an important step in the construction of a multi-layered capital market. Over the following 11 years, the GEM improved in both issuance and management. Still, problems remain — in particular, a high inventory of non-performing assets, and management systems that are not in line with international standards. On November 5, 2018, the Science and Technology Innovation Board launched its registration system pilot. The subsequent practice of nearly two years has provided a successful base of experience for the GEM registration system reform.

On March 30, 2020, the CPC Central Committee and the State Council issued the *Opinions on Building a More Complete Institutional Mechanism for Market-based Allocation of Factors*, which clarifies the importance of improving the market-based allocation of capital factors as well as the basic system of the stock market, formulating and issuing opinions on improving the basic system of the stock market, and improving the construction of the Main-Board, Science and Technology Innovation Board, SME board, GEM board, and NEEQ market. The newly revised *Securities Law of the People's Republic of China* took effect on March 1, 2020, laying a solid legal foundation for the deepening of registration system reform.

The GEM registration system pilot reform focuses on two issues. First is expanding the

---

① Author: Liu Yu, intern of the Program for China's Financial Policy Report, doctor of PBC School of Finance (PBCSF), Tsinghua University.

scope of the pilot registration system based on the Science and Technology Innovation Board to accumulate experience for implementation of the stock board registration system. The second is making the system more tolerant and inclusive for innovative start-ups, thereby highlighting the features of the board. The reform process will focus on "one major task" and "coordination in three aspects". The "one major task" refers to the implementation of the registration system for stock issuance with information disclosure as its core while improving transparency and authenticity and allowing investors to make value judgments on their own, truly giving the right of choice to the market. "Coordination in three aspects" refers to coordinating the reform of GEM with the construction of a multi-level capital market system, coordinating the registration system pilot with other basic systems' construction, and coordinating incremental reform with stock reform.

On June 12, 2020, the CSRC issued the *Administration Measures for the Registration of IPO of Shares on GEM (Trial)*, the *Administration Measures for the Registration of Securities Issuance by Listed Companies on GEM (Trial)*, the *Measures for Continuous Supervision of Listed Companies on GEM (Trial)*, and the *Administration Measures for Securities Issuance and Listing Sponsorship*, all effective on the date of issuance. Relevant supporting rules were simultaneously issued by the CSRC, Shenzhen Stock Exchange, China Securities Depository and Clearing Corporation Limited, Securities Association of China and other authorities.

On August 18, 2020, the Supreme People's Court issued the *Opinions on Providing Judicial Guarantee for GEM Reform and Registration System Pilot* (FF [2020] No.28). It proposes 10 measures to enhance awareness of judicial guarantee provisions for the GEM reform and registration system pilot, to ensure the smooth progress of the GEM reform and registration system pilot in accordance with the law, to increase costs for market entities' legal violations, and to effectively protect the legitimate rights and interests of investors in accordance with the law.

In reforming the GEM registration system, the requirements of the new *Securities Law* should be consciously applied, specifically in terms of increasing the cost of violation and preventing financial fraud in order to improve the quality of listed companies. At the same time, pilot reform experience should be summarized, studied, and formulated into an implementation program for the registration system's cross-market promotion to ensure the smooth advance of reform from the GEM to the whole market, to promote the construction of a differentiated capital market system, and to enable the capital market's overall high-quality and healthy development.

## Article 5

### Key-task focus and multi-pronged approach to enhance the quality of listed companies[1]

When it comes to the sustainable development of the capital market, listed companies are

---

[1] Author: Xu Kefei, Deputy General Manager of Cinda Securities, and senior project fellow of Program for China's Financial Policy Report.

the cornerstone. In the 30-plus years since China first established a capital market, the number of listed companies has grown significantly and their quality continuously improved. More and more, they are playing a prominent role in national economic development. However, there exist a number of salient problems with listed companies — irregular operation and governance and poor development quality, for example — so much remains to be done in building a modern economic system and raising the quality of economic development. Meanwhile, COVID-19 and other external factors have presented listed companies with new challenges in operation and the pursuit of quality development.

On October 5, 2020, the State Council issued the *Opinions Concerning Further Raising the Quality of Listed Companies* (the "Opinions"), which put forward 17 key initiatives in six areas and set down comprehensive and systematic arrangements for the quality improvement of listed companies.

The general objective of the "Opinions" is to significantly improve listed companies' standardization of operations, the quality of information disclosure, and the capacity and overall quality of sustainable development, while effectively resolving outstanding problems. Taking a problem-oriented approach, the "Opinions" makes clear arrangements for prominent problems like delisting snags, stock pledge risks, capital appropriation, and guarantee violations. It takes hold of two core issues — corporate governance and information exposure — and covers the entire capital market life cycle of listed companies. The "Opinions" seeks to smooth channels of entry and exit and support listed companies' growth and maturity via the support of the capital market.

To effectively carry out the "Opinions" and bring real improvements to listed companies' quality, the first and foremost actions are corporate governance and information exposure. As for the former, listed companies' governance needs to see improvements, with greater regulation and internal control and stronger code of conduct guidelines for directors, supervisors, controlling shareholders and the actual controllers of listed companies. As for the latter, information disclosure needs to see further improvement. Listed companies and other information disclosure obligees must be guided to follow the needs of investors more closely to ensure the disclosure of all information necessary to investors for making value judgments and investment decisions. Meanwhile, intermediaries should be motivated to fully utilize their roles and fulfil their due responsibilities, strengthening their capacity as gatekeepers for the capital market. The second action is to provide all-around support for listed companies' growth. We will continue to work on building a pool of enterprises in strategic emerging industries and manufacturing upgrades, to support the listing of high-quality enterprises through precise services and in-depth incubation, to encourage listed companies to utilize the capital market's comprehensive functions in financing and mergers & acquisitions to strengthen their main businesses and for overall optimization, and to assist listed companies in forming competitive industrial clusters. The third action is to strengthen the listed companies' delisting mechanism. Listed companies' exits will be supported through corporate mergers, pro-active delisting, bankruptcy restructuring and other diversified channels in accordance with the law, while proper delisting-related arrangements will be made to ensure the survival of the fittest. The fourth action is compelling institutional investors, small to mid-sized investors, and the media to play their proper roles in external oversight for the joint establishment of a sound external ecology. The fifth action is increasing penalties for legal violations. We will crack down on financial fraud, misappropriation of listed company funds, illegal guarantees, insider trading, market manipulation, and other illegal or unlawful acts. By the above measures, we aim to promote listed companies' quality development and strengthen the new development pattern for China's capital market.

## III. Development Policies for the Insurance Market[①]

2020 was the final year in the initiative to establish a "generally well-off society" and the last year in the "13th Five-Year Plan" period. Under the strong leadership of the Central Committee of the Communist Party of China with Comrade Xi Jinping at its core, the insurance industry worked hard to overcome the impact of the COVID-19 pandemic, manage risks and challenges, improve the quality and effectiveness of services for the real economy, improve abilities to prevent major risks, and maintain the momentum of sound development.

### (I) Main Policies for the Insurance Market in 2020

#### 1. Regulating administration of banking and insurance consumer complaints, maintaining the order of the financial market

In order to regulate the administration of banking and insurance consumer complaints and protect consumers' legitimate interests and rights, the China Banking and Insurance Regulatory Commission (CBIRC) issued the *Rules on Complaints Administration of Banking and Insurance Consumers* (hereafter referred to as the Rules) on January 14, 2020.

The Rules consists of six parts — namely, general provisions, organizational management, complaint handling, work systems, supervision management, and supplementary provisions — with the following main functions:

First is the clarification of matters of consumer complaint. The Rules identifies "consumer complaints" as the behavior of consumers possessing disputes with the banking and insurance institutions or practitioners thereof following from the purchase of banking and insurance products or related services and claiming their civil rights and benefits owed from banking and insurance institutions.

The second is specifying the responsibilities of banking and insurance institutions. The Rules clarifies that banking and insurance institutions are responsible for handling consumer complaints.

---

[①] Author: China Insurance Association Panel; Co-author: Wang Wei, Director, Life Insurance Department II, China Insurance Association.

Consumer complaints should be managed locally according to the principles of legal/regulatory compliance, convenience, and efficiency, a dual approach targeting both the symptoms and the root causes, and diversified solutions. Responsibility should be systematically graded, taking consumers' reasonable demands into full consideration. Complaints must be brought to a fair and legitimate conclusion.

The third is clarifying the complaint-handling procedure. The Rules clarifies the channels and scope of complaint acceptance, processing time limits, and other procedural requirements for banking and insurance institutions' complaint handling. In order to satisfy consumers' reasonable demands to the greatest possible extent and improve the efficiency of complaint processing, based on the actual situation of complaint processing, the Rules stipulates that, for consumer complaints with clear facts and simple disputes, banking and insurance institutions should complete handling and inform the complainant within 15 days of acceptance. For complaints entailing more complex situations, this period should be extended to 30 days. For complaints with highly complex or special circumstances, the processing period may be extended by another 30 days after undergoing necessary approval procedures. The Rules adds new requirements for the handling of complaints against the cooperative businesses of third-party institutions. Banking and insurance institutions should request the relevant third-party institutions' cooperation in handling consumer complaints, verify the matters of complaint, provide relevant information in a timely manner, and promote successful resolution.

The fourth is an emphasis on improving the complaint-handling mechanism. To address and replace the "simplistic and palliative approach" in current complaint handling, the Rules requires banking and insurance institutions to establish and improve systems for traceability, rectification, and accountability. Positive incentives and negative constraints are used in combination to urge banking and insurance institutions to improve their information disclosure as well as assessment and evaluation systems. In order to avoid conflicts of interest, banking and insurance institutions should establish a system for complaint handling avoidance and designate personnel with no direct investment in the matter to conduct handling.

The fifth is convenient and efficient complaint resolution. The Rules stipulates that institutions shall strengthen their responsibility and deal with complaints to the consumer's utmost convenience. This includes the simplification of acceptance procedures. The Rules provides that banking and insurance institutions should not reject complaints from consumers that are within reason and should not ask complainants to offer materials that the institution has already attained or can obtain through a search of internal files. In order to avoid problems such as branch institutions delaying the handling process or concealing or failing to report problems, the Rules specifies procedures for complaint verification. Higher-level banking and insurance institutions are responsible for verifying the complaint handling of lower-level institutions. What's more, when responding to opinions on complaint handling, they should inform consumers of the methods for appeal for verification, mediation, arbitration, litigation, and other remedies to fully protecting consumers' right to petition. To better protect consumers' legitimate rights and interests, banking and insurance institutions should verify complainant identities and guarantee the safety of personal and private information during the handling process. If it is discovered that the complaint is not made by the complainant (or his/her statutory agent or trustee), the banking and insurance institution involved should refuse to handle the case.

The sixth is stressing the importance of strong supervision and information disclosure. The Rules specifies that regulators must supervise the banking and insurance institutions' complaint handling with regular reports, disclosure, and transmission of consumer complaints. Banking and insurance complaint handling is integrated into evaluations of consumer rights protection. Supervisory actions must be strengthened. For banking and insurance institutions that fail to handle consumer complaints or to manage them in accordance with the Rules, strict measures should apply — for example, mandatory rectification and regulatory talks, the suspension of related business, and administrative fines — depending on the circumstances and in accordance with "the Law of the People's Republic of China on Regulation of and Supervision over the Banking Industry" and "the Insurance Law of the People's Republic of China".

The Rules will promote banking and insurance institutions' construction of a people-centered mindset and improve consumer satisfaction on complaint handling in the banking and insurance industry. At the same time, it will facilitate the CBIRC and its delegated institutions' to enhance their consciousness of supervision for the benefit of the people, to maintain order in the financial market, and to actively contribute to the modernization of the national governance system and governance capacity.

**2. Adherence to market-oriented reform, stronger market supervision, and a consolidated foundation for accident insurance**

In recent years, market insurance and other market-based means have greatly improved public awareness of risks and knowledge of risk prevention when it comes to accident insurance. Nevertheless, accident insurance itself remains incompatible with the demands of the modern insurance service industry. This is due to weak market infrastructure, unscientific pricing mechanisms, non-standard sales behaviors, and so on. In order to establish a mechanism for the market-oriented formulation of accident insurance rates, to better protect insurance consumers' legitimate rights and interests, and to promote the overall high-quality development of the accident insurance market, the CBIRC issued the *Opinions on Accelerating the Reform of Accident Insurance* (hereafter referred to as the "Opinions") on January 17, 2020.

The Opinions are divided into five sections. The first consists of the general requirements of accident insurance reform, including its guiding philosophy, basic principles, and main objectives. Sections 2 through 4 include the reform tasks for 2020 and 2021 — advancing market-oriented pricing reform, strengthening the supervision of market behaviors, and consolidating the foundation for development. The fifth section relates to work requirements.

The Opinions emphasize the reform tasks for 2020 and 2021, which mainly concern pushing forward the market-oriented pricing reform, strengthening the supervision of market conduct, and consolidating a foundation for the further development of accident insurance.

First, the Opinions require steps to promote the market-oriented pricing reform. These primarily consist of improving the actuarial system for accident insurance, accident insurance pricing assumptions, and the supervision of statutory liability reserves, as well as effectively preventing risks. The Opinions also makes provisions for a retrospective rate adjustment mechanism and the gradual elimination of products with excessively low compensation ratios, high channel costs, or unreasonable pricing. It compiles an accident insurance incidence table and explores and establishes a dynamic revision mechanism for accidental injury incidence tables.

Second, the Opinions require strengthening market conduct supervision. This includes the targeted rectification of key issues in the market such as tied and bundled sales, abnormally high service charges, and untruthful financial business data; the systematic improvement of a conduct supervision system for the accident insurance market and formulation of a unified system specific to accident insurance supervision; the establishment and improvement of a mechanism for information disclosure, the enhancement of transparency in the accident insurance market; the establishment and improvement of a mechanism for information sharing regarding accident insurance policies, and the study and formulation of criteria for a "blacklist" and "gray list" to strengthen the early warning of risks.

Third, the Opinions require consolidating a foundation for development. This includes quickening the pace of accident insurance standardization, studying and formulating risk rating standards and occupational classifications for accident insurance, improving assessment standards for unintentional injuries in the insurance industry, and striving to bring the industry into a national standard system. Accident insurance companies must also explore exemplary compilation methods for basic terms in accident insurance as a way to advance the standardization, streamlining, and popularization of product terms. Finally, a long-term cooperation mechanism should be established to combat insurance fraud.

The Opinions are of great significance to deepening reform of the accident insurance market, improving accident insurance's capacity to serve economic and social development, and enhancing public satisfaction.

### 3. Improving the life insurance actuarial system, upgrading risk protection products

On January 21, 2020, the CBIRC issued the *Actuarial Provisions on Ordinary Life Insurance Products* (hereafter referred to as the "Provisions"). Henceforth, ordinary life insurance newly developed by insurance companies must be implemented in accordance with the Provisions. Ordinary life insurance products which were approved or filed for approval prior to the issuance of the Provisions shall be exempt and permitted for sale. However, they must withdraw the liability reserves.

The Provisions cover five aspects — namely, the scope of application, insurance amounts, insurance premiums, cash value, and liability reserves — which highlight three aspects of product supervision. First is promoting the development of risk protection products to better protect the rights and interests of insurance consumers. The minimum cash value parameters of risk protection products are adjusted. Affected products include health insurance, accident insurance, term life insurance, and whole life insurance. Meanwhile, the upper limit on average surcharge rates for annuity products and most single-premium products is lowered and the minimum cash value threshold for long-term savings products such as annuities is raised. These adjustments will help lower said products' prices, making them more competitive and better able to satisfy consumers' insurance needs. Second is the integration and refinement of regulatory provisions and improvements to the actuarial regulatory system. The Provisions integrate the risk protection requirements of different insurance products; the scope of applicability covers all ordinary life insurance, annuity insurance, health insurance, and accident insurance. The document also applies to ordinary life insurance with a term of one year or less. The regulatory system is made more sound and regulatory policies clearer. Regulatory provisions are refined according to product features, setting different parameters to support the development of risk protection products correspondingly. The third is the adaptation to current circumstances and compensation for weak links in the regulatory system. The Provisions are a separate actuarial regulation in addition to that on participating insurance and universal life insurance. With "Actuarial Provisions on Participating Insurance", "Actuarial Provisions on Universal Life Insurance", and "Actuarial Provisions on Investment-linked Insurance", a generally sound and basically complete actuarial system has taken shape to cover the variety of product forms.

**4. Strengthening statutory reserve supervision for life insurance, improving off-site monitoring**

On January 21, 2020, the CBIRC issued the *Notice on Related Matters to Strengthening Actuarial Supervision of Life Insurance* (hereafter referred to as "the Notice").

The Notice focuses on further strengthening supervision of statutory reserves, standardizing the distribution of dividends and benefit demonstration of participating insurance, and improving the off-site monitoring mechanism. First, the Notice strengthens the supervision of statutory reserves. The coverage ratio of liability reserves serves as the starting point for incorporation into the off-site monitoring index and linkage to regulatory measures such as product supervision. Second, it better regulates the development of the participating insurance sector. Methods for demonstrating the distribution of dividends and benefits have been revised and improved. An upper limit is defined for the demonstration reference interest rate, and the dividend distribution ratio is uniformly set at 70%. Third, the Notice improves the mechanism for off-site monitoring. Relevant contents in the quarterly Liability Information Table required by *the Notice of the China Insurance Regulatory Commission on Submitting Relevant Data on Life Insurance Sector* have been adjusted. Information requirements have been added for the coverage ratio of liability reserves and basic information on universal life insurance accounts, unit-linked insurance accounts, etc. in order to strengthen supervision on insurance liabilities.

The Notice specifically strengthens supervision over statutory reserves and improves the mechanism for off-site monitoring in full accordance with the core principles of prudential supervision. It also enhances the scientificity and effectiveness of regulatory policies and guides the life insurance industry to build risk awareness and guard the bottom line for systemic risk. Holding that line will help protect against loss from divergent interest rates within the industry and promote the healthy, long-term development of the life insurance industry.

**5. Improving risk protection, increasing the long-term capital supply, and promoting the positive role of commercial insurance in social services**

In recent years, the insurance industry has followed the guidance of Xi Jinping Thought on Socialism with Chinese Characteristics for a New Era, adhered to a people-centered development philosophy, focused on supply-side structural reform, actively participated in the construction of multi-level medical and pension protection systems, explored innovative protection products in social services, and strengthened long-term financial support for pensions, health and other related industries, which has strongly promoted the development of the social service sector. But on the whole, certain problems remain — insufficient support, weak support, and weak guarantee mechanisms. In order to deepen supply-side structural reform in the financial sector and give full play to commercial insurance's ability to safeguard people's livelihoods, promote consumption, and boost domestic demand, 13 ministries and commissions — including the CBIRC, the National Development and Reform Commission (NDRC) and the Ministry of Education — jointly issued *the Opinions on Promoting the Development of Commercial Insurance in Social Services* (hereafter referred to as "Opinions") on January 23, 2020.

The Opinions clearly state that the following five foci for advancing the development of commercial insurance in social services, improving risk protection in related areas, and increasing the long-term capital supply.

First, health insurance products and services need to be improved. Insurance institutions are urged to provide comprehensive health insurance products and services in response to consumer needs. The goal is to expand the commercial health insurance market to over RMB 2 trillion by 2025. The operations and supervision of insurance institutions offering critical illness insurance also need to be improved, and commercial long-term care insurance further developed. Meanwhile, health insurance and health management must be further integrated.

Second, the Opinions call for strengthening the protective functions of commercial pensions and annuities. Diversified commercial annuities and personal account-based commercial pensions should be actively developed. For the sake of safety and prudence, the scope of commercial pension funds must be expanded. The goal is to accumulate no less than RMB 6 trillion in pension liability reserves for insured persons by 2025. Protections for the elderly (people aged 60 and above) must be improved. Actions must be taken to optimize policy support for the elderly citizens' reverse mortgage pension insurance, to improve the power of the notarization system to enforce contracts, and strengthen the role of notary institutions acting as estate managers. The elderly service industry must continue to develop.

Third, commercial insurance needs to be developed in the fields of education, child-rearing, housekeeping, culture, tourism, sports, etc., with the active creation of exclusive insurance products. Local governments and relevant government agencies are encouraged to further utilize insurance mechanisms to strengthen and improve social governance.

Fourth, insurance funds must be guided to invest in healthcare, elderly care, and other social services. Insurance funds are stable and long-term, so they are capable of providing more long-term equity financing for social services. This can help reduce financing costs and better serve innovation and entrepreneurship to support the development of private micro, small, or medium-sized enterprises.

Fifth, the Opinions state that the insurance market must be improved. Commercial insurance institutions are encouraged to moderately raise the pricing interest rate on term life insurance products within the range of controllable risks. Supervision of insurance market conduct must be strengthened to protect insurance consumers' legitimate rights and interests. The opening up of the insurance market will be accelerated and supporting policies improved.

Implementation of the Opinions will usher in new development opportunities for commercial insurance in social services — both in terms of enriching the product supply and expanding the scope of opening up to the outside world.

### 6. Promoting reform to streamline administration, delegate power, and optimize the business environment

In order to promote the reform of streamlining administration, delegating power, and optimizing the business environment, the CBIRC released the *Notice on Abolishing and Amending Some Normative Documents* (hereafter referred to as the "Notice") on February 4, 2020.

According to the Notice, 11 normative documents were revised, including the *Notice on Releasing "the Interim Rules on Information Disclosure Management of Trust and Investment Companies"*. At the same time, six normative documents were abolished, such as the *Notice on Designating Newspapers for Disclosure of Insurance Information*.

The release of the Notice is important to implementing the requirements of fair competition review and further improving the banking and insurance regulatory system.

### 7. Reshaping the regulatory framework of healthcare's entrusted management, meeting the people's diverse healthcare needs

With recent years' social and economic development, people's insurance consciousness has also improved, and more and more enterprises and institutions are providing their employees with healthcare services beyond basic medical care. Provision of these services is entrusted by insurance companies. The entrusted management of health care has made important contributions to the construction of a multi-level and diversified system of medical care. In order to strengthen the supervision of healthcare's entrusted management, the General Office of the CBIRC released the *Notice on Further Regulating Issues Concerning Entrusted Management of Health Care* on February 11, 2020 (hereafter referred to as the "Notice").

The Notice is the amendment to the *Notice on Issues Concerning Entrusted Management of Health Care* issued by the former China Insurance Regulatory Commission (CIRC) in 2008. This revision reshapes the regulatory framework for the entrusted management of healthcare, encourages the business to adhere to its original purpose, fills gaps in regulation, and prevents potential risks.

It does so first of all by clarifying operational conditions for the entrusted management business of healthcare and enriching the content of entrusted business. The Notice clearly states that insurance companies must meet the conditions for operating health insurance business stipulated in the "Rules on Health Insurance" to carry out healthcare's entrusted management business, and must establish branches or service cooperation agencies in the region where they are conducting such business. At the same time, it states that disease review and the payment of fees, disability income loss review and the payment of fees, nursing care review and payment of fees, and health management services, etc. can be included in entrusted matters.

Second, the Notice calls for a return to the original purpose of the business and cancels the requirement for product registration. The Notice stresses the original purpose of the entrusted management business of healthcare. Insurance companies no longer need to register such business with the regulatory authorities. They should conduct business prudently and in accordance with the relevant rules and regulations, sign contracts, and assume rights, obligations, and responsibilities accordingly.

Third, it cancels the investment function of entrusted businesses and standardizes management fees. The Notice forbids insurance companies from turning the entrusted management of health care into wealth management or providing various forms of value-added guarantees. It stipulates that management fees charged by insurance companies should go toward covering various costs of healthcare's entrusted management. The fees may float according to the actual management costs, but the method for fee floating must be specified in the contract.

Fourth, it strengthens business supervision for the prevention of potential risks. The Notice aims to strengthen the supervision of such business by clarifying prohibited acts, ensuring the main responsibility of insurance companies, and through other exploratory methods such as industry self-discipline.

The release of the Notice will guide the industry to carry out the entrusted management of healthcare in accordance with laws and regulations. This will have a positive effect in ensuring the legitimate rights and interests of all parties involved and meet people's needs for multi-level and diversified healthcare.

**8. Improving property insurance product supervision, deepening the reform of "streamlining administration and delegating power, improving regulation, and upgrading services"**

On May 12, 2015, the State Council held a national teleconference on the reform for streamlining administration, delegating power, and integrating functions. This meeting put forward the specific concept of "streamlining administration and delegating power, improving regulation, and upgrading services" for the first time. On May 22, 2020, Premier Li Keqiang stated in the 2020 Report on the Work of the Government that the "streamlining administration and delegating power, improving regulation, and upgrading services" reform is to be deepened. In order to do this in the property and casualty insurance industry, supervision priorities should be highlighted, supervision resources coordinated, supervision efficiency enhanced, and product quality improved. Thus the CBIRC released the *Notice on Issues Concerning Further Strengthening and Improving Property*

*Insurance Product Supervision* on February 19, 2020 (hereafter referred to as the "Notice").

This adjustment further improves the efficiency and effectiveness of product supervision. It adjusts the scope of product approval and registration given in the *Notice on Implementing the "Measures for the Administration of Insurance Clauses and Insurance Rates of Property Insurance Companies"* issued by the former CIRC for the demonstration products of property insurance, commercial motor vehicle insurance, one-year credit insurance and guarantee insurance, changing approval requirements to registration requirements (products originally under the registration requirement should continue to use registration management). At the same time, the CBIRC will continue to adhere to the principles of delegating power and strengthening regulation and strengthen its supervision over registration products.

In order to put each banking regulatory bureau's advantages — in particular, being near the front line and familiar with the market — into full play, and to form a joint force for supervision, the Notice stipulates that classified supervision and territorial supervision shall be conducted on the products offered by property insurance companies. First, products of commercial insurance for motor vehicles and agricultural insurance that are subsidized by central financial premiums (hereafter referred to as the "two product types") using demonstration products shall be registered and supervised by the CBIRC. Second, other products shall be registered and supervised by the relevant banking regulatory bureaus. Third, the CBIRC will adjust the scope of products registered and supervised by the banking regulatory bureaus in a timely manner according to changes in market conditions and product supervision needs.

Issuance of the Notice constitutes an important reform measure for the CBIRC in streamlining administration and delegating power, improving regulation, and upgrading services. It is also an important policy measure for the coordination of regulatory resources and the formation of a joint supervisory force. It is an important working regulation to standardize property insurance companies' product management and improve overall product quality, which is conducive to further improving property insurance companies' overall system of product supervision, stimulating the innovative product market's vitality, better meeting the people's growing insurance needs, and serving both high-quality economic and social development.

**9. Improving tools for insider financial crime prevention, strengthening corporate governance and systems-building**

In order to improve the working mechanism for the prevention of financial crimes committed by employees in the banking and insurance industry, and to prevent and control banking and insurance institutions' case risks, thus promoting the overall healthy development of the industry, the CBIRC released the *Guidance on Preventing Financial Crimes Committed by Employees in the Banking and Insurance Industry* on February 20, 2020 (hereafter referred to as the "Guidance").

The Guidance consists of four parts — namely: basic principles, the prevention of financial crimes in key areas, the strengthening of mechanisms for institutional internal control and industry self-discipline, strict penalties in accordance with the law, and the strengthening of supervision and coordination.

The Guidance puts forward four basic principles: strengthening party leadership and party building, equally valuing improvement measures for long-term mechanisms and key short-term penalties, taking a three-pronged management approach (internal control, industry self-discipline, and external supervision), and continuing to coordinate and link financial supervision departments with supervisory organs, public security organs, and judicial organs to form a joint force for prevention and penalty enforcement. The Guidance also lists 11 distinct areas of focus for the prevention of illegal and criminal acts: the credit business; interbank business, asset disposal; the asset management business, credit card business, cash management, insurance business, third-party cooperation, the financial market, money laundering, and terrorist financing, and information technology. It additionally puts forward six items to be improved or strengthened for better internal control within institutions and the construction of a mechanism for self-discipline within the industry: corporate governance, system process control, case risk monitoring and investigation, accountability, the education and training system, and industry discipline. The document contains five suggestions on enforcing strict punishments in accordance with the law, strengthening supervision, and improving linkage coordination: perfect the case prevention management system, strengthen the application of inspection and evaluation results, toughen punishment and tighten accountability in accordance with the law, make full use of the joint punishment & warning function, and strengthen linkage coordination.

Issuance of the Guidance will strengthen corporations' internal governance and systems-building, establish and improve a staff training mechanism, and cut down on occurrences of financial crimes by targeting the source, thereby ensuring the stability of insurance funds and safeguarding the financial security of investors and policyholders.

**10. Unifying regulatory standards for insurance asset management products to promote the business' healthy, sustainable development**

On March 18, 2020, the CBIRC issued the *Interim Rules on Insurance Asset Management Products* (hereafter referred to as the "Rules"). This was a move to regulate insurance asset management business products (hereafter referred to as "insurance asset management products"), unify the corresponding regulatory standards, guide insurance institutions to better serve the real economy, and effectively prevent financial risks.

The Rules consists of 66 articles across eight chapters, which cover: general provisions, asset management products' relevant parties, product issuance, renewal and termination, product investment and management, information disclosure and reporting, risk management, supervision and management, and supplementary provisions. Its main objectives are: first, to define product positioning and form. Second, to clarify the product issuance mechanism. Third, to strictly regulate products' operation. Fourth, to enforce accountability among product issuers. Fifth, to strengthen the responsibilities of service agencies. Sixth, to improve the product risk management mechanism. Seventh, to implement penetrating supervision.

The Rules' formulation constitutes an important measure in enacting the requirements of the *Guidance on Regulating Asset Management Business of Financial Institutions*. It improves the regulatory system for China's asset management business, which in turn helps standardize insurance asset management products' business development and broadens both the allocation space and investment channels of long-term funds like insurance funds. The Rules' policy is conducive to the unification of insurance asset management products' regulatory standards, compensating for supervisory shortcomings, and strengthening in-process and ex-post supervision. It helps deepen the financial sector's supply-side structural reform and makes good use of insurance asset management products' advantages. This will guide long-term funds to participate in the capital market, support infrastructure projects, and improve the quality and efficiency of service to the real economy.

**11. Encouraging the development of long-term medical insurance, protecting consumers' legitimate rights and interests**

As health insurance has developed rapidly in recent years, medical insurance, as one of the main types of health insurance, has also found a warm welcome among consumers and drawn wide attention in the market. However, in terms of timeframes, most medical insurance products operate on a yearly basis. There are few long-term medical insurance products. Thus, medical insurance is still unable to effectively meet the needs of the people for long-term health care. In order to enrich the supply of medical insurance products, encourage insurance companies to develop and sell long-term medical insurance products, and standardize related operations and management behaviors, the General Office of CBIRC released the *Notice on Issues Concerning Premium Rate Adjustment of Long-term Medical Insurance Products* (hereafter referred to as the "Notice") on March 25, 2020.

The Notice mainly sets the following requirements:

First, it defines the scope of long-term medical insurance products for which the rates can be adjusted. Taking technical and operational considerations into account, this scope currently includes only long-term medical insurance priced at natural rates, including medical insurance products with a coverage period of more than one year and medical insurance products with guaranteed renewal clauses (even though their coverage period is not more than one year).

Second, it clarifies the basic requirements for rate adjustment. Insurance companies should formulate rate adjustment policies that specify the trigger conditions, internal decision-making process, and work procedures for rate adjustments. The timeframe for the first-rate adjustment shall not be earlier than 3 years from the date when the products are sold in the market, and the interval for each rate adjustment may be no less than 1 year. Insurance companies are not allowed to implement differentiated rate adjustment policies based on differences in insured individuals' physical conditions.

Third, the Notice clarifies product terms and relevant product guide content. When offering long-term medical insurance products with adjustable rates, insurance companies are required to provide the applicant with a product guide. The products' terms and product guide shall specify conditions related to rate adjustment, including the specific conditions that trigger rate adjustments, the time intervals for rate adjustments, the upper limit for a single adjustment, the adjustment process, and the information disclosure requirements. The product guide shall also demonstrate its provided coverage with example cases, as well as any annual rate adjustments that the insured may face.

Fourth, it clarifies the information disclosure requirements for rate adjustment. The Notice stipulates that an insurance company should disclose rate adjustment policies and relevant product information on its website, making its rate adjustment information open to the public. For each instance of rate adjustment, the insurance company must notify the affected insured individual in the manner specified in the insurance policy contract.

Fifth, it standardizes the sales behavior of insurance companies and clarifies the regulatory measures for violations.

The Notice resolves institutional obstacles that have plagued the development of medical insurance, conveying encouragement for the development of long-term medical insurance. This will further deepen the supply-side structural reform of life insurance, effectively address the risk of non-renewable insurance contracts (due to changes in the insured's health or the suspended sale of products), and better protect the legitimate rights and interests of insurance consumers.

**12. Freeing the flow of capital in the industrial chain, assisting the return to work and production**

During the outbreak of COVID-19 in China, its banking and insurance industry conscientiously implemented the decisions and arrangements of the CPC Central Committee and the State Council. Their actions were based on the functional orientation of financial services toward the high-quality development of the real economy. Banking and insurance institutions accurately and forcefully promoted the resumption of work and production, business and market. They played a key role in epidemic prevention and control and supported the country's continued economic and social development. In response to the cash flow pressure faced by some enterprises upstream and downstream in the industrial chain during the return to work and production, on March 26, 2020, the CBIRC released the *Notice on Strengthening Financial Services for Coordinated Resumption of Work and Production across the Industrial Chain* (hereafter referred to as the "Notice").

The Notice covers the following six aspects: first, strengthening financial support for core enterprises in the industrial chain. Core enterprises were supported by appropriately reducing the occupying capital of upstream and downstream enterprises after applying financing through loan credit, bonds, and other means. Micro, small and medium-sized enterprises (MSMEs) in the upstream and downstream sectors of the industrial chain were supported to solve such problems as tight liquidity. Second, optimizing financial services for upstream and downstream enterprises in the industrial chain. Enhanced credit support was offered for MSMEs upstream and downstream in the industrial chain. This was achieved through account receivable financing, purchase contract financing, advance payment financing, inventory and warehouse receipt pledge financing, etc. Third, strengthening financial support for the coordinated development of global industrial chains. Banking institutions' role as "stabilizers of foreign trade" was enhanced. The supply of foreign trade credits was increased. Supporting policies included temporary postponement of loan principal and interest repayments for MSMEs. Insurance institutions were encouraged to further expand the coverage of short-term export credit insurance. Fourth, improving financial service technology in the industrial chain. Through a combination of online and offline service channels, enterprises were provided with convenient and fast supply chain financing services. Large and medium-sized banks and policy banks were encouraged to enhance their business cooperation with primarily internet-based banks in accordance with market principles and the relevant rules and regulations. Fifth, improving banking institutions' assessment incentives and risk control. Differentiated arrangements were made for granting credit related to the coordinated return to work and production in the industrial chain, and the relevant incentive mechanism was improved. Clear criteria were set for core enterprises, whose financing needs and loan objectives, as well as the background of supply chain transactions, were strictly examined. Sixth, increasing support from insurance and guarantee services. Under the premise of controllable risks, insurance institutions and policy guarantee institutions were encouraged to provide credit enhancement measures to MSMEs in the upstream and downstream sectors of the industrial chain to help them obtain financing. Life insurance companies could extend the terms of policy pledge loans and increase loan amounts as appropriate.

As one in a series of policies for the insurance industry to support epidemic prevention and control, the Notice has played an important role in guiding banks and insurance institutions to strengthen financial support and services, unblock the capital flow of the industrial chain, and enhance financial services for the coordinated resumption of work and production across the industrial chain

**13. Advancing the healthy development of market-oriented debt-to-equity swaps, standardizing financial asset investment companies' asset management business**

In accordance with the *Opinions of the State Council on Actively and Steadily Reducing the Leverage Rate of Enterprises, Guidance on Regulating Asset Management Business of Financial Institutions, Measures for the Administration of Financial Asset Investment Companies (Trial)*, and other relevant regulations, the CBIRC released the *Notice on Matters Concerning the Asset Management Business of Financial Asset Investment Companies* (hereafter referred to as the "Notice") on April 16, 2020. The Notice's release was intended to promote the sound development of market-oriented debt-to-equity swaps, standardize the asset management business of financial asset investment companies, and protect the legitimate rights and interests of investors in accordance with the law.

The Notice clarifies the relevant matters related to financial asset investment companies' asset management business from the aspects of general requirements, fundraising, investment operations, registration and custody, information disclosure and submission, and so on. According to the Notice, when a financial asset investment company conducts asset management business, that means it accepts the entrustment of investors, establishes a debt-to-equity swap investment plan and acts as a manager, and that it invests and manages the entrusted investor's property in accordance with laws and regulations as well as the contract of the debt-to-equity swap investment plan. Debt-to-equity swap investment plans should primarily invest in market-oriented debt-to-equity assets —

including creditor's rights, convertible bonds, special debt-to-equity swap bonds, ordinary shares, preferred shares, debt-to-preferred shares, and other assets — for the purpose of realizing market-oriented debt-to-equity swaps.

**14. Strengthening the supervision of credit and guarantee insurance, sustainably developing the credit insurance business**

In July 2017, the former CIRC released the *Interim Measures for the Supervision of Credit Guarantee Insurance Business* (hereafter referred to as the "Interim Measures"), which clarified the boundaries and principles of business development, rectified the chaotic behavior of the market at that time, and achieved certain results. With the development of new forms of financial business, and to further strengthen the supervision of credit insurance and guarantee insurance businesses (hereafter referred to as "credit and guarantee businesses"), the General Office of CBIRC issued the *Notice on Printing and Issuing the Measures for Supervision of Credit Insurance and Guarantee Insurance Businesses* (hereafter referred to as "Notice") on May 8, 2020. The Notice sets requirements for companies running financing-type credit and guarantee businesses. Beyond strengthening supervision, it is also intended to standardize business behaviors, prevent and resolve risks, protect insurance consumers' legitimate rights and interests, and promote the sustainable, healthy development of credit and guarantee businesses.

The revision of the Notice is focused on risk reduction and based on the concept of "supervision in accordance with differentiation and high-quality development". It also adheres to the principles of legal compliance, small-scale and wide diversity, and risk control. There are three main features: first, a focus on primary businesses, and supervision in line with differentiation. The Notice distinguishes between financing and non-financing credit and guarantee businesses, with a focus on the supervision of financing credit and guarantee business, which involves higher risks. It raises the regulatory requirements for financing credit insurance in terms of operating qualifications, underwriting limits, infrastructure, and so on. Second, it relaxes restrictions on certain businesses and tightens restrictions on others, simultaneously balancing supervision and development. On the one hand, it controls risk exposure and prevents business risks by reducing the underwriting limit for financing credit and guarantee businesses and expanding the scope of insurance types (i.e. commercial export credit insurance), among other means. On the other hand, it encourages insurance companies to provide financing and credit support for inclusive small and micro enterprises by setting flexible limits on financing and insurance businesses. Through an appropriate adjustment of business types, it supports insurance companies' exploration and development of new business areas under the premise of risk control. Third, it strengthens internal management and control, promoting high-quality development. According to the Notice, insurance companies are required to improve management and control capacities in order to advance the high-quality development of the credit insurance business. In terms of internal management and control, the areas in need of improvement are systems-building, liquidity management, early warning of risk, and so on, for the ultimate goal of business and liquidity risk prevention. Then, in terms of partnership management, systems of access, assessment, withdrawal, and consumer complaints must be established to lower potential risks in cooperation.

Therefore, implementing the Notice has far-reaching significance for — and will exert a positive influence on — risk prevention and the high-quality development of the credit insurance business. The Notice sets flexible underwriting limits allowing insurance companies to adjust their current business structures. The financing credit insurance business is expected to see a lower proportion of consumer credit services and a higher proportion of services for inclusive micro and small businesses. The financing business section should be assiduously supervised as internal management and control regulations concerning liquidity management, internal audits, and partnership management are further clarified, such that when existing risks are gradually removed, incremental risks are also better controlled.

### 15. Sales Force Management: Overall Improvement of Abilities and Image-building

On May 12th, 2020, the CBIRC released the *Notice on Implementing Insurance Companies Accountability and Strengthening Sales Force Management in the Insurance Industry* (hereafter referred to as the "Notice"). Within the legislative framework built by the Insurance Law and the "Insurance Agent Regulation and Insurance Assessor Regulation", the Notice focuses on problems discovered through intensive practitioner examination in 2019 — particularly concerning the management responsibilities of insurance institutions, which are carefully defined and clarified.

The Notice consists of 23 articles in total and can be divided into eight sections respectively focused on improving comprehensive awareness, strengthening strategic integration, the rigorous management of recruitment, training, qualifications, and employment, the consolidation of basic management, and strict supervision. A basic principle is established for legal and management responsibilities, on the basis of which institutions are asked to fulfill such tasks as building a solid management system, preventing high-risk sales force recruitment, continuous improvement of sales personnel professionalism, establishing a sales ability grading system, and team integrity system, data quality maintenance, and adoption of an accountability system with strict penalization in accordance with the law.

### 16. Strengthening Management of Professional Insurance Intermediary Practitioners

With the growing demand for insurance consumption, China is in the process of building a transformed, high-quality insurance market. Therefore, as a significant component of the insurance industry, insurance practitioners should be and must be subjected to stronger and more effective management. Only then will they be prepared for the new requirements of the industry and the new demands of consumers. Practitioners are those directly engaged with consumers through insurance sales and consulting services. Their quality and integrity standards are therefore highly consequential to insurance consumers' vital interests. Moreover, practitioners directly affect the image of the insurance industry. Since 2015, the industry has seen a rapid increase in the number of practitioners. Personal agents working in insurance companies alone number over 9 million. With so many practitioners, it is essential that insurance institutions fulfill their primary responsibilities as managers, improve their management consciousness, and optimize related mechanisms and systems. In 2019, the CBIRC planned and conducted a trial registration and examination of salespersons employed in insurance companies and of practitioners in professional insurance intermediaries. The results indicate the biggest problems are uneven levels of quality among practitioners, with some major inconsistencies in qualifications. The underlying causes were identified as errors in (or a lack of) principles, system-building, or staff management measures, resulting in the ineffective assumption of insurance institutions' primary management responsibilities.

To practically ensure professional insurance intermediaries are undertaking their main responsibilities and to comprehensively improve personnel/team management in terms of tightening management, improving quality, promoting transformation, image-building, etc., the CBIRC released the *Notice on Strengthening Management of Professional Insurance Intermediary Practitioners* (hereafter referred to as the "Notice") on May 12th, 2020.

Within the legislative framework built by the Insurance Law and the *Insurance Agent Regulation and Insurance Assessor Regulation*, the Notice focuses on problems discovered through intensive practitioner examination in 2019 — particularly concerning the management responsibilities of insurance institutions, which are carefully defined and clarified.

The Notice clarifies requirements on fully assuming the responsibility of the main management body, strengthening overall management, ensuring strict recruitment and training management, establishing a grading system for sales ability, consolidating basic management, and ensuring strict integrity management and supervision according to professional insurance intermediaries' characteristics and market positioning.

The Notice specifies regulatory requirements for sales ability grading, supports self-regulatory organizations in the insurance industry to leverage platforms' advantages, promotes sales ability grading among sales staff, urges insurance institutions to examine practitioners' qualities in a comprehensive manner — considering their educational level, work experience, knowledge of insurance products, records of integrity, etc. — and improve employees' overall sales qualifications.

The main thrust of the Notice is emphasizing insurance institutions' legal liability for insurance practitioners (including insurance sales staff) in accordance with the law and applies to corresponding business activities. It emphasizes that responsibility arises from legality and that insurance institutions' management requirements apply to practitioners throughout the whole process.

### 17. Expanding banks' capital replenishment channels and space for insurance fund use

In order to implement the guiding principles of the Financial Stability and Development Committee under the State Council and to further expand the replenishment channels of bank capital as well as space for the use of insurance funds, the CBIRC revised the existing *Notice on Matters Relating to Insurance Funds' Investment in Bank Capital Supplementary Bonds* to formulate a new version on May 20, 2020 (hereafter referred to as the "Notice").

The main contents of the Notice include: First, a loosening of conditions for issuers of capital supplementary bonds invested by insurance funds. The new version revises or removes a number of restrictions — requirements that the issuer's total assets shall not be less than RMB 1 trillion and net assets shall not be less than RMB 50 billion are removed; the limitation that the issuer's "core tier I capital adequacy ratio shall not be less than 8%, tier I capital adequacy ratio shall not be less than 9% and capital adequacy ratio shall not be less than 11%" is adjusted to "the capital adequacy ratio shall comply with regulatory requirements"; and the requirement that the issuer possesses an AAA level external credit rating is canceled. Second, removal of the limitation on investible bonds' external credit rating. The AAA level credit rating requirement for investible tier II capital bonds and the AA+ level credit rating requirement for open-end capital bonds are canceled. Third, insurance institutions' credit risk management is required to meet the CBIRC-set standard. The solvency ratio should not be less than 120% at the end of the last quarter. Fourth, insurance institutions are required to recognize their capital supplement bonds' equity or debt instruments as fixed-income or equity assets (according to the issuer's classification scheme) and include these in the corresponding regulatory ratio management.

The Notice facilitates enrichment of the varieties of insurance asset allocation, widening of the space for insurance fund allocation, and raising of insurance institutions' investment autonomy, giving them more rights to judge the value and risk of investments. It also helps support small and medium-sized banks supplement capital by multiple channels in order to optimize their capital structure, increase investors in capital supplementary bonds, and improve the market-based pricing mechanism. At the same time, the new version of the Notice requires insurance institutions to strengthen risk management and prudently judge investment benefits and risks. Insurance institutions should enhance their own risk awareness and risk management capacities, track and monitor investment risk, and fulfill reporting obligations in a timely manner.

**18. Clarifying conditions for operation and advancing supply-side structural reform in agricultural insurance**

At the eighth meeting of the Central Commission of Comprehensively Deepening Reform on May 29, 2019, the *Guiding Opinions on Accelerating the High-quality Development of Agricultural Insurance* was deliberated and agreed upon in principle. The "Guiding Opinions" indicates agricultural insurance's great significance — as an important tool for dispersing the risks of agricultural production and operation — to the development of modern agriculture. Its issuance was intended to promote the revitalization of rural industries, improve social governance in rural areas, and guarantee farmers' benefits. To carry out the guiding principles of the *Guiding Opinions on Accelerating the High-quality Development of Agricultural Insurance* as well as the *streamlining administration, delegating power and improving government services* reform and overall arrangements for developing agricultural insurance as set by the CPC Central Committee and State Council, the CBIRC issued the *Notice on Further Clarification of the Conditions of Agricultural Insurance Operation* (hereafter referred to as the "Notice") on June 12, 2020. The Notice is also intended to further the supply-side structural reform of agricultural insurance and develop a management mechanism for the operating conditions of agricultural insurance.

To address the issue of agricultural insurance market access which has been the focus of the industry, the Notice clarifies the conditions of agricultural insurance operation, strengthens dynamic supervision, establishes an assessment mechanism for agricultural insurance operation, improves the exit mechanism, develops a management system of agricultural insurance operation conditions which covers the whole process, and promotes the supply-side structural reform in agricultural insurance and the stable development of agricultural insurance market.

The Notice contains 19 articles in total, the main contents as follows: first, a clarification of the conditions of agricultural insurance operations. According to the *Regulation on Agriculture Insurance* (hereafter referred to as the "Regulation") issued by the State Council in 2012, the Notice sets respective conditions for the operation of agricultural insurance in terms of the head office and provincial branches. Any insurance institution meeting the conditions can carry out agricultural insurance in its region without needing to apply to the regulator for operation qualifications. Second, the Notice raises the standards for agricultural insurance operations. After its 2016 revision, the Regulation removes the need for approval to enter the agricultural insurance market but continues to require agricultural insurance businesses to meet certain standards for appropriate operation and comply with additional conditions stipulated by the insurance regulatory authority of the State Council. The Notice further improves these standards in terms of legal compliance, risk management, agricultural insurance service quality, and information technology capacities. The third is the development of an exit mechanism. In support of the reform and accordance with the Regulation, the Notice clearly specifies there must be an exit mechanism for agricultural insurance operations. In addition, it establishes a comprehensive tool for assessing agricultural insurance operations that can provide dynamic evaluations of insurance institutions' agricultural insurance operation management.

As an institutional arrangement crucial to the betterment of the agricultural insurance system, the Notice further improves the management mechanism of the conditions for agricultural insurance operation, optimizes its institutional layout, and regulates its market order, which effectively promotes the sustainable development of agricultural insurance, guides local authorities in formulating detailed rules in accordance with their own circumstances, improves the market access and exit mechanisms for agricultural insurance, and directs agricultural insurance to better address the issues of agriculture, rural areas, and farmers. At the same time, as insurance companies face increasing compliance management regulations, agricultural insurance will be brought to a new stage of high-quality development that is inevitably more legally compliant.

**19. Regulating internet insurance sales, protecting consumer rights**

The business resulting from the integration of the internet and insurance is experiencing rapid growth. As the still sparse and fragmented business of internet insurance begins to reach all types of consumers more expansively, issues of internet insurance infringing upon consumers' legitimate rights and interests have likewise exploded. In 2019, the CBIRC received 19,900 internet insurance consumer complaints, marking a year-on-year (YOY) increase of 88.59% and seven times the number of complaints in 2016. The issues, ranging from misleading sales to compulsory tying in disguise, have affected consumers' sense of benefit.

In response to the outstanding problems revealed by these complaints and based on new forms of internet and consumer behavior, the CBIRC issued the *Notice on Regulating the Retrospective*

*Management of Internet Insurance Sales* (hereafter referred to as the "Notice") on June 22, 2020. It is intended to regulate internet insurance sales by traceability management, taking behavior supervision as a starting point. The Notice consists of 26 articles in total, mainly covering the following five aspects.

First, the definition and scope of traceability management are clarified for internet insurance sales. For internet insurance sales to have "traceability" depends on sales page management and the recording of the sales process, insurance institutions should record and save transaction information for insurance products sold on their proprietary online platforms and enable this data to be checked. Traceability management should apply to commercial insurance products for which a policyholder is a natural person.

Second, clear definitions of sales pages and sales page management. There should be requirements in place for the boundaries of internet insurance sales, the scope of sales behavior, and the management and control over points of sales risk. The Notice emphasizes that sales pages may only be set up on the proprietary online platforms of insurance institutions and that these need to be separated from non-sales pages. Important terms and conditions must be displayed on separate pages to be confirmed by policyholders so as to protect consumers' right to know.

Third, requirements for insurance institutions' management of the internet sales process. This section covers protecting policyholders' freedom of choice, clarification of the responsibilities of insurance institutions for real-name verification, detailed standards for recording the sales process, and the principles of information collection. In terms of the collection and use of consumers' personal information, the Notice stresses that insurance institutions should act according to the law and out of legitimacy and necessity, taking effective measures to protect the information and consumers' information security rights.

Fourth, specifications on traceability internal control management. This section mainly stipulates the content, storage, protection, and related internal control system requirements for traceable data. It requires insurance institutions to establish a comprehensive, systematic, and standardized system of internal control. For investigation and inspection, the Notice specifically requires internet insurance sales' traceable data to be revertible to valid document formats able to be checked; sale pages should be revertible to valid pictures or videos.

Fifth, clarification of the management requirements for converged services and self-service terminal operation, including the related legal liabilities and timing of implementation.

Issuance of the Notice is conducive to maintaining market order, preventing operational risks, and further protecting financial consumers' basic rights — including the right to know, right to choose, and right to fair dealing.

**20. Consolidating the results of chaos management, winning in financial risk prevention and defusing**

The insurance industry has achieved remarkable results since 2017 in rectifying market irregularities, such as effectively curbing disorder in operations management, mitigating prominent risks in key areas in an orderly manner, and avoiding the diversion of funds out of the real economy.

Altogether this work has laid a solid foundation for finance to support the development of the real economy. In order to further consolidate and leverage the achievements of chaos management and solidify victory in the war against financial risks, the CBIRC issued the *Notice on the "Look Back" Work for Market Irregularities Rectification in Banking and Insurance Industries* (hereafter referred to as the "Notice") on June 23, 2020.

The Notice requires the reexamination of ("looking back" on) chaos management to focus on ensuring stability on the six fronts (employment, financial sector, foreign trade, foreign and domestic investments, and expectations) and maintaining security in the six areas (employment, people's livelihoods, market entities, energy and food, industrial and supply chains, and the normal functioning of primary-level governments). It also requires adherence to the guiding principles of the party's political work, with strict investigations and punishments in accordance with to law. Reexamination work should prevent the recurrence of market disorder and implement financial support and other policies for pandemic prevention and control as well as the resumption of work and production in industrial chains. Repeated investigations and violations will be significantly reduced through ongoing and intensive rectification; banking and insurance institutions will develop long-term compliance mechanisms for internal control mechanisms, and the quality and effectiveness of financial services in the real economy will noticeably improve.

The Notice clarifies that market disorder rectification work will be "looked back" on for the past three consecutive years. This reexamination should check the placement of entity liability, the benefits to the real economy, the effectiveness of rectification measures, the curbs on illegal violations, and the usefulness of compliance mechanisms. It also requires better political positioning throughout the entire industry, a deep understanding of the significance of financial support for micro, small, and medium-sized enterprises has for stability on the six fronts, and security in the six areas. In addition, chaos must be managed in the market while risks are prevented and stable growth is promoted. The Notice urges banking and insurance institutions to share the dividends of inclusive finance policy with private small and micro enterprises, reduces the overall cost of corporate financing, and cracks down on illegal capital arbitrage of loans obtained through the facilitation of financing policy. Investigations should be conducted for illegalities and irregularities in the fields of macro policy implementation, equity and corporate governance, business operations, shadow banking, and cross-financial business. Any violations wearing the guise of financial innovation will be dealt with strictly in accordance with the law.

The Notice emphasizes that banking and insurance institutions should conduct rectification from root causes, engage in self-examination, uphold effective rectification and a strict accountability system, develop a management system that applies to all staff, integrate financial chaos management with the cultivation of robust risk culture, and effectively improve operations' levels of legal compliance and risk management. Regulators at all levels should seriously investigate and punish irregularities such as violations of macro-control policy, infringements on the legitimate rights and interests of financial consumers, and repeated violations. They should apply severe punishments for financial corruption and illegal behavior that disrupts market order or causes significant losses or risks.

The Notice is a summary and consolidation of the insurance industry's work in market disorder rectification over the past three years. It marks the advancement of compliance construction in the insurance industry, which will strongly contribute to the insurance market order, guide the whole industry to focus on the nature of protection, and promote sustainable and high-quality development.

**21. Strengthening asset and liability management, enhancing risk resilience**

In order to support insurance funds' participation in the trading of government bond futures and to effectively prevent risks, the CBIRC issued the *Provisions on the Participation of Insurance Funds in Treasury Bond Futures Trading* on June 23, 2020. The "Provisions" were formulated according to the guiding principles of the *Announcement on the Participation in Treasury Bond Futures Trading on the China Financial Futures Exchange by Commercial Banks and Insurance Institutions*. At the same time, the CBIRC revised the *Measures for the Participation of Insurance Funds in Financial Derivatives Trading* and the *Provisions on the Participation of Insurance Funds in Stock Index Futures Trading*.

The *Provisions on the Participation of Insurance Funds in Government Bond Futures Trading* contains 17 articles in total, mainly covering the following content: first, it clarifies the purpose and participation term. Insurance funds should participate in government bond futures for the purpose of hedging risks rather than for speculation. Second, it specifies the mode of participation for insurance funds. Insurance funds should participate and open trading accounts in the form of asset portfolios and should conduct independent management in the fields of accounts, assets, transactions, and accounting, while strictly implementing measures for risk isolation. Third, it sets the amount limits of selling and buying contracts, control leverage ratio, and strengthen liquidity risk management. Fourth, it enhances the management of operations, technology, and compliance. Fifth, it clarifies relevant issues on supervision management and reporting.

The *Measures for the Participation of Insurance Funds in Financial Derivatives Trading* was amended from 36 to 37 articles. The adjustments are as follows: first, clarification of the purpose behind insurance funds' use of derivatives and removal of the term limit. The specific term is separately formulated according to the derivatives. Second, strengthening asset-liability management and solvency. Requirements of insurance companies' entrusted participation and self-participation are set respectively according to different risk characteristics. Third, adding a total leverage ratio requirement for insurance funds to participate in derivatives trading. Forth, requiring strict control of insider trading, manipulation of the securities market, and the transfer of benefits.

The *Provisions on the Participation of Insurance Funds in Equity Index Futures Trading* adjustments include: First, adjusting certain relevant requirements including the hedge period, liquidity management, and the amount limits for selling and buying contracts. Second, clarification of rights and obligations to be listed in the contract. The relevant issues of entrusted investment and asset management products — such as the purpose of transactions, proportion limits, valuation methods, information disclosure, risk control, and liability — should be included in the contract or guidelines. Third, added requirements for retrospective reporting. The insurance institution that participates in equity index futures trading must report deviation between the buying plan and the actual purchase every six months.

Issuance of the *Provisions on the Participation of Insurance Funds in Government Bond Futures Trading* effectively enriches risk hedging tools for insurance funds, which helps strengthen asset and liability management and enhance risk resilience. At the same time, revision of the *Measures for the Participation of Insurance Funds in Financial Derivatives Trading* and the *Provisions on the Participation of Insurance Funds in Equity Index Futures Trading* sets unified standards for supervision and improves the regulatory system for insurance funds participating in the trade of financial derivatives. This is beneficial for expanding insurance institutions' options, consolidating the main responsibilities of insurance institutions to conduct comprehensive risk management, reinforcing risk awareness, and building up risk management capacities.

**22. Proper off-site supervision of financing guarantee companies and standardized business practices**

In order to fully implement the *Regulation on the Supervision and Administration of Financing Guarantee Companies* issued by the State Council and conduct off-site supervision over financing guarantee companies, the Inter-ministerial Joint Meeting of Supervision over Financing Guarantee Business passed the *Regulation on Off-site Supervision over Financing Guarantee Companies* (hereafter referred to as the "Regulation"), issued by the CBIRC on July 14, 2020.

The Regulation requires financing guarantee companies to establish and implement an off-site supervision reporting system, and submit off-site supervision data/non-data information according to the requirements and time limits set by the regulatory authorities. The off-site supervision of financing guarantee companies should focus on changes in the external business environment, corporate governance, internal control, risk management capacities, guarantee business, relevant guarantee risks, asset quality, liquidity indicators, and investment. The Regulation stipulates that when a financing guarantee company encounters major risks, abnormal changes, or emergencies, the regulator should analyze the causes, promptly deal with the risk, and report to the people's government at the corresponding level as well as the CBIRC and the People's Bank of China according to the major risks reporting system. The Regulations stipulates that the supervisory and regulatory authorities may determine the appropriate response mechanism according to the severity of the risk posed by the financial guarantee company. They may then take regulatory measures in accordance with the law — such as increasing the frequency of reporting, urging self-examination, requiring the enrichment of risk management forces, issuing risk warnings and notices, holding regulatory talks, conducting on-site inspections, ordering the suspension of part of a company's business, limiting the scale and manner of its own capital use, and forbidding it from establishing new branches.

The Regulations focuses on the process and division of responsibilities in the off-site supervision of financial guarantee companies and makes provisions for the collection and verification of information, risk monitoring and assessment, information reporting and use, and regulatory measures. It improves interpretations of financial guarantee companies' regulatory indicators and statements, harmonizes regulatory indicator statistics with the requirements of the regulatory system, facilitates the supervision of financial guarantee companies' business conduct, promotes the regulatory system requirements' implementation and enforcement, and better supports the development of inclusive finance.

**23. Making space for autonomous decision-making on the use of funds and optimizing the regulation of equity asset allocation**

In order to further deepen the market-oriented reform of insurance funds' utilization, to guide insurance funds to better serve the real economy, to give play to the role of insurance institutions as key investors in the capital market, and to make space for autonomous decision-making on insurance companies' use of funds, the CBIRC formulated the *Notice on Matters Relating to the Optimization of Supervision of Equity Asset Allocation of Insurance Companies* (hereafter referred to as the "Notice") on July 17, 2020.

The Notice consists of 12 articles, and their main content as follows: First, the establishment of differentiated regulatory ratios for investment in equity assets. Second, strengthened supervision over key companies. Third, more concentrated risk regulatory indicators. Fourth, guiding insurance companies to make prudent and sound investments.

Issuance and implementation of the Notice constitute an important step in implementing the Party Central Committee and State Council's "stability on the six fronts", and hold great positive significance for the soundness of insurance funds' investments and the supervision of insurance funds' usage. This is conducive to furthering the market-oriented reform of insurance fund use and widening the independent decision-making space for insurance funds' investment. It is also conducive to the exploratory establishment of a differentiated regulatory mechanism, to improvements in the relevance, precision, and effectiveness of insurance fund use supervision, and preventing risks for key companies and key varieties. Finally, it is conducive to guiding insurance companies in their value investments, long-term investments, and prudent investments, and providing more capital funds for the real economy and the capital market.

**24. Harnessing the role of governmental financing guarantee institutions and establishing a sound system of governmental financing guarantees**

In line with the spirit of the *Opinions of the State Council on Promoting the Accelerated Development of the Financing Guarantee Industry*, as well as requirements of the *Guidance Opinions of the General Office of the State Council on Effectively Playing the Role of Governmental Financing Guarantee Funds to Effectively Support the Development of Small and Micro Enterprises and Agriculture, Rural Areas, and Farmers*, the CBIRC and seven other departments issued the *Notice on the Supervision of Governmental Financing Guarantee Institutions* (hereafter referred to as the "Notice") on August 5, 2020. The purpose of this Notice is to make full use of governmental financing guarantee institutions, significantly expand the coverage and reduce the rates of governmental financing guarantees, and to solidly ensure "stability on the six fronts" and "security in the six areas".

The main elements of the Notice are as follows.

First concerns the confirmation of government financial guarantee institutions. Confirmation work is the responsibility of the provincial finance departments of each region in conjunction with provincial financial guarantee companies' supervision and management departments. They should also formulate a list of government financial guarantee institutions and release it to the public. Second, the Notice requires government financial guarantee institutions to adhere to their quasi-public positioning, make up for market deficiencies, and focus on their main business of supporting small and medium-sized enterprises and agricultural businesses, steadily increasing the proportion of insured balance going to small and medium-sized enterprises and to agriculture, rural areas and farmers. Third, the Notice calls for the integration of internal and external factors to promote improvement in the quality and effectiveness of government financial guarantee institution services. Government financial guarantee institutions should strengthen their own construction, improve internal management, optimize incentives, innovate guarantee products, improve service efficiency, and promote the establishment of a long-term mechanism for "capability, willingness, and confidence" to bear. With regard to the external environment and policies, coordination should be strengthened to encourage banks' active cooperation with government financing guarantee institutions, to enact mechanisms for sharing risks, to improve the system for evaluating the performance of government financing guarantee institutions, and to implement policy on subsidizing reduced loan fees to support small-scale agriculture. Fourth, in order to strengthen supervision and guidance, supervision and management departments should coordinate the use of various means including on-site inspection and off-site supervision to strengthen the monitoring and analysis of government financial guarantee institution performance indicators including their support of small-scale agriculture, their comprehensive guarantee fee rate, and magnification. These institutions should be guided to focus on their main business of supporting small-scale agriculture, expand the scale of guarantees, and reduce the guarantee fee rate.

Issuance and implementation of this Notice constitute an important initiative in implementing the government work report and establish a sound system for government financing guarantees. As its next steps, the CBIRC will continue to improve the relevant rules and regulations as a means to direct government financial guarantee institutions' focus on their main business of supporting small-scale agriculture and their healthy, sustainable development.

**25. Enhancing the quality and effectiveness of corporate governance, building a corporate governance mechanism for a banking and insurance industry with Chinese characteristics**

On August 17, 2020, the CBIRC issued a *Three-Year Action Plan for Improving Corporate Governance of the Banking and Insurance Sectors (2020–2022)*" (YBJF [2020] No.40) (hereafter referred to as the "Plan"). The Plan's formulation and introduction constitute an important and conscientious CBIRC initiative to implement a series of Party Central Committee and State Council decisions on improving financial institutions' corporate governance. This move will comprehensively enhance the systemic, targeted, and forward-oriented qualities of corporate governance supervision and help improve the overall quality and efficiency of corporate governance in China's banking and insurance industries.

The Plan highlights the guiding importance of Xi Jinping Thought on Socialism with Chinese Characteristics for a New Era and emphasizes the strengthening of party leadership and the improvement of the modern financial enterprise system. It clarifies the need to follow a problem-oriented approach, addresses both symptoms and root causes, categorizes and carries out policies, promotes coordinated efforts, and focuses on the main problems, fills gaps in systems, strengthens differentiated supervision, and focuses on integrity and synergy of work. The Plan outlines three years of hard work for building a preliminary corporate governance mechanism in the banking and insurance industry with Chinese characteristics.

Consisting of ten parts, the Plan covers overall requirements (guidelines, basic principles, overall objectives), the integration of party leadership and corporate governance, corporate governance evaluation, the regulation of shareholder behavior, the performance of governance subjects such as boards of directors, incentive and restraint mechanisms, stakeholder protections, external market constraints, regulatory capacity building, and organizational guarantees. The Plan arranges key work series around various aspects of corporate governance. It is the designated action guide for the insurance industry's corporate governance regulation for 2020–2022.

While taking lessons from advanced foreign experience, the Plan also draws extensively on CBIRC evaluations of G20/OECD Principles of Corporate Governance implemented in China's banking and insurance industry. Where shortcomings are identified, targeted measures are proposed for their rectification — for instance, enhancing restraint mechanisms on the behavior of major shareholders, clarifying the requirement for all directors (including equity directors) to treat all shareholders equitably, improving the process of nominating and selecting directors, and encouraging institutions' strict enforcement of a high standard of professional ethics.

The Plan's release and implementation constitute an important CBIRC initiative to strengthen corporate governance supervision in the banking and insurance industry in accordance with the law. It will comprehensively enhance corporate governance's systematic, targeted and forward-oriented qualities, raise the overall quality and effectiveness of banking and insurance institutions' corporate governance, effectively enhance resilience to risks and the sustainability of operations, and provide strong support for major risks' resolution and the building of a moderately prosperous society.

**26. Supporting debt-to-equity operations based on the market and the rule of law**

On September 4, 2020, the CBIRC formulated the *Notice on Matters Relating to the Investment Plan for Insurance Funds to Invest in Debt-to-Equity Conversions* (hereafter referred to as the "Notice"). The Notice's creation aimed to implement the spirit of the Central Economic Work Conference and deployment of the government work report, to improve insurance funds' quality and efficiency in service to the real economy, to optimize the allocation structure of insurance assets, and to support debt-to-equity operations based on the market and the rule of law.

The major elements of the Notice consist of, first, clarification of the basis for regulation. Insurance funds' investment in debt-to-equity investment plans is regulated under the "Circular on Investment in Relevant Financial Products by Insurance Funds". The second is the clarification of conditions for issuers. Issuers of debt-to-equity investment plans invested by insurance funds must practice good corporate governance and prudent and sound operations; they must possess a good record of compliance with the law and strong investment management capabilities. The third is the clarification of the scope of investment. In principle, debt-to-equity investment plans invested by insurance funds should invest in market-based debt-to-equity assets with no less than 60% of their net assets. Other assets that may be invested include contractually agreed-upon deposits (including large certificates of deposit), standardized debt assets, and other assets approved by the CBIRC; if the debt-to-equity investment plans are subject to share grading, they shall be considered priority shares. The fourth is classification management in accordance with the principle of penetration. Debt-to-equity investment plans invested by insurance funds should be managed by incorporation as a proportion of equity assets or other financial asset investments in accordance with the proportion of equity assets. The fifth is strengthening concentration supervision. The Notice sets a limit of 50% for individual enterprises and 80% for groups.

The Notice constitutes an important measure in implementing supply-side structural reform, promoting cooperation between insurance financing and financial asset investment companies, advancing the development of market-based debt-to-equity business in line with the rule of law. Its issuance helps support financial asset investment companies' debt-to-equity swap business and expands the swaps' funding sources, enriches the types of insurance fund investment, puts the advantages of long-term insurance funds investment into play, and better serves the development of the real economy. The Notice is also conducive to lowering enterprises' leverage ratios, helps high-quality enterprises with good development prospects overcome difficulties, and enhances development resilience of the mid-to-long-term economy.

**27. Improving the insurance industry's health management services, enriching the content of health insurance products**

The *Report of the 19th CPC National Congress, Opinions on Promoting the Development of Commercial Insurance in Social Services* and other policy documents clearly propose "providing the people with comprehensive health services for the entire lifecycle" and "promoting the integrated development of health insurance and health management." In recent years, the insurance industry has actively explored health management services for the public, playing a positive role in the content enrichment of health products and overall better health of the people. However, the insurance industry's health management business remains immature, overall still in its early stage of development. In order to standardize the health management service behavior of insurance companies and advance the integrated development of health management services and the health insurance business, the General Office of the CBIRC issued the *Notice on Standardizing Health Management Service of Insurance Companies* (hereafter referred to as the "Notice") on September 6, 2020.

The main content of the Notice is as follows.

First, it defines "health management services" in terms of concept and purpose. The Notice defines the concept, content, and purpose underlying health management services, divides insurance companies' said services into seven categories (check-ups, health consultations, health promotion, disease prevention, chronic disease management, medical consultation services, and rehabilitation care), and stipulates that insurance companies' health management services should be for the prevention and control of incurring or developing the disease or the promotion of recovery from disease; to this end, said services should intervene in customers' health risk factors, reducing medical expenses by reducing the incidence of disease and improving overall levels of health.

Second, it sets forth principles and requirements that should be followed in health management services. Specifically, the principles insurance companies should follow when providing health management services are scientificity, rationality, safety, effectiveness, objectivity, and ethical compliance. The Notice also states that insurance companies must respect customers' right to informed consent, protect their privacy, ensure the security of relevant data and information, and provide timely feedback from service evaluations and complaint handling.

Third, it enhances rules for health management services' operations. The Notice clarifies requirements for insurance companies' organization and management, systems building, practitioners, personnel training, and information systems; for third-party service providers, it clarifies the scope of cooperation and qualification requirements, selection and assessment process, cooperation agreements, service supervision, and quality evaluation. In addition, it sets requirements on the content, principles, and means of information disclosure for health management services provided by insurance companies, as a means to effectively protect the legitimate rights and interests of consumers.

Fourth, it strengthens the supervision and management of health management services. The Notice clarifies compliance requirements and mechanisms for internal accountability among insurance companies providing health management services. It also consolidates the main responsibilities for these companies. There are requirements stipulated for information reporting, emergency response, and the reporting of major accidents or sudden mass incidents. In addition, the Notice emphasizes insurance industry associations' role as self-regulatory organizations, supporting these in explorations to establish a health management business exchange platform among insurance companies as well as an evaluation system for health management service providers, and to coordinate the establishment of industry standards for management, technology, data, and other relevant areas.

Against the industry trend of health insurance/health management integration, and insurance companies' general regard for health management as a new driver of growth in health insurance, the Notice improves health management service supervision. It will help standardize companies' service practices, improve the overall quality and level of services, and better protect consumers' legitimate rights and interests.

### 28. Standardizing on-site inspection procedures for higher efficiency

In order to standardize procedures for the establishment and implementation of on-site inspections and enhance their overall efficiency, on September 6, 2020, the CBIRC issued the *Regulations on the Establishment and Implementation Procedures for On-site Inspections of the CBIRC*

(*Trial*) (hereafter referred to as the "Trial Regulations").

The Trial Regulations, which is based on the 2019 *Measures for On-site Inspection of the China Banking and Insurance Regulatory Commission (Trial)* (hereafter referred to as the "Trial Measures"), concerns the CBIRC or its dispatched agencies' procedures for the on-site inspection of regulatory objects, covering five major aspects — the establishment of inspection, preparation for inspection, implementation of inspection, processing of inspection, and organization of inspection files. Under each aspect, the Trial Regulations also gives comprehensive and detailed provisions for workflow, work content, organizational structure, operating rules, and other items. It does so in accordance with the guiding principles of the Trial Measures on the seriousness, scientificity, and fairness of on-site inspection work. Issuance of the Trial Provisions simultaneously repeals the *Regulations of the China Banking Regulatory Commission on On-site Inspection* issued in 2007 and the *Regulations of the China Insurance Regulatory Commission on On-site Inspection* issued in 2009.

The Trial Provisions provides a clear scheme for putting the Trial Measures into practice. It not only creates a strong handle for scientific, standardized, and effective on-site inspections by the CBIRC; it will also lead the banking and insurance industries to better prevent financial risks, support the real economy, and maintain overall financial security and stability.

**29. Implementing the *New Regulation on Asset Management*, further regulating the business development of insurance asset management products**

In order to implement the *Guidance on Regulating Asset Management Business of Financial Institutions* (hereafter referred to as the "New Regulation on Asset Management"), to further regulate the business development of insurance asset management products, and to refine relevant provisions of the *Interim Measures for the Administration of Insurance Asset Management Products* (hereafter referred to as the "Product Measures"), the CBIRC issued three rules on September 7, 2020 — these include the *Implementation Rules for Portfolio Insurance Asset Management Products*, *Implementation Rules for Debt Investment Plans* and *Implementation Rules for Equity Investment Plans*.

The three rules adhere to the following principles: The first is holding a bottom line of strict risk control. The second is resolutely serving the real economy. The third is deepening reforms that "streamline administration and delegate power, improve regulation and upgrade services" to optimize the business environment. The fourth is creating parity among rules for similar private equity products in the broader capital management market.

The *Implementation Rules for Portfolio Insurance Asset Management Products* consists of 18 articles; the main provisions clarify the time limit for product registration, refine the scope for product investment, strictly regulate sales to qualified natural persons, and strengthen measures for post-event supervision. The Implementation Rules for Debt Investment Plans contains 18 articles; these primarily clarify the time limit for product registration, unify qualifying conditions and business management requirements for infrastructure/non-infrastructure real estate debt investment schemes, broaden the use of funds in debt investment schemes as appropriate, and improve the design of risk management mechanisms and transaction structures like credit enhancement. The Implementation Rules for Equity Investment Plans includes 17 articles; these primarily clarify the time limit for product registration, expand the scope of investment assets as appropriate, set requirements for product investment ratios, specify prohibited acts and strengthen requirements for information disclosure.

The three rules are a refinement of regulations found in the "New Regulation on Asset Management" and the "Product Measures", aimed to address different types of insurance asset management products. Such refinement is conducive to differentiating supervision over the three product types as well as the standardized and healthy development of insurance asset management products, the maintenance of a fair and healthy competitive environment in the asset management industry, and the protection of investors' legitimate rights and interests.

### 30. Improving the auto insurance actuarial system, preventing irrational competition

With the imminent launch of comprehensive auto insurance reform and liberalization of front-end prices, the CBIRC issued the *Model Commercial Auto Insurance Actuarial Provisions* (hereafter referred to as the "Actuarial Provisions") on September 9, 2020, as a means to improve the auto insurance actuarial system and prevent irrational competitive behavior.

The "Actuarial Regulations" mainly applies to two areas:

1. To resolve irregularities in the corporate auto insurance product rate filing and subsequent implementation, it imposes rate backtracking and product correction mechanisms;

2. To compel companies to operate rationally, it requires them to promptly reflect losses in financial statements and solvency indicators, and it clarifies the criteria for assessing premium deficiency reserves (PDR).

The "Actuarial Regulations" is divided into seven parts — first, the scope of application, which clarifies the provisions apply to commercial auto insurance products that use the industry model clauses. The second is the composition of premiums. Here the Actuarial Provisions specifies basic principles for determining premiums, formulas for their calculation, industry benchmarks in use, criteria for additional cost rates, and so on. The third is the retrospective rate and product correction. Here it stipulates that insurance companies shall establish mechanisms for retrospective rate and product correction, dynamically monitor and analyze the deviation of actuarial rate assumptions from actual company operations, and make timely adjustments to commercial auto insurance rates. The fourth is an assessment of premium deficiency reserves, which specify formula for the premium adequacy test and criteria for assessing PDR. The fifth is the duties of the chief actuary, which require that he or she regularly assess the rationality of pricing assumptions and promptly report to the regulator in the case of significant deviations between pricing assumptions and actual operating results, or if the insurer faces significant risks, such as in underpricing. The sixth is regulatory measures. To maintain strict discipline in the auto insurance market, it clarifies that the regulator can take certain regulatory measures, including ordering insurance companies to stop using products. The seventh is a by-law that clarifies matters such as document repeal.

The "Actuarial Regulations" was issued to improve the regulatory system and optimize the auto insurance industry's individual pricing system for premiums along with the supporting systems for retrospective rates, product correction, and PDR. This can effectively prevent and resolve risks in auto insurance operations, make for more reasonable matching between auto insurance rate prices and risks, and provide institutional safeguards for the smooth advance of comprehensive auto insurance reform. At the same time, the Actuarial Regulations clarifies operators' main risk prevention responsibilities through the form of a system, conveys regulators' resolute risk prevention and control and the Party's "zero tolerance" for violations through relevant penalty provisions, realizes the Party Central Committee's people-centered development ideology and deepens the supply-side structural reform, thereby better protecting consumers' rights and interests, giving the market a more decisive role in resource allocation, and furthering high-quality development of the auto insurance industry.

**31. Regulating emergency-response financial services, maintaining sound operations in banking and insurance**

In order to thoroughly implement Xi Jinping Thought on Socialism with Chinese Characteristics for a New Era and carry forth the spirit of the Fourth Plenary Session of the 19th CPC Central Committee, the CBIRC formulated the *Measures for the Administration of Financial Services of Banking and Insurance Institutions in Response to Emergencies* (hereafter referred to as the "Measures") on September 9, 2020. More specifically, the "Measures" responds to General Secretary Xi Jinping's urge to "pay close attention to filling shortcomings, plugging loopholes, and strengths and weaknesses" in response to the COVID-19 epidemic by regulating the business activities and financial services of banking and insurance institutions in terms of emergency response and consumer rights protection. The Measures will improve the relevance of supervision and help maintain the safe and sound operation of the banking and insurance industry.

The Measures' provisions follow these basic concepts: combining support for the real economy with stability maintenance of the financial system, combining convenient financial services with effective risk prevention, combining adherence to the bottom line of prudential supervision with flexible emergency response, adhering to a framework, adhering to principles and inclusivity. It offers regulators and bancassurance institutions comprehensive guidance for responding to emergencies. Its main elements are as follows.

First, the Measures clarifies the definition of "emergency", the basic principles of response, and institutional arrangements for organization and management. The system for organizing emergency response is clarified, effectively integrating requirements with other management systems (e.g. for business continuity) while emphasizing basic requirements such as the division of responsibilities, planning and drills, coordination and cooperation, and information reporting.

Second, beyond the requirement for basic financial services, it encourages the provision of additional measures of financial support. It stipulates that banking and insurance institutions should, in response to emergencies, ensure the continuity of financial services, and that insurance companies should develop targeted insurance products, increase business supply, and activate the role of insurance in risk prevention; it also advocates and offers further support for bancassurance institutions' active performance of social responsibilities.

Third, the "Measures" emphasizes the need of holding a bottom line of risk prevention in the course of providing financial services and support. It requires timely retrospection and post-assessment of business operations, the strict avoidance of infringement upon customers' legal rights, and enhanced monitoring, management, and response to public opinion.

Fourth, it provides targeted adjustments to the methods and requirements of supervision. Supervision must maintain continuity, effectiveness, and flexibility and must strengthen guidance and supervision as well as inspections of bancassurance institutions' response mechanisms, actions, and effectiveness in cases of emergencies.

**32. Regulating inquiries, freezing, and deduction for insurance companies' capital deposit accounts**

On September 11, 2020, the General Office of the CBIRC issued the *Notice on the Regulation of Banking Financial Institutions' Assistance to Authorized Authorities in Matters Relating to Inquiries, Freezing and Withholding of Capital Margin Accounts of Insurance Companies* (hereafter referred to as the "Notice"). The Notice is intended to further regulate banking financial institutions, thereby assisting the competent authorities in handling inquiries, freezing or making deductions from insurance companies' capital deposit accounts, and related matters for the smooth and healthy development of the insurance market.

The Notice contains six articles that define the scope of implementation as well as the capital margin. The Notice requires banking financial institutions to establish a system for managing insurance company capital deposit accounts and to properly handle such matters as accepting the relevant accounts for inquiries and regarding the freezing and deduction actions of the competent authorities. Banking financial institutions should verify the nature of account funds with their depositors and, during the deposit period, should not agree to depositors' requests to change the nature of the deposits, transfer the deposits' principal amount from the present bank of deposit, or other requests entailing disposal of the deposits in question. The system should specifically identify insurance companies' capital margin accounts, and relevant platforms and systems (such as the relevant network investigation and control platform and the electronic dedicated information transmission system) should place an overall restriction on freezing and deduction settings. When a banking financial institution receives instructions from a competent authority to either inquire about, freeze, or deduct funds from an insurance company's capital deposit account, the institution shall, in accordance with laws and regulations, inform the competent authority (either manually or through a relevant system) that accounts' funds may only be used for specific purposes such as settling debts in liquidation and that inquiries are allowed for it, but not freezing, deductions, or other arrangements. Banking financial institutions shall promptly report to the CBIRC when they encounter major abnormalities such as an insurance company's capital margin account being frozen or deducted from due to the improper activity of competent authorities.

**33. Standardizing security management and preventing security risks for regulatory data**

In order to standardize CBIRC's regulatory data security management, improve its capacity for data security protection, and prevent related security risks, the CBIRC issued the *Regulatory Data Security Management Measures (Trial)* (hereafter referred to as the "Measures") on September 23, 2020.

The Measures is divided into seven chapters with a total of 34 articles. The chapters respectively stipulate departmental work responsibilities, the collection, storage, and processing of regulatory data, and the entrustment and use of data, while standardizing data supervision, strengthening security management, and preventing security risks for regulatory data. The Measures requires that regulatory data's security management be centrally managed, with a department of statistics taking charge of overall planning and a business department reporting to the centrally managed department within 48 hours of discovering any major security risks. The Measures puts forward clear and standardized requirements on the collection, storage, processing, and use of regulatory data, such as data desensitization. In addition, it sets out access requirements for the management of regulatory data entrustment services.

In recent years, more and more attention has been drawn to personal information and financial data security regulation as network information and data security have come to impact people's lives. It is urgent that the financial industry do better work in financial data compliance.

**34. Deepening the market-oriented reform insurance fund use, strengthening interim and post-event investment supervision**

To continue streamlining administration, delegating power, optimizing the business environment, and deepening the market-oriented reform of the use of insurance funds, the CBIRC formulated the *Notice on Matters Relating to the Optimization of the Supervision of Investment Management Capabilities of Insurance Institutions* (hereafter referred to as the "Notice") on September 30, 2020, in accordance with the "Measures for the Administration of the Use of Insurance Funds" and related regulations.

The Notice consists of the main text and seven annexes; the body sets down basic requirements for the self-assessment, management, and information disclosure of insurance institutions in their investment management capacities; the annexes provide detailed requirements for the specific construction standards regarding each investment management function. For one, the new Notice optimizes and integrates insurance institutions' investment management functions and refines the requirements for capacity-building standards. After adjustment, there are seven categories of investment management functions: credit risk management, stock investment management, equity investment management, real estate investment management, derivatives application management, debt investment plan product management, and equity investment plan product management. For another, the new Notice deepens the reform of streamlining administration and delegating power, improving regulation, and upgrading services, abolishes the record management of investment management capacity, adjusts insurance institutions' management in this area to a combination of company self-assessment, information disclosure, and continuous supervision, clarifies the content, form, manner, and frequency of information disclosure, stipulates the circumstances and responsibilities of non-compliance, and comprehensively consolidates the insurance institutions' main responsibilities.

Issuance and implementation of the Notice constitute an important step by the CBIRC in deepening the Party Central Committee and State Council's reform on streamlining administration and delegating power, improving regulation, and upgrading services, and optimization of the business environment. It marks an improvement to the existing regulatory framework for insurance institutions' investment management capacity and holds great significance for the advance of market-oriented reform in the use of insurance funds. It will improve the efficiency of insurance institutions' independent investment decisions, assist in the continuous and comprehensive strengthening of insurance institutions' investment management capacities, stimulate insurance funds' investment vitality, and better support the development of the real economy and capital market.

**35. Supporting innovation-driven development and sci-tech research capacity-building in the insurance industry**

In order to implement an innovation-driven development strategy and promote the requirements of the *Special Program for the Reform and Innovation of Science and Technology Finance in the Wuhan City Circle* and the *Notice on the Issuance of the Overall Program of China (Hubei) Pilot Free Trade Zone* issued by the State Council and relevant ministries, the CBIRC and the People's Government of Hubei Province jointly issued the *Notice on the Issuance of the Overall Program of the East Lake Science and Technology Insurance Innovation Demonstration Zone* (hereafter referred to as the "Notice") on September 30, 2020.

The Notice specifies six tasks for the comprehensive construction of the East Lake Science and Technology Insurance Innovation Demonstration Zone: first, deepening innovation in science and technology (sci-tech) insurance products and services; second, creating a new institutional mechanism for insurance funds to invest in the sci-tech industry; third, innovating an organizational system for the sci-tech insurance market; fourth, advancing development of the sci-tech insurance market; fifth, refining the characteristics of sci-tech insurance through demonstration; and sixth, consolidating a foundation for the ongoing development of sci-tech insurance.

The Notice proposes policy support in three areas: one, reform of the financial support model for the technology insurance business; two, new subsidy and incentive policies for technology risk management and insurance institutions; and three, improving incentives and other policies for the cultivation of talents. The Notice introduces a number of new products and services in technology insurance, a set of mechanisms for insurance funds' participation in the development of technology enterprises, and a number of insurance institution and technology risk management platforms. It also gathers a group of high-end talents in technology risk management and insurance and builds a complete technology insurance market system and operational mechanism so that technology insurance can become an effective means of risk management for technological innovation.

Issuance of the Notice will further encourage the insurance industry to play a safeguarding role in the improvement of innovation and sci-tech research capabilities.

## 36. Contributing to the high-quality economic development of Anhui Province and its integrated development with the Yangtze River Delta

On October 12, 2020, the Anhui Supervisory Bureau of the CBIRC issued the *Guidance on Solidly Promoting the Integration of Anhui's Banking and Insurance Industry and Supporting Accelerated Integration into the Integrated Development of the Yangtze River Delta* (hereafter referred to as the "Guidance") to support Anhui Province's active participation in the integrated development of the Yangtze River Delta. The Guidance clarifies that, on the basis of establishing a sound mechanism for financial synergy that is adaptive to integrated development, the focus should go toward increasing financial support in key areas of sci-tech innovation and exploring innovative financial support for integrated development paths.

The Guidance focuses on industry leadership, guidance, and orientation, with an emphasis on the "two drives".

The first "drive" is to accelerate the integration of Anhui Province's banking and insurance industry into Yangtze River Delta integrated development. This involves establishing and improving a financial synergy mechanism that can adapt to integrated development, increasing the degree of financial services' regional co-location (i.e. same-city location), forming the initial experience of integrated financial development with Anhui characteristics, gradually building a multi-level, high-coverage, high-quality, differentiated and integrated system for banking and insurance development, and steadily improving the region's overall financial strength.

The second "drive" is to promote the banking and insurance industry as a pillar supporting Anhui's entry into the Yangtze River Delta's integrated development. To strengthen the optimal allocation of financial resources in the region and effectively connect industrial transformation and upgrading, the Guidance gives form to Anhui's mission — for its main indicators to realize faster growth than the national average, for significant loan growth in strategic emerging industries, scientific and technological innovation, advanced manufacturing and green industry areas, basic matching between the national credit to GDP ratio, a significantly higher premium income growth rate than the economic growth rate, and for gradually narrowing the gap between itself and Shanghai, Suzhou, and Zhejiang, reflecting the banking and insurance industry's greater role in building a new development pattern and accelerating construction of a better Anhui.

The Guidance stipulates the adherence to integrated development, a focus on improving the level of integrated development in the banking and insurance industry, and the direction of development in eight aspects — including accelerating institutional integration, strengthening capital supplements, innovating integrated operations, promoting credit cooperation, and improving co-location services.

The Guidance will lead the banking and insurance industry to assist in Anhui's high-quality economic development and support the province's participation in the integrated development of the Yangtze River Delta.

## 37. Improving risk diversification mechanism for major nuclear accident insurance, regulating the management of nuclear insurance catastrophe liability reserves

The *Nuclear Safety Law of the People's Republic of China* has been in effect since January 1,

2018. Nuclear power is developing rapidly in the country; China has already had the largest nuclear market under construction and is the world's third-largest producer of nuclear energy. With the rapid expansion of nuclear energy in power generation, nuclear safety has become an increasingly prominent issue. The government and party highly value nuclear safety, which is also regarded as a crucial component of national security.

Nuclear insurance is special risk insurance; it provides insurance services specifically for nuclear-related risks and is an effective means of diversifying risk coverage for major nuclear accidents. Under the *Nuclear Safety Act* (effective 2018), nuclear insurance is an integral component of nuclear safety and security. At the present stage, two main problems stand out in China's nuclear insurance operations: First, accumulated funds are insufficient for insurance companies to pay claims; profits from underwriting nuclear insurance premiums are converted into insurance company profits, thus failing to accumulate effectively. Second, management of nuclear insurance on a short-term, one-year business basis cannot accurately reflect the long-range risk characteristics of potential nuclear incidents. On October 30, 2020, the CBIRC, the Ministry of Finance, and the Ministry of Ecology and Environment jointly issued the *Measures for the Management of Nuclear Insurance Catastrophe Liability Reserves* (hereafter referred to as "the Measures"). The Measures aims to further improve the risk diversification mechanism for major nuclear accident insurance, to regulate the management of nuclear insurance catastrophe liability reserves, to promote healthy and sustainable nuclear insurance operations, and to better serve the development of nuclear power in China.

The Measures consists of six chapters and a total of 22 articles; these address the main issues in five areas — namely, the scope of the reserves' application, accrual criteria, conditions for use, daily management and supervision, and handling of the reserves for nuclear insurance catastrophe liability. First is the scope of application. The insurance business that provides coverage for property damage or third-party damage compensation during the transportation of nuclear equipment, nuclear materials, or radioactive waste associated with nuclear facilities must be included in the management of nuclear insurance catastrophe liability reserves. Second is the accrual criteria, specifying that the nuclear insurance catastrophe reserve is calculated as 75% of the nuclear insurance business's underwriting profit and is accrued from the annual net profit. The accrual criteria are generally in line with international specifications. Third, for the conditions of use, the nuclear insurance catastrophe reserves may be used when the estimated payout of the nuclear insurance industry's captive liability resulting from a single insurance incident exceeds RMB 300 million (or its equivalent in foreign currency) and the annual reported payout ratio of the nuclear insurance industry's captive liability exceeds 150%. At the same time, in terms of day-to-day management, it requires the permanent retention of the nuclear insurance catastrophe reserves and the inclusion of proceeds from the use of funds in reserve management; for supervision and handling, prohibitions are set for the reduction of underwriting profits by increasing costs or circumventing reserve provisioning and so on.

The Measures has had a positive impact by creating a long-term policy direction for the sound operation of nuclear insurance via the nuclear insurance catastrophe liability reserves. This move has enabled insurance companies to gradually accumulate nuclear insurance catastrophe liability reserves, strengthening their ability to cope with the risks of nuclear catastrophe. In addition, the nuclear insurance business has more standardized and scientific management practices, which solidify nuclear insurance's foundation, providing robust, long-term protection for nuclear energy risks. At the same time, insurance companies have contributed their industry experience to the protection of nuclear safety. Cooperation between the insurance and nuclear energy industries has drawn closer, forming a stronger, cross-industry foundation for a nuclear safety community better able to serve the development of the real economy.

**38. Accelerating the high-quality development of agricultural insurance in Anhui Province**

On May 29, 2019, General Secretary Xi Jinping presided over the eighth meeting of the Central Committee for Comprehensively Deepening Reform which deliberated and adopted the *Guidance on Accelerating the High-Quality Development of Agricultural Insurance*. Then, on September 19, the Ministry of Finance, the Ministry of Agriculture and Rural Affairs, the CBIRC, and the Forestry and Grassland Bureau issued a document to clarify the guiding ideology, basic principles, main objectives, and safeguard measures for the high-quality development of agricultural insurance, and requested the provinces to formulate respective work plans. In order to implement the relevant requirements, on October 26, 2020, the Anhui Provincial Department of Finance, Department of Agriculture and Rural Affairs, and Anhui Regulatory Bureau of the CBIRC jointly issued the *Notice on the Issuance of "Work Plan for Accelerating the High-Quality Development of Agricultural Insurance in Anhui Province"* (hereafter referred to as the "Notice").

The Notice puts forward a series of specific measures to effectively enhance the service capacity of agricultural insurance, continue to enhance its operating mechanisms, and continue to strengthen its infrastructure. The Notice proposes that by 2022, Anhui Province will have basically built a multi-level agricultural insurance system that is standardized, complete, sufficiently functional, and well-protected, compatible with the development stage of agricultural and rural modernization and able to meet farmers' risk protection needs, with a division of labor at all levels. The Notice's program consists of 17 articles across five sections. The first section covers general objectives. This section clearly defines the guiding ideology for the high-quality development of agricultural insurance in Anhui Province and identifies the main goals to be accomplished by 2022 and 2030. The second section concerns enhancing the capacity of agricultural insurance services. There are four paths in this regard: expanding insurance coverage, improving the level of insurance protection, broadening the supply of insurance products, and implementing people-friendly initiatives. The third section provides for the continuous optimization of agricultural insurance's operating mechanism. There are four requirements for said optimization: clarifying the boundary between the government and the market, improving the mechanism for catastrophe risk diversification, regulating the agricultural insurance market, and encouraging the development of "agricultural insurance plus". The fourth section is on strengthening agricultural insurance infrastructure. It covers four aspects — namely, improving the mechanism for formulating insurance terms and rates, establishing a mechanism for information sharing, optimizing the layout of insurance institutions, and improving the mechanism for risk prevention. The fifth section addresses the effective organization and implementation of the work. There are five areas of work to be strengthened and improved: organizational leadership, policy support, collaborative promotion, the development environment, and policy interpretation and publicity.

First, the Notice highlights goal-targeted leadership. It proposes stabilizing insurance coverage for the three main staple crops at approximately 90%, exceeding the central target by 20 percentage points, and maintaining a leading position. At the same time, the program increases the proportion target for special agricultural products insurance. The second highlight is coordination. Following the spirit of the four ministries and commissions' documents as well as the actual circumstances of Anhui Province, it proposes setting up a provincial agricultural insurance working group under the leadership of the Provincial Department of Finance; the Provincial Department of Agriculture and Rural Affairs, the Provincial Forestry Bureau, the Provincial Local Financial Supervision Bureau, the Anhui Banking and Insurance Supervision Bureau and the Provincial Meteorological Bureau shall also participate. According to the framework of the provincial financial work leading group, it will coordinate planning and promote the province's agricultural insurance work. The third highlight is policy supply. Making full use of the central government's policies, the Notice proposes measures to improve agricultural insurance policies in flood storage areas; comprehensively promote insurance for fattening pigs, reduce conditions and increase coverage, actively implement insurance for special agricultural products, work to incorporate advantageous varieties like greenhouse vegetables and tea into the scope of central government pilot financial subsidies, set reasonable insurance coverage standards and lower rates for forests, encourage the development of "agricultural insurance plus", and build a system of insurance products suited to the development of agriculture, rural areas, and farmers. The fourth highlight of the Notice is market regulation and risk prevention. There should be a sound mechanism in place for monitoring the use of agricultural insurance premium subsidy funds; meanwhile, daily supervision of insurance institutions should be strengthened. There should also be a scientific and standardized agricultural insurance operation mechanism featuring moderate competition, win-win cooperation, and smooth and orderly operation, as well as a service- and capability-oriented bidding and dynamic evaluation system for insurance institutions The establishment of a catastrophe insurance system should be explored, insurance institutions' main responsibility to prevent and resolve risks strengthened, and capacities for early warning, risk identification, and control enhanced.

**39. Strengthening the foundation for critical illness insurance and improving health insurance protections**

In China, critical illness insurance has undergone over 20 years of development; it is now one of the major insurance industries. Under the guidance of the former China Insurance Regulatory Commission (CIRC), the China Insurance Association and China Medical Doctor's Association jointly issued the *Code of Practice on the Use of Disease Definitions for Critical Illness Insurance* in 2007. The "Code" standardized the definition of "critical illnesses" in the insurance industry. In

2013, the China Society of Actuaries first compiled the *Table on the Experience Incidence of Critical Illnesses in China's Life Insurance Industry (2006–2010)*, which has played an important role in the development of critical illness insurance. However, rapid economic and social development and continuous innovations in medical technology have brought major changes to the disease spectrum and incidence of critical illnesses. Existing disease definitions and incidence tables, therefore, fail to meet the needs of the insurance industry's development and the diversified needs of consumers. To this end, the CBIRC has been guiding the industry to carry out relevant revision work since 2018. In 2020, the China Insurance Association and the China Medical Doctor's Association jointly revised and completed the *Specification for the Use of Disease Definitions for Critical Illness Insurance (2020 Revised Version)* and the China Society of Actuaries revised and completed the *Table on the Experience Incidence of Critical Illnesses in China's Life Insurance Industry (2020)*. Based on the above work, the CBIRC officially issued the *Notice on Matters Relating to the Use of the "Table on the Experience Incidence of Critical Illnesses in China's Life Insurance Industry (2020)"* (hereafter referred to as the "Notice") on November 5, 2020.

The Notice applies to long-term life insurance products that include liabilities for catastrophic illness. Its main elements are as follows.

First, it stipulates that the 2020 edition of the critical illness table is the minimum requirement for evaluation of the statutory liability reserve. The Notice requires insurers to use the 2020 edition of the critical illness table as the lower limit of evaluation basis for the incidence of critical illnesses when assessing the statutory liability reserve for life insurance products including critical illness insurance liabilities. In order to standardize the use of various tables, the Notice divides the applicable product categories into the 2007 edition-defined critical illness insurance, 2020 edition-defined critical illness insurance, 2020 edition-defined malignancy (severe) insurance, and 2020 edition-defined Guangdong-Hong Kong-Macao Greater Bay Area (GBA) exclusive critical illness insurance according to the time of filing or approval, the types of diseases covered, the sales regions, etc. It sets rules for determining lower limits in the assessment of incidences of major diseases and specifies that different tables should be used for different situations.

Second, the Notice clarifies the use of the 2020 edition critical illness table as a reference for product pricing. Insurers may use the 2020 edition of the critical illness table as a pricing guide for the incidence of major diseases when developing 2020 edition-defined critical illness insurance, 2020 edition-defined malignancy (severe) insurance, and 2020 edition-defined GBA exclusive critical illness insurance.

Third, the Notice establishes a dynamic revision mechanism for the table of empirical incidence of major diseases. The Chinese Society of Actuaries should coordinate updates to the table of incidence of major disease experience according to the development of major disease insurance. If the new incidence table is used to assess statutory liability reserves, the CBIRC must redetermine the relevant content and issue supporting regulatory provisions with respect to the new incidence table, and insurers must assess statutory liability reserves in accordance with the new incidence table and the corresponding usage norms.

To implement the Party Central Committee and State Council's strategic deployment for construction of the GBA, the CBIRC has also formulated a 2020 version of the regulatory rules defining critical illness insurance products exclusive to the GBA.

In terms of protecting consumers' interests, the Notice will helpfully consolidate bases for the development of critical illness insurance, improving the quality of the insurance product supply as well as health insurance's ability to complement the social security system.

**40. Rationalizing and strengthening insurance agent supervision**

An insurance agent is an organization or individual who receives entrusted by an insurance company that handles insurance business on that company's behalf and within the scope of that company's authorization. Insurance agents include professional agencies, part-time agencies, and individuals. As of today, 1,776 legal entities are professional insurance agencies, 32,000 are part-time insurance agencies, and there are 220,000 outlets, 9 million individual agents, and 3 million people working in insurance intermediaries. The concept of the insurance agent is clearly defined in the "Insurance Law", but at the level of departmental regulations and normative documents, the relevant requirements are widely scattered. To a certain extent, this has caused a lack of clarity in legal relations and regulation as well as inconsistencies in management standards for insurance agents.

To address the above-mentioned issues, consolidate recent years' achievements in chaos management, and improve access and exit management, the former CIRC has initiated and been drafting relevant systems since 2015, revising and consolidating documents such as the *Provisions on the Supervision of Insurance Professional Agencies*, the *Measures for the Supervision of Insurance Sales Practitioners* and the *Interim Measures for the Management of Insurance Part-Time Agencies* to rationalize legal relationships, unify regulatory yardsticks and form regulatory synergies. This work also encourages reform and innovation, strengthens agency self-control, and enhances supervision and management in the insurance intermediary market. On 12 November 2020, the CBIRC officially issued the *Regulations on the Supervision of Insurance Agents* (hereafter referred to as the "Regulations").

The Regulations consists of 7 chapters with 119 articles in total. It effectively brings professional and part-time insurance agencies and individual insurance agents into the scope for regulatory adjustments, establishes more unified basic regulatory standards and rules covering a large number of institutions and a wide range of personnel.

The Regulations' main requirements for insurance professional agencies are as follows: first, strengthen the management of market access. This involves strengthening the review of professional insurance agency shareholders and setting requirements for shareholders' ability to contribute capital as well as provisions for capital trusteeship, governance structure, internal control systems, and business models. The second is to strengthen branch control. In order to effectively prevent professional insurance agencies with weak internal control and high risk from indiscriminately establishing branches, specific conditions are set for branch establishment. Meanwhile, professional-agency legal entities' control responsibilities are further strengthened. The third is to rationalize the post-approval process. Professional insurance agencies are required to register relevant information in the regulatory information system promptly after obtaining a license; for those who fail to obtain a license or whose license has been canceled, they should promptly register the change and ensure that their name does not include the term "insurance agency". The fourth is to raise the minimum registered capital. Adjusting regional professional insurance agencies' minimum registered capital to RMB 20 million improves said agencies' ability to withstand risks, raises awareness of legal compliance, and promotes sound and long-term operations. The new standards must be strictly enforced for newly established regional agencies.

The Regulations adjusts requirements regarding professional liability insurance-related payments and security deposits, sets corresponding penalties for non-compliance in the sale of non-insurance financial products and the internet insurance business, and strengthens daily compliance management.

The Regulations' major requirements for part-time insurance agencies are as follows: first, a clarification of entry conditions stipulates the basic conditions for part-time insurance agencies' business entry. The Regulations clarifies that legal persons hold licenses and authorize branches' mode of operation. It also sets requirements for reporting matters and disclosing information and identifies persons responsible for insurance agency business. Second, the Regulations improves the withdrawal mechanism and stipulates the circumstances under which part-time insurance agencies can cancel their licenses in accordance with the law, as well as the process of business withdrawal. Third, the Regulations sets corresponding penalties for part-time agencies' violations in accordance with the law and within the scope of the regulatory authority.

The Regulations introduces the concept of "independent personal insurance agent" for the first time, indicating the trend of the market and orientation of supervisory leadership. The system relating to independent personal insurance agents will be developed and improved in accordance with practice. The Regulations introduces the concept of "independent personal insurance agent" for the first time. It includes insurance agency personnel engaged in the sale of insurance products, loss investigation, claims, and other businesses in the scope of its provisions, places restraints on their behavior, and institutes corresponding penalties for violations.

The Regulations abolishes licenses' three-year validity period, which is an important step in implementing "decentralization" and improving insurance supervision. Abolition of the license validity period will stimulate enterprises' vitality and accelerate the development of quality companies.

**41. Regulating insurance funds' direct investment in the equity of unlisted enterprises, increasing insurance funding support for various enterprises' equity financing**

In order to carry out the spirit of the executive meeting of the State Council, to increase insurance funding support for equity financing in the real economy, and to increase the proportion of direct social financing, the CBIRC formulated the *Notice on Matters Relating to Financial Equity Investment by Insurance Funds* (hereafter referred to as "the Notice") on November 12, 2020.

The Notice consists of ten articles. It removes sector restrictions on the financial equity investments made by insurance funds to enhance said funds' ability to serve the real economy via a "negative list plus positive guidance" mechanism. The main elements of the Notice are as follows: first is a clarification of the concept of "financial equity investment". In short, if the insurance institution and its related parties do not control or joint control over an invested enterprise, it is a financial equity investment. The second is a relaxation on the scope of the financial equity investment industry. The industry is no longer limited to insurance companies or non-insurance financial enterprises; it also covers specific insurance business-related enterprises such as those for pensions and medical care. This allows insurance institutions to independently choose the scope of their investment industries and expands options for insurance funds' equity investments. The third is the establishment of a negative list for financial equity investments. This list prohibits insurance funds from investing in enterprises of ten different statuses. At the same time, the Notice encourages insurance funds to conduct debt-to-equity projects based on the market and the rule of law. The fourth is a clarification on the nature of funds. Insurance institutions are now allowed to use their own funds and liability reserves to make financial equity investments. The fifth is a strengthening of risk control. Insurance institutions must assume primary responsibility for making financial equity investments, improve their equity investment management systems and capacity building, conduct prudent investment operations, and refrain from using equity investments for insider trading or the transfer of benefits. The sixth is a strengthening of supervision and management. The Notices stipulates that insurance institutions making financial equity investments must fulfill the relevant reporting obligations and that the CBIRC will take supervisory measures or impose corresponding administrative penalties if the investments are made in violation of the regulations.

While meeting the industry's asset allocation needs and diversifying investment risks, equity investments made by insurance funds should provide stable, long-term funds for the development of modern industrial systems — particularly for strategic emerging industries, etc. — and promote industrial integration, optimization, and upgrading.

### 42. Regulating the internet insurance business to effectively prevent risks

As the internet and related technologies continue to see in-depth use in the insurance industry, a new form of insurance sales and services has emerged to profoundly affect the industry landscape and industry regulation — the internet insurance business. The rapid development of the internet insurance business has revealed certain problems and potential risks, posing challenges to the industry and its regulation.

In order to regulate the internet insurance business, effectively prevent risks, protect consumers' legitimate rights and interests, and raise the level of service to society, people's livelihoods, and the real economy in the insurance industry, the CBIRC issued and implemented the *Measures for the Supervision of Internet Insurance Business* (hereafter referred to as "the Measures") on December 7, 2020.

The Measures consists of a total of 83 articles across 5 chapters — specifically, general provisions, basic rules of practice, special rules of practice, supervision and administration, and by-laws. Key regulations of the Measures include: first, a clarification of the essence of the internet insurance business, specifying system applications and convergence policy; second, requirements for internet insurance business operations, strengthening the principle of licensed operation, defining licensed institutions' self-operated online platforms, stipulating operating conditions for licensed institutions, and specifying prohibitions for of non-licensed institutions; third, regulations on the marketing and promotions of internet insurance, management requirements and standards of business conduct; fourth, regulation of the whole internet insurance after-sales service process and for improving consumer experience; fifth, regulation per operating entity type, with "special business rules" for internet insurance companies, insurance companies, insurance intermediaries, and internet enterprises acting as insurance agents, respectively, on the basis of "basic business rules"; sixth, innovations and improvements to regulatory policies and institutional measures, setting proper transitional arrangements for policy implementation.

The Measures implements the central government's requirements to strengthen financial supervision and prevent financial risks, helps regulate the internet insurance business, promotes supply-side reform of the insurance industry, and facilitates the industry's high-quality development.

**43. Actively responding to population aging, expanding pilots for long-term care insurance**

On December 15, 2020, according to the *Guidance of the National Health Insurance Administration Ministry of Finance on the Expansion of the Pilot Long-term Care Insurance System* (YBF [2020] No. 37), the General Office of the Tianjin Municipal People's Government issued the *Implementation Plan for the Pilot Long-term Care Insurance System in Tianjin* (hereafter referred to as the "Plan").

The Plan specifies basic policies regarding participation, financing, and payment of benefits, services, and settlements. First, it clarifies who is the insured. In the pilot phase, participants in Tianjin's basic employee medical insurance simultaneously participated in long-term care insurance. The program covered about 6.1 million people, including 3.9 million working employees (which included the flexibly employed) and approximately 2.2 million retirees. The next step will be to extend coverage widely to both urban and rural residents participating in basic medical insurance, eventually achieving full coverage. Second, the Plan clarifies participation contributions. In principle, work unit and individual contribution rates are respectively set at 0.16 percent of the employee's gross salary and the average salary of employees in the city for the previous year. During the pilot phase, employer contributions were RMB 120 per person per year and individual contributions were RMB 120 per person per year. Among these contributions, employers' were taken monthly from their basic medical insurance premiums (paid by employees), thus without increasing the burden on the work unit; individual contributions were taken monthly from the large medical assistance premiums paid by urban employees, without increasing the burden on the individual. Third, the Plan clarifies the procedure for disability assessments. Upon the Plan's implementation, disability assessments and their acceptance will be launched in batches. An assessment of disability will cost RMB 200 per person per time. If an assessment is unsuccessful, six months' interim is required before a new application can be submitted. Fourth, the Plan clarifies available reimbursement benefits. The long-term insurance care fund covers the costs of care services incurred by insured persons meeting the stipulated requirements. Among these, the insured who receive standardized institutional care services in designated nursing institutions are paid 70% by the long-term care insurance fund according to the standard of RMB 70 per person per day, or approximately RMB 18,000 per person per year; those who receive standardized home care services from designated nursing institutions are paid 75% by the long-term care insurance fund according to the standard of RMB 2,100 per person per month, or approximately RMB 19,000 per person per year. Fifth, the Plan offers detailed provisions on designated nursing institutions, disability assessment institutions, nursing service providers, methods for benefits settlement, and administration.

The Plan's introduction and piloting actively respond to population aging, actively address the issue of long-term care protection for the severely disabled, create a fairer and more sustainable social security system, and nurture and regulate the market for elderly care services.

**44. Standardizing the liability insurance business and protecting the rights and interests of involved parties**

As the development environment and its functions continue to be optimized, the scale of the liability insurance market has expanded and its operational capacity improved. Meanwhile, its roles of serving the economy, serving society, and assisting social governance have gradually taken shape. However, liability insurance's functioning and the healthy development of the market are highly dependent on the liability insurance market's degree of regulation. In the course of liability insurance's development, a small number of insurance companies offered some products to cover risks or losses like intentional acts, penalty fines, performance credit risks, definite losses, speculative risks, etc., crossing the boundary between liability insurance and other types of insurance (property damage, warranty, accident, etc.), which had a negative societal impact. On December 25, 2020, the CBIRC issued the *Measures for the Supervision of Liability Insurance Business* (the "Measures"), to go into effect on January 1, 2021.

For one, the Measures strictly limits the scope of liability insurance coverage; for another, it requires insurance companies to clarify the relationship between liability and three other categories of insurance so that types of insurance coverage can be determined in a reasonable manner. The Measures consists of 5 chapters with a total of 35 articles. Altogether there are four main objectives to the document.

The first is to standardize the boundaries of liability insurance coverage. In response to the expanding boundaries of liability insurance, the Measures tightens the range of coverage, making it clear that liability insurance shall cover the liability of the insured for damage caused to third parties in accordance with the law, and shall not cover damage from intentional acts, fines and penalties, performance credit risks, definite losses, speculative risks, and so on. In addition, the Measures requires insurance companies to clarify the relationship between liability insurance and property damage insurance, guarantee insurance, accident insurance, and other types of insurance, and determine proper types of insurance coverage as reasonable.

The second objective is to regulate the market's business conduct. In response to the current competition, which is unregulated, the Measures clarifies that there must be no failure to use approved or filed terms and rates, misleading sales, no unfair competition or illegal commitments, no material underwriting of financing credit risks in the form of underwriting the liability of guarantee institutions, etc., and no underwriting of motor vehicle third party liability under any primary or supplementary liability insurance other than motor vehicle insurance.

The third is to standardize insurance services. The Measures clarifies that insurance companies must provide services according to reason and necessity. Their main purpose should be to reduce the risk of paying claims; they may not arbitrarily expand the scope or content of insurance services. Insurance companies are required to develop systems related to insurance services and operate their accounts in strict accordance with accounting standards to ensure that data are accurate and true.

The fourth objective is to strengthen capital management. Requirements are further strengthened for business management, authorization systems, team building, business accounting, information systems, data statistics, risk management, and other aspects of the liability insurance business conducted by insurance companies.

Insurance market entities must strictly implement the Measures, continue to enrich liability insurance products, improve insurance services, enhance levels of protection, focus on major strategies, serve the real economy, and play an active role in social governance and conflict and dispute resolution, protecting and improving people's livelihoods.

### 45. Promoting decentralization and the effectiveness of supervision

In order to implement the Party Central Committee and the State Council decision on deepening the "management and administration" reform (to streamline administration and delegate power, improve regulation, and upgrade services), optimize the business environment, and promote the simplification of administration and decentralization and optimization of services in the banking and insurance industry, the General Office of the CBIRC issued the *Notice on Deepening the Reform of "Management and Administration" in the Banking and Insurance Industry and Optimizing the Business Environment* (hereafter referred to as the "Notice") on December 30, 2020.

The main elements of the Notice are as follows.

First is creating an open, fair, and equitable market access environment. The CBIRC and its dispatching agencies must set and implement administrative licenses according to the principles of openness, fairness, and impartiality and in strict accordance with the statutory authority, scope, conditions, and procedures, treating all types of market entities equally in accordance with the law, and taking initiative to publish the relevant administrative licensing provisions. The CBIRC strictly controls the scope of application for administrative licensing and makes specific provisions on administrative licensing matters set by the higher law.

The second is to continue simplifying and decentralizing banking and insurance supervision. The CBIRC and its dispatching agencies must, for the effective prevention of financial risks and safeguarding of financial security, optimally allocate regulatory resources and actively explore the cancellation or decentralization of administrative licensing matters that can instead be managed by innovative regulatory methods according to the principle of "canceling or decentralizing matters when they are ripe". For matters managed by administrative licensing, requirements on reducing links, materials, and time limits should be followed to continuously optimize approval services and efficiency, reducing the burden on market entities. Effective February 1, 2021, qualification examinations are abolished for directors, supervisors (insurance industry), and senior managers in the banking and insurance industry. Following the abolition of the examinations, the CBIRC and its dispatching agencies should, in order to verify qualifications for an appointment, examine whether the proposed appointee meets the basic conditions to perform the duties of the post through a review of application materials, inspection, and interview. At the same time, it should strengthen its performance supervision of directors, supervisors (insurance industry), and senior managers at banking and insurance institutions through on-site inspections and off-site supervision.

The third is enhancing the effectiveness of post-event supervision. Canceled or delegated administrative licensing matters should not be released into a management vacuum or released and then ignored; on the contrary, in the aftermath, the risk assessment should be stepped up and supervision increased to ensure that they are "released, accepted, and managed". The interface between approval and supervision needs to be strengthened; there needs to be clearer targets and scopes and better rules and standards of supervision, and the elimination of blind spots and vacuums. When it comes to small and medium-sized corporate banks establishing cross-regional institutions, pre-event communication needs to be strengthened, effective working arrangements explored, upward and downward linkage, and information sharing enhanced to form a synergy of work and improve the quality and efficiency of supervision. The institution's main responsibilities should be consolidated, violations should be more rigorously investigated and sanctioned, and the cost of violations should be raised. In addition, the CBIRC and its dispatching agencies should make full use of the internet, big data, and other technical means to promote "internet plus supervision" and credit supervision while enhancing supervision's overall effectiveness. Banking and insurance institutions need to improve their data governance, collection and sharing of regulatory information and correlation/integration, risk tracking and early warning systems, and levels of regulatory accuracy and intelligence.

The fourth is improving the quality and effectiveness of banking and insurance institutions' financial services. Banking and insurance institutions should continue to improve the quality and effectiveness of their financial services for private, small, and micro enterprises, while also improving the market financing environment. Banking institutions' conditions for granting credit must be reasonable and cannot discriminate against private enterprises and SMEs. In addition, banks and insurance institutions should assume the major responsibility for consumer rights protection, strengthen institutional mechanisms for consumer rights protection, and safeguard financial consumers' legitimate rights and interests. A mechanism for consumer rights protection review should be quickly established, while the internal assessment mechanism for consumer rights protection and the mechanism for information disclosure should be improved. Institutions should actively engage in financial literacy publicity and education, and do satisfactory work handling consumer complaints, thereby improving consumers' sense of access.

### (II) The Effects of Market Development Policies in China's Banking Industry in 2020

In 2020, the insurance industry withstood and actively responded to the new coronavirus epidemic and its effects. Risk resilience was improved throughout multiple channels; assets and liabilities and business steadily increased; quality and effectiveness in service to the real economy continued to improve; the industry made positive progress in reform and opening up.

**1. Overall operation of the insurance market**

In FY2020, the insurance industry's original insurance premium income came to RMB 4,525.734 billion, up 6.13% YOY, with a growth rate 1.03 percentage points lower than the first three quarters and 6.04 percentage points lower than the same period of the previous year (see Figure 1). Claims and benefits expenses were RMB 1,390.710 billion, up 7.86% YOY, with a growth rate of 1.72 percentage points higher than the previous three quarters and 3.01 percentage points higher than the same period of the previous year.

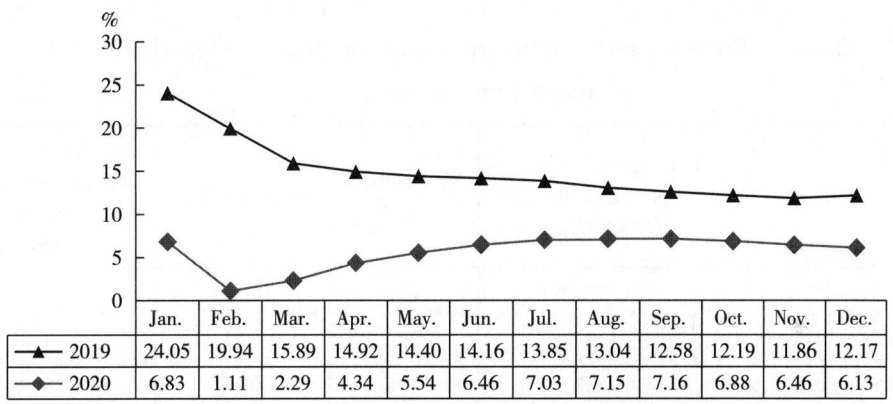

**Figure 1  Cumulative Premium Income Growth Rate by Month, 2019–2020**

To analyze the situation by business, original insurance premium income for the general insurance business was RMB 1,192.858 billion, up 2.40% YOY, with a growth rate 4.11 percentage points lower than the previous three quarters and 5.77 percentage points lower than the same period of the previous year; claims took in RMB 695.479 billion, up 6.97% YOY, with a growth rate of 0.68 percentage point lower than the previous three quarters and 3.28 percentage points lower than the same period of the previous year. The life insurance business' original premium income came to RMB 2,398.193 billion, up 5.40% YOY, the growth rate increasing 0.56 percentage point compared with the first three quarters and decreasing by 4.40 percentage points compared with the same period of the previous year; payout was RMB 371.511 billion, down 0.75% YOY, the decline narrowing by 2.65 percentage points compared with the first three quarters and 13.95 percentage points compared with the same period of the previous year. The original premium income of the health insurance business was RMB 817.271 billion, up 15.66% YOY, with a growth rate 1.75 percentage points lower than the first three quarters and 14.04 percentage points lower than the same period of the previous year; claims and benefits were RMB 292.116 billion, up 24.23% YOY, with a growth rate 4.63 percentage points higher than the first three quarters and 10.58 percentage points lower than the same period of the previous year. The accident insurance business' original insurance premium income came to RMB 117.411 billion, down 0.09% YOY, narrowing 1.43 percentage points from the first three quarters, demonstrating a growth rate of 9.26% compared with the same period of the previous year; claims came to RMB 31.604 billion, up 6.17% YOY, the growth rate increasing 0.40 percentage point from the first three quarters and down 5.02 percentage points from the same period of the previous year.

When analyzing by company, it is found that property insurers achieved an original premium income of RMB 1358.369 billion, up 4.36% YOY (see Table 1), a growth rate 4.07 percentage points lower than the previous three quarters and 6.36 percentage points lower than the same period of the previous year; claims expense came to RMB 788.042 billion, up 8.27% YOY, with a growth rate 0.31 percentage point lower than the previous three quarters and 4.49 percentage points lower than the same period of the previous year.

Table 1  Property and casualty insurance companies' original premium income by insurance type

| Insurance | Original insurance premium income (RMB 100 million) | YOY Growth (%) | Proportion (%) | Increase in percentage over the same period of the previous year (percentage points) |
|---|---|---|---|---|
| Total | 13,583.69 | 4.36 | 100.00 | — |
| Business property insurance | 490.26 | 5.64 | 3.61 | 0.04 |
| Home property insurance | 90.79 | −0.47 | 0.67 | −0.03 |
| Motor vehicle insurance | 8,244.75 | 0.69 | 60.70 | −2.21 |
| Engineering insurance | 138.41 | 17.45 | 1.02 | 0.11 |
| Liability insurance | 901.13 | 19.62 | 6.63 | 0.85 |
| Credit insurance | 204.88 | 2.46 | 1.51 | −0.03 |
| Guaranty insurance | 688.57 | −18.38 | 5.07 | −1.41 |
| Hull insurance | 57.71 | 3.96 | 0.42 | 0.00 |
| Cargo insurance | 135.96 | 4.49 | 1.00 | 0.00 |
| Special risks insurance | 72.16 | 4.75 | 0.53 | 0.00 |
| Agricultural insurance | 814.93 | 21.18 | 6.00 | 0.83 |
| Health insurance | 1,114.21 | 32.60 | 8.20 | 1.75 |
| Accident insurance | 540.90 | 2.72 | 3.98 | −0.06 |
| Other | 89.02 | 38.91 | 0.66 | 0.16 |

Personal insurance companies brought in an original premium income of RMB 3,167,364 billion, up 6.90% YOY (see Table 2), with a growth rate 0.25 percentage point higher than the previous three quarters and 5.92 percentage points lower than the same period of the previous year; claims and benefits totaled RMB 602.659 billion, up 7.33% YOY, with a growth rate 4.02 percentage points higher than the previous three quarters 3.89% lower than the same period of the previous year.

Table 2  Personal insurance companies' original premium income by insurance type

| Insurance | Original insurance premium income (RMB 100 million) | YOY Growth (%) | Proportion (%) | Increase in percentage over the same period of the previous year (percentage points) |
| --- | --- | --- | --- | --- |
| Total | 31,673.64 | 6.90 | 100.00 | — |
| Life insurance | 23,981.92 | 5.40 | 75.72 | −1.08 |
| General life insurance | 12,545.94 | 19.79 | 39.61 | 4.26 |
| Life insurance dividend | 11,327.18 | −6.90 | 35.76 | −5.30 |
| Investment-linked insurance | 4.33 | −1.57 | 0.01 | 0.00 |
| Universal insurance | 104.47 | −4.28 | 0.33 | −0.04 |
| Accident insurance | 633.21 | −2.37 | 2.00 | −0.19 |
| Health insurance | 7,058.50 | 13.38 | 22.29 | 1.27 |

The insurance amount was RMB 8,709.91 trillion, up 34.62% YOY; the number of new policies was 52.634 billion, up 6.25% YOY. The combined assets of property and life insurance companies amounted to RMB 22.32 trillion, up 15.95% from the beginning of the year.

**2. Insurance market development characteristics**

(1) The insurance market is generally stable with a continually optimized business structure

I. "Comprehensive auto insurance reform" underway, general insurance companies slowing growth to improve quality

2020 witnessed two inflection points in property and casualty insurance companies' premium growth — one a significant drop in revenue growth early in the year due to the epidemic outbreak. February's cumulative premium growth rate was 0.62%, the lowest of the year and down 13.07 percentage points from the same period the previous year. The growth rate started to pick up again in March and gradually normalized. The cumulative premium growth rate reached its annual peak in September, achieving 8.43%. The other inflection point marks implementation of "comprehensive auto insurance reform". Premium growth rate slowed after September, but the price cuts in auto insurance benefited people's livelihoods, and property insurance companies' annual premium income increased by 4.36%, down 6.36 percentage points compared with the same period of the previous year.

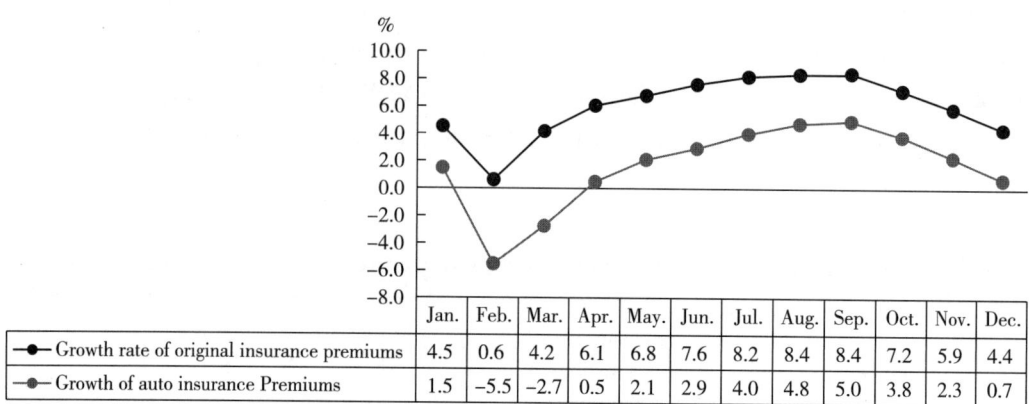

Figure 2  Cumulative Premium Income Growth Rate by Month for Property Casualty Insurers, 2020

Comprehensive auto insurance reform was officially implemented in September; the overall car insurance business saw "lower prices, more insurance, and better quality". For the whole year, auto insurance premiums increased 0.69% YOY, down 3.83 percentage points from the same period the previous year. In the fourth quarter, auto insurance premiums fell to a decrease of 10.43% from an increase of 5.96% in the same period the previous year. In October, November, and December specifically, car insurance premiums respectively fell by 6.50%, 11.35%, and 12.62% YOY, the rate of decline gradually increasing. Despite the slowdown in market size, coverage increased in the auto insurance business, better meeting consumers' needs for risk protection. Auto insurance provided RMB 32.380 trillion for risk coverage over the year, up 28.32% YOY, 8.87 percentage points higher than the same period the previous year.

II. Rapid growth in the non-auto business and more comprehensive general coverage

Property and casualty insurance companies maintained a high growth rate for non-auto insurance premiums, up 10.58% YOY, with health insurance, agricultural insurance, liability insurance, and engineering insurance growing rapidly — their respective growth at 32.60%, 21.18%, 19.62%, and 17.45%. The short-term health insurance business drove 2.10 percentage points of industry growth. The non-vehicle insurance market share for the year was 39.30%, up 2.21 percentage points from the same period the previous year. New companies are intensifying their non-auto insurance businesses, with some companies accelerating their transformation. Among the 84 general insurance companies, 32 have a non-auto insurance original premium income share higher than 20%, which is eight more companies than in 2018 prior to pilot implementation of the commercial auto insurance independent pricing reform.[①]

III. Life insurers' value business improves, begins to show signs of transformation

At the beginning of the year, the COVID-19 pandemic outbreak had a significant impact on

---

① This includes new companies formed since 2017.

life insurance companies with late "open door" plans. Throughout the year, life insurance companies' premium growth rate showed a trend of initial growth followed by stabilization.

In 2020, life insurance companies earned RMB 3,167.364 billion in premiums, up 6.90% YOY. Looking at the types of insurance, general life insurance was the main driver of industry growth. For the whole year, general life insurance achieved a premium income of RMB 1,254.594 billion, up 19.79% YOY, 4.96 percentage points higher than the same period of the previous year, contributing 6.99 percentage points to the industry's growth. From the perspective of business structure, although new business growth was lower than expected for the year (again, due to the impact of the epidemic) — annual new business premium income was at RMB 1,258.651 billion, down 2.08% YOY — the industry held to recent years' path of high-quality development, the proportion of value business increasing, with strengthened risk resilience and renewal premiums driving the industry to achieve growth. Annual renewal premium income was RMB 1,908.713 billion, up 13.79% YOY, and the effects of business structure optimization began to show. In terms of channels, premium income from the banking and postal channels achieved RMB 1,010.816 billion, up 12.61% YOY, an increase of 0.86 percentage point compared with the same period of the previous year. Premium income from individual agency channels achieved RMB 1,796.596 billion, up 4.27% YOY. The growth rate dropped by 7.23 percentage points compared with the same period of the previous year due to the impact of the epidemic and difficulties in offline business development.

IV. Steady, rapid growth and major social benefits from health insurance

The health insurance business developed rapidly in 2020, its premium income reaching RMB 817.271 billion for the year, up 15.66% YOY. This comes close to the volume of the auto insurance business, making health insurance the third-largest category in the market afterlife and auto insurance. In particular, property and casualty insurance companies health insurance business has maintained a trend of high growth over recent years, its annual premium income exceeding RMB 100 billion to reach RMB 111.421 billion, an increase of 32.60% YOY — the growth rate breaking 30% for four consecutive years from 2017. Personal insurance companies' health insurance business brought in RMB 705.850 billion, up 13.38% YOY, continuing to maintain a high growth rate but slowing down by 14.22 percentage points compared with the same period of the previous year. The business specifically includes short-term health insurance, with a premium income of RMB171.905 billion, up 11.11% YOY (slowing down by 19.65 percentage points compared with the same period of the previous year), and long-term health insurance with a premium income of RMB 533.945 billion, up 14.13% YOY (slowing down by 12.46 percentage points compared with the same period of the previous year). Since the November 2020 redefinition of critical illness insurance, life insurance companies have introduced services such as the option to purchase new or old terms and conditions prior to the date changes would take effect, allowing consumers to obtain better services and companies to achieve a win-win situation in 2021 "open door" plans.

For the whole year, health insurance provided risk coverage at RMB 1,833.11 trillion — an increase of 50.26% YOY — and payout and benefits expenses of RMB 292.116 billion — an increase of 24.23% YOY. Commercial health insurance played an active role in serving a healthy China, improving the health insurance system, and supporting the healthcare industry.

(2) The insurance market holds the bottom line of risk prevention and serves inclusive finance

The insurance industry is running soundly, with the solvency ratio remaining in a reasonable range. At the end of the fourth quarter, the average consolidated solvency margin of 178 insurers was 246.3% and the average core solvency margin was 234.3%.

The insurance industry performed its function of providing guarantees, with risk coverage of RMB 8,709.91 trillion for the year — an increase of 34.62% YOY — including RMB 7,511.89 trillion for property and casualty insurance companies (an increase of 39.92% YOY), and RMB 1198.02 trillion for personal insurance companies (an increase of 8.79% YOY). The insurance industry effectively contributed to Inclusive Finance and the three tough battles; RMB 4.13 trillion of agricultural risk coverage was provided for the year, up 8.57% YOY; RMB 59.252 billion was spent on agricultural insurance claims, up 12.25% YOY; RMB 39.511 billion was provided in liability insurance claims, up 15.64% YOY; and RMB 69.750 billion was provided in credit and guarantee insurance claims, up 42.31% YOY.

(3) The insurance market promotes openness; foreign enterprises are developing well

The insurance industry has steadily expanded its openness to the outside world. Since 2018, the first wholly foreign-owned insurance holding company Allianz (China) Insurance Holdings — and wholly foreign-owned life insurance company — AIA Life Insurance Co. — were approved for establishment. In 2020, the foreign-invested insurance market maintained its trend of growth, achieving an original premium income of RMB 352.444 billion for the year, an increase of 12.43% YOY, exceeding that of Chinese insurance companies by 6.80 percentage points, including RMB 317.672 billion in premium income from foreign-invested life insurance companies (an increase of 13.27% YOY) and RMB 34.772 billion in premium income from foreign-invested general insurance companies (an increase of 5.31% YOY). The market share of foreign insurers was 7.79%, an increase of 0.62 percentage point YOY. In both Beijing and Shanghai, foreign insurers have a market share exceeding 20%.

(4) Large insurers are generally stable, though small and medium-sized companies show discrepancies

Of the 88 property and casualty insurance companies, 48 grew faster than the property insurance industry average. Of the 91 personal insurance companies, 62 grew faster than the personal insurance industry average (see Table 3).

Table 3  Distribution of insurance company premium growth rates, FY2020

| Property and casualty insurance companies | | | | | | |
|---|---|---|---|---|---|---|
| Growth rate range | Negative growth | 0-4.36% | 4.36%-60% | 60%-100% | Over 100 percent | New companies |
| Companies | 31 | 8 | 46 | 2 | 0 | 1 |

Continued

| Personal insurance companies | | | | | | |
|---|---|---|---|---|---|---|
| Growth rate range | Negative growth | 0-6.90% | 6.90%-60% | 60%-100% | Over 100 percent | Other companies |
| Companies | 15 | 10 | 47 | 5 | 10 | 4 |

Notes: 1. [4.36%] is the average growth rate for property and casualty insurers; the growth rate is not calculable for newly added major property and casualty insurance companies.

2. [6.90%] is the average growth rate for personal insurance companies; the premium growth rate is not calculable for the four pension insurance companies with no insurance business.

The "old three"[1] property and casualty insurance companies showed steady development, with an original premium income of RMB 864.590 billion for the year, up 3.57% YOY, and an industry share of 63.65%, down 0.49 percentage point from the same period last year, while the original premium income of small and medium-sized property and casualty insurance companies[2] was RMB 493.779 billion, up 5.77% YOY. Against the double impact of the epidemic and "auto insurance reform", small and medium-sized property insurance companies demonstrated different levels of risk resilience and capacities for transformation, their business conditions differing significantly. Fifty-six companies had positive premium growth, including 26 companies whose growth rate was higher than it had been the same period last year, while 31 companies had negative premium growth[3], including 28 companies whose rate of decline expanded[4].

The "old seven"[5] personal insurance companies achieved a premium income of RMB 1,841.509 billion, up 3.33% YOY and accounting for 58.14% of the market, down 2.01 percentage points from the same period last year. Small and medium-sized personal insurance companies[6] achieved a premium income of RMB 1,325.855 billion, a YOY increase of 12.30%; 72 companies' premiums increased, among which 28 saw faster growth than they had in the same period the previous year, while 15 companies' premiums showed negative growth, including 11 companies whose rate of decline expanded.

(5) Property insurance underwriting profits are under pressure, but personal insurance profits show steady growth

Property and casualty insurers' businesses came under pressure, with a combined cost ratio of 100.90%, up 0.92 percentage point YOY. Among them, the credit insurance and auto insurance businesses were under particularly obvious pressure, partly due to the impact of the epidemic. Some company's and individuals' repayment abilities weakened, their credit and guarantee insurance

---

[1] The "old three" are PICC, Ping An Property & Casualty Insurance, and China Pacific Property Insurance.

[2] Property and casualty insurance companies other than the "old three".

[3] This includes companies whose premium income growth changed from negative to positive.

[4] This includes companies whose premium income growth changed from positive to negative.

[5] The "old seven" are China Life Insurance, Ping An Life Insurance, Pacific Life Insurance, New China Life Insurance, Taiping Life, Taikang Life Insurance, and PICC Life Insurance.

[6] Life insurance companies other than the "old seven".

underwriting margins at -22.52% and -15.05% respectively. Another source of pressure was the "comprehensive auto insurance reform", which caused a decline in auto insurance underwriting profits. For the year, said profit came to RMB 7.957 billion (down 23.19% YOY), with a profit margin of 1.01%, down 0.74 percentage point from the previous three quarters.

Personal insurance companies' resumed steady profit growth, estimated profits reaching RMB 277.210 billion, up 15.68% YOY, an increase of 11.54 percentage points from the first three quarters. Meanwhile, personal insurers improved their continuity of operations, with a surrender rate of 2.39% for the year, down 2.58 percentage points YOY.

(6) Fund use is becoming more efficient and investment income shows significant growth

The allocation structure of insurance funds was optimized in 2020, and by the end of the year, the balance of the industry's capital utilization was RMB 21.68 trillion, up 17.02% from the beginning of the year, with bonds accounting for the highest percentage at 36.59%, up 2.03 percentage points from the beginning of the year. The insurance industry took full advantage of long-term stable funds and further improved its investment capacity. Under the capital market's stabilizing influence and with the introduction of a series of policies such as the *Interim Measures for the Management of Insurance Asset Management Products*, the average return rate on capital utilization was 5.41%, 0.47 percentage point higher than that of the same period the previous year.

**(III) Insurance market development outlook for 2021**

2021 brings with it pressure and challenges, but the insurance industry retains hope and holds on to opportunities.

The first area posing opportunities is policy orientation. The *Outline of the Fourteenth Five-Year Plan of the National Economic and Social Development of the People's Republic of China and Vision 2035* uses the word "protection" 134 times and "insurance" 35 times. It includes clear recommendations for agricultural insurance, science, and technology insurance, environmental liability insurance, three-pillar pension insurance, and long-term care insurance, and proposes measures for the steady opening up of the financial sector, including insurance.

Second, there is a new landscape driving the development of insurance. The formation of a new development pattern with the domestic cycle as the mainstay and international dual cycles mutually promoting each other will accelerate, bringing new potential into play for domestic insurance demand and assisting the development of the insurance industry.

The third is digital transformation. Recurrent outbreaks of the ongoing pandemic have put pressure on the insurance industry's traditional offline presence, but the industry has accelerated its digital transformation and broadened its online channels to improve operational efficiency and its ability to serve consumers.

Fourth, health awareness has increased across the entire population. Under the long-term guidance of the Healthy China Strategy and the "alarm" sounded by the pandemic, the whole population has improved its level of health awareness and the demand for insurance products has increased.

Fifth, business transformation has accelerated. The "comprehensive auto insurance reform" and other measures have deepened reform and accelerated the industry's high-quality development. Some insurance companies have made the U-turn of business transformation; although it has added pressure in the short term, in the long term it will be conducive to insurers' diversification and ability to meet people's multi-level insurance needs.

In short, the insurance market is expected to develop in a generally stable manner over 2021.

## IV. Bond Market Development Policy[①]

China's bond market continued to develop effectively in 2020. It had secured a significant increase in the scale of issuance, an increasing market transaction activity, and some remarkable achievements in opening to the outside world; product and mechanism innovation were continuously strengthened, as was standardized management, and further improvements were made in the bond market's function of serving the real economy.

### (I) Overview of market development

First of all, in 2020, the bond index initially rose and then fell. The ChinaBond Total Wealth Index rose sharply at the beginning of the year reaching its highest point of the year — 202.1 points — at the end of April, then gradually fell and stabilized. Overall, the index rose slightly over the year, rom 192.1 points at year's start to 198.0 points at year's end, up by 3.1%. The Shanghai Clearing House (SCH) Interbank Debenture Bond Composite Index was basically in sync, initially rising, then falling, and then rising again, increasing from 126.8 points at year's start to 131.0 points at year's end, up by 3.3%. SSE Corporate Bond Index showed an overall upward trend, from 202.9 at year's start to 211.5 at year's end, an increase of 4.3%.

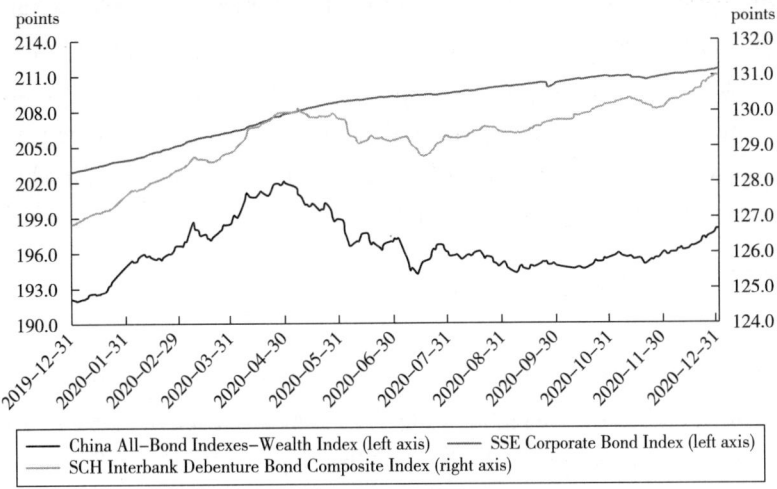

**Figure 1  Bond price indexes in 2020**

(Source: China Central Depository & Clearing Co., Ltd. (CCDC), Shanghai Clearing House, Shanghai Stock Exchange)

---

① Author: Rong Yihua, Deputy Director of Financial Market Management Department, PBC Shanghai Head Office.

Second, bond issuance increased substantially over the year. China's bond market issued RMB 57.3 trillion of bonds of all varieties in 2020, a year-over-year (YOY) increase of 26.5%; the growth rate increased by 23.4%. The national interbank bond market, for example, issued RMB 48.7 trillion in bonds, up by 27.9% YOY, accounting for 85.0% of total bond market issuance; the exchange bond market, meanwhile, issued RMB 8.6 trillion, up by 18.2% YOY and accounting for 15.0% of total bond market issuance. The top three most issued bonds were interbank negotiable certificates of deposit (NCDs), corporate debenture bonds, and financial bonds, with respective issuances of RMB 19.0 trillion, 12.9 trillion, and 9.3 trillion.

Third, transaction volume rose, but the rate of growth decreased. In 2020, the bond market accumulated RMB 253.0 trillion of transactions, up by 16.5% YOY; the growth rate fell by 22.1%. In terms of transaction volume, the interbank bond market achieved RMB 232.8 trillion, up by 11.5% YOY, accounting for 92.0% of the national interbank bond market; meanwhile, the exchange bond market achieved RMB 20.2 trillion, up by 141.6% YOY and accounting for 8.0% of the national bond market. As seen from the bond structure of the interbank bond market, the top three bonds were policy-based financial bonds, NCDs, and government bonds, respectively accounting for 36.7%, 20.1%, and 19.3%.

Fourth, 2020 saw the scale of bondholding by foreign institutional investors increase significantly. By the end of the year, a total of 905 foreign institutional investors had entered China's interbank bond market, making for an increase of 109 YOY. Foreign institutions held RMB 3.25 trillion in bonds, a YOY increase of RMB 1.05 trillion, or 47.7%, accounting for 3.2% of all bond trusteeship in the interbank market. Among these, RMB 1.88 trillion was held in government bonds, a net increase of RMB 570.8 billion or 167%.

Fifth, 2020 saw fewer instances of default in the bond market, but a higher amount involved in defaults. Throughout the year, 54 companies defaulted on 168 bonds in total. These figures were down by 23 and 15 respectively from the previous year, but the total default amount came to RMB 135.6 billion, up by 7.1%. Among the 54 defaulting companies, 36 were private enterprises (involving 84 bonds), with a default scale of RMB 54.37 billion, accounting for 43.5%, and 11 were state-owned enterprises (51 bonds), with a default scale of RMB 56.65 billion, accounting for 45.3%.

### (II) Main policies issued

#### 1. On market innovation

(1) Anti-epidemic bonds were introduced, including anti-epidemic government bonds, anti-epidemic financial bonds, and corporate bonds. In January 2020, the People's Bank of China (PBOC), the Ministry of Finance of the PRC, China Banking and Insurance Regulatory Commission (CBIRC), China Securities Regulatory Commission (CSRC) and the State Administration of Foreign Exchange (SAFE) jointly issued the *Notice on Further Strengthening Financial Support for COVID-19 Prevention and Control*, which emphasizes improving the efficiency of services like bond issuance and clarifies the establishment of a green channel for the registration and issuance of financial bonds, asset-backed securities (ABS), and corporate debenture bonds issued by financial

institutions and enterprises primarily raising funds for areas severely impacted by the epidemic. In 2020, China successfully issued RMB 1 trillion in anti-epidemic government bonds. These were mainly used for local infrastructure, covering 12 types of projects including for public health system construction, major epidemic prevention and control system construction, and industrial chain transformation and upgrading. There were also subsidies issued for local epidemic prevention and control expenditures (including rent subsidies, loan interest subsidies for key enterprises, interest subsidies for venture guarantee loans, subsidies for supporting enterprises and stabilizing posts, basic living allowance for people in need, and other anti-epidemic expenses). In 2020, China Development Bank, the Import-Export Bank of China and the Agricultural Development Bank of China issued RMB 64.5 billion in financial bonds for epidemic prevention and control, and the raised funds mainly went towards credit expansion in areas related to epidemic prevention and control. In particular, "Epidemic Prevention and Control ABS" propelled anti-epidemic financing. In 2020, "Epidemic Prevention and Control ABS" issued 44 bonds with a total scale of RMB 75 billion. This played a positive role in epidemic prevention and control while ensuring the smooth workings of production and operation. Altogether 110 corporate bonds for epidemic prevention and control were issued, totaling RMB 107.8 billion, which helped a number of companies ease liquidity pressure during the epidemic, and played a positive role in the resumption of production resumption and economic recovery.

(2) Bonds were also issued for poverty relief. In April 2020, China Development Bank issued RMB 11 billion in poverty relief bonds to the interbank bond market and the OTC market of commercial banks, mainly to issue poverty relief loans to seriously impoverished areas for major infrastructure, rural infrastructure, and industrial poverty alleviation. A total of 33 poverty relief corporate bonds, worth RMB 19.6 billion, were issued in impoverished areas over ten provinces/municipalities including Guizhou, Sichuan, Chongqing, Hunan, and Jiangxi.

(3) Policy-based financial bonds introduced a number of innovations in 2020. Over the year, the Agricultural Development Bank of China successively issued a variety of innovative bonds, such as for poverty alleviation, ecological protection, flood prevention and relief, western development, epidemic prevention and control, and consumption-based poverty alleviation, putting the bond market's financing function to full use as a way to support the implementation of national strategies. Aiming to improve bond markets' connectivity, China Development Bank issued green financial bonds to address climate change in multiple markets simultaneously. The Export-Import Bank of China innovatively issued themed bonds supporting new areas around ports with flexible bidding and also improved the issuance pricing mechanism.

(4) Green financial bond innovation continued to advance throughout the year. In April 2020, the Agricultural Development Bank of China issued "Liang Shan" ecological environmental protection financial bonds; in August, the green bonds of Chinese-funded banks issued by China Construction Bank debuted on the Nasdaq Dubai stock exchange; in September, the Bank of China successfully issued overseas the first dual-currency blue bond for Chinese-funded and international commercial institutions.

(5) Special bonds were introduced to supplement the capital of small to mid-sized banks. In December 2020, the Guangdong Provincial People's Government issued the country's first special bond to support the development of small and mid-sized banks; since then, many provinces have successfully issued special bonds to help enhance the ability of small- and medium-sized banks to guard against risks and serve the real economy. In addition, the issuing bodies of perpetual bonds were extended to cover small- and mid-sized banks. More than 30 small- to mid-sized banks issued perpetual bonds; private banks also issued perpetual bonds.

(6) Special enterprise bonds were introduced for the new urbanization of county seats. In August 2020, the General Office of the National Development and Reform Commission (NDRC) issued the *Guidelines on the Issuance of Special Enterprise Bonds for the New Urbanization in County Seats*, which introduced special enterprise bonds for the new urbanization of county seats. Its aim is to accelerate improvements to weak links in the urbanization of county seats and make full use of the active role corporate bonds play in the new urbanization of county seats.

**2. On bond issuance**

(1) A registration system was fully implemented for the issuance of enterprise bonds and corporate bonds. On March 1, 2020, a new *Securities Law of the People's Republic of China* officially took effect. NDRC made it clear that the system for issuing enterprise bonds had changed from an approval system to a registration system, while the CSRC clarified that the public issuance of corporate bonds would adopt a registration system. Both, meanwhile, put forward relevant requirements for bond issuance conditions and information disclosure. In July, China Central Depository & Clearing Co., Ltd. (CCDC) issued a supporting Rules for the Acceptance of Enterprise Bonds (Trial), officially launched the Enterprise Bonds Acceptance and Audit System, and jointly issued — with National Association of Financial Market Institutional Investors (NAFMII) — the *Rules for the Examination and Approval of Enterprise Bonds (Trial)* and the Questions and Answers about the Registration and Issuance of Enterprise Bonds. In November, the Shanghai Stock Exchange formulated the *No.1 Applicable Guide on the Examination and Approval Rules for the Issuance and Listing of Corporate Bonds at SSE — Application Documents and Preparation* and the *No.2 Applicable Guide on the Examination and Approval Rules for the Issuance and Listing of Corporate Bonds at SSE — Special Corporate Bonds* to regulate examinations and approvals for the issuance and listing of corporate bonds and applications for the issuance and listing of special corporate bonds.

(2) The issuance of local government bonds was standardized. In December 2020, the Ministry of Finance issued a *Notice on Printing and Distributing the 'Administrative Measures for the Issuance of Local Government Bonds'*. This document comprehensively regulates the issuance and administration of local bonds in terms of issuance amount and duration, as well as the credit rating, information disclosure, bond issuance and trusteeship. The *Administrative Measures for the Issuance of Local Government Bonds* clearly states that local financial departments shall issue local government bonds within the State Council-approved quotas; they shall reasonably determine the bond duration structure according to factors such as project duration, financing cost, matured debts distribution, investor demand, and bond market conditions. The document also reiterates relevant

provisions on local bonds' information disclosure.

(3) Supplementary channels for the bond capital of small mid-sized banks were expanded. In May 2020, the Financial Stability and Development Committee under the State Council issued the *Work Plan for Deepening Reform and Replenishing Capital at Small and Medium Banks* to strengthen bond market support for capital replenishment among small and mid-sized banks. In July, an executive meeting of the State Council decided to arrange a certain amount for local government special bonds by a new quota, allowing local governments to reasonably supplement small and mid-sized banks' capital by various means in accordance with the law. In November, the Ministry of Finance issued a new special bond quota of RMB 200 billion to help resolve risks faced by local small and mid-sized banks.

(4) Improvements were made to the system for registration and issuance of debt financing instruments for non-financial enterprises. In 2020, NAFMII revised and issued the *Working Rules on the Registration of Public Issue of Debt Financing Instruments for Non-Financial Enterprises*, the *Working Rules on the Registration of Directed Issue* and other measures to improve the arrangement of the hierarchical classification mechanism, facilitate shelf offering for enterprises, and integrate the registration workflow. It also revised and issued the *Guidelines for the Issuance of Debt Financing Instruments for Non-Financial Enterprises*, the *Working Rules for the Bookkeeping of Debt Financing Instruments for Non-Financial Enterprises*, and the *Notice on Further Strengthening the Matters Related to the Norms for the Issuance of Debt Financing Instruments* to further strengthen regulation requirements on the marketization of issuance pricing and optimize supervision and tracking mechanisms for bookkeeping, while strengthening market discipline by the prohibition of issuers' self-financing, strengthening the disclosure by related party subscriptions, and upgrading bookkeeping's operating norms. In addition, the authority revised and issued the *Selection Rules for Special Institutional Investors of Directed Debt Financing Instruments* to further facilitate directed issuance.

(5) The duty performance system of intermediaries was perfected. In June 2020, NAFMII revised and issued the *Rules on Intermediary Services for Debt Financing Instruments of Non-Financial Enterprises in the Interbank Bond Market*, which further improves the mechanism for group lead underwriters, strengthens requirements for the performance of responsibility for intermediaries, adds the role of trustee, and strengthens the main responsibility of duration management. In December, NAFMII revised and issued the *Guide on the Due Diligence of Lead Underwriters of Non-Financial Enterprise Debt Financing Instruments* to further clarify lead underwriters' due diligence responsibilities.

(6) The duration management system for debt financing instruments was revised and improved. In December 2020, NAFMII issued the *Working Rules on the Duration Management of Debt Financing Instruments for Non-Financial Enterprises in the Interbank Bond Market*, which integrates previous normative documents on duration management, further clarifies the responsibilities of duration management agencies, and further refines penalty clauses to severely punish duration-related violations.

### 3. Bond trading regulation

(1) Interbank bond market transactions management was also strengthened in 2020. Throughout the year, the interbank bond market improved system construction and discipline construction for trade, comprehensively revising rules for self-regulation in bond trading, money brokerage, bond market making, and so on, refining requirements for institutional businesses' internal control and code of conduct, and improving the self-regulation management framework for trade. At the same time, investigation and punishment were enhanced for irregularities in the trading of bonds. On-site investigation was conducted at more than 10 institutions — including banks, securities companies, fund companies, trust companies and futures companies — and self-regulation sanctions were imposed on five institutions for trading irregularities throughout the year.

(2) The interbank bond market's market making system was improved. In December 2020, the People's Bank of China issued the *Matters on Improving the Administration of Market Makers in the Interbank Bond Market* (Notice No.21 [2020] of the People's Bank of China). This document cancelled the administrative licensing for bilateral market makers in the interbank bond market. Subsequently, NAFMII revised the *Guidelines on Self-Discipline of Market Making Business in the Interbank Bond Market*, and the *Assessment Indexes for Market Making Business in the Interbank Bond Market*, which collectively set down requirements for the whole process of market making business and clarified business operation procedures, proposing multi-dimensional classified evaluations to guide market makers in improving quotation quality and information transparency, and applying the evaluation results to the market making authority's dynamic management so as to further improve the market making business' incentive and restraint mechanisms.

(3) Commercial banks actively participated in the exchange bond market. In January 2020, the Shanghai Stock Exchange and Shenzhen Stock Exchange respectively joined hands with China Securities Depository and Clearing Corporation Limited to issue notices further expanding the scope of banks involved in bond trading — from listed commercial banks to policy banks, national development banks, large state-owned commercial banks, joint-stock commercial banks, urban commercial banks, to foreign-funded banks in China and other banks listed in China. Eligible banks can now apply for the qualifications of bond trading or clearing participants, and can open their own trading units to enter the market directly (under the "direct clearing" mode) or indirectly (under the "broker clearing" mode).

(4) The system of self-regulation punishments was comprehensively revised. In August 2020, NAFMII issued the *Rules on Self-Regulation of the Interbank Bond Market*, the *Working Rules on Self-Regulation Meetings of the Interbank Bond Market*, the *Working Rules on Self-Regulation Investigation and Self-Regulation Inquiry on Violations of the Interbank Bond Market*, and the *Rules on the Experts Management of Self-Regulation Meetings of the Interbank Bond Market* to further optimize procedures for self-regulation punishment, introduce corresponding management measures, upgrade overall disciplinary standards, and establish an orderly mechanism for the convergence of self-regulatory punishments and administrative punishments to form a self-regulation punishment system with fair procedures, transparent rules, and the strict enforcement of law.

### 4. Strengthening market constraints

(1) Corporate debenture bonds' standards for information disclosure were made uniform. In December 2020, the PBC, NDRC and CSRC jointly issued the *Administrative Measures for Information Disclosure of Corporate Debenture Bonds*, as well as its supporting documents — the *Requirements for the Preparation of Offering Circulars* and the *Requirements for the Preparation of Periodic Reports* — to unify information disclosure standards for corporate debenture bonds, to clarify the basic and principled requirements for said disclosure, and to standardize disclosure documents, contents, timing, and frequency as means to regulate the corporate debenture bonds' information disclosure.

(2) Local government bonds' information disclosure management was also improved. In January 2020, the Ministry of Finance issued the *Notice on Enabling the Information Disclosure Template for New Special Bonds of Local Governments*. This notice stipulates that, starting from April 1, 2020, whenever local governments issue new special bonds, they must disclose the new special bonds' information and information relevant about the duration of each bond in accordance with given sample formats.

(3) Debt financing instruments' registration and issuance information disclosure was improved. In April 2020, NAFMII revised and issued the *Registration Documents and Forms System for the Public Issue of Debt Financing Instruments of Non-Financial Enterprises* and the Registration Documents and Forms System for the Directed Issue of Debt Financing Instruments of Non-Financial Enterprises. These effectively standardize information disclosure, make information disclosure more pertinent and differentiated, and make fuller use of information disclosure's function of risk disclosure. In September, the *Model Text on Investor Protection Mechanism in Offering Circulars of Non-Financial Enterprise Debt Financing Instruments* was issued to provide model statements on content closely related to investor protection in "Offering Circulars" as a way to improve the quality of information disclosure and effectively protect the rights and interests of investors.

(4) Self-regulation management was enhanced in the credit rating industry. NAFMII and Securities Association of China (SAC) strengthened communication and coordination to promote the unification of standards for evaluating marketization among credit rating agencies, to improve the evaluation system with rating quality as the core, to strengthen the monitoring and investigation of the credit rating business, and to intensify self-regulation violation sanctions.

### 5. Bond market connectivity

In July 2020, the PBC and CSRC jointly issued the *Notice of PBC and CSRC* ([2020] No.7) to promote connectivity between the interbank bond market, the electronic trading platforms of the exchange bond market, and infrastructure institutions such as bond registration, trusteeship and clearing institutions. Accounts of nominal holders shall be mutually opened by the interbank bond market's bond registration, trusteeship, and clearing institutions, banks, and the exchange market's bond registration, trusteeship and clearing institutions to record the balance of all nominal bonds held.

### 6. A new defaulted bonds disposal mechanism

(1) Building a unified framework for the disposal of defaulted corporate credit bonds. In June 2020, the PBC, NDRC and CSRC jointly issued a notice for the building of a unified institutional framework for the disposal of defaulted corporate debenture bonds. This move aims to promote the marketization and legalization of default disposal in the bond market. In July, the Supreme People's Court issued the *Minutes of the Forum on National Courts Hearing Bond Dispute Cases* to improve the flow in legal relief channels regarding bond disputes, to improve the efficiency of judicial remediation, and to comprehensively protect the rights of investors. In November, the 43rd Meeting of the Financial Stability and Development Committee under the State Council studied the process of standardization in the bond market and its stability maintenance, demanding a "zero tolerance" attitude to maintain fairness and order in the market. In December, the Central Economic Working Conference proposed improving the bond market's legal system and cracking down on illegal activities such as debt evasion or revocation.

(2) Active promotion of non-financial enterprises' trusteeship businesses' filing for debt financing instruments. NAFMII encouraged trusteeship management businesses carried out in the market in accordance with the *Guidelines on the Trustee Business for Non-Financial Enterprise Debt Financing Instruments in the Interbank Bond Market (Trial)* issued at the end of 2019. By the end of 2020, 77 institutions —covering securities companies, trust companies, financial asset management companies, and law firms — had completed trusteeship business filings.

(3) Improvement of the mechanism for bond default disposal. In August 2020, CCDC and the Shanghai Clearing House jointly issued the *Rules on the Transfer and Settlement of Maturing Defaulted Bonds of Bond Trusteeship and Settlement Institutions on the National Interbank Bond Market*, formally establishing the relevant business systems and mechanisms, and thereby marking the establishment of a mechanism for the transfer and settlement of maturing defaulted bonds in the interbank market.

(4) Activation of a regular push service for the bondholder roster. On June 30, 2020, the Shanghai Clearing House launched a regular push service for the bondholder roster. In 2019, the Shanghai Clearing House launched an inquiry service for the bondholder roster, expanded inquiry subjects and scenarios, and clarified the business process of bondholder roster queries for specific dates, thus providing strong support for duration management, bondholder meetings, and default disposal. The regular push service will help improve the efficiency of bondholder roster inquiries, as well as the overall bondholder roster service system and the service capacity of financial informatization.

### 7. Increased market openness to the outside world

(1) The overall institutional arrangement for the opening up of the Chinese bond market was clarified. On September 2, 2020, the PBC, CSRC, and SAFE jointly issued the *Notice on Matters Related to the Investment of Foreign Institutional Investors in China's Bond Market (Exposure Draft)* to clearly define the overall institutional arrangement for the opening up of China's bond market, to unify access management and funds management to align with international standards, and

to deepen cross-sector regulatory cooperation. On September 21, the PBC and SAFE issued the *Administrative Regulations on Foreign Institutional Investors' Investment in China's Bond Market (Exposure Draft)* to define rules for funds management in the bond market.

(2) QFII and RQFII systems were merged. In September 2020, the CSRC, PBC and SAFE jointly promulgated the *Administrative Measures for the Investment in Securities and Futures in China of Qualified Foreign Institutional Investors and Qualified Foreign Institutional Investors of Renminbi*. The CSRC simultaneously issued supporting rules to merge qualifications and systems for QFII and RQFII, cancel restrictions on the number of entrusted intermediaries, steadily and orderly expand the scope of investment, strengthen cross-market, cross-border and penetrating supervision, and increase penalties for violations.

(3) The panda bond issuance system was optimized. In December 2020, NAFMII issued the *Guidelines on Bond Business of Foreign Government Bodies and International Development Institutions (Trial)* to optimize the system through which foreign government bodies and international development institutions issue bonds in China, and to clarify institutional arrangements for registration and issuance, information disclosure, and intermediaries. At the same time, the *Business Guide on Debt Financing Instruments for Foreign Non-Financial Enterprises (2020 Edition)* was issued to optimize filing requirements, registration documents submission, and information disclosure requirements.

(4) Foreign-funded banks are now allowed to participate in the underwriting of local government bonds. In January 2020, the Ministry of Finance announced the lifting of qualification restrictions — on solely foreign-funded banks, Sino-foreign joint venture banks, and branches of foreign banks — on participation in the underwriting of local government bonds, allowing foreign banks to be absorbed into underwriting groups in accordance with procedure.

(5) Transaction efficiency was enhanced. In March 2020, the SCH and CCDC introduced rolling settlement and special settlement period services (T+N) for overseas institutional investors as a way to meet international investors' diversified settlement needs. In September, the China Foreign Exchange Trade System enabled new functionality. It became possible for either party to a transaction to independently choose to engage in "T+N" transactions online without submitting an application, thus improving settlement efficiency for foreign investors. On September 1, the National Interbank Funding Center began a direct trading services trial operation under a direct mode of investment. This allows foreign institutional investors to send quotation requests directly to domestic market makers to reach deals. Foreign investors can also make use of other convenient features like compartment and package deals to further improve the efficiency of their investment and trading in Chinese bonds. On September 15, a joint announcement by the National Interbank Funding Center, SCH and CCDC clarified that for a settlement cycle of T+1 or above, the bond trading period was extended to 20:00.

**(III) Policy assessment**

1. The scale of the bond market reached RMB 117 trillion. Under policy for optimizing and

standardizing the mechanism for issuing bonds, volume of issuance in said market has increased significantly and scale has increased further still. In 2020, the national bond market issued RMB 57.3 trillion in bonds of all varieties, an increase of 23.4 percentage points or 26.5% YOY. At the end of the year, the national bond market trusteeship balance was RMB 117.0 trillion, a YOY increase of 18.1%, ranking second in the world.

2. Support for the real economy was comprehensively strengthened. In 2020, the volume of corporate bond issuance continued to grow at a rate of over 30%. The total issuance of corporate bonds was RMB 13.6 trillion, an increase of 34.3% over the same period last year. This effectively played the bond market's role of direct financing and supported anti-epidemic work, enterprises' return to production, high-tech fields, advanced manufacturing, the green economy, private economy, SMEs and poverty alleviation, thereby driving sound development in the real economy.

3. Trading activity increased. In 2020, the bond market's trade volume continued to grow after breaking RMB 200 trillion, with an annual trading volume up to RMB 253.0 trillion, marking a YOY increase of 16.5%. The interbank bond market achieved a turnover rate of 269%, for a YOY increase of 50%. The top three types of securities with high transaction activity were policy-based financial bonds, NCDs, and book-entry government bonds — with turnover rates of 539%, 454%, and 288% respectively.

4. Market openness continued to show significant improvement. In terms of investment, 109 foreign corporate institutional investors entered the interbank bond market in 2020, further enhancing foreign institutions' trade activity. Annual trading volume reached RMB 9.16 trillion, representing a YOY increase of 72.5%. By the end of 2020, altogether 905 foreign institutions had entered the interbank bond market. Foreign institutions in the interbank market had a total bond trusteeship amount of RMB 3.25 trillion, an increase of 47.9% over the same period last year, accounting for 3.2% of the interbank bond market's total trusteeship. As for intermediary services, in May, Fitch (China) Bohua Credit Ratings Ltd. (Fitch Bohua) completed registration to conduct a Type B credit rating business in the interbank bond market. It thus became the second foreign rating agency (after S&P Global China Ratings) to conduct credit ratings in the interbank bond market. In October, S&P Global China Ratings finished filing its securities rating business with the CSRC, expanding its scope of practice from the interbank bond market to the exchange market. As for the introduction of international bond indices, on February 28, JPMorgan incorporated nine Chinese government bonds into its flagship Government Bond Index - Emerging Markets Series (GBI-EM); the incorporated bonds will reach the index's 10% weight limit. On September, FTSE Russell announced that it would include Chinese government bonds in the FTSE World Government Bond Index (WGBI). Thus at present, the world's three major bond indexes either have or plan to include Chinese bonds.

### (IV) Outlook

The year 2021 marks the beginning of the 14th Five-Year Plan period. The bond market will apply the spirit of the 19th National Congress of the CPC, the decisions and arrangements of the Central Economic Working Conference, and the new development concept for the new era, continuing to focus on serving the real economy and promoting the high-quality development of China's economy, adhering to the principles of marketization, legalization and internationalization, further strengthening institutional construction and product innovation, preventing and resolving financial risks, deepening financial reform, continuously promoting the opening up of the bond market, and further increasing the capacity and level of service to the real economy.

## Article 6

### Regulating the development and maintaining the stability of the bond market while promoting the healthy sustainable development of the capital market[1]

In recent years, China's bond market has developed well to become the most open and dynamic part of the country's financial market system. It plays an important part in increasing the proportion of direct financing, improving the efficiency of resource allocation in the market, and serving the real economy. That being said, problems also exist — the credit and legal systems, for instance, remaining incomplete. There has been an increasing number of credit bond risk events since 2014, and credit defaults in the bond market have become a major concern. On November 10, 2020, liquidity constraints forced Yong Mei Group's failure to make full payment of principal and interest on "20 Yong Mei SCP003" as scheduled, constituting a substantial breach of contract. On November 27, the CSRC opened a case against Yong Mei Group and Xigema Certified Public Accountants in accordance with the law. Yongmei's default caused the market re-price the government's implicit support, causing uncertainty (over whether future rigid payments of quasi-municipal bonds would break faith) and triggering continuous fluctuations in the capital market.

On November 21, Liu He, member of the Political Bureau of the CPC Central Committee, Vice Premier of the State Council, and Director of the Financial Stability and Development Committee, chaired the 43rd meeting of the Financial Stability and Development Committee to study the regulation and continued stabilization of bond market development. The meeting underscored the Party Central Committee and the State Council's high estimation of value on healthy and sustainable capital market development. The reform and opening up of China's bond market have been deepening, granting it ever-greater functionality in service of the real economy while keeping the market running steadily as a whole. The recent rise in cases of default is the combined effect of various cyclical, institutional, and behavioural factors. Progress should continue to be sought in a stable manner according to a market-based, law-based, and

---

[1] Author: Yang Chao, a senior fellow with China Galaxy Securities Institute, and a project researcher of the "Report on China's Financial Policy".

international approach in order to balance development and risk prevention and to promote the bond market's sustainable and healthy development.

The meeting firstly stressed the need to improve political positions and effectively fulfil responsibilities. Financial regulators and local governments should start from the big picture, advance the rule of law in a comprehensive way, resolutely uphold legal authority, carry out regulatory and local responsibilities, and encourage market players of every type to strictly fulfil their major responsibilities, establishing a sound local financial ecology and credit environment. Its second dictate is to maintain fairness and order in the market through "zero tolerance" enforcement. Fraudulent issuance, the false disclosure of information, malicious transfer of assets, misappropriation of issue funds and other types of illegal behaviour must be strictly investigated and dealt with, while all manner of "debt evasion" must be severely punished in order to protect the legitimate rights and interests of investors. Third, industry self-regulation and supervision must be strengthened, as must the mechanism for market discipline. Debt-issuing enterprises and their shareholders, financial institutions, intermediaries and other types of market entities must strictly adhere to laws, regulations, and market rules, as well as professional ethics; they must ensure diligence, honesty and trustworthiness, and must effectively prevent moral hazards. Fourth is to build up departmental coordination and cooperation. Efforts should go into risk prevention, detection, and early warning and disposal mechanisms. Risk mapping and screening should be enhanced to maintain sufficient liquidity while firmly safeguarding zero systemic risk as a bottom line. Fifth is to continue deepening reform. This applies to the bond market in terms of establishing a sound market system, improving the market structure, and enriching product services. SOE reform should also deepen to improve the quality and efficiency of operation.

Building effective systems for supervision and risk prevention and control, maintaining the stability of the bond market and promoting the healthy and sustainable development of the capital market will have far-reaching significance for the efficient development of China's real economy. As China's financial reform advances, direct financing will only play a more important role and the bond market will only be a stronger pillar for the development of the real economy. In one aspect, we should strengthen legislation, step up law enforcement, increase penalties, uphold zero-tolerance in bond market violations, and ensure a strict market discipline. In December 2020, the Central Economic Work Conference indicated that efforts were needed to improve the bond market's legal system. On December 24, the People's Bank of China held a symposium on the legal construction of the bond market, declaring that in consideration of problems in said construction, it would work with relevant departments, academic institutions and industries to improve the legal system and the rule of law in the bond market. These policy trends reflect the state and regulators' high valuation of risk prevention in the bond market; they also indicate that the legal construction of the bond market will accelerate in the future. In another aspect, in promoting the construction of a legal system and of effective supervision, there needs a comprehensive study is needed on implicit government guarantee and rigid payment in the bond market in order to improve the local governance model and deepen SOE reform, optimize market product structure, consolidate the bond market's credit foundation and enable its healthy and stable development.

## V. Policies for the Development of the Securities Investment Fund Market[①]

### (I) An Overview of Fund Industry Development

In 2020, the COVID-19 pandemic's continuous spread had severe impacts on the global economy. China, achieving great and strategic victories in pandemic prevention and control, was the only major economy to realize positive economic growth for the year. The country's supply-side structural reform in the financial sector and opening-up both deepened, while the basic environment for asset management continued to improve, the industry making remarkable progress.

According to statistics released by the Asset Management Association of China, as of the end of 2020, the total size of assets managed by fund management companies, their subsidiaries, securities companies, futures companies, and private equity funds management institutions stood at approximately RMB 58.99 trillion[②], increasing by RMB 6.76 trillion from a year earlier. Specifically, publicly offered funds accounted for RMB 19.89 trillion; private equity funds managed by securities companies and their subsidiaries came to RMB 8.55 trillion[③]; private equity funds managed by funds companies and their subsidiaries came to RMB 8.06 trillion; pension funds managed by fund companies amounted to RMB 3.36 trillion[④]; private equity funds managed by futures companies and their subsidiaries reached RMB 219.7 billion; private equity funds accounted for RMB 16.96 trillion and assets in support of special plans amounted to RMB 2.11 trillion.

Since 2020, public funds have been rapidly developed and their structure further improved, the functions of inclusive finance and purchasers in the capital market demonstrated yet further. In October 2019, the China Securities Regulatory Commission (CSRC) expanded pilot consultation projects for investment in the public offering of funds. At present, 18 institutions have obtained qualifications for pilot fund investment consultations and 15 have officially started their consultation business. Over 2020, new publicly offered funds raised RMB 3.16 trillion, a record high. As of the end of 2020, managed public funds stood at RMB 19.89 trillion, marking 34.7% growth from one year prior. The proportion of resident holders was 53%, up by 5 percentage points from a year prior,

---

① Author: Cai Hengpei, Senior Director of Investor Education and International Affairs Department (Research and Statistics Panel) of Asset Management Association of China.

② Any overlap between private equity fund management products and private asset management plans is exempted from the aggregate.

③ Pension funds managed by securities companies are not included.

④ Here, pension funds include social security funds managed by fund management companies, basic pensions, enterprise annuities, and occupational pensions, but excludes pensions for Chinese retirees overseas.

indicating wider investor coverage and increasing public support for inclusive finance. The product structure was further improved, with equity funds occupying 32.3%, up 10.7 percentage points from a year earlier. Public funds invested RMB 4.69 trillion in A-shares, accounting for 7.3% of the total circulating market values among the SSE and SZSE, its highest level since 2013. Publicly offered funds are playing an increasingly significant role in advancing direct finance and serving the real economy. Pension funds managed by fund companies amounted to RMB 3.36 trillion, up by 39.3% from one year earlier, indicating more effective asset allocation and application to elderly care services.

Securities and futures institutions' privately offered asset management continued to exhibit an improved business structure, with clear successes in deleveraging and shrinking channel businesses. Moreover, institutions in the industry improved their capacities for active management. As of the end of 2020, privately offered asset management reached RMB 16.83 trillion, decreasing by 13.7% from one year earlier. Channel business continually declined, down in 2020 by RMB 12.89 trillion, a decrease of 69.7%. The scale of asset-backed securitization products recorded by the Asset Management Association of China was RMB 2.11 trillion, up 28.2% from a year earlier. These products played an essential role in liquidizing remnant assets and improving the efficiency of capital utilization.

The steady and sound development of private equity funds significantly contributed to increasing direct finance and promoting innovative capital formation. As of the end of 2020, there were 24,561 private equity fund managers registered with the Asset Management Association of China with RMB 16.96 trillion in recorded private equity funds, up 20.4% from a year prior. The Asset Management Association of China had recorded 105,500 private equity fund-invested projects with a principal of RMB 8.10 trillion. Among this sum, RMB 2.20 trillion of principal was invested in 68,000 SME (small and medium-sized enterprise) projects and RMB 1.68 trillion was invested in 40,100 high-tech enterprise projects. Private equity funds' investment priorities were representative of industrial upgrading and new economy; they included internet and other computer applications, industrial capital goods like machine manufacturing, raw materials, pharmaceuticals and biology, medical devices and services, and semiconductors, with 67,700 projects invested and a principal of RMB 3.51 trillion. For the entire year of 2020, RMB 702 billion of private equity funds was newly invested in unlisted equities, amounting to 2.0% of all newly added private financing over the same period. These investments provided essential capital for enterprise development and strongly promoted supply-side structural reform and the growth of innovation. As of the end of 2020, 215 enterprises were listed on the Science and Technology Innovation Board. According to statistics of the Asset Management Association of China, among these 215, 176 had received capital support from private equity and venture capital funds during their development process, with an investment ratio of up to 81.9%.

### (II) Fund Industry Policy Analysis

The construction of a multi-level capital market and the comprehensive deepening of reforms have made profound progress since 2020. The asset management industry's institutional system and business environment have improved significantly while creating more space for further development. As a major component of the direct financing system aimed at serving the real economy and managing public finance, the regulatory authorities have persisted in "building a system, non-interference, and zero tolerance" to guide the industry back to its original purpose. For one, regulators improved industry compliance and strengthened risk prevention and control by imposing stricter supervision and institutional restrictions so as to fully protect investors' legitimate rights and interests. For another, regulators promoted continuous innovation, enriched product lines, and developed business layouts through institutional supply and effective guidance so as to cultivate the industry's professionalism and international competitiveness, pushing for more profound development.

### 1. Top-Level Design Consolidating the Industry's Legal Basis

The new Securities Law officially came into force. On March 1, 2020, the new Securities Law of the People's Republic of China officially went into effect. With the enforcement of the new Securities Law, progress has forged steadily ahead in registration system reform; investor protection and information disclosure have been strengthened; regulation and enforcement of the Securities Law have been tightened, with higher costs for violation; and the capital market environment has been purified. In particular, the new Securities Law clarifies that the State Council will set management rules for the issuance and trade of asset management products. The Law provides a legal basis and protection for the State Council to regulate the issuance and trading activities of relevant products.

Asset management's regulatory transition period was extended. On July 31, 2020, it was decided to prolong the *Guiding Opinions for Regulating Asset Management Business of Financial Institutions* transition period until the end of 2021 in order to more deeply implement the decisions of the Party Central Committee and the State Council in coordinating the COVID-19 pandemic prevention and control as well as economic and social development. This decision was made with the approval of the State Council, and through prudent discussions between the People's Bank of China (PBC) and the National Development and Reform Commission (NDRC), Ministry of Finance, China Banking and Insurance Regulatory Commission (CBIRC), China Securities Regulatory Commission (CSRC) and the State Administration of Foreign Exchange (SAFE). At the same time, the abovementioned authorities established and perfected the incentive and restrictive mechanism and improved related policies to facilitate and regulate the asset management industry's development in a stable and orderly manner. Appropriately extending the transition period helps steadily rectify the asset management inventory business and ease the rectification pressure on financial institutions. It also improves the environment and conditions for asset management institutions to enhance new products' investment research and innovation capacities while strengthening investor education and the long-term cultivation of capital.

Institutional investors were encouraged to make purchases to raise listed companies' quality. The *Opinions Concerning Further Raising the Quality of Listed Companies* was released on October 5, 2020. The "Opinions" clearly calls for the establishment of a quality communication mechanism between the board and investors, optimization of the channels and ways by which institutional investors participate in corporate governance, and full utilization of equity institutional investors' role in promoting better corporate governance, innovation, and start-ups, and industrial upgrading. The Opinions provides important guidance on harnessing the purchasing function of asset management institutions and facilitating institutional investors' active participation in the governance of listed companies.

**2. Toughening Supervision and Preventing Risks for Stronger Investor Protections**

The public funds investment in shares listed on the National Equities Exchange and Quotations (NEEQ) was standardized. On April 17, 2020, the CSRC released the *Guidelines on Publicly Offered Securities Investment Funds Investing in Stocks Quoted on the National Equities Exchange and Quotations*, which defines requirements for managers and on the types of funds open to investment. The "Guidelines" states that risks must be strictly prevented and controlled, demanding tougher management of liquidity risks, satisfactory information disclosure, and the proper management of investors so as to protect investors' legitimate rights and interests. Approving publicly offered funds to invest in NEEQ Select shares does not only improve the investor structure of the NEEQ and its market activity; it also expands the scale of the public fund investment and helps investors share the growth dividends of high-quality innovative startups.

The management of liquidity risks for publicly offered funds was tightened. In order to enhance publicly offered funds' risk prevention and control capacities and to better protect investors' legitimate rights and interests, the CSRC released the *Guidelines on Side Pocket Mechanism for Publicly Raised Securities Investment Funds (Trial)* on July 10, 2020. A side pocket is a tool for managing liquidity risk, whereby specific assets in a fund's investment portfolio are moved from the original account to a special account for independent management. The launch of the side pocket mechanism enriches the toolset of publicly offered funds for liquidity risk management, mitigating potential systemic risks caused by fund redemption under specific circumstances and preventing opportunistic early redemption so as to protect investors' legitimate rights and interests.

Requirements for fund custody and distribution were improved to optimize the industrial ecology. On July 10, 2020, the CSRC and CBIRC revised and jointly released the revised *Measures for the Administration of the Securities Investment Fund Custody Business*. The "Measures" allows the Chinese branches of foreign banks to apply for the qualifications to conduct fund custody business while strengthening related measures for risk control. It perfects regulations by combining requirements with regulatory practice to prevent risks in the fund custody business. It continues to streamline administration and delegate power to lower levels by simplifying application materials, making approval procedures more efficient, and implementing "approval before fundraising". Finally, it unifies access standards and regulatory requirements for commercial banks and other financial institutions. On August 28, the CSRC released the *Measures for the Supervision and Administration of Distributors of Publicly Offered Securities Investment Funds* (hereafter referred to as the "Measures") and related rules — the "Provisions on the Implementation of the Measures for the Supervision and Administration of

Distributors of Publicly Offered Securities Investment Funds" and the "Interim Provisions on the Administration of Publicity and Promotional Materials of Publicly Offered Securities Investment Funds". These releases aim to toughen requirements for licensed access and exit mechanisms for fund distribution, consolidate business regulation with institutional management, and enhance supervision over independent fund distributors. The "Measures" further improves the code of conduct for fund distribution and enhances fund distributors' compliance and internal control. It positively contributes to the protection of investors' rights and interests, optimizes the fund market ecology, and facilitates the industry's healthy development.

The supervision of private equity funds was strengthened. On December 30, 2020, the CSRC released the *Several Provisions on Strengthening the Regulation of Privately Offered Investment Funds* to strengthen supervision over private equity funds, crack down on all kinds of illegal behaviors, strictly control the existing risks of private equity funds, properly defuse inventory risks, advance the development of industrial standards, and better protect the legitimate rights and interests of investors and stakeholders. The "Provisions" applied ten prohibitions to private equity fund managers and other related workers. By reiterating and specifying bottom-line requirements for the regulation of private equity funds, it brings the private equity fund industry back to its true origins of "private equity" and "investment", thereby promoting a virtuous cycle of survival of the fittest and advancing the sustainable development of industrial standards.

### 3. Comprehensively Deepening Reform and Opening-up, Creating More Space for Industrial Development

REIT pilot programs were officially started for publicly offered funds in infrastructure. On April 30, 2020, the CSRC and NDRC jointly issued the *Notice of the Work Related to Promoting the Pilot Program of Real Estate Investment Trusts (REITs) in the Infrastructure Field* (hereafter referred to as the "Notice") which defines the basic principles, requirements, and arrangements for REIT pilot programs in the field of infrastructure. According to the Notice, the CSRC and NDRC will strengthen cooperation, adhere to the principles of marketization and legalization, and make full use of the capital market to actively support quality infrastructure projects in key regions and industries corresponding to national pilot REIT policy. On August 6, the CSRC released the *Guidelines for Publicly Offered Infrastructure Securities Investment Funds (Trial)*, clarifying the product definitions, the business model, and the distribution pattern of fund proportions, as well as stipulating fund investment restrictions, connected transactions management, borrowing arrangements, fundraising expansion, and information disclosure so as to facilitate the sound implementation of REITs in the field of infrastructure.

The capital market was further opened up. On September 25, 2020, the CSRC, PBC, and SAFE jointly released the *Administrative Measures for the Investment in Securities and Futures in China of Qualified Foreign Institutional Investors and Qualified Foreign Institutional Investors of Renminbi* (hereafter referred to as the "QFII and RQFII Measures"). At the same time, the CSRC released the related *Provisions on Issues Concerning the Implementation of the Measures for the Administration of Domestic Securities and Futures Investment by Qualified Foreign Institutional Investors and RMB*

*Qualified Foreign Institutional Investors*. The revised QFII and RQFII Measures and its related provisions consist of lowering the access threshold and facilitating investment operations, enlarging the investment scope, and allowing QFII and RQFII to invest in private equity funds and financial futures, enhancing continuous supervision, and so on. The QFII and RQFII Measures and its related provisions are beneficial to the establishment and perfection of an open, transparent, and convenient QFII and RQFII system with controllable risks, thus promoting the two-way high-level opening-up of the capital market.

### 4. Optimizing the Policy Environment, Guiding the Industry to Serve the Real Economy

Venture capital funds' reverse linkage policy was improved. In order to further improve venture capital funds' exit channels, to unblock a virtuous cycle of investment, exit, and reinvestment, and to facilitate the formation of venture capital, the CSRC revised and released the *Special Provisions for Shareholders of Listed Venture Capital Funds to Reduce Shareholdings* on March 6, 2020. The "Special Provisions" streamlines the applicable standards for the reverse linkage policy, increases the benefits of long-term investment-focused funds, widens the scope of the applicable policy beneficiaries, and includes private equity investment funds filed in accordance with the laws of the Asset Management Association of China. The CSRC's simplification and optimization of reverse linkage policy make better use of private equity and venture capital's ability to support the starting up and innovation of small and medium-sized enterprises as well as sci-tech innovation enterprises, thereby providing stronger support for the real economy.

Guidance and support were provided for the industry to effectively serve small and medium-sized enterprises. On May 26, 2020, the PBC worked together with the CBIRC, NDRC, Ministry of Industry and Information Technology, Ministry of Finance, State Administration for Market Regulation, CSRC, and SAFE to release the *Guiding Opinions on Further Strengthening the Financial Services for Micro, Small and Medium-Sized Enterprises* (hereafter referred to as the "Opinions"). The Opinions proposes explicit guidance for private equity and venture capital early investment in small and medium-sized enterprises (SMEs). Specifically, it includes a revision of the *Interim Measures for the Supervision and Administration of Privately Offered Investment Funds*, a strengthening of differentiated supervision and the self-discipline of venture capital funds, encouragement for asset management products increased support of venture capital and gradual increase in the proportion of equity asset management products. The Opinions holds great significance for the development of private equity and venture capital funds, growth in the proportion of direct financing, and offering of targeted service for the real economy.

### 5. Deepening Private Equity Fund Registration and Filing Reform, Modernizing Industry Governance

Pilot reforms of filing and spot-checking systems were conducted for private equity funds. In order to further improve dynamic credit management throughout the industry's entire private equity fund procedures, to lead managers to value the importance of credit accumulation and professional, honest business, to improve filing efficiency for institutions with good credit, and in adherence with the policy that supports the good and restricts the bad, on February 7, 2020, the Asset Management

Association of China first adopted pilot systems of differentiated filing and spot-checking for the private equity fund products of private equity fund managers exhibiting continuous compliance and good credit. This means that after eligible private equity fund managers submit filing applications, by publicizing the basic information of the private equity fund on the official Association website, all filing procedures can be completed within the next day. Once the filing is complete, the Association will then conduct spot checks for compliance. The pilot of the differentiated filing and spot-checking systems for private equity funds is an innovative reform measure that follows private equity funds' processual rule of filing after fundraising, indicating a substantial change to the industry's mechanism for the application of credit in the industry. It will help activate internal forces to strengthen the credit of private equity fund managers while establishing a system that encourages honesty, constrains defaults, and promotes the fiduciary duty to take root in the industry.

A private equity fund manager registry was opened disclosing the progress of registration procedures. In order to more fully deepening capital market reforms in accordance with requirements, better promote the openness and transparency of private equity fund managers' registration application procedures, and streamline the preparation of application materials, the Asset Management Association of China released the *Notice of the Matters Related to Facilitating the Application for Registration of the Private Equity Fund Managers* (hereafter referred to as the "Notice") on February 28, 2020. The Notice proposes separate lists of required application materials according to the type of private equity fund manager. It also discloses progress throughout the entire registration process. Members of the industry can make inquiries through the "Disclosure of Registration Procedures for Private Equity Fund Managers" on the Asset Management Association of China official website. In addition, as a way to strengthen social supervision and facilitate investors and market institutions' continuous and comprehensive understanding of managers' business development, the website discloses certain information on private equity fund managers to the public via its "Disclosure Platform for the Revelation of the Private Equity Fund Managers". This disclosure of the registry and the whole process improves transparency, helps applicants better prepare, and makes registration more orderly, efficient, and open, which ultimately strengthens social supervision.

### (III) Development Outlook for the Asset Management Industry

Through more than 20 years of development, the asset management industry has become an integral component of the modern financial system, providing public financial management with important tools and creating capital in the real economy. 2021 marks the first year of China's 14th Five-Year Plan, which includes requirements for high-quality development and an economic development paradigm of dual domestic and international circulation. Against this policy background, the advance of industrial transformation and upgrading and the cultivation of new drivers of growth in the domestic economy are all imperatives. A new economic development paradigm requires new modes of capital support. Thus, it is of the utmost priority to raise the proportion of direct financing, improve the financing structure, and promote the formation of innovative capital. The asset management industry will play a crucial role in achieving these goals.

The asset management industry's development is rooted in the real economy and real people's financial management needs. China's real economy led the way in escaping the negative effects of COVID-19, China becoming the only major economy to realize positive economic growth in 2020. The trend of sound economic development has continued to consolidate; industrial transformation and upgrading have continued to gain momentum; this is a solid foundation formed for the development of the asset management industry. China's per capita GDP has exceeded USD 10,000, with over 400 million of its population qualifying as middle-income. There is strong demand for financial management, meaning that necessary support is available for the development of the asset management industry. In particular, the comprehensive deepening of capital market reforms — such as the registration system reform higher-level two-way opening-up — have accelerated, providing a favorable environment and wider space for the industry's development. The asset management industry is expected to put its professional values into play and return to its original purpose, improve its level of professionalism and international competitiveness, keep to long-term value investments, focus on the development of equity products, and increase the proportion of direct financing, thus realizing industrial transformation and healthy, long-term development.

## Appendix

### Major Regulatory Policies for the Fund Industry Since 2020

| Issuing Date | Policy Name | Issuing Units | Issuing Number |
| --- | --- | --- | --- |
| February 28 | Notice of the Matters Related to Facilitating the Application for Registration of the Private Equity Fund Managers | Asset Management Association of China | |
| March 6 | Special Provisions for Shareholders of Listed Venture Capital Funds to Reduce Shareholdings | CSRC | CSRC Announcement [2020] No. 17 |
| April 1 | Instructions on the Recordation of Private Investment Funds | Asset Management Association of China | |
| April 17 | Guidelines on Publicly Offered Securities Investment Funds Investing in Stocks Quoted on the National Equities Exchange and Quotations | CSRC | CSRC Announcement [2020] No. 23 |
| April 30 | Notice of the Work Related to Promoting the Pilot Program of Real Estate Investment Trusts (REITs) in the Infrastructure Field | CSRC, NDRC | ZJF [2020] No. 40 |
| May 26 | Guiding Opinions on Further Strengthening the Financial Services for Micro, Small and Medium-Sized Enterprises | PBC, CBIRC, NDRC, Ministry of Industry and Information Technology of People's Republic of China (MIIT), Ministry of Finance of People's Republic of China (MOF), State Administration for Market Regulation (SAMR), CSRC, and SAFE | YF [2020] No. 120 |

Continued

| Issuing Date | Policy Name | Issuing Units | Issuing Number |
|---|---|---|---|
| July 10 | Measures for the Administration of the Securities Investment Fund Custody Business | CSRC, CBIRC | CSRC Order No. 172 |
| July 10 | Guidelines on Side Pocket Mechanism for Publicly Raised Securities Investment Funds (Trial) | CSRC | CSRC Announcement [2020] No. 41 |
| August 7 | Guidelines for Publicly Offered Infrastructure Securities Investment Funds (Trial) | CSRC | CSRC Announcement [2020] No. 54 |
| August 28 | Measures for the Supervision and Administration of Distributors of Publicly Offered Securities Investment Funds | CSRC | CSRC Order No. 175 |
| August 28 | Provisions on the Implementation of the Measures for the Supervision and Administration of Distributors of Publicly Offered Securities Investment Funds | CSRC | CSRC Announcement [2020] No. 58 |
| August 28 | Interim Provisions on the Administration of Publicity and Promotional Materials of Publicly Offered Securities Investment Funds | CSRC | CSRC Announcement [2020] No. 59 |
| September 25 | Administrative Measures for the Investment in Securities and Futures in China of Qualified Foreign Institutional Investors and Qualified Foreign Institutional Investors of Renminbi | CSRC, PBC, SAFE | CSRC Order No. 176 |
| September 25 | Regulation on Issues Related to the Implementation of the Administrative Measures for the Investment in Securities and Futures in China of Qualified Foreign Institutional Investors and Qualified Foreign Institutional Investors of Renminbi | CSRC | CSRC Announcement [2020] No. 63 |
| October 5 | Opinions Concerning Further Raising the Quality of Listed Companies | The State Council | GBF [2019] No. 49 |
| December 30 | Several Provisions on Strengthening the Regulation of Privately Offered Investment Funds | CSRC | CSRC Announcement [2020] No. 71 |

## Article 7

### China accelerates the opening-up of the capital market for a higher-level open economy[①]

At the opening of the 13th Summer Davos Forum on July 2, 2019, Premier Li Keqiang stated: "We will deepen the reform of finance and other modern service industries and remove restrictions on foreign shares in securities, futures, and life insurance by 2020 rather than 2021 as was previously stated."

In 2020, China accelerated the pace of opening up its capital market. On January 1, 2020, the China Banking and Insurance Regulatory Commission (CBIRC) canceled existing restrictions on the proportion of foreign investment in joint venture insurance companies engaged in the life insurance business; then, on March 13, the China Securities Regulatory Commission (CSRC) announced the cancelation of its existing restrictions on the ratio of foreign shareholding for securities companies starting April 1; next, on May 7, the People's Bank of China (PBC) and the State Administration of Foreign Exchange released the *Regulations on the Management of Foreign Institutional Investors in Domestic Securities and Futures Investment Funds*, which canceled the investment limit quota for foreign institutional investors and the remittance limit on investment income; on September 2, the PBC and two other departments jointly released the *Announcement on Matters Relating to Foreign Institutional Investors' Investment in China's Bond Market* (Draft for Comments), further facilitating the allocation of foreign institutional investors' renminbi bond assets; in October, a number of leading officials — including Liu He (member of the Political Bureau of the CPC Central Committee and Vice Premier of the State Council), Guo Shuqing (secretary of the Party Committee of the PBC and Chairman of the CBIRC), Yi Gang (governor of the People's Bank of China), and Yi Huiman (chairman of the CSRC) —lent their voices to promote the opening-up of the financial sector.

In 2020, China worked to advance the reform and opening-up of the capital market to shape a sound business environment. China means to demonstrate its ongoing commitment to financial and service-sector liberalization to the rest of the world, along with its resolve to expand the bidirectional opening of the bond market. The PBC has repeatedly stated that during this process it will maintain the stability of the renminbi's exchange rate within a reasonably balanced range and that China will not engage in competitive devaluation. China will further cut tariff levels, expand imports of goods and services, and continue to improve its legal system for opening-up. The country will speed up the formulation of supporting regulations for the *Foreign Investment Law* and cancel provisions no longer relevant. China will set down an initial layout for institution building to implement those supporting regulations together with the *Foreign Investment*

---

① Author: Xie Xuecheng, Assistant Dean of China Galaxy Securities Institute (Overall charge of the work), and senior project fellow of Program for China's Financial Policy Report.

*Law* in 2020. This will enable the construction of a sound business environment for China's macroeconomic structural reform, put in place adequate preparations for deepening supply-side structural reform, and lay down fertile soil for a new development paradigm with domestic circulation as the mainstay and domestic and international circulations reinforcing each other.

On November 3, 2020, the *Proposals of the Central Committee of the Communist Party of China on Formulating the Fourteenth Five-Year Plan for National Economic and Social Development and the Long-term Goals for 2035* was released. It details the implementation of a high-level opening-up breaking new ground for win-win cooperation. The "Proposals" indicates that China will build an institutional system and regulatory model that is in line with internationally accepted rules, will improve the management system of pre-entry national treatment plus a negative list for foreign investment, will further curtail the negative list for foreign investment access, will implement after-access national treatment, and will promote fair competition between domestic and foreign enterprises. China will also establish a sound negative list management system for cross-border trade in services and improve the technology trade promotion system; it will steadily promote the opening-up of banks, securities, insurance, funds, futures and other financial fields; it will deepen domestic-foreign capital market interconnection and improve the system of qualified foreign investors; it will promote the internationalization of the renminbi in a prudent manner, adhere to a market-driven approach and enterprises' independent choice, and create a new type of cooperative relationship based on the free use of the renminbi that is mutually beneficial; finally, it will improve entry and exit, customs, foreign exchange, taxation and other aspects of management services.

China is committed to accelerating its capital market's opening to the outside world. This move will have far-reaching significance in terms of developing a higher-level open economy. Amid frictions in global trade and the unexpected occurrence of the pandemic, acceleration of the capital market's opening-up is of great importance. Promoting reform through opening-up and, in turn, promoting greater openness through reform, will make full use of China's huge market and domestic demand potential to form a new pattern of the capital market opened at a high-level and better promote the overall development of domestic and international economic circulation. The capital market's opening is bidirectional; on the one hand, China will continuously open its product and capital market systems to the outside world — for example, expanding the scope and targets of scope for the Shanghai and Shenzhen Stock Connects, increasing the openness of the commodity futures market, and improving the convenience of investment in international funds; on the other hand, China will support domestic operators' "going global" regulators will actively participate in international financial governance, communication and policy coordination with overseas capital market regulators will be strengthened, cross-border capital market risks will be promptly prevented or resolved, and the vitality and resilience of capital market operations in an open environment will continuously be improved.

## Article 8

### Grasping the essence of the "Sci-Tech Innovation Finance 17 Articles" [1]

Science and technology innovation has always occupied a strategic position in Chinese policy. On December 11, 2020, the Political Bureau of the CPC Central Committee asserted the need to advance overall reform and opening-up to strengthen national strategic capabilities in science and technology. As major and key players in the latter regard, sci-tech innovation enterprises can effectively motivate innovations in the sci-tech field. As China enters a new stage of social and economic development, we are working faster to shape a new development paradigm with domestic circulation as the mainstay and domestic and international circulations reinforcing each other. This is a strategic development task for the "14th Five-Year Plan" period and beyond. Promoting financial supply-side structural reform is an important initiative and driver for the expansion and deepening of the new development paradigm. The strategic significance of financial supply-side structural reform for sci-tech innovation lies in the mobilization of financial resources, optimization of capital allocation, provision of sufficient capital for sci-tech innovation enterprises to best fulfill their strategic role, and optimization of the paradigm by which finance better serves the real economy.

In its position at the frontier of innovation-driven development, Beijing has utilized its advantages in sci-tech, finance, and other areas to improve its business environment and bring in more sci-tech innovation enterprises. In this context, on January 10, 2020, the Beijing Local Financial Supervision and Administration joined several other departments to formulate the *Measures on Increasing Financial Support for the Healthy Development of Science and Technology Innovation Enterprises* (the "Sci-Tech Innovation Finance 17 Articles"). This constitutes a major initiative in implementing the guideline of the Central Economic Work Conference, deepening the structural reform of the financial supply side, and vigorously promoting sci-tech finance. The Sci-Tech Innovation Finance 17 Articles consists of 17 measures addressing six different aspects; in essence, its purpose may be summarized as "EOSI" (expanding, optimizing, strengthening, and improving). It was designed to systematically strengthen the financial system's support for sci-tech innovation enterprises, comprehensively enhance the cohesiveness of different types of institutions serving sci-tech innovation enterprises, and optimize the allocation of funds to exert financial influence on sci-tech innovation finance. The detailed measures of the Sci-Tech Innovation Finance 17 Articles include: expanding the scale of credit financing, increasing capital market support, and better supporting the entire volume of the sci-tech innovation finance capital market; optimizing the financing guarantee system and solidifying its cornerstone for sound development; strengthening the interconnection of financial institutions and building a mechanism

---

[1] Author: Liu Yong, President of Zhongguancun Internet Finance Institute, and senior project fellow of Program for China's Financial Policy Report.

for mutual benefits in collaborative innovation-driven development; strengthening innovation among financial services, optimizing the government service environment, and continuously improving service capacity. The Sci-Tech Innovation Finance 17 Articles proposes quantitative indicators such as "15% of three indicators", "no less than RMB 15 billion", and an "RMB 3 billion capital increase". On one hand, these indicators clarify the strength, scope, and focus of policy support while providing targeted policies to support the development of sci-tech innovation enterprises in Beijing; on the other hand, the quantitative indicators are meant to pressure financial institutions to embrace new models while accelerating the formation of new drivers of development in the new era, and promoting the development of an innovation ecology in sci-tech innovation finance. Therefore, the issuance of the Sci-Tech Innovation Finance 17 Articles will not only provide policy support for sci-tech innovation finance companies; it will also explore new paths for financial supply-side structural reform.

## VI. Development Policy of the Money Market[①]

In 2020, in the face of fallout from the COVID-19 epidemic, thanks to sound monetary policy, China's money market was generally stable, the interest rate generally dropped, the market scale was further expanded, policies on the standardized development of the bill market were introduced, and market functionality was effectively improved.

### (I) The Interbank Lending Market

#### 1. Overview of Market Operations

In 2020, the interbank lending market was generally stable. Market entities continued to increase in number, transaction scale was stable (decreasing slightly), the interest rate declined, and the transaction structure continued to be dominated by short-term transactions. As shown in Figure 1, cumulative turnover in the interbank lending market was RMB 147.14 trillion in 2020, with a year-on-year (YOY) decrease of 2.96% and an average daily turnover of RMB 590.934 billion. The weighted average interest rate of interbank lending for the year was 1.64%, down 63 basis points YOY. There were 2,293 members in the national interbank lending market, with 26 new members over the previous year.

On the whole, the interbank lending market interest rate of the interbank went down. In 2020, the weighted average interest rate of interbank lending market dropped by 63 basis points compared with the previous year. At the end of 2020, the weighted transaction interest rates for overnight and seven-day lending closed at 1.34% and 2.55% respectively, down by 16 and 66 basis points from the beginning of the year. The range of the daily weighted transaction interest rate for the year was 207

---

① Author: Rong Yihua, Deputy Director of Financial Market Management Department, PBC Shanghai Head Office, and senior project fellow of Program for China's Financial Policy Report.

basis points, with a drop of 3 basis points from the previous year.

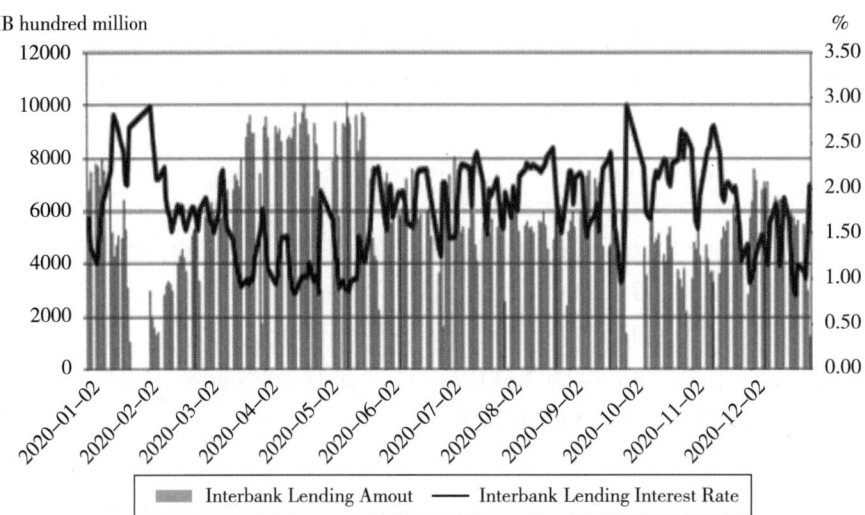

**Figure 1** China's interbank lending market transactions in 2020

(Data source: China Foreign Exchange Trade System)

In 2020, banking institutions still dominated the interbank lending market, accounting for 85.92% of all transactions. Considering capital flows among various financial institutions in the interbank lending market, large commercial banks, policy banks and joint-stock banks were the main capital lenders, while securities companies, city commercial banks and financial companies were the main capital borrowers.

**2. Prospects**

In 2021, the interbank lending market will continue to operate smoothly and orderly, the market interest rate will continue to fluctuate reasonably within the policy interest rate system of the People's Bank of China (PBC), and the standardized operation of market entities will be effectively improved, further highlighting the interbank lending market's liquidity adjustment function.

**(II) The Bill Market**

In 2020, the bill market's system construction was steadily advanced. Institutional policies were introduced in an orderly manner, the liquidity of bill assets was gradually improved, innovations in the bill business emerged one after another, and the market scale was further expanded. The bill market put the roles of policy transmission and targeted entity support into full play.

**1. Overview of Market Operations**

In 2020, the bill business continued to develop soundly; all business indicators registered positive growth, the market interest rate declined, and remarkable results were achieved in supporting the real economy.

The scale of bill acceptance increased, the acceptance of banks' acceptance bills rose steadily, and the proportion of commercial acceptance bills issued increased significantly. In 2020, enterprises issued a total of RMB 22.1 trillion in commercial bills of exchange, a YOY increase of 8.4%; the amount of commercial bills of exchange yet to reach their due dates at the end of the year was RMB 14.1 trillion, up 10.7% YOY. Among these, banks' acceptance bills in the market had an acceptance of RMB 18.5 trillion, a YOY increase of 6.4%; the amount of commercial acceptance bills issued was RMB 3.6 trillion, a YOY increase of 19.8% and occupying a market share of 16.4%.

Discounted bills increased, with banks' acceptance bills accounting for more than 90%. Bills discounted over the whole year amounted to RMB 13.4 trillion, a YOY increase of 7.7%. Specifically, the banks' acceptance bills discount came to RMB 12.4 trillion, accounting for 92.5%; commercial acceptance bills discount was RMB 1.0 trillion, up 9.9% YOY, accounting for 7.5%. The discounted balance at the end of the year was RMB 8.8 trillion, an increase of 7.3% from the beginning of the year.

The year witnessed active bill transactions and the enhancement of bill pledge and financing functions. The annual transaction volume of the bill market was RMB 64.1 trillion, up 25.9% YOY. To be specific, the transaction volume of interbank discounts was RMB 44.1 trillion, a YOY increase of 13.6%, and the growth rate had increased by 1.5 % over the previous year; meanwhile, the repo volume was RMB 20.0 trillion, a YOY increase of 64.9%.

Table 1    Scale of the bill market in 2020

Unit: RMB trillion

| Quarter | Acceptance | Discount | interbank discount | repo |
| --- | --- | --- | --- | --- |
| Q1 | 6.0 | 4.4 | 12.2 | 3.6 |
| Q2 | 5.6 | 3.5 | 13.3 | 5.7 |
| Q3 | 4.8 | 2.5 | 8.7 | 5.7 |
| Q4 | 5.6 | 3.1 | 9.9 | 5.0 |
| Total | 22.1 | 13.4 | 44.1 | 20.0 |

Data source: Shanghai Commercial Paper Exchange Corporation.

Bills' interest rate declined overall. The weighted average interest rate of discounted bills for the whole year was 2.98%, down 47 basis points YOY; the weighted average interest rate of interbank discounts was 2.71%, down 60 basis points YOY; and the weighted average interest rate of pledge-style repo was 1.87%, down 64 basis points YOY.

Greater efforts went into rediscounts. Over the year, the PBC increased the amount of relending and rediscounts by RMB 1.8 trillion three times in order to secure an adequate supply and help in the fight against the pandemic as well as in the return to work and production and the development of real economy — such as by targeting small and medium-sized enterprises. The rediscount balance at the end of the year was RMB 578.4 billion, an increase of 22.7% over the same period the previous year.

## 2. Main Policies

In February 2020, the PBC issued the Notice on *Strengthening the Support in Relending and Rediscount to Promote Orderly Resumption of Work and Production* (Yinfa [2020] No.53). A special limit on relending and rediscounts of RMB 500 billion was added to a special relending fund of RMB 300 billion for epidemic prevention and control set up in the early stage. In addition, the relending interest rate for supporting agriculture and small businesses was lowered by 0.25 % to 2.5%.

In April, the Shanghai Head Office, Hangzhou Central Sub-branch, Nanjing Branch and Hefei Central Sub-branch of the PBC jointly issued the *Work Plan for the Promotion and Application of Electronic Commercial Acceptance Bills in the Yangtze River Delta Region* (Hang Yinfa [2020] No.58) to further promote the application of electronic commercial acceptance bills in the region.

In April, the PBC issued the *Notice on Increasing the Relending and Rediscount Quota to Support Small and Medium-sized Banks in Increasing Credit Supply for Agriculture-related, Small and Micro Enterprises and Private Enterprises*, which increased the relending and rediscount quota by RMB 1 trillion.

In May, the China Banking and Insurance Regulatory Commission (CBIRC) and five other ministries jointly issued the *Notice on Further Standardizing Credit Financing Charges to Reduce the Comprehensive Cost of Enterprise Financing* (Yinbaojianfa [2020] No.18), which prohibited the classifying of credit lines as banks' acceptance bills regardless of enterprises' actual needs and the involuntary replacing of credit funds with non-cash forms such as banks' acceptance bills.

In June, the PBC issued the *PBC Announcement* [2020] No.6 (Measures for the Administration of Standardized Bills), which officially launched standardized bills and standardized the financing mechanism of standardized bills so as to better serve the financing of small and medium-sized enterprises and the development of supply chain finance.

In June, the PBC, CBIRC, China Securities Regulatory Commission and State Administration of Foreign Exchange jointly issued the *Rules for the Identification of Standardized Credit Assets* (PBC, CBIRC, CSRC & SAFE Announcement [2020] No.5), which clarified the boundaries between standardized and non-standardized credit assets as well as their respective identification standards and regulatory arrangements. It stipulated that standardized bills may only become standardized credit assets after their applications for confirmation have been approved.

In September, the PBC and seven other ministries jointly issued the *Opinions on Standardizing the Development of Supply Chain Finance to Support the Stable Circulation and Optimization and Upgrading of Supply Chain and Industry Chain* (Yinfa [2020] No.226), which proposed speeding up the implementation of the information disclosure system for commercial bills of exchange, improving the standardization and transparency of accounts receivable, and supporting the development of supply chain bills and standardized bill financing.

In December, the PBC issued the *PBC Announcement* [2020] No.19 (Regulating the Information Disclosure of Commercial Banks' Bills of Exchange), which clarified matters related to the information disclosure of commercial acceptance bills so as to improve the market credit environment and promote the functioning of commercial acceptance bills.

### 3. Analysis of Policies' Effects

Strong support for real enterprise development. Since the beginning of 2020, in response to the COVID-19 epidemic's impact on the real economy, the PBC arranged three instances of refinancing and rediscounting totaling RMB 1.8 trillion in a hierarchical and graded manner. This supported epidemic prevention and control, guaranteed stable supplies, facilitated the resumption of work and production, and promoted the development of micro-, small, and medium-sized enterprises and other forms of real economy, effectively solving urgent problems facing enterprises in terms of the return to work and production such as debt repayment, capital turnover, and financing expansion. By the end of 2020, the rediscounting balance was RMB 578.4 billion, with a YOY rise of 22.7%, which contributed to the precise injection of funds and supported the development of the real economy, especially private enterprises and micro-, small, and medium-sized enterprises.

Reinforcement of market mechanisms. Shanghai Commercial Paper Exchange Corporation Ltd. launched a commercial bill information disclosure platform on January 16, 2020, and the self-registration function on February 28. Commercial bill acceptance institutions are able to disclose bill-related information through the platform, and the platform discloses the credit status of acceptors' acceptance bills on a daily basis — including the acceptance amount, acceptance balance, accumulated overdue amount, and overdue balance. Twenty-one enterprises have become the first batch of pilot participants. At the end of 2020, the PBC issued an announcement on matters related to commercial acceptance bills' information disclosure based on the results of the pilot, establishing a commercial acceptance bills information disclosure system and effectively improving market transparency.

Reduction in corporate financing costs. In order to promote the effects of fee reduction, alleviate financing difficulties, and lower financing costs, the CBIRC and five other ministries and commissions jointly issued the "Notice on Further Regulating Credit Financing Charges and Reducing Comprehensive Financing Cost of Enterprises". The Notice focuses on various links in financing, puts forward a standard for determining whether or not to increase the comprehensive cost of financing, takes into account both supply and demand sides for credit funds, and regulates fee charging and management for credit, credit assistance, credit enhancement and credit assessment, thereby strengthening the role of internal control, external supervision and incentives, while clarifying interdepartmental cooperation on regulation and mechanisms of positive motivation. In terms of bills, in order to solve problems like linking deposits with loans and compulsory loan tying, the PBC required "not ignoring the actual needs of enterprises, not allocating part of the credit line as bankers' acceptances, and not forcefully replacing credit funds with bankers' acceptances or other non-cash forms" so as to effectively meet enterprises' actual financing needs.

Creation of an atmosphere conducive to development. Eight ministries and commissions jointly issued the *Opinions on Standardizing the Development of Supply Chain Finance to Support the Stable Cycle and Optimization of Supply Chain and Industrial Chain*. The opinions defines supply chain finance for the first time, clarifies the development objectives of supply chain finance, proposes policy measures to enhance the standardization and transparency of accounts receivable, and supports the development of supply chain bills and standardized bill financing, which in turn guides and promotes standardization and innovation in the bill market, improves the operational efficiency of the supply and industrial chains, supports the stable upgrading of the supply and industrial chains, and facilitates national strategic layout. Ten specific measures were put forward in the *Work Plan for the Promotion and Application of Electronic Commercial Acceptance Bills in the Yangtze River Delta Region*, including improving market efficiency, sharing market information, improving the credit system, supporting product innovation, strengthening rediscounting, and reinforcing the restraint mechanism. The Work Plan clearly stipulates that continuous efforts should be made to advance "Piaofutong" and "Tiexiantong" and carry out the pilot billization of accounts receivable. According to the "Measures for Standardized Administration of Bills", the bill market and the bond market are connected, which gives play to the professional pricing and investment capability of the bond market and improves the standardization of bill trade.

Innovations in bill products. As of the end of 2020, 57 standardized bills were successfully launched totaling RMB 6.118 billion, 31 of which have been redeemed for the total amount of RMB 3.226 billion. In addition, there were no failures of redemption. On April 24, a supply chain bill platform was launched and put into operation, which improved bills' payment circulation and offered new thoughts and channels for the billization of accounts receivable. On its very first day, 17 enterprises issued 17 supply chain bills which amounted RMB 1, 044, 200 and three supply chain bills for the endorsement transfer of two enterprises which totaled RMB 51, 000. On June 18, the first batch of rediscounting business for supply chain bills was successfully handled. Nine enterprises made 10 financing deals totaling RMB 5.0681 million via supply chain bill rediscounting, with rediscounting rates from 2.85% to 3.8%. All discounted bills were commercial acceptance bills. With the development of "Tiexiantong" and "Piaofutong" online, as of the end of 2020, a total of 7,819 enterprises had received bill broker services via "Tiexiantong" and 28,165 bills amounting to RMB 46.98 billion had expressed intentions to rediscount. The platforms promoted the sound and healthy development of innovative bills services and better satisfied the needs of private enterprises and small and medium-sized enterprises for rediscounting and financing. The quality and effectiveness of the bill market in serving the real economy were further improved.

### 4. Prospects

2021 marks the first year of "the 14th Five-Year Plan". Against the background of a new development paradigm featuring dual circulation in which domestic and overseas markets reinforce each other and with the domestic market as the mainstay, as well as further deepening of reforms in the financial sector, the Chinese bill market will continue to improve systems and structures, to strengthen infrastructure, to innovate systems and mechanisms, to promote transparency, to accelerate technological empowerment, to offer substantial support for the supply chain and industrial chain, and to play a more important role in promoting the high-quality development of the real economy.

## Article 9

### The State Council approves the Work Program for Deepening the New Round of Integrated Pilot of Expanding Opening-up of the Service Industry in Beijing and Building a National Comprehensive Demonstration Area of Expanding Opening-up of the Service Industry[①]

On August 28, 2020, the State Council formally approved the *Work Program for Deepening the New Round of Integrated Pilot of Expanding Opening-up of the Service Industry in Beijing and Building a National Comprehensive Demonstration Area of Expanding Opening-up of the Service Industry* (the "Program"), as was jointly reported by the Beijing Municipal People's Government and the Ministry of Commerce. The "Program" aims to implement major decisions from the Party Central Committee and the State Council to deepen the new round of comprehensive pilot projects meant to expand opening-up in Beijing's service sector and promote the service industry's quality development.

The Party Central Committee and the State Council see the expansion and opening-up of the service and financial sectors as highly important. On September 4, 2020, General Secretary Xi Jinping delivered an important speech at the China International Fair for Trade in Services. In it, he proposed Beijing play a leading role in opening up China's service industry. He also said the municipality should be supported in building a national comprehensive demonstration zone for the opening-up of the service industry in order for a more replicable experience. Greater opening-up in the financial services sector will drive the liberalization of the entire service industry —a concept which is also reflected in the 2021 government work report and the "14th Five-Year Plan" outline.

The Beijing Municipal Party Committee and Municipal Government are vigorously promoting service and financial industries' high-quality development. On February 22, 2021, Cai Qi, secretary of the Beijing Municipal Party Committee, conducted research on the promotion of high-quality development in the financial industry and held a forum in Beijing on financial work. He stressed the importance of following General Secretary Xi Jinping's important instructions for Beijing's reform and development. In the new stage of pursuing quality development, Beijing should embrace new development concepts and build a new development pattern to actively cultivate and develop a modern financial industry befitting the status of a large country's capital city and take the national lead in financial reform and development measures. Cai Qi has made a strategic plan for the deepening of reform and widening of opening-up for Beijing's financial industry. His plan approaches this task from three aspects: building financial infrastructure, strengthening the

---

① Author: Zhang Chen, Chief Researcher of Macro Situation and Financial Risk of the Research Department at China Cinda Asset Management, and project fellow of Program for China's Financial Policy Report.

construction of a multi-level capital market, and improving financial services for the real economy. Meanwhile, the plan puts forward three requirements: seizing the opportunity to build the "two zones" (that is, the national comprehensive demonstration zone for expanding the opening up of the service industry and the Beijing Pilot Free Trade Zone), further expanding financial opening-up, and strengthening the construction of the national financial management center.

The "14th Five-Year Plan" has repeatedly stressed that finance should provide factor support for the service industry and promote openness for the financial and service industries. The third section of Chapter 10 deals with deepening the reform and opening-up of the service sector. It proposes improving the policy system to support the development of the service sector, identifying new financial policies that serve new business models in the service sector or integrated industrial development, and promote comprehensive pilot reform and greater openness across the service industry. The second section of Chapter 13 deals with improving the level of international two-way investment, which will require improvement in overseas production and service networks and distribution systems, and accelerating financial services' international development. The third section of Chapter 41 deals with deepening pragmatic cooperation in trade and investment, proposing a "Belt and Road" financial cooperation network, the interconnection of financial infrastructure, and support for the joint participation of multilateral and national financial institutions in investment and financing.

The Program's approval fully affirms the strategic positioning of Beijing as the capital of China and requires under the premise of risk control that Beijing sets an example and provides experience for the rest of the country through the deepening of reform and expanding of opening-up in the service industry. The Program's approval requires Beijing to deepen market-oriented reform, expand high-level openness, adhere to international rules for advanced trade and investment, learn from the experience of mature economy, advance transformation in the character of openness from commodity and factor flow-type to that of rules and other institutional types of openness, create a good institutional environment for the high-quality development of the service industry, gain more replicable experience in the service industry's expanded opening-up and in building a new system of a higher-level open economy, set itself as a role model for the open and innovation-driven development of China's service industry, and make greater contributions to opening-up in an all-around way.

The "Program" is divided into four parts — respectively covering the general requirements, development goals, main tasks & measures, and organization & implementation for the new round of opening-up expansion for the integrated pilot in Beijing's service industry. The "Program" clarifies the strategic positioning of the capital city and puts forward general requirements to explore new business modes, new patterns, and new paths for the service industry's open development and to build a national comprehensive demonstration zone for the greater openness of the service industry.

In terms of development goals, the "Program" takes the years 2025 and 2030 as benchmarks, putting forward specific requirements for each of the two five-year periods regarding the institution and open system building. The "Program" dictates by 2025 a policy and institutional system should be established for trade & investment facilitation and the greater liberalization of the service industry. By 2030, Beijing should have realized free trade and investment, free cross-border capital flow, employment convenience, easy transportation, and a safe and orderly data flow, fundamentally setting down a system of openness for the service industry that meets a high international standard of economic and trade rules.

In terms of main tasks, the "Program" focuses on nine key sectors in the service industry — including, such as technology services, digital economy and trade, and financial services — and aims to increase service industry openness in seven major areas such as Zhongguancun Science Park, Beijing Financial Street, and the National Cultural and Financial Cooperation Demonstration Zone. It dictates six aspects of institutional innovation — including investment and trade, finance and taxation, and industry-supply chain synergy — seeks to optimize supply for four-factor types, i.e., capital, data, talent, and land, and proposes policy measures for open innovation in 26 fields, which include science and technology innovation, service industry liberalization, and the digital economy and digital trade.

Expanding openness in the financial service sector remains the top priority. Among the Program's 120-plus policies, 29 are related to financial services, which accounts for approximately one quarter. Especially notable are some policy breakthroughs in relaxing access to foreign capital and facilitating the cross-border flow of capital.

The introduction of the "Program" provides good institutional support for the opening-up of Beijing's service and financial industries. It will certainly contribute to a better business environment for foreign investors to engage in China's service and financial industries. It is also conducive to exploring new paths and setting a model for China's efforts to build a new higher-level open economy system so that the reform and opening up of China's service and financial industries can make steady and sustainable progress in the new era.

### VII. Trust and Wealth Management Market Development Policy[1]

### (I) Key policy elements in 2020

In 2020, the trust and wealth management market achieved outstanding results in development policy; one could say it was a pivotal year featuring policy developments.

**1. Guidance on Promoting Quality Development in Banking and Insurance Industries**

On December 30, 2019, the CBIRC issued the *Guidance on Promoting Quality Development in Banking and Insurance Industries* (YBJF [2019] No.52) (hereafter referred to as the *Guidance*).

---

[1] Author: Li Qingyun, President of Tianjin Minsheng Asset Management Co., Ltd., and senior project fellow of Program for China's Financial Policy Report.

As the Chinese economy transitions from a stage of high-speed growth to a stage of high-quality development, the imbalance and maladjustment between financial supply and demand are gaining prominence, and the banking and insurance industries' high-quality development is facing many challenges. In order to carry out the decisions and arrangements of the CPC Central Committee, promote the high-quality development of the banking and insurance industries, and better serve the construction of a modern economic system, the CBIRC formally issued the *Guidance*. An important programmatic document, the *Guidance* looks ahead to 2025, putting forward systematic requirements for such objectives as forming a differentiated multi-level banking and insurance institution system with wide coverage, perfecting the financial product system to serve the real economy and meet the people's basic needs, accurately and effectively preventing and defusing all kinds of risks in the banking and insurance system, establishing and perfecting the modern financial enterprise system with Chinese characteristics, realizing a higher level of opening up, and strengthening financial supervision and the construction of "clean finance".

The *Guidance* not only sets out objectives for the banking sector as a whole; it also sets out two direct objectives specifically for the trust industry:

(1) Regarding the construction of an institutional system, trust companies must return to their functional orientation of "entrusted by clients to manage money" and must actively develop their original businesses such as service trust, wealth management trust, and charitable trust.

(2) Regarding risk prevention and resolution, the industry must gradually clean up and reduce the scale of non-standard assets investment, on-balance sheet specific purpose vehicle investment, and interbank money management, and so on, and strictly control channel business in the banking and trust system.

**2. Interim Measures for Trust Company Equity Management**

On January 20, 2020, the CBIRC promulgated the *Interim Measures for Equity Management of Trust Companies* (hereafter referred to as the *Interim Measures*), which came into force on March 1, 2020.

The *Interim Measures* comprises six chapters and 78 articles in total: on general provisions, the responsibilities of shareholders in a trust company, the responsibilities of a trust company, supervision and administration, legal liabilities, and supplementary provisions. The *Interim Measures* relies on the *Interim Measures for the Equity Management of Commercial Banks* as a complete reference for penetrating supervision system design and the classified management of shareholders to clarify the responsibilities of shareholders of trust companies, trust companies themselves, and regulators in different stages of stock equity management. Specifically, the main contents of the *Interim Measures* are as detailed below.

(1) Shareholder liability

In this section, the *Interim Measures* makes clear provisions on shareholder qualifications, equity acquisition, equity holding, and equity withdrawal.

① Shareholder qualifications

The *Interim Measures* requires that "domestic non-financial institutions, domestic financial institutions, overseas financial institutions and other investors recognized by the banking regulatory body under the State Council may become shareholders of trust companies upon examination and approval by the banking regulatory body under the State Council or its agencies". For different types of institutions, the *Interim Measures* further clarifies requirements in terms of operating level, asset size, and other parameters. At the same time, the *Interim Measures* sets forth clear prohibition clauses for acting as the main shareholder of a trust company.

② Equity acquisition

The *Interim Measures* stipulates that "Investors may become shareholders of trust companies by investing in the establishment of a trust company, subscribing the additional capital of a trust company, obtaining the stock equity held by other shareholders of a trust company by agreement, bidding, or other means." For the principal shareholders of a trust company, a principle of upward penetration should be followed to "state its equity structure layer by layer until the actual controller and the ultimate beneficiary, as well as their relationship (related or concerted action) with other shareholders."

③ Equity holding

While putting forward norms on corporate governance, cross-shareholding, part-time employment, and risk isolation in trust companies, the *Interim Measures* particularly strengthens requirements for the information disclosure of trust company shareholders: If a shareholder "may have his shareholder qualification changed or have the equity he or she holds in a trust company changed", he or she must notify the trust company in writing within 15 days.

④ Equity withdrawal

The *Interim Measures* sets a time limit for equity withdrawal: "Any shareholder of a trust company shall not transfer the equity held by him or her within five years from the date of acquiring the equity." However, shareholders holding less than 5% of total shares are exempt.

(2) Trust company liability

In this section, the *Interim Measures* sets forth clear requirements in terms of change periods, equity affairs management, shareholder behavior management, and other areas.

① Change periods

The *Interim Measures* requires that during periods when "a trust company changes its equity or adjusts its equity structure, or merges, splits, or has other changes that affect its equity", the trust company must ensure effective corporate governance and strictly prevent insider control.

② Equity affairs management

The *Interim Measures* puts forward a number of provisions on daily equity management and requires trust companies "to establish and improve an equity management system and satisfactorily conduct equity information registration, related transaction management, and information disclosure". At the same time, the *Interim Measures* requires that trust companies establish an equity custody system — and, in principle — conduct intensive equity custody. In addition, the *Interim Measures* specifically sets forth provisions on persons responsible: "The chairman of the board of a trust company is the first person responsible for handling the trust company's equity affairs. The secretary of the board assists the chairman's work and is the direct person responsible for handling equity affairs."

③ Shareholder behavior management

The *Interim Measures* puts forward requirements on shareholder qualification review, related transaction management, and the corporate governance mechanism. In particular, it requires that each trust company strengthen qualification review of its shareholders, "verify the relevant information of principal shareholders and their controlling shareholders, actual controllers, related parties, persons acting in concert, final beneficiaries, and so on, grasp their changes and judge the principal shareholders' impact on the operation and management of the trust company".

(3) Supervision

The *Interim Measures* significantly strengthens supervision of trust companies' equity management and sets forth detailed provisions on the contents, measures, and means of supervision. In particular, the *Interim Measures* places special emphasis on penetrating supervision, requiring "stronger penetrating supervision over trust companies' shareholders, strengthening the review, identification, and confirmation of principal shareholders and their controlling shareholders, actual controllers, related parties, persons acting in concert and final beneficiaries".

**3. Notice on the "Look Back" Work for Market Irregularities Rectification in Banking and Insurance Industries**

On June 24, 2020, CBIRC issued the *Notice on the "Look Back" Work for Market Irregularities Rectification in Banking and Insurance Industries* (YBJF [2020] No.27, hereafter referred to as the Work Notice).

The *Work Notice* specifically sets forth the following requirements for trust companies:

(1) Macro policy implementation

The *Work Notice* particularly focuses on real estate trust, requiring special verification for the normalization of real estate development project loans, land reserve loans or working capital loans, other real estate-related loans, the illegal inflow of capital into the real estate market and providing financing for local government financing platforms and the guarantees of local governments and their subordinates.

(2) Corporate governance

The *Work Notice* puts emphasis on corporate governance, requiring self-inspection and rectification in terms of shareholder qualifications, contributions, information as well as shareholders' illegal pledges of equity, indirect transfers of equity, the abuse of shareholder rights or failure to fulfill shareholder obligations, related transactions, articles of association, job qualifications, key job vacancies, related party identification and updates, operations of the related transaction control committee, incentive and restraint mechanisms, and so on.

(3) Shadow banking and cross-financial business

Since shadow banking and cross-financial business are closely related to the trust industry, the *Work Notice* requires the inspection of non-standard fund pool business clean-up, rolling issuance, new non-standard fund pools in disguise, the acceptance of non-performing assets, penetrating management, and so on.

(4) Financing trust business

The *Work Notice* requires inspections of the financing trust business to focus on: due diligence, post-loan management, provision of allowances for asset devaluation, compression plans, and so on.

(5) Management of non-financial subsidiaries

The *Work Notice* places significant attention on the management of non-financial subsidiaries, requiring self-inspection and rectification for the establishment of non-financial subsidiaries, the liquidation of non-financial subsidiaries, quasi-trust or regulatory arbitrage, channel businesses, non-standard fund pool businesses, related transactions, organizational structure, and so on.

(6) Operation management

The *Work Notice* emphasizes the following in operation management: internet drainage and third-party promotion, the "dual admission" system, illegal commitments to principal preservation or earnings guarantees, implicit guarantees, information disclosure, and the transfer of risky assets.

(7) Innovative business

Innovative business is another concern of the *Work Notice*, which requires self-inspection and rectification of "projects that are classified as equity but are effectively analogous to debt", the yield of (beneficiary) rights or other "false innovations", beneficiary rights circulation, multi-layer nesting, innovation business qualifications, and so on.

**4. Rules on the Identification of Standard Credit Assets**

On July 3, 2020, the PBC, together with the CBIRC, CSRC and SAFE, issued the *Rules on the Identification of Standard credit Assets* (hereafter referred to as the *Identification Rules*).

In accordance with the 2018 *New Asset Management Regulations*' requirement that "the specific rules for the identification of standard credit assets shall be additionally formulated by the PBC in cooperation with departments of financial supervision and administration", the PBC and the CBIRC, CSRC and SAFE formulated the *Identification Rules* to clarify the boundaries, identification criteria, and regulatory arrangements for standard and non-standard credit assets (hereafter referred to as "non-standard assets") in order to guide the normative development of the market.

The *Identification Rules* provides a path for the identification of standard credit assets, which helps make the bond market more inclusive. For all types of credit asset that have been clearly identified as standard, there is no need to carry out the identification of standard credit assets procedures; for other new types of credit assets, these should be identified according to the relevant procedures; meanwhile, identified standard credit assets can be used by asset management products to replace stock non-standard assets.

The *Identification Rules* confirms "non-nonstandard assets" of wide concern, recognizing non-nonstandard assets at the Banking Credit Assets Register and Circulation Center, Beijing Financial Assets Exchange, Shanghai Insurance Exchange and other trading places as non-standard assets, but reserving their right to apply to become standard credit assets.

**5. Notice on Work Related to the Disposal of Risk Assets of Trust Companies**

On July 17, 2020, the CBIRC issued the *Notice on Work Related to the Disposal of Risk Assets of*

Trust Companies (hereafter referred to as the Notice on Disposal).

The *Notice on Disposal* mainly consists of three aspects: (1) requiring trust companies to increase the disposal and resolution of risk assets on and off the balance sheet; (2) setting clear requirements for crackdowns on the trust-related channel business; (3) requiring trust companies to crack down on the illegal financing trust business.

The *Notice on Disposal* further clarifies two key areas for crackdown: one, financial institutions using trust channels to conduct financing business for the purpose of regulatory arbitrage or to avoid policy restrictions; two, trust companies deviating from the position of the trustee to regard themselves as "credit intermediaries"; the risk is essentially borne by trust companies, and the financing business is carried out in violation of laws and regulations.

### 6. Announcement on Optimizing the Transition Period of the New Asset Management Regulations and Guiding the Smooth Transformation of Asset Management Business

On July 31, 2020, the PBC issued the *Announcement on Optimizing the Transition Period of the New Asset Management Regulations and Guiding the Smooth Transformation of Asset Management Business* (hereafter referred to as the *Transition Period Announcement*).

The core content of the *Transition Period Announcement* is the adjustment of the new asset management regulations transition period in accordance with changes in the actual situation. Considering the significant impact of COVID-19 on finance and the economy, the *Transition Period Announcement* clarifies: "In order to smoothly implement the new asset management regulations and normative transformation of the asset management business, the PBC, with the approval of the State Council and in cooperation with the NDRC, MOF, CBIRC, CSRC and SAFE, has carefully studied and decided to extend the transition period of the new asset management regulations until the end of 2021."

The *Transition Period Announcement* also states: "The extension of the transition period does not involve changes or adjustments to any regulatory standards related to the new regulations."

### 7. Notice on Carrying Out a New Round of Special Investigation of Real Estate Trust Business

On October 30, 2020, the Department of Trust Supervision under CBIRC issued the *Notice on Carrying out a New Round of Special Investigation of Real Estate Trust Business* (hereafter referred to as the *Notice on Investigation*).

The *Notice on Investigation* is obviously a successor of the "three red lines" policy for real estate companies. The *Notice on Investigation* requires all banking and insurance regulatory bureaus to earnestly fulfill their supervision responsibilities within their respective authoritative capacities, maintain high-pressure supervision over the real estate trust business, plan in advance for risk prevention and control, strictly investigate and deal with illegal activities, and improve the long-term mechanism for supervision of the real estate trust business. The specific objects of investigation are as follows.

(1) Investigation of the real estate trust business' continuous compliance and supervision. Investigation should focus on trust companies that are developing real estate trust loans in violation

of the rules, trust companies that are breaking regulatory requirements by improper "innovation" and other disguised forms, or providing channels for all kinds of funds to flow into the real estate market against the rules, and so on.

(2) Investigation of the real estate trust business' risk prevention and resolution. Investigation should particularly involve a case-by-case inspection of the real estate trust business, an analysis of risk mitigation measures in order to identify out risk status, a comprehensive look into the concentration of trust companies providing trust financing for real estate groups (including related parties) in order to evaluate the concentration risk, and the development and implementation of risk response plans.

(3) Rectification and implementation of accountability in the real estate trust business. Regarding the compliance and risk problems concerning trust companies' real estate trust business, a summary shall be made for the conditions of rectification and accountability since 2020 (including this special investigation).

**8. Implementation Measures for Administrative Licensing Items of Trust Companies by China Banking and Insurance Regulatory Commission**

On November 16, 2020, CBIRC released the *Implementation Measures for Administrative Licensing Items of Trust Companies by China Banking and Insurance Regulatory Commission* (YBJHL [2020] No.12, hereafter referred to as the *Implementation Measures*), which came into force on January 1, 2021.

The *Implementation Measures* contains seven chapters — General Rules, Institution Establishment, Institution Change, Institution Termination, Adjustment of Business Scope and Addition of Business Varieties, Qualifications of Directors and Senior Executives, and Supplementary Provisions — with a total of 76 articles. The *Implementation Measures* is a revised version based on the *Implementation Measures for Administrative Licensing Items of Trust Companies* by the China Banking and Insurance Regulatory Commission and is organically linked with the *Interim Measures for Equity Management of Trust Companies*. The revised content of the *Implementation Measures* mainly applies to four areas: shareholder qualifications, institutional changes, business qualifications, and director and executive qualifications. The details are as follows.

(1) Shareholder qualifications

① Trust company establishment

The *Implementation Measures* clearly stipulate that "contents regarding the management of shareholders and the rights and obligations of shareholders should be included in a trust company's articles of association in accordance with regulations". At the same time, it puts forward specific requirements for a trust company's "corporate governance structure" and "investor protection mechanism".

② A domestic non-financial institution as the shareholder

The *Implementation Measures* sets out corresponding requirements for non-financial institutions that intend to obtain a trust company's controlling rights, and the new content is consistent with the *Interim Measures for Equity Management of Trust Companies*. The number of trust company shareholders must also comply with the provisions of the *Interim Measures for Equity Management of Trust Companies* — that is, "The same investor and its related parties and persons acting in concert shall not be the shareholder of any more than two trust companies, or be the controlling shareholder of any more than one trust company".

③ A domestic financial institution as the shareholder

The *Implementation Measures* are a continuation of the old version, but add new requirements for domestic financial institutions as contributors of trust companies: "If a domestic financial institution intends to obtain the controlling stake, it must have made =consecutive profits in the last three fiscal years".

④ A foreign financial institution as the shareholder

The *Implementation Measures* removes the requirement that "the total assets at the end of the last fiscal year should in principle be no less than USD 1 billion" in line with the financial sector's policy direction of opening up to the outside world. Other new requirements are consistent with those for domestic non-financial institutions.

(2) Institutional changes

The *Implementation Measures* regulates possible changes in the course of a trust company's operations. The main items involved are: changes of name, changes of equity or adjustment of equity structure, changes of registered capital, changes of premises, modification to the articles of association, separation or merger, etc.

Notably, new amendments to this part of the *Implementation Measures* fully demonstrate an intention to simplify procedures. For example, a trust company should apply to an agency of CBIRC for listing; if the actual location of a trust company has not changed and the temporary premises are vacated within 6 months, the trust company need not apply for a change of premises; also, a trust company does not need to apply for an amendment to its articles of association as a result of adjustments in administrative divisions or changes to shareholders' names.

(3) Business qualifications

The *Implementation Measures* confirms the scope of business qualifications for trust companies, which mainly include enterprise annuity fund management qualifications, specific purpose trusts' trustee qualifications, entrusted overseas money management qualifications, stock index futures trading and other derivatives trading qualifications, and qualifications for engaging in the equity investment business with inherent assets. Among these, qualifications for engaging in the equity investment business with inherent assets are a new addition. Specifically, new content in these amendments to the *Implementation Measures* are mainly as follows.

① Specific purpose trust's trustee qualification

The revised *Implementation Measures* removes two items — "completion of re-registration for more than three years" and "good regulatory rating" — and appropriately relaxes the conditions of previous criteria. At the same time, the *Implementation Measures* eliminates the requirement for pre-issuance reporting on asset-backed securities and further simplifies the business processes.

② Qualifications for engaging in equity investment with inherent assets

The *Implementation Measures* adds this business qualification, its basic conditions almost consistent with those for trustee qualifications for specific purpose trusts. In distinction to other business qualifications, a company conducting a trust business should provide timely reports to regulators. Such reports should mainly contain the "basic situation and feasibility analysis of the project, scope and plan for the use of investment, description of project's main risks and risk management, equity investment project management teams and personnel", and so on.

Specific to business development, the *Implementation Measures* sets a number of operational requirements, such as no investments in related parties, no control over the invested enterprise, no holding equity for more than five years, and not exceeding 20% of net assets in the total amount of investment.

(4) Job qualifications

The Implementation Measures requires directors and executives to be licensed in their job qualifications. The board of a trust company mainly consists of "a chairman, a vice-chairman, an independent director, other board members, and secretary of the board"; a CRO is added to senior executives on the basis of traditional composition.

The *Implementation Measures* clearly states that "if a trust company applies for the approval of the qualifications of directors and senior executives, it shall submit an application to a CBIRC branch or local banking and insurance regulatory bureau". In addition, more stringent requirements are put forward for the chairman and the general manager: the chairman and the general manager (CEO and president) of a trust company must have their job qualifications licensed by the CBIRC.

**(II) Assessment of policy effectiveness for 2020**

**1. Tightening the monetary circuit and stabilizing macro leverage**

In 2020's trust-related policies, content restricting the financing/real estate trust business takes up the most space, mostly within the abovementioned *Work Notice*, *Notice on Disposal*, and *Notice on Investigation*. From a macroprudential point of view, restricting the scale of the financing/real estate trust business may have a certain impact on the money creation cycle, and may help in the long run to resolve the systemic problem of "high money scale and high capital cost". The value of trust-related policy is best understood from the correlation between bulk physical commodity demand and money demand in combination with the monetary creation mechanism.

Over the past 20 years, China's broad monetary (M2) growth rate has been significantly higher than that of GDP; in 2019, it reached the 200 trillion yuan level, far exceeding the scale of GDP. The horizontal comparison shows that China's M2/GDP ratio is significantly higher than those of other major economies. But from another angle, even though the M2 scale is obviously high, China's market interest rate has remained high as well, especially for private lending. A high market interest rate means a high capital cost, which is often called "costly financing". While the growth rate of M2 was much higher than that of GDP, the capital cost remained high, which obviously does not match the traditional definition of an "excessive currency issue". Under the premise of a huge money supply, it will remain difficult to finance. This suggests that shrinking the money supply is bound to cause a further increase in capital cost, which in turn may lead to a dilemma within the monetary policy orientation.

According to its classical theory, money creation is the synergistic result of base money and the required reserve ratio (RRR), and credit money is constantly derived from the deposit-loan cycle. It is important to note that it is lending behavior, not deposit behavior that initiates and drives this cycle. Only strong and sustained loan demand can drive the continuation of the money creation cycle. Furthermore, credit demand is highly correlated with heavy asset capacity demand and backed by real estate, infrastructure, and consumer durables. As a result, economies typically generate strong demand for credit during fast-growth periods of property and infrastructure demand, thereby increasing the money scale. It should be noted that an important prerequisite for realizing credit demand is value-matching pledges, which will be resolved after property prices rise and form a positive feedback loop. In the stage where real estate/infrastructure is the core demand, released funds inevitably flow to the areas of real estate/infrastructure, causing financing difficulties followed by costly financing in other industries.

This kind of demand structure will further aggravate this problem in terms of the velocity of money. According to the Fisher Equation, the velocity of money is inversely proportional to the supply of money. The lower the velocity, the greater the demand is for the money supply. In a demand structure where infrastructure/real estate/automobiles are the core, trading frequency is naturally low, and the velocity of money is in a slow period. Studies on the velocity of money in China have shown that it to have been declining steadily over the past 20 years. In comparison, real estate/infrastructure demand in the world's major developed economies peaked much earlier and has since entered a stage of stabilization. In the absence of new credit demand, even loose policies cannot lead to any significant increase in the money scale. Clearly, a substantial difference in demand structure is the fundamental reason that major developed economies' M2/GDP ratios are significantly smaller than that of China.

Data has shown that China's main rise in physical demand is coming to an end, so we can no longer allow the positive feedback loop of "real estate price – credit expansion" to grow any stronger. Although the trust business is not a standard banking business, it is a shadow banking business, and can cooperate with banks to expand credit in disguise. With the continuous strengthening of supervision on banks' on-balance sheet items, off-balance sheet items, or issuance of loans in disguise by means of trust have been expanding. In terms of asset size, the trust industry has long become the second-largest financial sub-industry after banking only. But the cycle of "real estate price – credit expansion" is unlikely to last forever; it must come to an end in one way or another. In order to prevent the emergence of real estate "gray rhinos", we should actively curb the cycle of monetary expansion. Tightening the efficiency of money creation by curbing the expansion of credit is clearly a prudent move. Therefore, 2020's firm policy of limiting the financing/real estate trust business is bound to help tighten the secondary gate of money supply, thus steadily resolving the problem of "high money scale and high capital cost".

## 2. Deepening risk prevention and promoting a return to origins

According to the *China Shadow Banking Report*, fund trusts and trust loans in the trust business are typical shadow banking businesses. Considering that shadow banking is often a source of risk, increasing the risk prevention and control for shadow banking is the most obvious measure for risk prevention. Generally speaking, repeated adverse changes in credit status and liquidity level are the root causes of financial asset risks. At present, China is in a key stage of shifting its economic growth rate as economic operations transform from the traditional to a new supply-demand cycle. In terms of industrial structure, the proportion of heavy asset industries will decrease steadily over a certain period, inevitably leading to gradual systematic adjustments in demand, capacity, financing scale, and leverage level.

Against this background, possible adverse changes to some enterprises' credit status and phased liquidity level should not be ignored, and there is an obviously higher level of risk with the shadow banking business. Therefore, the current stage is an important window for financial risk prevention, especially for preventing major risks like real estate gray rhinos. As a typical shadow banking business, financing trust — especially real estate trust — has long occupied the core position in the trust business scale. When it comes to risk prevention, we cannot continue to sit by and watch the financing/real estate trust business simply continue as it has been. Therefore, many policies in 2020 are highly targeted at preventing financial risks.

On the other hand, the abovementioned policies also have the distinct effect of returning the trust business to its origins. Trust companies, as entrusted professional asset management organizations, should focus on asset management, wealth management, and other business types in line with their original attributes. However, with strong credit demand in the background, the financing/real estate trust business obviously has a higher cost-performance ratio, which inhibits the trust industry's enthusiasm to develop its original business. Only with strict restrictions on the financing/real estate trust business will the trust industry finally put more attention on its original business.

## 3. Improving the institutional environment and preventing governance risks

Throughout the history of China's trust industry, there have been a number of large-scale rectifications, which is rare among other financial sub-industries. The reasons for said rectifications are complex and diverse, including the complexity of business attributes, the inadequate development of the financial market, and management ability shortcomings. However, it is undeniable that trust companies' deficiencies in corporate governance are also one of the important and even decisive factors that have led to development problems within the trust industry. Defects exist in corporate governance, the adverse effects of which will gradually manifest in specific business activities and have long-term adverse impacts on a daily business or even lead to the continuous accumulation of business risks. Historically, trust company risk events stemming from poor corporate governance were not rare, and some even had significant social impacts. Therefore, how to promote and urge trust companies to improve their mechanisms of corporate governance is highly important for the development of the trust industry.

In 2020, the CBIRC issued and revised the *Interim Measures* on equity management and the *Implementation Measures* on administrative licensing, which together formed a systematic institutional environment for improving trust companies' governance mechanisms and promoting the systematic regulation thereof. As long as corporate governance mechanisms are operating well, trust companies' normative levels on major issues such as development strategy, operations management, and compliance and risk control should improve significantly, which in turn will certainly help prevent the occurrence and accumulation of governance risks.

### (III) Policy Outlook 2021

#### 1. Reducing the scale of channel business

Affected by the population structure, the number of consumers with bulk physical commodities as the core is declining, and traditional industries' demand side will be adjusted accordingly. In the process of change from old demand to new, debt leverage and capital structure adjustments will also commence. Overall, the capital structure will demonstrate a long-term trend of a shrinking proportion of debt financing and an increasing proportion of equity financing. In this context, the scale of debt financing should be optimized in terms of either adaptation or risk prevention. We should remain wary of channel businesses with typical "shadow banking" characteristics. Therefore, in this year, steadily reducing the scale of channel business in trust industry will continue to be the policy focus.

#### 2. Promoting innovative business development

With the deepening development of social wealth status, society is focusing attention on wealth management needs. Trust, as a typical mechanism for asset management, is highly connected to the level of wealth ownership in terms of institutional needs and adaptability. Recent years have seen rapid growth momentum for wealth appreciation demand based on investment programs, wealth protection demand based on property security, and wealth inheritance demand based on inheritance arrangements. As traditional business gradually shrinks, we should accelerate the development of innovative trust businesses such as service trust and charitable trust.

#### 3. Encouraging the transformation of non-standard into standard assets

As the transition period of the *New Asset Management Regulations* is extended by one year to the end of 2021, trust products should strive to complete the corresponding standardization transformation by that deadline. There remain a large number of trust products under pressure for "changing non-standard assets into standard assets". To ensure the realization of this goal safely and effectively, we might consider the introduction of certain incentive measures — on the one hand, promoting trust companies' optimization or upgrading in product planning and business capabilities, on the other hand, urging trust companies to establish comprehensive and effective cooperation with other financial sub-industries — thus ensuring the smooth completion of "changing non-standard assets into standard assets".

## Appendix
### Main policies on the development of China's trust and wealth management market

| Date | Document name | Issued by |
| --- | --- | --- |
| December 30, 2019 | Guidance on Promoting Quality Development in Banking and Insurance Industries (YBJF [2019] No.52) | China Banking and Insurance Regulatory Commission |
| January 20, 2020 | Interim Measures for Equity Management of Trust Companies | China Banking and Insurance Regulatory Commission |
| June 23, 2020 | Notice on the "Look Back" Work for Market Irregularities Rectification in Banking and Insurance Industries (YBJF [2020] No.27) | China Banking and Insurance Regulatory Commission |
| July 3, 2020 | Rules on the Identification of Standard credit Assets | People's Bank of China, China Banking and Insurance Regulatory Commission, China Securities Regulatory Commission, State Administration of Foreign Exchange |
| July 17, 2020 | Notice on Work Related to the Disposal of Risk Assets of Trust Companies | China Banking and Insurance Regulatory Commission |
| July 31, 2020 | Announcement on Optimizing the Transition Period of the New Asset Management Regulations and Guiding the Smooth Transformation of Asset Management Business | People's Bank of China |
| October 30, 2020 | Notice on Carrying Out a New Round of Special Investigation of Real Estate Trust Business | China Banking and Insurance Regulatory Commission |
| November 16, 2020 | Implementation Measures for Administrative Licensing Items of Trust Companies by China Banking and Insurance Regulatory Commission (YBJHL [2020] No.12) | China Banking and Insurance Regulatory Commission |

# Article 10

## Harnessing spillover effects of the Shanghai International Financial Center to shape a new pattern of quality development where finance and the real economy thrive[1]
### ——Comments on the *Opinions on Further Accelerating the Building of Shanghai International Financial Center and Offering Financial Support for the Integrated Development of the Yangtze River Delta*

Construction of the Shanghai International Financial Center is a national strategy. With attention and support from the Party Central Committee and the State Council, significant progress and remarkable results have already been achieved in building the Shanghai

---

[1] Written by senior researchers of the project "Report on China's Financial Policy".

International Financial Center. The new development paradigm with domestic circulation as the mainstay and domestic and international circulations reinforcing each other has posed new requirements for the construction of the Shanghai International Financial Center. On the one hand, the financial industry is facing demands for its own reform and opening-up as a means to enhance internationalization, — for which it should participate in cross-border business, international financial order and rule-making, free convertibility under capital, and internationalization of the renminbi. On the other hand, the financial industry needs to serve the real economy. This entails investment and trade liberalization, the international deployment of industrial and innovation chains and value chains, and regional integration of the Yangtze River Delta. Such efforts will form a new pattern of quality development characterized by finance and the real economy in sound interaction and mutual support.

Within the context of pandemic prevention and control, the state issued the *Opinions on Further Accelerating the Building of Shanghai International Financial Center and Offering Financial Support for the Integrated Development of the Yangtze River Delta* (the "Opinions") not only as a way to support Shanghai and its financial industry but also to demonstrate to the entire world China's confidence and determination in expanding openness and accelerating financial reform. The focus of the "Opinions" is on integration of China (Shanghai) Pilot Free Trade Zone Lingang Special Area and the Yangtze River Delta, especially the comprehensive liberalization of the Lingang Special Area. The "Opinions" posits an overall requirement to serve the quality development of the real economy, deepen reform of the financial system and its mechanisms, and prevent systemic financial risks. In terms of specific measures, the "Opinions" declares that: First, financial trial reform should be actively promoted in the Lingang Special Area, with support for the Area to develop major, internationally competitive industries and the advancement of investment and trade liberalization and facilitation. Second, financial opening-up in Shanghai at a higher level and an accelerated pace, which includes expanding a high-level of openness within the financial industry, building renminbi financial asset allocation and risk management centers, and constructing a quality financial business environment in accordance with international standards. Third, financial support should be offered for the integrated development of the Yangtze River Delta. This entails cross-regional collaboration among financial institutions, an improved level of financial support services, and a sound mechanism for the coordination of financial policies and information sharing in the Yangtze River Delta.

To implement the "Opinions", in April the Shanghai Head Office of the People's Bank of China and other 11 departments issued the *Initiatives on Deepening the Early and Pilot Implementation of Financial Support Policies for the Ecological Green Integrated Development Demonstration Area in the Yangtze River Delta*, proposing 16 specific measures including the promotion of co-city financial services, piloting of cross-regional joint credit, and supported establishment of integrated financial institutions. Then on May 8, the China (Shanghai) Pilot Free Trade Zone Lingang Special Area Administration, the Shanghai Head Office of the People's Bank of China, the Shanghai Office of the China Banking and Insurance Regulatory Commission (CBIRC), the Shanghai Office of the China Securities Regulatory Commission (CSRC), and the Shanghai Financial Work Bureau co-issued the *Measures to Comprehensively Promote Financial Opening and Innovative Development in China (Shanghai) Pilot Free Trade Zone Lingang Special Area*, which put forth 50 specific measures for financial development in the Lingang Special Area.

With all departments' concerted efforts, substantial progress has already been made in the implementation of the "Opinions". Financial institutions have been settling in Shanghai at a faster rate, including some innovation-driven, functional signature projects. Notably, AIA Group officially opened, becoming the first wholly foreign-owned life insurance company to operate in the Mainland. Amundi BOC, the first foreign-owned wealth management company, was also approved to open. BlackRock, the second foreign-owned wealth management company in China, was approved for establishment as well. Also approved were the wealth management subsidiary of China CITIC Bank and the wealth management subsidiaries of China Guangfa Bank and Shanghai Pudong Development Bank. Bank of Communications established the subsidiary Bank of Communications Fintech Co. in the Lingang Special Area. The Shanghai Office of the CBIRC issued the *Management Measures for the Establishment, Relocation, and Withdrawal of the Record of Insurance Branches in China (Shanghai) Pilot Free Trade Zone (including Lingang Special Area)*, changing approvals into filings in instances of establishment, change of business premises, or the withdrawal of management for insurance branches and other subordinate branches in China (Shanghai) Pilot Free Trade Zone (including Lingang Special Area). It also aims to promote the reforms for the delegation of power, streamlining of management and optimization of government services, along with improvement of market vitality.

### Policy contents and features

The "Opinions" aims to enhance the Shanghai International Financial Center's capacities for financial innovation and its global influence with three highlights: first, following the highest international standards to reflect the needs of quality development. Focusing on the construction of "a special economic function area with international influence and competitiveness", the "Opinions" explores a more flexible financial policy system, regulatory model, and management system, extending the scope, range, and depth of the shanghai International Financial Center's high-level open development. Second, advancing the construction of renminbi financial asset allocation and risk management centers. Based on Shanghai's reform and opening-up to date, the "Opinions" seeks to strengthen pilots like cross-border renminbi business innovation, the cross-border transfer of renminbi trade finance assets, and renminbi interest rate options as a way to encourage and attract more overseas investors to allocate renminbi assets in the Shanghai International Financial Center. Third, strengthening risk prevention and control in financial reform and opening-up. The "Opinions" views the construction of a law-based financial environment as highly important while aiming to strengthen financial supervision and coordination, improve the risk prevention and control system, and safeguard financial stability.

One major task underlying the "Opinions" is the internationalization of the renminbi; another is international standardization of rules; thus it emphasizes the importance of internationalizing financial infrastructure to improve the internationalization of the Shanghai International Financial Center overall.

### Policy Outlook

The building of the Shanghai International Financial Center has already achieved major progress and remarkable results. Yet staunch support from all parties is still needed if the Shanghai International Financial Center is to lead Asia and reach out to the entire world. First, we need to build fully open financial market and financial institution systems: improving financial market levels and liquidity, financial market pricing power and resource allocation efficiency, and accelerating the concentration of various financial institutions and developing a higher-capacity headquarters economy. Second, we need to build world-leading financial infrastructure and financial technology systems as well as globally advanced financial infrastructure for payment, registration, settlement, clearing, and custody. Third, we need to improve the financial rule of law regulatory system in accordance with international rules and the modernized financial system risk prevention system, raising the level of financial rule of law and strengthening the capacity of financial supervision to promote the pilot rule of law and regulation in the Lingang Special Area. Fourth, we need to build a highly internationalized business environment and a top-flight talent team while improving legal services, internationalized urban management services, social credit, intermediary service system building, and financial talent policies.

## VIII. Financial Derivatives Market Development Policies[1]

### (I) Effects of Related Major Policies

#### 1. Exchange-traded Financial Derivatives Market

(1) Commercial Banks Receive Regulatory Approval to Participate in the China Government Bond Futures Market

With the consent of the State Council, on February 21, 2020, the China Securities Regulatory Commission (CSRC), the Ministry of Finance, the People's Bank of China (PBC), and the China Banking and Insurance Regulatory Commission issued a joint announcement allowing commercial banks and insurance companies to participate in the China government bond (CGB) futures market of the China Financial Futures Exchange (CFFEX) in a phased manner if meeting prerequisites for ensuring regulatory compliance, risk control, and business sustainability. Commercial banks' participation in the CGB futures market can promote the coordinated development of the CGB cash and futures markets, diversify the CGB futures market's investor structure, and facilitate the overall functioning of CGB futures.

---

[1] Author: Wang Qinhuai, General Manager, Research Department, China Foreign Exchange Trade System, and senior project fellow of Program for China's Financial Policy Report.

(2) CFFEX Releases the Notice on the Pilot Program of Commercial Banks Participating in CGB Futures Trading, and Amends Measures of China Financial Futures Exchange on Membership Management, Other Detailed Implementation Rules, and Guidelines of China Financial Futures Exchange on the Management of Futures-Company Member Qualifications

On March 1, 2020, the China Financial Futures Exchange (CFFEX) released the *Notice on the Pilot Program of Commercial Banks Participating in China Government Bond Futures Trading* along with 12 amended rules for detailed implementation including the *Measures of China Financial Futures Exchange on Membership Management*, as well as the amended *Guidelines of China Financial Futures Exchange on the Management of Futures-Company Member Qualifications*. The amended rules and guidelines took effect on March 9, 2020. This round of amendments mainly consists of the addition of the "non-futures-company member" concept to the existing membership framework, improvement to the membership management system, optimization of CGB futures' position limit system, and enhancement of regulation on qualification management for futures-company membership, so as to meet the evolving needs of market development.

(3) CFFEX Amends and Releases Regulatory Criteria and Handling Procedures for Abnormal Trading Activities Related to CGB Futures under the Measures of China Financial Futures Exchange on the Management of Abnormal Trading, and Guidelines of China Financial Futures Exchange on the Release of Information on CGB Futures

On April 8, 2020, the CFFEX amended and released the *Regulatory Criteria and Handling Procedures for Abnormal Trading Activities Related to China Government Bond Futures under the Measures of China Financial Futures Exchange on the Management of Abnormal Trading*, and the *Guidelines of China Financial Futures Exchange on the Release of Information on China Government Bond Futures* (the Guidelines). The above-amended rule and *Guidelines* took effect on April 9, 2020. Article IV (2) of the *Guidelines* took effect on September 14, 2020. The amendments of the above rule and *Guidelines* include clarifications on information disclosure arrangements for non-futures-company Clearing Members and the addition of non-futures-company members. Improving guidelines on information disclosure is conducive to protecting non-futures-company members' business secrets and further developing the CGB futures market.

(4) CFFEX Amends CGB Futures Contracts and Related Rules

On June 12, 2020, the CFFEX released amended CGB futures contracts and detailed trading rules. To facilitate the pilot program of commercial banks participating in the trading of CGB futures, the CFFEX delayed the CGB futures market's opening by 15 minutes. This will be conducive to the healthy and stable development of the CGB futures market. After this adjustment, the opening time of the CGB futures market was effectively synchronized with China's exchange-traded bond and equity index futures markets.

(5) CFFEX Optimizes Trading Limits for CSI 300 Index Options

On June 22, the CFFEX made adjustments to trading limits for China Securities Index (CSI) 300 index options. According to the keynote of stably seeking progress and following the law of gradual development for new products, the CFFEX further adjusted trading limits on CSI 300 index options to effectively prevent market risks. The adjustment is conducive market operation quality improvement, investor structure optimization, market ecology upgrading, and the effective functioning of the market.

(6) CFFEX Releases the Notice on Participation of Qualified Foreign Institutional Investors and RMB Qualified Foreign Institutional Investors in Equity Index Futures Trading

On October 30, 2020, the CFFEX released the *Notice on Participation of Qualified Foreign Institutional Investors and RMB Qualified Foreign Institutional Investors in Equity Index Futures Trading*, intended to implement the *Measures for the Administration of Domestic Securities and Futures Investment by Qualified Foreign Institutional Investors and RMB Qualified Foreign Institutional Investors* jointly issued by the CSRC, the PBC, and the State Administration of Foreign Exchange on September 25, 2020, as well as the *Provisions on Issues Concerning the Implementation of the Measures for the Administration of Domestic Securities and Futures Investment by Qualified Foreign Institutional Investors and RMB Qualified Foreign Institutional Investors* issued by the CSRC, and to coordinate with relevant policies. The notice further clarifies which financial futures varieties and trading methods qualified foreign investors may participate in, ensuring qualified foreign investors' orderly connection to participate in stock index futures trading.

(7) CFFEX Revises the Measures on the Management of Market Makers

On November 6, 2020, the CFFEX released a revised version of the *Measures of China Financial Futures Exchange on the Management of Market Makers*. The revised measures added a relevant provision that the exchange may adopt a tiered approach to market maker management. The revision of the system related to market maker management and the implementation of tiered market maker management will not only help improve relevant business rules, but also help stimulate the vitality of market makers.

(8) CFFEX Amends Detailed Clearing Rules

On December 11, 2020, the CFFEX released the *Detailed Clearing Rules of China Financial Futures Exchange (Amended)* and the *Guidelines of China Financial Futures Exchange on Using China Government Bonds as Margin (Amended)*. The amended rules took effect on December 14, 2020. After the revised detailed clearing rules and business operation guidelines were officially implemented, CGBs could then be disposed of by auction, negotiated sale, or regular sale through the collateral disposal platform of China Central Government Securities Depository and Clearing Co., Ltd. This significantly improved the disposal efficiency for CGBs posted as margin and enhanced the CFFEX's ability to quickly and effectively deal with clearing members' default risks.

(9) CFFEX Amends Risk Control Measures

On December 24, 2020, the CFFEX released the *Measures of China Financial Futures Exchange on Risk Control*. The measures refines and perfects the definition of extraordinary situations in the course of futures trading and relevant emergency actions that the exchange may take. The measures took effect on December 25, 2020. The amendments are mainly to provide rule-based support for the futures market's settlement risk segregation. The measures' implementation facilitates the exchange's rapid resolution of extraordinary situations such as IT system failure, and safeguards the normal and orderly operation of the market.

**2. Over-the-Counter (OTC) Financial Derivative Market**

(1) CFETS Launches the Interest Rate Options Trading, and Perfects the Product Offerings of the Interbank Market

In March 2020, the China Foreign Exchange Trade System (CFETS) launched trial trading in interest rate options linked to LPR, further diversifying the product offerings of the interbank interest rate derivatives market. Based on the management framework of the interbank derivatives market, the CFETS has formulated rules for trading interest rate options, thereby laying an institutional foundation for the sound operation of the market. At the same time, the CFETS has optimized trading services and provided services for the whole life cycle of interest rate option products. It independently develops the functions of the interest rate option trading system and provides institutions with one-stop services for options trading — including quotations and transactions, model pricing, exercise and delivery, risk management, mark-to-market valuation, and delivery amount proxy calculation — covering all aspects of the option business life cycle. In addition, the CFETS has established a bilateral quotation system for interest rate options, organized institutions that are capable and willing to make daily quotations for standard option contracts through the trading system, and formed the market's first complete volatility surface of LPR interest rate options based on institutions' final daily quotations, providing liquidity and pricing benchmarks for the market.

(2) CFETS Continuously Optimizes Standard Bond Forwards and Enhances the Market Activity

In March 2020, the CFETS improved the cash settlement mechanism of the standard bond forward market by reducing the number of quarterly (i.e. March, June, September and December) contracts to two per variety, and allowing investors to confirm deliverable bonds once the contracts are listed. Deliverable bonds are to remain unchanged during the listing period. The CFETS also arranged quotation institutions to provide bilateral quotations on standard bond forwards to the market via the trading system. Since the launch of standard bond forwards, the CFETS has continued to improve the trading mechanism and diversify trading varieties, while market activity has continued to increase. In October 2020, the CFETS launched standard forward contracts for bonds issued by the Agricultural Development Bank of China (ADBC bond forwards), which is significant for the diversification of standard bond forward contract strategies and enhancement of ADBC bond forwards' secondary market liquidity. In 2020, the cumulative turnover of the standard bond forward market was RMB 453.23 billion, with a year-on-year (YOY) increase of 3.8%.

(3) CFETS Adds Reference Rate for FX market Derivatives and Aligns with the New International Benchmark Rate

In order to ensure smooth connection between China's foreign currency interest rate market and the new international benchmark interest rate, the CFETS closely tracked the progress of benchmark interest rate reform and launched trading services for products related to the new foreign currency floating interest rate on April 20, 2020. Floating rates for foreign currency were first introduced to a series of products in the interbank FX market, including the RMB/FX cross-currency swap, G10 cross-currency swap, and foreign currency interest rate swap. Those newly introduced rates include the Secured Overnight Financing Rate (SOFR), CFETS Interbank Reference Offered Rate (CIROR), Sterling Overnight Index Average (SONIA), Euro Short Term Rate (ESTER), and Tokyo Overnight Average Rate (TONAR). The market has been receptive to the new benchmark rate and offers are active. The USD interest rate swap and RMB/USD cross-currency swap linked to the SOFR, USD interest rate swap linked to the CIROR, GBP/USD cross-currency swap linked to the SOFR and SONIA, and USD basis trading linked to the SOFR and CIROR O/N were successively included in the trading system, facilitating foreign currency interest rate risk management for market participants.

(4) CFETS Improves the Derivatives Market Trading Mechanism

In May 2020, the CFETS launched a new derivatives function on X-Trader, its new-generation RMB trading system, optimized X-Swap anonymous click system functions, and added new functions such as aggregated quotes and implied orders. It continued to enhance the efficiency and performance of negotiation while improving trading efficiency; it now maintains a steady market share of over 60%, constituting an important interest rate risk management tool for market members. In December 2020, the CFETS introduced the RFQ function for interest rate swaps that enables a requestor to request quotes from multiple institutions and decide whether or not to trade after receiving responses. This makes for a more efficient price discovery mechanism. In addition, the CFETS has continued to optimize interest rate derivatives functions and the trading mechanism. In 2020, the CFETS comprehensively improved the interface by adding quotation, negotiation, and transaction functions and thereby realizing a complete X-Swap trading interface covering a variety of credit, order, and trading data services. Interface trading has significantly increased the level of automation in derivatives trading and now accounts for nearly 80% of API volume on X-Swap.

(5) CFETS Launches a Bank-Enterprise Transaction Service Platform

On November 2, 2020, the CFETS launched a bank-enterprise transaction service platform (CFETS ONE) to support the development of the real economy and meet the needs of both foreign currency capital transactions and corporate risk management. CFETS ONE is an online trading platform where banks can exchange foreign currencies into Renminbi (and vice versa) for their corporate customers through a dedicated module independent of interbank transactions. Launch of CFETS ONE is an important CFETS initiative guided by regulators to comply with the financial sector's supply-side structural reform and to implement the requirements of financial services for the real economy. CFETS ONE provides safe, efficient, and low-cost services for foreign exchange transactions between banks and entity enterprises. It not only improves the timeliness of quotes and price transparency, it also helps ensure transaction compliance and data security. During the platform's preparation, the CFETS cooperated with regulatory authorities as well as a number of market makers and key enterprises to fully discuss the platform's trading methods, related institutional arrangements, and other content. CFETS ONE expands the scope of service for domestic electronic foreign exchange trading platforms from interbank business to customer business, while further optimizing the hierarchical structure of the FX market and facilitating the formation of renminbi exchange rates.

(6) CFETS Supports the Construction of Benchmark Interest Rate System and Promotes the Application of Benchmark Interest Rates

On November 11, 2020, the CFETS launched FDR001, a new interest rate swap (IRS) product created to implement the People's Bank of China's request for "Further Cultivating China's Interbank Benchmark Interest Rate System with DR (Depository-Institutions Repo Rate) as Representative." The FDR001 IRS product expands the scope of DR applications and increases their market recognition and influence. It also provides support for the issuance of DR benchmark floating rate bonds, thus meeting the needs of relevant bond issuers and investors for managing interest rate risk helping market participants manage and hedge interest rate risk, and providing favorable conditions for the construction of the benchmark interest rate system.

### (II) Financial Derivatives Market Development Outlook

1. We need to further enrich financial market products and bring market functions into play. It is necessary to provide a wider variety of interest rate derivatives to bolster derivative trading support on benchmark interest rates. The development of the interbank interest rate derivatives market has several important implications for the development of benchmark interest rates: first, it can expand the scope of application and enhance the influence of the benchmark interest rate for the money market; second, the validity of the benchmark interest rate can be verified through the price of derivatives, while a more reasonable equilibrium between various types of market prices can be maintained through derivatives trading; third, as the People's Bank of China adopts a price-based regulatory framework, the interest rate derivatives' price discovery function will only be further enhanced.

2. We need to strengthen risk prevention and the regulation of the financial derivatives market and maintain safe and smooth market operations. We should not only effectively fulfill our regulatory responsibilities and continue to strengthen financial derivatives market supervision and risk prevention in accordance with the law and regulations, we should also enhance the effectiveness of regulation and maintain the safe and smooth operation of the financial derivatives market by continuously improving operations and security capacities. We must intensify market risks monitoring and trading practices supervision in order to actively improve the regulatory system. In addition, we must perfect financial derivatives legislation to promote the healthy and regulated development of the financial derivatives market.

# Appendix

## Relevant Policies, Regulations and Announcements on Financial Derivatives Market in 2020

| Released on | Major Policies | Released by |
|---|---|---|
| January 22 | Announcement on the Enhanced Management of Foreign Exchange Risk for Foreign Institutional Investors in the Interbank Bond Market (CFETS Announcement [2020] No. 7) | China Foreign Exchange Trade System |
| February 14 | Notice on Exempting Hubei-based Market Members from Certain Trade and Insurance Fees (CFETS Notice [2020] No. 42) | China Foreign Exchange Trade System National Interbank Funding Center |
| February 14 | Notice on Publication of CFETS Bond Valuation Manual and CFETS IRS Valuation Manual | China Foreign Exchange Trade System |
| February 28 | Notice on Further Improving the Cash Settlement Mechanism for the Standard Bond Forward Market (CFETS Notice [2020] No. 52) | National Interbank Funding Center |
| February 28 | Notice on the Trial Operation of Interest Rate Option Business (CFETS Notice [2020] No. 51) | National Interbank Funding Center |
| March 1 | Notice on the Pilot Program of Commercial Banks Participating in China Government Bond Futures Trading | China Financial Futures Exchange |
| March 1 | Notice on Amending *Measures of China Financial Futures Exchange on Membership Management*, *Detailed Trading Rules of China Financial Futures Exchange*, and Other Rules | China Financial Futures Exchange |
| March 12 | Notice on Adjusting Services Related to Data Interface of RMB Derivatives Market (CFETS Notice [2020] No. 64) | National Interbank Funding Center |
| March 13 | Notice on the Provision of Services Related to Valuation of Interest Rate Options to Market Members | China Foreign Exchange Trade System |
| March 23 | Notice on Launching Spot Matching Business for Interbank G10 Currency Paris Market (CFETS Notice [2020] No. 75) | China Foreign Exchange Trade System |
| April 8 | Notice on Amending *Regulatory Criteria and Handling Procedures for Abnormal Trading Activities Related to China Government Bond Futures under the Measures of China Financial Futures Exchange on the Management of Abnormal Trading*, and *Guidelines of China Financial Futures Exchange on the Release of Information on China Government Bond Futures* | China Financial Futures Exchange |
| April 15 | Notice on Adding New Foreign Currency Floating Rates for Cross Currency Swap and Other Products in the Interbank FX Market (CFETS Notice [2020] No. 103) | China Foreign Exchange Trade System |
| April 27 | Notice on Launching the Repo Function of RMB Trading Platform for the Interbank Market and Derivatives (Phase I) (CFETS Notice [2020] No. 111) | National Interbank Funding Center |

Continued

| Released on | Major Policies | Released by |
|---|---|---|
| May 27 | Notice on the Launch of Prime Brokerage Business in the China Interbank FX Market (CFETS Notice [2020] No. 143) | China Foreign Exchange Trade System |
| June 3 | Notice on the Launch of Matching Mechanism for Swap Trading of G10 Currency Paris (CFETS Notice [2020] No. 150) | China Foreign Exchange Trade System |
| June 12 | Notice on Amending the *2-Year China Government Bond Futures Contract* and Related Rules | China Financial Futures Exchange |
| June 12 | Notice on Launching Confirmation Services for Spot, Forward, and Swap Trading of G10 Currency Paris (CFETS Notice [2020] No. 161) | China Foreign Exchange Trade System |
| June 15 | Notice on Launching FX Option Quotation Interface Services | China Foreign Exchange Trade System |
| June 18 | Notice on Adjusting Trading Limits for CSI 300 Index Options | China Financial Futures Exchange |
| September 24 | Announcement on the Implementation of the Enhanced Arrangements of the Currency Conversion and FX Risk Management under the Bond Connect Scheme (CFETS Announcement [2020] No. 45) | China Foreign Exchange Trade System |
| October 15 | Notice on Launching the New Generation of RMB Trading Platform for Anonymous Inquiry of Cash Securities (X-Bargain) and Derivatives (Phase II) and Other Functions (CFETS Notice [2020] No. 286) | National Interbank Funding Center |
| October 20 | China Foreign Exchange Trade System launched CFETS ONE, a Bank-enterprise Transaction Service Platform | China Foreign Exchange Trade System |
| October 30 | Notice on Participation of Qualified Foreign Institutional Investors and RMB Qualified Foreign Institutional Investors in Equity Index Futures Trading (CFFEX Notice [2020] No. 20) | China Financial Futures Exchange |
| November 6 | Notice on Amending *Measures of China Financial Futures Exchange on the Management of Market Makers* (CFFEX Notice [2020] No. 21) | China Financial Futures Exchange |
| November 11 | Notice on the Launch of FDR001 Interest Rate Swap Trading Service | National Interbank Funding Center |
| December 11 | Notice on Amending *Detailed Clearing Rules of China Financial Futures Exchange* and Related Guidelines (CFFEX Notice [2020] No. 32) | China Financial Futures Exchange |
| December 24 | Notice on Amending *Measures of China Financial Futures Exchange on Risk Control* (CFFEX Notice [2020] No. 36) | China Financial Futures Exchange |

Source: Compiled by the research group.

## Article 11

### Building a demonstration area for quality cross-border financial services cooperation in the Guangdong-Hong Kong-Macao Greater Bay Area[①]

In April 2020, the People's Bank of China, the China Banking and Insurance Regulatory Commission (CBIRC), the China Securities Regulatory Commission (CSRC), and the State Administration of Foreign Exchange (SAFE) jointly released the *Opinions on Financial Support for the Building of the Guangdong-Hong Kong-Macao Greater Bay Area* (the "Opinions"). The "Opinions" offers details on the financial section of the *Outline Development Plan for the Guangdong-Hong Kong-Macao Greater Bay Area* previously issued by the CPC Central Committee and the State Council; it also constitutes a companion piece for the *Opinions on Further Accelerating the Building of Shanghai International Financial Center and Offering Financial Support for the Integrated Development of the Yangtze River Delta*. With predictable and achievable contents, the "Opinions" asserts that the Guangdong-Hong Kong-Macao Greater Bay Area, as China's window to financial opening, will facilitate the strengthening of cross-border cooperation and strength complementarity between the three regions, demonstrating the state's determination to build the Greater Bay Area into a world-class urban agglomeration.

As a major engine for China's real economy, the Greater Bay Area boasts a solid financial-sector foundation. First, it has a high share of regional GDP and leads the country in terms of cross-border trade scale. In 2020, the total GDP of the Greater Bay Area was approximately RMB 11.59 trillion, accounting for 11% of the country. Of that, the GDP of Shenzhen alone reached RMB 2.7 trillion, while that of Guangzhou came to RMB 2.5 trillion, and that of Hong Kong to RMB 2.4 trillion. Also in 2020, the total value of Guangdong Province imports and exports based on Guangdong, Hong Kong and Macao was RMB 7.08 trillion, accounting for 22% of the national total. Second, the Greater Bay Area has a large population base and high per capita income, signs of its great consumption potential. In early 2020, the total population of the Greater Bay Area exceeded 70 million, while per capita GDP was approximately 2.3 times the national average. Third, the Greater Bay Area boasts a vibrant financial industry and leads the country in terms of market volume. By the end of 2020, the Area had 2,319 listed companies (including A-shares, Hong Kong shares and US shares), among which 608 were A-share listed companies with a total market value of RMB 15.66 trillion, accounting for 20% of the total market value of A-shares.

The "Opinions" puts forward five basic principles and 26 specific measures covering five

---

[①] Authors: Zhao Xianghuai, General Manager of the Planning and Operation Management Department at Everbright Securities and project fellow of Program for China's Financial Policy Report; Liu Sida, Manager of the Planning and Operation Management Department at Everbright Securities; Liu Jia, Head of the team of the Planning and Operation Management Department at Everbright Securities.

aspects of building quality cross-border financial services in the multi-center system of the Greater Bay Area; they may be summarized as follows:

The first aspect is the promotion of cross-border trade and the facilitation of investment and financing. First of all, this will improve the ease of trade payments, offering enterprises greater settlement flexibility and lowering the costs of cross-border financial transactions. The "Opinions" proposes to improve foreign exchange management for new forms of trade, promote the reform of capital project facilitation, and explore creating an account management system that would be compatible with the development of the Greater Bay Area. Secondly, it will enhance the Greater Bay Area enterprises' autonomy in investment and financing so they can better meet the financing needs of start-ups, innovation-driven and technology enterprises. The "Opinions" proposes to carry out cross-border loan business and pilot cross-border investment in private equity funds, and so on.

The second aspect is expanded openness in the financial sector. Firstly, expanded openness will assist domestic financial institutions to establish overseas operations. The "Opinions" proposes to create pilot programs for securities and futures operators' cross-border business. Secondly, it will attract overseas financial institutions to establish a presence in China. To this end, the "Opinions" proposes supporting banks and other financial institutions in Hong Kong and Macao to expand space for development in the Greater Bay Area's Mainland divisions. Thirdly, greater openness is conducive to producing more financial products and less expensive financial services for the residents of the Greater Bay Area while enhancing the vitality of the regional wealth management industry. The "Opinions" proposes to support commercial banks in the Greater Bay Area to initiate the establishment of financial asset investment companies and wealth management companies without a cap on foreign ownership, to support cooperation among insurance institutions in the Greater Bay Area to develop cross-border medical insurance and other innovative products, establish the cross-border Wealth Management Connect, etc.

The third aspect is the diversification of capital in Guangdong, Hong Kong and Macao's financing channels. First of all, the "Opinions" seeks to build an open economy through financial liberalization, increase institutional arrangements for easier domestic/foreign currency exchange and cross-border circulation and use, and build infrastructure for the two-way interconnection of cross-border asset allocation. In this regard, the "Opinions" proposes to support the development of offshore renminbi business in Hong Kong and Macao, promoting the convenience of cross-border renminbi circulation and exchange in the Greater Bay Area. It also extends encouragement for the financial industry in Guangdong, Hong Kong and Macao to create a new business model for effective differentiated development. The "Opinions" support Hong Kong's building of a green financial center in the Greater Bay Area, the building of a renminbi clearing center for Portuguese-speaking countries, and support for the development of featured financial industries in Hong Kong and Macao, and so on.

The fourth is raising the level of financial services innovation in the Greater Bay Area. One of the core strategic positionings of the Greater Bay Area is its evolution into "an international science and technology innovation center with global influence". After years of development, the Greater Bay Area can now boast robust industrial and technological advantages. It is home tech giants like Tencent, Huawei, and their incubated enterprises as well as financial companies like Ping An Group and China Merchants Bank; such entities — at the forefront of technological development — provide a foundation for finance-led technology development. The "Opinions" proposes strengthening financial services for technological innovation, support for Mainland banks to intensify cooperation with overseas venture capital institutions, actively explore diversified business models for the financial support of technological development, and enhance the level of innovation in financial services and the building of financial technology carriers in the Greater Bay Area.

The fifth aspect is the prevention of cross-border financial risks. For one thing, as financial cooperation continues to deepen between Guangdong, Hong Kong and Macao, cross-border financial innovation products are enriched and cross-border capital flows become more frequent, but the accumulation of financial risk entails higher requirements for cross-border financial supervision. For another, as a unified framework has not been formed for financial supervision in Guangdong, Hong Kong, and Macao, communication and coordination among the three locales' financial regulators need to improve to establish a sound long-term mechanism for cross-border financial risk management. The "Opinions" proposes toughening financial supervision and intensifying cooperation between Guangdong, Hong Kong and Macao, establishing a quality system for financial risk warning, prevention and resolution, and strengthening the protection of financial consumer rights and interests for those in Guangdong, Hong Kong, and Macao.

## IX. Development Policies for the Commodity Futures Market[1]

### (I) Main Policies for the Commodity Futures Market in 2020

#### 1. Supporting China's Battle against Poverty

In 2020, China achieved the goal of building a moderately prosperous society in all respects and attained a complete victory in the fight against poverty. The futures market ensured set prices through the "Insurance Plus Futures" policy for commodities from poverty-stricken areas including natural rubber, corn, soybeans, eggs, apples, cotton, white sugar and jujubes to help China win the battle against poverty. On January 2, 2020, the No.1 Central Document of the *Opinions of the Central Committee of Communist Party and the State Council of China on Doing a Good Job in the Key Areas of Agriculture, Rural Areas, and Farmers to Ensure the Building of a Moderately Prosperous Society in All Respects* proposed optimizing the pilot "Insurance Plus Futures" project. This was the

---

[1] Author: Gan Zhengzai, Deputy Managing Director of Guoyuan Futures Co. Ltd., and project fellow of Program for China's Financial Policy Report.

fifth consecutive year since 2016 that the No.1 Central Document had supported the "Insurance Plus Futures" project. Among various futures-based approaches to poverty alleviation, "Insurance Plus Futures" has increasingly become a key targeted measure in the futures industry and has already played a vital role in the fight against poverty by increasing farmers' incomes, facilitating rural revitalization, and serving the real economy. Meanwhile, following the No.1 Central Document of 2019, the 2020 document again proposed that we should "continue to promote the listing of produce futures and options". In addition to produce futures such as of apples and jujubes, which are included in efforts to reduce poverty, some other produce futures, such as of hogs, peanuts, dried chili and potatoes, have also been added to the listing agenda.

### 2. Serving the Guangdong-Hong Kong-Macao Greater Bay Area and the Belt and Road Initiative

In April 2020, the People's Bank of China (PBC), China Banking and Insurance Regulatory Commission (CBRIC), China Securities Regulatory Commission (CSRC), and State Administration of Foreign Exchange (SAFE) jointly issued the *Opinions on Financial Support for the Development of the Guangdong-Hong Kong-Macao Greater Bay Area*, which clearly proposed constructing and improving working mechanisms for green finance cooperation in the Guangdong-Hong Kong-Macao Greater Bay Area (GBA) in accordance with the Guangzhou Green Finance Reform and Innovation Pilot Zone. The China Emissions Exchange's role as a platform was put to full use, while a platform was established for environmental rights exchange and financial services in the GBA. Pilot projects for carbon emissions trading in foreign currencies were conducted, allowing foreign investors (both foreign institutions and individuals) that had passed the Guangdong-Hong Kong-Macao Greater Bay Area Mainland Carbon Emission Allowances Trading Center Co., Ltd. qualification review to trade carbon emission allowances in either Renminbi or foreign currencies in the Mainland area of the GBA. In addition, the Guangzhou Futures Exchange (GFE) was established. On July 28, the Guangdong Financial Supervisory Authority and other authorities issued the *Implementation Plan for Execution of the Opinions on Financial Support for the Development of the Guangdong-Hong Kong-Macao Greater Bay Area*, which proposed the formulation of mechanisms for assurance in the preparation and operation of the GFE as well as the further study of futures varieties for listing so as to build an important financial infrastructure platform in the Greater Bay Area. In September, the Guangzhou Financial Supervisory Authority dictated in the *Action Plan for Execution of the Opinions on Financial Support for the Development of the Guangdong-Hong Kong-Macao Greater Bay Area* that for the full facilitation of GFE establishment, the Guangzhou Financial Supervisory Authority shall proactively promote the implementation of related policies, cooperate with relevant authorities in preparation for GFE establishment, and study the futures varieties to be traded, vigorously advancing the establishment of the GFE and other similar institutions. In October 2020, the CSRC announced that a preparatory working group had been set up and the countdown begun for the unveiling of the Guangzhou Futures Exchange. Targeted at innovative, market-oriented, and international development, the Guangzhou Futures Exchange prioritizes serving the real economy and is of great significance to the improvement of China's capital market system, the development of the Greater Bay Area and the Belt and Road Initiative (BRI), and high-quality economic growth.

### 3. Increasing the Supply of Commodity Futures and Options Products

In 2020, in order to better meet the risk-hedging needs of the real economy and with the guidance of the market, the CSRC and three commodity futures exchanges launched a series of new futures and options varieties — including four commodity futures (liquefied petroleum gas, low sulfur fuel oil, staple fiber futures, and bonded copper futures) and eight commodity options (rapeseed meal, liquefied petroleum gas, linear low-density polyethylene, thermal coal, polypropylene, polyvinyl chloride, aluminum, and zinc). The liquefied petroleum gas futures and the low sulfur fuel oil futures were listed, which accelerated the construction of China's energy futures market system that is focused on oil, coal, and natural gas. Related derivatives in the textiles and chemical industry improved the industries' risk control instrument system as well as inter-sector agglomeration effects to accelerate optimal industrial integration and upgrading. In terms of different futures exchanges, the Shanghai Futures Exchange (SHFE) listed four varieties (low sulfur fuel oil futures and bonded copper futures plus aluminum and zinc options); the Zhengzhou Commodity Exchange (ZCE) listed three (staple fiber futures and rapeseed meal and thermal coal options); the Dalian Commodity Exchange (DCE) listed five (liquefied petroleum gas futures and options as well as polypropylene, polyvinyl chloride, and linear low-density polyethylene options). There are currently 90 futures varieties listed on China's futures market, 62 of which are commodity futures, and 22 of which are options.

### 4. Speeding Improvements to Current Rules and Regulations

On March 4, 2020, in order to regulate future companies' internet account-opening activities, the China Futures Association released the "Rules for Futures Companies to Open an Account on the Internet" (Amendment in 2020), providing standard guidance for the futures industry's online services. To provide regulatory support for the isolation of settlement risks within the futures market, the three commodity exchanges respectively amended the rules for risk control and management and refined specific unusual situations in futures trading along with possible emergency measures. Futures contracts were made more active in the futures market and a market making system was fully promoted. Throughout the year there were 32 new futures and options market making varieties, for a current total of 65 futures and options market making varieties. The liquidity of market making varieties and the continuity of active contracts were remarkably enhanced as well. In 2020, the three commodity exchanges took central government bonds as margin collateral. This practice not only helped broaden the scope of collateral in the margin; it also effectively lowered the cost of futures trading while increasing market liquidity. Amendments were made to existing varieties' contract rules, delivery warehouse layouts were optimized, and different varieties' trading margins were properly adjusted to reduce delivery costs and revitalize existing futures varieties.

### 5. Initial Success in the Over-the-Counter (OTC) Derivatives Market

With the rapid development of the risk control business, initial success was demonstrated in the construction of the OTC derivatives market. The three commodity futures exchanges successively launched platforms combining OTC futures and cash businesses — for warehouse receipts trading, basis trading, and commodity exchange. These platforms supplemented floor market instruments and connected futures with cash, the floor market with the OTC market, and online trading with offline trading to further promote the development of the derivatives market and effectively make room for serving the real economy. The DCE successively introduced six varieties for standard warehouse receipts trading to the OTC market, including soybean oil as well as iron ore and synthetic resin for non-standard warehouse receipts. It effectively set up circles for two varieties — coal coke and chemical products — and successfully launched the spot market for these two commodities, showing the outline of the OTC market. The ZCE saw increasing participation and an expanding market scale on its comprehensive platform, gradually revealing the role of the OTC market in serving the real economy. The standard warehouse receipts trading platform of the SHFE released standard warehouse receipts trading to invigorate the inventory of warehouse receipts and satisfy business entities' needs for individualized delivery. The OTC derivatives trading report led by the China Futures Margin Monitoring Center received a certificate of Financial Stability Board (FSB), becoming China's first report inventory to be officially certified by FSB. This report and achievement will play an important role in the stable development of China's OTC derivatives market.

### 6. Promoting the Opening Up of the Futures Market

First, specific varieties were expanded. Existing commodity futures varieties were pushed to internationalize and the number of specific varieties were further increased. On November 19, 2020, bonded copper futures were officially listed on the Shanghai International Energy Exchange (INE). As the first futures variety to be traded with two futures contracts in order to achieve internationalization, bonded copper futures are of great significance to the deepening integration of domestic and international cooper industrial and supply chains. With low-sulfur fuel oil and the palm oil futures successively made available to foreign investors, China now has a total of seven futures varieties open to foreign investors. Among these, iron ore futures have attracted trades from nearly 270 overseas clients coming from 21 countries to become the iron ore derivatives with the largest trading volume in the world. The prices of some varieties, such as pure terephthalic acid (PTA), natural rubber, and technically specified rubber (TSR) 20 futures have become price benchmarks in the market. Second, exchanges were supported to improve delivery mechanisms and explore mechanisms for the delivery of specific varieties overseas. The forced currency exchange based on daily profit and loss was managed and the value added tax (VAT) exemption for the bonded delivery of commodity futures was properly conducted. Forms of opening up were made more diverse with the introduction of the cross-border commodity futures Exchange Traded Fund (ETF), authorization of settlement prices, and trading orders for settlement prices. Third, futures companies' high-quality two-way opening up advanced at a faster pace, introducing wholly foreign-owned futures companies and foreign holding futures companies. In June, 2020, the first wholly foreign-owned and holding futures company was founded. On September 25, the CSRC granted permission for the Qualified Foreign Institutional Investor (QFII) and RMB Qualified Foreign Institutional Investor (RQFII) to invest in China's futures and options. Foreign investment in trade will deepen and catalyze market activity while broadening the international influence of China's capital market.

### (II) Achievements of Futures Market Policies in 2020

#### 1. Futures Market Trading Volumes Reach Record High

In 2020, the China futures market developed at a fast pace, its trading volumes reaching a record high and marking a consecutive two-year surge. In 2020, 6.153 billion lots were traded on the China futures market with a turnover of RMB 437.53 trillion, these figures marking respective year-on-year (YOY increases of 55.29% and 50.56%. In the global rankings of produce, metal, and energy trading volumes, China's futures varieties took the top ten places in produce, top four in metal, and had four energy futures in the top ten. The trading volumes of China's futures market accounted for 13.2% of the total global volumes, an increase of 1.7 percentage points from 11.5% in 2019. In terms of futures exchanges, the Shanghai Futures Exchange traded 2.129 billion lots and RMB 152.80 trillion, growing by 47.04% and 35.80% respectively YOY and accounting for 34.60% and 34.92% of the market. The Zhengzhou Commodity Exchange traded 1.701 billion lots and RMB 60.09 trillion, increasing by 55.74% and 51.97% respectively YOY and accounting for 27.65% and 13.73% of the market. The Dalian Commodity Exchange traded 2.207 billion lots and 109.20 trillion yuan, rising by 62.83% and 58.43% respectively YOY and occupying 35.88% and 24.96% of the market. In 2020, both the amount of funds and the volume of positions in the futures market hit record highs, further elevating the international prestige of China's commodity futures market.

#### 2. Achievements in the Fight against Poverty through Futures Industry Services

The futures market made full use of risk management and combined targeted assistance with poverty alleviation, the real economy, and issues related to agriculture, rural areas, and rural residents in an all-out fight against poverty. As of December 31, 2020, 123 futures institutions had paired with 242 poverty-stricken counties through the signing of 455 pairing agreements. The futures industry had invested a total of RMB 611 million on poverty reduction assistance. Futures institutions launched a total of 622 Insurance Plus Futures projects for poverty-stricken areas, coving natural rubber, corn, soybeans, eggs, apples, cotton, white sugar, and jujubes, providing farmers with price guarantees and underwriting 18.826 billion yuan of commodities. These institutions also helped turn 29 enterprises in poverty-stricken areas into delivery warehouses for futures exchanges, promoting industrial transition and upgrading in these localities and driving the development of local logistics. They also offered 119 risk management alternatives to entities and individuals in poverty-stricken areas — such as cooperation insurance, pricing, and OTC options — with a notional principal of 1.094 billion yuan. The futures industry thus employed a variety of practices to take an active role in raising farmers' income, promoting rural revitalization, and serving the real economy.

### (III) Outlook for Commodity Futures Market Policies in 2021

**1. Continued Increase in Futures Varieties**

In 2021, futures varieties in the futures market will continue to increase, thereby enriching the commodity futures and options system. In accordance with the listed peanuts variety, the Zhengzhou Commodity Exchange will gradually advance research and development on different varieties including p-xylene (PX), PET bottle flake, steel billet, caustic soda, chicken, sunflower seeds, and potatoes. On January 8, 2021, the Dalian Commodity Exchange listed live hog futures, China's first live-delivery futures variety. The DCE will continue to advance the listing of dried chili futures and investigate the possibility of listing such reserve varieties as ethanol, fructose syrup, and lumber. The Shanghai Futures Exchange, meanwhile, will focus on the international varieties such as Shanghai crude oil, copper, and natural rubber, will work on the listing of aluminum oxide, ferrochrome, and synthetic rubber futures, and will accelerate studies on the listing of refined oil and natural gas futures. In accordance with the development needs of the real economy, options coverage will gradually expand to all listed futures varieties. Greater efforts will be diverted to index futures research and development, such as on commodity index futures, shipping index futures, and electric power index futures.

**2. Continued Improvements to Operating Mechanisms**

In 2021, the futures market will be diversified with more trading orders. The introduction of block trade in futures will be studied and trading mechanisms for settlement prices will be explored. The market making system will see a larger extent of piloting, contract continuity will continue to be improved, and hedge efficiency will be enhanced for industry clients. In terms of lowering the market's trading costs, collateral management will be improved, portfolio margin requirements will be explored, and market funds will be utilized more efficiently. More futures varieties and more types of futures ETF products will gradually be introduced to increase market liquidity.

**3. Establishing the Guangzhou Futures Exchange**

On January 22, 2021, the CSRC announced that it had — with the approval of the State Council — officially authorized the establishment of Guangzhou Futures Exchange. On February 5, the Guangzhou Futures Exchange registered in the administration for industry and commerce in Nansha district, Guangzhou, with a registered capital of RMB 3 billion. The Guangzhou Futures Exchange currently has eight shareholders, including four futures exchanges under the CSRC, one state-owned enterprise and two private enterprises in Guangdong province, and an overseas company; it is China's first exchange to have mixed ownership. From the perspective of shareholder composition and holdings, the Shanghai Futures Exchange, Zhengzhou Commodity Exchange, Dalian Commodity Exchange, China Financial Futures Exchange and Ping An Insurance (Group) Company of China, Ltd. hold 15% each; Guangdong Pearl River Investment Co., Ltd. and Guangzhou Finance Holdings hold 9% each; Hong Kong Exchanges and Clearing Limited holds 7%. Introducing overseas and private capital will not only assist the development philosophy of economic integration between Guangdong province, Hong Kong SAR and Macao SAR; it also contributes to the exploration of market-oriented business theory, talent recruitment, and the exchange's business management. Carbon emissions allowances futures, the commodity index, and the electric power index will become optional varieties for listing on the Guangzhou Futures Exchange.

**4. Accelerated Enactment of the Futures Law**

The Futures Law is the fundamental legislation for the futures market, acting as legal top-down design for the reform and opening up of the futures market in China. The Futures Law clarifies the legal status of all participating entities as well as the basic legal relations, civil rights and obligations, and legal obligations of the futures market. The law also sets clear rules for market access, investor protections, and opening up to legally safeguard the opening up of the futures market along with cross-border regulation. According to the Report on the Work of the Standing Committee of the National People's Congress in 2021, the Futures Law has been listed in the legislative work plan for 2021, signaling maturation for the accelerated enactment of the Futures Law.

# Appendix

### Main Policies for the China Commodity Futures Market in 2020

| Released on | Major Policies | Released by |
| --- | --- | --- |
| January 2 | Opinions of the CPC Central Committee and the State Council on Making the Key Work in Agriculture, Rural Areas and Farmers a Success to Ensure the Realization of Moderate Prosperity in All Respects | The CPC Central Committee and the State Council |
| January 2 | Announcement on the Release of Guidance on Warehouse Receipts Trading of Zhengzhou Commodity Exchange and Guidance on Basis Trading of Zhengzhou Commodity Exchange (Amendment) | ZCE |
| March 4 | Rules for Futures Company to Open an Account on the Internet (Amendment in 2020) | China Futures Association |
| March 19 | CSRC's Reply to the Trading of Liquefied Petroleum Gas Futures and Options on Dalian Commodity Exchange | CSRC |
| March 25 | Announcement on the Release of Measures for the Management of Special Work on Investor Education of Zhengzhou Commodity Exchange | CSRC |
| March 30 | Measures for the Registration of Brands for Futures Delivery of Dalian Commodity Exchange | DCE |
| April 9 | Announcement on the Release of Detailed Rules of Futures Trading of Zhengzhou Commodity Exchange (Amendment) | ZCE |
| April 24 | Opinions on Financial Support for the Development of the Guangdong-Hong Kong-Macao Greater Bay Area | People's Bank of China, China Banking and Insurance Regulatory Commission, China Securities Regulatory Commission, and State Administration of Foreign Exchange |

Continued

| Released on | Major Policies | Released by |
|---|---|---|
| May 7 | Measures for Management of Options Trading of Dalian Commodity Exchange | DCE |
| May 15 | Measures for the Management of Standard Warehouse Receipts Trading of Dalian Commodity Exchange (for Trial Implementation) | DCE |
| May 28 | Reply to the Trading of Low Sulfur Fuel Oil Futures on Shanghai International Energy Exchange | SHFE |
| June 12 | CSRC's Reply to the Trading of Polypropylene, Polyvinyl Chloride, and Linear Low-Density Polyethylene Options on Dalian Commodity Exchange | CSRC |
| June 12 | CSRC's Reply to the Trading of Thermal Coal Options on Zhengzhou Commodity Exchange | CSRC |
| June 12 | CSRC's Reply to the Trading of Aluminum and Zinc Options on Shanghai Futures Exchange | CSRC |
| June 22 | Announcement on the Release of Thermal Coal Options Contract | ZCE |
| July 28 | Implementation Plan for Execution of the Opinions on Financial Support for the Development of the Guangdong-Hong Kong-Macao Greater Bay Area | Guangdong Financial Supervisory Authority and other authorities |
| August 7 | Measures for Designated Delivery Warehouses Qualification Management of Dalian Commodity Exchange | DCE |
| September 11 | Action Plan for Execution of the Opinions on Financial Support for the Development of the Guangdong-Hong Kong-Macao Greater Bay Area | Guangzhou Financial Supervisory Authority |
| September 24 | Circular on Posting Government Bonds as Margin Collaterals | SHFE |
| September 25 | Measures for the Administration of Domestic Securities and Futures Investment by Qualified Foreign Institutional Investors and RMB Qualified Foreign Institutional Investors | China Securities Regulatory Commission, People's Bank of China, and State Administration of Foreign Exchange |
| September 28 | Announcement on the Release of Rules of Options Trading of Zhengzhou Commodity Exchange (Amendment) | ZCE |
| September 28 | Announcement on the Release of Rules for the Management of Market Makers of Zhengzhou Commodity Exchange (Amendment) | ZCE |
| September 28 | Announcement on the Release of Staple Fiber Futures Contract and Related Rules (Amendment) | ZCE |
| December 7 | Announcement on the Release of Rules for Risk Control and Management of Shanghai Futures Exchange (Amendment) | SHFE |
| December 8 | Measures for the Management of Non-Standard Warehouse Receipts Business of Dalian Commodity Exchange (for Trial Implementation) | DCE |

| Released on | Major Policies | Released by |
| --- | --- | --- |
| December 8 | Measures for the Management of OTC Members of Dalian Commodity Exchange (for Trial Implementation) | DCE |
| August 31 | Live Hog Futures Contract of Dalian Commodity Exchange (DCE) | DCE |

# Article 12

Beijing Financial Court is established to strengthen financial judicial protection[1]

Finance constitutes a core competitive edge for any country, and financial security is essential to national security. As a financial hub with a high concentration of regulatory agencies, Beijing is the country's de facto center for financial management. In this respect, it is Beijing's mission to maintain national financial security and to promote the healthy development of the financial industry. When it comes to financial security and development, the rule of law is its fundamental guarantee, and financial justice is of great practical significance to the modernization of the financial governance system and governance capacity. On January 22, 2021, the 25th session of the Standing Committee of the 13th National People's Congress adopted the *Decision on the Establishment of the Beijing Financial Court*, determining that the Beijing Financial Court would exercise centralized jurisdiction over financial cases. This arrangement will facilitate the implementation of national financial strategy, the maintenance of financial security, the improvement of the financial trial system, the strengthening of financial judicial protection, and the creation of a sound law-based financial environment for the country's modernization.

I. Background

In recent years, General Secretary Xi Jinping's speeches have repeatedly emphasized the importance of finance and financial security. A number of China's strategic deployment documents have also clarified three main tasks in this regard — serving the real economy, preventing and controlling financial risks, and deepening financial reform — and have proposed the establishment of public prosecution and adjudication institutions specifically for finance. As the national financial management center, Beijing is home to important financial infrastructure and headquarters for large state-owned financial institutions; thus the municipality has a solid foundation for conducting financial judicial trials, with plentiful legal talent teams and sufficient cases. Considering the above circumstances, along with Beijing's unique functional positioning and features, the establishment of the Beijing Financial Court is a necessary step in the central government's major strategic deployment and crucial to the implementation of its financial

---

[1] Author: Shi Guanglong, Deputy Secretary-General of Tencent Financial Research Institute, and project fellow of Program for China's Financial Policy Report.

strategy. The Court will fulfil three major tasks in the field of finance: improving the financial trial system, preventing and resolving systemic financial risks, and providing strong judicial protection for the sustainable and healthy development of the national economy and society.

## II. Policy Content and Features

The Beijing Financial Court handles both civil and commercial cases as well as administrative litigation cases. Specifically, it specializes in financial civil and commercial cases and financial-related administrative cases in Beijing that should fall under the jurisdiction of intermediate people's courts. The jurisdiction of the Beijing Financial Court includes three types of first instance cases — namely, first instance financial civil and commercial cases that should fall under the jurisdiction of the intermediate people's courts in Beijing, first instance financial administrative cases in which a financial regulator is a defendant, and first instance financial civil and commercial cases and financial administrative cases in which a Beijing-based financial infrastructure institution is involved as the defendant or a third party in relation to the performance of its duties. This means that major financial civil and commercial cases of the first instance, cases in which a financial regulator is a defendant, and civil and administrative cases in which a financial infrastructure institution is a defendant or a third party will all be subject to the intervention of the Beijing Financial Court in order to determine a uniform scale of judicial decision-making. In addition, the Beijing Financial Court is also responsible for verdicts, retrials, appeals, and protests against judgments and rulings of the Beijing Basic People's Courts in financial civil and commercial cases or finance-related administrative cases, as well as in cases that should be enforced by the Beijing Financial Court in accordance with the law, and for other financial cases determined by the Supreme People's Court to be under its jurisdiction.

In terms of administration, the establishment of the trial division of the Beijing Financial Court is to be determined by the Supreme People's Court according to the type and number of financial cases. In terms of supervision, the Beijing Financial Court, once established in accordance with legal procedures, will be held accountable to and will report its work to the Standing Committee of the Beijing Municipal People's Congress; it is to be supervised by the Supreme People's Court and the Higher People's Court of Beijing Municipality; it will be subject to legal supervision by the People's Procuratorate in accordance with the law. As for the appointment and removal of judges, the deputy president, members of the Judicial Committee, the tribunal director and vice-director, and judicial officers of the Beijing Financial Court are to be appointed and removed by the Standing Committee of the Beijing Municipal People's Congress upon submission from the President of the Beijing Financial Court.

## III. Policy Outlook

Following the establishment of the Shanghai Financial Court in 2018, the Beijing Financial Court is China's second specialized financial judicial institution. It represents a new initiative within the judicial system to fully implement President Xi Jinping Thought on the Rule of Law. The establishment of the Beijing Financial Court will help enhance dialog and synergy between national financial regulators, national financial infrastructure, and Beijing financial judiciary for the joint resolution of financial risks and the healthy development of the financial industry. It will further improve finance's legal environment in Beijing while giving China more voice and influence internationally in the formulation of financial transaction rules and adjudication of financial disputes.

## X. Foreign Exchange Market Development Policies[①]

### (I) Policy List

**Major Chinese Foreign Exchange Market Policies, 2020**

| Released on | Released by | Major Policies | Document No. |
| --- | --- | --- | --- |
| January 13 | State Administration of Foreign Exchange | Notice on Issues Related to Improving Foreign Exchange Risk Management for Foreign Institutional Investors in the Interbank Bond Market | HF [2020] No.2 |
| February 13 | State Administration of Foreign Exchange | Notice on Revisions to Pilot Management Measures Concerning Domestic and Foreign Currency Exchange Franchise Services for Individuals | HF [2020] No. 6 |
| February 13 | National Interbank Funding Center | Rules for the Transfer of Maturing Defaulted Bonds on the Interbank Market of the National Interbank Funding Center | ZHJF [2020] No. 39 |
| February 28 | National Interbank Funding Center | Notification of Launch of Trial Interest Rate Options Business Operations | ZHJF [2020] No. 51 |
| February 28 | National Interbank Funding Center | Notice on Further Improvements to Cash Settlement Mechanisms in the Standard Bond Forward Market | ZHJF [2020] No. 52 |
| March 11 | People's Bank of China, State Administration of Foreign Exchange | Notice on Adjustment of Macroprudential Regulatory Parameters for Unified Cross-border Financing | YF [2020] No. 64 |
| April 10 | State Administration of Foreign Exchange | Notice on Optimizing Foreign Exchange Management to Support Development of Foreign-related Services | HF [2020] No. 8 |
| April 24 | People's Bank of China, China Banking and Insurance Regulatory Commission, China Securities Regulatory Commission, State Administration of Foreign Exchange | Opinions on Financial Support for the Construction of the Guangdong-Hong Kong-Macao Greater Bay Area | YF [2020] No. 95 |

---

① Author: Shang Xinxin, researcher of the Foreign Exchange Research Center of State Administration of Foreign Exchange.

Continued

| Released on | Released by | Major Policies | Document No. |
|---|---|---|---|
| May 7 | People's Bank of China, State Administration of Foreign Exchange | Administration of Foreign Institutional Investors' Domestic Securities and Futures Investment Funds | PBOC/SAFE Announcement [2020] No. 2 |
| May 9 | State Administration of Foreign Exchange China Securities Regulatory Commission, State Administration of Foreign Exchange | Notice on the Issuance of Content and Scoring Criteria for Assessment of Compliance and Prudential Management of Banks' Foreign Exchange Services (2020) | HZF [2020] No. 35 |
| May 20 | State Administration of Foreign Exchange | Notice on Support for Development of New Forms of Trade | HF [2020] No. 11 |
| May 26 | People's Bank of China, China Banking and Insurance Regulatory Commission, National Development and Reform Commission, Ministry of Industry and Information Technology, Ministry of Finance, State Administration for Market Regulation, China Securities Regulatory Commission, State Administration of Foreign Exchange | Opinions on Further Strengthening Financial Services for Small and Micro Enterprises | YF [2020] No. 120 |
| August 28 | State Administration of Foreign Exchange | Notice on Issuance of Guidelines on Foreign Exchange Current Account Operations (2020 Edition) | HF [2020] No. 14 |
| September 18 | State Administration of Foreign Exchange | Notice of Issuance of Business Guidelines on Foreign Financial Assets, Liabilities and Transaction Statistics (2020 Edition) | HZF [2020] No. 71 |
| September 25 | The China Securities Regulatory Commission, People's Bank of China, State Administration of Foreign Exchange | Measures for Administration of Domestic Securities and Futures Investment by Qualified Foreign Institutional Investors and RMB Qualified Foreign Institutional Investors | ZJHL [No. 176] |
| October 22 | National Interbank Funding Center, Interbank Market Clearing House Co., Ltd. | Notice on Launch of Standard Bond Forward Business for Agricultural Development Bonds | ZHJF [2020] No. 302 |
| December 14 | State Administration of Foreign Exchange | Foreign Financial Assets, Liabilities and Transactions Statistics Verification Rules (2020 Edition) | HZF [2020] No. 94 |

## (II) Effects of Policies

On January 13, the State Administration of Foreign Exchange issued the *Notice on Issues Related to Improving Foreign Exchange Risk Management for Foreign Institutional Investors in the Interbank Bond Market* (HF [2020] No. 2), in order to further facilitate the use of foreign exchange derivatives for foreign exchange risk management by foreign institutional investors in the interbank bond market, commencing February 1.

On February 13, the State Administration of Foreign Exchange issued the *Notice on Revisions to Pilot Management Measures Concerning Domestic and Foreign Currency Exchange Franchise Services for Individuals* (HF [2020] No. 6), seeking to promote the regulatory compliance and healthy development of franchised domestic and foreign currency exchange businesses for individuals.

On February 13, the National Interbank Funding Center issued the *Rules for the Transfer of Maturing Defaulted Bonds on the Interbank Market of the National Interbank Funding Center* (ZHJF [2020] No. 39), aiming to regulate behavior related to the transfer of maturing defaulted bonds in this interbank market, to protect the legitimate rights and interests of investors, and to provide services such as transaction quotations, market monitoring and quotation information regarding transfers of maturing defaulted bonds.

On February 28, the National Interbank Funding Center issued the *Notification of Launch of Trial Interest Rate Options Business Operations* (ZHJF [2020] No. 51), determining that the trial operation of interest rate options trading and related businesses would commence March 23, 2020, and that transaction fees for interest rate options would be temporarily waived during the first two years of their operation.

On February 28, the National Interbank Funding Center issued the *Notice on Further Improvements to Cash Settlement Mechanisms in the Standard Bond Forward Market* (ZHJF [2020] No. 52), seeking to optimize the settlement mechanisms for standard bond forward transactions from March 18, in order to enhance the liquidity of the standard bond forward market and to promote its development.

On March 11, the People's Bank of China and the State Administration of Foreign Exchange issued the *Notice on Adjustment of Macroprudential Regulatory Parameters for Unified Cross-border Financing* (YF [2020] No. 64), determining the adjustment of the macroprudential regulatory parameter in the *Notice of People's Bank of China on Matters Relating to Macroprudential Management of Full-scale Cross-border Financing* (YF [2017] No. 9) from 1 to 1.25.

On April 10, the State Administration of Foreign Exchange issued the *Notice on Optimizing Foreign Exchange Management to Support Development of Foreign-related Services* (HF [2020] No. 8), announcing optimization of the management of foreign exchange business from June 1, improvements in foreign exchange service methods and enhancements to cross-border trade and investment facilitation levels.

On April 24, the People's Bank of China, the China Banking and Insurance Regulatory Commission, the China Securities Regulatory Commission, the State Administration of Foreign

Exchange jointly issued the *Opinions on Financial Support for the Construction of the Guangdong-Hong Kong-Macao Greater Bay Area* (YF [2020] No.95), seeking to promote financial opening and innovation, to deepen financial cooperation between the mainland, Hong Kong and Macao, to increase financial support for the building of the Guangdong-Hong Kong-Macao Greater Bay Area, and to enhance the leading role of the Greater Bay Area in China's economic development and opening up to the outside world.

On May 7, the People's Bank of China and the State Administration of Foreign Exchange jointly issued *Administration of Foreign Institutional Investors' Domestic Securities and Futures Investment Funds* ([2020] No. 2).

On May 9, the State Administration of Foreign Exchange issued the *Notice on the Issuance of Content and Scoring Criteria for Assessment of Compliance and Prudential Management of Banks' Foreign Exchange Services (2020)* (HZF [2020] No. 35), stipulating the repeal of *Content and Scoring Criteria for Assessment of Compliance and Prudent Management of Banks' Foreign Exchange Services (2019)* (HF [2019] No. 15 Attached Table) as of its date of issuance.

On May 20, the State Administration of Foreign Exchange issued the *Notice on Support for Development of New Forms of Trade* (HF [2020] No. 11), aiming to promote the quality and efficiency of foreign trade, accelerate the development of cross-border e-commerce and other new trade formats, and improve the level of trade and foreign exchange receipts and payments facilitation.

On May 26, the People's Bank of China, the China Banking and Insurance Regulatory Commission (CBIRC), the National Development and Reform Commission, the Ministry of Industry and Information Technology, the Ministry of Finance, the State Administration for Market Regulation, the China Securities Regulatory Commission, and the State Administration of Foreign Exchange jointly issued their *Opinions on Further Strengthening Financial Services for Small and Micro Enterprises* (YF [2020] No. 120), aiming to streamline internal and external transmission mechanisms and promote a significant increase in the scale of SME financing while optimizing its structure, in order to achieve SME financing of an "increased amount, lower cost, higher quality, and wider scope", prompting faster resumption of normal life and economic activity and supporting the quality development of the real economy.

On August 28, the State Administration of Foreign Exchange (SAFE) issued the *Notice on Issuance of Guidelines on Foreign Exchange Current Account Operations (2020 Edition)* (HF [2020] No. 14). The SAFE consolidated the relevant regulations into the form of the *Guidelines on Foreign Exchange Current Account Operations (2020 Edition)*, effective the date of issuance.

On September 18, the State Administration of Foreign Exchange (SAFE) issued the *Notice of Issuance of Business Guidelines on Foreign Financial Assets, Liabilities and Transaction Statistics (2020 Edition)* (HZF [2020] No. 71). To facilitate reporting entities' more accurate understanding of the specific reporting requirements, the SAFE formulated the *Business Guidelines on Foreign Financial Assets and Liabilities and Transaction Statistics* (2020 Edition), on the basis of the *Rules for the Implementation of Measures for the Statistical Declaration of International Balance of Payments*

(State Council Decree No. 642) and the *Foreign Financial Assets, Liabilities and Transaction Statistics System* (HF [2018] No. 24).

On September 25, the China Securities Regulatory Commission, the People's Bank of China, and the State Administration of Foreign Exchange jointly issued the *Measures for Administration of Domestic Securities and Futures Investment by Qualified Foreign Institutional Investors and RMB Qualified Foreign Institutional Investors* (ZJHL [No. 176]) effective November 1, 2020.

On October 22, the National Interbank Funding Center and Interbank Market Clearing House Co., Ltd. jointly issued the *Notice on Launch of Standard Bond Forward Business for Agricultural Development Bonds* (ZHJF [2020] No. 302), announcing the launch of standard bond forward business for agricultural development bonds on October 29.

On December 14, the State Administration of Foreign Exchange issued the *Foreign Financial Assets, Liabilities and Transactions Statistics Verification Rules (2020 Edition)* (HZF [2020] No. 94), adding new contents such as multi-dimensional verification rules on inter-period balance linkage, and rules for verification of the consistency between name records and the corresponding department and country/region records.

### (III) Outlook for Foreign Exchange Market Development

2021 is the first year of the 14th Five-Year Plan. Foreign exchange authorities must adhere to Xi Jinping Thought on Socialism with Chinese characteristics in the New Era, and fully implement the guidelines of the 19th CPC National Congress and the second, third, fourth and fifth plenary sessions of the 19th Session, and the arrangements of the Central Economic Work Conference. They must maintain their political integrity, think in big-picture terms, follow the core of the leadership, remain in alignment with central Party leadership, and remain confident in the path, theory, system, and culture of socialism with Chinese characteristics. They must uphold General Secretary Xi Jinping's core position on the Party Central Committee and in the Party as a whole, and uphold the Party Central Committee's authority and centralized, unified leadership. They must pursue progress while ensuring stability, apply the new development philosophy during new stages of development to create a new pattern of development, and increase their efforts to ensure stability on the "six fronts" (keep employment, the financial sector, foreign trade, foreign and domestic investments, and expectations stable) and to maintain security in the "six areas" (ensure security in the six areas of employment, basic living needs, operations of market entities, food and energy security, stable industrial and supply chains, and the normal functioning of primary-level governments). They must strive to strike a balance between development and security, enhancing their awareness of opportunities and risks. They must deepen the reform and opening up in the field of foreign exchange in order to stimulate new vitality in development, and reform and improve foreign exchange management systems and mechanisms in order to adapt them to the new higher level systems of the open economy under new patterns of development. At the micro-level, efforts must be made to further facilitate and liberalize trade and investment, and at the macro level, national economic and financial security must be effectively maintained, such that the 100th anniversary of the founding of the CPC can be celebrated with outstanding achievements.

Major foreign exchange management tasks for 2021 include the following: First, the risks of abnormal cross-border capital flows must be prevented. Monitoring and assessment of the foreign exchange situation must be strengthened, with close attention paid to the impact of the epidemic and other external shocks, and guidance provided to financial institutions and enterprises to adhere to a principle of risk neutrality. Foreign exchange speculation must be combated, and management of market expectations and macro-prudential management strengthened, in order to avoid disorderly foreign exchange market fluctuations. Second, the reform and opening of the field of foreign exchange must be deepened, with a focus on two-way opening of the financial markets and promotion of the steady and orderly rollout of capital projects. The management of funds for domestic issuance of stocks and bonds by foreign institutions must be improved, pilot cross-border investment in private equity funds must be promoted, and foreign debt registration management reformed, in order to facilitate cross-border investment and financing. Pilot trade foreign exchange balance facilitation must be expanded, and the development of new trade forms promoted. An open, diversified, functional foreign exchange market must be constructed, supporting financial institutions' launch of further foreign exchange derivatives fulfilling market needs. Third, the "micro- and macro-prudential supervision" management framework of the foreign exchange market must be improved. Management of cross-border capital flows must be improved through a focus on strengthening macro-prudential supervision, the micro-regulation of the foreign exchange market must be improved through a transformation of supervision methods. The construction of a risk assessment-oriented classification-based credit risk management system must be completed, and off-site supervision capacity building strengthened. Illegal activities in foreign exchange, such as underground banking and cross-border gambling, must be suppressed with "zero tolerance" in order to maintain healthy, orderly foreign exchange markets. Fourth, management of foreign exchange reserves with Chinese characteristics must be improved, through adherence to market-oriented principles, forward-looking strategic allocation, and dynamic investment portfolio optimization. The safety and liquidity of foreign exchange reserve assets must be safeguarded to preserve or increase their value. Fifth, a solid foundation for foreign exchange management must be laid. The "14th Five-Year" periods reform concepts concerning foreign exchange management, promotion of "digital foreign exchange management" and "safe foreign exchange management", and improving the balance of payments statistics system, must be thoroughly researched, even as the conscientious implementation of regular epidemic prevention and control measures continues.

# Article 13

## The Regional Comprehensive Economic Partnership Agreement, a victory for free trade[①]

On November 15, 2020, the Regional Comprehensive Economic Partnership Agreement (RCEP), which covers 15 member countries, was signed during the fourth RCEP leaders' meeting. The RCEP constitutes the free trade agreement (FTA) with the most diverse membership structure and largest population coverage in the world. Thus with its signing was the FTA with the greatest development potential officially born.

As a regional FTA focused on developing economies, the RCEP was initiated in 2012 by the 10 ASEAN member states (Indonesia, Malaysia, the Philippines, Thailand, Singapore, Brunei, Cambodia, Laos, Myanmar, Vietnam). Six dialogue partners (China, Japan, South Korea, Australia, New Zealand and India) were invited to participate in the negotiations, which officially launched in November 2012. These consisted of three leaders' meetings, 19 ministerial meetings, and 28 rounds of formal negotiations. On November 4, 2019, the third RCEP leaders' meeting issued a joint statement announcing that the fifteen RCEP member countries had concluded negotiations on all 20 chapters of text and essentially concluded all market access issues. The legal text review process would thenceforth begin, in order to sign the agreement in 2020.

The RCEP Agreement consists of 20 chapters, their topics as follows: initial provisions and general definitions, trade in goods, rules of origin, customs procedures and trade facilitation, sanitary and phytosanitary measures, standards, technical regulations and conformity assessment procedures, trade remedies, trade in services, temporary movement of natural persons, investment, intellectual property, electronic commerce, competition, small and medium enterprises, economic and technical cooperation, government procurement, general provisions and exceptions, institutional provisions, dispute settlement, and final provisions. A number of the Agreement's initiatives, such as intellectual property rights and e-commerce, surpass the WTO's in terms of the level of commitment, marking an important step as the region takes real actions to uphold the multilateral trading system and build an open world economy.

Premier Li Keqiang was in attendance at the fourth RCEP leaders' meeting. On November 15 he stated: "This is not only a landmark achievement of regional cooperation in East Asia, but also a victory for multilateralism and free trade, and will certainly add new momentum to the development and prosperity of the region and contribute to the recovery of the world economy". Wang Shouwen, Vice Minister of Commerce and deputy representative for international trade negotiations added: "RCEP is not only the largest FTA in the world at present but also a comprehensive, modern, high-quality and mutually beneficial FTA".

---

[①] Author: Zhang Yansheng, chief research fellow with the R&D Center at Cinda Securities, and project fellow of Program for China's Financial Policy Report.

The signing of the RCEP is conducive to the integration of resources and coordinated economic development in East Asia but will promote the process of trade worldwide. Especially in the context of recent years' reverse globalization led by the US, the signing of RCEP is truly a victory for global free trade.

With its comparative advantage in manufacturing, China is often the party subjected to tariffs and increased costs when there are global disagreements over trade. This is not true for all commodities, however, especially resource goods. At present, China also has additional tariff policies for certain goods originating from RCEP initiating countries. The RCEP means new strength but also a new obligation for its signees, so all will have to work together to advance the process of free trade.

China's rapid economic development drives up national incomes, which in turn diminishes its labour cost advantage in manufacturing. Southeast Asian countries are now accelerating industrialization to take over some low-end manufacturing industries. The signing of RCEP bodes well for Southeast Asian countries' market prospects in these transferred manufacturing industries. As for China, improving the quality of economic development and upgrading the industrial structure are not only our people's needs; they are also mandatory tasks for our manufacturing industry.

## XI. Development of Gold Market Policies[1]

While actively combating the COVID-19 pandemic and steadily engaging in business, ongoing improvements have been made to the institutions and systems of the Chinese gold market. The market's infrastructure has thus continued to improve, operations have remained smooth and orderly, its scale of trading has continued to expand, and its service functionality has been further enhanced. The operation of the Shanghai Gold Exchange (SGE) has been stable and orderly, with safe, smooth clearing and delivery, and continued increases in the total scale of trading. The trading volume of gold futures on the Shanghai Futures Exchange (SHFE) has continued to grow, while the role of the gold market in China's financial infrastructure has been further enhanced.

### (I) Overview of Developments in the Gold Market

When the COVID-19 outbreak hit the global economy at the beginning of 2020, there was a general decline in stock and commodity prices. A shortage of market liquidity affected the precious metals markets, with the lowest international spot gold price reaching 1,451.13 USD/oz as a result. In March 2020, the US Federal Reserve (FED) began implementation of quantitative easing policies designed to allay fears of market liquidity shortages. Low real interest rates and inflation

---

[1] Author: Luo Jiang, Deputy General Manager, Research and Development Department, Shanghai Gold Exchange; and project fellow of Program for China's Financial Policy Report.

expectations propelled a sharp rebound in the spot gold price, with the international spot gold price reaching 2,075.14 USD/oz, and the Chinese domestic spot gold price reaching 449.00 RMB/g - both record highs - in early August 2020. During the fourth quarter of 2020, the gold price retraced to a high level reflecting progress in COVID-19 vaccine research and development and declining market uncertainty. At end-2020, the international spot gold price closed at 1,897.53 USD/oz, an increase of 380.35 USD/oz or 25.07% from end-2019. The opening price of SGE's AU9999 gold contract in early 2020 was 341.95 RMB/g. With a high of 449.00 RMB/g, and low of 327.60 RMB/g during the year, the contract traded within a 35.62% range in 2020, to close at 390.00 RMB/g at end-2020, up 14.44% year on year.

In 2020, the aggregate value of transactions on SGE reached RMB 43.32 trillion (bilateral), an increase of 50.66% year on year, with gold turnover of 58, 700 tons. The trading volume on SGE's international board reached RMB 8.26 trillion, up 125.24% year on year, with gold turnover of 8,028. 83 tons. SHFE's gold futures trading volume reached RMB 41.44 trillion (bilateral), up 38.16% year on year, with a cumulative trading volume of 104,800 tons.

By end-2020, the number of SGE members had reached 280, of which 156 were ordinary members - 31 financial members and 125 comprehensive members. There were 124 special members in total, of which 7 were foreign-funded financial members, 89 were international members and 28 security company, trust institution, and small and medium-sized bank-type special members. The main board had 11, 850 agency clients, of which 87 were international customers acting through international members, and 10.4683 million individual customers.

### (II) Industry and Market development Policies

In 2020, the gold market conscientiously implemented the gold market policies of the People's Bank of China (PBC), liberalized policies covering insurance asset management products' investments in gold, made further improvements to its financial infrastructure, continuously improved its anti-money laundering mechanisms, upgraded its market risk management system, took multiple measures to combat COVID-19, shouldering its social responsibility, and steadily promoted product innovation and improved its trading mechanisms. Thus, in 2020, further improvements were made to the gold market's policy framework.

**1. Liberalized policies on insurance asset management companies' gold investments**

On September 7th, 2020, China Banking and Insurance Regulatory Commission (CBIRC) issued the *Detailed Rules for the Implementation of Portfolio Insurance Asset Management Products* (YBJBF [2020] No. 85), allowing insurance asset management companies to invest in gold. Following on from the participation of trusts, securities and fund companies, and other financial institutions in the gold market, insurance asset management companies are now also permitted to invest in gold, marking the full interconnection of China's gold market with other financial markets. Investment in gold by large institutional investors such as insurance asset management companies can help fulfill their asset allocation needs, and they are now permitted to become qualified participants in the gold market, a change of great significance in the promotion of the market's sustained, steady and positive development.

## 2. Improvements in the gold market's financial infrastructure

In 2020, further improvements were made to the financial infrastructure of the gold market. In January, PBC officially certified SGE as a Qualified Central Counterparty, and in the same month, SGE was linked to the PBC's high-value payment system. The initial phase of the China gold market trading report database system went into operation in October 2020, with submission of business data starting smoothly.

SGE implemented two policy documents released by PBC's General Office, namely, the *Notice on Matters Related to Gold Asset Management Business* (YBF [2018] No. 215) and *Interim Measures for the Management of Online Gold Business of Financial Institutions* (YBF [2018] No. 221). Gold asset management business registration and custody was conducted in an orderly manner.

## 3. Modified Measures for the Administration of Import and Export of Gold and Gold Products

In April 2020, in accordance with the *Law of the People's Republic of China on the People's Bank of China*, the *Customs Law of the People's Republic of China*, and the *Decision of the State Council on the Establishment of Administrative Permissions for Administrative Examination and Approval Items Requiring Reservation*, the PBC and General Administration of Customs of China (GACC) modified the *Measures for the Administration of Import and Export of Gold and Gold Products* (PBC-GACC Order [2015] No. 1), issuing a revised version, *Measures for the Administration of Import and Export of Gold and Gold Products* (PBC-GACC Order [2020] No. 3), in order to standardize the importation and exportation of gold and gold products, strengthen the management of imports and exports of gold and gold products, further promote "streamlining government, delegating power and improving government services" reforms, and simplify the licensing process for the convenience of the public. In this revision, Item 7, Para 1, Article 10 was amended to "Banking financial institutions shall also provide materials related to their internal gold business risk control systems." Item 8, Para 1, Article 10 was amended to "Gold mining enterprises shall also submit copies of their pollutant discharge licenses and annual compliance inspection reports issued by provincial government environmental protection departments, copies of overseas investment approval documents issued by commercial departments, copies of bank remittance certificates, certification relevant to gold mining in overseas countries or regions, and their tax payment records for the preceding three years; enterprises applying to export gold shall also submit their spot gold exchange registration certificates, as approved by the State Council."

## 4. Improved anti-money laundering mechanisms

SGE is fulfilling its anti-money laundering obligations in accordance with the *Self-regulatory Guidelines on Anti-Money Laundering, Anti-Terrorist Financing and Anti-Tax Evasion for Members* issued by PBC and *Measures for the Implementation of Anti-Money Laundering and Anti-Terrorist Financing for Members of Shanghai Gold Exchange (Trial)*, and actively promoting continuous improvement in the precious metal industry's anti-money laundering systems. SGE has actively assisted the regulatory authorities in the performance of their duties, continued to follow up and implement rectification work related to Financial Action Task Force on Money Laundering (FATF) international mutual assessment, participated in drafting the *Report on Risk Assessment of Money Laundering in the Precious Metals Industry*, bolstered its internal systems, and disseminated the *Guidelines for Member Identification Work*, in order to ensure the continuous efficacy of member identification efforts, organized members' completion of the *Due Diligence Questionnaire of 2020* and carried out re-registration of member information. Anti-money laundering systems in the precious metals industry have thus gradually been established.

### 5. Upgraded market risk management system

In order to better implement the important task of mitigation of financial risk, assigned by the CPC Central Committee, in June 2020 the SGE set up a risk management department tasked with strengthening transaction risk management, standardizing transaction behavior, safeguarding the legitimate rights and interests of transaction parties, maintaining market order with respect to transactions, ensuring the market's stable operation, and improving market risk management systems. The SGE issued the *Comprehensive Risk Management Regulations of the Shanghai Gold Exchange* in November 2020, setting out principles of transaction risk management, leadership and supervision departments, and risk prevention resource management methods. It also set out clear and specific provisions regarding the systems governing margins, price limits, deferred compensation, overdue fees, position limits, trading limits, large account reporting, forced closure or positions, risk warnings and monitoring of abnormal transactions.

### 6. Combating COVID-19, shouldering social responsibility

After the outbreak of the COVID-19 pandemic, due to concern for members in the affected area, SGE reduced the annual membership, exchange seat, transactions, warehousing and receiving & shipping fees of Hubei member units in 2020, thereby lowering the operating costs of these members and related agencies.

The SGE has actively shouldered its social responsibilities. In July 2020, SGE released the first edition of its *Social Responsibility Report*, and in November, together with the China Gold Association and World Gold Council, released the *Chinese Gold Industry's Epidemic Prevention and Anti-Epidemic Social Responsibility Report*.

### 7. Promoted product innovation, improved trading mechanisms

The SGE has actively promoted innovation and development, enriched and improved its business systems, and, in 2020, achieved the listing of three traditional gold exchange traded funds (ETFs) and the first batch of four SGE ETFs, promoting insurance funds' participation in the gold market via investment in gold ETFs. SGE has continued to promote innovation in over-the-counter (OTC) products, completed the technical launch of performance guarantee "price inquiry" products, researched "SHAG" "price inquiry" derivative products, and promoted innovation in multilateral "price inquiry" products, creating a reserve of these.

## (III) Policy Evaluation and Outlook

The ongoing introduction of market systems is providing a strong guarantee for innovative development and further opening of, and risk prevention in, the gold market, to excellent effect.

Insurance asset management companies' gold investment plans are now complete. Since March 2020, under the guidance of PBC, SGE and financial institutions such as the Insurance Asset Management Association of China, World Gold Council, China Life Insurance Asset Management Company Ltd. and PICC Asset Management Company Ltd. have been running an insurance fund gold investment research group. Through unremitting efforts, this research group overcame the difficulties created by the epidemic to complete a series of research reports and gold investment product design plans, which received the CBIRC's affirmation in August. In September, the CBIRC issued three detailed regulations to further standardize insurance asset management product business development. The plan for "PICC Asset Management Gold-driven Asset Management Product", a PICC Asset Management Company Ltd. scheme for investment in gold index portfolio asset management products based on the *Detailed Rules for the Implementation of Portfolio Insurance Asset Management Products*, has been completed. This is the first insurance asset management gold investment product in the industry launched under the relevant provisions of the *New Asset Management Regulations* and the *Interim Measures for the Management of Insurance Asset Management Products*.

The gold market's financial infrastructure improved further with the SGE's recognition as a Qualified Central Counterparty. Under the PBC's guidance, the SGE has actively studied and promoted the financial standardization of the gold market; has completed overall planning for implementation of its fourth-generation system, has promoted construction of "two places and three centers", ensuring the system's safe and stable operation; and has increased overnight trading in the "price inquiry" market. After the latter change, overall "price inquiry" business trading hours were extended to 10.5 hours per day , and the online brokerage inquiry and negotiation function was launched. SGE's third-generation clearing system and international board system won the second and third prizes, respectively, in the 2019 Bank Science and Technology Development Awards. The first "Shanghai Standard", the "SHAU" gold ingot standard was successfully introduced. In accordance with the *Detailed Rules for the Implementation of Registration and Custody of Gold Asset Management Business of Shanghai Gold Exchange*, the SGE's gold asset management business registration and custody system completed registration for custody of 533 asset management products in 2020.

The fight against money laundering has yielded initial fruits. The SGE has encouraged members to fulfill their anti-money laundering obligations, has clarified system requirements, has integrated anti-money laundering requirements into membership reviews, has required members to establish anti-money laundering internal control systems, equipped with relevant personnel conscientiously fulfilling their obligations, and has encouraged members to establish qualifying anti-money laundering working systems through membership re-registration, investigation and discussion. The SGE has helped regulatory authorities deeply understand the precious metal market's business models and risk status, preliminary work which has been commended by the Inter-Ministerial Joint Conference on Anti Money Laundering. The SGE has fulfilled its "anti-money laundering, anti-terrorist financing and anti-tax evasion" obligations (the "Three Antis") and assumed responsibility for investor protection, conducted due diligence on member's anti-money laundering activities, successfully submitted four suspicious transaction reports to China Anti-Money Laundering Monitoring and Analysis Center, and was commended by the PBC for its anti-money laundering work.

Market risk management systems have been gradually improved. The SGE set up a risk control department and issued the *Comprehensive Risk Management Regulations of the Shanghai Gold Exchange*, significantly improving its level of market risk management. Under the effects of the international political and economic situation and COVID-19, precious metal market prices fluctuated violently, increasing associated investment and transaction risks. The SGE effectively responded to the precious metals market fluctuations that occurred under the influence of extreme market shocks in accordance with its risk prevention and control system. It took countermeasures, adjusted the price limits and margin ratios of deferred contracts many times, conducted timely window guidance interviews with members, collected personal customer risk information in real-time, issued timely risk alerts, handled extreme market and default events properly, and maintained stable market operations. SGE has optimized its membership management, strictly controlled OTC market risks, increased penalties for illegal activities in accordance with regulations, dealt severely with violating members, such as Shenzhen Gold Information Co., Ltd., Wuhan Kingold Jewelry Co., Ltd., and Jiangxi Yiniu Spot Gold Trading Co., Ltd., and introduced open warning and market prohibition measures. SGE has also optimized its full-cycle membership management, established a strict pre-admission approval mechanism, performed real-time risk monitoring, set post-event time limits for rectification and punishment, established a guidance period for members entering the market, begun membership re-registration, and has interviewed, warned and expelled a number of unqualified institutions.

The gold market has actively shouldered its social responsibilities. In 2020, under leadership of the PBC, the SGE engaged effectively in COVID-19 prevention and control, conducted business steadily, and effectively reduced transaction costs, ensuring the normal operation of the market in areas affected by the epidemic. The Chinese Expert Committee on CSR Report Rating awarded the "*Chinese Gold Industry's Epidemic Prevention and Anti-Epidemic Social Responsibility Report*" its five-star rating.

Looking ahead, the gold market is set to enter a new stage of development. We must adhere to new concepts of development, promoting risk prevention and control and business development as a whole, in order to meet varied challenges and promote high-quality development. The institutional foundations for the gold market's sustained and steady development are undergoing continuous consolidation. With the *Outline of the 14th Five-Year Plan for National Economic and Social Development of the People's Republic of China and the Long-Range Objectives Through the Year 2035* providing guidance, the market policies will promote the construction of a central node in the gold market's domestic circulation and the strategy of domestic and international circulation, enhancing the gold market's ability to serve the real economy, and building up China's gold market into a world-class, comprehensive, gold market.

## Article 14

### CAI and carbon neutrality facilitate China–EU strategy for common, long–term, green development[①]

The EU-China Comprehensive Agreement on Investment (CAI) was designed to establish a unified legal framework for China-Europe investment relations and to replace existing bilateral investment treaties between China and the 26 EU member states.

The CAI was finalized at the end of 2020 after 35 rounds of negotiations spanning a period of seven years. The agreement will provide strong support for the post-pandemic recovery of the global economy, promoting global trade in general as well as the liberalization and facilitation of trade and investment between China and EU member states specifically; it will accelerate green development and multilateral cooperation, and it will help build an open world economy characterized by two major markets — that of China and the EU.

The CAI's main clauses are to: (1) Ensure the protection of mutual investments and respect of intellectual property rights as well as the transparency of subsidies; (2) Improve market access conditions for both sides; (3) Ensure a clear, fair, and transparent investment environment and regulatory process; (4) Improve labour standards to support sustainable development.

Since 2018, under the pressure of unilateral US trade protectionism, both China and the EU have faced an increasingly challenging international trade environment. The combined value of direct investment between China and the EU reached approximately USD 100 billion over the past five years — this is equivalent to just 2-3% of their bilateral trade, indicating a sluggish pace of investment scale expansion. Trade protectionism and sector-specific security concerns in the wake of the pandemic continue to put pressure on bilateral investment.

In response to the massive global impact of COVID-19, particularly for longer-term green and sustainable development, China and the EU have focused negotiations on resolving their differences over fair competition and market access. Notably, China proposed realizing carbon neutrality by 2060. As this national goal aligns well with the EU's own targets, its inclusion significantly accelerated the negotiation process.

The CAI will promote direct investment growth between China and the EU, as both sides pledge to open up certain manufacturing and service sectors to investment. In terms of market access, the CAI adopts a model of pre-entry national treatment plus a negative list. This marks the first time that China has committed to opening up all sectors — both service and non-service industries — in the form of a negative list. Implementation of the CAI will promote European

---

[①] Author: Guo Jingpu, Deputy Director at Sinolink Securities Institute and project fellow of Program for China's Financial Policy Report.

capital investment in China's finance, construction, maritime, and aviation-related support services, attracting low-cost global capital via China's stable-return assets, reducing domestic financing costs, expanding sources of capital, and increasing the stability of China's financial system.

EU countries also hope to pique China's interest in their advanced manufacturing and service sectors. Looking for successful Chinese companies to invest in Europe, they especially aim to attract those with technological and first-mover advantages in the green energy and digitalization fields. This move will broaden Chinese companies' markets and field of investment opportunities, bringing them global and weak-cycle returns. At the same time, Chinese companies can learn the best practices from European companies in corresponding fields to promote China's GNP growth.

According to research from Frank L Klingberg and other scholars, US diplomatic policy follows an approximate half-century cyclical trend of alternation between introversion and outward expansion. Thus there is a significant chance of an inward and isolationist shift in US foreign policy between 2015 and 2035. This period offers China a strategic opportunity to broaden global influence, stabilizing its relations with the EU and strengthening bilateral economic and trade ties to find common ground and deepen cooperation in both global governance and long-term development.

In August 2020, the Chinese government announced its long-term goal to achieve carbon neutrality by 2060. This reflects the nation's responsibility as a world power and converges with EU countries' green development plans. Looking forward, carbon neutrality and the CAI herald constructive interaction, proactivity, and deepened cooperation for China and Europe. Each side will work with the other to create new opportunities, make new progress, and realize a strategy for common and green development.

# Major Financial Regulatory Policies

## I. Major Regulatory Policies of the People's Bank of China (PBC)[①]

### (I) Review of the PBC's Major Regulatory Policies in 2020

First, the PBC continued to build a comprehensive macroprudential policy framework. A counter-cyclical capital buffer mechanism was established, macroprudential stress tests were implemented in stages, and improvements were made to the monitoring, evaluating, and early warning of systemic risks. In addition, the macroprudential management framework for cross-border capital flows was established and improved and financial institutions/financial holding companies of systemic importance were placed under comprehensive supervision.

Second, significant phased achievements were made in the battle against financial risks. The PBC made timely adjustments to the foci and priorities of financial risk management in different stages, led coordination for the smooth takeover of *Tomorrow Holding's* nine core financial institutions, and properly dealt with default risks in the bond market. The PBC effectively curbed the rise of systemic financial risks, fundamentally reversing the situation of finance divorcing from the real economy and blindly expanding.

Third, international financial cooperation was strengthened by the orderly advance of financial sector opening-up. Involving itself in the coordination of international macro-policies in the face of COVID-19, the PBC actively participated in multilateral crisis prevention and relief. The PBC likewise involved itself in the formulation of the G20's Debt Service Suspension Initiative (DSSI) and relevant countries' applications for full debt suspension. In addition, the PBC assisted the International Monetary Fund (IMF) in the universal allocation of Special Drawing Rights (SDR) and offered support to low-income countries to lessen the impact of COVID-19. As a full participant in financial industry negotiations of the Regional Comprehensive Economic Partnership Agreement (RCEP), the PBC incorporated new financial services and financial information transfer into the Free Trade Agreement (FTA). Meanwhile, the PBC continued to actively promote international cooperation in green finance.

Fourth, new progress was made in financial reforms. The PBC chaired to the establishment of local coordination mechanism on provincial levels under the Office of Financial Stability and Development Committee (the FSDC Office). Two batches of 26 measures for financial reform and

---

[①] Author: Zhu Xiaochuan. Financial Law Research Association of Shanghai Law Society and project fellow of Program for China's Financial Policy Report. This part mainly refers to the official website of People's Bank of China. For details of PBC's monetary policy, please refer to the previous chapters.

opening up were put into practice, with further promotion of reform and opening up in the fields of foreign exchange and regional finance, as well as on pilot projects. Regulations for corporate credit bonds' default and information disclosure have been gradually unified and bond market infrastructures have become increasingly well-connected. In addition, the PBC helped deposit insurance companies and institutions fulfill their duties, advanced development financial institutions and policy financial institutions' classification management, and improved the asset management business' rectification during the transitional period.

Fifth, new foci emerged in financial services and management. To fully support epidemic prevention and control, a "green channel" for financial services was swiftly opened. The PBC made every effort to improve the performance of legislative duties essential to coordination of the financial industry. New progress was made in payment monitoring and services, Renminbi cash management, and pilot digital Renminbi; state treasury services also demonstrated continuous improvement. In addition, overall planning of the credit information system was completed. Breakthroughs were made in anti-money laundering monitoring to basically establish a "two-pillar" monitoring mechanism for risk assessment and law enforcement inspection. Remarkable results were similarly achieved in the analysis of anti-money laundering investigation and monitoring. When assuming chairmanship of the Financial Action Task Force on Money Laundering (FATF), the PBC successfully fulfilled its duties considerably advanced mutual evaluation and rectification. Finally, the PBC did more to crack down the violations of consumers' financial information security.

### (II) Evaluation of the PBC's Major Regulatory Policies in 2020

In 2020, under the centralized and unified leadership of the CPC Central Committee on financial work and guided by Xi Jinping Thought on Socialism with Chinese Characteristics for a New Era, the PBC upheld the people-centered philosophy of development and unswervingly implemented the decisions and arrangements of the CPC Central Committee and State Council. Under the overall coordination of the Financial Stability and Development Committee, the PBC remained committed to businesses' and employment's stability, fought hard to prevent and resolve major financial risks, and further deepened financial reform and opening up. The PBC conscientiously performed the duties of the FSDC Office and solicited opinions from the public in a timely manner prior to the introduction of major regulatory policies. Regulatory policies therefore became more deliberate, and social expectations of regulatory policies stabilized, making for better social results.

Areas of supervision still to be strengthened and improved include: the full utilization of important financial industry legislation's responsibility for coordination; the formation of a more sound financial regulatory system; and increased transparency and efficiency in supervision. A feasible method of supervision is to be formulated in accordance with the "Work Plan for Overall Supervision of Financial Infrastructure". In the meantime, understanding and the supervision of financial technology will be strengthened. The PBC will take full advantage of science and technology to advance supervision work and will standardize financial science and technology development through such supervision.

### (III) The Outlook for PBC Regulatory Policies

In 2021, under the overall leadership of CPC Central Committee in financial work, the PBC will continue to follow the guidance of Xi Jinping Thought on Socialism with Chinese Characteristics for a New Era, strengthen political construction, and advance the construction of a law-based central bank. The PBC will actively observe and reflect on economic and financial issues from a political perspective and prioritize the people's interests in improvements to financial management. Furthermore, the PBC will thoroughly implement Xi Jinping Thought on the Rule of Law and promote law-based governance to deepen reform, stimulate development, resolve conflicts and maintain stability. Revisions of finance legislation and law will be actively proposed, particularly in order to increase the costs of legal violations, clarify grey areas, and ensure transparency in the process of law enforcement.

First, major decisions and arrangements will be implemented regarding peak carbon dioxide emissions and carbon neutrality, with improvements to the green finance policy framework and incentive mechanism. The PBC will design and formulate policies that allocate more financial resources to — and thus stimulate — green development, will equip the financial system to better handle risks related to climate change, will establish the carbon emissions trading market with a reasonable price set on carbon emissions, and will progressively establish the green financial standard system. The PBC will also clarify financial institutions' requirements for regulatory and information disclosure, establish a system of policy incentives and restraints, improve green financial products and the green market system, and continuously promote international cooperation in green finance.

Second, the PBC will step up improvements to the macroprudential policy framework, incorporating major financial activities, financial institutions, financial markets and financial infrastructure under macroprudential management. Systematic financial risk monitoring and assessment will be strengthened, and the macroprudential stress testing system will be built up in increments. In addition, the PBC will accelerate the establishment of a sound macroprudential management framework in key areas such as cross-border capital flows and will improve financial holding companies' monitoring system.

Third, the PBC will continue to prevent and mitigate financial risks. In-depth risk investigations will be undertaken to deal with risks in a proper manner. Moreover, the PBC will regulate long-term risk-prevention and resolution mechanisms. It will also clarify the main responsibilities of financial institutions and shareholders, the territorial responsibilities of local governments, the regulatory responsibilities of financial supervision departments, and the responsibilities of lenders of last resort. Progress shall be made in the deposit insurance system and organization structuring. The prudential supervision of internet firms' financial activities will also be strengthened. The PBC will unfalteringly implement the decisions and arrangements of Party Central Committee and State Council on reinforcing anti-monopoly, preventing the disorderly expansion of capital, and coordinating financial development and financial security; at the same time it will pay close attention to correcting weaknesses within the regulatory system. With payment supervision toughened, personal credit information businesses will need to be licensed; the excessive marketing of financial products and inducing of excessive debts will be strictly prohibited; and illegal acts infringing on financial consumers' legitimate rights and interests will be seriously investigated and prosecuted. The PBC will ensure that financial innovation develops under prudential supervision and that the service level and competitiveness of inclusive financing steadily rise.

Fourth, out of its devotion to global financial governance, the PBC will rigorously prevent and control external financial risks and will steadily expand financial two-way opening up. Low-income countries' issues of debt will be coped with appropriately. The PBC will further expand the high-level opening up of the financial industry and fully implement the pre-establishment national treatment plus negative list administration system. Meanwhile, by its commitment to global financial governance, the PBC will faithfully uphold multilateralism.

Fifth, the Renminbi's internationalization will move forward steadily but cautiously. Here, focus will be on serving the real economy and following trends to promote trade and investment facilitation. The policy system related to the use of Renminbi will be improved and the high-quality two-way opening of financial markets continually advanced. The healthy and coordinated development of local and foreign currency and offshore-onshore markets shall also be promoted.

Sixth, the reform of financial markets and financial institutions will be deepened. The PBC will lead the formulation of a development plan for the bond market and work on perfecting its legal system, forge the interconnection of infrastructure, and improve the mechanism for multi-channel bond default disposal. The PBC will improve the bond market's unified law enforcement framework and intensify the investigation and punishment of illegal acts such as debt evasion and fraud in listing. Efforts will be made to improve real-estate's long-term mechanisms, real estate finance's prudent management system, and the housing leasing financial support policy system. The PBC will guide a shift in the service priorities of large banks and help small and medium-sized banks improve corporate governance and focus on main responsibilities and main businesses.

Seventh, foreign exchange management and services will be continually upgraded. The PBC will steadily open the Capital Account to the outside world in an orderly manner and will support enterprises' prudent and reasonable use of foreign exchange derivatives to manage exchange rate risks. Improvements to the two-pronged macroprudential and micro-regulatory management framework will be hastened. Meanwhile, the PBC will uphold a zero tolerance attitude toward illegal acts in the field of foreign exchange. Foreign exchange reserves will be well-managed in an intensive and efficient manner to maintain basic stability in the size of foreign exchange reserves.

Eighth, levels of financial service and management will be elevated. The PBC will formulate overall plans to promote the construction of financial legal system, extend the influence of PBC research, implement key financial tasks of the 14th Five-Year Plan, and formulate the 14th Five-Year Plan of Finance Industry. Achievements are anticipated in the financial industry's comprehensive statistics as well as the modernization of payment governance and the application and management of financial science and technology. The pilot test of digital currency electronic payments will be steadily conducted, and the application of credit information to digital finance and economic governance will be developed. While formulating a new development pattern for anti-money laundering work, the PBC will rigorously study and formulate a national anti-money laundering development strategy, move forward with revisions to the "Anti-money Laundering Law of the People's Republic of China", strengthen the construction of an anti-money laundering coordination mechanism, tighten up anti-money laundering supervision, and achieve better supervision results. In addition, the PBC will put anti-money laundering investigation and monitoring analysis to full use, participate in international anti-money laundering governance, and make adjustments after the FATF mutual evaluation.

## Appendix

### Major Regulatory Policies of the PBC in 2020

| Released on | Major Policies | Released by | Document No. |
|---|---|---|---|
| January 31 | Notice of PBC, MOF, CBIRC, CSRC and SAFE on Further Strengthening Financial Support for Containing Novel Coronavirus Outbreak | People's Bank of China (PBC), Ministry of Finance (MOF), China Banking and Insurance Regulatory Commission (CBIRC), China Securities Regulatory Commission (CSRC) and State Foreign Exchange Administration of the People's Republic of China (SAFE) | YF [2020] No. 29 |
| February 7 | Emergency Notice of MOF, PBC, NDRC, MIIT and NAO on Winning the Battle Against the Epidemic Outbreak and Strengthening Financing Support for Key Enterprises Engaged in Epidemic Prevention and Control | MOF, PBC, National Development and Reform Commission (NDRC), Ministry of Industry and Information Technology (MIIT) and National Audit Office (NAO) | CJ [2020] No. 5 |
| February 14 | Opinions on Further Accelerating the Development of Shanghai as an International Financial Center and Providing Financial Support for the Integrated Development of the Yangtze River Delta | PBC, CBIRC, CSRC, SAFE and Shanghai Municipal People's Government (SMG) | YF [2020] No. 46 |
| March 1 | Notice of CBIRC, PBC, NDRC, MIIT and MOF on Implementing Temporary Deferment of Loan Principal and Interest Repayments for Micro, Small and Medium-Sized Enterprises | CBIRC, PBC, NDRC, MIIT and MOF | YBJF [2020] No. 6 |
| March 5 | Work Plan for Overall Supervision of Financial Infrastructure | PBC, NDRC, MOF, CBIRC, CSRC and SAFE | None |

Continued

| Released on | Major Policies | Released by | Document No. |
|---|---|---|---|
| March 20 | The People's Bank of China-Measures of the People's Bank of China for the Implementation of Administrative Permits | The People's Bank of China | PBC Order [2020] No. 1 |
| April 16 | Notice on Revising the Administrative Measures of Importing and Exporting Gold and Gold Products | PBC and General Administration of Customs (GACC) | PBC and GACC Order [2020] No. 3 |
| April 24 | Opinions on Financial Support for the Building of the Guangdong-Hong Kong-Macao Greater Bay Area | PBC, CBIRC, CSRC and SAFE | YF [2020] No. 95 |
| April 29 | Decision on Revising the Administrative Measures of Education Savings and Other Regulations | The People's Bank of China | PBC Order [2020] No. 2 |
| May 26 | Opinions on Further Strengthening Financial Services for Small and Micro Enterprises | PBC, CBIRC, NDRC, MIIT, MOF, CSRC, SAFE and SMAR | YF [2020] No. 120 |
| June 1 | Notice of PBC, CBIRC, MOF, NDRC and MIIT on Extending the Policy of Provisional Deferred Repayment of Loan Principal and Interest for Micro, Small and Medium-Sized Enterprises | PBC, CBIRC, MOF, NDRC and MIIT | YF [2020] No. 122 |
| June 1 | Notice of PBC, CBIRC, MOF, NDRC and MIIT on Stepping up Credit Support for Micro and Small Businesses | PBC, CBIRC, MOF, NDRC and MIIT | YF [2020] No. 123 |
| June 2 | Notice on Revising the Detailed Rules for Implementing Administrative Rules of Payment Services of Non-financial Institutions and Another Five Normative Documents | The People's Bank of China | PBC Announcement [2020] No. 3 |
| June 15 | Notice of PBC, NDRC and CSRC on Issues Concerning the Default Resolution of Corporate Credit Bond | PBC, NDRC and CSRC | None |
| June 24 | Administrative Measures for Standardized Bills | The People's Bank of China | PBC Announcement [2020] No. 6 |
| June 24 | Rules for Recognition of Standard Debt-Based Assets | PBC, CBIRC, CSRC and SAFE | PBC, CBIRC, CSRC and SAFE Announcement [2020] No. 5 |
| June 29 | Joint Announcement on the Launch of "the Cross-Boundary Wealth Management Connect Pilot Scheme" in the Greater Bay Area | PBC, Hong Kong Monetary Authority (HKMA) and Monetary Authority of Macao (AMCA) | None |

Continued

| Released on | Major Policies | Released by | Document No. |
|---|---|---|---|
| July 19 | Issues Concerning the Interconnectivity Cooperation Between Relevant Infrastructure Institutions in the Interbank Bond Market and the Exchange-traded Bond Market | PBC and CSRC | PBC and CSRC Announcement [2020] No. 7 |
| July 23 | Notice on Printing and Distributing the Interim Provisions on the Administration of Issuing Common Commemorative Coins and Common Coins | The People's Bank of China | YF [2020] No. 173 |
| September 11 | Trial Measures on Regulation of Financial Holding Companies | The People's Bank of China | PBC Order [2020] No. 4 |
| September 14 | Notice of PBC and Relevant Departments on Printing Overall Plan of Inclusive Finance Reform Pilot Zone for Three Cities of Two Provinces | The People's Bank of China | None |
| September 15 | Implementation Measures of the People's Bank of China for Financial Consumer Protection | The People's Bank of China | PBC Order [2020] No. 5 |
| September 18 | Opinions of the PBC, MIIT, MOJ, MOFCOM, SASAC, SAMR, CBIRC and SAFE on Promoting Regulated Development of Supply Chain Finance in Support of Stable Circulation, Optimization and Upgrading of Supply Chains and Industrial Chains | PBC, MIIT, MOJ, MOFCOM, SASAC, SAMR, CBIRC and SAFE | YF [2020] No. 226 |
| September 30 | Notice on Establishing Countercyclical Capital Buffer Mechanism | PBC and CBIRC | None |
| October 26 | Notice on Regulating Collection Business | The People's Bank of China | YF [2020] No.248 |
| November 12 | Notice on Revising Normative Documents Involved in the Reform of Separating Operating Permits and Business Licenses | The People's Bank of China | PBC Announcement [2020] No. 15 |
| November 18 | Notice of Issues Concerning the Printing and Distribution of the Samples of Special Certificates and Seals for Counterfeit Currency Collection and Identification Business | The People's Bank of China | YF [2020] No.281 |
| December 2 | Notice of PBC and CBIRC on Issuing the Measures for the Assessment of Systemically Important Banks | PBC and CBIRC | YF [2020] No. 289 |
| December 9 | Announcement on Issues Concerning Cash Receipts and Payments of RMB | The People's Bank of China | PBC Announcement [2020] No. 18 |

Continued

| Released on | Major Policies | Released by | Document No. |
| --- | --- | --- | --- |
| December 18 | Regulating Information Disclosure of Commercial Acceptance Drafts | The People's Bank of China | PBC Announcement [2020] No. 19 |
| December 23 | Improving the Management of Market Makers for Spot Bond Trading in the Interbank Bond Market | The People's Bank of China | PBC Announcement [2020] No. 21 |
| December 25 | Administrative Measures for Information Disclosure of Corporate Debenture Bonds | PBC, NDRC and CSRC | PBC, NDRC and CSRC Announcement [2020] No. 22 |
| December 28 | Notice of PBC and CBIRC on Establishing the Real Estate Loan Concentration Management System for Banking Financial Institutions | PBC and CBIRC | YF [2020] No. 322 |
| December 31 | Notice of PBC, NDRC, MOC, SASAC, CBIRC and SAFE on Further Optimizing the Cross-Border RMB Policies to Stabilize Foreign Trade and Foreign Investment | PBC, NDRC, MOC, SASAC, CBIRC and SAFE | YF [2020] No. 330 |
| December 31 | Announcement on Transitional Arrangements for Pledge Registration of Four Types of Movables: Production Equipment, Raw Materials, Semi-finished Products and Products | PBC and SAMR | PBC and SAMR Announcement [2020] No. 23 |

Source: Official Website of the People's Bank of China. The release date shall be subject to the time when the document was signed; if there is no signing date, the date on which the document was published on the official website shall prevail.

## Article 15

### Building a regulatory framework to promote a virtuous circle[1]

On September 11, 2020, the State Council issued the *State Council's Decision on Implementing Access Management of Financial Holding Companies* (hereafter referred to as the "Access Decision"). That same day, the People's Bank of China (PBC) issued the *Administration Trial Measures for the Supervision of Financial Holding Companies* (hereafter referred to as the "Financial Holding Companies Measures"). Then on November 2, the PBC solicited public opinions for the *Interim Regulations on the Administration of Filing of Directors, Supervisors and Senior Management of Financial Holding Companies (Draft for Comments)* (hereafter referred to as the "Interim Regulations").

---

[1] Author: Tong Haoxiang, Assistant Researcher of Program for China's Financial Policy Report, a staff member of the Financial Market Department of China Construction Bank.

A financial holding company is a corporate group that operates in the financial industry against the backdrop of financial innovation and increased market competition; it provides one-stop integrated financial services through coordination of the group's various business subsidiaries. By expanding its business chain, diversifying its operations, and integrating industry and finance, a financial holding company can gain competitive strengths in comprehensive service, low business costs, and diversified profit sources.

The supervision-by-industry model entails a regulatory vacuum, which has created problems for both financial and non-financial institutional holdings: unclear corporate shareholding structures, unreasonable organizational structures, and the risk of large connected transactions within the group, the blind pursuit of large and comprehensive operations, imperfect risk management, and poor business synergy. There are even a few cases of shareholders interfering with financial institutions' operations, using connected transactions to covertly transfer benefits and siphon institutional funds, creating huge financial risks.

In accordance with the decision of the Party Central Committee and the State Council following the Fifth National Financial Work Conference in 2017, the PBC, together with the Ministry of Justice and other relevant authorities, began to implement access management and the continuous supervision of financial holding companies. The issuance of the *Access Decision*, the *Financial Holding Companies Measures*, and the *Interim Regulations* marks the official launch of supervision and management over financial holding companies.

The *Access Decision* consists of three parts. First, it defines the implementation of access management for financial holding companies as well as the scope of their subjects and establishment standards. Second, it clarifies conditions and procedures for the establishment of financial holding companies. Third, it makes provisions for other matters such as timing.

The *Financial Holding Companies Measures* refines the access conditions and procedures set down for financial holding companies in the *Access Decision* and further clarifies that the PBC shall supervise financial holding companies and that financial regulators shall supervise the financial institutions held by financial holding companies in adherence to the law and according to the division of financial supervision responsibilities. The *Financial Holding Companies Measures* puts forth regulatory requirements on key aspects such as shareholder qualifications, the source and application of capital, capital adequacy requirements, shareholding structure, corporate governance, connected transactions, risk management systems, and risk "firewall" systems.

The *Interim Regulations* clarifies the supervising subject of financial holding companies' directors, supervisors and senior management and dictates the strengthening of appointment management as well as pre- and post-event supervision. It also stipulates filing procedures and materials and clarifies management tools.

The *Access Decision*, the *Financial Holding Companies Measures*, and the *Interim Regulations* bring all financial holding companies within the scope of supervision but systematically separate the industrial from the financial sector, helping prevent the cross-contamination of risks and thus better meeting the needs of the whole society in terms of diversified, integrated, and convenient financial services, while promoting a virtuous cycle of economy and finance.

However, to fully moderate irregularities in the industry and contain blind expansion, more detailed regulatory rules, clearer ownership structures, and stronger internal corporate management are needed to highlight financial holding companies' main business and establish a mechanism for coordination. In the future, more emphasis must go on overall supervision, on the core of systemic risk prevention and mitigation, on the clarification of prudential supervision standards for financial holding companies' capital adequacy and corporate governance, and on reducing financial holding companies' complexity, contagiousness, and concentration of risks in order to promote financial holding companies' healthy and orderly development.

## II. Major Regulatory Policies in China's Banking Sector[①]

### (I) Major Regulatory Policies in China's Banking Sector in 2020

One: Financial services were improved for epidemic prevention and control and to fully support national economic recovery.

First, to ensure the stability of the financial order and uninterrupted services during the epidemic, the China Banking and Insurance Regulatory Commission (CBIRC) guided banks to improve financial services. Faced with the unexpected COVID-19 outbreak in 2020, the CBIRC properly responded to the epidemic and simultaneously advanced economic and social development, satisfying the financial needs of both the people and industrial and commercial businesses. On January 31, the People's Bank of China (PBC), joined the CBIRC and three other ministries and commissions to jointly issue the *Notice on Further Strengthening Financial Support for Epidemic Prevention and Control*. The notice focused on increasing credit support for enterprises engaged in epidemic prevention and control and providing severely impacted regions, industries and enterprises with differentiated and preferential financial services. On February 1, the PBC, CBIRC and two other departments jointly issued the *Ensuring Quality Financial Services after the Spring Festival Holiday*, emphasizing the need to effectively support financial services crucial to epidemic prevention and control, as well meet financial needs for people's livelihoods and thereby ensuring the smooth and orderly operation of the financial market. On March 26, banking regulators issued the *Notice on Strengthening Financial Services for Coordinated Resumption of Work and Production across the Industrial Chain*. The notice puts forward specific measures to strengthen financial support for core enterprises in the industrial chain, enhance financial support and services for enterprises in upstream and downstream sectors of the industrial chain, better coordinate the resumption of work and production throughout the industrial chain, and improve the quality and efficiency of financial services.

---

① Author: Zhou Jinfei, senior analyst of Strategic Development and Implementation Department of SPD Bank.

Second, the CBIRC enhanced support for financial inclusion and guided the financial sector to better serve the real economy. In 2020, the CBIRC coordinated efforts to promote the development of inclusive finance, guiding banks to strengthen financial support for key areas and weak links in micro- and small enterprises. On March 1, the CBIRC and four other departments jointly issued the *Notice on Extending the Policy of Provisional Deferred Repayment of Loan Principal and Interest for Micro, Small and Medium-Sized Enterprises*, which required banking institutions to implement the provisional deferred principal/interest repayment policy for micro-, small, and medium-sized enterprises within a certain period, provided enterprises in Hubei Province with a special credit scale, and offered fixed internal fund transfer preferences. On March 10, the CBIRC issued the *Notice on Optimizing the Change of Business Premises of the Branches of Banking Institutions*. This notice supported and encouraged banking institutions to continually optimize branches' network layout, increased financial services in weak service areas, and expanded the coverage of inclusive finance. On May 26, the PBC, together with the CBIRC and six other ministries and commissions, issued the *Guidance on Further Strengthening Financial Services for Micro, Small and Medium-sized Enterprises*. The guidance required banking institutions to offer credit support for the resumption of work and production in micro-, small, and medium-sized enterprises, required commercial banks to carry out projects for financial service capacity improvement targeting micro-, small, and medium-sized enterprises, optimized the external incentives of commercial banks' regulatory policies, and improved the system of performance evaluation for financial enterprises. On June 1, the PBC, CBIRC, and three other ministries and commissions issued the *Notice on Increasing Credit Support for Micro and Small-sized Enterprises*. This notice emphasized that banking institutions should allocate more credit resources to micro- and small- enterprises, helping more micro- and small enterprises to obtain collateral-free and non-guaranteed micro-loans; the same day, the PBC, CBIRC and three other ministries and commissions jointly issued the *Notice on Further Implementation of Phased Deferment of Capital and Interest Repayment for Micro, Small and Medium-sized Enterprises*, which aimed to ease the pressure of capital and interest repayments for enterprises over the year, especially for micro-, small, and medium-sized enterprises. It also further implemented the phased deferment of capital and interest for eligible enterprises. At the same time, appropriate incentives were given to local corporate banks that offered capital and interest deferments to micro- and small enterprises. On June 29, the CBIRC formulated and issued the *Provisional Rules on Supervisory Assessment of Commercial Banks' Financial Services for Micro and Small Enterprises* (*Trial*), which comprehensively and scientifically evaluated the development and effectiveness of financial services offered by commercial banks to micro- and small enterprises in terms of their evaluation systems, mechanisms, process, and application of evaluation results, and urged commercial banks to improve service quality and effectiveness for micro- and small enterprises. On August 5, the CBIRC and six other departments issued the *Notice on the Supervision over Governmental Financing Guarantee Agencies*, which required governmental financing guarantee agencies to adhere to a quasi-public positioning, make up for market deficiencies, to focus on supporting micro- and small enterprises as well as agriculture, rural areas, and farmers, to steadily increase the proportion of financing guarantees for micro- and small enterprises as well as "agriculture, rural areas and farmers" in outstanding balances, and to support the overall development of micro- and small enterprises as well as "agriculture, rural areas and farmers".

Third, the CBIRC supported the development of the supply and industry chains while reducing enterprises' comprehensive financing costs. In 2020, the CBIRC encouraged banking institutions to continue reducing fees and expanding concessions, standardize the development of supply chain finance, and alleviate financing difficulties and lower financing costs. On May 18, the CBIRC and five other departments jointly issued the *Notice on Further Regulating Credit Financing Charges and Reducing Comprehensive Financing Cost of Enterprises*. The notice further regulated fees and management for credit financing in four aspects — namely, credit, credit assistance, credit enhancement, and credit assessment — safeguarding enterprises' right to know as well as their right to independent choice and fair trade, and reducing the comprehensive costs of corporate financing. On September 18, the PBC, together with the CBIRC and six other ministries and commissions, jointly issued the *Opinions on Standardizing the Development of Supply Chain Finance to Support the Stable Cycle and Optimization of Supply Chain and Industrial Chain*. The opinions dictates clarifying the connotations and development direction of supply chain finance, advancing the standardized development and innovation of supply chain finance, strengthening the construction of supporting infrastructure in supply chain finance, improving its policy support system, preventing corresponding risks, and strictly regulating constraints on supply chain finance.

Two: Risk control in key areas was prioritized along with the healthy and stable development of the financial market.

First, the CBIRC established sound regulations in key areas and compensated for weaknesses in the regulatory system. In 2020, the CBIRC continued to prioritize compensation of weaknesses in the regulatory system, continuously striving to strengthen institutional safeguards for the banking industry's high-quality development. On February 20, the CBIRC issued the *Guidance on the Prevention of Financial Crime by Employees in the Banking and Insurance Industry*. The guidance clarified the basic principles of preventing financial crime within the banking industry, focused on requirements for the prevention of financial crime in key areas of the industry, and further emphasized the role of internal control and industry self-regulatory mechanisms in corporate governance along with other aspects of banking financial institutions. On May 26, the CBIRC issued the *Provisional Rules on Leasing Companies for Financing Purpose*. These provisional rules clarified the business scope, financing channels, the scope of leased goods, and prohibited businesses for financial leasing companies. It also specified supervisory rating factors for financial leasing companies. In view of such industry issues as "shell" or "lost-contact" companies along with those engaged in illegal operations, the rules put forward requirements for cleaning up such entities and clarified the division of supervision tasks. On June 30, the CBIRC issued the *Provisional Rules on Supervisory Rating of Financial Leasing Companies*, which included rating factors and methods, rating operational procedures, classified supervision, and other aspects, making overall arrangements for financial leasing companies' supervisory rating work in order to allocate supervisory resources and promote the sustained and healthy development of financial leasing companies. On July 12, the CBIRC issued *the Provisional Rules on Internet Loans of Commercial Banks*. This regulation targets commercial banks' internet loan business in terms of risk management system, risk data and risk modeling management, as well as IT risk management and loan cooperation management, aiming to promote the healthy development of commercial banks' internet loan business. On July 14, the CBIRC issued the "the Provisions on Off-site Supervision of Financing Guarantee Companies". These provisions focused on the division of responsibilities in the off-site supervision of financial guarantee companies and the off-site supervision procedures. It detailed information collection and verification, risk monitoring and assessment, information reporting and use, and supervisory measures. The provisions improved the interpretation of supervisory statements and indicators for financial guarantee companies, and for the supervision of financial guarantee companies' operating behavior. On September 7, the CBIRC issued the *Notice on Strengthening the Supervision of Micro-credit Companies*. The notice puts forward requirements on micro-credit companies in terms of business operations, management, market order, and policy support as a way to strengthen the supervision and management of microfinance companies and promote standardized and healthy development within the industry. On November 2, the PBC and the CBRC drafted the Interim Measures for the Management of Online Small Loan Business (Exposure Draft), which clearly stated in terms of business access, business scope and basic rules, operation management, supervision and management, and legal responsibilities to protect the legitimate rights and interests of small loan companies and their customers. On December 30, the CBIRC issued the *Notice on the Issuance of the Interim Measures on the Supervisory Rating of Consumer Finance Companies* (*Trial*). This notice set down rating components and methodology in terms of corporate governance and internal control, capital management, risk management, professional service quality, and information technology management.

Second, malpractice, misconduct and noncompliance in the financial market were rectified and financial consumers' legitimate rights and interests were safeguarded. In 2020, the CBIRC continued to rectify malpractice, misconduct, and noncompliance in the financial market so as to effectively protect the legitimate rights and interests of financial consumers. It furthermore urged market players to carry out financial activities in strict compliance with the law. On January 14, the CBIRC issued the *Rules on Complaints Administration of Banking and Insurance Consumers*. The rules clarified the channels and scope of acceptance, processing time limits, and other procedural requirements for the handling of consumer complaints by banking institutions. It required banking institutions to establish and improve traceability and rectification as well as the accountability and complaint handling recusal systems. It stipulates that banking institutions shall not refuse reasonable complaints and claims from consumers. On May 8, the CBIRC issued the *Notice on Strengthening Pawn Shop Supervision*. The notice put forward regulatory requirements to five distinct ends: improving market entry management, ensuring that pawnshops are operating in compliance with laws and regulations, guaranteeing supervision responsibility and strengthened supervision, improving the market order and the business environment so as to guide local authorities in strengthening ex-ante, in-process, and ex-post supervision of pawn shops, and standardizing the overall development of the industry. On October 26, the PBC issued the Notice of the People's Bank of China on Standardizing the Collection Business, which made it clear from the aspects of the authorization of the payer and the management of the opening institution of the payer, the management of the payee and the collection institution, the applicable scenarios of the collection business and the business specifications of the clearing institution, so as to protect the legitimate rights and interests of the parties. On December 9, the PBC issued the Notice on Regulating the Behavior of RMB Cash Receipt and Payment, which makes it clear from the aspects of the main body of cash receipt and payment, the main body of cash receipt and payment services, and the ecological norms of cash receipt and payment, so as to protect the public's rights and interests in the use of cash. On December 30, the banking regulatory department drafted the Measures for the Supervision and Administration of Anti-Money-Laundering and Anti-Terrorist Financing of Financial Institutions (Revised Draft for Comments), which clarified the internal control and risk management of anti money laundering, supervision and administration of anti money laundering and legal responsibility of financial institutions.

Third, the CBIRC steadily promoted risks disposal in key areas and maintained the bottom line of preventing systemic financial risks. In 2020, China was in the final push to meet its target of financial risk prevention and resolution. The CBIRC continued to dispose of problematic financial institutions in an orderly manner and effectively mitigate risks in key areas. On July 3, the PBC, CBIRC and other departments, jointly issued the *Rules for Standardized Identification of Creditor's Assets*. The rules clearly defined standardized creditors' assets and non-standardized creditors' assets, clarified the identification path of the former, and guided the transition of new creditors' assets to bonds and other standardized creditors' assets. On September 9, the CBIRC issued the *Financial Services Management Measures for Banking and Insurance Institutions in Response to Emergencies*. The measures clarified the definition of "emergencies", basic principles of response, and systems for organization and management. It put forward requirements on quality basic financial services and encouraged measures of financial support. The measures emphasizes maintaining the bottom line of preventing risks while simultaneously offering financial services and support. It also required targeted adjustments of supervision methods and requirements. On September 30, the PBC and CBIRC jointly issued the *the Notice on Establishing Countercyclical Capital Buffer Mechanism*. This notice specified methods of provision as well as the mechanism for coverage and evaluation of China's countercyclical capital buffer. The PBC and CBIRC will take into consideration such factors as macroeconomic and financial conditions, the level of leverage, and the soundness of the banking sector and will reevaluate and adjust countercyclical capital buffer requirements on a regular basis to forestall systemic financial risks.

Three: The financial sector's reform and opening up was deepened and the banking industry's high-quality development was advanced.

First, the CBIRC deepened supply-side structural reform in the financial sector and promoted the high-quality development of the banking industry. In 2020, the CBIRC comprehensively deepened supply-side structural reform in finance via multiple channels, promoting the construction of a financial services system in key areas and weak links. On March 5, the PBC and CBIRC jointly issued the *Work Plan for Coordinated Supervision over Financial Infrastructures*, which aimed to strengthen coordinated supervision and construction planning for China's financial infrastructure, including six types of facility and their corresponding operating agencies — namely, the financial asset registration and custody system, the clearing and settlement system, transaction facilities, transaction report repositories, important payment systems, and the basic credit system. On December 18, the PBC and CBIRC jointly issued the *Notice on the Establishment of Real Estate Loan Concentration Management System for Banking Institutions*. The notice specified the scope of the real estate loan concentration management system, management requirements, and adjustment mechanisms. According to such factors as asset size and banking institution type, the PBC and CBIRC specified caps for the proportion of outstanding real estate loans and outstanding personal housing loans in total outstanding loans. Banking institutions that currently exceed the caps specified in the management requirements should develop a plan for business adjustment according to their actual conditions during the transition period and establish mechanisms for regional differentiated adjustment. On December 30, the CBIRC issued the *Notice on Deepening the Reform of the Banking and Insurance Industry (Streamlining the Government, Delegating Power and Improving Government Services) and Optimizing Business Environment*, which aimed to create a market access environment that is open, fair, and equitable for the banking industry, to continue streamlining administration and delegating power to lower levels within the supervision of the banking industry, to enhance the effectiveness of in-process and ex-post supervision, and to improve the quality and effectiveness of services provided by banking institutions. On December 31, the PBC and CBIRC jointly issued the *the Notice on Further Optimizing Cross-border RMB Policy to Support Stabilizing Foreign Trade and Foreign Investment*. The notice covered five aspects: promoting the convenience of Renminbi settlements in trade according to the needs of the real economy, further simplifying the process of cross-border renminbi settlement, optimizing the management of cross-border renminbi investment and financing, facilitating cross-border renminbi receipts and payments under personal current accounts, and enabling the freer use of renminbi bank settlement accounts by overseas institutions.

Second, we supported major national strategies for regional development and deepened the financial sector's opening up to the outside world. In 2020, the CBIRC worked in conjunction with other departments to guide banking institutions in regional financial industries' opening up to the outside world in accordance with major national strategies for regional development. On February 14, the PBC, together with the CBIRC and two other ministries and commissions, as well as the Shanghai Municipal People's Government, jointly issued the *Opinions on Further Accelerating the Building of Shanghai into an International Financial Hub and Financially Supporting the Integrated Development of the Yangtze River Delta*. Thirty specific measures were put forward for the integrated development of the Yangtze River Delta in terms of increased financial support for the construction of the Lin-gang Special Area in China (Shanghai) Pilot Free Trade Zone (Lin-gang Special Area), driving the opening up of Shanghai's financial sector the outside world and promoting cross-regional collaboration among financial institutions in order to build a high-quality financial business environment adhering to international standards. On April 24, the PBC, CBIRC, and two other departments jointly issued the *Opinions on Providing Financial Support for the Development of Guangdong-Hong Kong-Macao Greater Bay Area*. Specific measures were put forward to better facilitate cross-border trade, investment, and financing in the Guangdong-Hong Kong-Macao Greater Bay Area (GBA), expanding the financial sector's opening up to the outside world, promoting connectivity among financial markets and infrastructures, raising the level of innovation in the GBA's financial services, and effectively preventing cross-border financial risks.

Four: The CBIRC improved regulatory methods and systems in the financial industry as well as the effectiveness and relevance of financial regulations.

First, the CBIRC continued to optimize regulatory methods in the financial industry and improve the effectiveness of financial regulations. In 2020, the CBIRC continued to improve supervisory rules for the financial industry and urged banking institutions to comply with laws and regulations and promote healthy development. On May 22, the CBIRC issued the *Notice on the Issuance of Measures for the Management of Criminal Cases Involving Banking and Insurance Institutions (Trial)*. The notice specified a classificatory scheme for case definitions and information reporting as well as definitions for risk events, information reporting, case disposal and supervision, which further regulated and strengthened the management of criminal cases involving banking institutions in a legal, timely and appropriate manner. On June 23, the CBIRC issued the *Notice on the Rectification of Malpractice, Misconduct and Noncompliance in the Banking and Insurance Industry*. Its main objectives were to guide judgments of whether main responsibilities were in place, whether the real economy truly brought about benefits, whether rectification measures were sufficiently strict and effective, whether violations had obviously been curbed, and whether compliance mechanisms were sound and effective. On August 17, the CBIRC issued *the Three-Year Action Plan for Improving Corporate Governance of the Banking and Insurance Sectors (2020–2022)*. Its objective was deepening corporate governance reform in the banking industry and strengthening corporate governance and supervision. The action plan covered general requirements — including CPC leadership and corporate governance integration — comprehensive evaluation of corporate governance, regulation of shareholder conduct, and performance of governance bodies (such as the board of directors), incentive and constraint mechanism improvement, and better stakeholder protection.

Second, the CBIRC developed differentiated regulatory policies and improved the relevance of financial regulations. In 2020, the CBIRC continued to improve differentiated regulatory policies to promote banking institutions' high-quality development. On September 30, the PBC and CBIRC drafted the *Measures for the Management of Total Loss Absorbing Capacity of Global Systemically Important Banks (Draft for Comments)*. The measures specified the basic principles of total loss absorbing capacity rules as well as the calculation methods and requirements for total external loss absorbing capacity risk-weighted ratios and leverage ratios. What's more, it specified the composition of total external loss absorbing capacity as well as deduction factors for said capacity. On December 2, the PBC and CBIRC jointly issued the *Assessment Measures of Domestic Systematically Important Banks*. The assessment measures proposed the establishment of an assessment and identification mechanism for domestic systemically important banks in terms of assessment purpose, method, and process. It indicated that special efforts should be made for differentiated supervision of systemically important banks according to the list and the improvement of China's regulatory framework for systemically important financial institutions. On December 18, the PBC issued the "Standardizing Information Disclosure of Commercial Acceptance Bills" to improve the marketization constraint mechanism, regulate the behavior of financial institutions in handling commercial acceptance bills and protect the legitimate rights and interests of holders.

### (II) Effects of Regulatory Policies in China's Banking Sector in 2020

First, the CBIRC supported the rapid recovery of the national economy from stagnation and decline to normal development. After the outbreak of COVID-19, the CBIRC prioritized protecting human lives above everything else. It formulated a series of policies, providing special emergency credit worth RMB 5.3 trillion to support the people's all-out war against the virus. As of the end of 2020, the value of corresponding loans had risen by RMB 19.6 trillion since the beginning of the year. Banking and financial institutions offered a total of RMB 6.6 trillion for deferred loan principal/interest repayments and granted RMB 24.27 billion in emergency loans. The goal of RMB 1.5 trillion of concessions to the real economy was realized; the concessions provided strong support for the resumption of work and production, ensured stability on "six fronts" and maintained security in "six areas". In 2020, RMB 2.2 trillion worth of new loans were extended to the manufacturing sector, which exceeded the previous five years' sum total. RMB 5.7 trillion worth of new loans were extended to the private enterprises, an increase of RMB 1.5 trillion compared with the previous year. The outstanding balance of loans given to micro- and small enterprises for inclusive financing reached RMB 15.3 trillion, up by more than 30%. Among these, loans granted by the five large commercial banks grew by 54.8%.

Second, the CBIRC properly resolved risk issues in high-risk financial institutions and key fields. Risks in the banking industry were gradually brought under control. The banking industry "has been better prepared and taken precautionary measures" against major hidden problems, thus resolutely maintaining the bottom line of preventing systemic financial risks. The CBIRC continued risk resolution on the Baoshang Bank case and took over six insurance and trust companies held by "the Mingtian Group". Takeover concluded for the Anbang Insurance Group. Risk resolution efforts were stepped up for high-risk small and medium-sized banks and trust institutions. Altogether, RMB 3.02 trillion worth of non-performing assets in the banking sector were disposed of, making the cumulative non-performing assets disposal volume from 2017 to 2020 higher than that of the previous 12 years combined. The high-risk shadow banking business was cut back in an orderly manner. Meanwhile, for the first time in eight consecutive years, growth in real estate loans was the lowest among all different loan types. All P2P lenders were closed down and anti-monopoly scrutiny was explored in the financial sector. The CBIRC worked with local governments to resolve large corporations' debt risks, and a number of major illegal fundraising cases were properly handled.

Third, the banking industry made positive progress in reform and opening up. The CBIRC made continual efforts to advance banking and financial institutional governance, deepen Party-building and corporate governance integration, strictly standardize equity management, and improve directors and supervisors' performance capacities. The CBIRC joined five government agencies to jointly issue the *Work Plan for Deepening Reform and Replenishing Capital of Small and Medium-sized Banks*. The CBIRC actively worked on the issuance of RMB 200 billion worth of local government special bonds to replenish capital for small and medium-sized banks and supported reforms to resolve risks for urban commercial banks and rural credit cooperatives. The CBIRC steadily expanded opening up in finance, promoted the implementation of additional measures for opening up to the outside world, and actively reviewed foreign-funded institutions' applications for market access. Since 2018, the CBIRC has approved foreign banks and insurance companies to set up nearly 100 entities in China. China's commercial banking system is currently undergoing continuous optimization. With adequate market competition, the four large commercial banks reached an advanced international level in terms of operating efficiency, some of them with key business indicators already at the advanced international level, including labor productivity, cost-to-income ratio, return on capital, and technological innovation.

Fourth, a good atmosphere has basically been formed for strong supervision and regulation. The CBIRC worked persistently to improve Party conduct, enforce Party discipline, and fight corruption. A number of corrupted officials engaged in the collusion of interests, tunneling, and illegal encroachment have been brought to justice. The CBIRC strictly promoted the separation of public and private sectors as well as the avoidance system and supervisory accountability. In 2020, a total of 164 people were disciplined within the CBIRC system. The CBIRC accelerated the mending of weak links in supervision and closure of loopholes in the system. Over the year, 61 rules and regulations were established. The CBIRC took positive measures to regulate malpractice, misconduct, and noncompliance in the banking industry. A number of major illegal fundraising cases were successfully handled. In 2020, the CBIRC and its local offices imposed a total of 3, 178 punishments on banking and insurance institutions and 4, 554 punishments on individuals, with fines and confiscations amounting to RMB 2.28 billion. The CBIRC promoted diversified settlement mechanisms for financial consumption disputes, with RMB 17.7 billion returned to consumers or dispensed to consumers as compensation, effectively safeguarding financial consumers' legitimate rights and interests.

Considering the current complexity of the economic and financial situation at home and abroad, supervision of the banking industry still needs to be improved. Efforts were made to accelerate the construction of an institutional mechanism for more effective service to the real economy, to improve the modern financial regulation system, to cut down the shadow banking business, to explore anti-monopoly scrutiny and prevent disorderly expansion of capital in the financial sector, to promote banking and financial institutions' corporate governance, to further improve the level of financial rule of law, to coordinate supervision and technology applications, and to continue improving the overall effectiveness of supervision.

**(III) Outlook on Regulatory Policies in China's Banking Sector in 2021**

2021 marks the start of a new journey to build a modern socialist country and the beginning of "the 14th Five-Year Plan". In view of this new stage of development, the CBIRC will implement new concepts on building a new development pattern and deepen supply-side structural reform in the financial sector. Efforts should also be made to enhance the effectiveness of serving the real economy, advance reform and opening up, and prevent and resolve financial risks, thereby maintaining economic, financial security, and social and political stability.

First, substantial support will be provided for the building of a new development pattern and enhancement of financial services' overall effectiveness. In 2021, the CBIRC will fully support the building of a new development pattern, explore all kinds of financial services to promote innovation in science and technology, expand domestic demand, and encourage and promote poverty alleviation achievements to revitalize rural areas. The CBIRC will actively develop green credit and trust, strengthen integrated financial services for foreign trade entities, and steadily pursue high-level opening up in banking and insurance. At the same time, the CBIRC will maintain the necessary level of support for economic recovery, strengthen financial support to micro-, small and medium-sized enterprises, and step up loan support for first-time homebuyers in terms of housing loans, credit renewals, credit loans, and medium-to-long-term loans. Finally, it will strengthen financial support for projects related to people's livelihoods and safeguard the legitimate rights of financial consumers.

Second, relentless efforts will be made to prevent and resolve financial risks and promote supervision over key activities. In 2021, the CBIRC will keep macro-leverage ratios largely stable, will stringently implement controls on loan concentration in the real estate sector as well as financing rules on financing for key developers, will properly dispose of non-performing assets, will accelerate the resolution of high-risk institutions, will improve processes and procedures for the handling major cases and risk events, will strengthen crackdowns on illegal financial activities and "unlicensed" activities, and will actively fend off external risks and shocks. At the same time, the CBIRC will continue to cut down on the shadow banking business as well as on any new form or variant of high-risk shadow banking activities wherever they emerge, will tighten oversight on institutions failing to effectively dispose of existing related wealth management assets in need of cutting back, and will crack down on malpractice, misconduct and noncompliance in the insurance industry as well as financial products whose names are inconsistent with their actuality.

Third, regulation will be enhanced for online platform financial activities and supply-side structural reform will be deepened in the financial sector. In 2021, the CBIRC will fully incorporate the supervision of financial activities in accordance with law, treat activities and entities of the same nature equally, tighten supervision over banking and insurance institutions' financial activities in cooperation with online platforms, and resolutely curb monopoly and unfair competition in aims of preventing disorderly expansion and barbaric growth of capital in the financial sector. At the same time, the CBIRC will further reform and optimize the system of banking and insurance institutions, support small and medium-sized banks to replenish capital via multiple channels, will further promote the issuance of local government bonds for capital replenishment, will encourage large banks to offer small and medium-sized banks risk control tools and techniques, advance the pilot reform of provincial credit unions in an orderly manner, and promote village banks' risk resolution by means of reform, merger, and acquisition.

Fourth, efforts will be made to improve corporate governance, corporate internal control, and the building of supervisory capacities. In 2021, the CBIRC will implement the shareholder commitment policy, strengthen penetrating shareholder examinations, regulate the conduct of major shareholders in accordance with law, further remove illegal shareholders, put mechanisms in place for the routine disclosure of illegal shareholders, strengthen the development of regulatory rules and systems for related-party transactions, enhance directors and supervisors' abilities to perform their duties, improve internal rules for the board of directors and supervisory committee, and encourage the development of a culture of compliance. At the same time, the CBIRC will improve the capacities of law enforcement to ensure strict enforcement and proportionality of punishment for major risks and cases, improve capacities for whole process supervision, strengthen ex-ante warning and early intervention, tighten ongoing intervention, improve ex-post risk resolution, and enhance the abilities of coordinated supervision and technology applications.

## Appendix

### Major Regulatory Policies in China's Banking Sector in 2020

| Released on | Major Policies | Released by |
| --- | --- | --- |
| January 14 | Rules on Complaints Administration of Banking and Insurance Consumers | China Banking and Insurance Regulatory Commission (CBIRC) |
| January 31 | Circular on Further Strengthening Financial Support for COVID-19 Epidemic Prevention and Control | The People's Bank of China (PBC), Ministry of Finance of People's Republic of China (MOF), China Banking and Insurance Regulatory Commission (CBIRC), China Securities Regulatory Commission (CSRC) and State Administration of Foreign Exchange (SAFE) |
| February 1 | Ensuring Quality Financial Services after the Spring Festival Holiday | The People's Bank of China (PBC), China Banking and Insurance Regulatory Commission (CBIRC), China Securities Regulatory Commission (CSRC) and State Administration of Foreign Exchange (SAFE) |
| February 14 | Opinions on Further Accelerating the Development of Shanghai as an International Financial Center and Providing Financial Support for the Integrated Development of the Yangtze River Delta | The People's Bank of China (PBC), China Banking and Insurance Regulatory Commission (the CBIRC), China Securities Regulatory Commission (CSRC), State Administration of Foreign Exchange (SAFE) and Shanghai Municipal People's Government |

Continued

| Released on | Major Policies | Released by |
|---|---|---|
| February 20 | Guidance on the Prevention of Financial Crime by Employees in the Banking and Insurance Industry | China Banking and Insurance Regulatory Commission (CBIRC) |
| March 1 | Notice on Extending the Policy of Provisional Deferred Repayment of Loan Principal and Interest for Micro, Small and Medium-Sized Enterprises | China Banking and Insurance Regulatory Commission (CBIRC), the People's Bank of China (PBC), National Development and Reform Commission (NDRC), Ministry of Industry and Information Technology of People's Republic of China (MIIT) and Ministry of Finance of People's Republic of China (MOF) |
| March 5 | The Work Plan for Coordinated Supervision over Financial Infrastructures | The People's Bank of China (PBC), National Development and Reform Commission (NDRC), Ministry of Finance of People's Republic of China (MOF), China Banking and Insurance Regulatory Commission (CBIRC), China Securities Regulatory Commission (CSRC) and State Administration of Foreign Exchange (SAFE) |
| March 10 | Notice on Optimizing the Change of Business Premises of Branches of Banking Institutions | China Banking and Insurance Regulatory Commission (CBIRC) |
| March 26 | Notice on Strengthening Financial Services for Coordinated Resumption of Work and Production across the Industrial Chain | China Banking and Insurance Regulatory Commission (CBIRC) |
| April 24 | Opinions on Financial Support for the Building of the Guangdong-Hong Kong-Macao Greater Bay Area | The People's Bank of China (PBC), China Banking and Insurance Regulatory Commission (CBIRC), China Securities Regulatory Commission (CSRC) and State Administration of Foreign Exchange (SAFE) |
| May 8 | Notice on Strengthening Pawn Shop Supervision | China Banking and Insurance Regulatory Commission (CBIRC) |
| May 18 | Notice on Further Regulating Credit Financing Charges and Reducing Comprehensive Financing Cost of Enterprises | China Banking and Insurance Regulatory Commission (CBIRC), Ministry of Industry and Information Technology of People's Republic of China (MIIT), National Development and Reform Commission (NDRC), Ministry of Finance of People's Republic of China (MOF), the People's Bank of China (PBC) and State Administration for Market Regulation (SAMR) |
| May 22 | The Notice on the Issuance of Measures for the Management of Criminal Cases Involving Banking and Insurance Institutions (Trial) | China Banking and Insurance Regulatory Commission (CBIRC) |

Continued

| Released on | Major Policies | Released by |
|---|---|---|
| May 26 | Opinions on Further Deepening Financial Services for Micro, Small and Medium-sized Enterprises | The People's Bank of China (PBC), China Banking and Insurance Regulatory Commission (the CBIRC), National Development and Reform Commission (NDRC), Ministry of Industry and Information Technology of People's Republic of China (MIIT), Ministry of Finance of People's Republic of China (MOF), State Administration for Market Regulation (SAMR), China Securities Regulatory Commission (CSRC) and State Administration of Foreign Exchange (SAFE) |
| May 26 | Provisional Rules on Supervisory Rating of Financial Leasing Companies | China Banking and Insurance Regulatory Commission (CBIRC) |
| June 1 | Notice on Increasing Support for Credit Loans to Micro and Small-sized Enterprises | The People's Bank of China (PBC), China Banking and Insurance Regulatory Commission (the CBIRC), Ministry of Finance of People's Republic of China (MOF), National Development and Reform Commission (NDRC) and Ministry of Industry and Information Technology of People's Republic of China (MIIT) |
| June 1 | Notice of PBC, CBIRC, MOF, NDRC and MIIT on Extending the Policy of Provisional Deferred Repayment of Loan Principal and Interest for Micro, Small and Medium-Sized Enterprises | The People's Bank of China (PBC), China Banking and Insurance Regulatory Commission (the CBIRC), Ministry of Finance of People's Republic of China (MOF), National Development and Reform Commission (NDRC) and Ministry of Industry and Information Technology of People's Republic of China (MIIT) |
| June 23 | Notice on the Rectification of Malpractice, Misconduct and Noncompliance in the Banking and Insurance Industry | China Banking and Insurance Regulatory Commission (CBIRC) |
| June 29 | Notice on the Issuance of Supervisory Evaluation Measures on Financial Services of Commercial Banks for Micro and Small-sized Enterprises (Trial) | China Banking and Insurance Regulatory Commission (CBIRC) |
| June 30 | Provisional Rules on Supervisory Rating of Financial Leasing Companies | China Banking and Insurance Regulatory Commission (CBIRC) |
| June 24 | Rules for Recognition of Standard Debt-Based Assets | The People's Bank of China (PBC), China Banking and Insurance Regulatory Commission (the CBIRC), China Securities Regulatory Commission (CSRC) and State Administration of Foreign Exchange (SAFE) |
| July 12 | The Provisional Rules on Internet Loans of Commercial Banks (Draft for Comments) | China Banking and Insurance Regulatory Commission (CBIRC) |

Continued

| Released on | Major Policies | Released by |
| --- | --- | --- |
| July 14 | Provisions on Off-site Supervision of Financing Guarantee Companies | China Banking and Insurance Regulatory Commission (CBIRC) |
| August 5th | Notice on the Supervision of Governmental Financing Guarantee Agencies | China Banking and Insurance Regulatory Commission (CBIRC), National Development and Reform Commission (NDRC), Ministry of Industry and Information Technology of People's Republic of China (MIIT), Ministry of Finance of People's Republic of China (MOF), Ministry of Agriculture and Rural Affairs of the People's Republic of China, Ministry of Commerce of the People's Republic of China and the People's Bank of China (PBC) |
| August 17 | Notice on the Three-Year Action Plan for Sound Corporate Governance in the Banking and Insurance Industry (2020–2022) | China Banking and Insurance Regulatory Commission (CBIRC) |
| September 7 | Notice on Strengthening the Supervision of Micro-credit Companies (the CBIRC General Office [2020] No.86) | China Banking and Insurance Regulatory Commission (CBIRC) |
| September 9 | Financial Services Management Measures for Banking and Insurance Institutions in Response to Emergencies | China Banking and Insurance Regulatory Commission (CBIRC) |
| September 18 | Opinions of the PBC, MIIT, MOJ, MOFCOM, SASAC, SAMR, CBIRC and SAFE on Promoting Regulated Development of Supply Chain Finance in Support of Stable Circulation, Optimization and Upgrading of Supply Chains and Industrial Chains | The People's Bank of China (PBC), Ministry of Industry and Information Technology of People's Republic of China (MIIT), Ministry of Justice of the People's Republic of China, Ministry of Commerce of the People's Republic of China, State-owned Assets Supervision and Administration Commission of the State Council, State Administration for Market Regulation (SAMR), China Banking and Insurance Regulatory Commission (the CBIRC) and State Administration of Foreign Exchange |
| September 30 | Measures for the Management of Total Loss Absorbing Capacity of Global Systemically Important Banks (Draft for Comments) | The People's Bank of China (PBC) and China Banking and Insurance Regulatory Commission (the CBIRC) |
| September 30 | Notice on Establishing Countercyclical Capital Buffer Mechanism | The People's Bank of China (PBC) and China Banking and Insurance Regulatory Commission (the CBIRC) |
| October 26 | Notice on Regulating Collection Service | PBC |
| December 2 | Interim Measures for the Management of Online Small Loan Business (Exposure Draft) | PBC and CBIRC |

Continued

| Released on | Major Policies | Released by |
|---|---|---|
| December 2 | Assessment Measures of Domestic Systematically Important Banks | The People's Bank of China (PBC) and China Banking and Insurance Regulatory Commission (the CBIRC) |
| December 9 | Notice on Regulating the Behavior of RMB Cash Receipt and Payment | PBC |
| December 18 | Standardizing Information Disclosure of Commercial Acceptance Bills | PBC |
| December 28 | Notice of PBC and CBIRC on Establishing the Real Estate Loan Concentration Management System for Banking Financial Institutions | The People's Bank of China (PBC) and China Banking and Insurance Regulatory Commission (the CBIRC) |
| December 30 | Notice on the Issuance of the Interim Measures on the Supervisory Rating of Consumer Finance Companies (Trial) | China Banking and Insurance Regulatory Commission (CBIRC) |
| December 30 | Notice on Deepening the Reform of the Banking and Insurance Industry (Streamlining the Government, Delegating Power and Improving Government Services) and Optimizing Business Environment | China Banking and Insurance Regulatory Commission (CBIRC) |
| December 30 | Measures for the Supervision and Administration of Anti-Money-Laundering and Anti-Terrorist Financing of Financial Institutions (Revised Draft for Comments) | PBC |
| December 31 | Notice of PBC, NDRC, MOC, SASAC, CBIRC and SAFE on Further Optimizing the Cross-Border RMB Policies to Stabilize Foreign Trade and Foreign Investment | The People's Bank of China (PBC), National Development and Reform Commission (NDRC), Ministry of Commerce of the People's Republic of China (MOC), State-owned Assets Supervision and Administration Commission of the State Council, China Banking and Insurance Regulatory Commission (CBIRC) and State Administration of Foreign Exchange (SAFE) |

# Article 16

## Targeted measures achieve results in the financial system[1]

In early 2020, China and the world were hit hard by the unexpected outbreak of COVID-19. The pandemic aggravated a global economy that was already in the process of recession. Data indicate that the global recession in 2020 was even more severe than the global financial crisis of

---

[1] Author Zhang Wei Associate Dean, National Institute of Financial Research (NIFR), Tsinghua University.

2008, making it second only to the Great Depression of 1929.

After the outbreak, the Party Central Committee and the State Council put a high value on both pandemic prevention and control and matters of economic development. Acting quickly, they delivered a series of timely and precise measures to control the spread of the pandemic. Meanwhile, efforts were made to preclude delays in the return to work and production. By these measures, China became the only major economy in the world to achieve positive economic growth in 2020.

Since the initial outbreak, the financial system has conscientiously implemented the Party Central Committee and State Council's decisions and arrangements. Focusing on the hardest-hit sectors, industries, enterprises, and residents, several financial departments have formulated and implemented targeted and effective financial measures as part of the anti-epidemic campaign to ensure the smooth operation of financial services, facilitate the resumption of production and social life, stabilize the economy, and provide the world with China's best practices in the financial sector.

Since January 26, 2020, the People's Bank of China, the China Banking and Insurance Regulatory Commission (CBIRC), the China Securities Regulatory Commission, the State Administration of Foreign Exchange, and other departments have proactively formulated and implemented a number of financial macro-control policies and have utilized monetary, interest rate, credit, investment, and other policy instruments to reduce interest rates and offer enterprises concessions, to cut corporate financing costs, broaden corporate financing channels, and maintain a reasonable amount of liquidity, thereby providing strong financial support for both economic recovery and pandemic prevention and control. In terms of the major measures, the first was to maintain a reasonable abundance of liquidity and help financial institutions offer more credit support through special refinancing and other means. The second measure is offering subsidized interest funds through central finance in order to cut corporate financing costs. The third is ensuring the rational allocation of financial resources in order to guarantee the public with daily financial services. The fourth is offering more targeted support to micro, small and midsize enterprises by allowing deferred capital and interest repayments, increasing credit loans, broadening financing channels, cutting loan interest rates, and other means. The fifth measure is to safeguard the security of financial infrastructure and maintain the financial market's smooth and orderly operation.

Effective implementation of the above series of anti-epidemic measures in the financial sector has significantly cushioned the negative effects of the pandemic across all fields, all industries, the majority of enterprises, and the majority of citizens. They have ensured stable supply and pricing, a smooth return to work and production, and the country's economic recovery. They have added strength to China's victories against the pandemic and in its economic and social recovery. As regards the anti-epidemic campaign, the domestic financial system has identified a proven Chinese model for fighting the "pandemic" in finance. It demonstrates not only China's institutional advantage of highly effective action within the financial system but also the ability of the financial policy sector to rapidly deploy financial resources. Practice has shown that China's financial system can ensure financial "arteries" are not "blocked" by the pandemic — and shown that it is quite capable of managing the relationship between economic recovery and pandemic prevention and control to achieve maximum results at a reasonable cost.

Although China has had huge successes in pandemic prevention and control and its economic growth has returned to normal, we must not ignore the reality: the pandemic is still spreading worldwide; the global situation remains critical; there are still weak links in domestic pandemic prevention and control; the foundation of economic recovery is not yet solidified; growth remains sluggish in consumption and investment; micro, small, and midsize enterprises are still in a tough position; and financial risk prevention still poses huge challenges. All these factors mean that in the context of normalized pandemic prevention and control, there is still a long way to go as we pursue economic recovery and growth through the precise and effective implementation of financial macro-control policies.

## III. Major Regulatory Policies for China's Securities Industry[1]

### (I) Key elements of regulatory policies for the securities industry in 2020

**1. Gradual promotion of basic system reform with the registration system as the core**

Reform of the Growth Enterprise Market and pilot registration system. On June 12, 2020, the China Securities Regulatory Commission issued the *Administration Measures for the Registration of IPO of Shares on GEM (Trial)* (hereafter referred to as the *GEM IPO Measures*), the *Administration Measures for the Registration of Securities Issuance by Listed Companies on GEM (Trial)* (the *GEM Refinancing Measures*), the *Measures for Continuous Supervision of Listed Companies on GEM (Trial)* (the *GEM Continuous Supervision Measures*), and the *Administration Measures for Securities Issuance and Listing Sponsorship* (the *Sponsorship Measures*). Meanwhile, the China Securities Regulatory Commission, the Shenzhen Stock Exchange (SZSE), China Securities Depository and Clearing Corporation Limited, and the Securities Association of China issued relevant supporting rules.

The revised *GEM IPO Measures* consists of seven chapters with 75 articles in total. As for its content of its objectives, first, it aims to streamline and optimize conditions for the IPO of shares on the GEM, to transform matters that can be judged by investors in the issue terms into more stringent requirements for information disclosure, and to emphasize the legal compliance and financial regularity of enterprises in accordance with the principle of materiality. Second, it makes institutional arrangements for the registration process, aims realize an electronic and open acceptance and review process, to ease the burdens on enterprises, and enhance the transparency

---

[1] Author: Jiang Jianrong, Vice President and Chief Researcher with SWS Research and project fellow of Program for China's Financial Policy Report; Xie Yunxia, Senior Fellow with SWS Research.

of review. Third, it aims to enhance requirements for information disclosure, strictly implement the responsibilities of issuers and other relevant entities in information disclosure, and formulate differentiated information disclosure rules in accordance with the characteristics of GEM enterprises. Fourth, it aims to clarify basic rules for market-based issuance and underwriting and stipulates that the pricing method, investor quotation requirements, the highest quotation rejection ratio, and other matters should comply with the relevant provisions of the Shenzhen Stock Exchange. Fifth, it aims to strengthen supervision and management as well as legal responsibility and increase the accountability of the issuer, intermediaries, and other market players for violations of the law.

The revised *GEM Refinancing Measures* consists of seven chapters with 93 articles in total. Its major contents are, first, meant to clarify the scope of the application. The *GEM Refinancing Measures* shall apply to listed companies that issue securities such as stocks, convertible bonds, and depositary receipts. Second, the revised *GEM Refinancing Measures* aim to streamline and optimize the conditions of issuance, distinguish between issuance to unspecified targets and issuance to specific targets, and set the refinancing conditions for various types of securities in a differentiated manner. Third, it aims to clarify the processes of issuance/listing review and registration, sets the review period for the Shenzhen Stock Exchange to two months, and sets the period for registration with the China Securities Regulatory Commission to fifteen working days. Meanwhile, it establishes simple procedures set for small-scale fast financing. Fourth, it strengthens information disclosure requirements, requiring targeted information disclosure regarding business models, corporate governance, development strategies, etc., to fully reveal risk factors having a potential adverse material impact on a company's core competitiveness, operational stability, or future development. Fifth, it makes special provisions for issuance and underwriting and special arrangements for issue price, pricing base date, and lock-up period, as well as the conversion period, conversion price and trading method of convertible bonds. Sixth, it strengthens supervision and management and legal responsibility, making listed companies, intermediaries and other market players more accountable for violations of the law.

The revised *GEM Continuous Supervision Measures* consists of 35 articles. Its major contents aim first of all to clarify the principle of application: GEM companies shall comply with the general requirements for continuous regulation of listed companies, except as otherwise provided in the *GEM Continuous Supervision Measures*. The second objective is to clarify requirements related to corporate governance and make special arrangements for companies with special voting shares. Third is to establish a system for targeted information disclosure, strengthen the disclosure of industry positioning and risk factors, and highlight key minorities' (e.g. controlling shareholders and actual controllers) information disclosure responsibilities. Fourth is to clarify requirements for shareholding reduction and appropriately extend the lock-up period for the shareholdings of unprofitable enterprises' controlling shareholders, actual controllers, directors, and supervisors. Fifth is to improve the system for major asset reorganization. The *GEM Continuous Supervision Measures* clearly stipulate that the M&A and reorganization of GEM listed companies involved in the issuance of shares shall implement the registration system and provide for the asset requirements for restructuring targets. The sixth objective of the document is to adjust the equity incentive system, expand the scope of persons who can become incentive targets, relax the price limit on restricted stocks, and further simplify procedures for granting restricted stocks.

Major revised contents of the *Sponsorship Measures* include ensuring consistency with the new *Securities Law of the People's Republic of China*, adjusting the terms of audit procedure, and improving sponsor representative management. It secondly aims to implement the requirements of GEM registration system reform, clarify requirements for issuers, their controlling shareholders, and actual controllers in cooperating with sponsorship work, refine requirements for intermediaries' practice, and urge intermediaries to cooperate and contribute to improvements in the quality of the sponsorship business. Third is to strengthen sponsors' internal control requirements, incorporate the sponsorship business into companies' overall compliance and comprehensive risk management, and urge the industry to ensure compliance, fulfill responsibilities, and guarantee self-discipline. Fourth is to increase accountability, enrich the variety of regulatory measures, and raise the costs of violations.

To carry out GEM reform and the specific implementation of registration system pilot well, the China Securities Regulatory Commission formulated and revised the *Special Provisions on Offering and Underwriting in the Securities of IPO on the GEM*, the *Code on the Content and Format of Disclosure for Companies Issuing Public Securities No. 28 - Prospectus for GEM Companies* along with four other normative documents; these were released together with the *GEM IPO Measures* and the *GEM Refinancing Measures*. The Shenzhen Stock Exchange formulated and revised business rules, involving listing conditions, review criteria, a share reduction system, and continuous supervision. The Securities Association of China has formulated self-regulatory rules on the underwriting of GEM offerings. China Securities Depository and Clearing Corporation Limited also formulated and revised its business rules on registration and settlement and refinancing business.

Refinancing methods of the Science and Technology Innovation Board were released to improve the major decision-making arrangements of the Science and Technology Innovation Board pilot registration system. In accordance with the *Securities Law* and the *Implementation Opinions on the Establishment of a Science and Technology Innovation Board and Pilot Registration System on the Shanghai Stock Exchange*, the China Securities Regulatory Commission issued the *Administrative Measures for the Registration of Securities Issuance by Listed Companies on the Science and Technology Innovation Board (Trial)* (the *Sci-Tech Innovation Board Refinancing Measures*) on July 3, 2020. The revised *Sci-Tech Innovation Board Refinancing Measures* consists of seven chapters with 93 articles in total. Its major contents include: firstly, clarification of the scope of application. If a listed company issues stocks, convertible bonds, depositary receipts, or other securities varieties, the *Sci-Tech Innovation Board Refinancing Measures* shall apply. Second, its provisions streamline and optimize the conditions of issuance, distinguish between issuance to unspecified targets and issuance to specific targets, and set refinancing conditions for various types of securities in a differentiated manner. Third is a clarification of the procedures for issuance/listing review and registration. The review period of the Shanghai Stock Exchange is two months and the registration period of the

China Securities Regulatory Commission is fifteen working days. Meanwhile, simple procedures were set up for small-scale fast financing. Fourth, it strengthens disclosure requirements, requiring the targeted disclosure of industry characteristics, business models, corporate governance, and other content, and full disclosure of the level of scientific research, research personnel, and research funds invested. Fifth, it includes special provisions for issuance and underwriting and makes special arrangements for issue price, pricing base date, lock-up period, as well as the conversion period, conversion price and trading method of the convertible bonds. Sixth, it strengthens supervision and management and legal responsibility while increasing listed companies, intermediaries, and other market players' accountability for violations of the law.

To ensure the steady implementation of various reform measures for NEEQ and improve supporting rules for NEEQ reform, the China Securities Regulatory Commission revised the *Guideline on the Content and Format of Information Disclosure by Unlisted Public Companies No. 3 - Prospectus for Directed Offerings and Report on the Status of Offerings* and the *Code on the Content and Format of Information Disclosure by Unlisted Public Companies No. 4 - Application Documents for Directed Offerings* (hereafter collectively referred to as the "directed offering format guidelines"), and formulated the *Code on the Content and Format of Information Disclosure by Unlisted Public Companies No. 9 - Annual Report of Innovative Tier Listed Companies* and the *Code on the Content and Format of Information Disclosure by Unlisted Public Companies No. 10 - Annual Report of Basic Tier Listed Companies* (hereafter collectively referred to as the "codes for the format of the annual report of the Innovation Tier and the Basic Tier") on January 13, 2020. On January 17, the China Securities Regulatory Commission issued the *Code on the Content and Format of Information Disclosure by Unlisted Public Companies No. 11 - Prospectus for Public Offering of Shares to Unspecified Qualified Investors* and the *Code on the Content and Format of Information Disclosure by Unlisted Public Companies No. 12 - Application for Public Offering of Shares to Unspecified Qualified Investors 12 Pieces* (hereafter collectively referred to as the "public offering format codes").

The revision of the codes on the format of directed offerings is mainly based on the *Measures for the Supervision and Administration of Unlisted Public Companies*, with the following contents revised. First, this revision unifies the requirements for directed offerings and extends the application of information disclosure and filing requirements to all public companies; second, it improves the content of information disclosure, clarifies disclosure requirements for the issuance of shares to purchase assets, etc., and refines disclosure requirements for the use of funds raised, etc.; third, it encourages intermediaries to exercise due diligence and supplements requirements for intermediaries' expression of views; fourth, it further streamlines administration and delegates power, clarifying that if a listed company applies for a directed issuance and needs to fulfill an administrative license, NEEQ Co., Ltd. shall first issue a self-regulatory opinion; this constitutes a required document in administrative license applications.

The formulation of codes for the format of the annual report in the Innovation Tier and the Basic Tier is mainly based on the *Measures for the Administration of Information Disclosure by Unlisted Public Companies*, and aims to detail the annual report disclosure requirements for innovation tier and basic tier listed companies. Specifically, the first aim is to clarify differentiated disclosure requirements for the innovation and basic tiers' respective annual reports and simplify disclosure content as appropriate. The second aim is to draw on the results of the Science and Technology Board reform to improve the readability and usefulness of the annual report disclosure focusing on the needs of investors. The third aim is to strengthen the disclosure of risk factors that have a significant impact on innovation- and basic-tier companies' operating performance based on the characteristics of SMEs.

The release of the public offering format codes is mainly based on the *Measures for the Supervision and Administration of Unlisted Public Companies*, with the following contents regulated. First, it puts forward general requirements on public offerings' information disclosure and to clarifies the main responsibilities of issuers and intermediaries' related parties; second, it clarifies the disclosure content and chapter setting requirements for the public offering prospectus, requiring issuers to focus on the disclosure of information regarding business and technology, corporate governance, finance and accounting, as well as the use of raised funds and other information; third, it specifies production and submission requirements for public offering application documents and lists an application documents directory.

Establishment of an NEEQ transfer mechanism. On June 3, 2020, in order to regulate transfer and listing, coordinate system rules among different listing paths, and do a good job of regulatory convergence, the China Securities Regulatory Commission issued the *Guidance on the Transfer and Listing of Companies Listed on the NEEQ* (hereafter referred to as the *Guidance*). The establishment of the transfer and listing mechanism is an important measure to implement the decisions of the Party Central Committee and the State Council; it will enrich listing paths for listed companies, open up channels for SMEs to grow in size and strength, strengthen connections among multi-level capital markets, and make financial services better serve the real economy. The *Guidance* contents cover three major aspects. The first is a general principle. It dictates that in implementing the mechanism for transfer and listing, we should take a market-oriented approach, ensure balance and coordination, work to prevent and control risks, and implement the mechanism on a trial basis. The second aspect concerns main institutional arrangements. It sets down principles for the scope of a transfer to the board, transfer and listing conditions, procedures, sponsorship requirements, share restrictions and other matters. The third aspect is regulatory arrangements. This content clarifies the responsibilities of stock exchanges, NEEQ Co., Ltd., intermediaries, and other relevant parties. Those engaged in illegal or irregular behaviors in the transfer of listing will be subject to strict investigation and punishment according to the law and regulations. The Shanghai Stock Exchange, the Shenzhen Stock Exchange, NEEQ Co., Ltd., China Securities Depository and Clearing Corporation Limited, and other parties shall formulate or revise their rules of in accordance with the *Guidance* to further clarify and refine specific institutional arrangements.

Further improvement of the NEEQ disclosure system. On July 22, 2020, in accordance with the unified arrangements of the Party Committee of the China Securities Regulatory Commission on deepening the NEEQ reform, the China Securities Regulatory Commission issued the *Supervisory*

*Guidelines for Non-listed Public Companies No. 5 - Guidelines for Ongoing Supervision of Listed Companies on Selected Tiers (Trial)* (hereafter referred to as the *Supervisory Guidelines*) and five codes on the format of listed companies' periodic reports. The *Supervisory Guidelines* is formulated for three purposes: first is to establish a continuous supervision system suited to the characteristics of selected tier companies and the realities of the NEEQ market; second is to strengthen regulatory requirements for the selected tier companies in the form of administrative regulatory documents, to lay an institutional foundation for strengthening the administrative supervision of selected tier companies, and to implement classification supervision in conjunction with market stratification; third is to draw on the experience of listed companies' supervision and establish a "three-in-one" working mechanism for the China Securities Regulatory Commission, dispatched institutions, and NEEQ Co., Ltd. for selected tier companies. The five codes on the format of periodic reports for listed companies include guidelines on the format of annual, interim, and quarterly reports for the Selected Tier as well as guidelines on the format of interim reports for the Innovation Tier and Basic Tier. The following principles were followed in the process of formulation: first, disclosure requirements among the selected, innovation and basic tiers were graded to decrease in turn; second, these codes focus on interconnections among tiers' internal rules, and requirements for interim report disclosure are lower than those for annual reports but higher than those for quarterly reports; third, the formulation is based on existing NEEQ regulatory rules while drawing on listed companies' institutional concepts to fully reflect listed companies' characteristics.

Regulation of NEEQ in equity incentive and employee stock ownership plan implementation. In order to deepen NEEQ reform, to encourage the innovation-driven development of the private economy and SMEs, and to prompt the NEEQ market to better serve the real economy, on August 31, 2020 the China Securities Regulatory Commission issued the *Supervisory Guidelines for Unlisted Public Companies No. 6 - Supervisory Requirements for Share Incentives and Employee Stock Ownership Plans (Trial)* (hereafter referred to as the *Supervisory Guidelines*). Following the principles of marketization and the rule of law, the *Supervisory Guidelines* expands corporate autonomous decision-making power, enriches employee stock ownership plan formats, strengthens mechanisms for market restraint, fulfills a supervisory role via host brokerage firms, and clarifies supervision rules on equity incentives and employee stock ownership plans that conform to the practices of the NEEQ market and the characteristics of listed companies. The *Supervisory Guidelines* consists of three parts: the first identifies targets for equity incentives, incentive methods, pricing methods, stock sources, conditions, necessary contents and the arrangement of rights and obligations of each party, performance evaluation indexes, phased exercise information disclosure and implementation procedures. Among these, incentive methods are mainly in the form of restricted stock and stock options, and the sources of stock mainly consist of the issuance of new shares, repurchase of shares, and gifts from shareholders. The second part identifies the sources of funds and shares, forms of shareholding, management methods, and information disclosure requirements for employee stock ownership plans. Management methods are divided into two types: entrusted management and self-management. Entrusted management should be filed as financial products and held for more than

12 months, and self-management should have "closed-loop operation" for at least 36 months; both types of employee stock ownership plan are considered as a single shareholder when participating in the issuance and no penetration or reversion are required. The third part is the by-law, which mainly prohibits the use of equity incentives and employee stock ownership plans for insider trading and other illegal and unlawful activities.

These policies will support listed companies in accessing refinancing. In order to deepen finance's supply-side structural reform, improve market-based restraint mechanisms for refinancing, enhance the capital market's ability to serve the real economy, and help listed companies respond to the epidemic and resume production, the China Securities Regulatory Commission issued the *Decision on Amending the Measures for the Administration of Securities Issuance by Listed Companies*, the *Decision on Amending the Interim Measures for the Administration of Securities Issuance by Listed Companies on the Growth Enterprise Market*, and the *Decision on Amending the Rules for the Implementation of Non-public Offering of Shares by Listed Companies* on February 14, 2020. The provisions which adjust the refinancing system consist of the following: first, streamlining the conditions for issuance and broadening the coverage of GEM refinancing services. This amendment removes the condition that the asset-liability ratio should be higher than 45% at the end of the latest period of a public offering of GEM securities; it also removes the condition that companies must make a profit for two consecutive years for a non-public offering of shares on the GEM; finally, it adjusted as a disclosure requirement the condition that companies should basically exhaust previous funds raised in GEM and should ensure basic consistency between the use of prior funds-raised and the effect of the capital use and disclosure. Second is optimizing non-public institutional arrangements to support the introduction of listed companies' strategic investors. If the listed companies' board of directors resolves to determine in advance all issue targets and strategic investors, etc., then the pricing benchmark date may serve as the announcement date of the board of directors' resolution on the non-public offering, the announcement date of the shareholders' meeting resolution, or the first day of the issuance period; this amendment adjusts the pricing and lock-up mechanism of the non-public offering of shares, changing the issue price from no less than 10% to 20% of the average price of the company's shares for the 20 trading days prior to the pricing reference date; this amendment also shortens the lock-up period from 36 months and 12 months to 18 months and six months, respectively, and does not apply the relevant restrictions of underweight rules; the amendment uniformly adjusts the number of issue targets for the non-public offering of shares in the Main Board (SME) and GEM from no fewer than ten and five to no more than 35. Third is the appropriate extension of the approval period to facilitate listed companies' decision of issuance window. Refinancing approval validity was extended from six months to 12 months.

**2. Comprehensively enhanced investment functions via improvement of the investment ecosystem**

(1) Improving the quality of listed companies

The quality of listed companies was improved in six aspects. On October 9, 2020, the State Council issued the *Opinions Concerning Further Raising the Quality of Listed Companies*, which included requirements and instructions in six aspects: one, to improve listed companies' governance level; two, to prompt listed companies' growth in size and strength; three, to improve listed companies' listing mechanism; four, to resolve salient problems facing listed companies; five, to raise the costs of violations by listed companies and related entities; six, to form synergy for the quality improvement of listed companies. In order to implement relevant requirements of the State Council on enhancing the governance of listed companies in the *Opinions Concerning Further Raising the Quality of Listed Companies*, the China Securities Regulatory Commission launched a special campaign for listed companies' governance. The special campaign aims to solidify the foundation for quality development of listed companies by strengthening self-examination for issues of corporate governance, improving the rules of the corporate governance system, building a good ecosystem of corporate governance, and improving the corporate governance structure among listed companies that people may perform their own responsibilities while coordinating with one another. Listed companies' self-examination of corporate governance issues constitutes an important part of this special campaign. When listed companies encounter problems and difficulties in the process of self-examination, they can communicate with jurisdictional securities regulators in a timely manner to ensure smooth operations. On December 31, 2020, the Shanghai Stock Exchange issued the *Shanghai Stock Exchange Risk Warning Board Stock Trading Management Measures (revised in December 2020)*. This document was meant to improve delisting standards, simplify delisting procedures, strengthen delisting regulation and protect investors' rights and interests. It was the second revision of the year, after a revision in May 2020. To improve the mechanism for market-oriented and normalized delisting, better fulfill the functions of the capital market, and protect the rights and interests of investors, the Shanghai Stock Exchange revised the *Implementation Measures for the Relisting of Delisted Companies on the Shanghai Stock Exchange (Revised in August 2018)* (SZF [2018] No. 99).

(2) Regulation of shareholder and investor behavior

To protect the legitimate rights and interests of investors, the behavior of corporate shareholders was regulated for companies listed on the Science and Technology Innovation Board through shareholdings reductions by way of inquiry transfer and placement to specific institutional investors. According to the *Implementation Opinions on the Establishment of a Science and Technology Innovation Board and Pilot Registration System on the Shanghai Stock Exchange*, the *Measures for Ongoing Supervision of Listed Companies on the Science and Technology Innovation Board (Trial)*, the *Shanghai Stock Exchange Rules for the Listing of Science and Technology Board Stocks*, and other regulations, the Shanghai Stock Exchange formulated the *Rules for the Implementation of Shareholding Reduction by Shareholders of Listed Companies on the Science and Technology Innovation Board of the Shanghai Stock Exchange through Quotation Transfer and Placement to Specific Institutional Investors*, effective on July 22, 2020.

The proper management requirements were clarified for investors in companies' conversion of convertible bonds listed on the Science and Technology Board. On December 4, 2020, the Shanghai Stock Exchange issued the *Notice on Matters Relating to the Appropriateness Management of Investors* in the Conversion of Convertible Bonds Issued to Unspecified Objects by Listed Companies on the Science and Technology Innovation Board, clarifying investor suitability management requirements for the conversion of convertible bonds' non-directed issuance on the Science and Technology Innovation Board, and dictating their implementation in accordance with the investor suitability management requirements for the Science and Technology Innovation Board stocks. Only investors who meet the suitability management requirements for investors of the Science and Technology Innovation Board stocks can participate in the conversion of convertible bonds' non-directed issuance on the Science and Technology Innovation Board.

(3) Cultivation of medium and long-term funds and institutional investors

Public funds were permitted for investment in NEEQ Selected Tier stocks to improve the investor structure of the NEEQ. On April 17, 2020, the China Securities Regulatory Commission issued the *Guidelines for Publicly Raised Securities Investment Funds to Invest in Listed Stocks on the National Small and Medium Enterprise Stock Transfer System* (hereafter referred to as the *Guidelines*). The *Guidelines* makes the following arrangements: first, it clarifies the management requirements and the types of funds that can participate in investment. The fund manager is required to be capable of investment research and the investment research staff must be adequate. The types of funds that can participate in investment are equity funds, hybrid funds, and other funds recognized by the China Securities Regulatory Commission. Second is strict risk prevention and control. The *Guidelines* provides that funds' investment scope is limited to Selected Tier stocks. Fund managers are required to strengthen liquidity risk management in the areas of institutional internal control, product design, investment restrictions, redemption management, liquidity risk management tools, valuation disclosure, etc., adopt fair methods for valuation, and activate the side pocket mechanism under statutory circumstances in accordance with regulations of the China Securities Regulatory Commission. Fund managers are also required to satisfactorily perform information and risk disclosure and to effectively manage investor suitability. It also requires stock public funds to comply with statutory procedures before they can invest in Selected Tier stocks.

The *Guidelines* seeks to improve venture capital funds' reverse linkage policy to guide investment in early-stage enterprises, SMEs, and high-tech enterprises. On March 6, 2020, the China Securities Regulatory Commission revised and issued the *Special Provisions for Shareholders of Listed Venture Capital Funds to Reduce Shareholdings* (hereafter referred to as the *Special Provisions*), effective on March 31, together with the implementation rules revised by the Shanghai Stock Exchange and the Shenzhen Stock Exchange. To improve venture capital funds' exit channels, smooth the virtuous cycle of "investment–exit–reinvestment", promote the formation of venture capital, better fulfill venture capital's role to support SMEs as well as the science and innovation of sci-tech enterprises, help prevent and control the epidemic through private equity and venture capital funds, and increase support for the real economy, the China Securities Regulatory Commission revised and improved the reverse linkage policy in the following ways: first is simplification of the reverse linkage policy's application criteria It clarifies that venture capital fund projects meeting one of three conditions — "early-stage enterprises", "SMEs" or "high-tech enterprises" — can enjoy inverse linkage policy; at the fund level, it also removes the requirement that "more than 50% of the total investment amount in early-stage SMEs and high-tech enterprises." Second, it activates transferee trading motivation under block trading, simultaneously revising the stock exchange implementation rules to improve the reverse linkage policy in block trading and eliminate the limitation on the lock-up period for the reduction's transferee. Third, in order to reduce the unrestricted holding of shares after the expiration of the lockup period, the preferential level for funds dedicated to long-term investment is expanded, and venture capital funds with an investment term of more than five years are allowed. Fourth, a reasonable adjustment is made to period calculation. The investment deadline is amended from "the date of issuance application materials' acceptance" to "the date of the issuer's IPO". Fifth, the range of applicable subjects who can enjoy the reverse linkage policy is broadened. The private equity investment funds filed in accordance with the law in the Asset Management Association of China apply.

(4) Enriched investment varieties to improve the product system

The Pilot Program of Real Estate Investment Trusts (REITs) was launched in the Infrastructure Field. On April 24, 2020, in order to implement the decisions of the Party Central Committee and the State Council on risk prevention, deleveraging, stabilizing investment, and shoring up weak links, to support the implementation of major national strategies, to deepen the structural reform of the financial supply side, to strengthen the capital market's ability to serve the real economy, to identify new investment and financing mechanisms, and to liquidize remnant assets and promote high-quality infrastructure development, the China Securities Regulatory Commission and the National Development and Reform Commission issued the *Notice on the Promotion of the Pilot Program of Real Estate Investment Trusts (REITs) in the Infrastructure Field Related Work*. Related actions are arranged as follows: In the early stage of the pilot, eligible securities or fund management companies that have obtained qualifications for public fund management shall set up publicly-offered infrastructure securities investment funds in accordance with the law, and, after registering with the China Securities Regulatory Commission, shall publicly offer fund shares to raise funds and complete acquisition of the underlying infrastructure by purchasing infrastructure asset-backed securities set up and issued by the manager belonging to the same beneficial owner, and shall carry out infrastructure REITs business. Publicly offered infrastructure securities investment funds may apply for stock exchange listing and trading if they comply with the provisions of the *Securities Law of the People's Republic of China* and the *Securities Investment Fund Law of the People's Republic of China*. Provincial development and reform commissions shall issue special opinions on such aspects as whether the project conforms to major national strategies, macro-control policies, industrial policies or fixed asset investment management regulations and systems, as well as encouraging the recovery of funds for use in infrastructure and other weak areas. Provincial development and reform commissions shall strengthen guidance, liquidize remnant assets, promote the recovery of funds for the construction of infrastructure projects to shore up weak links, and form a virtuous cycle of investment. Based on the special opinions of provincial development and reform commissions, the National Development and Reform Commission shall recommend eligible projects to the China Securities Regulatory Commission; then the China Securities Regulatory Commission and Shanghai and Shenzhen Stock Exchanges shall, in accordance with the law, follow market-oriented principles to independently perform the procedures for registration and review and thereafter make autonomous decisions. Dispatched institutions of the China Securities Regulatory Commission — and the Shanghai and Shenzhen Stock Exchanges and provincial development and reform committees — shall all strengthen collaboration and satisfactory perform project selection and recommendation. The China Securities Regulatory Commission shall formulate rules related to publicly-offered infrastructure securities investment funds to regulate the requirements on the performance of fund managers and other participating entities, as well as of product registration, share offerings, investment operations, information disclosure, etc. The Shanghai and Shenzhen Stock Exchanges shall establish a review system for the issuance of infrastructure asset-backed securities in accordance with relevant requirements for the public issuance of securities. Relevant units of the China Securities Regulatory Commission, the Shanghai and Shenzhen Stock Exchanges, the Securities Association of China, the Asset Management Association of China and other relevant units have urgent need to establish a working mechanism for the acceptance, examination, filing, information disclosure, and continuous supervision of infrastructure asset-backed securities, to perform well in investor education and market cultivation, and to strengthen supervision and management of parties involved in the issuance of infrastructure asset-backed securities with reference to the relevant requirements for the public issuance of securities, to prompt intermediaries to fulfill their responsibilities and implement regulatory requirements. On August 6, 2020, the China Securities Regulatory Commission officially issued the relevant supporting rules — namely, the *Guidelines for Publicly Raised Infrastructure Securities Investment Fund (Trial)* (hereafter referred to as the *Guidelines*). The *Guidelines* includes 51 articles. Its first objective is to clarify definitions of products and modes of operation. The Publicly Raised Infrastructure Securities Investment Fund (the *Infrastructure Fund*) is a listed and traded closed-end public fund that must meet the following conditions: more than 80% of the fund assets are invested in infrastructure asset-backed securities; full ownership or operating rights for infrastructure projects are acquired through special purpose means such as asset-backed securities or project companies; fund managers actively operate and manage infrastructure projects to generate stable cash flows and distribute more than 90% of the consolidated fund's annual available distribution amount to investors as required. Its second objective is to ensure that institutions fulfill their responsibilities and to strictly control the quality of infrastructure projects. The *Guidelines* enhances requirements on fund manager and custodian expertise, as well as on their fiduciary duties of honesty, trustworthiness, prudence and diligence. It focuses on quality infrastructure assets and strict project quality control and makes use of external management agencies, accounting firms, and evaluation agencies' professional roles. Third, it clarifies how fund shares are to be offered: The subscription price of fund shares shall be determined by means of offline inquiry, and public investors shall participate in the subscription of fund shares at the price determined by the inquiry. Fourth is the regulation of fund investment operations, strengthening of risk control, and solidifying of the mechanism for investor protection.

The *Guidelines* clarifies restrictions on fund investment, the management of connected transactions, borrowing arrangements, fund expansion, information disclosure and other requirements, putting the "information disclosure-centered" policy to full use so as to ensure investors' full rights to information. It also clarifies the supervision and management responsibilities of the China Securities Regulatory Commission and the management responsibilities of relevant self-regulatory organizations to strengthen violation restraints.

(5) Expansion of main participants in the government bond futures market

The structure of entities in the treasury bond futures market was improved and commercial banks and insurance institutions were allowed to participate in the trading of treasury bond futures in the China Financial Futures Exchange. With the approval of the State Council, the China Securities Regulatory Commission, the Ministry of Finance, the People's Bank of China, and China Banking and Insurance Regulatory Commission issued the *Announcement on the Participation of Commercial Banks and Insurance Institutions in Treasury Bond Futures Trading on the China Financial Futures Exchange* to improve the structure of market entities. The document stipulates that eligible commercial banks may participate in the trading of treasury bond futures in the China Financial Futures Exchange (on a pilot basis) for the purpose of risk management; insurance institutions with investment management capabilities may likewise participate in the trading of treasury bond futures in the China Financial Futures Exchange for the purpose of risk management; commercial banks and insurance institutions may participate in the trading of treasury bond futures under the premise of legal compliance, risk control, and commercial sustainability; commercial banks and insurance institutions participating in the trading of treasury bond futures shall establish comprehensive risk management and internal control systems and business processing systems with professional management teams and standardized business operations in order to prevent and control trading risks; the China Securities Regulatory Commission, the Ministry of Finance, the People's Bank of China, and the China Banking and Insurance Regulatory Commission will play the role of inter-ministerial coordinator, strengthening regulatory cooperation and information sharing and promoting the participation of commercial banks and insurance institutions in treasury bond futures market transactions by batches in order to promote the healthy development of the treasury bond futures market.

**3. Strengthened prudential supervision of intermediaries**

The effectiveness and adaptability of securities companies' risk control index system was enhanced as a means to promote the sustainable and sound development of the securities industry. On January 23, 2020, the China Securities Regulatory Commission issued the *Regulations on the Calculation Criteria for Risk Control Indicators of Securities Firms* (hereafter referred to as the *Calculation Criteria*), effective June 1, 2020. On June 16, 2016, the China Securities Regulatory Commission issued the *Measures for the Management of Risk Control Indicators of Securities Firms* (hereafter referred to as the *Risk Control Measures*) and supporting standards for the calculation of risk control indicators, which improved securities firms' risk control indicator system with net capital and liquidity as the core. More than three years of practice shows that the current risk control index system has effectively improved securities companies' risk management and effectively enhanced the industry's ability to withstand systemic risk. At the same time, with development and changes in both the capital market and securities industry specifically, further improvements to the risk control index system are needed — especially to certain new businesses' calculation standards — if the needs of risk management and industry development are to be met under the new circumstances. To this end, the China Securities Regulatory Commission drafted the *Calculation Standards* in the second half of 2019 and made it available for public comment from August 9 to September 9. Following the principles of "unchanged framework, risk-oriented, partial improvement, leniency and strictness", the *Calculation Standards* makes differentiated adjustments according to different businesses and products' risk characteristics, thereby making the index system more scientific and complete, and further enhancing its guidance of securities companies in capital allocation. Compared to the current risk control indicator system, there are adjustments and improvements mainly falling within the following five areas: First, the encouragement of value investment and the introduction of long-term incremental capital. Restrictions are reduced on securities company investments in policy financial bonds, index funds, constituent stocks, etc., and the introduction of long-term incremental capital into the capital market is encouraged. Second, the adjustments cover targeted measures to strengthen capital constraints and prevent outstanding points of risk; they regulate high-risk businesses such as equity pledging, private equity asset management, private equity fund custody and distribution services; and they optimize criteria for calculation in specific situations such as high-leverage/high-concentration capital management products, a high percentage of pledges by the first-largest shareholder, or the low-performance guarantee ratio. Third, they further complete the indicator system in accordance with the practices of market development. Combined with the "new asset management regulations" and the new businesses launched over recent years (including the Shanghai-London Stock Connect, the Science and Technology Innovation Board, credit derivatives, and stock index options), calculation standards are clarified for risk control indicators to achieve full coverage of securities companies' business and risks. Fourth, they meet the needs of differentiated development and open up capital space according to merit. Based on the results of security companies' classification evaluations, the risk capital provision adjustment factor for "securities companies with a Class A, AA rating or above for three consecutive years" is reduced from 0.7 to 0.5 to further enhance the efficiency of high-quality securities firms' capital utilization. Compared to the Draft for Comment, the *Calculation Standards* features relaxation in three aspects: first, to guide the industry in the prevention of stock pledging business' incremental risk and to properly resolve stock risk, an "old and new zoned off" arrangement is set up for this business' credit risk calculation standard; second, it optimizes calculation criteria for debenture bond investment, reduces the calculation ratio of market risk for AA-rated credit bonds from 50% to 15%, reduces the calculation ratio of BBB-rated credit bonds from 80% to 50%, and appropriately relaxes the calculation criteria for liquidity indicators of the above credit bonds to support the industry — especially private enterprises in bond financing — under the premise of risk control; third, to meet parent and subsidiary securities companies' reasonable risk management needs, the inclusion of liquidity guarantee commitments provided by securities companies for their securities subsidiaries — such as investment banking and capital management — is permitted in the transfer of the subsidiaries' available liquid assets. In addition, to facilitate a smooth and orderly transition, the *Calculation Standards* sets a certain transition period, which effectively begins on June 1, 2020.

Support was provided to securities companies to enrich their capital and improve their risk resilience. On May 26, 2020, the China Securities Regulatory Commission issued the *Decision on Amending the Regulations on the Administration of Subordinated Debt of Securities Firms*. The revision of the *Regulations on the Administration of Subordinated Debt of Securities Firms* covers the following content: first, allowing securities companies to publicly issue subordinated bonds; second, to reserve space for securities companies that they may issue other bond varieties such as write-down bonds; third, the uniform application of regulations. In the *Management Measures for the Suitability of Securities and Futures Investors*, the definition of institutional investors in the regulations is uniformly revised, and requirements are adjusted relating to the sale of subordinated bonds. Said adjustments are made in accordance with the *Measures for the Administration of Corporate Bond Issuance and Trading*. Fourth, the revision adds the *Notice of the General Office of the State Council on the Implementation of the Revised Securities Law* and the *Measures for the Administration of Corporate Bond Issuance and Trading* as the basis for upper-level legislation.

Efforts shall be made to effectively implement the prudential supervision of securities companies and ensure that such companies' business activities are in line with their governance structure, internal control, compliance management, risk management and other circumstances to achieve sustainable and standardized development. On July 10, 2020, the China Securities Regulatory Commission issued the *Decision on Amending the Regulations on the Classified Supervision of Securities Firms*. The revision maintains, unchanged, the overall framework for the classified supervision system, but adapts to the development of the securities industry and needs of prudential supervision, focusing on optimizing the classification and evaluation index system to solve outstanding problems in practice. The main changes are as follows. The first change is to further strengthen the orientation of compliance and prudent business. This revision improves securities companies' point deduction rules (as well as such rules for their related personnel who are subject to administrative supervision and self-regulatory measures) to more accurately reflect their status of compliance and risk control; it also clarifies the basis for downgrading the classification level for cases of serious failure in corporate governance or internal control and improves indicators and standards for evaluating securities companies' capacities for risk management. The revision optimizes the risk management capability bonus point index to motivate securities companies to realize stronger capital constraints, more effective comprehensive risk management, and complete risk management coverage. The second change is a further adaptation to the need for specialized and differentiated development. To adapt to developments in the securities industry, the revision optimizes business development status evaluation indicators from such perspectives as investment banking, asset management, institutional customer service and trading, wealth management, profitability, and information technology input. This optimization reflects supervision's support for securities companies, that they focus on their main business, grow in size and strength, and pursue differentiated characteristic development. The revised *Regulations on the Classified Supervision of Securities Firms* re-emphasizes that classification and evaluation results are primarily for use by the China Securities Regulatory Commission and its dispatching agencies. Following the principle of prudential and classified supervision, the China Securities Regulatory Commission sets different standards of risk control indicators and risk capital reserve ratio for different types of securities companies, conducting targeted resource allocation regulation. Securities companies are not allowed to use the results of classification for commercial purposes such as advertising, promotion, or marketing.

**4. Promotion of high-level opening-up in the capital market**

The QFII and RQFII systems were improved and the national treatment of foreign capital was promoted. On September 25, 2020, the China Securities Regulatory Commission, the People's Bank of China, and the State Administration of Foreign Exchange issued, with the approval of the State Council, the *Measures for the Administration of Domestic Securities and Futures Investment by Qualified Foreign Institutional Investors and RMB Qualified Foreign Institutional Investors* (hereafter referred to as the "QFII and RQFII Measures"); at the same time, the China Securities Regulatory Commission issued supporting rules, the *Provisions on Issues Concerning the Implementation of the Measures for the Administration of Domestic Securities and Futures Investment by Qualified Foreign Institutional Investors and RMB Qualified Foreign Institutional Investors*. The QFII and RQFII Measures and its supporting rules came into effect on November 1, 2020. The revision of the QFII and RQFII Measures and the supporting rules mainly involve the following aspects: First, lowering the threshold of entry to facilitate investment operations. The QFII and RQFII qualifications and system rules are combined into one, entry conditions are relaxed, application documents are simplified, approval times are shortened, and procedures for administrative licensing are simplified; the limit on the number of commissioned intermediaries is abolished, filing matters management is optimized, and data reporting requirements are reduced. Second is the steady and orderly expansion of the scope of investment. QFII and RQFII are allowed to invest in listed securities, private investment funds, financial futures, commodity futures and options on the NEEQ, and are allowed to participate in bond repurchase and securities margin trading on the stock exchange, as well as refinancing securities lending. QFII and RQFII may also participate in financial derivatives and other specific varieties and methods of trading, which will be opened gradually in a prudent and orderly manner and will be announced by the China Securities Regulatory Commission after consultation with the People's Bank of China and the State Administration of Foreign Exchange. Third is the strengthening of continuous supervision. Cross-market supervision, cross-border supervision, and penetrating supervision will all be improved, non-compliance penalties will be increased, regulatory measures applicable to specific non-compliance situations will be refined, and so on. Shortly after the revisions' issuance, the Shanghai Stock Exchange officially issued the *Guidelines for the Application of Securities Trading Rules of the Shanghai Stock Exchange No. 1 - Qualified Foreign Institutional Investors and RMB Qualified Foreign Institutional Investors* (hereafter referred to as the "Guidelines"), and the Shenzhen Stock Exchange issued the newly revised *Implementation Rules for*

*Securities Trading by Qualified Foreign Institutional Investors and RMB Qualified Foreign Institutional Investors of Shenzhen Stock Exchange* (hereafter referred to as the "Rules"). In general, the revised QFII, RQFII rules and guidelines are characterized by the following changes: First is an expansion in the scope of investment. Qualified foreign investors are now allowed to invest in depositary receipts, stock options, government-backed bonds, etc., and are allowed to participate in bond repurchase, securities margin trading, and refinancing securities lending. Secondly, the initial disclosure ratio of foreign ownership was lowered from 26% to 24%; this is mainly out of foreign investors' increasing enthusiasm and confidence in A-shares investment over recent years with the inclusion of A-shares in important international indices such as MSCI and FTSE Russell. In communications with foreign investors and financial institutions, many expressed hopes that they could keep abreast of the overall level of foreign ownership of listed companies and have more sufficient time to react.

### 5. Financial risk prevention and mitigation

The transition period for the "new asset management regulations" was extended by one year. On July 31, 2020, the People's Bank, together with the National Development and Reform Commission, the Ministry of Finance, the China Banking and Insurance Regulatory Commission, the China Securities Regulatory Commission, and the State Administration of Foreign Exchange — with the approval of the State Council — after prudent deliberation decided to extend the transition period of the "new asset management regulations" by one year to the end of 2021 for the smooth implementation of the "new asset management regulations" and the standardization and transformation of capital management. This was a strong response amid the outbreak of the epidemic.

Promotion of the convertible bond market's standardized development and avoidance of excessive speculation on convertible bonds. On December 31, 2020, to implement the provisions of the new *Securities Law of the People's Republic of China*, to improve the system of convertible corporate bonds (hereafter referred to as convertible bonds), to prevent risks and to protect the legitimate rights and interests of investors, the China Securities Regulatory Commission issued the *Management Measures of Convertible Corporate Bonds* (hereafter referred to as the *Management Measures*). The *Management Measures* consists of 23 articles, covering trading transfer, information disclosure, conversion, redemption, resale, trustee management, regulatory penalties, and rules convergence. First, looking at the trading system, it requires securities trading venues to improve existing trading rules according to convertible bonds' risks and characteristics in order to prevent and curb excessive speculation; it also requires them to formulate corresponding management rules for investor suitability according to the relevant requirements of the stock's underlying sector; it requires them to clarify issuers' information disclosure requirements before and after the mandatory redemption clause is triggered; and it requires them to clarify securities trading venues' risk monitoring responsibilities, etc. Second is regarding information disclosure: Based on the provisions of Article 80 and Article 81 of the *Securities Law of the People's Republic of China* on information disclosure, and taking into account the characteristics of convertible bonds and the actual regulatory experience of the Exchange, the *Management Measures* improves the provisional disclosure of material events. Third is conversion price: Taking into account the rights and interests of issuers, shareholders, and convertible bondholders, the determination, amendment and adjustment of the conversion price of convertible bonds issued by listed companies are improved in conjunction with existing refinancing methods. Fourth, the fiduciary management system: The *Management Measures* establishes a trustee management system for convertible bonds in accordance with Article 92 of the *Securities Law of the People's Republic of China* to clarify the duties of trustee managers, etc. Fifth is regarding regulatory penalties: For violations of the *Management Measures,* the China Securities Regulatory Commission will take the corresponding regulatory measures; for those subject to administrative penalties, said penalties shall be faced in accordance with relevant provisions; in serious cases, the responsible personnel will be subject to securities market entry measures; those suspected of a crime shall be transferred to the judicial organs and subject to criminal prosecution. Sixth is the convergence of rules: The *Management Measures* does not change convertible bonds' existing issuance rules while leaving certain institutional space to listed companies for the issuance of convertible bonds to specific targets for the purchase of assets. Seventh is about the "old and new zoned off" arrangement: The *Management Measures* shall apply to convertible bonds whose applications for issuance are accepted on or after the effective date, but its requirements and integration as regards trading rules, investor suitability, information disclosure, redemption and resale, and other trading aspects shall apply to both issued and unissued convertible bonds.

Improved public funds risk prevention and control capacities to better protect investors' legitimate rights and interests. Drawing on the mature experience of overseas markets, the China Securities Regulatory Commission issued the *Guidelines on Side Pocket Mechanism for Publicly Raised Securities Investment Funds (Trial)* (hereafter referred to as the "Guidelines") on July 10, 2020. The revised Guidelines consists of 17 articles. First, it clarifies that the "side pocket" mechanism for separating risk assets that are difficult to reasonably value from the fund portfolio assets for disposal and liquidation under statutory conditions in order to ensure the normal operation of the remaining fund assets. Second, it specifies conditions for the side pocket mechanism's activation, implementation process, and operational requirements for the main links in implementation. Third, it dictates that fund managers perform risk control duties, standardizes links in investment operations such as fee collection, information disclosure, and related internal controls, while clarifying the responsibilities of the custodian and accounting firm and forming a mechanism of internal constraints, public supervision, and checks and balances by external professional institutions for the manager. The launch of the side pocket mechanism will enrich public funds' liquidity risk management tools, mitigate potential systemic risks arising from fund redemptions under specific circumstances, and prevent acts that take advantage of the system (such as by the redemption of back funds) to protect investors' legitimate rights and interests. As a next step, the China Securities Regulatory Commission will, in accordance with the *Guidelines* and relevant laws and regulations, urge fund managers to improve their abilities and build a firm line of defense, enhance public funds' risk control capacities, and summarize practical experience in a timely manner, for the optimization of the regulatory system.

Coordinated efforts shall be made to strengthen the regulation of private equity funds and promote the standardized and sustainable development of the industry. Along with the private equity industry's rapid development come a variety of chaotic phenomena; these include public or disguised public fund-raising, circumvention of requirements for qualified investors, failures to fulfill registration and filing obligations, complex group operations, capital pool operations, transfer of benefits, self-financing and self-assurance and even embezzlement, misappropriation of fund assets, illegal fund-raising, and other serious violations of investor interests. Industry risks have emerged gradually over recent years. One example of such typical risk event is that which happened within Fuxing Group and Gold Finance, which had a significant negative impact on the industry's reputation and overall ecosystem. On December 30, 2020, the China Securities Regulatory Commission issued the *Provisions on Strengthening the Supervision of Private Investment Funds* (hereafter referred to as the *Provisions*. The *Provisions* includes 14 articles, which form 10 prohibitions for private equity fund managers, practitioners, and other subjects. Major contents are as follows. First, the *Provisions* regulate private equity fund managers' names, scope of business, and the "old and new zoned off" arrangement. Second, it aims to optimize the supervision of group private equity fund managers, to support good performers and restrict poor performers. Third, it reiterates that private equity funds should be solicited from qualified investors in a non-public manner. Fourth, it clarifies the requirements for private equity property investment. Fifth, it aims to strengthen requirements for private equity fund managers, practitioners, and other subjects in order to standardize associated transactions. Sixth, it clarifies legal responsibilities and transitional arrangements.

Improving and unifying the fund custody industry's regulatory. On July 10, 2020, the China Securities Regulatory Commission and the China Banking and Insurance Regulatory Commission jointly issued the *Measures for the Administration of Custody Business of Securities Investment Funds* (hereafter referred to as the *Custody Measures*). From May 9 to June 23, 2020, the *Custody Measures* were opened for public comments. At the same time, the China Securities Regulatory Commission and the China Banking and Insurance Regulatory Commission listened to various parties' views by consulting relevant ministries, holding seminars, conducting video research, and other forms. The revision of the *Custody Measures* covers the following aspects: First, in accordance with the national financial industry's unified opening up, the China branches of foreign banks are allowed to apply for securities investment funds (hereafter referred to as "funds") custody business qualifications; financial indicators such as net assets may be calculated according to overseas head offices; responsibilities to be assumed by the overseas head office are clarified in the revised *Custody Measures*, and supporting risk control arrangements are strengthened. In practice, these measures apply to all China subsidiaries of foreign banks. Second, fund custodian net asset access standards shall be adjusted appropriately based on the requirements of regulatory practice; the fund custodian business' centralized and unified management shall be strengthened; continuous compliance requirements for fund custodians shall be improved; measures for administrative supervision shall be further enriched; and the implementation of effective supervision shall be strengthened. Third, the revised *Custody Measures* continues to streamline administration and delegate power, simplify application materials, optimize the approval process, and realize "approval before fundraising". Fourth, it unifies commercial banks' (and other financial institutions') entry standards and regulatory requirements and integrates relevant provisions for non-banking financial institutions to conduct fund custody business into the *Custody Measures*. After the measures' introduction, the China Securities Regulatory Commission accordingly updated the service guide for matters of administrative licensing related to fund custody qualifications. Eligible financial institutions — including branches of foreign banks in China — can now submit relevant applications in accordance with the law. The China Securities Regulatory Commission will work with the China Banking and Insurance Regulatory Commission to strengthen the daily supervision of fund custodians and the fund custodian business, strengthen law enforcement, and punish violations to effectively protect investors' legitimate rights and.

To promote the sound development of the funds industry, the regulatory system for the sale of public funds was optimized, the regulation of fund sales practices further improved, the compliance of fund sales organizations and internal control were strengthened, as was the protection of investors' rights and interests, and the ecosystem of the fund market was optimized. On August 28, 2020, the China Securities Regulatory Commission issued the *Measures for the Supervision and Administration of Sales Institutions of Publicly Raised Securities Investment Funds* (hereafter referred to as the *Sales Measures*) and supporting rules, effective October 1, 2020. The amendments to the Sales Measures and supporting rules mainly involve the following aspects. First, they aim to strengthen the requirements for licensed access to fund sales activities and clearly define the responsibilities of fund sales organizations and related fund service providers. They also clarify the connotation and denotation of the fund sales business, define the boundaries of the business and bottom-line requirements for cooperation between fund sales institutions and internet platforms, supporting fund managers and fund sales institutions in standardizing the use of internet platforms to expand their customer bases. Second, they optimize exit mechanisms and access to fund sales institutions, striving to build an orderly and healthy ecosystem for the fund sales industry. The amendments also adjust and optimize the process for qualification registration and implement "approval before fundraising", integrate registration requirements for various financial institutions, and further improve access requirements for independent fund sales institutions and their shareholders. They moreover introduce a renewal system for the validity of fund sales business licenses and strengthen institutional arrangements for the cessation of business and revoking of licenses. Third, to consolidate business norms and institutional control, and promote the institutional mechanism-building focused on investors' interests, the *Sales Measures*' amendments highlight bottom-line requirements for fund sales practices, refine and improve investor protections and service arrangements, encourage fund sales institutions to create assessment systems focusing on investor interests, and promote long-term rational investment; they also strengthen the regulation of private equity fund sales, add a special chapter on "internal control and risk management", and require various fund sales institutions to improve their internal systems to conform to the fund sales business. Fourth, they improve the supervision of independent fund sales institutions, and promote the professional, sound, and law-based development of independent fund sales institutions. They improve requirements for equity management and independent fund sales institutions' and internal governance, emphasize the independence of business development, and put forward targeted requirements for compliance and risk control, branch management, and the scope of business development.

### (II) Effects of securities industry regulatory policy in 2020

The capital market progressed steadily over 2020, with various regulatory policies gradually delivering results.

First, the capital market's ability to serve the real economy was significantly enhanced. There were 396 IPO companies in 2020, raising a total amount of RMB 469.963 billion, an increase of 95.07% and 85.57% YOY, respectively, strongly supporting the real economy's; meanwhile, the number of refinancing companies reached, involving a total amount of RMB 885.434 billion, a YOY increase of 46.15% and 26.10%, respectively.

Second, the stock market maintained healthy development. First of all, stock market capacity steadily expanded, with a total of 4,154 listed companies at the end of 2020, marking an increase of 9.98% from the end of the previous year; second, stock market prospects indicate positive developments, with significant growth in market capitalization and a total market capitalization of RMB 79.7 trillion at the end of 2020, marking an increase of 34.46% from the previous year; third, the stock market exit mechanism continued to improve, with 20 companies delisted in 2020, the number of delisted companies increasing by 66.67% compared with the same period of the previous year, while supervision was also strengthened.

Activity grew in the treasury bond futures market. Treasury futures delivered in 2020 on a unilateral basis came to RMB 20.90 billion, an increase of 128.7% YOY.

The rule of law in the capital market continued to improve. In 2020, the China Securities Regulatory Commission handled 740 cases — among which, 353 were newly initiated investigations (including 282 cases filed for investigation); 84 major cases were processed, a figure that is up 34% YOY; and 116 case leads were transferred and notified to public security authorities throughout the year, a YOY doubling.

### (III) Securities industry regulatory policy outlook in 2021

The world today is facing changes rarely seen in a century. In the current period and looking just ahead, China is and still continue to be in an important period of strategic opportunity. Domestically, China's economy has entered a new era of quality development, and a new development pattern with domestic circulation as the mainstay and domestic and international circulations reinforcing each other has rapidly taken shape. As a hub of economic activity, the capital market connects and leads economic transformation in the new stage and shoulders an important historic mission for the reform of China's economic and financial systems.

On January 28, 2021, the System Work Conference of the China Securities Regulatory Commission was held in Beijing. This conference studied and deployed key tasks for capital market reform, development, and stability in 2021: first among these is to combine the advantages of the Party's leadership and the laws of capital market development; second is to staunchly promote comprehensively deepened reform of the capital market; third is to maintain the capital market's steady development momentum in a complex environment; fourth is to fully implement the "zero tolerance" law enforcement concept and crackdown campaign; fifth is to resolutely win the battle in preventing and resolving major financial risks; sixth and last is to accelerate the deep integration of business and technology. The following policies are expected to be issued in 2021.

**1. Full implementation of the registration system and continued improvement to the supporting system**

A full implementation of the registration system is expected for 2021. With the registration system implemented in the Science and Technology Innovation Board and the GEM, the 2021 government work report again proposed to "steadily promote the registration system reform", signifying an expectation that the registration system be fully implemented. From the "establishment of the Science and Technology Innovation Board and pilot the registration system" in 2019 to the "reform of the Growth Enterprise Market and pilot the registration system" in 2020, and then to "steadily promote the registration system reform" in 2021, this is the third consecutive year that "the registration system" has been written into the government work report. As the time is ripe for said system's full implementation, capital market reform is expected to continue to deepen, which entails the improvement of the registration system's supporting system.

Also expected is the improvement of investor relations management. Strengthening investor relations management is an important step to improve the quality of listed companies and an important component of investor protections. In July 2005, the China Securities Regulatory Commission issued the *Guidelines on Investor Relations for Listed Companies* (hereafter referred to as the *Guidelines (2005)*) as a basic guide for listed companies in their management of investor relations. Since its implementation, it has played a positive role in guiding listed companies in investor relations management, promoting the standardized operation of listed companies and protecting investors' legitimate rights and interests. In recent years, as the reform of the capital market is comprehensively deepened and the basic system of the securities market is continuously improved, new requirements have been put forward for listed companies to strengthen investor relations management; listed companies have thus accumulated new practices and experiences in investor relations management; however, certain new situations and problems have emerged. In this regard, investor relations management needs to be further connected with overseas markets amid the two-way opening of the capital market. The development of the internet has also brought new changes to investor relations management. It is therefore necessary to sort out and summarize the practices of listed companies in recent years and revise and improve the *Guidelines (2005)*, which is also an important measure for the optimal implementation of the new *Securities Law of the People's Republic of China*. On February 5, 2021, the China Securities Regulatory Commission revised the

*Guidelines (2005)* to form the *Guidelines on Investor Relations Management for Listed Companies (Draft for Public Comments)*.

Listed companies' disclosure management is expected to see further enhancement. To implement the new *Securities Law of the People's Republic of China,* which became effective on March 1, 2020, and strengthen the regulation of information disclosure, the China Securities Regulatory Commission issued the *Measures for the Administration of Information Disclosure by Listed Companies (Revised Draft)* (Draft for Public Comments) for public comments on July 24, 2020. The *Measures for the Administration of Information Disclosure by Listed Companies (Revised Draft)* (Draft for Public Comments) mainly revises the following contents: First, it improves provisions for information disclosure. The revised version adds new requirements for concise, clear, and understandable information disclosure, improves the principle of fair disclosure, and clarifies the relevant requirements for voluntary disclosure to better encourage it. Second, it improves matters of interim reporting. Provisions for interim report matters are improved in accordance with the new Securities Law of the People's Republic of China; such matters include, for example, "significant changes in the situation where the company's actual controller and other enterprises under their control are engaged in the same or similar business as the company" and "changes in the company's dividend distribution, capital increase plan, and shareholding structure". For listed companies issuing corporate bonds at the same time, interim bond disclosure is required and the requirements of disclosure are clarified. Third, it further emphasizes the responsibility of relevant subjects such as directors and supervisors. It strengthens responsibility for the board of directors regarding the disclosure of periodic reports, clearly requiring that such reports' content be considered and approved by the board of directors, and that when directors, supervisors, and senior management cannot guarantee the truthfulness, accuracy, or completeness of said content, or if they disagree, they shall express their opinions and state their reasons for difference in a written confirmation opinion, which shall then be disclosed by the listed company. It further clarifies the obligations of controlling shareholders and actual controllers in cooperation. In addition, in accordance with the relevant provisions of the new *Securities Law,* the amendment adjusts disclosure requirements for designated media, related expressions of accounting firms, legal liabilities and other related provisions, while improving disclosure requirements for issuance documents in accordance with the registration system and drawing on the relevant provisions for information disclosure during non-trading sessions of the Science and Technology Innovation Board.

### 2. A big step in cultivating institutional investors

(1) Improvement to the supporting rules of new asset management regulations

Securities companies' capital management public offering business licensing and liberalization. On July 31, 2020, the China Securities Regulatory Commission publicly solicited comments on the *Supervision and Administration Measures for Managers of Publicly Raised Securities Investment Funds (Draft for Comments)* (hereafter referred to as the *Managers Measures*) and supporting rules. To enhance the public fund industry's ability to serve the real economy, to support industry institutions grow stronger and improve performance, and to create a favorable industry ecosystem, the China

Securities Regulatory Commission revised the *Management Measures for Securities Investment Fund Management Companies* and renamed it the *Supervision and Administration Measures for Managers of Publicly Raised Securities Investment Funds*. Article 2 of the *Managers Measures* clearly defines what constitutes a public fund manager. The first major category of public fund managers consists of securities companies' fund management subsidiaries approved to obtain the qualification of public fund manager. Second, it optimizes the public offering license system, and appropriately relaxes the "1+1 principle" (i.e. that an institution can be the equity participant of no more than two fund management companies, and the controlling shareholder of only one of them). The *Managers Measures* allows the same entity to control both a fund company and a public offering licensee. The number of other public fund managers controlled by the same subject or by different subjects that are in turn controlled by the same subject shall not exceed one; the number of companies with equity participation in fund management shall not exceed two — of which the number of companies controlling fund management shall not exceed one, while the regulatory arrangements for public offering licensees and fund companies shall be leveled in terms of corporate governance and other aspects.

Further regulation of securities and futures institutions' private asset management business. To effectively prevent and control financial risks, better play the role of asset management business in promoting capital formation, and deepen direct financing in service of the real economy, the China Securities Regulatory Commission decided to amend the *Measures for the Administration of Private Asset Management Business of Securities and Futures Institutions* and the *Regulations for the Operation of Private Asset Management Plans of Securities and Futures Institutions*, drafted and released the draft for public comments on October 23, 2020. Major contents of the draft are detailed below.

First, the amendment aims to further improve the ratio limit of debt leverage (total assets/net assets) in private equity management plans and strengthen reverse repo risk management. It requires capital management plans to set reasonable debt ratio caps and maintain sufficient cash or other highly liquid financial assets for the repayment of debts as they fall due. It clarifies regulations related to high-proportional investment in single assets and highly leveraged products; it requires collective management plans to reasonably diversify the maturity of reverse repo transactions, counterparties and the concentration of repo securities, strengthens counterparty management in accordance with the principle of penetration, and improves the pledged collateral management system.

Second, it draws on the characteristics of private equity investment and fund investment operation to optimize the relevant institutional arrangements. This mainly consists of: subjecting the exemption of private equity investment funds to the restriction "all pooled asset management plans managed by the same securities and futures institution may not invest more than 25% of the same asset"; improving installment payments, open participation, and other institutional arrangements to meet the needs of private equity investment funds and other phased, step-by-step investment; integrating with venture capital and government industrial investment funds' existing special provisions; leaving room for indirect investment in the equity of unlisted enterprises through special purpose means; relaxing restrictions on the participation ratio of managers' own funds to further meet the practical needs of managers' follow-on investment.

Third, investment restrictions related to futures management institutions are relaxed appropriately. This involves allowing futures companies and their subsidiaries — whose last two classification evaluations were A-Class, AA — to establish capital management products that invest in non-standard assets such as standard warehouse receipts and OTC derivatives and selecting head futures companies for pilot projects to give full play to the professional advantages of futures operators, enhance their service capacities and professionalism, and meeting real enterprises' risk management needs.

Fourth, checking against the new "Securities Law", relevant provisions' statement "accounting firm with securities-related business qualifications" was amended to become "accounting firm in line with the provisions of the Securities Law". The amendment aims to streamline administration and delegate power, to further streamline the filing and reporting of relevant matters, and to effectively resolve the issue of submission to multiple departments.

Fifth, checking against the extension of working arrangements during the transition period in the new asset management regulations, the transition period in the supporting rules was extended to the end of 2021.

(2) The comprehensive regulation of securities and funds investment advisory business

Investment advisory business is a basic capital market intermediary service, helpfully eliminating information asymmetry in the capital market, promoting the professional division of labor among intermediaries, and improving investor education. At the same time, due to the rapid development of the market and changes in the internal and external environment, the development of the investment consulting business has also revealed some outstanding problems. It is necessary to develop unified sector-based regulations according to the development of the industry, and to comprehensively regulate the investment consulting business to ensure the industry's long-term standardized development. In order to regulate the securities fund investment advisory business (hereafter referred to as the "investment advisory business"), to protect the legitimate rights and interests of investors and related parties, and to maintain the order of the capital market, the China Securities Regulatory Commission solicited public comments for the *Management Measures for Securities Fund Investment Advisory Business* (hereafter referred to as the *Management Measures*) on April 17, 2020. The *Management Measures* includes the following contents: First, in order to clarify the business' classification and connotations, the securities investment consulting business stipulated in the *Securities Law* and the *Interim Measures for Securities and Futures Investment Advisory Management* was consolidated with the fund investment advisory business stipulated in the Securities Investment Fund Law; they became the securities fund investment consulting business, which was then divided into categories such as the securities investment advisory business, fund investment advisory business, and publishing securities research report business. Second is the classification of access arrangements, which clarify that engaging in the securities fund investment advisory business shall be approved by or registered with the China Securities Regulatory Commission in accordance with the law and with the provisions of upper-level legislation, and specifying detailed entry requirements and application approval procedures. Third is to strengthen compliance and internal control requirements, requiring investment advisory institutions to improve compliance management, internal control, and risk management. Fourth is to establish a business organization that primarily provides services by institutions and improves the quality of services in general. Fifth is to improve personnel management and code of conduct requirements, ensure strict qualification management for practitioners and executives, and require honesty, trustworthiness, diligence and responsibility among investment advisory institutions and practitioners. Sixth is to establish a sound exit mechanism to strengthen ex-post supervision, and so on.

**3. Improved legal and regulatory system for capital market construction**

It is expected that rules for the implementation of regulatory measures are to be optimized. On March 27, 2020, in order to further standardize implementation procedures for supervision and management measures, fully utilizing supervision and management measures' role in preventing market risks and maintaining market order, the China Securities Regulatory Commission drafted the *Measures for the Implementation of Supervisory and Regulatory Measures in the Securities and Futures Market (Trial)* (hereafter referred to as the *2008 Trial Measures*) on the basis of the new *Securities Law*, and drafted the *Measures for the Implementation of Supervisory and Regulatory Measures in the Securities and Futures Market* (hereafter referred to as the *Implementation Measures*) based on the provisions of the new *Securities Law*, and published it for public comments. The *Implementation Measures* includes 31 articles, which cover the following contents. First, it clarifies the type and setting of supervisory and management measures. After combing through existing system rules, it defines 16 common types of supervisory and management measures, with "other supervisory and management measures stipulated in laws, administrative regulations, rules and regulations" as the basis, leaving room for the subsequent introduction of new types of supervisory measures. Meanwhile, to improve law-based administration and strengthen self-regulation, it clarifies that regulatory documents other than SEC regulations shall not set regulatory measures. Second, it clarifies the application of regulatory measures, allowing regulatory measures to be applied individually or in combination. Third, it clarifies general procedures for the implementation of supervision and management measures, stipulating that the implementation of regulatory measures should be based on sufficient evidence and have sufficient basis, and that before implementing part of the supervision and management measures, ex-ante notification procedures should be performed and relevant units should be informed. Fourth, it clarifies specific implementation procedures for various types of regulatory measures — including implementation steps, modalities, corrective goals, time frames, and other content. Fifth, it clarifies requirements for the taking of supervisory and management measures. The enforcement body shall conduct supervisory measures promptly, and no supervisory measures shall be taken for violations not found within two years. It furthermore clarifies supervision and management measures' decision letter content, publicity requirements, and delivery procedures.

In addition, the *Implementation Measures* standardizes law enforcement behavior, seeking to promote strict, standardized, fair, and civilized law enforcement, and prevent law enforcement risks. In accordance with the requirements of comprehensive promotion of the rule of law, law-based government construction is strengthened. In order to regulate law enforcement behaviors related to securities and futures administrative penalties, maintain market order, protect the legitimate rights and interests of relevant citizens, legal persons, and other organizations, in accordance with the practice of securities and futures market supervision and enforcement, the SFC built on the basis of the *Administrative Penalty Law* in combination with the relevant provisions of the new *Securities Law* to solicit public comments for the *Administrative Punishment Measures for Securities and Futures Violations* (hereafter referred to as the *Punishment Measures*) on July 17, 2020. Consisting of 39 articles, the *Punishment Measures* covers the following contents: First, it clarifies the conditions and authority of investigation. The *Punishment Measures* stipulates that the SFC and its dispatching agencies shall, upon approval, open a case for investigation if they find suspected violations of securities and futures laws, regulations, or rules that meet relevant conditions. Meanwhile, to ensure the smooth implementation of administrative penalties in accordance with the law, in combination with the new *Securities Law*, the *Punishment Measures* further clarifies and refines the SEC and its dispatch agencies' enforcement authority and measures, as well as the circumstances and consequences of non-cooperation with investigation. Second, it standardizes investigation and evidence collection procedures. Such standardization is directly related to the outcome of a case, and thus key to administrative punishment. In combination with relevant legal provisions and law enforcement practices, the *Punishment Measures* further clarifies forensic requirements and investigative measures. Third, it optimizes the investigation and review processes. It explores diversified and differentiated modes of investigation and trial and classifies different treatments to improve the efficiency of case investigation and processing. Fourth, it clarifies procedures for cohesive execution. In combination with actual law enforcement, it points out three procedural modes: "direct criminal transfer", "punishment first and then criminal transfer", "synchronous punishment and criminal transfer" — this in aims to strengthen connection between securities administrative enforcement and criminal justice. Fifth, the *Punishing Measures* implements a record system for law enforcement public disclosure and law enforcement full process, dictating that the entire process of law enforcement shall be recorded and administrative penalty decisions are made public in accordance with the provisions of government information disclosure. Sixth, it strengthens protection of parties' rights as well as supervision over law enforcement officers.

### 4. Continued promotion of the capital market's high-level opening up

The bond market's opening up will continue to be promoted. In order to make the opening up of China's bond market more systemic, holistic, and synergistic, and to simultaneously promote the gradual unification of relevant market rules, the People's Bank of China, together with the China Securities Regulatory Commission and the State Administration of Foreign Exchange, drafted the *Announcement of the People's Bank of China and the China Securities Regulatory Commission and the State Administration of Foreign Exchange on Matters Relating to Foreign Institutional Investors'*

Investment in China's Bond Market (Draft for Comments) on September 2, 2020. The aim of the draft is to clarify overall institutional arrangements for the opening up of China's bond market and further facilitate the allocation of RMB bond assets by overseas institutional investors. On September 21, 2020, in order to promote the overall opening of China's bond market, the People's Bank of China and the State Administration of Foreign Exchange drafted the *Regulations on Funds Management for Foreign Institutional Investors to Invest in China's Bond Market (Draft for Comments)*, which aims to unify rules on funds management in the bond market and further facilitate foreign institutional investors' investment in China's bond market.

## Appendix

### List of Major Regulatory Policies for China's Securities Industry in 2020

| Released on | Major Policies | Released by |
|---|---|---|
| February 14 | Decision on Amending the Measures for the Administration of Securities Issuance by Listed Companies | China Securities Regulatory Commission |
| February 14 | Decision on Amending the Interim Measures for the Administration of Securities Issuance by Listed Companies on GEM | China Securities Regulatory Commission |
| March 6 | Special Provisions for Shareholders of Listed Venture Capital Funds to Reduce Shareholdings | China Securities Regulatory Commission |
| March 13 | Provisions for the Formulation of Securities and Futures Regulations | China Securities Regulatory Commission |
| March 20 | Decision on Amending Some Securities and Futures Regulations | China Securities Regulatory Commission |
| April 17 | Guidelines for Publicly Raised Securities Investment Funds to Invest in Listed Stocks on the National Small and Medium Enterprise Stock Transfer System | China Securities Regulatory Commission |
| June 12 | Administration Measures for the Registration of IPO of Shares on GEM (Trial) | China Securities Regulatory Commission |
| June 12 | Administration Measures for the Registration of Securities Issuance by Listed Companies on GEM (Trial) | China Securities Regulatory Commission |
| June 12 | Measures for Continuous Supervision of Listed Companies on GEM (Trial) | China Securities Regulatory Commission |
| June 12 | Administration Measures for Securities Issuance and Listing Sponsorship | China Securities Regulatory Commission |
| July 3 | Administrative Measures for the Registration of Securities Issuance by Listed Companies on the Science and Technology Innovation Board (Trial) | China Securities Regulatory Commission |
| July 10 | Measures for the Administration of Custody Business of Securities Investment Funds | China Securities Regulatory Commission, China Banking and Insurance Regulatory Commission (CBIRC) |

Continued

| Released on | Major Policies | Released by |
|---|---|---|
| July 10 | Decision on Amending the Measures for the Administration of IPO and Listing of Stocks | China Securities Regulatory Commission |
| July 10 | Decision on Amending the Measures for the Administration of Registration of IPO of Shares on the Science and Technology Venture Exchange (Trial) | China Securities Regulatory Commission |
| July 10 | Guidelines on Side Pocket Mechanism for Publicly Raised Securities Investment Funds (Trial) | China Securities Regulatory Commission |
| August 6 | Guidelines for Publicly Raised Infrastructure Securities Investment Fund (Trial) | China Securities Regulatory Commission |
| August 28 | Measures for the Supervision and Administration of Sales Institutions of Publicly Raised Securities Investment Funds | China Securities Regulatory Commission |
| September 25 | Measures for the Administration of Domestic Securities and Futures Investment by Qualified Foreign Institutional Investors and RMB Qualified Foreign Institutional Investors | China Securities Regulatory Commission, the People's Bank of China, State Administration of Foreign Exchange |
| October 30 | Decision on Amending and Repealing Some Securities and Futures Regulations | China Securities Regulatory Commission |
| December 10 | Announcement on the Special Campaign on the Governance of Listed Companies | China Securities Regulatory Commission |
| December 31 | Management Measures of Convertible Corporate Bonds | China Securities Regulatory Commission |

# Article 17

## New delisting rules to improve market constraint[①]

The Shanghai and Shenzhen stock exchanges released revised delisting rules on December 31, 2020. The new rules will put a stricter delisting system in place for China's listed companies while improving standardization and operability, promising to have a profound impact on the long-term healthy development of China's capital market.

The China Securities Regulatory Commission has conducted a total of four reforms since the delisting system framework was founded in 1999 with the *Securities Law of the People's Republic of China*. It has established a relatively complete system with delisting rules appropriate to the current stage of market development. Yet when compared with mature markets, China's capital market is still clearly troubled by unsystematic and superficial delisting, and the average annual delisting rate remains low.

---

[①] Author: Du Shuming, Assistant Dean of China Galaxy Securities Institute and General Manager of the Research Department, and senior project fellow of Program for China's Financial Policy Report.

On December 28, 2019, the plenary session of the 15th session of the Standing Committee of the 13th National People's Congress adopted the newly revised Securities Law, which went into effect on March 1 the following year. The new *Securities Law of the People's Republic of China* eliminates specific requirements for delisting, leaving the formulation of delisting standards up to the exchanges. This opens up ample operating space for the streamlining and all-around better implementation of the delisting system. On October 5, 2020, the State Council issued the *Opinions Concerning Further Raising the Quality of Listed Companies*, which prioritizes improvements to listed companies' exit mechanism, requires higher standards for delisting, simplifies delisting procedures, and intensifies delisting supervision. Then on November 2, the Central Commission for Comprehensively Deepening Reform adopted the *Implementation Plan for a Sound Delisting Mechanism of Listed Companies*, re-emphasizing the importance of a sound and complete delisting mechanism for listed companies in the context of comprehensively deepening capital market reform. Likewise, the *Proposal of the Central Committee of the Communist Party of China on Formulating the Fourteenth Five-Year Plan for National Economic and Social Development and the Visionary Goals for 2035* issued on November 3 also proposed "the establishment of a regular delisting mechanism". On December 14, the Shanghai and Shenzhen Stock Exchanges released a draft of supporting delisting rules for public comment. On December 31, the Shanghai and Shenzhen Stock Exchanges officially released a number of supporting regulations including the newly revised *Rules for the Listing of Stocks on the Shanghai Stock Exchange*, the *Rules for the Listing of Stocks on the Shenzhen Stock Exchange*, as well as the *Rules for the Listing of Stocks on the Science and Technology Innovation Board of the Shanghai Stock Exchange* and the *Rules for the Listing of Stocks on the Growth Enterprise Market of the Shenzhen Stock Exchange*.

The new rules strengthen the synergy between delisting and registration system reform, reflecting experience absorbed from pilot delisting reforms of the Science and Technology Innovation Board and the Growth Enterprise Market while drawing extensively on the experience of mature markets. They target and rectify loopholes in the previous delisting policy and detail standards and procedures for trading, financial, and regulatory delisting as well as mandatory delisting for major violations, significantly improving both standardization and operability. The rules also abolish single continuous loss delisting indicators in all sectors and formulate a combined indicator for deducted net income with an RMB 100 million operating income; they clarify that business income separate from the main business and income that does not have commercial substance should be deducted from the operating income. The rules further shorten the delisting process - for financial delisting indicators, the process is shortened to two years. While retaining "face value delisting" and other delisting standards for trade, they set an "RMB 300 million market value" standard; they add a new standard, namely, for information disclosure and standardized operations refusing to correct significant deficiencies. The rules detail the determining circumstances for major illegal delisting; they establish risk warning boards and optimize corresponding trading arrangements. Meanwhile, they also cancel the suspension or resumption of listing and optimize the delisting consolidation period to enhance efficiency.

The delisting system for listed companies is a fundamental component of the capital market. Delisting rule improvement and strict enforcement will get market entries and exists moving more quickly, clearing the market of underperforming, "garbage", and "zombie" companies. In the long run, this will purify the market environment, strengthen constraints, promote a healthy "metabolism", and make better use of the capital market's ability to allocate resources.

## IV. Major Regulatory Policies in China's Insurance Industry[①]

### (I) Analysis of major regulatory policies of China's insurance industry in 2020

In 2020, the China Banking and Insurance Regulatory Commission further strengthened financial supervision to prevent financial risks. It focused on risk control in key areas, and firmly held the bottom line of risk. The relevant systems cover solvency management of insurance companies, management of criminal cases involving banking and insurance institutions, supervision of internet insurance business, and supervision of corporate governance. At the same time, efforts were made to deepen insurance reform and openness, strengthen the use of insurance funds, comprehensive reform of auto insurance and accident insurance reform, promote the reform and development of commercial pension insurance and the steady growth of health insurance, to promote high-quality development. The relevant system covers the business reform of insurance institutions and the implementation of opening up. The main regulatory policies for the year are as follows:

**1. Strengthen the supervision of fintech to guide the healthy development and compliance of new business forms**

The rapid digitization in the financial industry has brought about problems in network security, market monopoly, unclear data ownership, and consumer rights protection, affecting market equity and financial stability. In the second half of 2020, regulations for fintech were tightened across the board, with regulators introducing new rules in internet insurance, internet deposit and loan, anti-monopoly, financial holding groups, and protection of financial consumers' rights and interests. Fintech converges with traditional financial business and has fully integrated into the regulatory system, focusing on strengthening constraints on disorderly capital expansion and maintaining fair competition and financial market order.

In the field of insurance, the integration of the internet and insurance was accelerating and problems were gradually emerging, such as illegal operation, marketing gimmicks, and the risk of misleading sales. Regulators have introduced new regulations to regulate the internet insurance business and promote its healthy development.

---

① Author: Tan Liang, senior fellow with the project "Report on China's Financial Policy", Partner, Strategic Client and Marketing Leader, Deloitte China; senior project fellow of Program for China's Financial Policy Report; Xu Qianqian, Senior Manager, Financial Services, Deloitte China.

The first, to tighten market access. On December 7, the China Banking and Insurance Regulatory Commission issued the *Rules of Internet Insurance Business* (Order of the CBIRC[2020]No. 13), which clarifies the nature of internet insurance business, stipulates the operating requirements of internet insurance business, strengthens the principle of licensed operation, and emphasizes that "internet insurance shall be carried out by insurance institutions established by law, and other institutions and individuals shall not carry out internet insurance business"; defining the self-operated Internet platform of licensed institutions, stipulating the operating eligibility requirements of licensed institutions, and specifying the prohibited activities of non-licensed institutions, including but not limited to "providing insurance product consulting services, comparing insurance products, premium trial calculations and quotations; designing insurance plans for policyholders; handling insurance procedures on behalf of policyholders; collecting premiums on behalf of insurance institutions". It stipulates that sales promotion, technical support, etc. are the main responsibilities of insurance institutions, and substantive and core functions are no longer allowed to be outsourced, to ensure the serious fulfillment of insurance institutions' main responsibilities.

Second, to standardize marketing activities. On October 28, 2020, the China Banking and Insurance Regulatory Commission issued the *Warning on Risks Related to Live Stream Marketing of Financial Products* (Risk Alert No. 5 of 2020). It reminds the public to be aware of the risks of misleading sales that may be hidden in live stream marketing and also re-emphasizes that "financial institutions should implement the main responsibility of financial marketing activities and promotional activities, and effectively regulate the financial marketing activities and promotional activities behavior of those institutions and their partners", reflecting the requirements of regulating business activities and creating a healthy and compliant internet insurance marketing environment.

The *Rules of Internet Insurance Business* further strengthens the management responsibility of licensed institutions, stipulating that insurance institutions should establish a series of management systems for internet insurance marketing and publicity, conduct marketing and publicity information review, monitoring and inspection, and assume the main responsibility for compliance; regarding the marketing and publicity of practitioners, it is clearly required that practitioners should carry out internet marketing and publicity within the authorization of insurance institutions, and the content of marketing and publicity should be produced by the insurance institutions to which they belong; regarding the content of marketing and publicity, it is also stipulated that the content should be clear and accurate, easy to understand, in line with the public order and good customs, and be consistent with the terms of the insurance contract.

Third, strengthen the protection of internet consumer rights. First, emphasize the full protection of the consumer's right to be informed, the right of independent choice and the right of fair trade. For example, the China Banking and Insurance Regulatory Commission issued the *Notice on Regulating Retrospective Management of Internet Insurance Sales Activities* (YBJF[2020]No.26) on June 22, which clearly stipulates that sales webpage should fully explain the insurance products and disclose accurate and complete information; to ensure that the insurance behavior is the true meaning of the consumers, and policyholders should read it independently before entering the insurance process to ensure that the act of buying insurance is the true intention of the consumers; and set up a separate page to explain policyholders important clauses such as exemption of insurer's liability. Secondly, it is further required that internet insurance sales should have traceability. The above-mentioned regulatory provisions (YBJF[2020]No.26 and Order of the CBIRC[2020]No.13) both emphasize that "key behavioral information such as sales and service is tamper-proof and should be traceable throughout the process", clarify internet insurance sales activities, page content and interaction methods, and strictly control internet insurance sales page management and sales process records, to ensure that sales practices are reversible, effectively mitigating risks of misleading sales, and protect the legitimate rights and interests of consumers. In addition, the protection of customer information was regulated. The *Rules of Internet Insurance Business* requires insurance institutions to establish a customer information protection system covering the whole life cycle to prevent information leakage.

**2. Refine regulation of key business areas to promote high-quality development of the industry**

With the development of the new financial industry, Non-car insurance business is growing rapidly. Business risks have changed, and the aggregation, crossover and contagion of financial risks have become increasingly complex, with the aftermath of brutal growth ensuing. On May 8, the China Banking and Insurance Regulatory Commission issued the *Rules of Credit Insurance and Guarantee Insurance Business* (YBJBF[2020]No.39), setting out clear requirements for credit guarantee insurance in terms of business rules, internal control management, supervision, and management. First, focus on the supervision of high-risk financing credit insurance business. It distinguishes between financing and non-financing credit insurance business and raises the regulatory requirements for financing credit insurance business in terms of operating qualifications, underwriting limits, infrastructure, etc. Second, it relaxes restrictions on some businesses and tightens restrictions on other businesses, while balancing supervision and development. On the one hand, it seeks to compress the underwriting limit of the financing credit insurance, expand the scope of insurance types (i.e. commercial export credit insurance), etc. to control the risk exposure; on the other hand, it aims to set flexible limits to encourage insurance companies to provide financing credit enhancement support for inclusive small and micro-enterprises. By moderately adjusting the type of business, it supports the exploration and development of new business areas under the premise of risks being controlled. Third, strengthen internal control management to promote high-quality development. It requires insurance companies to enhance their management capabilities and further strengthen institutional improvement, system building, liquidity management, and risk warning in terms of internal control management.

On the other hand, the *Operational Guidelines for Pre-insurance Management of Financial Credit Insurance* and the *Operational Guidelines for Post-insurance Management of Financial Credit Insurance* (YBJBF[2020]No.90) issued on September 14 refine the requirements of establishing standardized operation specifications for two major aspects: pre-insurance risk management and post-monitoring and management of financial credit insurance. First, it refines the operational requirements. The *Operational Guidelines for Pre-insurance Management of Financial Credit Insurance* refines the requirements on sales management, underwriting management, partner management, product management, system and information management; the *Operational Guidelines for Post-insurance Management of Financial Credit Insurance* refines the requirements on post-insurance monitoring, overdue collection, claims handling, subrogation recovery, and complaint handling. The second is to establish operational standards for the current outstanding problems. These two documents clarify the operational standards of sales management, such as "to do a good job of the reminder insurance prompting in the sales process, with the reminder of prompting content including but not limited to the functions and attributes of guarantee insurance, key information of the product, debt recovery after default, and uploading information of the credit system of the People's Bank of China", etc.; they clarify the requirements of underwriting and system functions. For example, "insurance companies are required to establish underwriting module management and anti-fraud review rules in the system according to underwriting rules and process requirements". Strengthen the requirements and process management of partners, such as "insurance companies should develop sales, funds, collection and recovery of the partner management system, at least to clarify the partner entry criteria, evaluation system and exit mechanism."

Besides, the China Banking and Insurance Regulatory Commission issued the *Rules of Liability Insurance Business* (YBJBF[2020]No.117) on December 22. As China's first liability insurance regulatory method, it regulates underwriting boundaries, market conducts, insurance services, internal control management. On the one hand, it is emphasized that insurance companies should clarify the relationship between liability insurance and property damage insurance, guarantee insurance, accident insurance and other types of insurance, reasonably determine the types of insurance, standardize insurance services, strengthen internal control management, etc. On the other hand, it emphasizes that insurance liability should be regulated by specifying the risks or losses that should not be covered through a negative list. It emphasizes that "not to underwrite the financing credit risk in the form of underwriting the liability of the guarantee institution" and "no liability insurance to cover performance credit risk or loss".

In general, these "overhaul" regulations on Non-car insurance business are conducive to preventing and resolving business risks, giving play to the role of credit enhancement, promoting high-quality business development, and a greater role of the business in the process of financial inclusion.

**3. Promote the reform of "delegating power, streamlining procedures, improving supervision and services" in the use of insurance fund, and strengthen the hard constraints on insurance asset and liability management**

In 2020, regulators issued a series of supervision policies in terms of insurance fund investment, promoting the market-oriented reform in the use of insurance funds, enhancing the efficiency and supervisory effectiveness in the use of insurance funds, emphasizing risk control and structure adjustment, ensuring the safety of insurance funds, and better serving the development of the real economy.

First, to promote the reform of "streamlining the government, delegating power and improving government services". On September 4, the China Banking and Insurance Regulatory Commission issued the *Notice on Relevant Matters Concerning Insurance Fund Investment in the Debt-to-equity Swap Investment Plans* (YBJBF[2020]No.82), clarifying that insurance funds can invest in debt-to-equity swap investment plans set up by financial asset investment companies, reflecting the direction of enhancing the quality and efficiency of the financial industry in serving the real economy and optimizing the allocation structure of insurance assets. On September 7, the China Banking and Insurance Regulatory Commission issued the *Detailed Rules for the Implementation of Portfolio Insurance Assets Management Products*, the *Debt Investment Plan Implementation Rules*, and the *Equity Investment Plan Implementation Rules* (YBJBF[2020]No.85), clarifying the registration mechanism, investment scope, risk management and supervision and management of the three types of products and other requirements. By streamlining administration and delegating power and reforming the registration mechanism of insurance asset management products, the registration efficiency of these three types of products has increased; by improving the capital investment and credit enhancement requirements for debt investment plans, the investment scope of the equity investment plan has been expanded to expand effective social investment. Besides, in the *Notice on Relevant Matters Concerning Insurance Fund Financial Investment in Equity Rights* (YBJF[2020] No.54) on November 12, it was proposed that "For investment in financial equity with insurance funds, under the conditions of safety, liquidity and profitability, and taking into account factors such as solvency, risk appetite, investment budget, assets and liabilities, the industry scope of investment enterprises can be selected independently according to the law and regulations", and the requirement that financial equity investment industries be limited to insurance companies, non-insurance financial enterprises and insurance business-related pension, medical and other specific companies should be removed, to allow insurance institutions to independently choose the scope of investment industries; By introducing the mechanism of "negative list + positive guidance", efforts should be made to broaden the space for independent decision-making of insurance funds investment and enhance the ability of insurance funds in serving the real economy.

Second, to reform the filing of the investment management capabilities of insurance institutions, focusing on strengthening ongoing and export supervision. On September 30, the China Banking and Insurance Regulatory Commission issued the *Notice on Optimizing the Supervision of Investment Management Capability of Insurance Institutions* (YBJF[2020]No.45), which clarifies the standard requirements for investment management capacity building of insurance institutions. After the adjustment, there are seven categories of investment management ability of insurance institutions: credit risk management, stock investment management, equity investment management, real estate investment management, derivatives application management, debt investment plan product management, and equity investment plan product management. In terms of competence standards, detailed regulations are made in the organizational structure design, professional team composition, system building, investment operation mechanism, risk control system, and information system building of insurance institutions, together with differentiated requirements for different investment management capabilities; the adjustment canceled the management of investment management capacity filing and adjusted the management of investment management capacity of insurance institutions to a combination of corporate self-assessment, information disclosure, and continuous supervision. This will further enhance the efficiency of independent investment decision-making and investment initiatives of insurance institutions, forming a regulatory system in which insurance institutions, self-regulatory organizations and regulators have their own roles and support each other. It will not only enable the market-oriented reform, but also stimulate the vitality of insurance funds investment; and by rousing insurance institutions' compliance awareness and prompting the supervision and management of self-regulatory organizations, it will enhance the supervision dimension, frequency and coverage, and ensure the fulfillment of insurance institutions' main responsibilities.

Third, under the premise of effective risk control, differentiated supervision is implemented for insurance companies' equity asset allocation. On July 17, the China Banking and Insurance Regulatory Commission issued the *Notice on the Notice on Optimizing the Supervision of Equity Asset Allocation of Insurance Companies* (YBJBF[2020]No.63), which supports companies with strong investment ability to increase equity investment. Based on the indicators of insurance companies, such as solvency adequacy, asset and liability management capability and risk profile, the regulatory ratio of eight classes of equity assets is clarified, and the investment balance of equity assets can account for up to 45% of the total assets at the end of the last quarter; It strengthens the supervision of key companies, specifying that "insurance companies should immediately stop investing in new equity assets if their comprehensive solvency ratio is less than 100% at the end of the last quarter."; At one of the following circumstances, the regulatory ratio of equity assets shall not exceed 15%: "life insurance companies with less than 100% liability reserve coverage at the end of the previous quarter, major risk events occur in the use of funds in the previous year, weak asset-liability management ability and poor matching, being penalized by the CBIRC for major violations of law in the previous three years, the existence of major hidden risks or being listed as a key supervisory target by the CBIRC". Through classified supervision and moderate increase in investment ratio, it guides insurance companies to carry out value investment, long-term investment and prudent investment, promoting the return of equity investment to its original source of service insurance protection business.

**4. Improve the regulatory framework system for unified insurance sales force and sales channel management**

At present, the insurance industry is moving toward high-quality development, and the insurance needs of consumers are becoming diversified and complex. The competence level of practitioners (insurance salespersons, employees of corporate insurance intermediaries, insurance agents, etc.) must match the insurance needs of consumers as well as the complexity of insurance products, therefore, it is necessary to implement more refined management of practitioners. In 2020, regulators issued a number of relevant regulatory policies, aiming to establish a salesperson management system and clarify the main responsibility of insurance institutions; and to consolidate the achievements of rectify the financial market disorder in recent years, transform the insurance marketing development model and deepen the reform of the insurance intermediary market.

First, to strengthen the management of insurance sales staff and professional insurance intermediaries. Practitioners are directly engaged in insurance sales and consulting services to insurance consumers, and their quality level and integrity status are directly related to the vital interests of insurance consumers. On May 12, the China Banking and Insurance Regulatory Commission issued the *Notice on Strengthening Main Responsibilities of Insurance Institutions and Management of Insurance Sales Personnel* (YBJBF[2020]No.41), which puts forward requirements for strengthening the management of insurance sales persons in terms of improving the management structure system, rejecting "sick" sales personnel, improving the professionalism of sales personnel, building a grading system for sales personnel, establishing an integrity system for sales personnel, and imposing severe penalties according to the law. On the same day, the China Banking and Insurance Regulatory Commission issued the *Notice on Effectively Strengthening Management of Employees of Corporate Insurance Intermediaries* (YBJBF[2020]No.42), putting forward clear requirements on the characteristics and market positioning of insurance professional intermediaries, fully assuming the main responsibility of management, strengthening the overall management, ensuring strict recruitment management, establishing a sales ability grading system, and ensuring strict integrity management and supervision. The two Notices specify the regulatory requirements for sales capability grading, refining the regulations around the main links in the process chain of practitioner management, as well as the key links in the process from entry to exit.

Second, improve the system of insurance intermediary supervision. On November 12, the China Banking and Insurance Regulatory Commission issued the *Rules on Insurance Agents* (Order of the CBIRC[2020]No.11), which brings corporate insurance agents, sideline insurance agencies and individual insurance agents into the regulatory adjustment and establishes relatively unified basic regulatory standards and rules. First, it has clear requirements for corporate insurance agents: strengthening the review of shareholders of corporate insurance agents making requirements for shareholders' capital contribution ability. At the same time, it makes provisions in capital trusteeship, governance structure, internal control system and business model to strengthen market access management; strengthen branch control, set out the specific conditions that should be met for the establishment of branches, while further strengthening the control responsibilities of legal entities; and rationalize the post-approval process. It requires that after obtaining a license, the insurance professional agency should promptly register the relevant information in the regulatory information system; enhances the minimum registered capital, and adjusts the minimum registered capital of regional insurance professional agencies to RMB 20 million. Secondly, it has clear requirements for sideline insurance agents, mainly including clear entry conditions, as well as legal person holding a license, the model of authorizing branches to operate; improves the exit mechanism, providing for the circumstances where a sideline insurance agent can cancel licenses in accordance with the law, as well as the business exit process. In addition, it introduces the concept of "Independent Individual Insurance Agent" for the first time, clarifies the concept of insurance agency employees, people in insurance agency engaged in the sale of insurance products or loss investigation, claims and other business personnel are included in the provision, and their behaviors are restrained, and corresponding penalties are provided for violations.

At the same time, the China Banking and Insurance Regulatory Commission issued the *Notice on Relevant Matters Concerning Independent Individual Insurance Agents* (YBJBF[2020]No.118) on December 23. As a regulatory document supporting the *Regulations on Insurance Agents*, it refines and supplements the content of "establishing an independent individual insurance agent framework", with specific requirements on the positioning of independent individual insurance agents, eligibility requirements and standards, professional conduct, selection and hiring mechanism, management, supervision and regulation. It clarifies the essential characteristics of independent individual insurance agents who are not affiliated with a team and carry out insurance sales independently, strictly stipulates the basic conditions of personnel and the selection mechanism, focuses on regulating the practice of personnel, and emphasizes management responsibility of insurance companies and the supervisory responsibility of regulators. The Notice also stipulates that corporate insurance agents, insurance brokerage institutions and their employees may refer to the Notice for rules governing independent individual insurance agents.

**5. Improve the corporate governance mechanism of insurance institutions and prompt the insurance industry to effectively improve the quality and efficiency of corporate governance**

Good corporate governance is a prerequisite and foundation for the long-term sound operation of insurance institutions. On July 3, 2020, the Economic Daily published the article To Improve Corporate Governance is the Top Priority in Financial Institutions Reform authored by Guo Shuqing, Secretary of the CPC Committee of the People's Bank of China (PBC) and Chairman of the China Banking and Insurance Regulatory Commission (CBIRC). The article proposes that efforts should be made to improve the corporate governance system, ensure the fulfillment of financial enterprises' main responsibilities, authorities should regard corporate governance as a fundamental regulatory requirement, strengthen party leadership and party building, clean up and regulate the equity relationship of financial enterprises in accordance with the law, and give full play to the monitoring role of the market, intermediaries and stakeholders in all aspects. On July 15, Liang Tao, Vice President of the China Banking and Insurance Regulatory Commission published the article "Work to build a corporate governance mechanism for the banking and insurance industry with Chinese characteristics" on *China Finance*, noting that strengthening the board of directors building is the next priority for sound corporate governance in the banking and insurance industry. In addition, problems in shareholders' equity and connected transactions are the root causes of the irregularities in small and medium-sized financial institutions in recent years; good market discipline and stakeholder rights protection mechanisms are important components of corporate governance in the banking and insurance industry with Chinese characteristics. At the same time, on July 23, the official website of the China Banking and Insurance Regulatory Commission published a signed article of Cao Yu, Vice President of the China Banking and Insurance Regulatory Commission: "Optimize the building of institutional mechanisms, strengthen investor protection, and comprehensively improve the corporate governance of banking, insurance, and capital management institutions". The article notes that efforts should be made to improve corporate governance mechanism in line with the characteristics of China's asset management industry. The focus is to protect the interests of investors, and continuously improve the effectiveness of the board of directors in performing its duties; strengthen information disclosure to enhance the transparency of operation and management; strengthen the management of connected transactions to strictly prevent the transfer of interests; improve the regulatory system to strengthen supervision and management, etc.

In recent years, the China Banking and Insurance Regulatory Commission has attached great importance to corporate governance oversight and continued to improve the regulatory system to rectify shareholder equity irregularities. It has established a nationwide unified record of bad equity management of investors in banking and insurance institutions and made public for the first time a group of shareholders in serious violation of the law in July 2020. In December, it made public the second group of major shareholders in violation of the law. All those show that the CBIRC prioritizes strengthening corporate governance as the key to transform the institutional mechanism of the banking and insurance industry.

On August 17, the China Banking and Insurance Regulatory Commission issued the *Three-Year Action Plan for Improving Corporate Governance of the Banking and Insurance Sectors (2020–2022)* (YBJF[2020]No.40) (hereafter referred to as the Plan). The Plan features the principle of being problem-oriented, tackling both symptoms and root causes, differentiated policies and coordinated promotion. The first is to focus on the major problems of current corporate governance in the banking and insurance industry and propose targeted rectification measures; the second is to solve existing risks in a timely manner while working to build a sound, long-term mechanism of corporate governance; the third is to fully consider the differences of corporate governance among different types of institutions; the fourth is to follow the system theory to improve the integrity and synergy of all aspects of corporate governance. The ultimate goal is to implement the *G20/OECD Principles of Corporate Governance* and build a corporate governance mechanism of the banking and insurance industry with Chinese characteristics.

The Action Plan consists of ten parts, covering general requirements (including philosophy, basic principles and overall objectives), integration of the CPC leadership and corporate governance, corporate governance evaluation, regulation of shareholders' conduct, duty performance of governance subjects such as the board of directors, incentive and constraint mechanism, stakeholder protection, external market constraint, regulatory capacity building, and enforcement of work and responsibilities. It is the action guide for corporate governance supervision of the insurance industry in 2020–2022. Efforts will be made to prioritize the integration of party leadership and corporate governance, make the integration of party leadership into corporate governance more institutionalized, standardized and procedural, continue to explore ways to improve the integration of party leadership and corporate governance and ensure that Party organizations of state-owned institutions follow the right direction, manage the overall situations well, and ensure full implementation. Drawing on international best practices, the Action Plan fully absorbed the assessment results on the implementation of the G20/OECD Principles of Corporate Governance in China's banking and insurance industries. The CBIRC worked on the gaps and deficiencies identified in the assessment, and put forward targeted improvement measures. For example, the constraint mechanism on major shareholders' conduct should be improved, all directors, including directors with equity interests, should treat shareholders fairly, the nomination and selection process of directors shall be enhanced, and high ethical standards shall be set up.

**6. Risk management of financial holding groups, including the insurance industry, enters the era of full-caliber regulation**

The year 2020 witnessed the study, validation and testing of phase-II of China Risk Oriented Solvency System under an intense schedule. So the official document on phase-II has not been released. However, the regulatory requirements for strengthening financial supervision, preventing financial risks, focusing on key risk control and firmly guarding the risk bottom line have become stricter. On September 11, the People's Bank of China issued the *Trial Measures on Regulation of Financial Holding Companies* (Order of the PBOC[2020]No. 4), which dictates that financial holding companies, including insurance companies, should establish a comprehensive risk management system that is commensurate with their organizational structure, business scale, complexity, reputation and influence; should exercise comprehensive and continuous control over the corporate governance, capital and leverage of the institutions they hold within the scope of consolidated management, and effectively identify, measure, monitor and control the overall risk profile of the financial holding group. This includes credit risk, market risk, liquidity risk, operational risk, reputation risk, strategic risk, IT risk and other risks such as concentration risk. Moreover, they should establish a group risk appetite system that is compatible with the purpose of serving the real economy, determine risk management objectives, determine risk tolerance and risk limits for various types of risks, and establish an over-limit disposal mechanism. The *Measures* makes it clear that the capital, behavior and risks of financial control groups are subject to comprehensive, continuous and penetrating supervision to prevent the transmission of financial risks across industries and markets.

### (II) Outlook on insurance regulatory policy in 2021

In January 2021, the China Banking and Insurance Regulatory Commission held the 2021 CBRC Work Conference. Guided by Xi Jinping's thought of socialism with Chinese characteristics for a New Era, fully implement the guiding principles of the 19th CPC National Congress, the Second, Third, Fourth and Fifth Plenary Sessions of the 19th CPC Central Committee and the spirit of the Central Economic Work Conference, the supervisory work in 2020, analyzed the current economic and financial conditions, and map out the priorities for 2021.

According to the spirit of the conference, the insurance industry regulatory policy in 2021 will likely be strengthened and breakthroughs may be made in the following areas: First, substantial support will be given for the building of a new development pattern. For example, consolidating the results of poverty eradication and integrating poverty eradication into rural revitalization, developing green insurance, and steadily promoting the high-level opening of the insurance industry.

Second, to further enhance the overall effectiveness of financial services. For example, strengthening financial support to projects related to people's livelihood; promoting the development of pension, health, liability and catastrophe insurance; and protecting the consumers. Third, be committed to preventing and resolving financial risks. For example, improving the processes and procedures for handling major cases and risk events; strengthening the crackdown on illegal financial activities and "unlicensed" activities; and actively fending off external risks and shocks. Fourth, Supervision over key activities will be promoted. For instance, rectify irregularities in the insurance market and cracking down on financial products having names that are inconsistent with what they are. Fifth, to effectively strengthen the supervision of financial activities on online platforms. For example, tighten the supervision of financial activities of banking and insurance institutions in cooperation with online platforms. Sixth, continue to deepen the supply-side structural reform in the financial sector. For instance, continuously, promote the regulated development of the third pillar of the pension system; consolidate the reform of auto insurance; further advance the reform of personal accident insurance and health insurance; and promote the market-oriented reform for investment of insurance companies and the reform in insurance agents. Seventh, continue to improve the level of corporate governance and internal control management.For example, implement the shareholder commitment policy; strengthen look-through examination of shareholders, regulate the conduct of major shareholders in accordance with law, further remove illegal shareholders, and put in place the mechanism for routine disclosure of illegal shareholders; strengthen the development of regulatory rules and systems for related-party transactions; Enhance directors and supervisors' capabilities to perform their duties, and improve the internal rules on the board of directors and supervisory committee; and encouraging the development of the culture of compliance. Eighth, strengthen the regulatory capacity building. For instance, improve the law enforcement capability and the ability to supervise the whole process, strengthen ex-ante warning and early intervention, tighten ongoing intervention, and improving ex-post risk resolution.

In 2021, the starting year of the "14th Five-Year" Plan, the CBIRC is focusing on making new progress in the quality development of the banking and insurance industry and promoting the building of a new development pattern for the national economy. From the beginning of the year, the CBIRC has issued a series of regulatory policies or drafts for comments:

First, improve the level of corporate governance. For example, the *Code of Corporate Governance of Banking and Insurance Institutions (Draft for Comments)* is viewed as a programmatic system of corporate governance for the insurance industry; *Measures on the Performance Evaluation of the Performance of Directors and Supervisors of Banking and Insurance Institutions (Trial, Draft for Comments)* will regulate the conduct and evaluation of directors and supervisors of banking and insurance institutions in performing their duties. The above two documents were issued as specific measures to implement the above-mentioned three-year plan, meaning an upgrade in the supervision of corporate governance. As planned by the China Banking and Insurance Regulatory Commission, in 2021 the major task is to study how to improve the horizontal and vertical collaboration mechanism of corporate governance supervision and make the authority and responsibility of corporate governance supervision clearer, coordinated, efficient, and regulated. Continue to strengthen system building, refine the equity supervision methods of banks and insurance institutions, optimize the rules of operation of the board of directors, and improve the regulatory regulations on remuneration and performance assement.

Second, strengthen the level of risk prevention and control and internal control management. For example, the China Banking and Insurance Regulatory Commission revised and issued the draft of the *Insurance Company Solvency Management Regulations* to make a comprehensive revision of the current rules of C-ROSS, and formed a revised draft of 20 regulatory rules (draft for comments) and revised instructions for the Phase 2 of China Risk Oriented Solvency System (C-ROSS). Currently, comments from the industry are being solicited and they are expected to be issued at the end of April 2021. Based on the progress of the Phase 2 of China Risk Oriented Solvency System (C-ROSS), the above-mentioned Regulations clearly defines the three-pillar framework of solvency regulation, makes the insurance solvency supervision system more targeted toward risks, and enhances the risk coverage. It can reflect risk changes in the insurance industry more scientifically and effectively from both qualitative and quantitative perspectives, thus guiding enterprises to make targeted improvements and management tools, optimize product structure, adjust investment strategies, etc., improve insurance companies' risk management capacity and risk resilience, and thus ensuring the long-term stable development of the insurance industry. Besides, the China Banking and Insurance Regulatory Commission issued the *Rules on Reputational Risk Management of Banking and Insurance Institutions (Trial)*, which clarifies the full-process system and routine building of reputation risk management of insurance institutions, and other important elements. It will promote organizations to pay more attention to consumer experience and strive to enhance service awareness and service capabilities.

Third, promote the reform of "delegating power, streamlining procedures, improving supervision and services". Promote the reform of Promote the reform of Main Supervisory Responsibilities and expand industrial supervision to lower-level institutions. From functional regulation to institutional regulation, insurance company regulation is aligning with that of banks. In January 2021, the China Banking and Insurance Regulatory Commission issued the *Reform Plan on the Main Supervisory Responsibilities of Life Insurance Companies*, which clearly defines the regulatory responsibilities of the China Banking and Insurance Regulatory Commission and Banking and local offices. The China Banking and Insurance Regulatory Commission is responsible for coordinating the overall supervisory policies; the CBIRC headquarters and local offices undertakes respective administrative licensing matters and daily supervisory duties for centrally- and locally-supervised companies. the Notice on Releasing the Reform Plan of Supervisory Responsibilities of P&C Insurance Companies and Reinsurance Companies in July 2020 marks that the insurance industry has entered the era of territorial supervision.

Fourth, Supervision over key activities will be promoted, such as cooperation with online platforms for financial activities, and strengthen the fight against illegal finance and illegal fund-raising, and the release of the *Regulations for the Prevention and Disposal of Illegal Fund-raising*; consolidate the reform of auto insurance and continue to deepen the reform of personal accident insurance and health insurance, such as the issuance of the *Notice on the Regulating Short-term Health Insurance Business*, focusing on the outstanding problems in the development of short-term business in the industry to promote the high-quality development of the insurance industry.

Fifth, deepen the supply-side structural reform in the financial sector: promoting institutional building in insurance market entry and exit, auto insurance reform, and the insurance marketing system reform, especially, promote steady progress in the Independent Individual Insurance agent system; accelerate digital transformation with financial technology; further promote the two-way opening of the financial service industry, etc.

## Appendix

### List of Major Regulatory Policies of China's Insurance Industry in 2020

| Released on | Name of Policy Document | Issuing Units | Document no |
|---|---|---|---|
| January 3 | China Banking and Insurance Regulatory Commission Normative Documents Management Measures | China Banking and Insurance Regulatory Commission | Order of the CBIRC (No.1 in 2020) |
| January 14 | China Banking and Insurance Regulatory Commission Letter and Visit Methods | China Banking and Insurance Regulatory Commission | Order of the CBIRC (No.2 in 2020) |
| January 14 | Rules on Complaints Administration of Banking and Insurance Consumers | China Banking and Insurance Regulatory Commission | Order of the CBIRC (No.3 in 2020) |
| January 17 | Opinions on Accelerating the Reform of Accident Insurance | China Banking and Insurance Regulatory Commission | YBJBF[2020]No.4 |
| January 21 | Notice on Related Matters to Strengthening Actuarial Supervision of Life Insurance | China Banking and Insurance Regulatory Commission | YBJBF[2020]No.6 |
| January 21 | Notice on the Actuarial Provisions on Ordinary Life Insurance Products | China Banking and Insurance Regulatory Commission | YBJBF[2020]No.7 |
| January 23 | Opinions on Promoting the Development of Commercial Insurance in Social Services | China Banking and Insurance Regulatory Commission, National Development and Reform Commission, Ministry of Education, Ministry of Civil Affairs, Ministry of Justice, Ministry of Finance, Ministry of Human Resources and Social Security, Ministry of Natural Resources, Ministry of Housing and Urban-Rural Development, Ministry of Commerce, National Health Commission, State Taxation Administration, National Healthcare Security Administration | YBJF [2020] No. 4 |

Continued

| Released on | Name of Policy Document | Issuing Units | Document no |
|---|---|---|---|
| January 31 | Circular on Further Strengthening Financial Support for COVID-19 Epidemic Prevention and Control | People's Bank of China, Ministry of Finance, China Banking and Insurance Regulatory Commission, China Securities Regulatory Commission, State Foreign Exchange Administration | YF[2020] No. 29 |
| February 1 | Notice on the Work of Financial Services after the Spring Festival Holiday | People's Bank of China, China Banking and Insurance Regulatory Commission, China Securities Regulatory Commission, State Administration of Foreign Exchange | YF[2020] No. 30 |
| February 4 | The Interim Rules on Insurance Asset Management Products | China Banking and Insurance Regulatory Commission | YBJF[2020] No. 5 |
| February 7 | Notice on Promoting Electronic Return Visit of Life Insurance | China Banking and Insurance Regulatory Commission | |
| February 11 | Notice on Further Regulating Issues Concerning Entrusted Management of Health Care | China Banking and Insurance Regulatory Commission | YBJBF[2020]No.13 |
| February 14 | Opinions on Further Accelerating the Construction of Shanghai as an International Financial Center and Providing Financial Support for the Integrated Development of the Yangtze River Delta Region | The People's Bank of China, China Banking and Insurance Regulatory Commission, China Securities Regulatory Commission, State Administration of Foreign Exchange and Shanghai Municipal People's Government (SMG) | YF[2020] No. 46 |
| February 14 | The Announcement on the Participation in Sovereign Bond Futures Trading on the China Financial Futures Exchange by Commercial Banks and Insurance Institutions | China Securities Regulatory Commission, Ministry of Finance, People's Bank of China, and China Banking and Insurance Regulatory Commission | Notice of the CSRC[2020]No.12 |
| February 19 | Notice on Issues Concerning Further Strengthening and Improving Property & Casualty Insurance Product Supervision | China Banking and Insurance Regulatory Commission | YBJBF[2020]No.17 |
| February 20 | Guidance on the Prevention of Financial Crime by Employees in the Banking and Insurance Industry | China Banking and Insurance Regulatory Commission | YBJBF[2020]No.18 |
| March 18 | Interim Rules on Insurance Asset Management Product | China Banking and Insurance Regulatory Commission | Order of the CBIRC(No.5 in 2020) |
| March 25 | Notice on Issues Concerning Premium Rate Adjustment of Long-term Medical Insurance Products | China Banking and Insurance Regulatory Commission | YBJBF[2020]No.27 |

Continued

| Released on | Name of Policy Document | Issuing Units | Document no |
|---|---|---|---|
| March 26 | Notice on Strengthening Financial Services for Coordinated Resumption of Work and Production across the Industrial Chain | China Banking and Insurance Regulatory Commission | YBJBF[2020] No. 28 |
| April 9 | Notice on Banking and Insurance Sectors Better Serving Key Work Priorities in Agriculture, Rural Areas and Farmers in 2020 | China Banking and Insurance Regulatory Commission | YBJBF[2020]No.31 |
| April 16 | Notice on Issues Concerning the Development of Asset Management Business by Financial Asset Investment Companies | China Banking and Insurance Regulatory Commission | YBJF[2020] No. 12 |
| April 24 | Opinions on Financial Support for the Development of the Guangdong-Hong Kong-Macao Greater Bay Area | The People's Bank of China, China Banking and Insurance Regulatory Commission, China Securities Regulatory Commission and State Administration of Foreign Exchange | YF[2020] No. 95 |
| May 8 | The Rules of Credit Insurance and Guarantee Insurance Business | China Banking and Insurance Regulatory Commission | YBJBF[2020]No.39 |
| May 12 | Notice on Strengthening Main Responsibilities of Insurance Institutions and Management of Insurance Sales Personnel | China Banking and Insurance Regulatory Commission | YBJBF[2020] No. 41 |
| May 12 | Notice on Effectively Strengthening Management of Employees of Corporate Insurance Intermediaries | China Banking and Insurance Regulatory Commission | YBJBF[2020] No. 42 |
| May 18 | Notice on Further Regulating Credit Financing Charges and Reducing Comprehensive Financing Cost of Enterprises | China Banking and Insurance Regulatory Commission, Ministry of Industry and Information Technology, National Development and Reform Commission, Ministry of Finance, the People's Bank of China, State Administration for Market Regulation | YBJF[2020] No. 18 |
| May 20 | Notice on Issues Concerning Insurance Fund Investment in Bank Capital Replenishment Bonds | China Banking and Insurance Regulatory Commission | YBJF [2020] No. 17 |
| May 22 | The Notice on the Issuance of Measures for the Management of Criminal Cases Involving Banking and Insurance Institutions (Trial) | China Banking and Insurance Regulatory Commission | YBJF[2020] No. 20 |
| May 24 | Provisions on Implementation Procedures of Administrative Licensing | China Banking and Insurance Regulatory Commission | Order of the CBIRC (No.7 in 2020) |

Continued

| Released on | Name of Policy Document | Issuing Units | Document no |
|---|---|---|---|
| May 26 | Guiding Opinions on Further Strengthening the Financial Services for Micro, Small and Medium-sized Enterprises | The People's Bank of China, China Banking and Insurance Regulatory Commission, National Development and Reform Commission, Ministry of Industry and Information Technology, Ministry of Finance, State Administration for Market Regulation, China Securities Regulatory Commission, State Administration of Foreign Exchange | YF[2020] No. 120 |
| June 1 | Notice on Further Clarifying the Operating Conditions for Agricultural Insurance Business | China Banking and Insurance Regulatory Commission | YBJBF[2020]No.51 |
| June 15 | The Administrative Punishment Measures of the China Banking and Insurance Regulatory Commission | China Banking and Insurance Regulatory Commission | Order of the CBIRC (No.8 in 2020) |
| June 22 | Notice on Regulating Retrospective Management of Internet Insurance Sales Activities | China Banking and Insurance Regulatory Commission | YBJF[2020] No. 26 |
| June 23 | Notice on the Rectification of Malpractice, Misconduct and Noncompliance in the Banking and Insurance Industry | China Banking and Insurance Regulatory Commission | YBJF [2020] No. 27 |
| June 23 | Policies on Insurance Funds Participating in Trading of Financial Derivatives, Treasury Bond Futures and Stock Index Futures | China Banking and Insurance Regulatory Commission | YBJBF[2020] No. 59 |
| July 16 | Notice on the Reform Plan of Supervisory Responsibilities of P&C Insurance Companies and Reinsurance Companie | China Banking and Insurance Regulatory Commission | |
| July 17 | Notice on Optimizing the Supervision of Equity Asset Allocation of Insurance Companies | China Banking and Insurance Regulatory Commission | YBJBF[2020]No.63 |
| July 22 | The Three-year Action Plan for Promoting High-quality Development of the Property Insurance Industry(2020-2022) | China Banking and Insurance Regulatory Commission | YBJBF[2020]No.68 |
| August 17 | Notice on the Issuance of the *Three-Year Action Plan for Improving Corporate Governance of the Banking and Insurance Sectors* | China Banking and Insurance Regulatory Commission | YBJF[2020] No. 40 |
| September 9 | Notice on the Guiding Opinions on Implementing Comprehensive Reform of Auto Insurance | China Banking and Insurance Regulatory Commission | |

Continued

| Released on | Name of Policy Document | Issuing Units | Document no |
|---|---|---|---|
| September 4 | Notice on Relevant Matters Concerning Insurance Fund Investment in the Debt-to-equity Swap Investment Plans | China Banking and Insurance Regulatory Commission | YBJBF[2020] No. 82 |
| September 6 | Notice on Regulating the Health Management Services of Insurance Companies | China Banking and Insurance Regulatory Commission | YBJBF [2020] No. 83 |
| September 6 | Notice on the Issuance of the Regulations on the Establishment and Implementation Procedures of On-site Inspections by the China Banking and Insurance Regulatory Commission (Trial) | China Banking and Insurance Regulatory Commission | YBJBF[2020]No.84 |
| September 7 | The Supporting Rules of the Interim Measures on Insurance Asset Management Products | China Banking and Insurance Regulatory Commission | YBJBF[2020] No. 85 |
| September 9 | The Actuarial Provisions on Model Commercial Vehicle Insurance | China Banking and Insurance Regulatory Commission | YBJF[2020] No. 42 |
| September 9 | Financial Services Management Measures for Banking and Insurance Institutions in Response to Emergencies | China Banking and Insurance Regulatory Commission | Order of the CBIRC(No.10 in 2020) |
| September 9 | Notice on Adjustment of Liability Limit and Rate Fluctuation Factor of Compulsory Traffic Insurance | China Banking and Insurance Regulatory Commission | |
| September 11 | Notice by the General Office of the China Banking and Insurance Regulatory Commission of Regulating the Matters Concerning Banking Financial Institutions' Assistance in the Competent Authorities' Inquiry about, Freeze of and Deduction from Accounts of Deposits for Capital Recognizance of Insurance Companies | China Banking and Insurance Regulatory Commission | YBJBF[2020] No. 91 |
| September 11 | The Interim Measures for the Supervision and Administration of Financial Holding Companies | People's Bank of China | PBOC Order [2020] No. 4 |
| September 14 | Notice on the Operational Guidelines for Pre-insurance Management of Financial Credit Insurance and the Operational Guidelines for Post-insurance Management of Financial Credit Insurance | China Banking and Insurance Regulatory Commission | YBJBF[2020]No.90 |
| September 23 | Notice on the Issuance of Regulatory Data Security Management Measures (Trial) | China Banking and Insurance Regulatory Commission | YBJF[2020] No. 43 |

*Continued*

| Released on | Name of Policy Document | Issuing Units | Document no |
|---|---|---|---|
| September 30 | Notice on Optimizing the Supervision of Investment Management Capability of Insurance Institutions | China Banking and Insurance Regulatory Commission | YBJF[2020] No. 45 |
| October 15 | The Rules on Nuclear Insurance Catastrophe Liability Reserve | China Banking and Insurance Regulatory Commission, Ministry of Finance, Ministry of Ecology and Environment | YBJF[2020] No. 47 |
| November 5 | Notice on Relevant Matters Concerning Applying the Table of Experience Incidence Rate of Major Diseases for China's Life Insurance Industry (2020) | China Banking and Insurance Regulatory Commission | YBJF[2020] No. 51 |
| November 12 | Notice on Relevant Matters Concerning Insurance Fund Financial Investment in Equity Rights | China Banking and Insurance Regulatory Commission | YBJF[2020] No. 54 |
| November 12 | Insurance Agent Regulatory Regulation | China Banking and Insurance Regulatory Commission | Order of the CBIRC(No.11 in 2020) |
| December 7 | Regulation of Internet Insurance Business | China Banking and Insurance Regulatory Commission | Order of the CBIRC(No.13 in 2020) |
| December 22 | The Rules on Liability Insurance Business | China Banking and Insurance Regulatory Commission | YBJBF[2020]No.117 |
| December 23 | Notice on Relevant Matters Concerning Independent Individual Insurance Agents | China Banking and Insurance Regulatory Commission | YBJBF[2020]No.118 |
| December 30 | Notice on Deepening the Reform of the Banking and Insurance Industry (Streamlining the Government, Delegation and Decentralization) and Optimizing Business Environment | China Banking and Insurance Regulatory Commission | YBJBF [2020] No.129 |
| December 30 | Supervision and Administrative Measures on Anti-money Laundering Institutions and Counter-terrorism Financing by Financial Institutions (Revised Draft for Comments) | People's Bank of China | |

## Article 18

Several local authorities roll out financial supervision and administration regulations

At the 5th National Financial Work Conference in 2017, General Secretary Xi Jinping called for the strengthening of weak links and coordination in financial supervision. To this end, he said, local governments should take more responsibility handling risks within their jurisdiction under the premise of central authority and in accordance with the unified rules of the central government. On

January 16, 2020, the People's Bank of China held a teleconference on the rule of law in finance. The meeting dictated that accelerating local financial supervision and administration legislation would be a priority for the year. Indeed, 2020 saw the intensive rollout of financial supervision and administration regulations in Shanghai, Zhejiang, Guangxi, Inner Mongolia, Xiamen, Jiangxi, Beijing, Guizhou, and other areas across the country. As a whole, these regulations exhibit the following characteristics — in terms of positioning, the objects of supervision, the means of supervision, the mechanisms of supervision, and functional coordination:

1. Positioning. The regulations may be taken as "basic law" for local financial supervision, as they lay out local financial organizations' basic and institutional arrangements. They also clarify the scope of local financial organizations, issue codes of conduct, authorize regulatory methods, and provide a basis for future amendments to supporting documents. In the past, the supervision of local financial organizations mainly relied upon departmental regulations and normative documents as the legal basis for local financial supervision was lacking. The issuance of provincial regulations has resolved this issue.

2. Objects of supervision. The regulations all focus on the emerging financial sector, their regulatory objects basically consisting of the following institutional types: microfinance companies, financial guarantee companies, regional equity markets, pawnbrokers, financial leasing companies, commercial factoring companies and local asset management companies, as well as regional investment companies, specialized mutual credit farmer cooperatives, social crowdfunding institutions and various local exchanges.

3. Means of supervision. The new regulations come with new regulatory models. In Shanghai, Guangxi, Xiamen and other areas, local financial regulators are authorized to conduct on-site inspections and to shut down, detain, or take other measures; these may include regulatory talks, the presentation of risk warning letters, notification of criticism, and orders to rectify. Shanghai authorities also clarified that local financial regulators should establish credit files for local financial organizations, collect credit information on the organizations and their practitioners, and publish a list of entities committing serious failures. Jiangxi authorities, meanwhile, urged local financial regulators to use big data, cloud computing, and other modern financial technology tools to analyze, evaluate and manage the business activities and risk profiles of local financial organizations.

4. Mechanisms of supervision. The regulations take into account the local characteristics of financial development. Therefore, to promote the high-quality and integrated development of financial regulation in the Yangtze River Delta, the *Shanghai Municipal Financial Supervision and Management Regulations* stresses the importance of: improving cooperation mechanisms for regional financial regulation; establishing an interconnected mechanism for risk monitoring, early warning, oversight and enforcement; and strengthening the sharing of information and coordination of processing. The *Financial Regulations of Zhejiang Province* states that Zhejiang will support the use of cloud computing, big data, AI, blockchain, and other emerging technologies in the field of financial services and financial supervision and administration, and that it will encourage compliance innovation in financial technology products, services, and business

models. Zhejiang also situates private financing companies within the scope of regulation. The *Financial Regulations of Xiamen Special Economic Zone*, then, identifies the Xiamen Area of the China (Fujian) Pilot Free Trade Zone and the Cross-strait Financial Center (among other areas) as leaders for institutional mechanism and policy measure experimentation in the field of local finance, as well as in exchanges with Taiwan, so as to promote innovations in local finance business and in businesses' interaction with regulatory mechanisms.

5. Functional coordination. The regulations do not only emphasize coordination between the central and local governments; they also aim for "regulatory interaction" among various levels and departments of local government. Authorities of Shanghai, Zhejiang, Beijing, and other localities have evidently strengthened collaboration with the Office of the State Council Financial Stability and Development Committee's local coordination mechanism in terms of financial supervision, risk management, information sharing, and the protection of consumer rights. To clarify local financial organizations' supervisory and administration responsibilities, authorities in Zhejiang, Jiangxi, and elsewhere have set up financial regulation institutions at three levels — province, county, and city (specifically, cities divided into districts or counties). Meanwhile, authorities of Shanghai, Guangxi, Inner Mongolia, and other localities have standardized risk management and the division of responsibilities for local financial supervision and administration departments, public security organs, market supervision departments, network security and information technology departments, communications management departments, people's courts, people's procuratorates, and other relevant industry authorities.

These regulations will make up for shortcomings in supervision, avoid regulatory vacuums, enhance the authority and effectiveness of coordination in financial supervision, professionalize and unify financial supervision, improve supervision capacities for innovation-driven development, promote the stable development of regulation, and forge a strong synergy between financial development and supervision.